Montrose
Cavalier in Mourning

ABOUT THE AUTHOR

Ronald Williams was born in Rawalpindi, Pakistan, in 1942. Educated at Rossall School in Lancashire, and a History Exhibitioner at Selwyn College Cambridge, he won a Trevelyan Scholarship for a thesis on the Marquis of Montrose in 1960. Between 1964 and 1979 he was a member of the Diplomatic Service and served in Jakarta, Singapore, Budapest and Nairobi. From 1980 to 1997 he worked in the forestry sector and from 1987 to 1997 was Executive Director of the Forestry Industry Council of Great Britain. In 1998 he became Chief Executive of the Publishers Association.

He was appointed OBE in 1991 and is a Fellow of the Royal Society for the Encouragement of Arts, Manufactures and Commerce (FRSA). In addition to Scottish history, he has a passion for fly-fishing and his interests include archaeology, photography, walking, travel and Real Tennis. When not in Scotland, Ronald Williams lives in a small Hampshire village in the valley of the River Test.

Montrose: Cavalier in Mourning was his first book. Other works by Ronald Williams and published by House of Lochar include *The Lords of the Isles: The Clan Donald and the Early Kingdom of the Scots*, *The Heather and the Gale: Clan Donald and Clan Campbell during the Wars of Montrose*, and a sequel *Sons of the Wolf: Campbells and MacGregors and the Cleansing of the Inland Glens*.

Montrose
Cavalier in Mourning

Ronald Williams

British Library Cataloguing in Publication Data
A catalogue record of this book is available from the British Library

ISBN 1 899863 59 1

This edition published by House of Lochar 2001

Printed in Great Britain
by SRP Ltd, Exeter
for House of Lochar
Isle of Colonsay, Argyll PA61 7YR

Contents

List of Illustrations

Plates (between pages 214 and 215)

Page 1   *1st Marquis of Montrose* (1644), from the portrait by Dobson in the Scottish National Portrait Gallery
1st Marquis of Montrose (1649), from the portrait by Honthorst in the Scottish National Portrait Gallery

Page 2   *Archibald, 1st Lord Napier*, from an engraving of the portrait by Jameson in the possession of Lord Napier and Ettrick
Archibald, 2nd Lord Napier, from an engraving of the portrait by Jameson in the possession of Lord Napier and Ettrick

Page 3   *George Gordon, 2nd Marquis of Huntly*, from an engraving of the portrait by Vandyke in the possession of The Duke of Buccleuch
George, Lord Gordon, from an engraving of the portrait in the possession of The Duke of Hamilton

Page 4   *The Marquis of Argyll* (1652), from the 'Newbattle Portrait' in the possession of the Marquis of Lothian

Maps

Acknowledgements

His Grace The Duke of Hamilton
His Grace The Duke of Buccleuch
The Most Honourable The Marquess of Lothian
The Late Earl of Southesk
The Right Honourable The Earl of Dalhousie
Colonel Charles Napier, CBE MC
The Scottish National Portrait Gallery
The Scottish Record Office
Mr John Imrie, Keeper of the Records of Scotland
Mr D. MacArthur, Librarian, University of St Andrews

Preface

Even such is Time, which takes in trust
Our youth, our joys, our all we have,
And pays us but with earth and dust;
Who, in the dark and silent grave
When we have wandered all our ways
Shuts up the story of our days:
But from that earth, that grave and dust
My God shall raise me up, I trust.

Sir Walter Raleigh

When the Stuart James VI of Scotland succeeded to the throne of the Tudor Elizabeth, he inherited a country at a point of change. The Elizabethans, with their aggressive and extrovert attitudes towards life, were giving way to a Jacobean generation of doubt and redefinition. The change was artificially personified by the strongly contrasting characters of the monarchs themselves. The benevolent despotism which had seemed acceptable at the hands of Elizabeth was revealed as a medieval anachronism when administered by her more inept successor. The old queen's spell was broken: James was a stranger, less known, and less beloved. But the change was something more than that. History had as yet afforded no parallel to the metamorphosis that was creeping over Britain. Men were beginning to question certain hitherto fundamental doctrines, to raise up new interests, to substitute new ways of thinking. In this uneasy atmosphere, the sanctions of the old world began to crumble, the old compromises were questioned and found deficient. It was a hesitating and halting process in which the mind set free by the Reformation struggled within the confines of its medieval experience, and the Age of Faith made a last effort to perpetuate itself. As it made for discontent, so also it produced intolerance. As the security of the old world diminished, the pressure on the individual personality increased, and in their uncertainty men turned again to dogma. And since religion and politics were inextricably mingled, this in turn produced that dangerous hybrid of the seventeenth century–the 'Political Religionist'. It was not an isolated phenomenon. The seeds of change came on a wind out of Europe, and the continent itself was soon to be engulfed by the Thirty Years War. In England, under the Stuarts, the dragons' teeth would also render up their harvest of contending men.

The conflict of the seventeenth century has been interpreted in a variety of ways and from many standpoints. Ironically, the issue was settled, in the short term at least, not by the parliamentarian, nor by the preacher, but by the soldier; and the new commonwealth was established by sword right in a manner as old and as pagan as early kingship itself. When the parties finally divided and the English Civil War began, the most effective protagonists on either side were often considerably less noble than the ideals which they claimed to represent. In such a crisis the extremists had the easy choice. But there were many who were lost between the extremes.

In such a situation it is the moderates who exercise the greater fascination–the men whose loyalty belongs to neither extreme; who would improve what is unjust or obsolete, but who will not commit themselves blindly to the uncompromising structures which revolutionaries would impose. Moderation is too easily associated with apathy and silence. But there are occasions when the principle of moderation, if it is to mean anything, must be defended as singlemindedly, and possibly even as violently, as the extremist doctrines that threaten to destroy it. And there can come a time when the moderate himself has got to choose. If, during the progress of a state, the constituted authorities resort to open war against each other, a man may be compelled to draw his sword for what he believes to be the best inheritance of his country. There follows one further distinction–whether the hand that reaches for the sword is guided by determination or despair. During the English Civil War the second alternative found brief expression in Falkland; in Scotland the first was personified in Montrose.

Few men can have been so admired or so vilified in their time. Clarendon regarded him as 'one of the most illustrious persons of the age in which he lived'. For de Retz he recalled the great classical heroes of a bygone, better age. Carlyle later described him as the 'Hero Cavalier'. To his enemies, however, he was a 'bloody murderer' who loosed the savage gaels upon his Christian Lowland kindred; a man who, contrary to his professed ideals, joined the Covenant out of pique and deserted it for ambition. This caricature has been perpetuated–partly through the bias of the Whig historians, and partly perhaps because the Restoration for which Montrose fought did not produce an heroic age. The true cavaliers had no inheritance.

The controversy over his consistency lingers still, and it cannot be resolved by simple generalizations. Montrose must stand on his record–by what he did and said, and by the Declarations which he signed. In the last analysis it hangs on the question of whether a man who joins a party for reasons that he believes initially to be right is thereafter obliged to continue to support it even to excess. Is loyalty to faction more important than loyalty to country–or to an ideal? The quality of consistency is more truly measured, not in terms of political shift, but in the continuity of principle. It is on this basis that Montrose should be judged, and the individual must read the record and decide.

Many things have been claimed of him–some rightly, some exaggerated. He was, by common consent, one of the greatest soldiers of his age. Sir John Fortescue, in his *History of the British Army*, described him as 'perhaps the most brilliant natural military genius disclosed by the Civil War'. He ranks with Condé and Turenne, and as a tactician puts Cromwell in the shade. Certain of his detractors have tried to suggest that he may have been a coward, always 'careful of his own person'. Similar theories have been put forward concerning Marlborough and Wellington with as little charity and as little truth. Montrose commanded caterans who would never have followed a man whose courage was in question. He was the only lowlander to become a legend in the Highlands alongside Alastair–the greatest of all the MacDonald fighting men. There was no place for cowards in the gaelic battle-line.

He was neither statesman nor politician. As Gardiner, one of the greatest historians of the Civil War, once wrote of him: 'He never could have been a statesman because he had no eye for the complexity of life. The simplicity of his conceptions did not fit him for the guidance of his nation in the sore straits into which it had fallen. It did something far better than anything the statesman can achieve. He gave to those who are immersed in the struggles of this world an example of one who kept his heart pure and his eye clear for the reception of every truth he was capable of admitting.' To be cynical is not necessarily to be wise. The idealist may fail in his practical endeavour, but the greatest causes of mankind are never altogether lost. The ideals remain, to be taken up again and passed through generations.

Nor, by the same tokens, was Montrose a political philosopher in the conventional sense of the term. He did not set out to design a new polity but to interpret the constitution as he believed it already existed. He drew his inspiration from the past, and it is this antique cast of mind that lends a peculiarly romantic aspect to his character. He rode to war like the paladin of medieval romance, and he left behind him 'an inspiration and a name which would survive the ruin of his hopes'.

It is a story of strange contrasts and contrarieties–of triumph and failure, of the pursuit of honour against a background of feral savagery, of genuine conviction and religious bigotry, of integrity in a milieu of corruption and intrigue. And for those who are not ashamed to call themselves romantics, who would read of causes lost and battles won, of heroes facing fearful odds, of an idealist, soldier, poet–it is a story such as dreams are made of.

PART I
Prelude

1

Premonitions
(1612–1636)

To the heart of youth, the world is a highwayside
Passing forever, he fares; and on either hand
Deep in the gardens, golden pavilions hide,
* Nestle in orchard bloom, and far on the level land*
Call him with lighted lamp in the eventide.

Robert Louis Stevenson

He was a man, not very tall, nor much exceeding a middle stature, but of exceeding strong composition of body, and incredible force, with excellent proportion of feature. Dark brown haired, ruddy complexion, a swift and piercing grey eye, with a high nose–somewhat like the ancient sign of the Persian King's Magnanimity. He was of a most resolute and undaunted spirit which began to appear in him to the wonder and expectation of all men even in childhood.

He was a man of a very Princely courage, and excellent addresses, which made him for the most part be used by all Princes with extraordinary familiarity. He was a complete horseman and had a singular grace in riding.

He was exceeding constant and affable to those that did adhere to him, and to those whom he knew very affable, though his carriage, which indeed was not ordinary, did make him seem proud. Nor can his enemies lay any greater fault to his charge, than this insatiable desire of honour which he did pursue with as handsome and heroic action as ever any ever did.[1]

According to the old legends, the family of Graham traced its descent from Graym or 'Gramus', who was the father-in-law of Fergus II, King of the Scots, and had come over with that monarch from Denmark. Some accounts state that he was the son of an exiled Albain nobleman and a Danish mother, while others claim that he was a Briton who had rebelled against the Roman rule and fled to Denmark where he married a princess of the royal house and through his daughter became grandfather to a king. As Fergus's general, he is chiefly remembered for having attacked and demolished part of the wall of Antoninus which the Romans had built between the Forth and the Clyde to check the inroads of the wild Caledonians, and which, in commemoration of this exploit, later became known as 'Graeme's

3

Dyke'. But all this is too remote in time to admit of convenient proof.[2]

Another theory, which is possibly more accurate if less romantic, is that the Grahams were of Norman stock, from the family Lez Grames who may have come to Britain with the Conqueror. However, modern genealogists prefer to go no further back than the twelfth century, and take as the first authentic ancestor the knight William de Grame, who witnessed the charter of the Abbey of Holyrood in 1128 and received from David I the lands of Abercorn and Dalkeith in Midlothian. It was from this William's second son, John de Grame, that the Earls of Montrose claimed their descent.

From William de Grame the family also inherited the lands of Kynaber, Charlton and Borrowfield, to which were added during the thirteenth century the Barony of Dundaff and Strathcarron in Stirlingshire, and that of Kincardine near Auchterarder in Perthshire, with the castle of Kincardine which for many generations was the principal seat of the Grahams. Sir David Grame of Dundaff and Kincardine (sixth in line from William de Grame) was sheriff of the county of Berwick and added the lands of Strathblane in Stirlingshire and Mugdock in Lennox to his growing patrimony, and in 1325 another Sir David[3] obtained the house and estates of Auld Montrose from Robert the Bruce in exchange for the castle of Cardross on the Clyde (where the Bruce subsequently retired to die). In 1445 Sir Patrick Graham,[4] who had been a Lord of Regency during the minority of James III, was raised to the peerage with the title of first Lord Graham, and in 1504 his grandson, William, third Lord Graham, was created first Earl of Montrose by James IV.

The Grahams had cause to be proud. The family had three times intermarried with the royal line and they could claim the blood of kings. A Graham had been the first primate of Scotland. Moreover, if their rise to pre-eminence had been gradual, they were conspicuous among their peers in that their record was an honourable one and relatively unstained by the deeds of savagery and treason which punctuate the early history of Scotland. There had been renegades, such as Sir Robert Graeme of Kinmont, a younger son, who murdered James I, but apart from such rare exceptions the family had developed a tradition of service and loyalty to the national cause. Sir Patrick Graeme[5] had been killed by the English at Dunbar in 1296. His younger brother, Sir John de Graeme, was the trusted friend of William Wallace and fell at Falkirk two years later. Sir David Graeme of Montrose, Patrick's son, had been a supporter of the Bruce, a signatory of the famous letter of independence to the Pope, and one of the few Scots excluded from amnesty by Edward I of England. William, first Earl of Montrose, led a division of the Scottish vanguard at the battle of Flodden and died in the steel ring around the body of the King. A later Graham was killed by a cannon ball at Pinkie. John, third Earl of Montrose, and the most distinguished of his line to date, had been chancellor of the jury that condemned the regent Morton, and thereafter held successively the offices of Lord Lieutenant of the

4

Border, Lord High Treasurer, Lord Chancellor and, when James VI went south to claim the English throne, Viceroy of the Kingdom.

In contrast to his illustrious predecessor, John, fourth Earl of Montrose, apart from being involved in a notable affray in Edinburgh during his youth, appears to have preferred the quiet life of a country gentleman, spending most of his time between his three principal dwellings of Mugdock, Kincardine and Auld Montrose and devoting his leisure hours to golf, hunting with the bow and smoking prodigious quantities of tobacco. He occasionally took a part in public affairs. He supported the Palatinate cause, and was a royal commissioner at the General Assembly at Aberdeen in 1616; and Charles I on his accession appointed him president of the Scottish Privy Council, but he was soon obliged to relinquish the office on account of his deteriorating health. He married Margaret Ruthven, daughter of the Earl of Gowrie, whose ill-fated house was associated with necromancy and dark deeds of violence. Her grandfather had been the grim old Lord of Ruthven who led the murderers of Rizzio. Her father had died on the scaffold for conspiracy, the victim of Arran's intrigue, and her two brothers had been killed at Huntingtower under suspicious circumstances and in the presence of the King. She bore him five daughters and a single son—James Graham—who was born in 1612, possibly in the month of October, and by tradition in the town of Montrose.[6]

It was said that his mother consulted witches at his birth, and the Earl, his father, is alleged to have told a neighbour that the boy 'would trouble all Scotland'. It was also claimed that as a baby he swallowed a live toad, but the same had been said of Morton and the tale was probably intended for an allegory. Such references to strange premonitions possibly originated in the pious superstition of his later opponents, yet in the seventeenth century the belief in witchcraft was very real. As a young man Montrose is said to have visited astrologers in France, and some who knew him afterwards would maintain that he was inspired at least in part by certain prophecies that had been made concerning himself. In the nearer future, a more sinister form of necromancy would cause the ruin of his sister.

If indeed she consulted witches concerning her son, Margaret Ruthven did not live to watch their prophecy mature. She died in 1618. The two eldest daughters married soon after, Margaret Graham in 1619 to Archibald Napier of Merchiston, then Treasurer Depute of Scotland, and Lilias (the elder) to Sir John Colquhoun of Luss the following year. The remaining children, James, Dorothea, Katherine and 'the bairn Beatrix', were brought up by their father who appears to have been genuinely devoted to all of them. However, possibly some time after his wife died, the old earl sired another, bastard, son who was called Harry Graham. As there is no mention of him in the family's accounts of this time, he was probably put out to foster parents, but in later years he would become one of his brother's trusted and loyal lieutenants.

Kincardine Castle was situated near Blackford in the old stewardry of Strathearn, a wild and beautiful district lying in the great valley between the Grampians and the Ochils. It stood on a slightly elevated plateau, surrounded by a moat, looking northwards across the broad, fertile vale of Perthshire to the blue outlines of Schiehallion and the Grampians in the further distance. On its southern side the walls were built on the edge of a steep, wooded bank which descended sharply into the Glen of Kincardine and the rushing Ruthven Water, and its towers and parapets commanded a broad view of Craig Rossie and the Ochils a mile or so away. In this country of hills and glens on the border of the Highlands, the child James Graham learned to ride, wearing out his horse's shoes on the high muirs, and trotting down through Auchterarder and the King's Wood to the smith at Aberuthven whose extant accounts record the shoeing of the Lord James's 'twa naigs' and his favourite white pony. It was a healthy outdoor life, and he grew into a strong and active boy, learning fencing and archery and acquiring the co-ordination and competitive instinct of a sportsman. Most of the time he seems to have stayed at Kincardine, and his earliest companions were probably drawn from the cadet branches of his family–Braco, Orchill and Inchbrakie–who lived nearby. But after he was nine he would sometimes ride with his father to visit his sister Lilias and Sir John Colquhoun of Luss at their house in Rossdhu, where he learned to hunt roebuck with a bow and arrows on the hills above Loch Lomond.

When he was twelve his father decided that it was time to begin his education, and he was entrusted to a certain Master William Forrett, pedagogue, to be prepared for the College of Glasgow. Since the Grahams did not own property in that city, the Earl arranged for him to live at the house of Sir George Elphinstone of Blythswood, the Lord Justice Clerk, near the Townhead, where he was allowed a small but sumptuous establishment suitable to the young son of the nobility. This included a modest stud, since the little household travelled on horseback, a valet, and two pages–William and Mungo Graham–in scarlet liveries. The Lord James was provided with several 'stands' of new clothes, and his personal effects were carefully inventoried:[7] red and green chamber counter cloths, red *figurato* curtains and a red counterpane for his bed, yellow curtains and a yellow counterpane sewn with red, two cushions of arras work, a red embroidered cushion, another of green velvet, and a brown velvet cushion for kneeling on in kirk. For his board he had a red counter cloth, a plain silver cup and another of dimplest work, double gilt, eight silver spoons, 'the knaps whereof were gilt', a silver 'satfatt' of raised work 'one tyre in height' with 'ane lid double over gilt', a quantity of linen and a cabinet to put them in. His personal possessions, which were also itemized, included a gilt sword which had been given to him by Archibald Napier, a scarf of silk and silver tissue–a present from his father–a crossbow set with mother of pearl, and a brazen hagbutt.

For his studies the Earl gave him a number of books from his library which included Sabellicus's *Universal History* in Latin, Camerarius—his living library: *A Treatise on the Order of Knighthood*, Xenophon's *Hellenics*, Stanvage's *Life and Death of Mary, Queen of Scots*, Seneca with Lipsius's commentary, and Fairfax's translation of Tasso's *Gerusalemne Liberata* with a life of Godfrey de Bulloigne. The selection was probably Master Forrett's, but as a mixture of history and romance it was ideally suited to the mind of his young pupil. There is some truth in the old adage that books and presents evince the man.

The Lord James's favourite book, both now and for long afterwards, however, was Sir Walter Raleigh's *History of the World*, which he kept separate from the others and insisted on carrying himself. Raleigh, of course, was dead seven years since, beheaded by an ungrateful king—to the distress of many Englishmen and for the satisfaction of the papist Gondomar—though what the young Graham thought of this one cannot say. But to a boy whose mind even now drew inspiration from the past, the book was an antique echo of a bygone age of spirit and adventure, and there were to be several moments in his life, and most particularly before his own execution, when Montrose would seem to recall some strange affinity with his childhood hero.

During his second year at Glasgow, the old Earl (though still in his prime) fell seriously ill, and Lord James hurried back to Kincardine, arriving two days before his father died on 14 November 1626. The body was lapped in lead to lie in state, while the Grahams gathered to drink the dredgie in the hall and attend the burial feast. The 'funeral' lasted for more than six weeks, and the old Earl's burial was not finally 'accomplished' until 3 January 1627, when he was laid to rest in the family vault at Aberuthven. It was the occasion for a huge family gathering, and it enabled the young heir to meet the many cadet branches of his house. The Earl of Wigton, his cousin-german was there, and his brothers-in-law Lord Napier of Merchiston and Sir John Colquhoun of Luss, and probably the Earl of Menteith and his son Kilpont, and a host of Grahams—Inchbrakie, Braco, Monzie, Gorthy, Fintry, Claverhouse, Garvock, Balgowan, Morphie, Auchincloich, Tamrawer and many others.

And there was considerable family business to transact. The new Earl was barely fourteen and therefore still a minor, and Sir Robert Graham of Morphie, John Graham of Orchill, Sir William Graham of Claverhouse and Lord Napier were nominated as his curators or guardians to manage his affairs until he came of age. While the first three seem to have been mainly involved with administrative detail and the supervision of his estates, Lord Napier deserves further mention as the person who, more than anyone else, now took the place of his father, and was to have the greatest influence during the formative period of his life.

Archibald, first Lord Napier, was the only son of John Napier of Merchiston, the famous philosopher and mathematician, by his first wife Elizabeth, daughter of Sir James Stirling of Keir. He had been seventeen years gentleman of the bedchamber to James VI, a senator of the College of Justice, and subsequently Lord Justice Clerk. James VI had described him as a man 'free of partiality and any factious humour', and recommended him to his son Charles I who created him a baronet of Nova Scotia and raised him to the peerage in 1627 (giving rise to the popular pun–'Napier hath nae peer but yet a peer is he'). He was a member of the Scottish Privy Council from 1615 to 1641, and served both monarchs as Treasurer Depute of Scotland. As such, he had become the target of a smear campaign launched by the Earl of Traquair, who hoped to obtain the lucrative office for himself. Napier successfully defended his innocence before the King, but subsequently resigned from the post, having become sickened by the envy and corruption of court officials. 'There was nothing I desired more in my secret thoughts than to be rid of that place, long before my troubles', he wrote in his Memoir; '. . . having had experience of the chief of Council and Session: and of their manners to which I could never fashion myself; and considering the place I held could never be profitable to a man who had resolved fair and direct dealing.' Wishart called him the wisest head in Scotland–'a man of most innocent life and happy parts; a truly noble gentleman'.

In 1619 he had married Montrose's sister Margaret, whom he described as 'a woman religious, chaste, and beautiful, and my chief joy in this world'. She died sometime after 1628, but the bond between the two families if anything grew stronger. Wishart, Montrose's first biographer, who knew them both, would later write of their relationship: 'This man, when a boy, Montrose looked on as a most tender father; when a youth a most sage monitor; and when a man as a most faithful friend.' His son, also Archibald, would become Montrose's lieutenant and companion in exile. Napier was a staunch Presbyterian, but also a loyal servant of the Crown, and though in the Troubles that followed he opposed the policies of Charles and his archbishop, he was cautious or prescient enough to abstain from the Covenant, which he saw must ultimately threaten the proper prerogatives of the sovereign. His political quarrel, if one can call it that, was against corruption in high office and those who for their own ends deliberately misinformed the king. This set of values he imparted to his young Graham protégé, and those who later accused Montrose of self-seeking and lack of integrity would have done well to study further the character and personal memoranda of his mentor.

After his father's interment the young Montrose stayed for a short time at the home of Lord Kilpont. His eldest unmarried sister, Dorothea, went to live with the Napiers at Merchiston, and Katherine and Beatrix went to their sister Lilias's house at Rossdhu. It was decided that James should not return to Glasgow, and on 26 January 1627 he was installed at St Salvator's College at the University of St Andrews,[8] signing himself in the *Nomina Incorporatorum*–Jacobus Gramus, Comes Monterouse. Master William Forrett was paid off with the sum of 400 merks, with which he declared himself 'completely payit'. In time he was to become tutor in turn to his pupil's two eldest sons. On 28 March the young earl went to Edinburgh to be served heir to his father's title and estates, a legal formality carried through by Mr Thomas Hope, at that time the family's lawyer and subsequently the Covenanting Lord Advocate of Scotland.

During his time at St Andrews Montrose's household was managed by his 'pursemaster', Mr John Lambie, whose detailed accounts provide a remarkable picture of his life at university, although by their nature the emphasis is on recreation rather than on studies. His favourite sport was archery—at the butts and in the field—and his room in college was hung with bows. He played golf on the links (paying five Scottish shillings for a ball) and tennis at the court of Leith. Like others of the nobility he kept a falconer to tend his hawks, hunted regularly (his horse was fed a pint of ale after a day's riding after hounds), and was a frequent visitor to Cupar Races. For indoor games he preferred billiards, chess and cards.

His studies were not altogether neglected, however, since there are references to the purchase of Greek and Latin grammars, and '29/- to a poor scholar who wrote my Lord's notes in school'. Bills for book-binding show that he acquired a copy of Buchanan's works, and Barclay's *Argenis*,[9] and he probably read the Latin and Greek authors— Caesar, Lucan, Plutarch, Livy, Sallust, Catullus, Tacitus, Suetonius (many of these in translation)—through which he acquired, possibly by choice, the classical knowledge of a poet as much as of a scholar. He may have made his own first attempts at lyric verse at this time, and to poor poets he was a sympathetic patron, since the accounts record a gift of 18s. to 'ane rymer called Croter' and 58s. to 'ane Hungarian poet who made some verses to my Lord'.[10] He subscribed to William Lithgow, author of *Adventures and painful peregrinations of long nineteen years travel from Scotland to the most famous kingdoms in Europe, Asia, and Africa*—an imaginative work that lost nothing in the telling; and Lithgow also submitted to him for comment a manu-script called 'The Gushing Tears of Godly Sorrow, containing the causes, conditions, and remedies of Sin, depending mainly upon con-trition and confession; and they seconded with sacred and comfortable passages under the mourning canopy of tears and repentance'—which, notwithstanding its terrifying title, later appeared in print with a suit-able dedication to the young editor.

The Graham was not thrifty, since the sums of money given to the poor exceed the rest. His winnings at the races of over 100 merks were so distributed according to the Statute of 1621, and whenever he rode abroad, at the 'onlouping and lichting' a handful of silver was scattered to the unfortunates who collected near the mounting step, or at the houses which he visited. Drummers and 'pyperers' were his special favourites, and it seems that the young earl, when he rode through town or village, enjoyed a grand entry. His companions of this time from among his own order were Wigton, Colville, Kinghorn, Sinclair, Sutherland and Lindsay of the Byres. (Some of them, ironically, would later be conspicuous among his enemies.) During the holidays he rode to Rossdhu to visit Colquhoun and his sisters, or toured the Graham cadets, or the houses of his friends; and the poor at the gates of Cumbernauld, Glamis, Balcarres and many other places are recorded as having benefited accordingly. While at university he was also a frequent visitor to the Castle of Darsay, home of John Spottiswoode, Archbishop of St Andrews and later Primate. There he probably got to know his son, Sir Robert Spottiswoode, 'the good President' and his devoted friend during the Troubles.

In April 1628 he went to Edinburgh for the marriage of his sister Dorothea to Sir James Rollo of Duncruib. The wedding celebrations lasted from 22 to 29 April, when the party adjourned to Carnock in Fife where the feasting continued until 2 May. On 3 May Montrose rode to Stirling, and back the following day for kirk at Kincardine, two days at Orchill, then to St Andrews on the seventh and the hectic round of Hungarian poets, archery and golf. It seems that he had overdone it, since the accounts record 24 May as the first day of his sickness. On 28 May a Dr Maal from Dundee was sent for, who charged £26 13s. 4d. (Scots), but on 3 June the patient was still ill and a second opinion was required in the person of Dr Arnot, a leech, and from his bill an altogether superior being. Chess and cards were called for, a curtain was hung across his window, and the young earl's hair was shaved off. Dr. Arnot charged £80 (and £16 16s. 0d. for his colleague) and apparently prescribed a diet of 'fresh-water flooks', trout, pigeons, capons, drapped eggs, grouse (out of season), milkbreads and calf's foot jelly, washed down with liquorice, possets, whey, aleberry and claret, and all served up by James Pett's daughter. (James Pett made my lord's golf clubs.) In spite of this, the young earl appears to have made a rapid recovery since on 4 July he won the silver arrow for archery at the butts, which, till the end of his time at St Andrews, he held against all comers.

In October 1628 he gave a great housewarming at Kincardine— possibly to celebrate his sixteenth birthday—and the following March he was formally introduced to Edinburgh society, appearing with gilded spurs and newly 'dichted' sword to pay his respects to the Lord Chancellor and Lord Justice General, the Earl of Kinnoul.

In the summer of 1629 he left St Andrews to get married. The pace of life was quicker in those times, the future more uncertain; and though still a boy he was an only son, and it was his duty to beget an heir who would secure his line. Since August 1628, he had been a frequent visitor to Leuchars and Kinnaird, the houses of David, Lord Carnegie, where he met and grew to know Carnegie's sixth and youngest daughter Magdalen. She was not the first lady of his acquaintance since it seems that during his college days he was something of a gallant and his enemies were later to embarrass him by discovering a casket of letters 'strewn with arcadian compliments' to the young student from the daughters of certain other noble families. But it has the appearance of a love match, since from August 1629 until their marriage in November he was constantly at Kinnaird. Mr Lambie's accounts show too that he began to take a greater interest in fine clothes than hitherto, and bought new gloves, clasps, spurs, combs, waxed boots, a new rapier, laces, masks, carkanets and necklaces, and gilt paper–all somewhat suggestive of a young cavalier embarking on the courtship of his lady.

In dynastic terms, the Graham could have looked higher than a youngest daughter, but his curators supported the marriage. The Carnegies were an old family,[11] and Sir David, the first Lord, was a distinguished man in Scottish affairs. Always a strong supporter of the Crown, he had been chosen to accompany Queen Ann to England when James VI succeeded to the English throne, and on his subsequent visits to Scotland the King had been a guest at Kinnaird. In 1610 he had been appointed commissioner to the Court of High Commission, and at the General Assembly of Aberdeen in 1616 he had been one of the assistants to Montrose's father who was then Royal Commissioner to the Assembly. Carnegie had actively supported James VI's ecclesiastical policy and the following year he had been one of the commissioners who helped secure the passage of the Five Articles by the Assembly at Perth.[12] In that year he was also raised to the peerage for his services to the Crown. Between 1616 and 1625 he was an Extraordinary Lord of Session and from 1617 a member of the Scottish Privy Council, resigning his seat on the bench in accordance with the statute of Charles I that no one could be a Privy Councillor and a Lord of Session at the same time. As Parliamentary Commissioner for Fife he was extremely active in the committees of Parliament and in the various commissions appointed by that body. He was not a statesman or a politician so much as an administrator, and as such he had much to teach the young Montrose–if the pupil had patience enough to learn. Later, perhaps, it would seem that the two were temperamentally not a match, and that Magdalen was closer to her father, but this was for the future and could not spoil the marriage of the moment.

Carnegie's wife, Margaret Lindsay of Edzell, had died in 1614, having given him four sons and six daughters. Of the latter, Margaret, the eldest, was married to Lord Dalhousie, the second, Agnes, to the future Lord Abercrombie and the third, Katherine, to the Earl of Traquair with whom Carnegie jointly administered the estates of Lennox. Now he seems to have welcomed an alliance with the Graham. (The two families were already connected through the marriage of Carnegie's sister Euphemia to Montrose's curator, Graham of Morphie. Indeed, this may have been how the young couple first came to meet each other.)

There is a story that Magdalen was originally betrothed to the Master of Ogilvie, Lord Airlie's son, who until 1626 had lived part of the time at Farnell Castle, barely two miles from Kinnaird.[13] It is said that young Ogilvie was on his way to Kinnaird to ask her hand in marriage when his horse pecked in a stream, and that being superstitious (or, if he fell off, very wet), he decided to proceed no further. The tale has often been dismissed as apocryphal, but the basis at least is true, since Magdalen's rejection of Ogilvie was keenly felt by some members of the Airlie family. This one may gather from a letter written by Margaret Hamilton to her sister the Countess of Airlie in which, referring to a meeting with Carnegie of Balnamoon (Lord Carnegie's nephew), she remarked: 'Drawn Balnamoon upon that purpis to get him ane affront as that family got befor be ye refusal of my Lady Montrose for My Lord youre son.'[14] But the incident does not appear to have soured the relationship between Montrose and Ogilvie since they became comrades in arms and the closest of friends.

A few days before his marriage, Montrose rode north to Aberdeen to receive the freedom of the city. He also had his portrait painted by Jamieson, the Scottish Van Dyck. It was to be Graham of Morphie's wedding present to the bride, and it has hung in Kinnaird Castle ever since. It is a gentle portrait, showing the innocent unmarked face of a boy, with a long Scottish nose, wide grey eyes and chestnut hair with a slight tint of auburn that would grow darker with age. The young earl is magnificently dressed in an olive velvet doublet slashed with silk and edged about in gold. In one corner is the date, 'Anno 1629', and the words 'Aetatis 17'. The artist required only a few sittings and after two days in Aberdeen Montrose rode back via Arbuthnott (the home of another of Carnegie's married daughters— Marjory) to spend the last few days before the wedding at his house of Old Montrose. On Tuesday, 10 November, he and Magdalen Carnegie were married in the parish church of Kinnaird.

Under the terms of the marriage contract, Lord Carnegie was to 'entertain and maintain in home' the young couple until Montrose should come of age, and so the next three years were spent at Kinnaird. They were to be the most peaceful of Montrose's life, and during this time his two eldest sons, John and James, were born.

Kinnaird, as now, was a beautiful place. In 1655 Sir John Ochterlony would describe it as 'A great house, having excellent gardens, parks with fallow deer, orchards, hay meadows wherein are extraordinary quantities of hay, very much planting, an excellent breed of horse, cattle, and sheep, and extraordinary good land; without competition the finest place altogether in the shire'. Montrose's life followed a pleasant and leisurely routine – riding and hunting on the Moor of Monrommon, flying his hawks, golf (often with Colquhoun, who was an occasional visitor), and attending kirk on Sunday. But most of all they were years of quiet and serious study.

And yet, beneath the calm, they were years of impatience, the boy wanting to be a man and about great things. It is reflected in a short verse which he possibly wrote at this time:

> *I would be high; but that the cedar tree*
> *Is blustered down while smaller shrubs grow free.*
> *I would be low; but that the lowly grass*

> *Is trampled down by each unworthy ass.*
> *For to be high, my means they will not do;*
> *And to be low, my mind it will not bow.*
> *Oh Heavens! Oh Fate! When will you once agree*
> *To reconcile my means, my mind, and me?*

The first four lines were not original, but the whole contains the germ of his awakening ambition. He was also fond of epigrams and would copy them or add thoughts of his own inside the covers of his books. As in his copy of Lucan:

> *As Macedo his Homer, I'll thee still*
> *Lucan, esteem thee as my most precious gem;*
> *And though my fortune second not my will,*
> *That I may witness to the world the same*
> *Yet if she would but smile even so on me*
> *My mind desires as his, and soars as high as he.*

and in Caesar's *Commentaries*:

> *Though Caesar's paragon I cannot be*
> *Yet shall I soar in thought as high as he.*

But Alexander was his greatest hero, and in his edition of *Quintus Curtius* he wrote:

> *As Philip's noble son did still disdain*
> *All but the dear applause of merited fame*
> *And nothing harboured in that lofty brain*
> *But how to conquer an eternal name;*
> *So great attempts, heroic ventures shall*
> *Advance my fortune or renown my fall.*

and here perhaps is the origin of the most famous of his later lyric verses:

> *As Alexander I will reign*
> *And I will reign alone.*
> *My thoughts did ever more disdain*
> *A rival on my throne.*
> *He either fears his fate too much*
> *Or his deserts are small*
> *Who dares not put it to the touch*
> *To win, or lose it all.*

In June 1633 Charles I was to come to Scotland to be crowned, but for some reason Montrose did not stay for the coronation. His absence is strange, since he had much to hope for at such an occasion. At the end of 1632 he had entered his twenty-first year and so attained his majority, and it would have been an excellent opportunity at the very start of his career for the young earl to be presented to the King. His antecedents seemed to assure him of the royal favour. His father had been President of the Privy Council, and his grandfather Viceroy of the Kingdom. Nor could he have asked for better sponsors at the time. His father-in-law was high in the royal esteem and about to be created Earl of Southesk, and Napier was to be one of the four peers chosen to hold the canopy over the King's head. Moreover he was widely thought of as one of the rising stars of the young generation, and William Lithgow, in his poem 'Scotland's welcome to her native son and Sovereign Lord, King Charles', written in advance for the occasion, had singled out the Graham as a young man of great expectations:

> *As for that hopeful youth, the young Lord Graham,*
> *James, Earl of Monterose, whose warlike name*
> *Sprung from redoubted worth, made manhood try*
> *Their matchless deeds in unmatched chivalry,*
> *I do bequeath him to your gracious love;*
> *Whose noble stock did ever faithful prove*
> *To thine old-aged ancestors, and my Bounds*
> *Were often freed from thralldom by their wounds;*
> *Leaving their root, the stamp of fidele truth,*
> *To be inherent in this noble youth;*
> *Whose heart, whose hands, whose swords, whose deeds, whose fame,*
> *Made Mars for valour canonize the Graham.*

But in 1633 Montrose was on the continent.

The reason for his departure from Scotland was almost certainly not political, though there were many Scots who expressed dissatisfaction at the King's delaying eight years before coming north to be crowned in his second kingdom and the land of his birth. It may have been partly due to impatience – a desire on coming of age to get away from the now dull routine of Kinnaird and see something of the world. In those days an extended continental tour was regarded as an essential part of a young Scottish nobleman's further education, and with his fondness for Raleigh and the fantastic works of Lithgow, Montrose had developed a thirst for foreign travel. Yet, had that only been the case, Napier and the other members of his family would surely have persuaded him to wait until after Charles's coronation.

A more likely reason for his leaving when he did was a particularly unpleasant and sinister scandal involving his younger sister Katherine, who was seduced and carried off by her brother-in-law, Colquhoun of Luss. But Colquhoun was charged with necromancy, not incest, since it was said that he had accomplished his evil design through the agency of a German servant called Carlippis–'ane necromancer'– who had used certain love philtres and 'a jewel of gold set with divers precious diamonds or rubies which was poisoned and intoxicat' to bewitch the girl and bring about her ruin. Colquhoun and his 'familiar' were excommunicated and publicly put to the horn. Montrose probably took it badly, since Rossdhu had been a favourite haunt of his childhood, and Katherine the closest of his sisters, while Colquhoun

14

he had trusted as her guardian and his supposed friend. Possibly he felt tainted by it and was unwilling to face the King with such a recent stain, as he saw it, upon his family honour. More probably he set out to find his sister, and, given his spirited temperament, to avenge himself upon Colquhoun. (The couple had fled from Scotland the previous year, but it was known that they had lived in London for a while before going to the continent.) In the event, he never found them. When Colquhoun returned in 1647, things had changed and he received a full pardon. Katherine disappeared forever.[15]

Comparatively little is known about Montrose's travels in Europe. He set out some time in the beginning of 1633, accompanied by Mr John Lambie, young Graham of Morphie, Basil Fielding (Lord Denbigh's son) and a young clerk called Thomas Saintserf, who recorded that they visited France and Italy,

> ... where he made it his business to pick up the best of their qualities necessary for a person of honour. Having rendered himself perfect in the academics his next delight was to improve his intellectuals, which he did by allotting a proportionable time to reading and conversing with learned men; yet still so that he used his exercise as he might not forget it. He studied as much of the Mathematics as is required for a soldier. But his great study was to read men and the actions of great men.

In France he attended the famous school of arms at Angers where he first began to study seriously the military art. The Thirty Years' War still raged in Europe, and the continent was a breeding ground for soldiers. This was where Montrose's inclinations lay, and his own campaigns in later years show that he made a special study of the tactics developed by Gustavus Adolphus (who had been killed at Lützen only a few months before). He became skilled in the use of weapons. Saintserf recalled of him: 'As he was strong of body and limbs, so was he most agile, which made him excel most of others in those exercises where these two are required. In riding the great horse and making use of his arms he came short of none. I never heard much of his delight in dancing though his countenance and his other bodily endowments were equally fitting the court as the camp.'

The young Denbigh later told Burnet[16] that, while they were in France, he and Montrose consulted a number of astrologers. 'I plainly saw that the Earl of Denbigh relied on what had been told him to his dying day; and the rather because the Earl of Montrose was promised a glorious future for some time, but all was to be overthrown in conclusion.' Burnet wrote with the advantage of hindsight, and where Montrose is concerned he is rarely to be trusted, but there may be some truth in the story since in later years Montrose appears to have had a belief in destiny which is otherwise almost inexplicable. It was not uncommon for people of quality to consult astrologers, and it is quite possible that the young man with his burning ambitions looked to make a conscious compact with his fate.

Some time during his travels he acquired a little French Bible, which has survived, much rat-eaten, at Innerpeffray. His large bold signature is on the first three pages, and as usual the fly leaves are covered with epigrams (though there are signs that he was growing older):

La vita passa, la morte viene; Beato colui chi havra fatto bene.
(Life passes, death comes; Blessed is he who shall have done the right.)

Honor mihi vita potior.
(I prefer honour to life.)

Ardito e presto.
(Courageous and swift.)

Aut solvam, aut diruam.
(If I cannot untie it, I shall cut the knot.)

And on one page, a strange doodle combining the letters J, M and E above a drawing of roses set among thorns and transfixed by a cross, with the lines: '*Non crescunt sine spinis*' (They do not grow without thorns) and, below, '*Pro jocundis, aptissima quoque Deus dat*' (God gives us those things which are most fitting for us).[17] The Italian quotations are an echo of his time in Italy where early in 1633 he dined with Lord Angus (later the Douglas) and others at the English College in Rome.

'Thus,' said Saintserf, 'he spent three years in France and Italy: and would have surveyed the wonders of the East, if his domestic affairs had not obliged his return.' Important developments were taking place in Scotland, and probably Napier and his other friends were anxiously calling him home. In 1636 he returned via London, where he approached the Marquis of Hamilton to be his sponsor at court, stating that he wished 'to put himself in the service of the King'.

Of Hamilton, more anon, since he was to play a disastrous part in the Troubles to come. The Hamiltons were the senior branch of the Stewart family besides the royal line, a fact of ancestry that made the Marquis a prey to uneasy yet undefined ambition, since he stood next in succession to the Scottish throne after the descendants of James VI. He and Charles had been brought up together, and after Buckingham's assassination and Charles's accession he had succeeded to the position of royal favourite as Master of the Horse and Gentleman of the Bedchamber. He had more recently been made a member of the privy councils of both kingdoms and the King's principal adviser on Scottish affairs, a post more appropriate to his rank than to any intellectual ability that he might have possessed. He was by nature melancholic, tortuous and pessimistic in his thought, and given to irresolute intrigue, but his natural taciturnity led many to think him wiser than he was. As he had held a minor command under Gustavus and had a tendency to expound on matters military, he was also reckoned to be a soldier, but in fact his sole experience of war had consisted of a prolonged and somewhat inglorious period of garrison duty, since Gustavus (who was a judge of men) had not thought to employ him in the field. He was the victim, in a sense, of overestimation, and the King believed him to be more able and trustworthy than he was, while his enemies looked on him as being more dangerous than he deserved. Buchan, following the verdict of Hamilton's contemporary Clarendon, sums him up as a man whose 'life was one long pose, but the poses were many and contradictory, and the world came to regard as a knave one who was principally a fool'.[18]

Yet it was natural for Montrose to have asked him to be his sponsor. Hamilton was the senior member of the Scottish nobility at the English court, and could guarantee the patronage of the King. Moreover, Montrose had toured the continent with Denbigh, who was Hamilton's brother-in-law, and who may even have helped effect the introduction.

According to Heylin,[19] who claimed to have had much of his information from Napier and is therefore a good authority, Hamilton however viewed Montrose's presence with alarm. The young Graham was altogether too prepossessing, and the nervous Marquis looked on him as a potential rival in the King's affections. He therefore agreed to present Montrose to Charles but warned him that 'the King was wholly given up to the English, that he discountenanced and slighted his own countrymen', and that he wished to reduce Scotland to the state of a mere province. As for himself, he said, but for the hope of doing his country some small service he would not remain where he was a day longer, so many were the indignities put upon him!

'This done, he repairs to the King, tells him of the Earl's return from France, and of his purpose to attend him at the time appointed, but that he was so powerful, so popular, and of such esteem among the Scots by reason of an old descent from the royal family that if he were not nipped in the bud, as we used to say, he might endanger the King's interest and affairs in Scotland.' When Montrose was presented to the King in front of the court, Charles merely extended him a hand to kiss and coldly turned away. The young earl's hopes of entering the royal service were thus dashed at the outset, and the snub was the worse in that it was public.

It was afterwards alleged by Montrose's critics that, angry and disappointed by this personal slight, he returned to Scotland and at once allied himself with the King's opponents in that country, so that he has often come to be represented as a man who was motivated, not by those grand ideals which he later claimed to possess, but by injured vanity, pique and plain ambition. This, however, is a distortion, both of his character and of his actions immediately after the event. It is true that he returned to find that he had become a figure of considerable interest to the Scottish faction leaders, who hoped to secure for their cause the prestige which his name alone would bring as well as the talent and the enthusiasm which the King had so carelessly rejected. But he did nothing that could be called impetuous, since almost a year elapsed before he emerged as the protégé of the Covenant party. The intervening months were spent in quiet seclusion with his wife and family on one of his country estates, although he was probably lobbied and flattered continually by the Earl of Rothes and other leaders of the Presbyterian interest. When he finally decided to support the cause of the National Covenant, his commitment was total: such was his nature. And it is also true that, in reaching his decision, the personal affection for Charles, which was to influence him later, was non-existent. But the real importance of the incident at court was that it seemed to confirm what Hamilton had told him. He had been snubbed not for himself, since he had done nothing to offend (apart from missing the coronation), but because he was a Scot. Patriotic sentiment would therefore blend with constitutional principle, but he had neither the experience nor the perspective to appreciate that the politics of some of his contemporaries were less clear-cut. As for Hamilton, who had been responsible for this unfortunate and unnecessary gesture, the enmity and contempt came later.

2

Prelates and Presbyters, and the Distemper of the Scots

I know nothing but that Kings and armies and Parliaments might have been quiet at this day if they would have left Israel alone.[1]

In order to understand the situation in Scotland in 1637, and the decision that now confronted Montrose, it is necessary briefly to look back over eighty years of Scottish history, to the Scottish Reformation, and to the quarrel and the policy begun by James VI which had matured into the fateful inheritance of Charles.

Prior to the sixteenth century, Scotland had no recognizable tradition of religious radicalism, and the early heresies such as Lollardry had gained few adherents in the North. Nor did Presbyterianism as a mature creed or theory of church government come suddenly into being with the first Band of 1557, which denounced the Papacy and demanded the introduction of the English Prayer Book. The Scottish Reformation, as an event, was largely a political affair, and in contrast to England, where the Crown itself provoked the breach with Rome, it was imposed upon a reluctant monarchy by a nobility whose motives in most cases were other than religious.

By comparison with Marian England, there had been few Protestant martyrs. In 1528 Patrick Hamilton was burned at the stake for proclaiming Luther's doctrine of justification by faith, and in 1546 George Wishart was similarly executed for preaching the Swiss Protestant doctrine, which rejected all beliefs and practices that were not directly founded upon Scripture. During the 1530s Protestant ideas continued to spread, and despite a series of Acts against heresy the movement grew apace. The illegal importation of Tynedale's English Bible encouraged it, and small congregations who used the English Prayer Book were sustained by the resolution of a new generation of preachers such as John Knox who had broken with the Old Church and the authority of Rome. From the beginning the movement

19

contained a strongly iconoclastic element, and there was much smashing of images and stained glass windows, but in the corruption and wealth of the Romish Church there was much to provoke a destructive reaction. Yet though Protestantism found strong popular support in the towns, the reformers and their variegated congregations had not the strength in themselves to precipitate a revolution against a French and Catholic regent who had the backing of an army of foreign mercenaries. The Reformation came about because a large section of the nobility, drawn mainly from the lesser baronage and certain magnates out of favour, saw in the movement a means to advance their secular interests and enhance their material prosperity. Their motives were various, but they led to the same end. Many cast covetous eyes upon the rich lands of the Old Church, or resented the payment of tithes to an institution that had become too ostentatiously wealthy and corrupt. Others, without the necessary influence at Court and so without hope of having a relative nominated to a lucrative benefice, looked to participate directly in the spoliation of monastic lands, while greater lords, out of favour and neglected in the councils of state, saw here a vehicle which could carry them to influence and power. Xenophobia too played an important part—an anti-French feeling directed against the French regent, Mary of Lorraine, and an absent French queen (who was to become Mary Queen of Scots), so that by some twisted irony to be patriotic was to be pro-English which was to be Protestant, and so to be Protestant was to be patriotic and anti-French. It was a jumbled equation, but for the moment it was effective.[2] In 1559 the Lords of the Congregation swore to defend Protestantism and to free the country from 'the bondage and tyranny of strangers'. In 1560, following the defeat of the regent through the intervention of an English fleet, the Scottish Parliament accepted Knox's 'Confession of Faith'.

So, then, was Presbyterianism born, but it was a still uncertain thing. Beneath the surface was the Calvinistic dynamism of an emergent and victorious faith; yet outwardly it was cautious, its way unclear. The later characteristics of a dogmatic and intolerant theocracy may have existed in embryo, but they had not yet grown into a hard body of doctrine. It had gained recognition, but little more. By its nature the alliance with the nobles was temporary and could not last – at least, not on the nobles' terms. They had not pulled down one ecclesiastical tyranny only to replace it by another. Nor were they prepared to disgorge the lands of the Old Church to support the new. Knox's grand design for a system of education and welfare under the aegis of the Kirk survived only in his own 'devout imagination'.

It has sometimes been supposed that the entire scheme of a Presbyterian polity existed in the mind of Knox from the beginning, but this was not the case. The first Presbyterian institutions developed in an almost haphazard way. Moreover, the theological content of the Kirk in its early days was comparatively low. The preoccupation was with organization and with the participation of the people rather than with academic doctrine, and the early liturgy (a set of guiding principles rather than a list of formal rules) was modelled on that of England. It was 'Congregationalism with a dash of episcopacy',[3] for although Knox rejected papal theories of apostolic succession, he did not altogether reject an hierarchical system of church government. The ministers were elected by their congregations, but over them were superintendents who in many ways were similar to bishops in everything but name. In 1572 the Concordat of Leith recognized the continuation of episcopacy in Scotland. The Catholic bishops, deprived of spiritual power and authority, had been permitted to reside in their old dioceses for their lifetime, and the Concordat now provided for the nomination of Protestant bishops to sees as they became vacant. Knox, despite his fears that bishops could become mere instruments of the Crown, yet gave the Concordat his blessing. It was a limited episcopacy, and compatible with Scottish practice.

Yet at the same time, there were a number of factors peculiar to the situation in Scotland which would shape the future attitudes of the Presbyterians and predetermine the direction which the new Kirk would take. In England the Crown had arrogated to itself the power of which the Papacy had been deprived. The King had become supreme head of the Church, defender of the faith, and the consequent government of the Church remained hierarchical and essentially authoritarian. The initial royal impulse had been as much schismatic as heretical, and the austerities of Calvinism did not appeal. The high Anglicans of the seventeenth century still appealed to other authority than the bare scriptures. They held that the Reformation had not involved a complete breach of continuity with the past. They believed in a 'catholic and apostolic Church' and one which, being national and uniform, was closely connected to the authority of the Crown. In Scotland, however, the Reformed Church came into being in spite of, and in opposition to, the monarch. The Catholic Mary Queen of Scots could not be its head, and for lack of a Protestant prince the vacuum at the top was filled by a system of government through a General Assembly, which in these early days was a genuinely representative body of clergy and laity together. This, and the system of lay elders, enhanced the lay aspect of the Kirk and gave it an essentially democratic appearance. The nature of the Reformation and the hostility of the Crown also made it suspicious of the civil authority which it came to judge in terms of whether or not it ruled 'in accordance with the Word of God' – and in practice this ultimately came to mean whether or not it was friendly to the interests of the Kirk.

Once the Kirk had become established, in its own eyes at least, the apologetics of its creed were bound to harden. In theory, the idea of the Reformers was to restore the purity and simplicity of the early Church whose teachings were based on the divine revelation of the Bible, and to re-emphasize the direct relationship which the individual soul was at liberty to achieve with God. However, in practice the intellectual legacy of the Middle Ages still enthralled them, and the pioneers of Presbyterianism were not yet able to distinguish between individual liberty of conscience and more sinister conceptions of religious anarchy. They drew from their medieval inheritance the concept of a universal Church and the right to enforce a uniformity of religion in the genuine belief that theirs was the only system that was divine. Carried to extremes, it could follow that coercion was the duty of the faithful, and it could also lead to an internal discipline as dogmatic and oppressive as that which had seemed so intolerable before. Presbyterianism was to share the characteristic of many developing ideologies in that, when the founders of the movement had departed from the scene, those who came after tended to expand their claims, or imprison within rigid definitions concepts which the early reformers had voiced none too coherently, until finally they would come close to the very doctrine of an external infallible canon which their predecessors had rejected.

When Knox died, a new and rigidly academic theology entered the Kirk which was to determine and shape the later extreme doctrines of Scottish Presbyterianism. Its protagonist was Andrew Melville, who in Geneva had been a disciple of Theodore de Bèze, the religious revolutionary who had disrupted Calvin's own reformed church in Switzerland. Its most immediate impact was on the system of church government and the relationship between the Kirk and the civil power. Knox had accepted an hierarchical element in church government, and, though often contradictory in his public statements, he seems also to have accepted that, in a Christian state, the last word lay with the civil authority. Melville rejected both. He denounced episcopacy as having no basis in the Scriptures and preached instead the parity of ministers. To him, the basic concept of Presbyterianism was of a free autonomous community under the headship of Jesus Christ – whose authority could overrule any lesser sanction. It followed that the authority of the Church was different from and superior to that of the civil power which must conform to the Kirk in matters of conscience and religion. Melville's Second Book of Discipline put forward the extreme doctrine of the 'Twa Kingdoms': the kingdom of the monarch, and the kingdom of Christ in which the Prince on earth was but God's 'silly vassal'. 'To Discipline must all the Estates within this realm be subject, as well Rulers as they that are ruled.' The ministers of the Kirk exercised no civil jurisdiction, yet they were to instruct the civil magistrates as to how it should be exercised. The actions of all men, the King included, were ultimately to be measured against a concept of divine law. Not least, behind this theoretical authority of the Kirk was the practical weapon of excommunication and the additional civil penalties that accompanied it.

It had the merits of democracy had it not been theocratic, and theocracy in practice cannot be democratic. Taken out of time and space it was a claim to spiritual leadership. But in the sixteenth century it was also a claim to political power, for in an age where politics and religion were so closely intertwined, within such a doctrine it would become increasingly difficult to differentiate between the things of God and of Caesar. It was a claim to be the *'imperium in imperio'*, and as such it was a danger which princes could not long ignore. In 1590 Elizabeth of England wrote to James VI:

> Let me warn you, there is risen in both your realm and mine, a sect of perilous consequence, such as would have no Kings but a Presbytery, and take our place while they enjoy our privileges, with a shade of God's Word, which none is judged to follow right without by their censure they be so deemed.

James had already encountered Andrew Melville and needed no such warning to remind him of the Kirk's pretensions. 'A Scottish Presbytery agreeth as well with Monarchy as God with the Devil.' The compromises and conflicts of the next fifty years revolved around the Crown's counter-claim to be God's viceroy, and its attempts to bring the leaders of the Kirk within the body politic and responsible to their sovereign on earth. Episcopacy was the keystone of the royal policy, since only through an hierarchical system of church government and the institution of bishops could the Hildebrandine authoritarianism of the new Kirk be contained and the prerogative of the Crown preserved in matters ecclesiastical.

As opposed to the growing solidarity and organization of the early Presbyterian Church, before James VI came to the throne there was no strong apparatus of secular government in Scotland. In a feudal society such as existed in Scotland during the sixteenth century, the monarchy was strong only when a strong king occupied the throne. But a series of regencies and royal minorities had seriously weakened the power of the Crown. Since the death of Robert III in 1406, six kings and a queen had succeeded to the throne, each of them a minor at the time of his accession. Each of them, on coming of age, had found the government in the hands of a group of powerful magnates, and three had won back their power by defeating the dominant faction in arms. The monarchy was not hedged about by any particular aura of reverence or concept of divine right, and the common origin of the Stuarts made their position particularly weak in dynastic terms. The nobles supported the Crown when they did not happen to be rebelling against it–and they did both in furtherance of their individual feudal ambitions. Traditional politics in Scotland followed a pattern of struggle between groups, or 'bands', of nobles for control of the means of government–which often meant securing the person of the sovereign. Yet their attitude towards the Crown was considerably more flexible than their relationships with one another, and the craft of a king lay in having a sound knowledge of the feudal relationships between the great lords and the lesser baronage, and in the successful exploitation of conflicting groups.[4] For there were no strong institutions for the monarch to fall back on. The Crown was poor, with an inherent executive weakness which stemmed from a conciliar form of government. Parliament was essentially the passive instrument of whichever faction happened to be in power. To this uneasy amalgam the growing power of the Reformed Church brought a new and volatile dimension.

James VI was considerably more competent than many history books would give him credit for. The picture has come down of a grotesque, slobbering, rheumy-eyed, frog-like figure, in turns pedantic, timorous, coarse, besotted and possibly homosexual. But although he was the least attractive and perhaps the least accomplished of the Stuarts, he was the luckiest, and in many ways the most successful. Having survived his minority (no mean feat), he set out to revive the power and the concept of monarchy, and he developed for the purpose a theory of 'kingcraft'—which, when he practised it, stood him in good stead—and a notion of divine right—which was to prove fatal to his successor who believed in it.

James's notions of absolute monarchy were fundamentally incompatible with the theocratic pretensions of the new Kirk and a struggle between the king and the extreme Presbyterians became inevitable. The ministers' persistence in meddling in political affairs upon the most specious of excuses, their inflammatory sermons against the King and his Council in language that was both indecent and prejudicial to the dignity of the Crown, and the Kirk's support of the faction who kidnapped James in what was known as the Raid of Ruthven, all served to convince him that the concept of presbytery was basically inimical to the establishment of monarchy. But at first, circumstances compelled him to act prudently, and while he was king of Scotland only, his fortunes fluctuated according to his varying grip on power. External factors, and not least the policies of Elizabeth, whom one day it was his ambition to succeed on the English throne, also obliged him in the early years to proceed with caution and restraint.

However, despite early setbacks, James's determination to control the Kirk remained undiminished, and the middle years of his reign saw the application of his 'kingcraft' at its best. By 1596 Elizabeth, freed from the immediate Catholic threat which hitherto had obliged her to sustain the Protestant garboil in Scotland, was beginning to persecute puritans on her own account, and James could launch his political offensive against the Kirk without fear of English interference. By degrees he arrogated to himself the right to appoint the time and place for the meetings of the General Assembly, and used this advantage to remove it from Edinburgh which was the main centre of the extremists' support. This gave him a greater opportunity to exploit the divisions among the moderate Presbyterian ministers, not all of whom shared Melville's extreme views, and to beguile those who seemed susceptible to royal flattery or the sacerdotal vanities which episcopacy had to offer. The better to obtain control over the business transacted in the Assembly, he induced it to accept a standing commission which in time was to become 'the King's led horse'. He also supported the suggestion that the Kirk should be represented in Parliament, and in 1597—on a petition of the Commission of Assembly–that body enacted that such ministers as the king should promote to the dignity of prelate should take their seats in the Estates as representatives of the vacant sees. The next year, at a General Assembly at Dundee (from which Melville was excluded), James gave an assurance that it was not his wish 'to bring in Papistical or Anglican Bishops, but only to have the best and wisest of the ministers appointed by the General Assembly to have a place in Council and in Parliament'. A small majority voted in favour of fifty-one ministers (the traditional number allotted to the second Estate) being given seats in Parliament. This was the nucleus of a future episcopacy, and though in 1600 an Assembly at Montrose tried to limit the position of the new bishops by a number of caveats, the Trojan Horse was within the city walls.

In 1603 James succeeded to the English throne and with it to the strong machinery of central government created by the Tudors. This sudden improvement in his situation and the increase of power which he acquired thereby served to encourage his already exaggerated notions of sovereignty and enabled him to give freer reign to those despotic tendencies which he had hitherto been forced to curb and restrain. The instruments of absolute monarchy felt attractive to his touch. The English nobility had lost the habit of rebellion. The smooth flattery of the English clergy contrasted pleasurably with the rude polemics of the Scottish brethren. Come thus from poverty to wealth, James plainly found the change agreeable, and it was characteristic of him that he was not content merely to use his new power but felt obliged to theorize about it. One of his Scottish domestics who accompanied him to England is said to have remarked with considerable prescience: 'A plague of these people. They will spoil a good King.'

Scotland now had an absentee monarch and was to derive but little comfort thereby. At first there was a certain element of pride that a Scottish King should have succeeded to the throne of the 'auld enemy', but in the long term the union of crowns was to have a prejudicial effect on Scotland's independence since while both countries persisted in maintaining their own laws and institutions, the poorer of the two–and Scotland was by very much the poorer–must ultimately come into subjection. Despite his promise to return every three years, James inevitably became more absorbed in the affairs of his wealthier kingdom and preferred to govern Scotland as if it were a province– through a Privy Council which in time came to consist almost entirely of royalist officials who in turn controlled the Scottish Parliament through its administrative committee known as the Lords of the Articles. He was wont to boast that 'Here I sit and govern by my pen. I write, and it is done, and by a clerk of the Council I govern Scotland now, which others could not do by the sword.' But James could get away with it because of his Scottish experience and his knowledge of the interplay of faction and interest which governed Scottish politics. Subsequently the gradual estrangement of the monarchy was to be an important factor in 'the Troubles'. It created a vacuum in Scottish politics which had always depended upon contact. Admittedly the King was safer than he had been hitherto, but he was also inaccessible and out of touch. Finally, it was inevitable that Scotland, as the weaker partner, should become increasingly sensitive about its traditions, rights and privileges, as distinct from those of England. English 'encroachments' would be particularly resented and a highly conservative and suspicious sense of nationalism developed in defence of what were regarded as Scotland's institutions–and in particular of its own 'peculiar institution', the Kirk.

The accession of power and patronage which he had acquired with the English throne now enabled James to put his long cherished designs into effect. From the security of his new kingdom he proceeded to reorganize the Scottish Church and his methods were considerably more authoritarian than hitherto. He did not convene the General Assembly in 1603 or 1604, and when in 1605 a group of ministers attempted to hold an Assembly of their own, the meeting was banned by the Privy Council and the nineteen clergy who were bold enough to attend were either fined or exiled for high treason. In 1606 James summoned Melville and seven other Presbyterian ministers to Hampton Court for a lecture on the merits of episcopacy, after which six only were allowed to return home to Scotland and Melville was imprisoned and subsequently exiled for life. Also in 1606 the Scottish Parliament enacted legislation restoring 'the estate of Bishops', and in the same year a convention at Linlithgow (which the King later claimed had the authority of an Assembly) agreed to the nomination of 'constant moderators' for provincial synods as well as Presbyteries, thus giving bishops power over the clergy in their dioceses. An Act of 1609 returned to prelates the jurisdictions they had lost at the time of the Reformation, and in 1610 each archbishop was given a Court of High Commission. In that year a subservient General Assembly agreed to the innovations and in 1612 they were ratified by an equally subservient Parliament.

James had been remarkably successful, but the measure of his success lay not in the application of those theories of kingship to which he pretended, but in the elements of compromise and compatibility that existed within the settlement and in the techniques by which he achieved it. Despite his personal propensity towards despotism, he acted through institutions and not by royal warrant alone. His favourite method seems to have been to obtain concessions from the Scottish Parliament or from informal and nominated bodies of the clergy and then to enlarge these concessions with a vigorous use of the prerogative before confronting the General Assembly with a *fait accompli* and extracting its acquiescence.[5] But though he was often tortuous and dishonest in his dealings, and though the institutions that served his will were on occasion subjected to outrageous pressure, the resultant measures were, by a reasonable stretch of the imagination, con-stitutional since it could be claimed that they had the sanction of Scottish law. Moreover, James was generally open to persuasion and argument in matters concerning policy and administrative convenience. The pedant could give way to the politician.

The episcopacy thus established was a limited and parliamentary one only–a superstructure added to a Presbyterian foundation–and did not affect the lives and worship of the common people. It enraged the extremists, but the moderates accepted bishops even though they may not really have wanted them. Moreover, the Jacobean prelates had themselves grown up in the Presbyterian tradition and shared with the ministers a common dread of popery. Consequently 'they took little upon them', and their appointment, though unwelcome in extreme Presbyterian circles, aroused no great religious controversy.

But unfortunately James was not content, and he now embarked on a further series of measures which he would not have dared to attempt had he still been king of Scotland only. Since arriving in England he had been exploring the possibilities that being head of the Church might afford, and he found much in the doctrine and ritual of the Anglican Church that appealed to his conception of the divine right of kings. Aware of the influence of religion in the minds of his subjects, he thought to gain control too of that principle, and when he announced that his aim was to establish 'One worship of God; one kingdom entirely governed; one uniformity of law', it was a uniformity on the English model that he had in mind. This now led him to embark on the dangerous experiment of introducing Anglican rituals and ceremonies into the Scottish Kirk.

In 1617 he returned to Scotland accompanied by a number of Anglican advisers including one William Laud, the dean of Gloucester. The English service was introduced into the Royal chapel and the officiating ministers wore white surplices and served communion to the King upon his knees in the High Church fashion. Such papistical customs greatly alarmed the Scots, and Archbishop Spottiswoode and other moderate bishops tried to warn James that the time was not yet ripe to introduce any changes in ritual. But the following year, against their advice, he coerced a General Assembly at Perth into accepting a number of innovations known as the Five Articles. These provided that the Sacrament should be received kneeling and that it should be available to the sick in private. Baptism was also permitted in private houses; children were to be confirmed by a bishop; and the birth, passion, resurrection and ascension of Jesus Christ were to be commemorated on the appointed days. The Assembly was subjected to outrageous pressure. The King's letter was read several times to bully the fainter-hearted, and as the members voted the commissioners (of whom Carnegie was one) reminded each in turn: 'Remember the King: Have the King on your mind', while the names of the dissenters were ostentatiously recorded. In 1621 the Articles were ratified in Parliament.

Well might the extremists claim that they could hear the footsteps of popery without the door. The Articles aroused the deep suspicion of the Scottish people and were to remain a smouldering grievance in the North. Yet they were not overtly opposed. Though English impositions, they had been imposed however arbitrarily under Scottish law and their practical effect was small since they were more honoured in the breach than in the observance. Even in later troubled times Spottiswoode could refer to them as 'a matter of moonshine'. James wisely went no further. 'I promised that I would try their obedience no further anent ecclesiastical affairs, nor put them out of their own way which custom has made pleasing to them.' Unfortunately, while James's pretensions were remembered by his son, this particular promise was forgotten.

Perhaps the dragon's teeth were sown, but the harvest was not in reckonable view. Though the attitude of the Presbyterians was hardening they had neither the leadership nor the muscle to resist, nor the right allies to provoke an open revolt. James had kept the nation divided, and the nobles who had allied themselves with the Kirk at the Reformation now sided with the King. Many favoured bishops to discipline the clergy. More had acquired church lands they did not intend to disgorge. Beneath the surface was a murmuring suspicion, an essential vitality within the Kirk, a watchful nationalism. But James knew his people, and while the acquaintance lasted, a semblance of peace yet ruled in Israel.

In 1625 James died of a tertian ague, and a stranger came to the throne of the two kingdoms. Although Charles I had been born in Scotland,[6] he had left the country at the age of four and did not return for nearly thirty years. He knew little about the land of his birth, its institutions or the life of its people. His only contact was with the Scots who came to Court, but he knew them as individuals, and understood little of their heritage, their family connections or the subtle ties that attached them and others of their kind together. His horizon was bounded by the protracted and artificial limits of the Court, where formal protocol protected him from the harsh realities of life outside and disguised the true abilities of the courtiers and advisers whose judgement, through lack of confidence, he trusted rather than his own. And like others of his ill-fated house he had the unfortunate habit of placing his faith in those who were themselves unfaithful.

It is perhaps one of the ironies of history that he became king by accident of death, since, had his elder brother Henry lived, he might have entered the Church (as the old King may have intended) or at least been free to pass his life in some other aesthetic quiet removed from the complexities of seventeenth-century politics. He had been the neglected second son, of an introverted and religious turn of mind, a fragile child who stammered, isolated from the world and fellow men by a natural shyness and reserve. Yet like many of the Stuarts he had a strange attraction, and even in the retrospect sympathy and judgement run counter and conflict. He had undoubted courage, and the determination to conquer his debility. He had perseverance and a constancy of purpose, but it was a constancy that made him obstinate and a purpose that was not tempered by comprehension or human understanding. He had that inflexibility which is wrongly associated with strength of character and it concealed a strange sense of inferiority and incompetence in government. He had the manners and bearing of a king that his father had lacked, but he had neither the practical worldliness nor the shrewd political sense that had been the old King's greatest attributes.

He saw himself as completing James's work, and he pursued this end with an implacable sense of duty. He succeeded to the exaggerated notions of divine right which were James's dangerous legacy to monarchy, but though he had inherited the theory he could not inherit the hard experience of practical government. His inflexible thought made no distinction between principle and policy and what James had pursued for a political reason Charles now followed as an act of faith. The pedant gave place to the zealot. He was resolved that the Kirk of Scotland should conform to the Church of England, and the Scots were to discover that their new King did not admit of compromise.

Quite apart from his own religious inclination, it was natural that Charles, under pressure from the parliamentary Puritans in England, should have indulged that institution which supported the concept of royal absolutism which he believed to be the rightful legacy of the Tudors. But while under the Tudor monarchs the Church had been virtually a department of state, during Charles's reign it was elevated to a sort of sacred partnership.[7] The association would ultimately prove fatal to both, since the humour of the nation was running clean contrary to the old superstitions, while it was Charles's fate to face the inevitable reaction to four generations of Tudor absolutism. James himself had been increasingly attracted to the rituals of high Anglicanism, but he had used churchmen as advisers only. Charles tended to use them as guides–and none more so than William Laud.

James had taken Laud to Scotland with him in 1617, but he had kept him on a tight leash. 'He was a restless spirit who could not see when matters are well, but loves to toss and change, and bring things to a pitch of Reformation floating in his own brain which may endanger the steadfastness of that which is in a good pass.' 'Laud knows not the stomach of these people [the Scots].' And when solicited for Laud's promotion, the old King had remarked: 'Take him since you will have him, but ye will surely repent it!' Under Charles he rose from Dean of Gloucester to become Bishop of London (1628) and finally Archbishop of Canterbury (1633).

Laud has been described as 'a virtuous man if severity of manners and abstinence from pleasure deserve that epithet'.[8] He was not particularly gifted, since his vision if anything was confined to the short term, while his intellect was narrow and devoid of human consideration. He is said to have had an unfortunate manner–temperamental, easily roused to anger when crossed, brusque and often rude in his dealings with people; and, like Charles himself, he had a tendency to give

29

offence without realizing how or why he did so. Above all, he was zealous and unrelenting in the cause of his religion. He was pre-occupied with decency and orderliness, with ritual and the form and garments of religion, and he was fanatic in the cause of uniformity which he was determined to impose upon recalcitrant Presbyterians and Puritans whose irregularity of worship and propensity for *ex tempore* utterance he found offensive and abhorrent. But the genius of his religion was more akin to Rome than to the developing Protestantism of the British people. It was said of him that he would have been prepared to recognize the Mother of Churches had Rome in turn been willing to recognize her daughter. He demanded a Romish aspect to the sacerdotal character, the same submission to a fixed creed, the same pomp and ceremony in service, the same exclusion of the laity, the same spiritual authority for the ecclesiastical hierarchy. And in return for Charles's indulgence he magnified the royal authority and was satisfied perhaps that his enemies were also the King's.

Laud saw Scotland as a challenge. In the northern kingdom the form of religion was irregular and rude. Some congregations followed a liturgy of sorts, but the Presbyterians detested most vestiges of ecclesiastical ritual. Their altar was 'The Table', while candles, organs, surplices, images, devout gestures and all that Laud held dear were accounted abominations, and any theology short of theirs was Romish or Arminian. Though as yet comparatively impotent, the extremists had shown their savage temper and their undoubted talent for invective. The bishops were already dubbed 'Bellie Gods', and 'knobs and wens and bunchy popish flesh'. Charles's marriage to Henrietta Maria, Frenchwoman and Papist, 'the daughter of Heth', was blamed as the cause of the plague which was beginning to sweep the North, and Laud himself was the target of threats and abuse; 'Laud look to thyself; be assured thy life is sought.' These may have been the howling of prophets in the wilderness who had passed long since from simple faith into a devout darkness of their own, but behind them among the Scottish people as a whole was a genuine pride in their Kirk and a deep-rooted fear of popery which Laud would overlook only at his peril. Nor should he have underestimated the Scottish capacity for hatred.

The change in the monarchy and Laud's elevation were also to be reflected in the changing nature of the ecclesiastical hierarchy in Scotland. The Jacobean bishops had been moderates who had risen within the Scottish system and many of them had had a Presbyterian background. And though James had counted it a political victory when he won the right to appoint his nominees to the vacant dioceses, at least he had selected experienced men who, though royalist, were qualified for the job. But in Charles's reign the seat of Scottish preferment was transferred to England, and more particularly to the Court and Canterbury. The new generation of prelates were children of Laud's favour, and having no obligation to their elders for their advance-ment they remained bound to England for reasons of religious and self-interest. Young in office, they were quick to obey instructions, and since many were anti-Calvinistic and had hierarchical views it was inevitable that they should have found much in the Anglican system that appealed and they displayed an unfortunate impatience of the Scottish compromise which allowed them an appearance but not the reality of ecclesiastical power. Their attitudes and behaviour served to increase the growing suspicions of the average Presbyterians, and as they became identified as mere instruments of the royal power, in the ensuing political conflict they came to symbolize the despotic methods that Charles and Laud employed in their policy of 'crushing the consciences' and violating the national independence of an increasingly sensitive people.

Charles's first blunder came at the very commencement of his reign. He had inherited an uneasy peace, and one that had been achieved by keeping the land divided—which in practice meant keeping the nobles and the Kirk, those original allies of the Reformation, apart. In theory it should not have been too difficult to keep it so since the key factor involved was not hard to see. However much James might have exasperated the Presbyterians by his episcopalian proclivities, so long as he left the nobles' property alone he was safe. But now Charles rushed in where James had feared to tread. In October 1625, by an Act of Privy Council he recalled to the Crown all property alienated since the accession of Mary in 1542. Similar Acts of Revocation had been passed before—at the beginning of a reign or at the end of a minority—but this Act involved most of the wealth that had passed from the Old Church since the Reformation—including the religious houses that had been 'erected' into temporal lordships, and the tithes or teinds which had been taken into secular hands. There had been so many confiscations of church lands, forfeitures and alienations of estates since Mary's accession that few of the nobility were not affected. To do Charles justice, the Act was intended to be beneficial and had much to recommend it. (The historian Gardiner called it 'the one successful Act of Charles's reign'.) Tithes were an open scandal. The feudal lords to whom they had passed levied them in kind upon tenants who were obliged to leave their crops rotting in the fields until the lord condescended to take his toll. Charles wanted only to stop this abuse and to provide a living wage for the ministry for whose support the system of tithes had originally been devised. The nobles reacted immediately in defence of their privileges, led by the Lord Chancellor himself. A deputation was sent to the King, inflammatory reports were circulated among the people, and the King's Commissioner was threatened with violence. Charles withdrew and a Commission of Surrender of Superiorities and Tythes, sitting between 1627 and 1629, effected a compromise whereby holders of lands and tithes were able to secure their property upon payment of stipulated sums. This too was a fair procedure and was praised by the honest and moderate Napier who was one of the commissioners. But the nobles were hardly interested in justice, and Charles had incurred their deep displeasure. Nor did he get any gratitude from the Kirk, which had no great desire to see money wrung back from the nobility to pamper an idolatrous and prelatical Church. The malcontents, lay and clerical, began to band together and neither party was over-particular as to the causes of the other's dissatisfaction.

Yet had the King let well alone thereafter the conflict might still have been averted. Unfortunately, he had only just begun.

When Charles ascended the throne in 1625 he told the Privy Council that in Scotland 'matters shall continue and go forward in the same course wherein they now are', and for eight years he governed the country from a distance, though each year he promised to come north for his second coronation. The Scots resented these postponements which they took for neglect, and when Charles proposed that the Crown of Scotland should be sent south to England there to be solemnly placed upon his head, the Keeper of the Regalia replied that, though Scotland was loyal enough, 'if the Crown was not worth a progress there might be some other way of disposing of it.' In 1633 Charles eventually came north, and Scotland, whatever her misgivings, gave him a brave welcome.

He was crowned in the chapel of Holyrood House by the Bishop of Brechin, who chose for his sermon the somewhat inappropriate text, 'And all the people cried God save King Solomon!' All the people, however, were suspiciously recording the antics of Laud who was seen to displace the Archbishop of Glasgow from the King's side 'with indecent violence', and anxious and jealous eyes were noting the papistical trappings which the Englishman had introduced into the service. It was marked that a table had been placed:

> . . . in the manner of an altar . . . having thereon two clasped books [particularly terrifying these] . . . with two candelabra and two wax candles which were unlit, and ane basin wherein there was nothing. At the back of this altar . . . was ane rich tapestry on which the crucifix was curiously wrought and as the Bishops who were in service passed by this crucifix they were seen to bow their knees and beck, which with their habit[9] was noted and bred great fear of inbringing of Popery.

Thereafter, Charles proceeded to Parliament. He had just had a rough passage with its English counterpart, and with the characteristic reaction of a weak man had come determined that in his poorer kingdom there would be no similar nonsense. On the morning he entered Edinburgh the Earl of Rothes as spokesman for the dissatisfied nobility, approached him with a petition addressed to the King and Parliament asking for a redress of grievances. In order to convince Charles of the nobles' reasonable attitude, Rothes explained that, before giving it to the Clerk of the Register, he had thought it 'decent' to show it first privately to the King. Charles read it and then returned it to Rothes with the peremptory reply: 'No more of this my Lord, I command you!' In Parliament the subservient Lords of the Articles forced through without debate no less than 168 Acts in a single day, including the Act of Revocation, an Act providing for the payment of an income tax, and an Act confirming all the ecclesiastical innovations of James including the Five Articles of Perth. When the votes were taken Rothes accused the Clerk Register of making a false return but was promptly told that he would imperil his life if he demanded a scrutiny and did not thereby prove his case. Any further resistance was prevented by the interference of Charles himself, who noted down the names of each of the nobles as they were called up, observing: 'I shall know today who shall do me service.' During the remainder of his stay he refused a petition of the ministry, created a new episcopal see at Edinburgh, snubbed Rothes in his official capacity as hereditary sheriff of Fife, and refused a town provost a kiss of the hand because he was a 'dissenter'.

In August 1633 Laud became Archbishop of Canterbury and embarked on a vigorous policy designed to bring the Kirk into conformity with the Anglican Church. In 1634 the Court of High Commission was established by royal warrant, and the number of bishops on the Privy Council increased to seven. The prelates were openly accounted the political instruments of the Crown, having a disproportionate influence over the nomination of the Lords of the Articles, while in the Estates they represented a solid vote for the King. Charles now thought to appoint them to high secular office. In 1626, when the new Privy Council was formed, he had demanded precedence for Archbishop Spottiswoode whom he appointed President of the Exchequer ('the first and last President the Exchequer ever had'), and the Chancellor, Hay of Kinfauns, in refusing it had declared that 'never a ston'd priest in Scotland should set a foot in front of him so long as his blood was hot'. In 1635 Charles capped this by making Spottiswoode Chancellor, the first time since the Reformation that the office had been bestowed on a churchman. The appointment was intolerable to the baronage who were bound to resist any encroachment upon the secular authority which they regarded as theirs by right. In the eyes of the nobility and the Presbyterian extremists alike the bishops were now the principal enemy since both parties would benefit by their elimination.

An incident in 1634 lent fresh colour to the nobles' fears. Lord Balmerino, one of the Lords of Erection, circulated a written protest against certain of the new Acts and the document fell into the hands of Spottiswoode who sent it to the King. Charles promptly had Balmerino indicted for high treason, and on his conviction by a majority of one he was condemned to death. He was subsequently pardoned, but Charles gained nothing by this demonstration of royal clemency (which some extremists construed as weakness) while his high-handed action only further aroused the temper of the nobles. They blamed the bishops as the instigators of it, and the word went abroad that under Charles and his creatures the old liberties of Scotland were being systematically destroyed. Even moderate theoreticians like Drummond of Hawthornden were provoked to vigorous remonstrance.

But uncaring, uncomprehending, Charles and Laud continued to foist on Scotland the political and ecclesiastical emblems of England in their most unappealing form. They wanted to bring order and decency to a popular, and to their mind indecent, ministry, to restore the Churches after decades of neglect, and to recreate the aesthetic mystery and beauty of religion. It might be argued that their illusion, though impolitic, was comparatively blameless, but not so the despotic methods by which their innovations were thrust upon a reluctant nation. In May 1635, without reference to General Assembly or Parliament, the King authorized by royal warrant a Book of Canons designed to regulate the government of the Scottish Kirk. Published in January 1636, the book had been drafted by a committee of Scottish bishops and subsequently edited by Laud. It re-enacted the Articles of Perth which were now to be more strictly enforced, forbade *ex tempore* prayer and proclaimed the King head of the Church. It also commanded the exclusive use of a new liturgy or prayer book which was still in preparation, and in the fly leaf it contained a warning that anyone who did not accept and follow the new liturgy when it appeared would be liable to automatic excommunication.

This was to be the spark to ignite the powder train. James had toyed with the idea of a new liturgy but wisely dropped it. Not all the bishops supported it because it had no ecclesiastical sanction, and since the intention was first mooted many had practised a policy of delay. To the Scottish Presbyterians it was to be 'the Mass in English', though in that atmosphere of heightened tension and suspicion their fears were much exaggerated. Charles 'lost three kingdoms and his head, not for a mass but for a surplice.'[10]

Charles had now succeeded in antagonizing the vast majority of the Scottish nation. He had insulted Scottish national sentiment. He had aroused widespread apprehension–among the nobles who feared for their lands, among the Presbyterians who saw their faith imperilled, and among the moderates who supported a constitutional monarchy but felt bound to resist an arbitrary and despotic rule which threatened to destroy what they held to be the established laws and customs of their country. The feeling of resentment was almost universal and now resistance began to take on a definite shape.

In previous reigns the nobility could have resorted to brigandage, a *coup de main* or even an attempt upon the person of the king. But times had changed. Charles sat secure in London and the initial opposition tried to justify itself in legal and constitutional terms. Lack of experience in such matters obliged the nobles to turn to the Advocates, a new and distinct class which had arisen in Scotland,[11] who were to play a vital role in the events to follow. This group of lawyers came to form an intermediary element between the nobles (for whom they acted as city agents) and the Presbyterian leadership, to whom they were closely connected through the medium of lay elders in the ministry. For the most part they were Presbyterians, but they were in the unique position of being trusted by both sides, and while nobles such as Rothes appeared to be the front-runners in the opposition movement, it was the Advocates who provided the machinery of resistance and indeed shaped the course of the immediate conflict. In time, however, by virtue of their Presbyterian leanings and the power of the clerical laity in the Calvinist polity, they would be instrumental in turning an initially conservative opposition into more revolutionary paths, and some would stamp their personality more clearly on the covenanting movement then ever did Rothes or those other lords who thought to begin it.

Two of these Advocates in particular deserve specific mention. The first was the Lord Advocate of Scotland, Sir Thomas Hope of Craig-hall. In 1637 he was almost seventy, having practised law for over forty years, and was adjudged the finest legal brain in Scotland. A man of profound intellect though irritable temper (and not without self interest), he fell entirely within the Presbyterian pattern, being a bitter Puritan whose diary records his secret dialogues with God each night (and the miscellaneous borrowings of his debtors in the morning). His judgements had the force of law, but his politics were governed by his Presbyterian outlook and a narrow faith. His ruling that Charles's actions were unconstitutional would provide the legal basis for the Scottish revolt.

The second was Archibald Johnston of Wariston. He came from a family of small border gentry (had not Knox?), and though still in his twenties was already a leading advocate at the bar. Wariston may have had a brilliant legal mind, but behind it was the tormented soul of a fanatic. He believed that God had called him to a high destiny to be the salvation of His Kirk in Scotland. Like others of the more devout Presbyterians he would spend whole nights upon his knees in prayer, but his was the jealous God of old Israel and his fervour was not tempered by breadth of vision or any element of human compassion. Like Sir Thomas Hope, he kept a diary of his inmost thoughts and it reveals a mind swaying perilously on the brink of madness. The archetype extremist, he was capable of inhuman hatred and ferocious superstition. And yet twenty years after, Cromwell would prove him as venal as a megalomaniac can be. He was to be the draftsman of the Covenant—and later its high executioner.

It should also be said that, whereas the popular reaction to Charles's measures was in the main spontaneous, from the beginning there was an element in the Scottish revolution (as in most other revolutions) that was not. There are always some who, in Napier's phrase, being 'pressed with necessity at home are glad of any occasion or pretext to trouble the public quiet, and to fish in troubled waters to better their own fortunes'. Although the initial opposition to Charles had a conservative aspect, inspired by a determination to resist the English innovations and the autocratic and illegal methods by which they were introduced, there was within the movement a small minority calculating ahead of events, who saw in the forces of popular discontent a possible vehicle that could carry them from a position of comparative impotence to one of influence and power. These were the real revolutionaries, whose aim was not merely the preservation of ancient liberties of which they were already impatient but the curtailment of monarchy itself. Their intention was not merely to preserve the Presbyterian faith in Scotland, but ultimately to establish a uniformity of their own upon their howsoever reluctant neighbours. And while others protested openly, in 1637 these were already conspiring in secret.

A number of contemporary writers, notably James Gordon and John Spalding, refer to a document known as The Clandestine Band:[12]

> Whereupon followed ane Clandestine Band drawn up and subscribed secretly between the malcontents, or rather malignants of Scotland *and England*: that each should concur and assist others while they got their wills, both in Church and policy; *and to bring both kingdoms under ane reformed religion*; and to that effect to root out the Bishops *of both kingdoms,* crop and root, whereby His Majesty should lose one of his three estates; and likewise they should draw the King to dispense with diverse points of *his own prerogative,* in such degree as he should not have arbitrary government as all his predecessors ever had, conform to the established laws of both kingdoms, as on the said Clandestine Band at length reports; as was said.[13]

This was the beginning of a greater conspiracy and also of a fallacy which would lead not only to the ruin of the King but ultimately to that of Scotland also. Unfortunately no copy of this Clandestine Band is extant, but in such reports of its content one may trace the origin of that later Solemn League and Covenant to which moderates such as Montrose objected, and which would one day cause the national humiliation of those who had been conceited enough to believe that they could enforce Scottish Presbyterianism upon England. For having accepted the theories of predestination and convinced themselves that they were the elect of God, the Presbyterian leadership took this to the dangerous extreme of concluding that it was also their duty to convert their southern neighbours. When later they signed the Solemn League and invaded England in support of their parliamentary allies, they did so on the naïve assumption that, when the revolutionary party in England agreed to reform the kingdom 'according to the Word of God and the example of the purest Churches', they had been referring only to the reformed religion established in the Kirk of Scotland. It was to be a grave miscalculation. English sympathy for the Scots did not stem from a desire to emulate the Scottish form of worship. It was rather that the opposition in Scotland came to propagate successfully a conception of the responsibility of rulers which the English revolutionary group found particularly apposite to their own situation. It was the Scots' technique of insurgency that was in demand—not their Book of Discipline.

In the meanwhile, however, the Scots were well placed to pursue their intrigue with the English. The King's presence chamber, the privy chamber and the bedchamber were filled with Scottish lords. The Earl of Haddington, Rothes's brother-in-law and later a Covenanter, remained in Whitehall and in touch with dissident English peers such as Holland, Say, Brook and Wharton. A Mr Eleazor Borthwick, an able agent of the Covenanters who was to spend twelve years in London, had almost daily communication with Pym and other Puritans. A number of English malcontents also went north to consult with the Scots as to how they could best concert against the King, and Wariston in later times used to pride himself on the part he played in these intrigues. The Puritans had a propensity for secret societies and there was a cloak and dagger aspect to the whole affair. Meetings were held at Lord Say's house in Oxfordshire in a room accessible only through a secret passage, or at a Mr Knightley's house in Northampton, at Lord Mandeville's lodgings in Chelsea and other discreet places in London.

The Scots always had excellent intelligence as to the King's intentions. Like his father, Charles had retained his Scottish domestics who now proved more loyal to their countrymen than to their master. They watched him in his unguarded hours, recorded his private or accidental remarks and ransacked his pockets at night for official documents which he had carelessly left upon his person. One of these, a groom of the bedchamber called William Murray—the man who warned the 'five members'—will appear several times in this story, and always in a sinister light.

In 1637 the plotters in Scotland were moving to create the explosion which their aims required. According to Spalding:

> The Lord of Lorne convened the Earls of Rothes, Cassilis, Glencairn, Traquair [a great enemy of the Bishops], Lindsay, Loudoun, Balmerino, Couper, and diverse others... together with ane mengzie of discontented Puritans of whom Mr Alexander Henderson [Minister at Leuchars], Mr David Dickson [Minister at Irving], and Mr Andrew Cant [Minister at Pitsligo] were the ringleaders ... [to a private meeting at which they discussed measures against the increasing power of the Bishops]. . . . And after much resolving *they conclude to see a Reformation shortly* and to that effect draws in a great number of the nobility quietly to their opinion, and only wanted a time to begin, as was concluded in the Clandestine Band.[14]

They were interested in recruiting men who would be a credit to their cause—men popular and respected, whose energy and force of character marked them out as desirable leaders in a dangerous enterprise. Not surprisingly, their eye fell on the young and promising Earl of Montrose.

PART II

Protagonists

3

The Covenanter
(1637–1638)

We are those fools who could not rest
In the dull earth we left behind,
But burned with passion for the West,
And drank a frenzy from its wind;
The world where small men live at ease
Fades from our unregretful eyes,
And blind across uncharted seas
We stagger on our enterprise.

The Ship of Fools

'The Clandestine Band thus past,' wrote Spalding,[1] 'our nobles lay quiet while they found occasion to break the ice and begin the bargain, as was concluded.' The introduction of the new Liturgy provided them with their opportunity.

The new prayer book had been completed in April 1637, but it was not due to come into use until Sunday, 23 July. During the intervening months it became the object of a carefully engineered agitation. By preachers and pamphlets[2] the people were induced to believe that it 'was nought but the Mass in English brought in by the craft and violence of the Bishops'–until, wrote the Rev Robert Baillie (whose *Letters and Journals* provide one of the principal commentaries on this period), 'these things were the table talk and open discourse of high and low'.[3] It was important, however, that a popular disturbance should at least appear spontaneous since the Privy Council would have been obliged to take order with any prominent persons who were actually seen to be instigating a riot. The agitators therefore decided to invoke the Edinburgh mob–which in those times used to consist principally of the 'kail wives' that congregated at the gallows and the market place, and who, since the Reformation, had achieved a reputation for their violence in religious causes. According to Guthry,[4] some time before the Liturgy was due to be introduced, Alexander Henderson and Mr David Dick met Balmerino and Sir Thomas Hope 'at the house of one Nicholas Balfour in the Cowgate, with Euphame Henderson, Bethia and Elspa Craig[5] and several other matrons, and recommended to them that they and their adherents should give the first affront to the Book, assuring them that men should afterwards take it out of their hands'.

The resulting tumult has passed into legend. On the morning of

41

Sunday, 23 July, the High Kirk of St Giles was packed to over-
flowing. The Privy Council, the magistrates and the lords, lay and
ecclesiastical, filled the galleries, while the main body of the church
was thronged with the commoners–including a large number of serving
women with their portable 'creepie stools' whose job was usually to
reserve places for their betters. The service began without incident,
but as soon as the dean, Dr Hanna, started to read from the new
Liturgy pandemonium broke loose. The women began clapping and
cursing, and shouted him down with yells of 'Beastly Belly God!',
'Crafty fox!', 'The Devil colic the wame o' ye!', 'Ill hanged thief!',
'Fie if I could get the thrapple out of him!', 'Witches' breeding
and the Devil's get!', 'False anti-christian wolf!' and other virtuous
ejaculations of religious fervour. The wretched dean was pelted with
'whole pockfulls' of clasped Bibles, and one harridan, since immortalized in the name of Jenny Geddes, picked up her creepie
stool and flung it at his head. The Bishop of Edinburgh and even
Spottiswoode himself tried unsuccessfully to calm the rabble, and
finally the provost and his bailies were obliged to clear the church
and lock the doors against the mob outside, who continued to shout
curses and throw stones through the windows. When the service was
over, the godly women of Edinburgh set out to lynch the prelates,
and the unfortunate Bishop of Edinburgh, who was twice caught in
the streets, owed his life on both occasions to the timely intervention of members of the nobility.

Those who had not been party to the plot were genuinely surprised by the violence of the reaction. Baillie, who previously had
decided that he would receive the Liturgy 'quietly', thought that the
people were 'possessed of a bloody Devil. . . . All the people think
Popery at the doors . . . no man may speak anything in public for
the King's part except that he should have himself marked down for
sacrifice to be killed one day . . . [it is] far above anything that
even I could have imagined though the Mass in Latin had been
presented.' He added, rather sententiously, that 'I think it base and
wicked to be moved and carried down with the impetuous spirit of the
multitude; my judgement cannot be altered by their motion. . . .'[6]
Baillie, like the majority, would be swept along with the tide.

The Privy Council were at a loss. Feebly they asserted the King's
authority, but did–and could do–nothing to support it. The position
of individual councillors was equivocal. Sir Thomas Hope was probably
one of the instigators of the riot. The Earl of Traquair, Lord High
Treasurer and technically the most powerful official in Scotland, was
a known enemy of the prelates since he feared to lose his post to
the Bishop of Ross and, according to Spalding, had already been
conniving with the plotters. On 23 July he had been conspicuously
absent from Edinburgh. Lord Lorne had also been suddenly and conveniently indisposed. The majority of their colleagues, however loyal,
resented the recent intrusions of the bishops into civil office, and all
of them, whatever their degree of knowledge, signed a dispatch to the

King stating that the 'barbarous tumult' was 'occasioned for anything we can learn as yet by a number of base and rascally people', and blaming the imprudence and precipitation of the bishops. The Liturgy was temporarily suspended since preachers bold enough to use it were being assaulted and systematically beaten up.

Since there was nothing in the Council's report to convey the impression of a national revolt, the King, who was in any event pre-occupied with English affairs (notably Ship Money), seriously under-estimated the gravity of the situation. His initial reaction was as much one of anger at the pusillanimity of the Privy Council, who had apparently failed to take order with 'the insolent rabble', and he sent peremptory instructions that the use of the Service Book was to be resumed immediately and the principal rioters arrested for treason. Overconfident, misinformed and uncomprehending, Charles seems to have calculated that the Scots could be subdued by the mere expression of the royal will. But the Council no longer had the effective power to carry out his orders, and the people were more angered at his reply than terrified by it.

Meanwhile the agitators maintained the momentum of resistance by bombarding the Privy Council with petitions and supplications against the Liturgy, while the populace were kept at a high pitch of excitement by the perfervid eloquence of the political preachers. From '24 July to 10 August,' wrote Baillie,[7] 'the posts ran thick betwixt the Court and the Council.'

In September the Duke of Lennox, who had recently been married in London, was obliged to return to Scotland on account of the death of his mother, and the King asked him to investigate the matter and report on the true state of affairs. Like the other great magnates, Lennox was not directly associated with any particular faction, and though somewhat slow-witted he could be relied on to give nothing away. When they heard that he was coming, the agitators decided to impress him with a demonstration of solidarity, and in arranging this they were helped by the fact that the summer had been particularly dry and the harvest early, so that yet more supporters from Lothian and the surrounding shires were now flocking into Edinburgh. When Lennox went to attend the meeting of the Privy Council the nobles and ministers lined the street and, having 'saluted him very low', presented a petition for consideration by the Duke and the Privy Council. After a face-saving delay, the councillors eventually sum-moned the Earls of Sutherland and Wemyss and told them that Lennox had read their petition and would report on the situation to the King. On the last night before the Duke's departure, Rothes visited him at his lodgings to impress upon him the seriousness of the discontent and the need for a reasonable answer. 'All we want is that the Book may be abolished and that we may have fair play from the King.'

Lennox returned to court and almost a month passed. The Scots spent the time in fasts and solemn prayers, while the agitators con-tinued to recruit adherents to 'the good cause'. On 17 October,

Charles's formal reply to their petition was read at the Mercat Cross of Edinburgh. The Service Book was to be enforced; the 'Supplicants' were to disperse and leave the city within twenty-four hours; the Privy Council and Court of Session were to remove to Linlithgow. This last sanction had previously been used by James VI with considerable effect since the economy of Edinburgh was largely dependent upon the government institutions established in the capital, but the result on this occasion was another more serious riot during which the Bishop of Galloway (Sydserf) was assaulted and Traquair himself manhandled by the infuriated mob. 'The Lord give this business a fair end,' wrote Wariston in his diary, 'for it has a fair beginning.'[8] On 19 October a new petition–'Scotland's Supplication and complaint against the Book of Common Prayer, the Book of Canons, and the Prelates' (the demands were increasing), was sent to the King in London.

It is the first petition in which Montrose's name appears among the list of signatories.

On 20 September the malcontents had held a 'convention' which was attended by the Lords Rothes, Cassilis, Eglinton, Home, Lothian, Wemyss, Lindsay, Yester, Balmerino, Cranston and Loudoun, and a number of ministers and burghers from Fife and the western shires. Among the subjects discussed was the need to secure more widespread support outside of Edinburgh. Mr Henry Pollock was sent 'to deal with those of Lothian, Merse, and Teviotdale': Mr Andrew Ramsay was 'to take the like pains with those of Angus and the Mearns': Mr Andrew Cant was 'to use the like diligence in the North': and Mr Robert Murray, Minister of Methven (and incidentally the uncle of William Murray of the King's bed chamber), was 'to travail with them of Perth and Stirling shires'. 'And so the ministers disbanded for a time.'[9] Mr Murray was conscientious in his travails. Kincardine Castle and the Graham estates along Strathearn came within his province, and Montrose later named him 'as an instrument of bringing me to this cause'.[10]

However, Baillie, reflecting subsequently on the somewhat inadvised recruitment of the young earl, recorded that 'the canniness of Rothes brought him in'.[11] This too is possible, since it was as Rothes's protégé that Montrose first emerged.

John Leslie, sixth Earl of Rothes, had by now established himself as the natural leader of the middle-ranking nobility outside the Privy Council who formed the core of the lay opposition to Charles. Clarendon later called him 'the chief architect' of the rebellion, though Rothes's motives seem to have been somewhat cynical and less extreme or clear cut than those of his clerical colleagues who were to carry the movement to its conclusion. Although he came from a strongly Protestant background (his father had been one of the murderers of Cardinal Beaton), and as a young man (he was now thirty-seven) had voted against James's Articles of Perth, he was a political Presbyterian and had little in common with the fanatics. Burnet[12] states that 'there was much levity in his temper, and too much liberty in his course of life', while Clarendon described him as 'pleasant in conversation, very free and amorous, and unrestrained in his discourse by any scruple of religion which he only put on when the part he was to act required it, and then no man could appear more conscientiously transported'.[13] Self-interest seems to have played a not inconsiderable part in determining his career in opposition, since despite a long minority his estates were permanently burdened with debts and he stood to lose heavily by the Act of Revocation. Charles was known to dislike him personally and Rothes may well have calculated that he had little to gain by acquiescence and good behaviour. Three years afterwards, had not consumption struck him down, he seems to have been ready to change sides for a suitable price. He was well aware of the subterranean ambitions of the extremists and had been one of the signatories of the Clandestine Band, but he possibly promoted this as an instrument to serve the purpose of the moment, and cynically reckoned that the forces on which he rode would later prove conveniently susceptible to control. Like others of his class, he completely underestimated the significance of the ministers, while for their part the extremists did not much trust him either. It is a point for speculation as to who was effectively gulling whom. Yet to all appearances, Rothes was the key figure of the opposition. And he had all the requisite skills. He was an adroit diplomat, an eloquent speaker, an efficient organizer, a politician who had espoused a dynamic cause and perhaps the most popular man in Scotland.

He seems to have been genuinely fond of Montrose, whom he appears to have indulged rather like a younger brother. Perhaps the energy and enthusiasm of the young earl amused him, while for his part the Graham may have felt flattered by the attentions of Rothes and the distinguished role at the forefront of affairs which the older man shrewdly offered to him.

However, since Montrose's political consistency–and thus his personal integrity–were later to be disputed by his enemies in their effort to discredit him, his original motives for joining Rothes's party as and when he did are worth discussing in some detail. He did not, as his critics have alleged, oppose the King merely out of pique at his cold reception at court; for nearly a year he seems to have lived quietely among his family at Kincardine. (His third child, Robert, was probably born at this time.) Nevertheless, Kincardine was not so remote that he was isolated from events, and during these months he must have taken a growing interest in the affairs of the country and been in frequent communication with Napier and others of his friends who were already politically involved. It seems certain, therefore, that his decision to enter the political arena on the side of Rothes and the opposition was taken quite deliberately and after considerable thought– and indeed his readiness in later years to defend his action largely confirms this. But the process of deliberation is affected to some degree by experience, and of political experience Montrose had none. He was young, romantic, idealistic, in search of an heroic cause; and Rothes, by appealing to his patriotism, to the national religion that was his birthright and even to his loyalty, was sure of attracting an emotional response which was to some extent the measure of the young man's political *naiveté*.

In this context there was a significant contrast between the behaviour of Montrose and Napier at this time even though their political beliefs were virtually identical and they were later to become closely associated in opposition to the Kirk extremists. Both were staunch Presbyterians, and both were agreed on the necessity to defend their national religion against the arbitrary innovations of the Anglican archbishop. However, neither was a fanatic and they were both to display a religious tolerance towards other men which was unusual in the seventeenth century. Both were strongly anti-clerical and fiercely resented the intrusion of the prelates in secular affairs. Napier was the author of a succinct Memorandum on the subject:

> That Churchmen have competency is agreeable to the laws of God and man. But to invest them into great estates, and the principal offices of state is neither convenient for the Church, for the King, nor for the State. Not for the Church, for the indiscreet zeal and excessive donations of princes were the first causes of corruption in the Roman Church, the taste whereof did so inflame the avarice and ambition of the successors as they have raised themselves above all secular and sovereign power, and to maintain the same have obtended to the world certain devices of their own for matters of faith. Not to Kings nor states, for histories witness what troubles have been raised to Kings, what tragedies among subjects in all places where Churchmen were great. Our reformed Churches having reduced religion to the ancient primitive truth and simplicity ought to beware that corruption enter not in their Church at the same gate. . . .[14]

Montrose echoed these views, and it was consistent with his anti-clerical standpoint that he later opposed the theocratic pretensions of the Kirk extremists.

Both were Royalists who believed in the constitutional authority of the King subject to the established laws of the country. And both could justify opposition to Charles's ecclesiastical measures on the grounds that 'the causes of God's true religion and His Highness's authority are so joined as the hurt of one is common to both.' Although they realized that resistance could be dangerous to the peace of the kingdom, they still held that such resistance, if constitutionally justified, was compatible with loyalty to the King. The preservation of constitutional liberty and of the King's lawful prerogatives was indivisible. Both envisaged a state of affairs in which a constitutional king could govern at peace with a Presbyterian Church, and neither realized that Charles could not share their ideal. However, Montrose's own theory of sovereign power had not yet crystallized. This creative impulse emerged out of his frustration two years later, and then probably under the influence of Napier. For the moment his actions were determined by a desire to fight against what he believed to be wrong, rather than to establish what he held to be right.

Yet while Montrose joined the opposition movement and later signed the Covenant, Napier did not. It is possible that his position on the Privy Council prohibited him from direct participation, but it is as likely that he was too shrewd and cautious to entrust himself and his conscience to such as Rothes–who fitted almost too exactly into the category of those who 'hard pressed at home are glad of any occasion . . . to disturb the public quiet . . . to better their own fortunes'.[15] Where the young and impetuous Montrose saw only a cause, the older and experienced Napier may have suspected faction. It is possible that he even urged caution, but Montrose was always difficult to persuade against his feelings. The young man was impatient of advice and he had the fault of being hyper-conscious of his own integrity. There was also a generation between them.

His enemies have accused Montrose of being ambitious. This indeed was true, and grist to Rothes's mill. But his ambitions were always within the bounds of honour and he had no secret sympathy with the agitators.

Unfortunately, having joined a faction, Montrose himself became factious, and for a time he was to be carried away by the heady atmosphere of insurrection. Modesty and humility were not among his early virtues and in time he would regret some of the high-handed actions of the next twelve months. However, for their part, the agitators who regarded his recruitment as something of a *coup* did not yet realize that they had acquired a dangerous liability. The Graham was not the sort of person who would be content simply to do as he was told.

Montrose first appeared publicly on the opposition side at a large convention of the malcontents on 15 November 1637. He seems to have caused something of a stir, and some of the bishops with whom he had been on friendly personal terms were disheartened–'having that esteem of his parts that they thought it time to prepare for a storm when he engaged'.[16] The Privy Council, having failed to find accommodation at Linlithgow, was at that time sitting at Dalkeith, and on the advice of Sir Thomas Hope they agreed to the nomination of commissioners who could negotiate on behalf of the dissidents. Traquair would have challenged this procedure, being aware of its significance, but Hope pronounced it legal,[17] and it was the only way of persuading the mob to disperse.

The agitators therefore elected four Tables[18] of Commissioners representing the nobles, the lairds, the burgesses and the ministers, which now came to form something similar to a committee of public safety. Opposition had become institutionalized–and one step closer to revolution.

It was a measure of Montrose's popularity that at this, his first appearance, he was voted on to the Table of the nobility, his three colleagues being Rothes, Loudoun (a Campbell of Lawers about whom a Graham might have had some reservations) and Lindsay of the Byres (his old friend from college days). It is noticeable, however, that these other three had all been in the movement from the beginning, so that effective control remained in the hands of the early agitators. Sir George Stirling of Keir, who had married Margaret Napier, Montrose's niece, was also elected to the second Table representing the lairds.

Early in December the Earl of Roxburgh brought a message from the King in which Charles declined to answer any further petitions, but declared that he contemplated no innovation upon the national religion as 'professed at present'. This last phrase intimated that he intended the continuation of episcopacy and therefore failed to satisfy the opposition. The bishops, meanwhile, had withdrawn from the Privy Council and began to correspond independently with the King while petitions against them continued to be served upon the lay members by the Tables.

On 21 December it was decided, with the agreement of the King, that Traquair should go to London and give Charles a full report on the situation. Unfortunately Spottiswoode, the President of the Court of Session (and son of the Archbishop) got there before him, and Traquair found the King unsympathetic to any version of events that tried to lay the blame on the bishops. Charles was coming to realize that he had a serious revolt on his hands, but felt that it was already too late to turn back since any leniency on his part might be taken as a sign of weakness and so encourage the growing Puritan opposition in England. Traquair got a cold reception, and in February was ordered to return to Scotland with a new royal proclamation in which Charles took complete responsibility for the publication of the Service Book. The proclamation also stated that the Scots' petitions were derogatory to the royal authority, and ordered all 'petitioners' to disperse upon pain of treason.

Traquair did not relish his task. He was fast losing credibility with both sides and could profit little from this commission.[19] In order to prevent a further riot he was told to keep the proclamation secret until the day of publication, and so, on arriving at Dalkeith on 14 February, he weakly told Cranston that he had no directions. This unlikely statement was accepted at its face value, but covertly the malcontents kept a close watch upon his movements. On 19 February, shortly after midnight, having kept a straight face for a week, he made a bolt for Stirling where he hoped to get the proclamation read and done with without interference from the Tables. But servants' gossip gave them warning, and Home and Lindsay overtook him on the road and were ready at the Mercat Cross to make the now customary protestation. The other supplicants followed them to Stirling next day, the nobles with substantial retinues of armed men, and Traquair was forced to return meekly to Edinburgh on the twenty-second to reread the proclamation in front of a hostile crowd. On this occasion Wariston read an impassioned protestation in reply, and during the tumult that followed, Montrose enthusiastically climbed onto a large barrel and addressed the people. Rothes, who was standing beside him, is said to have jokingly exclaimed: 'James, you will never be at rest until you are lifted up above the rest on three fathoms of rope'–a remark that was no doubt more illustrative of a macabre sense of humour than of any gift of prophetic foresight.[20]

The opposition leaders now 'fell upon the consideration of a Band of union to be made legally'. 'It was', said Rothes, a 'Band with Jehovah'; and 'it was' (wrote a later historian of the Kirk) 'an expedient admirably devised, the success of which exceeded even their own most sanguine expectations'.[21] A band was an old device of the rebellious nobility, but this was exceptional in that it was to be legal. For some months Wariston and Henderson had been planning to revive the old covenants of 1580–1 against popery–with 'certain additions', and their draft, after some revision by Rothes and Loudoun, was now produced as the National Covenant of 1638, which must rank as one of the most important documents of Scottish history.

In its content, the text of this Covenant fell into three parts. The first was a repetition of the covenant against popery signed by the young James VI in 1580 which renounced and condemned the Romish religion. The second consisted of a lengthy recitation of all the Acts of Parliament passed at and since the Reformation in favour of the Reformed Church–including the Golden Act of 1592 which excluded episcopacy. However, it is the third–the operative and obligatory part– that requires the closest attention. It contained a pledge to defend the true religion against all innovations 'already introduced', and all corruptions of public government 'till they be tried and allowed in the Assemblies and in Parliaments', and it concluded with the crucial paragraph as follows:

> . . . We declare before God and men that we have no intention nor desire to attempt anything that may turn to the dishonour of God, or to the diminution of the King's greatness or authority. But on the contrary we promise and swear that we shall, to the utmost of our power . . . stand to the defence of our dread Sovereign, the King's Majesty, his person and authority, in the defence and preservation of the foresaid true religion, liberties, and laws of the kingdom; as also to the mutual defence and assistance, everyone of us another in the same cause of maintaining the true religion, and His Majesty's authority . . . against all sorts of persons whatsoever . . . so that whatsoever shall be done to the least of us for that cause shall be taken as done to us all in general and to every one of us in particular. . . . Neither do we fear the foul aspersion of rebellion . . . seeing that what we do . . . ariseth from an unfeigned desire to maintain the true worship of God, the Majesty of the King, and the peace of the kingdom. . . .

The document was superscribed with the words: 'For God and the King'.

The Covenant has been described as 'a candid and straightforward document, temperately expressed and accurately directed to the grievances which it was designed to remedy. The claim was to both spiritual and religious freedom, and the formidable sanction behind it was at once ecclesiastical, feudal, and democratic'.[22] So it seemed certainly to the vast majority of Scots who subscribed it. But the last section is capable of various and possibly ominous interpretations. While promising to defend the King's authority, the phrase 'in the defence and preservation of the foresaid true religion' could be taken to mean that the promise was valid only if the King espoused Presbyterianism—or in effect signed the Covenant, which is what the Covenanters later tried to force him to do. And in the clause that bound the signatories to mutual defence '. . . against all sorts of persons whatsoever', this last could be construed as including the King. Similarly, the Covenanters could also later conclude that their military alliance with the English Parliament and the invasion of England were justified by their 'unfeigned desire to maintain the true worship of God, the Majesty of the King, and the peace of the kingdom'.

Defenders of the Covenant have been quick to resent any suggestion that the professions of loyalty which it contained were entirely hypocritical and insincere. But there is a crucial distinction—between the spirit in which the document was signed by thousands of people throughout Scotland, and the spirit in which it may have been drafted by Archibald Johnston of Wariston. Nor were these more ambiguous interpretations apparent only in the retrospect. They were noticed at the time—by Charles, obviously, and also by the ministers and professors of Aberdeen and a number of other Scots who refused to sign the Covenant for precisely this reason. Rothes and his friends seem to have been aware of the possibility that some people would express reservations about the 'additions'. On 27 February the Covenant was 'propounded' by the Tables to some two to three hundred clergy in the Tailors' Hall at Edinburgh. A number of ministers did object to certain points and were taken privately aside to a summer house in the adjoining garden and lectured on the necessity of mutual concession for the sake of the general cause. (The argument is not entirely unfamiliar.) Yet if the Covenant was intended purely and solely as an expression of mass solidarity, such phrases, if they caused doubts, could have been deleted or the wording changed. They were not.

The following day (28 February) the document was taken to the Church of Greyfriars. Loudoun, as the most accomplished orator, made a speech in which he said that the nobility, gentry and the other commissioners had all agreed on the form of the Covenant as absolutely necessary both for the temporal and spiritual welfare of the State and as the only means of saving the country from ruin. He ended with a statement that he and his brethren called on God to witness that, whatever might be thought of their motives by 'the agents of tyranny', they intended nothing to the dishonour of God or to the diminution of the King's honour—but wished they might perish all who did so. Wariston then read the document aloud, after which Rothes announced that anyone who still had any doubts could withdraw to either end of the church where he, Loudoun, Henderson and Dick would be happy to discuss their objections with them. The Covenant was then taken out into the churchyard where, amid scenes of deep popular emotion, it was first signed by the Earl of Sutherland and then by the vast concourse of nobles and commoners–who 'all fell a swearing and subscribing', some, it was said, in their own blood.

Montrose was among the first to sign, and his large holograph is prominent immediately below the text. He had no reservations, and to the end of his life he would defend this action and the principles embodied in the document to which he had set his name. He took the Covenant to be based on constitutional law and within the bounds of loyalty to the King. He had engaged in a solemn undertaking to defend the religious and constitutional liberties of Scotland, and he would later oppose the Covenanters, not because he retracted from that path, but because in his eyes they were perverting the Covenant of their country and the principles that he had sworn to uphold. And had he in later years been accused of self-deception, or of having been mistaken, he would have as strenuously denied it, since he always defended the Covenant not as others may have casuistically interpreted it, but for what he believed it to be.

Yet if it is true that Montrose was deceived, then so was most of Scotland, for his belief in the Covenant was shared by the vast majority of his fellow countrymen. Robert Baillie could tell his cousin in Holland:

> I do not only believe that there is no word in it that makes against the King's full authority so far as either religion or reason can extend it, or against the office of Bishops or any power they have by any lawful Assembly or Parliament . . . not only do I believe this, but have professed to say as much before the whole meeting at Edinburgh. . . . If any presently or hereafter shall abuse any claims of this write, to overthrow the King's authority etc. . . . I can make it evident before the world that the write has no such errors . . . else would I never have subscribed it.[23]

But if the Covenant were accepted, episcopacy was doomed.[24] Baillie would change colour with the times and remain silent. Montrose could not.

Among the list of signatories, Napier's name was again conspicuously absent. Yet Montrose could refer to him as 'a true Covenanter'–and perhaps he was 'too true to the spirit of the real Covenant to be deceived by its specious copy'.[25] When the issues became confused, it was to the principles of the 'true' Covenant that they both adhered, and in the last analysis it is upon the sincerity of his oath and not the mere form of it that Montrose too should finally be judged.

Through March, April and May the Covenant 'flew like fire about'. The Tables ordained that a copy should be sent to every shire, stewartry and bailliery within the kingdom to be signed by the chief men, and also to every parish for subscription by the common people. It became a crusade. The nobles rode about the country with sheepskin copies in their saddlebags, pressing everyone they met upon the road to sign. And gradually an element of coercion began to infect the movement. 'The greater the number of subscribers grew, the more imperious they were in exacting subscriptions from others who refused to subscribe', and in certain districts which proved recalcitrant the Covenant was 'obtruded upon people with threatenings, tearing of clothes, drawing of blood'.[26]

In Edinburgh, the significance of the Covenant's success became immediately apparent. The Privy Council and the principal officers of state effectively ceased to function. Spottiswoode and a number of bishops fled the country. The power of the Tables was firmly established and they now began to take on the role of a provisional government and issue edicts upon their own authority. A voluntary subscription of one dollar per thousand merks of rent was demanded to defray public expenses. Thirty-four nobles contributed a total of 670 dollars and Montrose headed the list with a donation of 25 dollars. The Covenanters began purchasing arms.

In London, Charles not unnaturally regarded the Covenant as yet another act bordering on outright rebellion. He had no illusions as to its implications for episcopacy, and insisted that any compromise on his part would be conditional on its being rescinded, since while it remained in force he had 'no more power than the Duke of Venice'. (Nor could he have it condemned in the courts as he would have wished since Sir Thomas Hope and the Scottish bar had already pronounced upon its legality.) A more astute man might have manoeuvred for an opportunity to divide the unnatural alliance between the nobles and the Kirk, but Charles, pressed by the Archbishop and his Catholic queen, and increasingly apprehensive of the Puritan opposition in England, now inclined towards the delusion that he could suppress the Covenant by armed force. In May he called Traquair, Roxburgh and Lorne to London and, having heard their version of events, announced that he would send a special Royal Commissioner to negotiate with the Scots.

The lot fell on Hamilton, who was perhaps the worst, but in some ways the only possible, choice. The great magnates had so far held aloof, but Lennox was known to have Roman Catholic connections, Lorne for various reasons was unsuitable and Huntly (who had just succeeded to the title) was virtually a stranger and held in some contempt in Scotland. Hamilton was most reluctant to accept the responsibility, being characteristically pessimistic of the outcome, and agreed to go to Scotland only on receiving the King's assurance that, whatever might result, he would not suffer in Charles's favour. Having thus obtained the royal amulet he was free to act as equivocally as he pleased.

Charles entrusted Hamilton with two alternative proclamations and

orders that he was to use his discretion as to which he should publish.
Both stated that the Liturgy and the Book of Canons would not be
pressed 'except in a fair and legal way', but while one demanded the
surrender of the Covenant, the other did not. However, Traquair and
Roxburgh told him that the first would only cause a fresh disturbance,
and since the terms of both were already known in Scotland,
Hamilton's position was prejudiced at the outset. Not that it really
mattered, since the Commissioner's instructions reveal only too clearly
the King's real purpose. 'I expect not anything can reduce that people
to their obedience but only force,' wrote Charles on 11 June:

> I give you leave to flatter them with what hopes you please . . .
> except that . . . you consent neither to the calling of Parliament or
> General Assembly until the Covenant be disavowed and given up. . . .
> Your chief end now being *to win time,* that they may not committ
> public follies until I am ready to suppress them. . . . But when I
> consider that not only now my crown but my reputation for ever lies
> at stake . . . [I] will not yield to those impertinent and
> damnable demands for it is all one as to yield to be no King in a
> very short time . . .[27] [And two days later:] I shall follow your
> advice in staying the public preparations for force; but in a silent
> way I will not leave to prepare that I may be ready upon the least
> advertisement.[28]

The King wanted six months. He was planning on an army of 14,000
foot and 2,000 horse and 40 pieces of artillery. Meanwhile, arms were
being imported from Holland, the fleet was at sea, and the lords
lieutenant of the six northern shires were ordered to muster the
trained bands. The castles at Edinburgh and Stirling were already
effectively invested by the Covenanters, but Carlisle and Berwick were
to be secured and the defences of Hull and Newcastle strengthened.

Such preparations could not go unnoticed. Nor were the Covenanters
idle. In the spring Rothes had sent for his cousin, General
Alexander Leslie, who came from Europe to put matters in hand for
the raising of an army, then returned to Germany with a copy of the
Covenant to recruit among the Scottish mercenaries there. Around
Edinburgh the nobles were arming their followers and provisioning
their castles. Arms and munitions from the continent were being landed
at the Port of Leith. War was in the air. Men smelled it, and if
some trembled, many were exhilarated. There was no shortage of
strange portents and forebodings. Prophets saw visions of ghostly
armies marshalled in the sky. The rumble of unearthly cannon was
said to echo in the hills, and among the old Pictish trenches at
Banuckyne of Echt, throughout the winter of 1637–8 men heard the
touking of drums and claimed that they could distinguish the battle
hymns of many nations. Events began to march inexorably towards
the inevitable conflict.

The Covenanters were determined not to allow Hamilton any
advantage. The followers whom he had summoned to meet him—in the
hope of effecting a grand entry—were sent home, and at Berwick he

was greeted instead by the unfriendly trio of Roxburgh, Lindsay and Lauderdale. He arrived at Dalkeith in the first week of June and would have proceeded to business, but Traquair had rather foolishly stocked the palace with gunpowder,[29] and the Covenanters, with suitable allusions to Kirk o' Field, refused to meet with him there. He was therefore obliged to continue to Edinburgh where a show of force had been arranged for his benefit. A crowd of over 60,000, the greatest ever assembled in the capital, awaited him outside the city gates, at which reception Hamilton wept copious crocodile tears and 'professed his desire to have had King Charles present at that sight of the whole country so earnestly and humbly crying for the safety of their liberties and religion'.[30] After preliminary discussions with the Council and a private conversation with Rothes, he realized that the King's terms were not likely to provide even a basis for negotiation. The Tables stated that they would accept no *particular* concessions from Charles and would not be satisfied with anything less than a free General Assembly and a Parliament. As for renouncing the Covenant, 'they would not abate one word or syllable of the literal sense thereof'. The Commissioner, still playing for time, asked leave to return to England for fresh instructions.

Shortly before he left an incident occurred which seems to have prejudiced Montrose against Hamilton whom he thereafter held in contempt, regarding him as two-faced and a potential if not an active traitor. Some time during the first week in July, together with Rothes, Loudoun and a number of clerics, he was present at a conference with Hamilton and the lords of the Privy Council at Holyrood House. Nothing noteworthy seems to have taken place during the conference itself, but when it was over Hamilton drew a number of the Covenanters (including Montrose) aside and said: 'My Lords and Gentlemen, I spoke to you before as the King's Commissioner, but now there being none present but ourselves, I speak to you as a kindly Scotsman: if you go on with courage and resolution you will carry what you please, but if you faint or give ground, you are undone.' Having an extremely precise sense of duty, Montrose regarded this as a piece of outright duplicity. He recounted the incident to Henry Guthry[31] over supper that night, saying that 'it wrought an impression that my Lord Hamilton might intend by the business to advance his own design, but that he would suspend judgement until he saw further and in the meantime look more narrowly in his walking'. He may have been referring to the old allegation that Hamilton was ambitious for the Crown, and his reaction seems to suggest that he was not aware that Hamilton had for some time past been encouraging the 'Supplicants' through the medium of the Covenanters' agent Eleazor Borthwick.[32] But it may also have caused him to wonder for a moment (and then suppress the thought) whether there was rather more to the business than he had so far supposed.

The Covenanters availed themselves of Hamilton's absence to consolidate their position. Glasgow, Edinburgh and the South East were solidly for the movement, but in the North, at Aberdeen and among the Gordon tenantries, they had met with less success. This was partly due to Huntly's influence. Rothes was inclined to dismiss him as 'not worth a salt cytron', but with the growing possibility of war the Covenanters became rather more apprehensive of the northern threat since the Gordon, though impoverished, could field a substantial force of cavalry. In July they therefore sent a Colonel Robert Monro (a professional soldier who had fought under Gustavus) to Huntly with miscellaneous threats and promises. If he would join the Covenant they offered to make him general of the army and to pay his debts (which amounted to over £100,000 sterling). If he remained obdurate, however, Monro was to tell him that they had the King's forces outnumbered and 'would know how to undo him'. Time was to demonstrate Huntly's shortcomings as a man of action, but he was a staunch royalist and always good for a gesture. 'My House', he told Monro, 'has risen by the Kings of Scotland. It has ever stood for them and with them shall fall. Nor will I quit the path of my predecessors. And if the event be the ruin of my Sovereign, then shall the rubbish of his House bury beneath it all that belongs to mine.'

At the same time, Montrose was commissioned to treat with the city of Aberdeen and the country round about, and he rode north accompanied by Graham of Morphie, Henderson, Dick, Cant and about thirty other itinerant agitators. The provost, Patrick Leslie, was another of Rothes's cousins to whom he wrote about 'a Great Work to be done which will shortly be seen. Do ye all the good ye can in that town . . . ye will not regret it . . . and attend My Lord Montrose who is a noble and true hearted cavalier.' Unfortunately, the scholars of Aberdeen were stubborn, and Montrose's behaviour hardly commensurate with chivalry. The delegation were hospitably received (Montrose was popular in Aberdeen–he had received the freedom of the city shortly before his marriage in 1629), but they rudely refused to touch the proffered banquet until their hosts had signed the Covenant. The Aberdonians, however, would not be bullied, and the wine was distributed among the poor.[33]

On the Sunday following, the three Covenant ministers demanded to be allowed to preach in the city churches, but the local clergy had no intention of being lectured from their own pulpits and refused to be displaced. On Monday Henderson, Cant and Dick were eventually offered the use of a balcony overlooking a courtyard at the house of Lady Pitsligo (the Earl Marischal's sister, and a precise Presbyterian), where they took it in turns to address the curious but generally sceptical crowd. Eloquence having failed, the Covenanters resorted to argument but were overmatched by the scholars of the university. The ministry of Aberdeen declared their adherence to the Reformed Kirk of Scotland, but they refused to condemn episcopacy or admit the 'immutability of Presbyterian government'. In order to allay the doubts which many openly expressed, Montrose drafted a supplementary declaration–'that we neither had nor have any intention but of loyalty to his Majesty, as the Covenant bears', and with the addition of this caveat, a few signatures were obtained. But the mission was generally accounted a failure, and in early August the Covenanters left–after being presented with a paper containing fourteen written objections composed by the clergy of Aberdeen which the apologists in Edinburgh were to find extremely difficult to answer. When next Montrose had occasion to ride north it would not be with a gospel trumpeter.

Hamilton returned from England at about the same time, armed with a number of fresh concessions and proposals for the restoration of order. However, he now kept himself more remote (he had been severely criticized in London) and 'after four or five days parleying no one could get his mind'. Charles's preparations had not proceeded as rapidly as he had hoped, and Hamilton was instructed to procure a further delay. The King offered a General Assembly and Parliament under certain conditions, and when the Tables objected that they would be satisfied only with a free Assembly without preconditions of any sort, Hamilton asked for a further twenty days in which to obtain yet more instructions. He returned on 20 September with Charles's permission to call a General Assembly for the following month. In an attempt to rally support, the King now issued a covenant of his own, based on the negative confessions of 1580–1. (It seems to have taken the Covenanters initially by surprise, since Sir Thomas Hope himself signed it to the great mortification of Wariston.) It had only a moderate success however. The Privy Council (including Napier and Lorne) signed it. Southesk persuaded a number of the Angus gentry to subscribe, and Huntly obtained two thousand signatures in the North. But the King still swore to maintain 'religion as professed at present' and as the Covenanters interpreted this as implying the preservation of episcopacy, the King's covenant was vilified from every pulpit in Edinburgh. The agitators also discovered a useful instrument of propaganda in the person of a prophetess called Margaret Mitchelson who was installed in Wariston's house where she lay face downwards on a bed and 'groffled' her words of revelation–speaking of Covenanting Jesus, and of how the true covenant was approved in heaven but the King's was the invention of the devil. A number were sceptical, but the multitude believed. 'Lord make me thankful,' wrote Wariston, 'and her presence useful to me and mine.'

During the intervening weeks the energy of the Tables was directed at 'packing' the 'freely constituted Assembly' which they had demanded of the King, and in this Montrose was (one might say, 'regrettably') most active. They were determined to keep the power of election as far as possible within lay hands, and a large proportion of lay elders were nominated to represent the presbyteries (most of the nobles sat in this capacity). This caused a certain amount of jealousy among the ministry, from which Hamilton tried to gain some advantage, but those who complained were again brought into line by the admonition that solidarity was the most important thing. The Tables instructed presbyteries as to whom they were to elect and simply overruled the nomination if this was not complied with.

Hamilton had cause to be pessimistic. 'I know well', he wrote to Charles on 14 October, 'that it is chiefly monarchy which is intended by them to be destroyed, and I cannot say but that it hath received so great a blow as it never can be set right till the principal actors have received their just punishment.' The Assembly would precipitate the crisis. The King would not agree to the abolition of episcopacy, which he held to be the only bulwark against anarchic theocracy, and the Covenanters were intent on the impeachment of the bishops.

On 21 November the Cathedral of Glasgow was packed to the doors. Beneath the high throne of the King's commissioner 240 delegates (142 ministers and 98 lay elders) took their places around the central aisle below the Lords of the Privy Council, the numerous assessors and other officials. (Montrose sat as a lay elder representing his parish of Auchterarder.) Hamilton had chosen Glasgow because it was in this region that his own strength principally lay, but his adherents could not gain an entrance. The Covenanters had minted leaden billets of admission and distributed them only to their own supporters, who now filled all available space in the church. There was much jostling and pushing, and such lack of reverence that Baillie (who attended as a clerical representative) was moved to exclaim that 'they might learn from Canterbury or the Pope–or even from pagans'. Contrary to Hamilton's injunction, many of the delegates had come armed–for fear, as they said, of an anti-Covenant brigand called MacGregor–and though most had left their pistols in their lodgings, many had swords and daggers prominently displayed.

The Assembly began with a procedural wrangle, after which Alexander Henderson was appointed moderator and Wariston clerk to the Assembly. Hamilton tried to challenge the legality of the convention as long as the bishops were excluded (those that had not fled were under his protection in Glasgow) but was informed that, in view of the popular petition that the 'pretended' bishops should be tried for their crimes, it would be improper for them as accused persons to take their seats before they had been acquitted. The Commissioner then questioned the competence of the lay members to discuss theological matters, but had his position suddenly and completely undermined by Wariston, who produced a series of old registers which he claimed were copies of the original records (now lost) of the first General Assemblies before they came under the influence of James VI. This enabled the Covenanters to win any argument over precedent. (Whether the registers were genuine or forgeries is a matter of conjecture since Wariston refused to divulge where or how he had himself obtained them. Twenty years later, in an attempt to save his life, he offered to reveal a secret concerning their discovery, but by then the legality of the 1638 Assembly was of no concern to anyone.)[34]

57

Most of the second day was taken up with arguments and protestations—in which Rothes spoke more than the rest together—and only latterly did the Assembly get on to 'proving' the commissions of the individual delegates. At this stage an incident occurred in which Montrose played a prominent and discreditable part.

The Presbytery of Brechin had been directed by the Tables to elect Erskine of Dun, but in the event Lord Carnegie, Montrose's brother-in-law, received the greater number of votes. The minority group had sent Erskine's commission to Edinburgh asking for advice and it was returned with a note on the back signed by Montrose, approving Erskine's nomination as directed and declaring Carnegie's election void.

When, in the Assembly, Montrose handed Erskine's commission to Wariston, the clerk 'inadvertently' read out not only the commission itself but also part of the note as well, and then . suddenly realizing how compromising it was, broke off in mid-sentence. Hamilton immediately demanded to see the commission, but Henderson refused, stating that the declaration on the back was an accident and not meant to be read in public. After an eloquent protest the Commissioner was forced to give in.

At this point Mr David Dick got to his feet and spoke of the 'backwrit as having some negligence in it'. This infuriated Montrose, who resented such criticism from a presumptious cleric, and he declared hotly that he was ready to 'avow the least jot that was writ'. Southesk, who was one of the assessors, now unfortunately entered the argument in defence of his son:

> Montrose disputed for Dun and by 80 persons attested Dun's election. Southesk disputed for Carnegie, his son, with whom the Commissioner, in Carnegie's absence, took part; but the Assembly sided with Dun. The sture grew so hot that the Moderator wished both the commissions to have been annulled before such noise should have been. To this Southesk did answer sharply. The Moderator replied that he had been his minister 24 years (at Leuchars) yet he had never wronged him. Loudoun then said that no lord should upbraid a Moderator; and Southesk excused himself and qualified his words. The contest between Montrose and Southesk grew so hot that it terrified the whole Assembly so that the Commissioner took upon himself the Moderator's place and commanded all to peace.[35]

It is possible that a quarrel between them had been brewing for some time, but in the event it was made worse by being public. Montrose in particular had behaved rather badly.

By 28 November all hope of achieving a settlement had collapsed. When Hamilton saw that nothing could prevent the Covenanters from proceeding to the trial of the bishops, he decided to dissolve the Assembly. After 'a sad and sorrowful discourse', acted with many tears, he expressed his sincere grief at having to depart without obtaining a peaceful solution, and he declared the Assembly dissolved because of 'the spoiling of the Assembly which he had obtained most free by their most partial directions from the Tables'. The Covenanters now stood at the brink of revolution.

The previous evening, Hamilton had composed a long and significant dispatch to the King:

> It is more probable [he wrote] that these people have somewhat else in their thoughts than religion, but this must serve as a cloak to rebellion wherein for a time they may prevail; but to make them miserable and bring them again to dutiful obedience I am confident Your Majesty will not find it the work of a long time nor of great difficulty. . . . I have missed my end in not being able to make Your Majesty so considerable a party as will be able to curb the insolence of this rebellious nation without assistance from England and greater charge to Your Majesty than this miserable country is worth . . .
> . . . Now for all the Covenanters I shall say only this: in general they may be all placed in one roll as they now stand; but certainly Sire, those that have broached this business and still hold it aloft are Rothes, Balmerino, Lindsay, Lothian, Loudoun, Yester, Cranston. There are many others as forward in *show*—amongst them none more vainly foolish than Montrose.[36]

Though it may have contained an element of spite, the last comment is largely justified. Montrose had done himself no good with either party. His carelessness and lack of tact had revealed the whole disreputable business of the elections and given Hamilton the excuse he needed. His hot-tempered reaction and ill-considered outburst had demonstrated that 'more than ordinary evil pride' with which the Covenanters were later to reproach him. And he had humiliated his father-in-law in public when he himself had been demonstrably in the wrong. But more than this, Hamilton had seen what Montrose could not: that the Graham was to the fore, but only in 'show'. The direction of the movement was firmly in others' hands.

The Glasgow Assembly had been formally dissolved. However, it was not yet over, and for Montrose it was to have another significance not yet apparent, since from it there would emerge a new protagonist who was to become the Graham's mortal enemy—a person whom Hamilton described as 'the dangerousest man in Scotland'.

4

The Campbell

For close designs and crooked counsels fit,
Sagacious, bold, and turbulent of wit,
Restless, unfixed in principle and place,
In power unpleased, impatient in disgrace.
Absalom and Achitophel

'Before His Grace's departure,' wrote Baillie, 'Argyll craved leave to speak, and that time we did not well understand him; but his actions since have made his somewhat ambiguous speeches plain.'[1]

There has been a tendency among later royalist historians to present Argyll in caricature–the villain of the piece, religious bigot, 'craven, a man of plots, craft, poisonous counsels, wayside ambushings, accursed who strikes nor lets the hand be seen'. Yet as the man who was to become Montrose's lifelong enemy, who would in a sense play Caesar to the Graham's Pompey, and who overmatched his rival in political ability in as great a degree as he was himself outshone by the other's romantic chivalry and military flair, he deserves a rather better introduction–if only that their enmity might be brought more sharply into focus, their backgrounds and their talents set in opposition. A simple comparison, however, will not serve. Argyll's was an exceptionally complex character, introverted, and a blend of strange and powerful contrasts. Part Douglas by blood, more Campbell, part feudal magnate, part gaelic chief, a highlander trusted in the Lowlands, a skilful and pragmatic politician shackled to a fanatical and obscurantist creed, a subject powerful enough to have been an independent prince–the Campbell was different, his position unique, his clan close-knit, a race apart.

Physically, he was not cast in the heroic mould. His build was slight: his hair light brown with that reddish tinge common among the Campbells; the nose long, becoming pendulous with age, a heavy chin, thin lips and a pursed mouth, and his eyes, which were grey-blue, 'ill-placed' so that he was often called the 'gley'd Argyll'. Portraits of him differ considerably. As a young man he looks dull and rather sour. The later Castle Campbell portrait (now destroyed) showed a tired and melancholy face, but in middle age he reappears severe and resolute. Only the last portrait has a truly malevolent aspect which seems to personify the character that his enemies have put upon him. The clothes of the noble have been exchanged for the black gown and skull cap of a cleric. The squint is more pronounced, and the mouth is twisted, giving him a dour and sinister appearance as if the crooked face were a symbol of a crooked mind within.

Patrick Gordon of Ruthven, the Gordon historian and Argyll's contemporary, wrote of him:

> For his external and outward disposition, he was of a homely carriage, gentle, mild, and affable, gracious and courteous to speak to. Internally, he had a large and understanding heart, a jealous and far reaching apprehension, and yet his presence did show him of such plain and homely aspect, as he seemed rather inclined to simplicity than any way tainted with a lofty and insatiable ambition, although he proved the deepest statesman, the most crafty, subtle, and over-reaching politician that this age could produce.[2]

Gordon was a royalist, and his description reveals the two faces of the Campbell. By his friends and by his clan Argyll was well loved. By his enemies he was hated, and he had the long memory of a gael, who never forgot a wrong done to him and never forgave the man who did it. But unlike the gael, he had no joy or skill in battle, and he is generally considered to have been a coward. Burnet wrote of him that he was cruel in cold blood,[3] and certainly, when he had the power to be so, he was brutally vindictive.

He had had a bitter childhood. He was probably born in 1607,[4] the youngest child and the only son among five daughters. His mother, Anne Douglas, a daughter of William, seventh Earl of Morton, died either at his birth or shortly afterwards. His father abandoned him three years later.

Argyll's father, the seventh Earl of Argyll, known as Gillesbuig Gruamach or Gillespie the Grim, had a chequered career, and after his first wife died he went to London where he married Anne Cornwallis, a minor heiress in her own right (her mother had inherited Earls Court) and an ardent Roman Catholic. Unlike the majority of the highlanders, the Campbells were a Protestant clan and had done well out of the Reformation, but under her influence Gillespie now embraced the Catholic faith, for which indiscretion he was declared traitor and rebel and formally put to the horn. He was forced to leave Scotland and in 1618 he went to western Flanders where he took service under the Catholic Philip III of Spain. In 1627, however, Charles I had the sentence against him reversed and he returned to London and spent the last ten years of his life in somewhat reduced circumstances in Drury Lane.

From the age of three, his son the Lord of Lorne was brought up by curators of whom the chief was his uncle, the Earl of Morton. He underwent a secluded and solitary education at the hands of a pedagogue who instructed him in the classics and the Protestant religion. At the age of sixteen he was entered at St Leonard's College at the University of St Andrews, where like Montrose five years later he won the silver arrow for shooting at the butts. But unlike most of his contemporaries he did not make the continental tour. Consequently he was neither 'marred nor fashioned' by foreign influences or the English Court, and the omission was later to prove an important factor in that the Presbyterian ministers were the more inclined to trust him.[5] In later life he took little or no interest in foreign affairs, and the French envoy, M. de Boisivon, once remarked of him that 'The Marquis of Argyll is intelligent in the highest degree as to what concerns Scotland but nothing more.'[6] This concentration of his expertise was also to be a prime reason for his influence.

From an early age, albeit under the guidance of his curators, he was burdened with responsibility for the welfare of his house. Before his second marriage the seventh Earl had conveyed the fee simple of his hereditary estates to his son and thereafter enjoyed the income from the property as a life tenant. At the time of his disgrace, however, only the timely intercession of Morton and other friends of the family averted the forfeiture of all the Campbell honours and estates as well. The young Lorne thus inherited a precarious patrimony and the years of his minority were one long struggle to keep it.

Although his estates were seriously burdened with debt (and much of the income was absorbed by the old earl in London), so that he was at once preoccupied with pressing financial problems, Lorne was nevertheless extremely conscious of the Campbell power, and like others of that race he regarded the preservation and extension of it as a duty as well as an ambition. The Campbells were originally of Norman–Irish stock, tracing their ancestry on the gaelic side from the O'Duins, who claimed descent from Diarmid, a nephew of Fionn MacCual, son of the High King of Ireland. From this Diarmid they drew their Highland appellation.[7] In early times they had settled in Garmoran in Argyllshire, where the tribe divided into two branches–the MacArthurs and the MacCailein Mhor. The latter branch grew strong under the patronage of Robert the Bruce, and when the MacArthur was executed by James I and in 1493 the Lords of the Isles were put down also, the MacCailein Mhor as chief of the Clan Campbell became paramount in the western Highlands. By good fortune, well judged policy and predatory enterprise, the Campbells continued to extend their power and in 1457 their chieftain was created Earl of Argyll by James II. Lorne inherited lands more extensive than any other feudal baron in Scotland, larger and richer than any other highland chief. Yet it was not only the extent of the Campbell territory but its position, geographic symmetry and the hereditary jurisdictions that passed with it that made his power significant. The country of Argyll was a compact block of land, bounded on the West by the sea, to the North by mountains, and in the East stretching into Breadalbane and the headwaters of the Tay. It was a buffer between the civilization of the Lowlands and the barbaric mountain country of the gael, a situation from which the Campbells derived much advantage since they undertook the police work of the North-West. They could thus pursue a policy of aggrandizement in the Highlands at the expense of their turbulent but weaker neighbours whose chiefs they subdued and whose lands they annexed under the authority of the Lowland writ. They were the clan who 'Birses yont'. So Lorne as a young man exercised his hereditary jurisdiction to suppress the MacIans and continue the pursuit of the unfortunate Clan MacGregor. He seems also to have dreamed of extending his power to the Hebrides since in 1633 he sponsored a voyage of exploration to annex a remote and fabulous island in the Western seas.

Within his territory the MacCailein Mhor also exercised authority over the other branches of his clan. The Campbells were a close-knit race, and unlike their gaelic neighbours possessed a strong sense of solidarity in time of peace as well as war. So Lawers and Glenorchy, chieftains in their own right, would take their orders from Inveraray. 'Their power of co-ordinated action was exemplary.'[8] In military terms, the MacCailein Mhor could put five thousand swordsmen into the field.

While the seventh Earl lived in London, father and son were continually at feud over the inheritance, and most of Lorne's energy was directed at preventing his estates from falling into the hands of his father's children by his second marriage. While Gillespie was alive therefore there was some need for caution since there was always a chance that an indulgent King might allow the deed of conveyance to be reversed or support the father against the son. (In the event, the peninsula of Kintyre which had been acquired as lately as 1617 and so was not entailed with the rest, did pass to his step-brother, Robert, later Earl of Irvine, who later sold it back to Lorne and went to seek his fortune overseas.)

The quarrel made it politically advisable for Lorne to go to London. He proved a competent courtier and the King quite liked him. So did the Queen, despite the fact that he was a Presbyterian, since she had a shrewd appreciation of his power in Scotland and his ability to use it, and she advised that the young man should be entered on the royal payroll. Charles arranged for him to marry Elizabeth Stewart, Lennox's sister, but she eloped with Lord Maltravers, son of the Earl of Arundel, preferring, said the gossips, a crooked marriage to a crooked man. Lorne does not seem to have been unduly distressed since four months later he married Margaret Douglas, daughter of his guardian Morton. It was probably a better choice since she was devoted to him, while he too was always indulgent to his own family and took a benign interest in the welfare of his relations as later he also became preoccupied with their spiritual salvation. In 1628 he was made a Privy Councillor. In 1631 the seventh Earl was required to renounce his life rent in exchange for a fixed subsistence, and the Parliament of 1633 confirmed Lorne in his full inheritance. The old Gillesbuig Gruamach was greatly put out, and is said to have complained bitterly to the King: 'Sir, I must know this man better than you can do; you have brought me low so that you may raise him; which I doubt not you will live to repent. For he is a man of craft, subtlety, and falsehood, and can love no man; and if he ever has it in his power to do you mischief, he will be sure to do it.'[9] Father and son hated each other cordially and the remark was possibly splenetic rather than indicative of the old man's foresight.

Secure in his estates, Lorne could now devote greater attention to national politics. He was aware of the trouble that was brewing in Scotland but his position was rather different from that of Rothes and the other protagonists. Unlike the other Scottish earls, he had no material ambitions in the Lowlands. The sphere of Campbell aggrandizement was in the Highland north and west. The Act of Revocation therefore did not affect his interest. Moreover, as one of the great magnates and a member of the Privy Council, he remained somewhat aloof from the middle-ranking baronage who formed the opposition.

He was, however, extremely anti-clerical, and strongly opposed to the secular pretensions of the prelates. This was partly due to his strict Presbyterian upbringing and partly to political interest. In 1635, when the office of Chancellor became vacant with the death of Kinnoul, Lorne 'dealt' for it. But the King appointed Spottiswoode, thus passing over the most powerful subject in Scotland in favour of a priest. The following year Lorne was involved in a violent dispute with the Bishop of Galloway, who had fined and banished the Laird of Earlstoun, a Campbell client; and he also defended a non-conformist minister called Samuel Rutherford who was arraigned before the Court of High Commission for preaching against the Articles of Perth. It was shortly after this that he convened a meeting of Rothes and the other malcontents to discuss what steps should be taken to curb the importunities of the bishops.[10] His relations with the opposition, however, appear to have been discreet and largely covert. But he began to draw closer to the ministry and may have been a frequent though probably secret visitor at the house of Archibald Johnston of Wariston. He possibly had warning of the riot in St Giles, and in the months that followed he may have supplied Wariston with information concerning the proceedings of the Council. He did not sign the Covenant, however, and to most men he remained an enigma.

In May 1638 he accompanied Traquair and Roxburgh to London to report on the situation to the King. There is no detailed record of this conference, but Lorne appears to have spoken his mind in criticism of the bishops. Charles was extremely displeased and there was a rumour that Lorne would be arrested, possibly on the advice of his father, who told the King that his son 'would wind him a pirn'. He left ahead of the others, however, and returned safely to Scotland.

Charles is said to have distrusted Lorne from this time. Indeed, he had good cause to think that Lorne might join the opposition since he was himself playing the Campbell false. The King was now fixed on the idea that the Covenanters could be put down by force, and his strategy included a scheme whereby an army of Irishes were to invade the West of Scotland under Ranald MacDonald, Earl of Antrim, who, as the son of the rebel Tyrone, had been brought up at the English Court and married to the Duke of Buckingham's widow. Antrim was an empty-headed but engaging scoundrel, and he was a great favourite with the King, the Queen and the Archbishop, whom he regaled with extravagant projects of invading Scotland with a host of Irish MacDonalds. His reward was to be Kintyre–which had been granted to the Campbells in 1617. In Ireland, Wentworth, the most able of the King's administrators, vehemently opposed the scheme–'He is as much able to do it as I to take upon me the Cross with so many for the Holy Land'–and he argued that Lorne's doubtful loyalty should be strengthened and not undermined. But Charles was beginning to display that callous and misdirected cunning that was to bring them all to ruin, and the frivolous Antrim was promised Kintyre. It was a foolish plan and the first of a sequence of events which would lead to the Irish Rebellion–perhaps the greatest single disaster of Charles's career.

Inevitably the secret got out, and in Scotland Lorne complained to Hamilton and told him that if Antrim invaded Kintyre he would defend his land. In Argyll the Campbells began to muster in readiness. For his part, Hamilton, in his serpentine way, wrote to Charles encouraging him to use Antrim as an instrument to harass the Lord of Lorne. However the Campbell was a cautious politician. He signed the King's covenant with other members of the Privy Council and his correspondence with Hamilton gave no indication of the action that he contemplated. It was now that he best demonstrated that 'close and false carriage' of which the King so indignantly complained.

In describing Lorne's action at the Glasgow Assembly, the historian Gardiner stated merely that he chose to join 'the many against the few'. It is an unjust and unnecessary distortion. In considering the Campbell's motivation, it seems more likely that there were two principal factors that led him to make his decision and so initiated the political calculations that determined the timing and manner of his actions. The first was inherent in his position as the MacCailein Mhor– the duty to protect his patrimony against whosoever might threaten it. Regardless of whether he was in league with the Covenanters or not, Charles had been prepared to play him false and promise Kintyre to Antrim, his hereditary enemy. The King did not necessarily reward loyalty, it seemed. The second was religious, since although he had been brought up a Presbyterian, it was only at this time that he was 'converted' in the full emotive sense of the word, and the religious quarrel immediately became of prime importance. During the early sessions of the Glasgow Assembly, Alexander Henderson conducted nightly prayer meetings which the Campbell is reported to have attended, and, according to his friends, it was at one of these that his conversion took place. Royalists have been quick to suggest that the occasion was too convenient for this conversion to be true, but his private life thereafter seems to confirm the sincerity of his professed belief. The charlatan such as Rothes could drop the mask, but Lorne never did. As he grew older his preoccupation with religion took on a more sinister aspect, and it was one of the strange contradictions of his character that a man with such a clear political brain could be so chained to a medieval intolerance and a fanatical creed. Yet it was this contradiction which enabled him to become the leader of the Covenanting movement. Greater than the other secular lords who were ranged against the King, his interests were not the same, or so obvious as theirs, while his beliefs gave him more in common with the extreme Presbyterians who trusted him as they would no other noble.

Political calculation determined the detail of his actions. In mid-1638 his father died and he became the eighth Earl of Argyll. The need for caution was thus past. The decisive moment was approaching. His power could tip the balance. He knew the doubts of the majority of the Scots, but he knew also, having been in London, the impotence of the King. He knew who on the Council were secret Covenanters and he knew that only he was ideally qualified to seize the leadership.

There was much that he could not have foreseen. Though he took his place at the forefront of the movement, he never actually controlled it but was also carried by its momentum. Alone among the nobles he realized the crucial significance of the ministers and the power of Presbyterianism among the Lowland people and he was aware of the strength of the forces about to be unleashed. But he seems to have miscalculated (at least in 1638) just what the end would be. He did not count on war itself (it was not his element) but saw no further than the probable efficacy of a demonstration of strength upon the border. And to say that he already aimed at being dictator is possibly premature. There is a strong element of drift in the development of a country's affairs. If a man is ambitious his ambition evolves with events and he marks his way accordingly. The ambition and the end result may only seem clear in retrospect. So Argyll could tell his son: 'I never thought of those dire consequences which presently followed.' Seen through Montrose's eyes, as in this account he must be, the Campbell is the enemy, the traitor, perjured and foresworn. Yet when the wheel had turned full circle and Argyll faced the fate that he had meted out to others, he alone could look back on events with a perspective that Montrose and other men more single-hearted than the Campbell never could have shared.

As Hamilton prepared to leave the Cathedral, Argyll asked leave to speak. His voice was low, and he addressed himself only to the Covenanters. He had been commanded by the King, he said, to attend the Assembly as one of the royal assessors, and he had acted justly and honourably in that capacity. But he could never be moved by private ambition to flatter the King or persuade him to 'run violent courses'. He was surprised by Hamilton's decision to dissolve the Assembly since 'in his humble opinion' the objection to the inclusion of lay elders was insufficient reason for so drastic a step. The Assembly, he thought, ought to consist of laymen as well as clerics since 'these two made up one complete body'. He exhorted them to stand by the Confession of Faith of 1581, 'and to suffer no other expositions to be put upon it', and he wished them all to understand that he had himself signed the King's covenant only 'with the express reservation that it should be interpreted according to the minds of those who had subscribed it in 1581'.[11]

While the delegates were pondering the significance of this, Hamilton (after some embarrassment while the door was unlocked) left the Cathedral. That afternoon he met with the Privy Council and asked them to subscribe a proclamation declaring all members of the Assembly traitors if they continued to sit after its formal dissolution by the Commissioner. Hope and Argyll refused to sign it.

Back in the Cathedral, the Covenanters had embarked on revolution. 'We are at war,' said Henderson, 'with the Kingdom of Satan and Anti-Christ'. By a large majority the members voted to defy the King's authority and continue the Assembly.

The next morning, alone of the Privy Councillors, Argyll returned to his seat. Though he had not been elected to represent a parish, his right to sit and speak in the Assembly was granted by common consent, and Henderson himself asked him to remain 'for the common interest he had in the Church'. Many still could not divine his purpose:

> No one thing did confirm us so much as Argyll's presence [wrote Baillie]: not only the man was the most powerful subject in the kingdom but also at that time being in good grace with the King and the Commissioner, we could not conceive but his stay with us was with the allowance of both . . . to keep matters in some temper, and hold us from desperate extremes . . . yet afterwards we found that nothing was more against the stomach of the Commissioner and the King than Argyll's stay.[12]

Baillie did not know about Antrim perhaps. (Argyll it is true, was subsequently to have a private interview with Hamilton, after which they are said to have parted on terms of great cordiality—but this apparent rapproachement was something else again.) In a short speech he urged them also to be careful to abstain from criticisms injurious to the royal authority and any unnecessary provocation of 'the powers that be'. He may have been keeping the back door open for himself, or he may have believed that a modified form of revolution was possible. If so, he did not realize that such movements once started are hard to limit, or that Charles, however weak, would react in kind. The Assembly immediately began to defer to his advice, and his influence is best indicated by a subsequent remark of Baillie's—

that on 5 December '. . . they did nothing of moment because of Argyll's absence at a funeral.'[13]

'Now that there were none to curb them', the Assembly 'went on at a great rate.' The last six Assemblies were declared invalid. The Service Book, the Book of Canons and the Court of High Commission were condemned, the Articles of Perth annulled. episcopacy abjured and abolished and salmon-fishing prohibited on Sundays. Because a number of broadsheets had attacked the Covenant, a system of press censorship was organized under the direction of Wariston. Charles called this last 'A pretty Act, that he might print nothing concerning ecclesiastical polity and govern except Wariston gave him leave'.[14]

On 13 December sentence was pronounced upon the bishops. The hierarchy were formally deposed and many of them excommunicated. Since the prelates had declined to appear, no defence was offered. They were convicted of corruption, debauchery, Sabbath-breaking and every conceivable iniquity. Few of the charges would have stood up in a court of law. 'The mere fact of episcopal office was held to afford proof presumptive of moral delinquency.'[15]

The most important piece of legislation, however, came at the very end. On 19 December a permanent Commission of the Church was established and invested with the full powers of the Assembly. This opened the door to a future theocracy since in theory it enabled the Kirk to interfere in any department of civil and religious life. 'In following Assemblies it was licked into a shape, midwifed by politicians, and its power added to it by piece-meal, in a surreptitious way; not all at once for that would have startled the creators of it . . . who did begin to quarrel with its usurpations too late. . . .'[16]

Finally, the delegates proposed a vote of thanks to the King for allowing them 'a free and lawful Assembly', and when this had been passed another special vote of thanks was given to Argyll. He replied at some length, begging them not to misunderstand his delay in declaring himself, since from the beginning he had been 'set their way'. By remaining a member of the Privy Council he had hoped to be more useful than he would have been otherwise. 'But now of late, matters had come to such a height that he found it behoved him to join himself openly to their society except he should prove a knave.' He ended by stressing the need for unity, and 'entreated all the ministers to consider what had brought the Bishops to ruin, *viz* pride and avarice; and therefore willed them to shun these two rocks if they would avoid shipwreck'.[17]

It was a judicious warning.

'We have now cast down the walls of Jericho,' concluded Henderson. 'Let him that rebuildeth them beware of the curse of Hiel the Bethelite.'

5

'Invictus Armis . . .'

His honour rooted in dishonour stood,
And faith unfaithful, kept him falsely true.
Idylls of the King

'Now about this time, there came out of Germany home to Scotland a gentleman of base birth born at Balveny, who had served long and fortunately in the German Wars and called to his name, Field Marshal Leslie, His Excellency.'[1] He was appointed commander-in-chief of the Covenant forces. 'We were feared', wrote Baillie, 'that emulation among our Nobles might have done harm when they should be met in the field; but such was the wisdom of that old, little, crooked soldier, that all with an incredible submission from the beginning to the end, gave over themselves to be guided by him as if he had been the Great Solyman.'[2] Leslie brought with him a number of other Scottish veterans of the continental wars, mercenaries happy to find employment in their native country and in their national cause, who trained the fresh levies and formed the nucleus of a professional officer corps.

The country prepared for war. Arms and equipment were shipped from Holland, and a cannon foundry was established at Potterow. The Covenanters already had a modest war chest, but the ministers did good work in persuading people to shake out their purses to pay for the army, and a further 200,000 merks were borrowed from William Dick, the richest merchant in Edinburgh. (A number of nobles including Montrose and Napier stood surety for its repayment.) In January 1639 the citizens were organized to dig entrenchments and fortify the Port of Leith. Committees of War were established in every county, and Montrose, who was appointed colonel for the shires of Perth and Forfar, now found work more congenial to his temper. In late January he was raising a regiment from the tenantry of Angus and Strathearn.

In parallel with the practical preparations for defence, the volume of Covenant propaganda also increased. The Scots published a manifesto laying their case before the English people in which they blamed the bishops for precipitating the crisis–an argument calculated to appeal to the Puritan opposition in the South. The King recited his own version of the quarrel in a 400-page volume entitled *The Large Declaration* which was published at the beginning of the year. Neither document was inducive to rational negotiation, and as salvoes in a paper war they tended to act as irritants and not much else.

On 27 February, Charles issued a proclamation commanding the nobility and their vassals to meet him in arms at York on 1 April. The English fleet was ordered to intercept Scottish vessels on the seas. Scottish ships in English harbours were seized and their cargoes impounded. The King planned a co-ordinated invasion of Scotland from three separate directions. While the main army was to muster at York and then advance on the border, Hamilton was to take 5,000 troops by sea and make a landing on the East Coast, in Lothian or Fife. He was then to link up with the northern Royalists under the Marquis of Huntly, who was appointed the King's Lieutenant for the North. In the West, Antrim was to invade Kintyre, while Wentworth, with another Irish force, would first occupy the Isle of Arran and then advance to Dunbarton.

The plan looked impressive on paper, but in reality Charles had neither the ability nor the means to carry it out. For almost ten years now he had ruled in England without a Parliament, and although he had so far managed to 'live of his own', there were insufficient funds in the Exchequer to finance a war of any long duration. The King had money only for a short campaign, which meant in effect that he would have to gamble on the mere threat of invasion by an army on the border being enough to frighten the Scots into submission. But this was foolishly optimistic. Nor did the English army come up to his original expectation. The war was not popular, and the level of recruiting was correspondingly low. The old system of the feudal muster had become antiquated and inefficient. It was ninety years since the last major campaign across the border,[3] and two generations of peace had eroded the warlike habits of the northern English. Even the borders had grown quiet, and the old moss troopers had all but vanished as a breed. Consequently, the quality of the levies was extremely poor. They were miserably paid and arrangements for provisioning the army were almost non-existent. The proportion of experienced officers was small at every level of command, and the generals–Holland and Arundel–who led the cavalry and the infantry respectively were no match for a professional like Leslie who had learned his trade under Gustavus Adolphus.[4]

Of the proposed diversions, the one in the North was by far the more promising–as the Covenanters were quick to realize. The northern Royalists–Gordons, Ogilvies, Setons, Urquharts–could possibly raise a force of 4,000 men, which if joined by Hamilton's 5,000 and supported by a fleet could pose a serious threat to the Covenanters' rear and oblige them to divert troops away from the border. Huntly had commanded the Scottish Archer Guard in France and so had at least some military experience. However, the supreme command in this theatre of operations had been assigned to Hamilton, and, fearful as ever that a rival might usurp his place in the King's favour, he successfully conspired to restrict Huntly's freedom of action. He described the Gordon to Charles in equivocal terms as 'much misliked'–'to be trusted by you but whether fitly or no I cannot say'–and, having thus cast doubts upon Huntly's reliability, he proposed that he should be instructed to take no offensive action until specifically ordered to do so. Charles, who had complete faith in Hamilton's military ability, agreed. 'I mean not to put any other in the chief trust in these affairs but yourself.' To what extent Hamilton's subsequent conduct justified this trust will shortly be seen. One contemporary account went so far as to state that he sent a secret message to the Covenanters hidden in the barrel of a pistol advising them 'to curb their Northern enemies or expect no quarter from the King'.[5]

A further weakness of the plan was the co-ordination required between the three attacking forces. It was envisaged that the Irish invasion and the rising in the North should be launched so as to coincide with the arrival of the main army on the border. But since the King's advance was extremely slow, the Covenanters, who were suitably forewarned by their spies at Court, had ample time in which to take pre-emptive action to secure their flanks. Argyll, as Warden of the West, garrisoned the peninsula of Kintyre and seized Hamilton's Castle of Brodick on the Isle of Arran. Having thus neutralized the threat from Ireland, he then took a band of highlanders, and in temporary alliance with the Camerons (for once on the Lowland side), went raiding into Huntly's lands of Badenoch.

During March, the royal castles of Edinburgh, Dumbarton, Dalkeith and Tantallon were surprised and taken, leaving Caerlaverock only in Charles's hands. In Clydesdale and Tweeddale, Traquair, Roxburgh and the Douglas made a half-hearted effort to raise support for the King, but having little success gave up the attempt. The South of Scotland was lost to Charles 'without stroke of sword'.

Since the most immediate threat was from the North, the Covenanters decided to send a force to Aberdeen and settle accounts with Huntly, whose commission as King's Lieutenant was already known in Edinburgh. Command of the expedition was given to Montrose, who was thus gazetted general for the first campaign of his career. However, since he was still only twenty-seven and had no previous experience of war, Leslie (whose commission as commander-in-chief was not issued until 9 May) was deputed to accompany him as adviser with the rank of adjutant-general.

The first day of February had found Montrose presiding over a committee of war at the tolbooth of Forfar and involved in a fresh quarrel with his father-in-law. Having received a summons to attend, Southesk (himself a power in Forfar), with the Master of Ogilvie, young Spynie, and the Constable of Dundee, rode in to demand by what authority the Graham was attempting 'to stent the King's lieges'.[6] Montrose produced his warrant from the Tables (which had been signed by Lord Carnegie, among others, who was in the process of becoming a Covenanter), but Southesk refused to accept its validity, and, having further declined to subscribe the latest edition of the Covenant,[7] he departed in high dudgeon to Kinnaird.

Montrose had also summoned a committee of the northern Coven-anters – Forbeses, Frasers, Crichtons – to meet him at Turriff in Aber-deenshire on 14 February. Huntly heard of it and decided to occupy the town with 2,000 of his Gordons and prevent the muster. Montrose now gave first proof of his ability. News of Huntly's in-tention reached him a few days before, and taking 200 cavalry he hurriedly crossed over the Grangebean to the rendezvous where he was joined by 800 men of the northern Covenanters. He took up a strong position in a walled churchyard, and when the Gordon eventu-ally arrived at the head of his army it was to discover the Coven-anters firmly in possession and obviously prepared to fight. A number of the younger Gordons were for attacking but, mindful of Hamilton's orders, Huntly was not ready to risk an assault, and after the two forces had 'glared at each other' for a while, the Royalists withdrew to Strathbogie.[8] Having thus won the first round, Montrose concluded his arrangements with the northern Covenanters for an advance on Aberdeen, and then returned to Angus, where Leslie was occupied in licking the county levies into shape.

Huntly now contemplated a defence of Aberdeen, but he was still paralysed by the instructions which he had received from Hamilton. Nor, apart from 100 cavalry, had he received the help from England that had been promised. He decided therefore to parley for time, and sent Gordon of Straloch[9] to the Covenant general asking him to forbear from any military action until it were seen whether the King would be prepared to negotiate. For his part, he undertook to keep within the bounds of his jurisdiction and not to interfere with the Covenanters in any way. Montrose was anxious to reach the city before Huntly could have time to fortify it. He replied that he was under orders from the Tables to march on Aberdeen, but that he would pay for what his soldiers took and would not commit any un-provoked act of aggression. Huntly thereupon advanced as far as Inverurie but continued to make peaceful overtures.

The Covenanters appear to have believed that a Royalist attack was imminent since Huntly's commissioners reported that the enemy were very nervous and the camp disturbed by nightly alarms. Montrose, who was possibly unaware of the Gordon's dilemma, also seems to have thought that it would come to a fight, and he spent his last days at home putting his affairs in order, providing among other things for 20,000 merks to be paid from his estate or by his heirs as a marriage portion for his youngest sister Beatrix. The army moved on 28 March.

Huntly meanwhile had briefly occupied Aberdeen where he enlisted all loyal citizens and began to construct a series of defensive

earthworks. However, when he learned of Montrose's advance his resolution failed him, and, either on orders from Hamilton or for lack of
them, he abandoned the town again and withdrew to his castle at the Bog
of Gight. The unfortunate burghers, thus deserted, viewed the Covenanters' approach with considerable dread. 'They began to be heartless
and comfortless, and entirely to despair, not knowing what course to
take.'[10] Many of the ministers and members of the university fled,
while a few loyal lairds and their followers hastily took ship and
sailed south to join the King. The rest abandoned their trenches and
opened the gates to the Covenanters.

The army reached the vicinity of Aberdeen on the evening of 29
March where it was joined by a force of northern Covenanters whom
Huntly's withdrawal had enabled to march south unmolested. Montrose firmly rejected suggestions that the city should be given over to
rapine, and camped outside the town. The following day he led his
troops in good order, with colours flying and banners displayed,[11]
through the centre of Aberdeen and on to the Queen's Links beyond.
The Covenant force numbered about 6,000 horse and foot, excellently
appointed. As a distinguishing badge each man wore a bunch of blue
ribbon in his hat, or, if a trooper, a blue scarf bandolier-wise across
his chest from which he hung the spanner for his firelock. The
ministers were somewhat critical of the fashion[12] and referred to them
as 'Montrose's whimsies', but the idea caught on and the blue bonnets
or 'jockies', as the English called them, became the standard insignia
of the Covenant armies.

While his soldiers breakfasted in the fields, the General held an
informal council of war with Leslie and the other Covenanting lords—
Marischal, Kinghorn, Elcho, Erskine, Forbes, Carnegie and the Master
of Fraser. The ministers took immediate possession of the pulpits.
Orders were given for the trenches to be filled in, and the burghers
were summarily fined 10,000 merks for recusancy. Then, leaving
Kinghorn with 1,800 men to garrison the town, Montrose set out to
deal with Huntly.

The Gordon was still anxious to treat, and Straloch was sent from
Strathbogie to request a further parley. On 4 April the two leaders
met at the village of Lewes of Fyvie, accompanied by only eleven
followers armed with walking swords. When each side had searched
the other for concealed firearms, Montrose and Huntly drew aside
to talk. Exactly what passed between them is not known, but after
a long and earnest conversation,[13] Huntly, without giving any explanation to his suite, mounted his horse and rode with Montrose
to the latter's camp at Inverurie. There he signed a bond, which
may have been an amended version of the Covenant, 'to maintain the
King's authority together with the liberties both of Church and State,
Religion and Laws', and which was possibly dictated by Montrose. He
also agreed to allow members of his clan to subscribe the Covenant
should they wish to do so, while for his part Montrose promised that
the Covenanters would not molest the northern Catholics so long as

they observed the laws and liberties of Scotland. Montrose conducted this negotiation on his own authority and seems to have been satisfied that Huntly had been effectually neutralized.

It is impossible to establish precisely what happened next, since contemporary accounts differ in apportioning responsibility or blame. It appears that the next day, or shortly after, Huntly came to a second conference at Inverurie and was alarmed to discover that a number of his hereditary enemies—Forbes, Fraser, and particularly Crichton of Frendraught, with whom he was at feud over the suspected murder of his kinsmen—had meanwhile taken quarters in the Covenant camp. He sent Straloch to advise Montrose that such men intended mischief and that any attempt to detain him prisoner would be deeply resented by the Gordons. Montrose is said to have replied: 'I shall do my utmost for Huntly's satisfaction, . . . but there is this difficulty, that business here is all transacted by vote and a committee; nor can I get anything done of myself.'[14] This not only implied that their agreement would have to be confirmed by the committee, but it also contained a warning which Huntly could not have missed.

A few days later Montrose broke camp and returned to Aberdeen, where he was joined by 500 of Argyll's highlanders whom he quartered on the lands of absent Royalists but would not permit to enter the town. By now all the northern Covenanting barons had come in, including the Earl of Seaforth (who thus makes his first appearance in the first of several changes of coat), and a large committee was convened 'to take a final course for the settlement of the North'. At this, Montrose was severely criticized for his leniency towards Huntly and it was decided by the majority that the Gordon should be required to come to Aberdeen and give satisfaction to the committee in person.

According to Spalding's account,[15] Huntly obeyed the summons and went to Aberdeen under a promise of safe conduct which had been personally guaranteed by Montrose. He attended a session of the committee at which nothing untoward seems to have occurred, and afterwards had supper with some of the leading Covenanters, all of whom behaved in a friendly and sociable way. When the meal was over he took his leave of them, since he intended to depart home in the morning (he had already sent an *avant courier* to arrange horses on the road), and returned to his lodging. Some time during the night, however, the Covenanters put a guard around the house, and when Huntly emerged unsuspecting in the morning he was informed that he must again appear before the committee. On arriving at Marischal's house, where the meeting was to be held, he was met by Montrose who, having greeted him normally enough, then proceeded to demand that he should make a substantial contribution towards the repayment of the 200,000 merks loaned by William Dick to finance the northern expedition. Huntly indignantly replied that, since he had not incurred the expense, the reimbursement of an Edinburgh merchant was no concern of his. He was then asked to undertake the suppression of a band of highland robbers who had been raiding Covenant property, but he excused himself on the grounds that such work did not fall within his jurisdiction. Finally he was required to become reconciled with Crichton of Frendraught, but he replied categorically that he would not even consider it. Montrose then closed the meeting and turning to Huntly said: 'My Lord, seeing we are all now friends, will you go South with us?' The Gordon answered that he had already made arrangements to return to Strathbogie, whereupon the General repeated in a rather firmer tone: 'Your Lordship would do well to go with us!' Catching his drift, Huntly hotly protested that he had come under a safe conduct and demanded that the bond that he had signed should be returned to him. This was done, and he then asked: 'Whether will you take me with you south as a captive or willingly by my own mind?'–to which Montrose answered shortly: 'Take your choice.' Huntly then said that he would prefer to go 'as a volunteer', and he was accompanied south by his eldest son, Lord George Gordon. (His second son, the Viscount Aboyne, was released on parole to collect some money and other necessaries from Strathbogie.) At Edinburgh Huntly was summoned before the Tables and asked to sign an unamended copy of the Covenant. He refused to do so, and was escorted, protesting eloquently, to a prison in the Castle.

If this is indeed what happened, then Huntly had cause to feel aggrieved. The historian Gardiner, writing two hundred years after the event, concluded that 'Montrose played but a mean and shabby part . . . the only mean action of his life.' Huntly certainly bore a grudge against the Graham ever after. 'He could never be gained to join cordially with him nor to swallow that indignity . . . whence it came to pass that such as were equally enemies to them both . . . in the end prevailed so far as to ruinate and destroy both of them and the King by a consequent.'[16]

Yet whether 'Montrose was content to be overborne by votes so that it might be to his greater glory to lead Huntly into Edinburgh as a trophy of his conquest',[17] or whether he was simply powerless to prevent what happened remains uncertain. Straloch, who was better placed than Spalding to know what occurred, put the responsibility for the quarrel and Huntly's arrest on Alexander Leslie, and Monteth, writing some years afterwards, maintained that 'Montrose opposed with all his might their determination to break the parole which had been given: nevertheless his single authority being insufficient to prevent it.'[18] In England it was reported that Huntly had been arrested by Leslie. It is significant too that Lord George Gordon and Aboyne, who were also witnesses to the proceedings, do not seem to have shared their father's grudge since both, and especially the former, were later among Montrose's closest and most trusted companions in arms.

It has been suggested also that Huntly was not an unwilling captive but was glad enough to escape from the impossible situation in which

Hamilton had placed him. Charles wrote to his favourite at this time describing the Gordon as 'feeble and false'. His confinement at Edinburgh does not seem to have been particularly rigorous, since two of his daughters were married there during his period of incarceration. Nor did Montrose's own report to the Tables of 15 April say anything about his having been 'persuaded' or otherwise constrained, but stated only that 'the Marquis of Huntly was come in and subscribed the Covenant and gave his eldest son as a pledge for his conduct.' It is a matter for speculation perhaps whether the Gordon's resentment of Montrose stemmed from the fact that the Graham had been the instrument of his betrayal, or because he had been the contemptuous witness of his humiliation. It is certain, however, that he never forgave, and the quarrel was to have fatal consequences for them both.

On the day that Montrose returned to Edinburgh, Charles arrived at York with an army estimated at 12,000 foot and 2,000 horse.

On 1 May Hamilton appeared in the Firth of Forth with 19 sail and 5,000 troops, but finding the approaches to Edinburgh fortified and the Scots mustered along the shore, he did not attempt a landing. The fleet anchored between the little islands of Inchkeith and Inchcolm where the bulk of the soldiers disembarked, while Hamilton sat on board his flagship and opened a lugubrious correspondence with the King. Daunted perhaps by the warlike preparations of the Scots (and possibly by his mother, the Dowager Countess, who rode into Edinburgh with a brace of pistols at her saddle-bow swearing that she would be the first to shoot him if he set foot as an invader upon Scottish soil), he decided that action was impossible and advised Charles to come to terms. At the same time, he wrote to a number of leading Covenanters to inform them that he was 'a lover of his country', that this employment had been forced upon him, and that 'he had accepted it with the resolution to manage it for the greatest advantage that his loyalty to his Prince would permit him'. In the event, he allowed himself considerable latitude.

Charles, on reaching Newcastle, was already at his wits' end for money, and in the first week in May his proclamations, which had been merely truculent hitherto, became more conciliatory in tone. He promised the Scots 'all just satisfaction' in Parliament as soon as the troubles had subsided, and to call off his invasion 'if all civil and temporal obedience were shown him'. Since there was no reference to 'ecclesiastical' obedience, this seemed to open the way for negotiation.[19]

The Scots, however, were determined to treat from strength. On 20 May Leslie mustered the army at Leith and then advanced as far as Dunglass at the eastern end of the Lammermuir. The Scottish force numbered something over 20,000 men, accompanied by a large number of ministers including the Rev Robert Baillie, who, somewhat carried away by the pomp and circumstance, went armed to the teeth with a train of henchmen – 'having taken leave of this world . . . and resolved to die in that service without return'. Baillie's description of the state of the army is over-idealistic, and it appears from Wariston's account that, initially at least, there was some confusion and difficulty over provisions and the supply of elementary equipment such as entrenching tools. However, the morale of the Scots was undoubtedly higher than that of the English, engaged as they were in a national cause and constantly fortified by the sermons of their ministers. They were also better armed, better officered and drilled, and paid a regular 6d. a day.

Neither army was anxious to engage. Both sides were in something of a fright, and since a negotiation was the ultimate object of both the two forces kept a wary distance. Charles's hesitation allowed Leslie to advance to Dunse Hill unopposed where he took up a strong position and might have cut Charles off from Newcastle had he chosen to do so. Psychologically, the King had fallen back on to the defensive. But the Scots did not want to cross the border. Charles, outnumbered, could not do so. Nor, however, could he defend the Tweed indefinitely, and his situation became daily more critical.

But in the meanwhile there were fresh developments in the North. When Aboyne returned to Strathbogie to collect Huntly's effects, the Gordon barons persuaded him to break his parole on the grounds that the clan could not be left without a leader at so critical a time. As Huntly's third son, Lord Lewis, was still only thirteen and something of a scamp, Aboyne decided to go south and seek help from the King, and sometime early in May he appeared at the royal camp at Newcastle. Charles agreed to appoint him Lieutenant of the North in Huntly's absence but referred him to Hamilton for support since he himself had no troops to spare.

While Aboyne was in England, however, the northern Royalists, led by Ogilvie of Banff, with Urquhart, Foverane, Seton and a number of the younger Gordons–Haddo, Abergeldie, Gight and others–took matters into their own hands. In a cavalry raid known afterwords as the Trot of Turriff (the first actual engagement of the Civil War), they attacked and dispersed the Covenant garrison in that town, and then proceeded to Aberdeen, which they retook and occupied from 15 to 20 May.

That Hamilton failed to react at all to this event was indicative either of extreme incompetence or deliberate treachery. According to the King's original instructions it was one of his principal tasks to support a rising in the North, and on 8 May Charles had written again advising him that, if he could not land his 5,000 troops on Lothianside, 'then it may be counsellable to send most of your landsmen to the North to strengthen my party there'. The Trot of Turriff took place on 14 May. News of it reached Edinburgh on 18 May and Newcastle on 24 May. Yet although Hamilton was in touch with the Covenanters on shore, and barely a hundred miles (no more than two days by sea) from the scene of action, he seems to have been completely unaware that the Royalists had taken Aberdeen, since on 21 May–seven days after its capture–he wrote to the King advising the *withdrawal* of two of his regiments to reinforce the army at Newcastle, and on 23 May, with Charles's consent, 3,000 troops were duly detached from the fleet and sent south.

Aboyne arrived in the Firth of Forth on 29 May to be told regretfully that there were no troops to spare—since the greater part had returned to the main army. Hamilton entertained the young Gordon lavishly on board his flagship[20] and offered him four field pieces together with the services of a certain Colonel Gunn, who had apparently served with great distinction in the German wars and in whom he placed the greatest trust. With this, and a vague promise of help later, Aboyne had to be content, and he hastily put to sea again and headed north for Aberdeen. Hamilton wrote to Charles describing the Gordon in somewhat disparaging terms and asking for reinforcements, but otherwise remained inactive though in daily correspondence with the Covenanters. ('It was evident', wrote Baillie, 'he eschewed all occasion of beginning the war; he did not trouble a man on shore with a shot.')

The Covenanters had first learned about the fresh disturbance in the North through an intercepted letter from Ogilvie of Banff to the King. Montrose was again detached from the main army, which was about to start south, and ordered to march on Aberdeen. On 18 May he was still at Edinburgh raising a force, but Marischal was at Dunnottar with 800 Covenanters where he could be relied upon to delay any Royalist advance until Montrose arrived.

The Gordons spent some days carousing in Aberdeen where they were joined by several hundred highlanders from Deeside and Glentanner led by Donald Farquharson, Huntly's Baillie of Strathawine, and by Lord Lewis Gordon who had escaped from the care of his grandmother in order to join the army. After some considerable discussion, the leaders decided to march south to settle with Marischal, and they sent Straloch (who was much against the venture) to see what the Covenanters would do. Marischal was content to parley for time and told Straloch that, unless he received orders from the Tables to march against them, he would fight only if attacked. The Royalists plundered Durris, but then fell to quarrelling among themselves, and after a night in the fields and a glimpse of the defences at Dunnottar, they eventually thought better of it and retired to Strathbogie. From there they conducted a quick raid across the Spey and, having cornered Seaforth, Innes and the other northern Covenanters at Elgin, forced them to disband. But Ogilvie of Banff, who was the most effective leader among them, now fell sick of a fever and the rest dispersed to defend their separate strongholds.

Marischal took advantage of their withdrawal to advance on Aberdeen, which he occupied on 23 May. Montrose arrived two days later with an army of about 4,000 horse and foot. The ministers and others of his Covenant colleagues now pressed the General to make a savage example of the city by turning it over to pillage, but he firmly rejected the suggestion and spared the town upon payment of a further 10,000 merks. This 'too great leniency' caused some dissatisfaction among the soldiery, who felt cheated of their rightful spoil, and there were a large number of desertions. The troops satisfied their bloodlust by slaughtering all the dogs found in the streets who, during the Royalist interim, had been decked out with blue rosettes in mockery of the Covenanting ribbon.

On 30 May Montrose led the army out of Aberdeen and as far as Udny, where he quartered his cavalry in the church – 'a practice then unusual', says Rothiemay, 'though afterward it grew to be more in fashion . . . especially after Oliver Cromwell'.[21] Bypassing Haddo's place of Kellie, which was too strong to be taken without a proper siege train, he then invested the Castle of Gordon of Gight. But after two days, news that Aboyne had been sighted off the coast obliged him to raise the siege and withdraw south again through Aberdeen to Stonehaven. He assumed, reasonably, that Aboyne had obtained a force of troops from Hamilton, and in the face of this more serious threat his first consideration was to protect his communications with Edinburgh.

On 2 June Aboyne appeared in Aberdeen Roads with two small warships and a Newcastle collier. Though he seems to have waited in hope, further reinforcements from Hamilton were not forthcoming. However, at the news of his arrival the Gordons began to reassemble, and by the end of a week he had collected a force of 4,000 foot and 600 cavalry. On 14 June he started to move south, and early on the morning of 16 June came up with Montrose and Marischal who had entrenched themselves in front of Stonehaven.

Aboyne, who was still only eighteen and had no previous experience of command, entrusted the disposition of his army to the veteran Gunn whom Hamilton had recommended to him as a professional soldier of some distinction – though in the event he turned out to be a splenetic and temperamental character of questionable ability whose loyalty became more doubtful as the short campaign progressed. The Royalists had no artillery since Gunn had sent the few field pieces ahead by sea and a storm had driven the ships away from the coast. He now drew up the infantry (which included a large body of highlanders) on an exposed hillside within range of Montrose's guns, for the purpose as he afterwards explained of making them 'cannon-proof'.

The Covenant artillery promptly opened fire on the defenceless Royalists massed in front of them. Fortunately for Aboyne's men, the standard of gunnery was poor and most of the shots went wide. But when a few balls did plough home the highland contingent, who were unused to cannon fire and could not abide 'the musket's mother', turned and fled. The rest of the infantry started to mutiny and call Gunn a traitor. They began to leave the field in increasing numbers and only the Gordon cavalry continued to maintain some kind of order and covered the general retreat. That evening at Aberdeen, of the 4,000 who had set out, barely 1,000 answered to the muster.

The Gordons now besought Aboyne to dispense with 'Traitor Gunn', but the young man (whom time was to prove a dashing cavalry commander in his own right) had not yet the confidence to do so. The Royalists did have one thoroughly competent professional soldier, however, in Colonel Johnstone, the son of the town provost, who now rallied the citizen militia and prepared to defend Aberdeen. Montrose meanwhile was advancing towards the River Dee, and on 17 June there was a small cavalry skirmish in which the Royalists came off best. In fact, only seven troopers were engaged on each side, but the Royalist vedette, commanded by Johnstone with Nathaniel Gordon (who later was to make a name for himself in Montrose's wars), succeeded in capturing two of the enemy without loss to themselves. Johnstone begged Aboyne to let him take 150 cavalry and harass the Covenanters on the march, but Gunn refused to permit it and threatened to resign if his order was overruled.

On 18 June the Royalists marched out of Aberdeen and took up a strong position at the Bridge of Dee. The river was at that time swollen by rain and impassable for cavalry. A gate at the southern end of the bridge was hastily fortified with turf and earthworks, and manned by the citizen regiments under Johnstone. The cavalry under Gunn remained on the open ground to the north to cut off any Covenanters who might succeed in getting across the river.

The earthworks had barely been completed when the Covenant army came in sight and took up a position on some high ground about a quarter of a mile from the bridge. Montrose ordered the artillery to begin bombarding the breastworks, but on this occasion the cannonade had little effect and the militia under Johnstone put up a spirited resistance. Two assaults against the bridge were successfully beaten off, and by nightfall the Covenanters had suffered numerous casualties without having been able to make any impression upon the defence.

Under cover of darkness, Montrose moved his artillery closer to the bridge to a spot where his guns would be able to pound the breastwork from point-blank range. Soon after daybreak he paraded his cavalry in view of the enemy and then sent them up-river as if to look for a fording point. Although he was told that no such ford existed, Gunn fell for the trick and diverted the Royalist cavalry to shadow the Covenant horse. As he left, the cannonade resumed and from close range the Covenant shot began to demolish the earthwork. Soon after, a cannon ball striking the parapet of the bridge dislodged a piece of masonry which fell on top of Johnstone crushing his leg, and he had to be carried from the field. When word of this reached Gunn he told his troopers that Johnstone was dead and the bridge lost, and that their only chance was to ride for Aberdeen. His panic communicated itself to the rest, and, abandoning the wretched infantry at the bridge, the cavalry began to leave the field. A number of young Gordons rode furiously up to Gunn and protested that it was not their custom to leave a battle without engaging the enemy, and one of them told him to his face that he was a villain and a traitor. 'He swallowed all very quietly.' But the Gordons did not charge, and when the Covenant assault under Middleton[22] finally carried the bridge, they turned and dispersed towards Strathbogie.

Montrose advanced on Aberdeen and camped outside the town. He was this time under definite orders from the Tables to sack the city, and Marischal and the other Covenanting lords who were present argued with him to allow the army to plunder loose inside the town. But he still opposed it and eventually persuaded them to desist for one night at least and reconsider the matter in the morning. Next day a courier arrived with news of the Treaty of Berwick which had been signed between the King and Covenanters on 18 June. The timely message saved Aberdeen. However, Montrose, who was learning how to manage the committee, took the precaution of persuading his colleagues to sign a document stating that they had concurred in his decision to defy the original order of the Tables and not pillage the town. He then fined the burghers another £4,000 (Scots), released his prisoners and, having withdrawn his army to a safe distance, disbanded it in accordance with the terms of the Treaty.

Riding south again to Edinburgh, he was possibly well content. He had won his first battle and emerged from the campaign with credit. Yet in refusing to sack Aberdeen he had also shown that he reserved the right to disobey, and certain of the Covenanters were already becoming critical. 'The discretion of that generous and noble youth was but too great,' wrote Baillie. 'A great sum was named as a fine on that unnatural city, but all was forgiven.'[23]

(The young Gordons lived to fight again, some with great distinction. Gunn returned to England where Johnstone later accused him publicly of treachery and challenged him to a duel. But the King exonerated Hamilton's protégé, and shortly after he was knighted and appointed a Gentleman of the Bedchamber. He did not fight in the Civil War but returned to Germany, where he married an heiress and rose to the rank of major general in the Imperial Army, ending his days a baron of the Holy Roman Empire.)

6

'. . . *Verbis Vincitur*'

O watchman leaning from the mast,
*   What of the night? The shadows flee,*
The stars grow pale, the storm is past,
*   A blood-red sunrise stains the sea.*
At length, at length, O desperate wills
*   Luck takes the tiller and foul tides turn;*
Superb amid majestic hills
*   The domes of Eldorado burn.*

The Ship of Fools

The Pacification of Berwick was no more than a temporary truce. At best it offered a breathing space. At worst it was, in Hallam's words, 'indefinite, enormous in concession, yet affording a pretext for new encroachments'. Clarendon wrote of it: 'There were not two present who did agree in the same relation of what was said and done, and which was worse, not in the same interpretation. An Agreement was made in which nobody meant what others believed he did.' The only clear stipulation in the treaty–that both armies should disband[1]–was not adhered to by the Scots, who kept their officers and many of their troops in pay. Edinburgh Castle was duly handed over to the Royalist General Ruthven, but the ordnance, heavy cannon and ammunition were retained by the Covenanters. The fortifications at Leith were not dismantled. The Tables remained in existence. When Charles remonstrated, the Scots published their own version of the treaty– 'Some Conditions of His Majesty's Treaty . . . set down for Remembrance'–which the King described as 'in most parts full of falsehood, dishonour, and scandal', and ordered the document to be burned by the common hangman. Barely a week had passed before the Covenant ministers were denouncing Charles as a truce-breaker.

Moreover, the main point in contention had been left pending. The King had refused to ratify the Acts of 'the late pretended Assembly in Glasgow'–which had not only expelled and excommunicated the Scottish bishops, but had declared that episcopacy was itself unlawful. Aware of the implications in England and Ireland, this was something that Charles could not countenance, and the Covenanters were under no illusions but that he would seek to reverse the enactments of the Glasgow Assembly by one means or another. This suspicion seemed justified when the royal proclamation of 1 July, convening a new

General Assembly for 12 August (as promised in the treaty), decreed also that the prelates should take their places as before. Legally speaking, Charles was in the right, since if the Assembly was to try their case it was proper that the bishops should be present to defend themselves. But the Covenanters not unnaturally interpreted it as a clear sign that the King not only refused to accept the resolutions of the Glasgow Assembly but, possibly with the aid of the bishops' votes, was still seeking some way to perpetuate episcopacy.

On 2 and 3 July there were fresh riots in Edinburgh during which Aboyne and some of Huntly's household were roughly handled by the mob, and a coach in which Traquair and Kinnoul were travelling was thrust through with swords. Loudoun went tongue in cheek to the King to apologize, but Charles was extremely angry and summoned Argyll, Cassilis and a dozen other Covenanting lords to attend him at Berwick with a full explanation. Some like Argyll refused to go, while others made a great pretence of being persuaded by their friends not to trust the King's safe conduct. In the event, five lords only—Montrose, Rothes, Loudoun, Lothian and Dunfermline—went to the new conference at Berwick, accompanied by Alexander Henderson who had not been invited.

Charles, in fact, was more preoccupied with the forthcoming Parliament than with the Assembly because any enactments passed by the latter would require ratification by the Estates—where his own power to influence events would turn on how the fourteen places vacated by the bishops on the Committee of the Articles would be filled. The Scottish lords were expected in Berwick on 18 July, and on the seventeenth the King instructed Hamilton (who was still very much in favour and sharing the royal bedchamber) to use all means he could to find out from Rothes, Montrose and the rest 'which way they intend the estate of Bishops shall be supplied in Parliament . . . for which end you will be necessitated to speak that language which, if you were called to account for by us you might suffer for it'.[2] The role was not unfamiliar, but it is unlikely that Hamilton, if he tried, was able to elicit anything so definite since events were to show that the Covenanters were themselves divided on this question. However, his probings may have alerted Montrose at least to the constitutional issues surrounding the royal prerogative which could no longer be postponed.

The conference itself was a complete failure. Charles accused the Scots of breaking the treaty and demanded punishment of the rioters, the dissolution of the Tables, restoration of the castle guns, the cashiering of Leslie and the suppression of the Covenanters' interpretation of the Pacification of Berwick. He quarrelled violently with Rothes over the resolution of the Glasgow Assembly that episcopacy was unlawful, to whom he pointed out the impossibility, with England and Ireland in view, of his agreeing to ratify any Act so worded. Rothes argued that the Covenanters had no intention of going beyond Scotland, but when Charles twice called him a liar to his face, the

Earl lost his temper and stated that if the King insisted on the merits of episcopacy in his other dominions 'our people' would 'rip up' the iniquities of the English and Irish bishops. The threat of an alliance with the Puritan opposition to establish Presbyterianism in England was implicit. The talks broke down after six days.

Charles, offended by the attitude of the Scots and their professed distrust of his safe conduct, decided (unwisely) to return to London on pretence of important business and so not attend the Scottish Parliament. Instead, he appointed Traquair to be Commissioner on his behalf, and on Hamilton's advice instructed him that, as bishops were constitutionally one of the estates of the realm, any Act abolishing them could not be held to be binding. To Archbishop Spottiswoode he wrote that he 'gave way for the present yet shall not leave thinking in time how to remedy . . . what was prejudicial . . . both to the Church and our own Government'.

As to what effect this meeting with the King had upon Montrose, there is no precise information. According to Burnet, 'he was much wrought upon, and gave His Majesty full assurance of his duty in time coming, and upon that entered into a correspondence with the King'. Bishop Guthry also records the suspicion that 'the King had turned him at Berwick'. However, although this view subsequently gained currency, it seems unlikely, and more probably reflects later speculation among the Covenanters after Montrose had moved into opposition. Montrose was still a Covenanter, and would remain one until the objects of the Covenant had been achieved. On the religious issue in Scotland his standpoint had not changed; but neither had those principles of monarchy to which he adhered and which he believed that the Covenant sustained. It is possible that he was already becoming a prey to doubts – engendered in part by the speed of the revolutionary current which, ingenuously, he had not anticipated, by the growing arrogance of the Kirk, the subterranean ambitions which he seemed to detect among certain of his Covenant colleagues and the gradual erosion of the central authority of the Crown, which, if constitutionally defined, he held to be the essential foundation upon which the natural political order depended. The meeting with Charles did nothing to resolve such doubts, but as a personal encounter it probably did have a profound effect upon the young earl, whose romantic cast of mind always inclined him to respond to people as much if not more than to institutions.

Charles had inherited to the full the fatal attraction of the Stuarts, and there were few, even among his enemies, who were not affected by it. To Montrose, he was now a very different man from the disdainful monarch whose hand he had kissed two years before, or the distant English tyrant who had threatened to extinguish the religion and liberties of Scotland. But whatever the emotions that may have been aroused during this second meeting with Charles, they did not of themselves induce him to change sides. Montrose's principles remained constant. But he now thought rather differently of Charles.

The long, almost mournful, face and stately carriage came to personify his ideal of a gentle, constitutional sovereignty–to which he believed that the true Covenant was not antagonistic. He also came to make a clearer distinction between the King, whom he held to be essentially innocent, and those advisors–Hamilton, Laud and Strafford –whom he distrusted and saw as the evil counsellors of the royal autocracy. He did not know about Charles's secret instructions to Traquair and Hamilton, nor of the guile, the weakness and the stubborn fanaticism that lay concealed behind the gentle and melancholic manner of the King. He returned to Scotland a Covenanter still, but with something new to ponder.

The General Assembly met on 12 August 1639, and without reference to the Glasgow Assembly re-enacted all its work 'at a gallop', including the offensive resolution that episcopacy was unlawful. Traquair as Commissioner ratified this measure without demur– probably because he knew that Charles had no intention of recognizing any future ratification by Parliament. The King's *Large Declaration* was condemned in violent language, and the Privy Council agreed to order the compulsory signing of the Covenant throughout Scotland. This measure (and by implication the element of coercion involved) was supported by both Montrose and Alexander Henderson.

Parliament met on 31 August, and, as predicted, difficulties at once arose concerning the allotment of the fourteen seats vacated by the bishops. During the period of its existence, the Committee of the Articles had been formed in a number of ways, so that arguments based on precedent were not worth much. The recent custom, however, had been for the nobles to elect the churchmen, and for the bishops to elect the nobles, while both together elected the lairds and burgesses and the King added a further eight nominees of his own. By means of the bishops the Crown had thus been able to secure a majority. Charles now proposed that the bishops' places should be filled by fourteen ministers chosen by the Crown or, failing that, by fourteen laymen. The first of these propositions was obnoxious generally, the ministers suspecting that the fourteen clergy so nominated were intended to constitute the nucleus of a new hierarchy, while the nobles voted against out of jealousy of the clerical interest *per se*. A temporary compromise was reached whereby Traquair as commissioner chose the nobles who in turn chose the lesser barons and burgesses.

The Estates proceeded to ratify all the Acts of the General Assembly including the resolution that episcopacy was unlawful, before going on to pass a number of measures designed to reduce the royal prerogative. These included the transfer to Parliament of control of the Mint and of the power to appoint officers of state. However, the most significant point in the proceedings came when Argyll, returning to the vexed question of the Committee of the Articles, put forward a motion that in future each estate, nobles, barons and burgesses, should elect its own Lords of the Articles without reference to the King. In retrospect, the importance of this lay not only in the sweeping constitutional change proposed, but also in the fact that it placed Montrose squarely in opposition to the revolutionaries and constituted in effect the first major clash between the two men who were to become the main protagonists in Scotland during the decade that followed. It was a formative factor that in this, their first encounter, Montrose was defeated.

He had been an active member of the General Assembly in which he had voted for the abolition of episcopacy and for the compulsory signing of the Covenant. But when the constitutional issue came to a head he balked, and in the 'Altercating Parliament' he acted and voted with the minority. In his view, the objects of the Covenant had been largely achieved in the Assembly. The prelates had been removed, the Court of High Commission abolished, and religion in Scotland was in the hands of her own recognized tribunals. It remained only to confirm and secure the King's agreement to the advantages they had gained. But at the same time he believed that the Scots were bound in honour to adhere to the promises of the Covenant also – that they would not 'attempt anything that might turn to the diminution of the King's greatness and authority'.

On the question of the Lords of the Articles, Montrose had opposed Charles's suggestion that the vacant places should be filled by clergy, and proposed instead that the ecclesiastical lords should be replaced by a corresponding number of nobles chosen by the King. He had no mind to see the authority of the Crown reduced to a cypher, nor to deprive the King of a voice in the selection of the Lords of the Articles. The changes proposed by Argyll would have given Parliament power corresponding more nearly to that which it has today. But the present system and the democratic ideas behind it are the product of evolution. Argyll had no democratic motive. He moved directly against the royal prerogative and in one stroke would have silenced the voice of the King in Parliament forever. His scheme also promised advantage to anyone such as himself who was uniquely placed to influence the burgesses and the middle classes who would elect the third estate. To Montrose such a reform was unacceptable since it removed the central pivot of authority as constituted in the sovereign, and his arguments drew much support, not least from Sir Thomas Hope, who protested that by law only the King could elect the nobles and only nobles in turn could elect the barons and burgesses. Notwithstanding, Argyll's motion was passed by one vote.

On 14 November Charles ordered Traquair to prorogue a Parliament which seemed bent on threatening the very existence of monarchy. Had he at this point made it clear that it was the attacks on the prerogative that alone determined his action, he might have obtained the fixed support of Montrose and other moderates. But popular instinct realized that it was the question of episcopacy that vexed him most, and Montrose was left to 'wrestle between extremities',[3] reluctant to break from those whom he had joined in Covenant, and unwilling to submit to the King 'in what still seemed doubtful'. Charles, advised by Hamilton, saw only two alternatives–to abandon bishops (which he would not) or to renew the war.

Montrose's behaviour during the Altercating Parliament caused considerable speculation among Covenanters and Royalists alike, and it was at this time that the rumour gained currency that he had been seduced by the King at Berwick. Someone pinned a notice to the door of his lodgings which read: '*Invictus armis, verbis vincitur*'. His defence of the prerogative also gave the Scottish Royalists some reason to hope that he could be induced to change sides, and in September 1639 the Earl of Menteith and Airth (his cousin and a cadet of the Graham family) wrote to the King that Montrose 'hath carried himself both faithfully and is more willing to contribute to his uttermost in anything for your Majesty's service than any of these Lords Covenanters'. Airth suggested that the King should write personally to Montrose to encourage him in the royal service and advised that it would be more prudent for any such letter to be sent under cover of one to himself. Charles's reply contained no reference to this proposal but shortly afterwards Montrose received directly an invitation to Court. This may have caused him some embarrassment since he took the precaution of showing it to Wariston.[4] He also declined the invitation and his reply to Charles is interesting since it would seem to mark his position at this time (26 December 1639). Having courteously thanked the King for doing him this honour he continues:

> Which coming to be known here did so put aloft the minds of most part (being still filled with their usual and wonted jealousies) that I could expect but more peremptory resolutions, nor is fit to trouble Your Majesty withal–or me (in thinking to do Your Majesty service) to have occasioned; . . . I chose rather, before matters should have been made worse and the gap enlarged by my means, to crave Your Majesty's humble pardon for my stay, and make you acquainted with the necessity of it; hoping Your Majesty will do me the honour to think that there is no shift (for all of that kind is too much contrary to my humour, chiefly in what Your Majesty or your service is concerned in) but that as I have been ever bold to avow, there is nothing Your Majesty shall be pleased to command me in (persuading myself that they will be still such as befits and do suit with all most incumbent duties) that I shall not think myself born to perform. . . .[5]

The growing disillusionment and irritation with his Covenant colleagues are apparent, but the proviso at the end also indicates that Montrose was not yet prepared to trust the King entirely or to offer him unconditional obedience.

The winter passed in barren diplomacy. Everything pointed to a renewal of the war. Loudoun and Dunfermline were sent to London, but Charles refused to see them on the grounds that their embassy had not been sanctioned by his Commissioner in Scotland. Traquair himself was rebuked by the King for his docile and indifferent behaviour in ratifying the Acts of the General Assembly, and to ingratiate himself into the monarch's favour again he produced an intercepted letter from the Covenanters (it bore Montrose's signature among others) to Louis XIII seeking French aid. In London, Loudoun and Dunfermline were intriguing with Bellievre, the French ambassador, to whom they proposed that in any new treaty with Charles the suggested alliance between Scotland and France should be formally recognized, while a clause was to be added allowing the Scots a place on the Committee of Foreign Affairs – which they could occupy in the French interest. Richelieu, however, would have none of it. In January 1640 Loudoun was sent to the Tower but formal charges could not be brought against him since he was covered under the Act of Amnesty of 1639. In April 1640 Charles, on Strafford's advice, summoned the Short Parliament, and in the belief that the intercepted letter would establish beyond question the treasonable nature of the Scottish movement had the document read before both Houses. But it did not produce the desired effect, since the English Parliament was intent only upon its own grievances and the Puritan politicians had no mind to interfere in a matter that made for their own interests. Parliament was dissolved after three weeks. In the Tower, Loudoun entered into a fresh conspiracy with Lord Savile, an English peer who pursued an hereditary feud against Strafford – of which more hereafter.

In Scotland the Covenanters were refurbishing their war chest, and by the Blind Band levied fresh taxes and 'voluntary' subscriptions. Leslie was methodically organizing the army. The propaganda war of pamphlets and protestations increased in tempo. In Edinburgh the citizens refused to allow supplies and material to reach the Castle, and the garrison occasionally fired upon the town.

The King, paralysed for want of money, needed more time. By mid-summer Leslie would be able to field an army of over 20,000 foot and 3,000 horse. Charles could count on barely half that number – and they undisciplined and reluctant recruits. The northern counties could not be pressed again and he was obliged to levy men in the South. Only the Roman Catholic communities genuinely supported his cause. Strafford suggested employing an army from Ireland – and it was this proposal, deliberately misconstrued, that later led to his impeachment and execution. In England opposition to Laud was growing more vociferous, and the sympathies of the people tended largely towards the Scots. Riots in London had to be suppressed by the Trained Bands. The Scottish Parliament was due to reconvene on 2 June. In May Charles prorogued it for another month in the hope of securing a further delay. His legitimate excuse was that Traquair, as Royal Commissioner, could no longer return in safety to Scotland since, after the affair of the letter to the French king, he had been branded as the Great Incendiary and an enemy of the Covenant.

The Scots refused to accept the King's order and on the basis of a technical fault in the wording Sir Thomas Hope pronounced that 'Parliament could not be prorogued for want of Commissioner'. The Covenanters thereupon elected Lord Burleigh as their President and the session opened on the day appointed. The fiction of loyalty was still maintained. The Covenanters declared that they were acting by His Majesty's 'tacit consent' and 'presumed allowance', and that they were only 'receiving and making use of that benefit which His Majesty in his justice had publicly granted to us and never recalled'. But to Montrose this was revolution indeed, and he argued vehemently with Rothes, Argyll, Balmerino and Wariston that Parliament could not lawfully sit without the King or his appointed Commissioner. Argyll returned the sinister reply that 'to do the less [i.e. dispense with the royal permission] was more lawful than to do the greater [depose the King]'.[6] Montrose found little support. The Campbell could claim that he was arguing from necessity. The King was preparing for war and there was no time to cavil over constitutional niceties. Montrose was put in an equivocal position. Resignation would have meant forgoing any power he still had to influence events, or possibly even exile, while he still supported a defensive war since not until the King was made fully to understand the resolution of the Scots on the question of religious freedom would the Covenant be safe and its aims secured.

The Parliament ratified all the Acts of the General Assembly, passed a Triennial Act and organized a general mobilization for a new war against the King. It adjourned on 12 June, but before doing so it appointed a large and heterogeneous Committee of Estates which included persons of every rank from earls to tradesmen to act as the government when Parliament was not sitting. Montrose, together with Napier and Stirling of Keir, was appointed a member of the committee–possibly with the intention of stifling his opposition. Argyll, however, for his own ends declined to sit on it. This deference was not out of modesty. 'All saw', wrote Gordon,[7] 'that he was *Major Potestas,* and though not formally a member, yet all knew that it was his influence that gave being, life, and motion to these new-modelled governors; and not a few thought that this *junctio* was his innovation.' As a member of the committee that was all he would have been, and the Campbell preferred to manipulate events from behind the scenes while by a series of bands he began to gather a party of his own. It seems possible that he intended the committee to be a temporary expedient only, since it was large and unwieldy for the management of a war. Argyll's ambition was beginning to run high and in Edinburgh he consulted leading lawyers and divines as to whether a king might, under certain circumstances, be deposed. They appear to have returned a cautious but generally favourable answer.

Montrose commanded two regiments in the new army, but he did not march south with the main host. The Covenanters were anxious to secure their rear and Colonel Monro was again sent to Aberdeenshire to complete the pacification that Montrose had begun, as was said too leniently, in 1639. Monro showed no such weakness and his record in the North was one of cruelty and extortion. In Aberdeen, heavy fines were imposed, citizens pressed into the army, homes plundered, women raped, money extracted under torture and the whole country about Strathbogie left 'almost manless, moneyless, homeless and armless'.[8]

A second area to give concern was Angus, where Lord Ogilvie held Airlie Castle for the King. Argyll procured a Commission of Fire and Sword from the Estates against the Earls of Athol and Airlie and covering the whole district in which their influence was acknowledged. On 18 June he marched from Inveraray with a strong body of his clansmen and 'a pretty camp and cannon'. The highlanders were held in great dread by the Lowland communities, Covenanters and non-Covenanters alike, and the town of Perth sent a formal request to the Estates that Montrose and his two regiments should remain as a protection against the depredations of the clansmen until Argyll's expedition had passed through Perth and Angus. Although he had been a signatory to Argyll's commission, Montrose probably supported the petition. He had lands in both the shires, was a friend of Ogilvie and was possibly alarmed by the tales of injustice and oppression in Aberdeen. Permission seems to have been granted since at the end of June he marched to Airlie Castle and obtained Ogilvie's formal surrender. He then garrisoned it with a detachment of his own troops and wrote to Argyll advising him that the Castle had been duly handed over 'to the public service'. Having thus, as he thought, forestalled the Campbell, he marched south to join the main army at Dunse Muir.

Argyll was exasperated by Montrose's intervention. He had obtained a legal commission to pursue a dynastic feud against the Ogilvies and did not intend to be cheated of his revenge. He marched directly upon Airlie, dismissed Montrose's garrison, plundered the house of everything that was movable and then burned it to the ground. Twenty years later he was to deny the crime, but his orders to Dugald Campbell of Inverawe were explicit enough at the time: 'See how ye can cast off the iron gates and windows, and take down the roof, and if ye will find it will be longsome, ye shall fire it well, that so it may be destroyed. . . . But ye need not let know that ye have directions from me to fire it.'

He proceeded next to the Ogilvie house at Forthar, which he also burned (having callously turned out Lady Ogilvie who had been confined there in an advanced state of pregnancy), together with Craig, a small unfortified house in the district. When one of his lieutenants questioned the legality of this he was brusquely told to finish the work and treated to one of the Campbell's favourite epigrams— *Abscindantur qui nos perturbant.*

Argyll then marched into Breadalbane where at the Ford of Lyon he trapped Atholl with the offer of a conference under a flag of truce.

Before the captured earl was sent to Edinburgh a strange conversation took place (witnessed by a number of Athol's followers, including Stewart of Ladywell and Stewart of Grandtully), during which Argyll boasted of being 'the eighth man from The Bruce' and talked of certain circumstances under which the King might be deposed. Private 'bands' were mentioned, while in the camp the clansmen claimed openly that they followed 'King Campbell' and sang a gaelic verse: 'I gave Argyll the praise, because men say it is truth, for he will take gear from the Lowland men and he will take the Crown perforce and he will cry King at Whitsunday.'[9]

Finally, having settled accounts with some MacDonalds and wasted all Badenoch from Lochaber to Braemar, Argyll returned to Edinburgh where he obtained a complete indemnity under the King's authority exempting him and his heirs for the violence, arson and murder which he and his clan had perpetrated under the authority of his commission. But no such document could alter the legacy of hatred which he had left behind him in the Highlands.

Still not content, he also struck openly at Montrose and demanded that he should be impeached for having dealt too leniently with Ogilvie. The charge was monstrous and Montrose, arraigned before Leslie, was completely exonerated. But the enmity was in the open and a number of events now combined to confirm the Graham's worst suspicions.

While the army lay at Dunse, Montrose was approached, probably by Archibald, brother of Sir James Campbell of Lawers, and asked to sign a band, the purport of which was that, since the Committee of Estates was unsuited to the conduct of a war, the government of Scotland should be transferred to a triumvirate. Argyll was to rule all the country north of the Forth, and Mar and Cassilis the country south of it, while this triumvirate would be seconded by a new committee of which Montrose would be a member. The Graham had no intention of supporting a Campbell dictatorship in the north and he succeeded in having the draft commission altered so that, besides Argyll, there were added his own name, those of Cassilis and Mar and two others. He then posted to Edinburgh where he had a significant conversation with Lindsay of the Byres (his old college friend and one of Argyll's creatures) who told him of a scheme to make 'a particular man' dictator of all Scotland 'after the Roman fashion'.[10]

This, and rumours of what had passed at Ford of Lyon, had Montrose thoroughly alarmed. He rode to Cumbernauld near Glasgow where at his cousin Lord Wigton's house he convened a clandestine meeting of those moderates who like himself believed that a point had been reached at which some action was necessary to save the Covenant from the extremists and from Argyll. They agreed to sign a band:

> Whereas we, the under-subscribers, out of our duty to Religion, King, and country, were forced to join ourselves in a Covenant for the maintenance and defence of eithers, and every one of other in that

behalf; Now finding how that by *the particular and indirect practising of a few* the country and Cause now depending does so much suffer, as heartily hereby bind and oblige ourselves, out of our duty to all these respects above mentioned, but chiefly and namely that the Covenant already signed, to wed and study all public ends which may tend to the safety both of Religion, Laws, and Liberties of this poor kingdom, and as we are to make an account before that Great Judge at the last day, that we shall contribute one with another . . . to the hazard of our lives, fortunes, and estates. . . . And like as we swear and protest by the same oath that in so far as may consist with the good and weal of the public, every one of us shall join and adhere to the others' and their interests, against all persons or Causes whatsoever. . . .[11]

Besides Montrose (who drafted it and whose view it chiefly represents) there were eighteen other signatories to this band. But though numerous, the party of moderates included no men of any great power. It was indicative of their own sense of weakness that the existence of the Cumbernauld Band was kept a secret.

Montrose rejoined the army as it prepared to invade England. The decision to cross the border had partly devolved upon Loudoun's intrigue with Lord Savile, mentioned earlier. Savile had proposed to Loudoun that the Scots should begin a new war, and on 23 June, while Leslie was still mustering the army, Wariston had written to the English malcontent, putting forward the idea of extending the Covenant to England. Savile and five other peers replied through Loudoun (who was released in June) that they could not lend treasonable aid since the opportunity was not yet ripe, but that they confessed to a common cause. Argyll, who trusted nobody, demanded a band, and so Savile 'sent them what they wanted'—a letter signed by himself and the other peers, inviting a Presbyterian invasion of England. It was concealed in a hollow cane, to be read only by Argyll, Rothes and Wariston, who for their part were to give out that they were confident of 'a very great and unexpected assistance'. Not until the Scots met the supposed signatories at Ripon did they learn that the document was a forgery.

On 20 August 1640 the Scottish army arrived at the Tweed. The crossing was likely to be dangerous since the river was swollen and the current strong, and lots were cast as to who should lead the host across.[12] The lot fell upon Montrose, who promptly waded across alone to prove the passage and then returned to lead his own regiments through the river. A week later the Scots reached the Tyne at Newburn where Lord Conway with 4,500 men tried to prevent a crossing. The Scots brought up their heavy cannon and the raw English levies were routed after a short bombardment. Elated by their easy victory, the Covenanters advanced to Newcastle. (In one of the cavalry skirmishes which took place during this advance, the Royalist Wilmot mistakenly reported that Montrose had been killed.) Charles, marching north with a feeble army of undisciplined recruits, fell back on York, and negotiations between the two sides were opened at Ripon.

Their occupation of Newcastle gave the Scots a strong bargaining position since they controlled the main supply of coal to London and thus £50,000 of royal revenue. They continued to preface their demands with protestations of loyalty, in which the rank and file genuinely believed. Robert Baillie also recorded his emotions in particularly purple prose, picturing Charles as a man misled, at 'the wicked hands of an evil faction . . . divided these sixteen years or more from his best minded subjects . . . by a handful of miscreants'.[13] 'We pant', he wrote, 'for the trials of Laud and Strafford.'

Much of the early negotiations at Ripon concerned money, and the Scots (who regarded themselves as being there by invitation) were permitted to levy £25,000 a month from the northern counties for the maintenance of their army until a formal treaty should be concluded. In November 1640 the talks were transferred to London and the Covenanters, whose ambitions had been fed rather than satisfied by their success, raised their demands. As a direct result of the invasion, on 3 November 1640 Charles had been forced to call the Long Parliament and was now fatally trapped between the hammer and the anvil. Strafford was imprisoned and Laud was soon to follow. The Puritan opposition in both Houses welcomed the Scots as friends and allies, and Henderson and Wariston were in close touch with Pym and others of his faction. The idea of forcibly introducing Presbyterianism into England was discussed in depth. Wariston had been plotting this for a long time, and Alexander Henderson, who was the best and most sincere of the extreme Covenanters, was also convinced that the only way of safeguarding Presbyterianism in Scotland was to secure its adoption south of the border. The demand was duly presented by the commissioners in London:

> In the paradise of nature, the diversity of flowers and herbs are useful, but in the paradise of the Church, different and contrary religions are unpleasant and hurtful; it is therefore to be wished that there were one Confession of Faith, one form of Catechism, one Directory for the parts and public worship of God, one form of Church Government in all the Churches of His Majesty's dominions.

The argument was hardly new. Charles and Laud had said something very similar in justification of their own policy—and perhaps with more right. The 'Root and Branch' Petition was rejected in the English Parliament, but support for the Scots was such that the Covenanters were given cause to hope. (Henderson's submission was finally to bear fruit in the Solemn League and Covenant.)

Montrose openly opposed the demand for the abolition of episcopacy in England, and stated that it was 'contrary to the mind of the most part of the subscribers of the National Covenant'. He also spoke against another of the Covenanters' demands—that Traquair, Sir Robert Spottiswoode and a number of other prominent Royalists should be excluded from the Act of Oblivion which would form part of the treaty. Charles too would not stomach this and stated that if the Scots persisted in their demand he would on his side exclude a like number of them. The King also talked of going himself to Scotland to preside over the next Parliament—a proposition which did not suit the extreme Covenanters. Wariston, whose habit was to brand all opponents as 'plotters' (a trick of phraseology which had much advantage in propaganda terms), spoke of 'this plot of reserving some of us and this plot of causing the King to declare his intention to go home to Scotland', which he attributed by implication to the intrigue of certain Royalists—not excluding Montrose.

The Earl of Rothes passes from the story at this time. He had been one of the commissioners sent to London to conclude the negotiations begun at Ripon, and when the Pacification was finally agreed he remained in England. It seems that 'the gaiety of the English court was congenial to him' and he had some hopes of obtaining a position in the royal household and the hand of the wealthy Countess of Devonshire—which would have provided him with an income of £4,000 per annum. In the following year he was to have accompanied Charles to Scotland where he might have used his influence to raise a party for the King, but he was seized by a rapid consumption and died at Richmond in Surrey on 23 August 1641.[14]

While the army was at Newcastle, Montrose got himself into serious trouble. Sensitive perhaps to the equivocal nature of his position, and yet wishing to distinguish between the twin principles of loyalty and liberty which he believed could still be reconciled as in the original Covenant, he wrote a short letter to the King expressing no more than his dutiful affection to His Majesty. The document was picked from the King's pocket by Will Murray or another of the spies in the royal bedchamber and a copy sent to General Leslie. When news of this leaked out there was considerable excitement in the Covenant camp and many of the ministers treated the incident as if the army had only narrowly escaped being betrayed to the enemy. Montrose was arraigned before Leslie on charges that could have led to his impeachment for treason. Before crossing the Tweed, Leslie had issued a General Order of the Day forbidding any correspondence with the enemy except under his warrant and any secret contact would thus be accounted treasonable.

Though taken at a disadvantage in that the moment was not of his own choosing, Montrose possibly welcomed the opportunity to provoke an issue. He admitted writing the letter, and protested his right—and that of any other subject—to express duty and obedience to the Sovereign. The Articles of War under which he was charged stated also that: 'If any man shall open his mouth against the King's Majesty's person or authority or shall presume to touch his sacred person he shall be punished as a traitor.' By what, and by

94

whose interpretation, then could the King be called an 'enemy'?

This bold counter-attack had his accusers at a loss. Leslie may have muttered something to the effect that he had known princes lose their heads for less, but the leading Covenanters were not yet ready to admit the inconsistency between practice and profession at which he pointed. Montrose was known to have a following among the moderates, and the extremists did not feel strong enough to deny their own law, or to challenge in public debate the interpretation that had been put upon it. The matter was allowed to drop, but Montrose was a marked man thereafter.

Worse was to follow. In November 1640 Lord Boyd, one of the signatories of the Cumbernauld Band, died of a fever and in his delirium he uttered something about the existence of a secret association, of which, being reported to Argyll, the Campbell began an immediate investigation. It happened that Lord Almond, another signatory, was at that time in Callander on leave from the army, and under pressure he revealed the details of what had passed at Cumbernauld. Montrose and the other nobles concerned were summoned to appear before the Estates to answer a new charge of treason.

Montrose took the same bold course as before, avowing what he had done and stating that his action had been justified by the dangers that threatened Scotland and her National Covenant. The case became something of a *cause célèbre*, with extreme Presbyterian ministers demanding the death penalty, but the number of signatories to the band made Argyll hesitate since, apart from Montrose, others such as Marischal were popular with the army. Nor could the wording of the document be called treasonable, and the Committee had to be content with censuring it as a 'divisive movement'. The band was ordered to be burned and the subscribers signed a declaration to the effect that they had intended nothing against the common weal. The destruction of the evidence enabled Covenant propagandists to put whatever interpretation they liked upon the 'conspiracy' and the subsequent smear campaign against Montrose convinced many that there had indeed been some wicked and treasonable plot against the cause of religion and liberty—a view shared even by later historians since it was not until the last century that a handwritten copy of the band was discovered among Lord Balfour's papers. Covenant writers such as Baillie, who had hitherto praised Montrose, now referred to that 'Damnable Band' and described the Earl as a man 'whose pride long ago was intolerable and whose meaning very doubtful'.[15]

It was a severe blow to Montrose's hopes of forming a moderate constitutional party in Scotland since many were no longer willing to support him openly against the power of Argyll. However, there was some small consolation to be derived from the fact that the Cumbernauld Band did not altogether fail in its object, since Argyll was made aware of the breadth of the opposition to a triumvirate and the scheme was dropped.

At the end of 1640 Montrose had reached the critical point of his career. He was a man who had lost his way. He believed in the Covenant but could no longer trust the Covenanters. He wanted to, but could not, trust the King. He knew that, by defending the prerogative and pressing for a just reconciliation between King and people on the basis of the Covenant, he was honestly seeking the best solution for his country. He was extremely conscious of his own integrity and it made him see only dishonesty in those around him. He heard himself branded as an unscrupulous, self-seeking traitor by men whom he had recently esteemed. He thought he saw with dreadful clarity the treachery of Argyll and it galled him that the Campbell should be followed in blind confidence by the mass of the clergy and people. He was stung by the falsehood and injustice that seemed to prevail—when honest men were slandered as conspirators and ambitious schemers lauded as devoted patriots. The country was moving towards anarchy and nobody seemed to realize what was happening.

Perplexed and frustrated, he began clumsily to seek a means of escape from the false position in which he found himself. He could find few men apart from Napier who thought as he did. There were fewer whom he could trust, and he chafed under the suspicions and misconstructions that surrounded him. In this *impasse* he fixed his enmity upon Argyll, and his hatred blinded him to the greater conspiracy that was being acted out in London. He talked rashly to anyone who would listen—and even to some who would not.[16] He spoke of a conspiracy to depose the King and set up the Campbell as dictator in his place. He referred to rumours and he mentioned proof. And here he entered upon dangerous ground.

7

The Plot, and the Incident

Tell men of high condition
That manage the estate,
Their purpose is ambition,
Their practice only hate.
And if they once reply
Then give them all the lie.
         Sir Walter Raleigh

About 'the time of Yule', 1640, a small group comprising Montrose, Napier, Sir George Stirling of Keir and Sir Archibald Stewart of Blackhall took to meeting of an evening, usually at Montrose's lodgings in Edinburgh or at Napier's castle of Merchiston. It was a family gathering, since Keir was married to Napier's daughter (Montrose's niece) and Blackhall was Keir's brother-in-law. Politically they were of the same mind, and their discussions turned on the deteriorating situation in Scotland and on what steps might be taken to remedy it.

During the course of these conversations, the constitutional philosophy which has come to be attributed to Montrose was evolved, and, it seems, committed to paper in an 'Essay on Sovereign Power'. The provenance of this document rests on a copy in Wodrow's handwriting (but omitted from his *Analecta*) which was found among a collection of manuscripts in the Advocates' Library[1] in Edinburgh. In 1639 Drummond of Hawthornden, a Scottish philosopher of conservative views, had written a pamphlet for private circulation called 'Irene' in defence of the monarchy and against those, Covenanters and Puritans, who sought to subvert it. Drummond sent a copy of his pamphlet to a certain 'Noble Lord' (thought to have been Montrose) with a superscription—'Force hath less power over a great heart than duty', and the 'Essay', addressed 'Noble Sir', is generally taken to have been Montrose's reply. In some respects the two documents resemble each other quite closely, but there are certain significant points of difference between the theories expressed. Moreover, Napier, not Drummond, was Montrose's principal mentor, and in the 'Essay' it is his influence that is most apparent. The order of argument appears to correspond to a set of notes in Napier's handwriting listing 'The Axioms of Government',[2] which may have been used as a basis

97

for the draft, while a number of phrases recur verbatim in a 'Memorandum' (also in Napier's handwriting) relating to the meetings of the group in Edinburgh.[3] However, even though it may thus represent a composite effort, the 'Essay on Sovereign Power' is of considerable significance in determining those constitutional tenets that influenced Montrose's actions at this time and throughout the remainder of his life.

The document begins with a statement of the main premise–that 'Civil Societies cannot subsist without government, nor government without a Sovereign Power, to force obedience to laws and just command, to dispose and direct private endeavour to public ends, and to unite and incorporate the several members into one body politic . . . that they may better advance the public good.' All types of government, republics as well as monarchies, are said to have this power in some form, but howsoever it exists it should not be 'bounded, disputed, or meddled with . . . by subjects, who can never handle it . . . without disturbing the public peace'. This sovereignty is seen as a power over the people, sacred and inviolable–a reflection of the power of God on earth; but at the same time 'it is limited by the laws of God and of Nature, and some laws of nations, and by the Fundamental Laws of the country . . . which are those upon which Sovereign Power resteth, in prejudice of which the King can do nothing'. (This is quite different from the doctrine of divine right.) Sovereign power 'is strong and durable when it is temperate', that is when it is possessed and used with moderation and in accordance with those same laws of God and nature and the fundamental laws of the country. However, despotic princes, encouraged by courtiers and wicked counsellors of 'hasty ambitions', may seek to extend it, and rebellious subjects may try for their part to restrain it. Of these two, the second is by far the worse. Restraint of the sovereign power leads to the oppression and tyranny of the subject–'the most fierce, insatiable, and insupportable tyranny in the world' (a favourite phrase of Napier's). The lawful power of a king can be restrained only through violence, and thereafter it may only be recovered by the same. A despotic prince however, may be induced to return to a moderate course by good advice, a sense of conscience, by 'the pens of writers', or by events.

The State is seen as an organic unity. Prince and people do not represent the contrarieties, but are both part of the ordered whole, and are therefore interdependent on each other. 'Let a King command never so well . . .': if the people do not obey, anarchy will result. Nor is it for the people to take upon themselves the limitation of the royal power. 'It requires more than human sufficiency to find the middle road between the Prince's prerogative and the subject's privilege . . . for they can never agree upon the matter . . . and where it hath been attempted . . . the sword did ever determine the question, which is to be avoided by all possible means.' The proper way to procure moderate government is to 'endeavour the security of Religion and just Liberty' as contained in the established laws of the country and in parliaments ('which have ever been the bulwarks of subjects' liberties in monarchies'). Parliaments can advise new laws against emergent situations which may prejudge the liberty of subjects, and, if frequently and rightly constituted, they act as a curb on politicians who seek to mislead the king.

The 'Essay' then attributes the present controversy to the ambitions and specious arguments of certain men, and it lists and contradicts the several theories which they had promulgated in support of their designs. It is wrong, it argues, to claim that the 'constitutor' has more power than the 'constituted', since when people gave power to the monarchy they did so 'unconditionally'. Nor is the sovereign power transferable. Power and privilege are intersupporting, and power taken from the king does not automatically pass to the people. It ends with a warning. 'If their first act be against the King, their second will be against you.' When the monarchy has been pulled down, the great ones will fight for power among themselves – with the blood and fortunes of those whom they have deluded. The result will be anarchy and oppression, with 'all those mischiefs, massacres, and proscriptions of the *Triumvirate* of Rome'. And after the anarchy will come a dictator – 'the ONE who will tyrannize over you'.[4] (Though it names no names, this last prediction of course, refers to Argyll. No one had yet heard of Cromwell.)

Rather too much has been made of this 'Essay on Sovereignty' by those later supporters of Montrose who have sought to portray him as a political philosopher in advance of his time. He was not a metaphysician, and he was not indulging in an amateur exercise in metaphysics. The concept of constitutional sovereignty was not new. He may have been influenced by certain philosophers of his age, and some of his ideas may be similar in part to those that came after, but he founded no school and made no impact upon the mainstream of political thought. Neither was he 'original' in the sense that he set out to define a new constitutional theory, since rather he was endeavouring to interpret the constitution as he believed it already existed. Nevertheless, the concept of the organic unity of the State was a modern one, and the significance of the 'Essay' is perhaps that it asserted the middle position between the doctrines of the extreme Covenanters on the one hand and the theories of extreme Royalists such as Strafford on the other. This indeed was its intention, and it was a practical one. Montrose was attempting to define the framework in which the present quarrel (and the Covenant) operated, to warn against the dangers of anarchy towards which he believed that the Covenanters were headed, and thereby to justify his own personal standpoint.

The group in Edinburgh also determined upon a course of action. They decided that the only way to remedy the situation and to thwart the extremists was for the King to come to Scotland and at the next Parliament to satisfy the Covenanters in person on the question of religion and liberties. In this way they hoped that the popular suspicion so assiduously fostered by Argyll and Wariston would be allayed while the King would be brought to realize the resolution of the Scots. A permanent reconciliation might then be achieved. At the same time, Montrose intended formally to accuse Argyll and Wariston of treason and demand that they be tried before Parliament and in the presence of the King. In the meanwhile it was essential that certain offices of state such as the chancellorship (left vacant by the death of Archbishop Spottiswoode on 26 November 1639) and the lord treasurer (hitherto held by Traquair) should not be filled until the King was able to make the appointments in person. The group almost certainly had their own opinions as to who could best perform these functions in the royal interest.

The main difficulty lay in getting their proposals through to Charles, and they decided to try to open a channel of communication through the Duke of Lennox, who was generally considered to be 'a man of honour and fidelity in all places'[5] and not involved in Covenant intrigues. They found a means of doing this when Blackhall discovered an old acquaintance of his in Edinburgh called Colonel Walter Stewart, a cousin and servant of Traquair, who boasted of having excellent contacts at Court. Stewart was invited to Montrose's lodgings where, after supper, he was taken into the bedchamber and entrusted with a message for Lennox. Although he was in no sense a 'member' of the group, the use of him as a courier meant that he became privy to certain of their conversations and intentions. It also meant involving Traquair, albeit indirectly.

Stewart made the journey to England safely and returned with cautious answers from Lennox and Traquair. However, the response was generally favourable. There was a practical difficulty in that the Scottish army lay between the King and Scotland, but since Parliament was not due to meet until July, the group were not over-optimistic in hoping that some sort of treaty would be patched up before then. Accordingly, Montrose (who was said to have been the prime mover in this) sent Stewart back to Court .with the following letter to the King, stating their proposals and directly yet courteously offering his advice. In a sense it was also a statement of the terms under which he was prepared to serve:

Your ancient and native kingdom of Scotland is in a mighty distemper. It is incumbent on your Majesty to find out the disease, remove the cause, and apply convenient remedies. The disease in my opinion is contagious, and may infect the rest of your Majesty's dominions. It is a falling sickness, for they are like to fall from you, and from the obedience due to you, if, by removing the cause, and application of wholesome remedies, it be not speedily prevented. The cause is a fear and apprehension, not without some reason, of changes in religion, and that superstitious worship shall be brought in upon it, and therewith all their laws infringed and their liberties invaded. Free them, sir, from this fear, as you are free from any such thoughts; and undoubtedly you shall thereby settle the State in a firm obedience to your Majesty in all time coming. They have no other end but to preserve their religion in purity, and their liberties entire. That they intend the overthrow of monarchial government is a calumny. They are capable of no other, for many and great reasons; and ere they will admit another than your Majesty, and after you your son and nearest of your posterity, to sit upon your throne, many thousands of them will spend their dearest blood. You are not like a tree lately planted, which oweth a fall to the first wind. Your ancestors have governed theirs, without interruption of race, two thousand years or thereabouts, and taken such root as it can never be plucked up by any but yourselves. If any others shall entertain such treasonable thoughts, which I do not believe, certainly they will prove as vain as they are wicked.

The remedy of this dangerous disease consisteth only in your Majesty's presence for a space in that kingdom. It is easy to you in person to settle their troubles, and to disperse these mists of apprehension and mistaking—impossible to any other. If you send down a commissioner, whatever he be, he shall neither give nor get contentment, but shall render the disease incurable. The success of your Majesty's affairs, the security of your authority, the peace and happiness of your subjects, depend upon your personal presence. The disease is of that kind which is much helped by conceit and the presence of the physician. Now is the proper time and the critical days. For the people love change, and expect from it much good—a new heaven and a new earth; but, being disappointed, are as desirous of a re-change to the former estate.

Satisfy them, sir, in point of religion and liberties, when you come here, in a loving and free manner; that they may see your Majesty had never any other purpose, and doth not intend the least prejudice to either. For religious subjects, and such as enjoy their lawful liberties, obey better and love more than the godless and the servile, who do all out of base fear, which begets hate. Any difference that may arise upon the Acts passed in the last Parliament, your Majesty's presence, and the advice and endeavour of your faithful servants will easily accommodate. Let your Majesty be pleased to express your favour and care of your subjects' weal by giving way to any just notion of theirs for relief of the burdens these late troubles have laid on them, and by granting what else may tend to their good; which your Majesty may do with assurance that therein is included your own.

Suffer them not to meddle or dispute of your power. It is an instrument never subjects yet handled well. Let not your authority receive any diminution of that which the law of God and Nature and the fundamental laws of the country alloweth; for then it shall grow contemptible: and weak and miserable is the people whose prince hath not power sufficient to punish oppression and to maintain peace and justice.

On the other side, aim not at absoluteness. It endangers your estate and stirs up trouble. The people of the western parts of the world could never endure it any long time, and they of Scotland less than any. Hearken not to Rehoboam's counsellors. They are flatterers, and therefore cannot be friends; they will follow your fortune, and love not your person. Pretend what they will, their hasty ambition and avarice make them persuade an absolute government that the exercise of the same (may be put) on them, and then they know how to get wealth. . . .

Practise, sir, the temperate government. It fitteth the humour and disposition of the nation best. It is most strong, most powerful, most desirable of any. It gladdeth the heart of your subjects, and then they erect a throne there for you to reign. *Firmissimum imperium quo obedientes gaudent.* Let your last act there be the settling the offices of State upon men of known integrity and sufficiency. Take them not upon credit and other men's recommendation; they prefer men for their own ends and with respect to themselves. Neither yet take them at a hazard, but upon your own knowledge, which fully reacheth to a great many more than will fill those few places. Let them not be such as are obliged to others than yourself for their preferment; not factious nor popular; neither such as are much hated; for these are not able to serve you well, and the others are not willing if it be prejudice to those upon whom they depend. They who are preferred and obliged to your Majesty will study to behave them well and dutifully in their places, if it were for no other reason yet for this, that they make not your Majesty ashamed of your choice.

So shall your Majesty secure your authority for the present, and settle it for the future time. Your journey shall be prosperous, your return glorious. You shall be followed with the blessings of your people, and with that contentment which a virtuous deed reflecteth upon the mind of the doer. And more true and solid shall your glory be than if you had conquered nations and subdued a people.

> . . . *pax una triumphis*
> *Innumeris potior.*

This then, was the origin of the Plot.

All might yet have proceeded to advantage had Montrose not now been guilty of a gross indiscretion. In March he visited Lord Stormont (a signatory of the Cumbernauld Band) at his home of Scone Abbey. The other guests included the Earl of Atholl and John Stewart of Ladywell, and the discussion centred on Argyll's treasonable statements at Ford of Lyon to which both, as prisoners, had been witnesses. Such a meeting of well-known dissidents aroused speculation among the neighbourhood and particularly among the busybodies of the Kirk— including Robert Murray, Minister of Methven, and John Graham, Minister of Auchterarder, who were determined to find out what was going on. Montrose knew both well and he agreed to meet Murray by appointment at the house of one Margaret Donaldson in Perth. In the course of this interview, the Earl became very angry at some of Murray's insinuations and told the minister: 'You were an instrument of bringing me to this cause. I am calumniated and slandered as a backslider, and I desire to give you and all men satisfaction anent my carriage therein. I am wronged by the scandal raised upon the bond that was burnt.' He then tried to explain that the Cumbernauld Band had been in defence of the Covenant against the 'indirect course' of a few powerful men, and out poured all his suspicions of Argyll, the statements made at Ford of Lyon, the bond which he had been asked to sign, the proposal to set up a triumvirate, and the conspiracy to depose the King and make the Campbell dictator in his place. He also told Murray that, when he had succeeded in clearing his own name, he intended to accuse the persons concerned in open Parliament.

Murray entreated him to 'keep unity' and, referring to a current rumour, asked Montrose whether he meant to bring about a session of Parliament in order to get rescinded those Acts restricting the royal prerogative which had been passed the previous June. Montrose replied that since he had subscribed those Acts he would maintain them, but that he intended to get certain 'able men' nominated to the Committee who were at present left out.

Murray was considerably alarmed, and next day he pursued the Earl to Scone to ask for an assurance that these were no more than threats to be carried out only in 'unavoidable extremities'. Montrose replied that there was nothing 'conditional' about what he had said and that his purpose was fixed. Murray again pleaded with him not to cause a split in the Covenant party, but Montrose was abruptly called away to supper and the conversation ended.[6]

Murray repeated the whole story to John Graham of Auchterarder who had seen the two men in heated argument and was bursting with curiosity to know what was toward. He in his turn repeated it around his presbytery (of which Montrose was a member), whence it came to the ears of Argyll who summoned him before the Council. When questioned John Graham gave the minister of Methven as his authority, and so Murray was also summoned to appear in Edinburgh on 27 May 1640. He faced the Committee in something of a fright since Montrose himself was present at the inquiry, but the Earl, seeing his embarrassment, told him to speak out boldly. Murray therefore told them of the conversations at Perth and Scone, and when he had finished Montrose stood up and confirmed the truth of his deposition. The Earl then gave Stewart of Ladywell as his authority for the statements at Ford of Lyon in reference to the deposing of the King, Lindsay of the Byres as the man who had told him of the plot to make Argyll Dictator, and Mar, Cassilis, Archibald Campbell and Hepburn of Humbie as witnesses to the treasonable bond which he had been asked to sign at Berwick. The Earl of Argyll, he suggested, should be asked to explain what he knew about the business.

The Campbell reacted violently and swore that he would prove that the man who had made these allegations was 'a liar and a base ****'. The challenge had been thrown down and accepted, and the Committee began a full inquiry into the accusations made by Montrose.

Stewart of Ladywell appeared before the Committee on 31 May. He stuck stoutly to his story, and when Argyll, with 'many great oaths', denied that he had ever said anything that could be interpreted as treasonable, he replied: 'My Lord, I heard you speak those words in Atholl in front of a great many people, whereof you are in good memory.' The Campbell could not afford to let this pass, and at the conclusion of his deposition Ladywell was arrested and imprisoned in the castle. This was done on Argyll's authority alone, and it was an ominous demonstration of his power.

Lindsay's testimony might also have been embarrassing to the Campbell since he was a strong Covenanter and a known friend of Argyll, and his evidence could not lightly be brushed aside. Consequently he was questioned less severely by the Committee and was allowed to extract himself from a difficult situation by saying that he did not remember mentioning Argyll's name in connection with the idea of a dictatorship. The Committee promptly passed a resolution that 'it was possible that the Earl of Montrose had mistaken Lord Lindsay's expression'. The allegation concerning the treasonable bond which Montrose had been asked to sign at Berwick was conveniently ignored and neither Mar nor Cassilis was called upon to give evidence, although from Argyll's point of view they, like Atholl, remained a potential threat—should Montrose be allowed the opportunity to repeat his accusations in open Parliament before the King.

Meanwhile, Ladywell in prison was persuaded to retract his former evidence. Since he was unable to walk for a while thereafter, it is possible that he was put to the torture, but this is not specifically stated in contemporary accounts and it is more likely that a mixture of threats and promises was sufficient to extract the necessary confession. He was charged with 'leasing-making'—of bringing false and calumnious accusations against Argyll—and although the original statute defining this crime referred only to slander against the King, nobody questioned the substitution and it was generally thought that he had been persuaded to recant in the hope of mercy. He made a fresh deposition before the Committee in which he admitted to having deliberately misquoted certain 'innocent speeches' referring to kings in general and not, as he had previously stated, to Charles in particular, for the purpose of falsely and maliciously accusing Argyll. This was as far as he could plausibly go, but it was not enough for Argyll, who took the extra precaution of securing counter-depositions from several of his own clansmen who had been present at Ford of Lyon, and who swore that they could not remember any allusions whatsoever to kings or parliaments. Argyll also produced six private bonds, all dated prior to the Cumbernauld Band and professing 'duty to the public' but bearing no relation to the one that Montrose had been asked to sign at Berwick. The Committee accepted these as evidence that no other bond existed and pronounced that 'the taking of these Bands was good service to the public'.

This was a fair way towards suggesting that Montrose himself was guilty of leasing-making also. However, Ladywell refused in his recantation to implicate the Graham as being party to a deliberate slander but said that Montrose had specifically warned him 'rather to keep within bounds than to exceed'. This did not suit Argyll, who could not afford to let matters rest there. It was essential to the

Campbell that Montrose should not be permitted to remain at liberty to bring a case before Parliament where the evidence of new witnesses such as Atholl, Cassilis and Mar would seriously prejudice the issue. Argyll therefore moved to the attack.

Under interrogation Ladywell had also revealed that on Montrose's advice he had sent written copies of his original deposition to Traquair by hand of Walter Stewart. It was known from spies at Court that Stewart was on the point of returning to Scotland and arrangements were made to intercept him. On 4 June he was arrested between Cockburnspath and Haddington by someone 'sent expressly to meet him' and taken to Balmerino's house in Edinburgh for questioning. Stewart at first proved uncooperative but a search revealed a letter hidden in the lining of his saddle from the King to Montrose dated 22 May (presumably Charles's answer to Montrose's letter quoted above):

> I conceive [Charles wrote] that nothing can induce more to a firm and solid peace and giving full contentment and satisfaction to my people than that I should be present at the next ensuing session of Parliament. This being the reason of my journey and having a perfect intention to satisfy my people in their Religion and just Liberties I do expect from them that retribution of thankfulness as becomes grateful and devoted subjects: which being a business wherein not only my service, but likewise the good of the whole Kingdom is so much concerned, I cannot but expect that your particular endeavours will be herein concerning—in confidence of which I rest your assured friend. . . .[7]

There was nothing in this that could be used against Montrose, but it confirmed Argyll's suspicions that the Graham had reached an accommodation with the King. However, in Walter Stewart's pockets a number of curious strips of paper were also found containing notes in his own handwriting interspersed with a number of code-names and hieroglyphics. At first Stewart would offer no explanation, but it seemed likely that they were a series of notes in a kind of short-hand cypher of his own devising which he used to record verbal instructions which had been entrusted to him. (They also reflected his somewhat romantic interpretation of the work in which he was engaged.) Under pressure he divulged the details of the code, and the following extract is illustrative of the evidence which had thus fallen into Argyll's hands (the words in brackets represent the Covenanters' interpretation of the code):

- How necessary it is that *R* [the King] come to the Parliament.
- To desire that *H* [offices of state] be kept till it be seen who deserves them best.
- That *H* [offices] be not bestowed by advice of the *ELEPHANT* [Hamilton]. . . .
- To assure *D* [Lennox] and *T* [Traquair] except they take *GENERO* [Montrose] by the hand they will be trod upon at home and made naked.

- To assure *L* [King] and *D* [Lennox] that *G* [Montrose] will take him by the hand and lead him through all difficulties, *R* [Religion] and *L* [Liberties] being granted. . . .

And from the King's answers:

- That all means be used for trying the Information against the *DROMEDARY* [Camel = Campbell = Argyll] and what further can be found of his carriage with *MACDUFF* [Atholl] or any other in those parts wherein *SIGNIOR PURITANO* [Seaforth] and some of the *REDSHANKS* [Clanranald] friends can best inform and instruct. . . .
- To let . . . know how well *L* [King] takes their care and in the discreetest way to inform yourself of their desires, and particularly if *RIEK* [Keir] aim upward that its business goes right. . . .

There was enough here, if not to prove a plot, then at least to create the suspicion of one. Walter Stewart was brought before the Committee and encouraged to 'adjust' his evidence to suit the case that Argyll was now preparing. Whereas at his first interrogation he claimed only to have shown the hieroglyphs to Montrose and Napier, he subsequently stated that the notes had actually been dictated by Montrose. The testimony was also contradictory in other respects and some of the code-names were changed to allow a more sinister interpretation. Though somewhat confused, Stewart proved an easy tool and he was preserved in prison as an important witness for the prosecution.

On the night of 11 June, Montrose, Napier, Keir and Blackhall were arrested and imprisoned in the Castle by Argyll's order. They were not informed of the charges against them, nor were they permitted to see one another. (However they did manage to confer together on one occasion at least, for which their warder was subsequently dismissed.) Rumours were circulated among the people that they had been involved in a dangerous conspiracy against the Covenant and the liberties of the country, and the fact that no official charges were published only seemed to make the plot more sinister. While they were given no chance to defend themselves in public, Covenant propaganda saw to it that their reputations were damaged beyond repair. Pamphlets were printed in Edinburgh and London quoting the evidence of Walter Stewart's notes arranged in a suitable order to arouse the maximum suspicion. Reports were circulated throughout both kingdoms that, in collusion with the incendiary Traquair, they had conspired the overthrow and ruin of the country and the destruction of Hamilton, Argyll and other true Covenanters. The King was also said to have been implicated.

These rumours provoked Charles to remonstrance, and he wrote to Argyll (12 June) protesting that his journey to Scotland was not to promote division but to reach a settlement in accordance with the articles of the recent treaty. He denied having promised to appoint Montrose and his friends to the vacant offices of state as the Covenanters alleged and said that it was his intention to dispose of them 'to the best advantage of his service and the satisfaction of his subjects'. But he readily admitted having corresponded with Montrose: 'I do avow it, both for the matter and for the person to whom it is written, who for anything I yet know is no ways unworthy of such a favour.' The King's letter disproved the evidence of Walter Stewart and Argyll did not produce it in front of the Committee.

Montrose and his friends were now subjected to 'private examinations' at which the interrogators tried to get them to contradict each other. After their initial questioning Montrose and Keir refused to reappear before the Committee and demanded a public trial before their peers. They were brought to the chamber under armed guard and when they still refused to answer any further questions they were pronounced disobedient and contumacious. Napier, however, avoided the charge of contumacy by submitting to the summons. But he would give nothing away: 'As I told Lord Balmerino in the Castle yesterday [22 July] I have deponed all I know freely and ingenuously. Would you have me depone that I know not?' Like the others, he denied any knowledge of Walter Stewart's code and declared that he had never seen the strange notes and hieroglyphs before. Nor had he any knowledge of another paper carried by Stewart purporting to have come from Traquair.

The Committee had no particular desire to press the case against Napier. His reputation for loyalty and integrity was well known throughout Scotland and his presence among the 'conspirators' was something of an embarrassment. After some speeches in praise of his past life and known character they therefore offered to release him on condition that he should reappear before them if required to do so. Napier, however, refused the offer, saying that, though they no doubt meant it as a favour, it would in fact be a double disgrace. He had been imprisoned as a traitor and would be satisfied with nothing less than a proper and public acquittal. 'I am as guilty as any of the rest. They knew nothing which they did not impart to me and they had my approbation. . . . If I were to obtain my release by favour and without a trial, all the world will think that I had taken a way separate from Montrose and Keir and that I had deponed something to their prejudice.' In some private memoranda recording his several interrogations Napier concluded that the Covenanters were trying to prove that Montrose was involved in some conspiracy with Traquair. But both he and Montrose had denied communicating with Traquair, and Napier noted that, even had they done so, this in itself would have been insufficient grounds for arrest and imprisonment.

The Covenanters were indeed intent upon dragging the Great Incendiary into the net, and, possibly on Charles's instructions, Traquair wrote a humble submission to the Scottish Parliament contradicting the evidence of Walter Stewart (whom he described as 'a fool, or at least a timid half-witted body') and demanding a public trial. He also denied collusion with Montrose and his colleagues and criticized the Committee's bias in setting up the questionable evidence of Stewart against the consistent testimony of the King, Napier, Montrose, Keir, Blackhall and himself. His request for a trial was rejected and a charge of treason was drawn up and read before Parliament in his absence.

In the search for further evidence against Montrose, Argyll now sent Lord Sinclair to ransack the Graham's houses and search among his private papers for any other documents that might incriminate him. Sinclair found only a collection of love letters from Montrose's college days and a copy of the Cumbernauld Band with a short memorandum which Baillie described as being full of 'vain humanities magnifying to the skies his own courses, debasing to the hells his opposites'. The old issue of the Band was thus revived against him and the 'tenor' of it read before the General Assembly. But this body still could not condemn it as being treasonable and merely passed a new resolution stating that the Band was 'unlawful and not obligatory upon any'. The General Assembly also suggested that, for the sake of unity, the several protagonists should attempt to resolve their differences (an admission almost that there was no proper case against Montrose and his friends), and Alexander Henderson offered to act as peacemaker. Argyll, however, was determined to keep his enemy in prison until the King had come and gone, and under his influence Parliament ignored the Assembly's proposal.

On 15 July Charles announced that he would have to postpone his journey to Scotland for another month, and so to prolong the process against the 'Plotters' a huge 'libel' or indictment was drawn up by Wariston. It was a *mélange* of every possible accusation that the Covenanters could devise. Montrose was accused of perjury and of breaking his oath to the Covenant; of conspiring secretly with Walter Stewart; corresponding with the enemy in time of war; associating with Traquair; of dilatoriness in bringing his regiments to join the army; of criminal leniency in his dealings with Lord Ogilvie over the surrender of Airlie Castle; of divisive motions and false accusations against the Committee of Estates; of leasing-making; of seeking preferment for himself; of speaking dishonourably of the King; and of plotting with the King to obtain an amnesty or Act of Oblivion which would include those Royalists excluded by the Covenanters. Montrose wrote a long and spirited defence, answering each of the charges in turn, describing some as 'senseless lies' and the whole as 'nothing but a rhapsody of forethought villainy'.[8] But the defence was not made public and there was no mention of a proper trial.

On 28 July Stewart of Ladywell was beheaded. On the scaffold he confessed to Henry Guthry that his original deposition had been true and that he had been persuaded to alter his evidence in the hope of mercy. It was many years since anyone had actually been executed for the crime of leasing-making, but Ladywell was too dangerous to be allowed to live. His death was a precaution, and 'it served as a warning that for all practical purposes Argyll was King in Scotland'.[9]

It was a warning too that the struggle was in deadly earnest.

During July and August Montrose was made to appear several times before Parliament at the bar for common delinquents. He remained courteous and self-assured. Concentrating on the charge of leasing-making, the Committee tried to trap him into making fresh accusations against Argyll, but while he would not withdraw his earlier statements he refused to be drawn into any further indiscretion, and he continued to demand a public trial before his peers. In a speech that was polite but defiant he told them:

> I am heartily sorry that it should be my misfortune to show myself in this condition; for as it has been far from my intention to fail in my duty to the public, so it was as much from my thoughts that I would have appeared here upon the present terms. . . . For what I have done for the public is known to a great many, and what I have done against it is unknown even to myself. However, as truth does not seek corners, it needs no favours, neither will I trouble your Lordships with long discourses, but resolutely rely upon my own innocency. . . . My resolution is to carry along with me fidelity and honour to the grave. . . .

On 14 August Charles arrived at Holyrood with a small retinue which included both Lennox and Hamilton. The latter was, as usual, 'most active in his own preservation' (the King's words) and shortly after their arrival, both he and Lennox signed the Covenant. Charles told Parliament that he had come 'to perfect' whatever had been promised but the Covenanters were intent on nothing short of the King's complete capitulation. The ensuing sessions were humiliating for Charles. 'There was never King so insulted over,' wrote Sir Patrick Wemyss. 'It would pity a man's heart to see how he looks; for he is never at quiet among them, and glad he is when he sees any man that he thinks loves him.'

On 21 August a petition from Montrose was read in Parliament. But Argyll took the situation in hand by ordering the Committee to discover whether the Graham was prepared to sign 'an accommodation and humble submission' to the King in Parliament (thus by implication acknowledging the justice of the proceedings against him). Montrose refused and said that he desired only a speedy and just trial, whereupon Parliament set his case aside until they 'had dispatched their more weighty affairs'.

These were mainly concerned with appointments to the vacant offices of state which the Covenanters wanted brought entirely under the control of Parliament. Charles finally compromised to the extent of agreeing that he would only nominate to the Privy Council with the approval of Parliament. There followed an unseemly scramble over the spoils. The King, however, remained adamant in his refusal to grant any office to Argyll. He nominated Morton to the Chancellorship, but when Argyll objected that his father-in-law was too 'decrepid' for the post, it went instead to Loudoun, whose popularity was such that the Campbell thought it unwise to cavil further. Charles also wanted to appoint Lord Almond to the Treasureship, but on account of Argyll's opposition to this also, the functions of the office were divided among a committee of five. Sir Thomas Hope was confirmed as Lord Advocate, and Sir Alexander Gibson was made Clerk Register (at Argyll's suggestion and to the considerable chagrin of Wariston, who had wanted that lucrative office for himself). Honours were scattered among the King's enemies. Argyll was created a Marquis. Leslie became Earl of Leven. Wariston was knighted.

Throughout, Charles was very sensible of Montrose's dangerous situation, but was too weak to insist on justice. He believed that any direct interference on his part would only provoke Argyll and so do more harm than good. In early September, Endymion Porter of the Household wrote to Secretary Nicholas:

> The King is yet persuaded to hold out, but within two or three days must yield all, and here are legislators that know how to handle him, for they have his bosom friend [Hamilton] sure and play their game as he directs them that sees both. . . . Though Montrose be in hold, he is so gallant a gentleman and so well beloved as they will be fearful to meddle with him, but will keep him up so long as the King is here.[10]

Nicholas was of the same opinion and wrote to Charles:

> . . . as for Montrose and the rest, some here (they pretend to understand the condition of the case) are of the opinion that their innocency is such that they will not fare the worse for Yours Majesty's leaving them to the ordinary course of justice there.

But the King was not so sure and noted in the margin:

> This may be true that you say, but I am sure that I miss somewhat in point of honour if they be not all relieved before I go hence.

Sir Patrick Wemyss reported:

> His Majesty has engaged his Royal promise to Montrose not to leave the Kingdom till he comes to trial. For if he leave him, all the world will not save his life.

In early October 1641 occurred a conspiracy – or perhaps a number of conspiracies – known as 'the Incident'. The subsequent depositions of those involved were so confusing and contradictory that it has never been possible to determine precisely what happened. The Incident seems to have been preceded by rumours of a possible Royalist *coup d'état*. Charles was still quite popular among the people and a number of the lords such as Crawford, Ogilvie, Almond and Perth staunchly took his part. As Perth stated: 'If this be what you call liberty, God give me the old slavery again,' and the Royalist Kerr brought 600 borderers to Edinburgh – for what purpose people could only guess. Possibly to counteract this, or to further some scheme of their own, Argyll and Hamilton summoned 5,000 of their own supporters to the capital. It began to look as if the Scots were about to revert to their old practice of kidnap and street affrays, and the new Chancellor, Loudoun, protested at the sudden 'confluence' of armed men whose presence in Edinburgh seemed to indicate some ominous intent.

At the beginning of October, Montrose was visited in the castle by William Murray of the royal bedchamber, who offered himself as a channel of communication to the King. Just how Murray obtained access to Montrose has never been satisfactorily explained, but it seems impossible that he could have seen the prisoner without the connivance of Argyll. There is an abundance of evidence to suggest that Murray was the Campbell's creature and his role in this affair was probably that of *provocateur*. However, at least two messages passed from Montrose to the King before 10 October in which the Earl stated that he had some 'high' matters to reveal. Murray deponed later that the King had considered the substance of these messages as 'neither so home nor so high', but it seems possible that Charles was considering possible means of bringing Montrose's case into the open.

On 10 October, Crawford, Ogilvie, Gray and Almond were asked by Murray if they had heard of a letter from Montrose to the King offering to accuse Hamilton and Argyll of treason. They answered that they had not. The same night Murray mentioned the possibility of sequestrating Hamilton and Argyll to Colonel Cochrane and asked him how his regiment was disposed at Musselburgh. Cochrane told him that he would have nothing to do with 'the cutting of throats'.

On 11 October Montrose wrote a third letter to the King stating that 'he would particularly acquaint His Majesty with a business which not only did concern his honour in a high degree, but the standing and falling of his Crown likewise'. Montrose later told Clarendon that Murray, having been 'a principal encourager of what had been proposed to the King, and had undertaken to prove many notable things himself', now revealed the contents of this correspondence to Hamilton. This Marquis became alarmed and, approaching the King in the garden at Holyrood, spoke 'in a philosophical and parabolical kind of way', complaining that he had been maligned and traduced to the Queen, and that because of the slander of his enemies he felt obliged to withdraw from Court for a while. According to popular gossip as recorded by Spalding, Hamilton then went to Argyll, told him what he knew, and said that he was so deeply engaged to the Covenant that he feared for his life and estate. Argyll agreed to stand by him and the two of them decided to concoct a rumour that there was a plot against their lives in which the King himself was implicated. To give substance to the tale they also decided to 'flee' out of Edinburgh.

The same night, a small group of professional soldiers – Colonel Hurry (of whom much more in later years), Captain William Stewart and Colonel Alexander Stewart, met for a drink at Colonel Cochrane's lodging. Hurry left the party early as he was dining with the Earl of Crawford, and when he had gone Colonel Stewart tried to enlist the Captain in a plot to murder or kidnap Argyll, Hamilton and the latter's brother Lanerick. The three victims were to be summoned to the King's apartments, and when William Murray had enticed them into the withdrawing chamber, Almond and Crawford, who would have been waiting in the garden, were to enter suddenly and either kill them or carry them off to a ship which was anchored in the roads.

Captain Stewart, much excited, hurried to inform General Leslie of the plot. Leslie called Hamilton, Lanerick and Argyll to his house and quickly informed them of the threat to their lives. (In his subsequent deposition he stated that he had not reported the matter to the King because 'he thought it was a foolish business and therefore omitted it'!)

Argyll, Hamilton and Lanerick fled to Kinneil and the rumour spread behind them that there had been a dreadful conspiracy against the lives of 'the chief patriots and pillars of the Kirk of God'. It was said that the King was deeply involved, that Crawford had planned to release Montrose, and that Mar, Home, Roxburgh and Almond had been ready to raise their counties against the Covenant. Crawford and Cochrane were arrested and guards posted within the city.

Next morning the King, much agitated, addressed Parliament, and recounted the 'strange story' of his conversation with Hamilton the previous day. With tears in his eyes he read out a list of the favours which he had bestowed upon his favourite, and demanded a full inquiry into the affair. He expressed his horror at 'such base treacheries as were spoken of' and requested a trial before Parliament for 'the clearing of his innocence'. But although this request was seconded by both Lennox and Sir Thomas Hope, the Covenanters agreed only to an investigation by a private committee—at which the King was not permitted to be present. The subsequent report was not made public, but a copy was sent to the King and to the Privy Council in England who declared that there was nothing in it that reflected upon Charles's honour.

During the course of these investigations, Montrose was again interrogated. According to one rumour he had personally offered to assassinate Hamilton and Argyll. (Clarendon recorded this at the time but subsequently expunged it from his *History* after he had the true story from the King.) But no evidence could be found that could link him with the alleged murder plot. On 30 October he was questioned about his correspondence with the King but he 'did so cunningly carry himself in this perplexity that no ground or argument could be gathered from his speeches do what they could'.

On 2 November Hamilton and Argyll returned to a heroes' welcome. Meanwhile the Committee's refusal to publish the official report on the Incident worked to confirm the popular rumours that the King had been implicated. The final mystery was that shortly afterwards William Murray, for reasons known only to Charles, was promoted from groom to gentleman of the bedchamber.

In November news of the Irish Rebellion caused Charles to cut short his visit and leave Scotland. It was a disaster of the first magnitude. After Strafford left Ireland, the country went awry. The Irish Catholics had watched the rise of the Puritans in England and, finding neither justice nor mercy at the hands of their new rulers, rebelled. Terrible atrocities occurred and many English and Scottish settlers were brutally massacred. Worse, the rebels had acquired a copy of the King's privy seal (the Scottish one which was in Lanerick's keeping) and attached it to their proclamation. It was being said openly that the rebellion had been encouraged by the Queen with Charles's approval and connivance.

But before he left, Charles kept his promise to Montrose. On 16 November, after an imprisonment of over five months, Montrose, Napier, Keir and Blackhall were 'ordered to be liberated on caution, and on promising to carry themselves soberly and discreetly' and to appear before the Committee for trial on 4 January 1642. The proceedings of the Committee were to be concluded before 1 March and the sentence remitted to the King, who, in consideration of this 'concession', agreed not to employ them in any office of court or state without the approval of Parliament, or to allow them access to his person. Crawford and others arrested during the Incident were unconditionally discharged.

At the end of January, Montrose and the others were served with a formal list of charges and ordered to submit their defence before 4 February. Montrose, who was 'very unwell in his health', had gone to Old Montrose, and, owing to bad weather, arrived in Edinburgh with only one day in which to prepare his formal answer. But the Committee brought no case against them, and upon their entering a final protest at the injustice that had denied them a fair trial, they were again released. Argyll had achieved his purpose and could now afford to let the process go by default.

In defence of their personal honour, Montrose and Napier procured letters of exoneration under the Great Seal, in which their absolute innocence was attested. But it was empty consolation. Covenant propaganda had done its work. They were still suspected by their countrymen and barred from public life.

Montrose retired to his castle of Kincardine, broken in health and depressed in spirit. In later years Argyll probably wished that he had killed him while he had the chance.

The King's Commission

The worn ship reels; but still unfurled
Our tattered ensign flouts the skies:
And doomed to watch a little world
Of petty men grown mean and wise,
The old sea laughs for joy to find
One purple folly left to her
When glimmers down the riotous wind
The flag of the Adventurer.

The Ship of Fools

Charles left Edinburgh on 18 November 1641, departing, so Loudoun told him, 'a contented King from a contented people', and returned to England to face the crisis of his reign. The details of the quarrel between the King and his English Parliament may be found elsewhere. Now, as the situation polarized and both sides manoeuvred to force an issue, the possibility of compromise was passed and lost, and England slithered into civil war. On his return from Scotland, Charles was confronted by the Grand Remonstrance. On 4 January 1642, on the advice of the Queen, he made a foolish and blundering attempt to arrest five members of the House of Commons, and four days later he was forced to leave London. On 23 April Sir John Hotham shut the gates of Hull in his face, and although the opposing armies did not actually take the field until the autumn, with this incident hostilities between King and Parliament effectively began.

To these events Montrose was a remote spectator. For some months after his release from prison he lived quietly with his wife and children at his castle of Kincardine in Strathearn. Very little is known of his family and domestic circumstances except that of his four sons the eldest was now about twelve years old and the youngest still an infant. The heavy expenses incurred during his imprisonment had left him somewhat impoverished and his estates burdened with debt, and as he rapidly regained his health it is likely that much of his energy was directed towards recouping his personal affairs. During these early months of 1642 there was time too for study and reflection—and for composing poetry. His bitter verse on 'False Friends' possibly belongs to this period, and also the famous lyric, 'I'll never love thee more'—part allegory, part love poem that has perplexed precisians since.[1] However, although he had been excluded from any part in public affairs he did not lose touch with events, and Napier, Keir and Lord Ogilvie were frequent visitors to Strathearn. (Napier's son, Montrose's nephew, was married at about this time to Elizabeth Erskine, a daughter of the Earl of Mar.) But he had learned prudence and the Covenanter Baillie afterwards spoke of him as having been 'very quiet... that long while'.

In January 1642 Charles had written in terms of sympathy and gratitude, but for advice on Scottish affairs the King had again turned to Hamilton to whose diplomacy he trusted to keep the Covenanters neutral in the coming war. Notwithstanding all that had gone before, the favourite was given another chance to vindicate himself. 'Hamilton', the King is said to have told him, 'this is the time to show what you are.' The Marquis had given his assurance that 'he would at least keep that people from doing anything that might seem to countenance the carriage of Parliament'. And Charles believed him.

Montrose was not so deluded. Hamilton was now on terms of great intimacy with Argyll, and his optimism was either ingenuous or insincere. Under his nominal leadership the dwindling band of Royalists in Scotland received neither encouragement nor direction, and the King's cause was failing through default. Nor would Charles's temporizing policy content the Covenanters since they were aware of his weakness and intended to exploit it without scruple. Fresh military preparations in Scotland added a sinister aspect to their protestations of 'contentment'. In November 1641 the King had appealed to the Scots for help in Ireland, and a force under Monro had sailed the following February. Leslie was mustering a greater army, ostensibly also for Ireland, but for what use it was really intended was a matter of conjecture. It did not require the advantage of retrospect to realize that the Covenanters could not afford to remain neutral since if Charles were to emerge victorious in England it was likely that he would then withdraw the concessions granted at Edinburgh also. The safety of Presbyterianism in Scotland could be guaranteed only by the abolition of episcopacy south of the border. This at least was the extremists' view and Alexander Henderson had expressed his conviction of it after Ripon. But the Covenanters were no longer thinking in purely defensive terms, and the war in England could work to their advantage. Theirs could be the 'redder's part'–with the power to mediate or intervene decisively at a favourable moment and for a price. That price was the establishment of rigid Presbyterian government in England.

In May 1642 Charles was at York, and Montrose, Ogilvie and Keir rode south to inform him about the position of the Royalists in Scotland and to ask what he wanted them to do. But, fearful of offending the Covenanters, and mindful of his promise not to see Montrose, the King refused to allow them to approach within twenty miles. He did, however, write:

I know I need no arguments to induce you to my service: duty and loyalty are sufficient to a man of so much honour as I know

115

you to be; yet as I think this of you, so will I have you to believe of me, that I would not invite you to share of my hard fortune if I intended you not a plentiful partaker of my good. The Bearer will acquaint you with my designs. . . .[2]

Montrose and the others returned to Scotland where, possibly on the instructions conveyed by the King's messenger, they drew up a petition to the Privy Council (convened for 25 May) referring to the rebellious conduct of the English Parliament and reminding the councillors of their oath of allegiance embodied in the Covenant. Argyll reacted by spreading rumours of a fresh 'plot' against himself, and the 'Banders' (as the Royalist party were now called) were not permitted to enter Edinburgh. Wariston returned from London to plead the English Parliament's case, and the petition, presented by Montgomery (who previously had been a strong Covenanter), was ignored by the Council. The General Assembly subsequently censured it and passed a resolution 'to prevent such presumption in time to come'.

This Assembly, which met at St Andrews on 27 July 1642, provided further indications of the true state of affairs. 'The Marquis of Hamilton and Argyll', wrote Baillie, 'kept down the malcontents [Royalists] from any stirring.' Charles had ordered Argyll to attend as a member of the Privy Council and assistant to the Commissioner Dunfermline, but the Campbell publicly announced his refusal to participate as a crown official and sat only as an elder for Inveraray—in which capacity he opposed and obstructed the Commissioner throughout. At the end of the session, Argyll sent Lord Maitland (then a new face among the Covenant hierarchy but who later as Earl of Lauderdale was to become Montrose's bitter enemy) to acquaint the King and the English Parliament with the enactments of the Assembly and to 'supplicate' for uniformity of religion. The Covenanters were making their terms quite plain.

On 22 August Charles raised the royal standard at Nottingham, and five days later he wrote again to Montrose:

I send Will Murray to Scotland to inform my friends in the estate of my affairs, and to require both their advice and assistance. You are one whom I have found most faithful, and in whom I repose greatest trust, therefore I address him chiefly to you. You may credit him in what he shall say both in relation to my business and your own, and you must be content with words while I am able to act. I will say no more. . . .[3]

The King still clung to Hamilton's 'diplomacy' and it was Montrose's duty to endure.

William Murray, somewhat predictably, went first to Hamilton and Argyll, to whom he probably showed this letter. (He found them in the process of negotiating a marriage contract between Hamilton's eldest daughter and Argyll's heir, Lord Lorne.) Neither could have been much in doubt as to what Montrose's advice to the King might be. The

Graham was still a potential nuisance, and the Covenanters now made the first of a series of attempts to entice him back into their party. At first sight it may seem a strange manoeuvre, but they probably calculated that it would do no harm. Argyll subscribed to the cynical view that every man has his price; Montrose, having been broken, might now be bought. It was accordingly hinted that a commission as lieutenant-general with command of the army under Leslie could be his if he wanted it. Montrose did not accept, but Argyll took the precaution of putting it about that the Graham was considering the offer.

After Edgehill, the English Parliament made a direct appeal to the Scots, and although Hamilton stirred himself into publishing the King's counter-appeal, Montrose was more than ever convinced that Charles had to take some positive and pre-emptive action in Scotland before it was too late. In February 1643, together with Ogilvie and Aboyne, he again left Kincardine and rode south across the border. While the others continued to Oxford, Montrose went to Newcastle, where he learned that the Queen, who had been in Holland buying arms and war material, had just landed at Bridlington Bay and he hurried there to meet her.

He arrived at a bad moment. The Queen had been exhausted by the stormy crossing, and during the night a parliamentary flotilla had bombarded the house in which she was staying and forced her to take refuge in the open fields. She was too tired and shaken to discuss matters of importance and asked Montrose to wait until they reached York. The delay was unfortunate. When Montrose eventually obtained an audience with Henrietta Maria he clearly and forcefully described the deteriorating situation in Scotland as he saw it. The Covenanters, he said, were only waiting for a favourable opportunity to join forces with the English rebels. Such an alliance would have fatal consequences for the royal cause in both countries. He argued that the only way to prevent this was by bold, pre-emptive action – that was, by immediately raising a Royalist force to defend the King's interests in Scotland. Leslie would not dare to march south while such a threat existed to his rear. The Covenanters were already levying men and, if given time to mobilize, they would soon be strong enough to suppress any Royalist initiative before it had properly begun. In the meanwhile, the Scottish Royalists were themselves become increasingly dispirited and their numbers dwindled with every week that passed.

The Queen might have been persuaded but for the intervention of Hamilton and Traquair, who came hurrying south from Edinburgh, ostensibly to pay their respects but in reality to thwart Montrose. Hamilton dismissed the Graham's advice as rash and imprudent. He admitted that the situation in Scotland contained an element of danger but maintained that Montrose had grossly exaggerated it. The solution lay in careful diplomacy and not, as Montrose had proposed, in a violent course of action which would succeed only in driving the Covenanters into the arms of the English rebels. It was not in the King's interest to extend the Civil War to Scotland. The Marquis concluded by saying that, if the King would appoint him Royal Commissioner with all the authority vested in that office, he would personally undertake to keep Scotland out of the war.

Hamilton's plausibility prevailed. The English advisers who surrounded the Queen did not know Montrose. He was considered young and headstrong–and possibly tainted by his Covenant past, while Hamilton, though not much liked, still had the reputation of being a man of sagacity and experience. 'Montrose', recorded one witness, 'was a generous spirit but . . . he had not so good a headpiece as Hamilton.' The young earl was dismissed with brief thanks for wishing well, while Hamilton was appointed Royal Commissioner and promised a dukedom for his services to the Crown. The Scottish Royalists had no choice but to acquiesce in the continued policy of diplomatic inaction.

Montrose, greatly depressed, returned to Kincardine where, with Napier and Keir, he committed his proposals to paper and sent them secretly to the King. But the Queen now had Charles's ear, and they were again rejected. However, the fact that there had been a confrontation between Montrose and Hamilton at York was soon common knowledge, and a number of Royalists were disturbed that the Graham might have been given such offence that he would withdraw from the King's cause. On 8 May 1643 Sir Robert Poyntz wrote to Ormonde that 'Montrose is the only man to be head and leader of the King's Party, and being of a high spirit, he cannot away with affronts,' while Nithsdale, in a letter of the same date, expressed the opinion that 'I am not altogether desperate of Montrose, but grant he were changed, I am in good hope that you will not lack good affected subjects in Scotland.' Both these letters fell into the hands of the Covenanters and confirmed their suspicions that, when it came to the point, many Royalists would take their lead from Montrose and not from the King's Commissioner. They too were aware of his rebuff by the Queen and of his unconcealed contempt for Hamilton,[4] and they renewed their offer of a high command in the army. Rumours of Montrose's possible defection reached as far as Oxford, and may have prompted the Queen to write in defensive yet conciliatory terms (31 May):

I . . . perceive that you consider affairs in Scotland to be in a very bad state . . . and this owing to my own neglect of certain propositions submitted to me when I first arrived. In that I followed the commands of the King. But I am still of the opinion that if His Majesty's faithful servants would only agree among themselves and not lose time, all the evil to be dreaded from that quarter may be prevented. For my own part, I shall contribute to the utmost of my power. . . . And my confidence in you is not the least diminished, although I too, like yourself, have been disturbed by rumours that you have formed an alliance with certain persons, which might well create apprehension in my mind. But my trust in you . . . is not

built upon so slippery a foundation as mere rumour. . . . Be
assured that neither shall I fail in my promise to you. . . .[5]

But expressions of trust, even if genuine, could not stem the
quickening march of events.

In June 1643 the Scots sent commissioners to treat with the King at
Oxford. Charles had agreed to triennial parliaments, the next being
due in June 1644, but the Covenanters now asked that the date
should be advanced by one year because of the urgent necessity, as they
put it, of establishing a uniformity of religion throughout the King's
dominions. Charles, however, would not submit to this demand since
he would never agree to the destruction of the Church of England
which their idea of uniformity entailed. He told the commissioners that
he could and would not permit them to interfere in English affairs;
nor would he authorise a parliament in Edinburgh before the day
appointed. The Covenanters then asked, ominously, for a safe conduct
to London. The implication of blackmail was not lost upon Charles and
this request was also refused.

Argyll reacted by calling a Convention of Estates upon his own
authority. Hamilton made some show of opposing this action, but then
asked the loyal lords to attend with him – 'in the King's name' – promising
that if the vote were to go against them he would declare the
proceedings illegal and leave the chamber. He made a particular point
of trying to persuade Montrose to attend, but the Graham felt that
if he were to do so he would again be putting himself in a false and
equivocal position. He finally agreed to be present on one condition –
which was that Hamilton should promise, upon his honour, that if
the loyalist party failed to secure fair and reasonable terms for the
King in the debate, he would thereafter endeavour to obtain them by
force of arms. Hamilton demurred. He would protest, he said; but he
would not fight. Montrose flatly refused to attend. In the event, the
extreme Covenant faction had a large majority and carried every
measure which they proposed. Hamilton neither protested against the
proceedings; nor did he walk out of the chamber.

A few days after this convention, the Earl of Antrim was captured
in Ireland by Scottish soldiers of Monro's army, and from a number of
letters found upon his person, Covenant propaganda was able to concoct
evidence of a new popish plot 'to extirpate the Protestant Religion in
England, Ireland, and Scotland'. This fabrication caused great
excitement among the godly in London – as it was intended that it
should. It was said that Charles was negotiating with the Irish rebels,
that the Scots in Ulster were to be massacred, that Monro was to be
bribed to carry an Irish army to England, that an invasion force was to
land in the Solway while the Irish MacDonalds were to attack
Kintyre, and Montrose, Huntly, Aboyne and Marischal were to raise a
rebellion in the North. 'Great probability for all this,' wrote Baillie,
'albeit no certain evidence can be had for some parts of it.' In fact,
the only piece of hard evidence was that Montrose, Marischal and

Ogilvie were known to have met with Huntly at Kelly near Aberdeen in early June. It was not known what had transpired there, but Baillie recorded a rumour that the Royalist conference had broken down owing to the obstructive attitude of Huntly, who had so infuriated Montrose that he now seriously contemplated deserting the King's cause.

Although Baillie, as usual, misinterpreted Montrose's motive, there may have been an element of truth in this, since in June 1643 the Covenanters made their third and most determined attempt yet to 'buy' Montrose, and this time he did not refuse the offer outright. Instead he said that he could not accept unless 'certain doubts' were removed, and he asked for a private meeting with Alexander Henderson 'to solve these scruples'. The Covenanters, believing that the fish was already on the hook, agreed.

However, the whole truth was somewhat different. Montrose had come to the conclusion that the only way to convince the King of Hamilton's incompetence – or duplicity – was to obtain positive intelligence of the Covenanters' intentions and, if possible, to obtain it in front of witnesses. Of all the Covenanters, Henderson was most likely to speak freely. He had been Southesk's chaplain at Leuchars and had known Montrose since he was a boy. And though a convinced Covenanter, he also had a reputation for integrity.

They met informally on the banks of the River Forth not far from Stirling. Henderson was accompanied by Sir James Rollo, who had previously been married to Montrose's sister Dorothea (and subsequently to a sister of Argyll). Montrose was accompanied by Napier, Keir and Ogilvie, who could later bear witness to the conversation that followed. The Earl came quickly to the point. Referring to his own enforced 'retirement' from public affairs, he asked Henderson to explain 'freely and ingenuously' how matters now stood, what his proposed commission as lieutenant-general would actually involve, and indeed why the Covenanters were prepared to offer a position of such rank and responsibility to one who had so recently incurred their severe censure. Henderson, who had been led to believe that he was talking to an apostate come to repentance, answered with equal frankness. He told Montrose that the Covenanters were about to send a powerful army to the assistance of 'their Brethren in England'. The Presbyterians of both countries, he said, were resolved to bring Charles to their terms or die in the attempt. He urged Montrose to throw in his lot with the majority of his fellow nobles – and if he did so, the obdurate few who still resisted would follow his example. Montrose could name his price. He would be appointed lieutenant-general with command of the army under Leslie, and furthermore, the Estates would undertake to pay all his debts (which Henderson knew were considerable) including all the legal expenses incurred during his imprisonment.

Montrose had his proof, but he had to remain at liberty to take it to the King. He therefore stalled for time by asking Henderson whether this offer had been made officially by the Estates, or whether it came merely from certain individuals. Rollo explained that Henderson did not actually have the terms in writing but that the Committee of Estates would make good all that he had said. Montrose replied that he would return home and consider the matter while he waited for the Committee's formal offer.

On 19 July four members of the English Parliament came to Edinburgh with a specific request that a Covenant army should march into England. The tide of war was turning against the parliamentarians. In June, Hampden had been killed at Chalgrove Field. Fairfax had been defeated in Yorkshire. Sir Ralph Hopton had cleared the Roundhead garrisons out of Devon, and the Royalist armies had won two victories at Lansdowne and Roundaway Down. Bristol was about to fall to Prince Rupert. The parliamentary leaders were ready to pay the Covenanters' price.

Montrose did not await the issue. The time had come to show his hand, and accompanied only by Lord Ogilvie he rode south to join the King. They reached Oxford sometime in early August to discover that Charles was absent at the siege of Gloucester. The Queen listened to what Montrose had to say but steadfastly refused to credit any statement that conflicted with the reports that had been received from Hamilton. Seeing that he was making no impression, Montrose went to Gloucester to see Charles, but he was equally unsuccessful in his attempts to persuade the King. He found himself snubbed by the courtiers in the Council, who attributed his actions to jealousy of the Hamiltons, and it was no consolation to know that when he was finally vindicated by events it would already be too late. However, in the early autumn a number of other Scottish Royalists, disgusted by Hamilton's extraordinary acquiescence during the Convention, also came to Oxford and endorsed Montrose's accusations against the favourite. Finally, at the end of the year, Hamilton himself wrote to Charles from Scotland, confessing that he could not prevent the Scottish army from marching south to join the parliamentary forces in England. It was significant that he delayed making this admission until Leslie reached the border.

Between August and October the Scots had agreed and signed a Solemn League and Covenant with the English Parliament. It was a document of fatal consequence for it exchanged the original policy of simple defence embodied in the first Covenant for one of aggression and interference in the religion and liberties of others. 'The Estates of Scotland' entered 'into a mutual league and Covenant with the Kingdom of England for the defence of the true Protestant religion in the Kirk of Scotland and the reformation of religion in the Kirk of England, *according to the Word of God and the example of the best reformed Churches,* and as may bring the Kirks of both kingdoms to the nearest conjunction and uniformity of religion in Church government.' Lanerick, probably with the full knowledge of his brother Hamilton, even affixed the royal signet to the announcement of the treaty and to the commissions of array for levying troops to fight against the King.

If the Covenanters thought that they had obtained their price they were the more deceived. Few of the English signatories had any sympathy with the main object of the Scottish treaty. They needed a Scottish army, but when the time of reckoning arrived they would not tolerate a Scottish Kirk. The insertion of the phrase 'according to the Word of God and the example of the best reformed Churches . . .' is said to have been the work of the younger Vane, and it was designed to provide the necessary loophole. The Scots should have seen it and been warned. Had they merely entered into a. military association with the Roundheads, Scotland might have emerged from the war with her liberty intact and her Kirk secure. But she had presumed to impose her own particular kind of religion upon England, and for this Cromwell and his sectaries would exact their own retribution. Scottish liberty was staked against a bigot's whimsy.

Charles's eyes were finally opened. He sent for Montrose and gave him two days in which to submit his proposals as to what should be done. The Graham responded by promising the King that he would reduce the rebels in Scotland to obedience or die in the attempt. He did not minimize the difficulties. A year ago there had been a chance of success. Now the situation was virtually beyond hope of recovery. The Covenanters were mobilized and enemy troops blocked the approaches to the borders. The Covenanters had garrisons in every castle in the North. But he believed that it might yet be done–if a man had the courage and determination, and above all the faith. He told the King that, though he himself had neither men nor money, 'yet he would not distrust God's help in a righteous cause'. He would require some outside help–an Irish landing in the West, some German cavalry from Denmark if these could be obtained, and arms from abroad. He also asked that the Marquis of Newcastle (who commanded the Royalist forces in the North) should supply him with a party of horse with whom he would cut his way across the border into Scotland. 'The rest must be left to God's good Providence.'[6]

Considered rationally as a military operation, it was attempting the impossible. To fight his way through enemy country with a few troops of cavalry–where even an army might not succeed in forcing the passage; to trust for support on local Royalists, many of whom were too cowed or dispirited to fight; to operate without a base–no mere soldier would have proposed this. It took an adventurer, a knight errant–or a man of destiny. But for Montrose it had come to this. He had always had that premonition of destiny that affects some men, and it grew stronger in adversity. He could endure no longer the frustration of doubt and inaction, of looking on while his cause disintegrated, or the stifling atmosphere of corruption and intrigue that hung about the royal Court. The issue was now clear, his position unequivocal. He knew the path which he had to take, and there was a certain safety in not knowing what lay across it.

Charles was willing to clutch at the straw. Antrim (who had been released) was summoned, and he promised to land 2,000 Irish MacDonalds on the coast of Argyllshire by 1 April 1644. Orders were drafted for the Marquis of Newcastle requesting cavalry and any other support which he could give, and commissions were made out to the loyalist lairds along the Scottish border requiring them to join Montrose with whatever men they could muster. A special commission as Lieutenant of the North was prepared for Huntly, since the Gordons would be the essential nucleus for a Royalist rising in Scotland. (Rumours were already reaching Oxford that Huntly had called his clan to arms.) The King offered to appoint Montrose lieutenant-governor of Scotland and commander-in-chief of all the Royalist forces in that kingdom, but, aware of the jealousies that this could cause, the Earl asked instead that the supreme command should be conferred upon Prince Maurice–a move that also secured the support of the Palatines. Montrose's own commission as the King's Lieutenant in Scotland was signed on 1 February 1644.

Preparations took several weeks, and in late December 1643 Montrose was disturbed to learn that Hamilton and Lanerick were on their way to Oxford. He was particularly worried that the King would again weaken and take them back into his favour since he suspected that Hamilton would defeat the Scottish venture if he possibly could. He therefore went to Charles and warned him that if Hamilton and Lanerick were restored to their old positions on the Council, he would request permission to resign his command and retire abroad. He was not, Montrose maintained, demanding that they should be punished but merely that they should be prevented from doing any further mischief. He would no longer stand by and see his country ruined.

Similar submissions were made by other genuine Royalists, and when the Hamiltons arrived they were placed under guard. They came with 'a fair though lamentable tale', and numerous excuses for their behaviour, but the facts were against them. The depositions of Montrose, Ogilvie, Nithsdale, Kinnoul and others, under oath, attested to their duplicity. Hamilton's acquiescence over the Convention was indefensible. Lanerick's use of the royal signet on Covenant commissions of array was undeniably treason. Charles proposed to try them in front of the Council Board and they were given copies of the charges against them so that they could prepare a defence. However, on the second night Lanerick escaped and fled to London, where the enthusiastic welcome which he received from the parliamentarians and the Scots commissioners served to heighten the suspicions against his brother. Lanerick now became an open Covenanter. Hamilton was imprisoned at Pendennis and later at Cariston Castle in Cornwall.

This incident aroused Montrose's fears as to the possibility of further treachery among the Scots at Oxford, and he therefore drew up another band which condemned in strong terms the Solemn League and Covenant and the consequent invasion of England by a

Scottish army as being both illegal and treacherous. The band was not enforced by any threats or penalties, but he asked all the Scots at Court to sign it. Significantly, Traquair and William Murray refused to do so. The document also caused great offence among the Covenanters in London.

Montrose started north at the end of February accompanied by Ogilvie, Aboyne and several other Scottish cavaliers. He stayed two days at York and on 13 March met the Marquis of Newcastle at Durham. Newcastle was friendly but could offer little help to the enterprise. The Royalist forces in the North of England were on the retreat. Leslie had forded the Tweed on 19 January and, after spending three weeks before the town of Newcastle, the bulk of his army forded the Tyne at the end of February. On 2 March he was across the Wear, and on 4 March the Scots occupied Sunderland. The Covenant army mustered over 18,000 foot and 2,000 horse, and the Marquis of Newcastle, with less than half that number, fell back on Durham. Leslie was currently besieging the town of Newcastle, while Fairfax and Manchester with another parliamentary army were advancing from the South. On 23 March Montrose was probably a witness to the poor Royalist performance at Bowdounhill, after which Newcastle's army withdrew to York. Despite his own predicament, however, Newcastle did give Montrose 100 'ill-appointed troopers' and two small brass field pieces, together with permission to call out the militia of Cumberland and Westmorland. But the King's Lieutenant had less luck among the Scottish cavaliers in the Royalist camp, and when the Earl of Carnwath threw the King's commission on the ground and refused to serve under the Graham upstart, it was an ominous indication of things to come.[7]

Montrose moved into Cumberland, where with the help of Newcastle's commissions of array he obtained 800 foot and 3 troops of horse together with a further 200 gentlemen volunteers. With 1,300 men he crossed the border on 13 April and advanced along the River Annan, but after only two days the Cumberland militia deserted and returned home. With his remaining troops Montrose pushed on to Dumfries (which surrendered without a fight) and there raised the royal standard.

Here, he seemed to hesitate. His original plan had been to penetrate deep into Scotland to Strathearn and Angus, where his and Napier's influence would offer the greatest hope of support. But he now had insufficient troops to cut his way through the Covenanting Lowlands. No help was forthcoming from the border earls. Home, Roxburgh, Hartfell and Annandale, like Carnwath, declined to accept the King's commission. Nor was there any news of Antrim's landing in the West.

However, while he was waiting at Dumfries, a courier arrived with a token from his niece, Margaret Napier, Lady Keir, together with an urgent message inviting him to advance on Stirling where the garrison was ready to desert the Covenant cause. Despite Lady Keir's assurance, Montrose was suspicious, not least because the commander of the

Stirling garrison was Lord Sinclair, whom he remembered as a strong Covenanter and one of Argyll's minions.[8] He also heard, almost simultaneously, that a Covenant force of 5,000 men under Callander (previously Lord Almond, and a signatory of the Cumbernauld Band on whose support he had counted) was marching on Dumfries via Stirling. Under these circumstances it was impossible to advance upon Stirling or to hold Dumfries against such numbers, and Montrose had no alternative but to retreat across the border to Carlisle. The first attempt had been a failure.

Many Scottish Royalists subsequently claimed (in extenuation of their own behaviour) that Montrose had missed his chance. The offer from Stirling had been honestly intended, though whether or not it would have been practicable is a matter of doubt. Sir James Turner, a soldier of fortune who was Sinclair's second in command, later recorded in his *Memoir:* 'thus by Montrose's negligence and Callander's perfidy was lost the fairest occasion that could be wished to do the King service.' However, it was not quite so simple. Montrose was discovering that his small invasion force had not the flexibility which he had at first envisaged. He was too weak to risk a major engagement and yet he had many of the logistic problems attendant upon an army. Nor was his force small enough to slip through unnoticed. It was becoming clear that if he was to pass safely through the Lowlands he would need a diversion—a successful Royalist rising north of the Forth or an Irish landing in Kintyre—and he decided to wait in the vicinity of the border in the hope that a favourable opportunity for a second attempt might soon present itself.

In the meanwhile he could make himself useful by keeping Callander pinned on the border and away from Leslie, and he took to harassing the Covenant forces in the North of England. The main Covenant army had invested Newcastle, and Montrose also kept his soldiers busy by convoying supplies through to the beleaguered town. In order to weaken the enemy stranglehold about the city, on 10 May he attacked the castle of Morpeth which was garrisoned by a Scottish force under the command of an experienced old soldier called Somerville of Drum.[9] Here he won an indifferent victory. The Royalists had no siege train and an assault with scaling ladders was beaten off with heavy loss. Montrose spent twenty days erecting breastworks around the fort while his troopers held off a Covenant relief force, but it was not until he was able to bring up heavy cannon from Newcastle to open a breach in the walls that the garrison agreed to surrender upon generous terms. A Covenant fort at South Shields fell more easily.

On 6 May Montrose was created a marquis.

In late June, while still engaged in skirmishing about the border, he received an urgent summons from Prince Rupert, who had marched north to fight the combined Scottish and parliamentary forces about York. Montrose hurried south at once but arrived one day after the disaster at Marston Moor. He and Rupert met at an inn in

Richmond, and the Prince, who was now himself desperate for troops, commandeered the rest of Montrose's recruits leaving him with less than 100 cavaliers.

The small column rode slowly back through Lancashire to Carlisle. There was still no news of Antrim and they heard a disturbing rumour that a Gordon rising in Aberdeenshire had miscarried. A letter from Montrose to Sir Robert Spottiswoode of 15 July reflects the feeling of depression which had settled over the little band of Scottish Royalists:

> I hope with God's Grace you shall have some good news from us soon. The Marquis of Huntly was once very strong; and as I am informed, about 5,000 horse and foot; but business was unhappily carried; and they all disbanded as unfortunately as heretofore, without stroke stricken. Traquair is coying upon the border; but takes no notice of me and none of the King's party. . . .[10]

Ogilvie and Sir William Rollo slipped over the border into Scotland to scout for further news of the Gordon insurrection and to listen for any intelligence of an Irish landing. They returned with a dismal account. The Gordons had indeed risen and been savagely put down by Argyll. All passes, towns and castles throughout the Lowlands were in Covenant hands and strongly held against an attempt by Montrose. The Scottish Royalists were cowed or beaten. None dared say a word for the King for fear of Argyll. The cavaliers were too few, and Montrose had come too late.

Ogilvie's report was the final blow. At Carlisle Montrose called a council of war among his friends, and listened without argument when they urged him to abandon the enterprise. Some advised that he should return to Oxford and explain to the King that the mission had become impossible. Others recommended that he should return his commission to Charles in a letter and then go abroad to await a more favourable opportunity. It seemed an ignominious ending.

Montrose heard them out in silence, and then sadly gave the order for the column to begin the long retreat south.

PART III

Phoenix

9

The Coming of the Gael
(August 1644)

He either fears his fate too much,
Or his deserts are small
That dares not put it to the touch:
To win or lose it all.

Montrose

But Montrose did not intend to return to Oxford himself. Although he had admitted the probable accuracy of Ogilvie's report, he had for some weeks been haunted by the grimmer truth that, if the present venture were abandoned, there could be no second attempt. Amidst the pessimism at Oxford that vision of a noble chance was irredeemable, and after Rupert's defeat at Longmarston Moor the King had not the resources to waste on another such expedition to Scotland. Romantic notions of a forlorn hope breaking through the Lowlands were a fashion of the past. Yet, all other controversy notwithstanding, it was one of Montrose's particular qualities that, no matter how difficult or disheartening the situation in which he found himself, whether his predicament was the result of accident, treachery or adverse events, if the smallest prospect remained of retrieving what was lost and of overcoming the disappointment, he never resigned himself to defeat or gave up in despair.

If events had proved the impracticability of the original plan, his present purpose was dangerous in the extreme. The time was unsorted, friends uncertain. A chain of Covenant troops spanned the borders and strangers were not allowed to pass through any of the Lowland towns without first being subjected to interrogation.[1] Yet where a force of armed cavaliers could not pass, it was just possible that one man—or, better, three— might slip by unseen. It was a desperate chance to take, but to Montrose's mind at least there was no alternative left to him.

Apart from Sir William Rollo and Colonel Sibbald, whom he had chosen to accompany him in a dash across the border, Montrose told only Ogilvie of his decision. The latter was to lead the remaining cavaliers back to Oxford and there to tell the King what had happened, and, even if no more troops could be spared, to press for a supply of arms to be landed in Scotland at the first opportunity. To support his case, Montrose also gave Ogilvie a list of detailed instructions in the form of a written memorandum which he could recall upon his arrival at Court. Ogilvie was to inform Charles that the border earls—Hartfell, Annandale, Morton, Roxburgh, Traquair, Crawford, Nithsdale and the rest—had refused *utterly* to support the venture, and he was to explain that Montrose's present action, though desperate, was the only course left open to him. Help from England was essential if there was to be any hope of success. Yet Ogilvie was to be careful not to paint too dark a picture.

(1) The possibility of the business, had it been done in time, evidently does appear by that at the least which we have done, which shews clearly that his Majesty hath formerly been but betrayed by those whom he trusted.

(2) With what good reason we did undertake it. Since, if any point of the capitulation had been observed to us—as money, supplies from Newcastle, arms and ammunition from Denmark; Antrim fallen in the country himself with 1,000 men, and much of that kind— we could easily have done the business. Nay, though nothing was held good to us, yet we could easily have effected it notwithstanding, had either we not stayed at Dumfries, or had retreated to Stirling, whereas we went to Carlisle, and by whose means all that befell.

(3) That till we were called away by the Prince [Rupert] by two peremptory orders from off the Borders, Callander did not come in, nor could not, so long as we had stayed. And how, when we came to the Prince, his occasion forced him to make use of the force we brought along with us, and would not suffer him to supply us with others; so that we were left altogether abandoned and could not so much as find quartering for our own person in these counties.

(4) Forget not to shew how feasible the business is yet and the reason thereof, if right courses be taken.[2]

The small force left Carlisle on about 12 August and began the long journey south. Ogilvie rode at the head of the column while Montrose and his two companions kept to the rear, but since his servants, horses and baggage were with the main body the others had as yet no cause to think that anything was untoward. On the second day the three dropped still further behind until the rear-guard also were finally out of sight. Then they turned their horses' heads about and galloped back towards Carlisle.

The rest of the cavaliers continued southwards unsuspecting and, as it happened, to disaster. On 15 August they met up with 400 of Rupert's horse who had been scattered after Marston Moor, and were now riding hard for Lathom House in Lancashire, pursued at some distance by a force of parliamentarians. Their commander brought the unwelcome intelligence that the road south was blocked by the Roundheads who held the Ribble Bridge (near Preston) in strength. Ogilvie did not hesitate, but assumed command of their united forces and at once led an attack on the parliamentary position.

Unfortunately, however, he was not aware that another strong detachment from Fairfax's army was also in the neighbourhood and moving to the relief of the defenders. Ogilvie's party had no sooner carried the bridge than a second force of ironsides surprised them from the rear, and, winded and disorganized after their own assault, the Royalists were surrounded and captured to a man.[3] They were escorted first to Fairfax's camp at Hull. There the Scots were separated from the rest and sent under guard to Newcastle, where Leven was beleaguering the city. Of Montrose's company some ninety-five cavaliers were now prisoner including the Master of Airlie, three Ogilvies, Harry Graham (his natural brother), Sir John Innes (his colonel of horse) and Patrick Melville. Leven sent them north to Edinburgh, some to fret a twelvemonth in the castle and the rest to the Thieves' Hole in the Tolbooth. All their papers had been seized, and so Montrose's memorandum intended for the King was in Covenant hands within a week of its being written. On the basis of this intelligence the Covenanters could guess accurately at Montrose's true weakness, and, although Ogilvie's instructions fortunately contained no specific reference to his plan to enter Scotland alone, they now knew for certain that he had not returned to Oxford but was somewhere in the North of England.

In the meanwhile, however, the King's Lieutenant had vanished. In fact, he was back in Carlisle and talking with Huntly's second son, Viscount Aboyne.[4] Despite the failure of the recent rising in the North, Montrose was still convinced that the key to the situation lay with the Gordons, around whose military nucleus he could most effectively rally the loyal gentry of Angus and the Mearns. It seemed proper therefore to consult with Aboyne—Huntly being inaccessible—and it was eventually agreed between them that Montrose would take with him Huntly's commission as lieutenant-general in the North, while, rather than risk putting two heads into the one noose, Aboyne would wait in Carlisle until the Graham sent him word. Having thus mooted, apparently satisfactorily, the principle of Gordon co-operation in the North, Montrose, Rollo and Sibbald hastily made their final preparations for the attempt on the border.

They left Carlisle on 18 August. Rollo and Sibbald rode together, dressed in the buff jackets of Leven's troopers, while Montrose followed some distance behind in the guise of their groom, mounted on 'a lean jade' and leading another horse on a long rein. They had cause to hurry. It is possible that word had already reached them of Ogilvie's capture, and they knew that the normal routes across the Scottish march were strictly guarded by Covenant patrols. But two chance incidents before they reached the border reminded them of the extreme urgency of their situation, and, according to Wishart, so alarmed Montrose that he 'resolved to push forward with the utmost speed to anticipate the rumour of his coming, and spurred on without sparing horse flesh'.[5]

In Netherby Woods they fell in with a servant of Sir Richard

Graham of Esk who noticed nothing strange about the modest trio and their rather sorry looking horses, and regaled them, as servants will, on the business of his master and his influence thereabouts. This Sir Richard Graham was an adventurer who had begun his career as confidential attendant and master of horse to the late Duke of Buckingham, whom with Charles I he had accompanied in their mad attempt upon the Infanta in 1623. The King had rewarded this service to the monarchy by making him a baronet in 1629, since when Sir Richard contrived to change his spots and had more recently distinguished himself on the Roundhead side at the Battle of Edgehill. At the present, the gillie confided, his master was on excellent terms with the Covenant authorities and had undertaken, as their spy, to provide information about anyone passing that way whom from personal recollection he suspected of favouring the King. The three eventually found some opportunity to rid themselves of this importunate fellow, but the conversation had worried them considerably.

A little further on they caught up with a soldier—a Scot who had campaigned with Newcastle's Whitecoats but was now contracting out of the war. Unfortunately, he recognized Montrose. Though the others greeted him civilly enough, he ignored them altogether and respectfully saluted the embarrassed groom. Montrose hoped even now to keep up his disguise and took no notice of him, but the man was persistent and exclaimed: 'Do not I know my Lord the Marquis of Montrose well enough? But go your way and God speed you!' It was an anxious moment. They were within a few miles of the border where a careless word would put up the hue and cry. What were the chances that the secret would not come spilling out in the nearest ale-house, and what price then á drunken deserter's honour? This man lived at their peril, and they must have been tempted to stick a pike in his throat and have done with it. But although he was much disturbed that the disguise had been seen through so soon and by such a one as this, Montrose would not allow the others to harm the man and gave him some gold to send him on his way. As it turned out, the soldier did not betray the trust.[6]

Now they rode hell for leather, across the middle march, up Liddel Water and through Roxburgh for the North. With no thought to the horses, or pause for food or rest, they made it, incredibly, in four days to Tayside and the house of the Grahams of Inchbrakie at Tullibelton. It was almost home for Montrose and excellent for his purpose. The old curator Patrick Graham (who had arranged his library at Kincardine fifteen years ago) was unquestionably loyal, and so too his son Patrick Graham the Younger, called Black Pate (after an accident with gunpowder) who now became Montrose's first recruit. His own lands lay to the south, and the favourite haunts of 'ancient Kier'; to the north, the braes of Atholl. This was a good centre from which to gather intelligence and, if it suited, to call a rendezvous.

But he could hardly afford to relax. It was logical to assume that the Covenanters would look for him among his own, and he still did not dare send word to his wife and his sons that he was again in Scotland, and very near. During the daytime he hid in a small cottage on the estate or in Methven Wood close by, and when night fell (fortunately it was high summer) he walked up into the safety of the hills above Tullibelton. At first there was little else to do but brood. Rollo and Sibbald rode off to give the news to Napier, and to canvass once more among the Royalist gentry, delivering letters which purported to come from the King's lieutenant in Carlisle. Montrose's approach to the problem was still conventional, and they concentrated their energies within the undulating country along the eastern seaboard, since it was from among the Royalists of Angus and the Mearns, together with the Gordons in the North, that he yet looked to win back Fifeshire and the Lothians–the true centres of political power–from the Covenant.

The better part of a week dragged by and the signs grew steadily more discouraging. Rollo and Sibbald returned 'corby messengers' with news as dismal as before, and answers that were detached and cold. As ever in war or times of unease there was rumour, and much that was unreal. Men claimed to have heard the 'touking of drums' at the dead of night. Phantom armies fought on Manderlee, and at the muir of Forfar contending hosts were seen to muster in the air. People took such visions to be dreadful omens which, as Spalding remarked 'fell out over true', but in the daylight Argyll's grip was tight around the land. Rollo and Sibbald could tell only of the ruinous fines, imprisonment or even death that had been meted out to those who would have stood for King Charles, and how the rest, dismayed, had either submitted to King Campbell or withdrawn into a frightened neutrality. They also brought the depressing story of the rising in the North, how Huntly had fumbled at Aberdeen and the Gordons' strength was wasted and their leader fled–'without a stroke stricken'–as Montrose himself had ruefully put it.

The Cock of the North had strutted prematurely and his crowing had been sadly out of tune. When the main Scottish army had crossed into England, the more ardent of the northern Royalists urged Huntly to raise his clan and strike immediately for the King. The Marquis himself agreed that some sort of decision was called for since his Royalist past marked him down as deserving of particular attention and in the face of the unconcealed threats of the Covenanters it seemed only prudent to protect himself. The revolutionary authorities had cast covetous eyes over Gordon lands, and promptly announced their intention of forcing him to contribute a ruinous proportion to their war chest, while he, on the grounds that any such levy was nothing short of treason, was equally resolved not to disgorge. On 16 March 1644 he issued a declaration defending his position and protesting that, without legal trial or condemnation, the Committee of Estates had ordered the sheriffs of Aberdeen and Banff to seize his person, houses, rents and goods.[7] Because he had resisted the illegal commission to levy men and money for the invasion of England (a course that was incompatible with his conscience and duty to the King), an armed force was even now being raised against him in the South. Though his protest was eloquent, as a declaration of the Royalist cause in Scotland it was somewhat tentative. But he had rattled his broadsword to show he meant business, and he now set to calling up the Gordons.

Unfortunately, the main movers in this affair had been somewhat optimistic in overestimating the strength that Huntly was able to muster. The Master of Gordon was at this time on the Covenant side and a reckonable portion of the clan's fighting strength went with him. Moreover, although initially Huntly must have counted on the support of prominent Royalists such as Airlie, Southesk, Atholl or Seaforth, outside of the Gordon country the gentry were, in the event, ominously reluctant to commit themselves under his leadership unless he could produce a formal commission from the King. He therefore sent a messenger off on the hazardous journey to Oxford to ask the royal pleasure, and resolved not to move decisively until he got an answer.[8]

However, for the young fire-eaters in the Gordon camp this was nowhere near good enough. In the early hours of 19 March, the young Laird of Drum (who was married to Huntly's fourth daughter), Robert Irving his brother, Gordon of Haddo, the Lairds of Gight, Tibbertie and Scethin and Nathaniel Gordon, with about 60 horse, rode into Aberdeen and carried off four of the most notorious covenanters,[9] including the town provost. Having casually robbed a few more who favoured that faction, they then galloped up and down the Gallowgate to see if there was anyone who cared to dispute the issue, while Haddo went into the Old Town and collected his children from school (all but the eldest returned next morning). At about 10 a.m. they rode leisurely out through the Loch Wynd, stopped to celebrate at Kintore and reached Leggitsden by nightfall. Next morning they returned in high fettle to Strathbogie where, like it or not, Huntly was now committed by their precipitous action. Consequently, he had the four prisoners incarcerated in his fortress of Auchindoune and hastily published another declaration justifying the raid.

The Covenanters of Aberdeen were thoroughly alarmed. One of the remaining bailies hurried to the Committee of Estates in Edinburgh with the story of the kidnapping and a demand for redress,[10] while some forty-eight others of the brethren hastily packed up what gear they could and sought comparative safety among the Presbyterian communities of Angus. At Dunnottar Castle, the Earl Marischal told Huntly's messenger that he would take no action unless compelled to do so, but meanwhile gave shelter to some of the fugitives and cautiously waited upon events.

On 20 March the town of Aberdeen was put in a state of defence, but as all its able-bodied men of serviceable age had been drafted into the Scottish army, it had neither the will nor the wherewithal to resist when Huntly's force arrived before the gates on the twenty-sixth. At the same time, however, the citizens were in no mood to help, since their previous experience of the Marquis's martial enterprise led them to rate his chances of success as none too high, whereas the likelihood of summary retribution at the direction of Argyll seemed as certain as it was unpleasant to contemplate. Since he could obtain no material satisfaction from the burghers, Huntly felt justified in helping himself to any war materials that could be found, and a search of the town provided a reasonable haul of arms – muskets, hagbutts, carrabines, swords, pistols, pikes, spears, forks, corslets, powder and ball – with which to equip his followers. Bands of Gordons scoured the countryside for further supplies and munitions, and Haddo rode off to Turriff to seize four pieces of ordnance that were known to be there. About this time the messenger returned from England with assurances that help was on its way, and that Aboyne would follow shortly bringing with him the royal commission for which Huntly had asked. Montrose, Crawford, Nithsdale, Kinnoul and Ogilvie were said to be on the borders with a strong force and poised to attack the Lowlands while he held his ground in the North. The Covenant armies would have to concentrate in the South to meet this latest threat and it was therefore unlikely that any formidable expedition could be mounted against the Gordons. Apparently reassured, Huntly left Aberdeen on 28 March to continue recruiting among his own tenants, leaving the town in the hands of Haddo, Drum and Gight.

During the next week these three went raiding in the surrounding district, ostensibly for arms and horses, and to discomfort any local Covenanting gentry. Straloch, Turriff, Tollie Barclay and Sir John Burnet of Craigmyllis property at Blackhills were visited and robbed, and young Drum for good measure looted his cousin John Irving of Kincousie's house at Auchquhorters. When the supply ran short they lifted horses belonging to such of the local citizenry as had been foolish enough to walk them in the street, and one Sunday captured a fine animal in the possession of the Laird of Meldrum when this worthy attended Kirk at Bathelny. Huntly, however, had already four prisoners too many and, though glad of the beast, restored the outraged gentleman to liberty – 'for he wes a preceis puritane and wold not follow the Marques'.[11]

Meanwhile, time was slipping away and the Gordons' chance had almost come and gone. The separate agencies of the Covenant had recovered from their initial surprise and were gathering to launch a decisive counter-attack. On 20 March Argyll had arrived in Edinburgh and received a commission from the Estates to assume command of an army which was to be raised and employed in the suppression of the northern rebellion. Lothian's regiment was recalled from Ireland. Perthshire could send 800 men, Fife 500 more; 1,000 Campbell swordsmen were marching from Argyll, and at Dunnottar the Earl Marischal, for all his cautious words to Huntly's courier, was meeting with the Committees of Angus and the Mearns to co-ordinate the muster there. In the North the gentry of Moray were gathering at Elgin, while Huntly's other enemies of long-standing–Forbes, Frasers and the barons of Buchan, Mar and Gareoche–sat secure behind their castle walls waiting only for the moment when they might assist in Argyll's victory and scavenge among the ruins of Strathbogie for their share. Given two weeks more, the Covenant could count on 5,000 troops for an offensive in the North.

Incredibly, however, Huntly continued to maintain his forces in arms and idleness. His friends would later assert in his defence that he was still short of supplies and money to equip and sustain an army, but, apart from the loot from his raiding expeditions, it is reckoned that he already had some £100,000 in his war chest while some of the individual barons who had joined him had undertaken to maintain their own contingents. He was able to billet 250 of his soldiers at the Aberdonians' expense, but the rest of his adherents from Strathbogie, Strathavan and Engzie were costing him nearly 600 merks per day with nothing to show for it. Ammunition there was for the taking.

On 3 April Huntly returned to Aberdeen in person and opened negotiations with the Covenanting Committees of Angus and the Mearns. He had heard that they were raising a force to come against him, but instead of moving immediately to destroy them as his friends advised, he sent repeated assurances that his principal motive in the matter was still one of self-preservation, and that although he might at some stage require passage through the area he would do them no damage unless he was forced to. Co-ordinating with Marischal, who by now had the measure of his adversary, the representatives of the committee replied that they would disband their forces if Huntly would do likewise, and when he demurred for prudence's sake they protracted the discussions still further by pausing to ask for fresh instructions from their masters, the while playing for time until Argyll should have drawn his forces to a head.

This inactivity was taking a severe toll of the Gordons' morale. The younger officers were highly critical of Huntly's conduct of the war, but tempers were short everywhere, and the lieutenants were also quarreling among themselves. Haddo was wounded in a duel (his opponent went home) and Nathaniel Gordon, who was perhaps the ablest soldier of them all, fell out with Huntly over a herring boat which he had seized, and threatened to leave the Marquis's service. Discipline was very poor. Throughout early April the precious days were wasted in more uncoordinated raids upon Covenanters' property. In the South, Argyll made his final preparations unmolested.

At last, on Saturday 13 April, a month all but three days after his original declaration, Huntly called a general muster at Inverurie, where a rough count put his force at 400 horse and 2,100 foot. On Monday the fifteenth he rode once more into Aberdeen to have the standards made–on each side a lion rampant with a gold crown above its head and the initials C.R. (for Carolus Rex). The motto was 'For

God, the King, and against all Traittouris' and beneath it, 'God save the King'. Other pincels were made for the barons while Huntly and his followers purchased lengths of black taffeta to bind around their 'crag' to signify their solemn determination to fight to the death. (However, as Spalding remarked: 'But it provit uthervayes'.[12]) This finished, he called another muster at Inverurie for the eighteenth when he appointed some companies of foot to garrison Aberdeen, and sent 240 men under Donald Farquharson, McRanald and the Tutor of Struan on an expedition into Angus. He then returned to his lodgings in Aberdeen, and on the Saturday held a grand review of his remaining troops (160 horse and 700–800 foot) on the links outside the town.

The same day a band of younger Gordons rode out on the only foray of the entire campaign that could be said to have resembled a military operation in the proper sense of the word. Young Drum, Robert Irving his brother, Nathaniel Gordon, Ardlogie, Gight the younger and some others left Aberdeen with about 75 horse and on 22 April crossed the Dee to ride south over Cairn O' Mount until they linked up with Donald Farquharson and his 240 foot on the Northesk. Despite the proximity of the Covenant musters at Fordoun and Forfar, their purpose was to seize the town of Montrose and capture the two brass cannons which they knew were there. They then proposed to ship the cannon and themselves back to Aberdeen on board a vessel in the harbour belonging to one Alexander Burnet who was party to their plan.

They reached Montrose at about 2 a.m. on 24 April to find that the provost had had word of their coming and the town was in a state of defence. Drum promptly led one party in a frontal assault on the gates while the rest scaled the garden walls and fought their way in the darkness towards the market place. The burghers and apprentices put up a fierce resistance but were overwhelmed. Their bailie, Alexander Pearson, was shot down at his stairhead by Nathaniel Gordon[13] and the Royalists '. . . dang the toune's people fra the calsey to thair houses, and out of the foirstaires thay schot desperatelie, bot thay war forssit to yeild by many feirfull schotes schot aganes thame.' Unfortunately, when they trundled the two cannon down to the harbour, things began to go awry. Burnet must have previously betrayed the plan as a policy of reinsurance, for when the expected ship approached the quay it was manned by the town's provost with 40 musketeers, and on coming within range it discharged its broadside at the group of waiting Royalists, killing two and wounding several more. Drum was beside himself with rage, and had the wheels broken and the cannon tipped into the sea. For the next ten hours the Gordons plundered the town.

They finally left Montrose in some disorder in the early afternoon, and by nightfall Drum and others had ridden as far as Cortachy Castle. There they invited Airlie to join the uprising, but the old earl's reputation for prescience was not for nothing, and he ran a cool eye over their undisciplined band and politely declined. Next morning Drum returned to Aberdeen at his own pace, leaving the rest of his expedition to follow as best they pleased. Casualties in the fight had been quite light and, incoherent as they were, surprisingly no one molested them as they straggled through Kincardine. However, some 52 highlanders who had had difficulty in disengaging themselves from the wine cellars of Montrose did not get back, but were captured by the Covenanting forces who were deploying into the area, and sent under guard to Edinburgh to suffer for their insobriety.

On 26 April Argyll rode into Dunnottar. The Clan Forbes now emerged from their strongholds and took the field in strength.

On 29 April Huntly was forced to face the truth. His followers were by now thoroughly demoralized, and while Argyll's encircling forces were growing each day in numbers and in confidence, his own army was rapidly melting away. At a council of war he defended his inactivity. If he had followed the advice of his lieutenants and attacked the Covenanters in Angus before they could consolidate, the Frasers, Forbeses and other malcontents in Aberdeen itself could have fallen in a pack upon his unprotected rear. There had been, he maintained, sound reason to delay. His messenger, John Gordon of Berwick, had promised that the royal commission was on its way, and it was right that he should have waited for it. Charles had hoped to have an army in Scotland by the end of March but Montrose had turned back from Dumfries and his hopes of the loyalist gentry rising for the King had all been disappointed. Nothing, he confessed, had turned out as he had reckoned, and the situation was already beyond saving, for his depleted forces could no longer hope to offer battle to the invincible army that had been gathered against them.

Huntly's friends now urged him to fight a guerilla war against the Covenant authorities. Although not strong enough to confront Argyll's army in the field, he could still hang around its flanks and savage it. The Lowland troops could not match the Gordons in the high country. The Marquis agreed to this suggestion, and, because the Covenanters' net was already drawn too tight for comfort, he left Aberdeen and called a muster at Strathbogie.

At this point Nathaniel Gordon, still discontented, left the Gordons' leaguer for good. Ever the soldier of fortune, he offered his sword to Lord Gordon, who was still a Covenanter and would have none of it, before riding off into the wild mountain country to shift for himself. The others would follow soon enough.

On 30 April Huntly was temporarily diverted by news that his son and a party of his friends were at Banff, and he hurried north to surprise them, or perhaps to win them to his cause. He arrived too late, however, and returned dispirited to the muster at Strathbogie where he learned that his entire force had now dwindled to 1,500 foot and 300 horse. Haddo, Drum and Gight, as usual, pressed him to issue some positive orders for the subsequent campaign, but a feeling of hopelessness had by now overtaken him and he answered that he could not begin to fight in any way with so few men as were now left. The young Gordons' disillusionment was final. 'We have schawing our selfis foolishlie, and will leave the fieldis schamefullie. We thocht never better of it,' Drum shouted at Huntly as he left.

It was time enough to look to his own safety. At Auchindoune Huntly released the four prisoners from Haddo's raid before going on to the Bog of Gight to get several chests of treasure which he kept there. Having taken what he needed, he sent the keys to his son Lord Gordon, who was with Argyll, rode the waters of Spey, and eventually got a boat to Caithness where he took refuge with his cousin german, Francis Sinclair. From there he found another ship to take him to Strathnaver, where he hid 'in ane island callit Toung'.

Argyll was now master of the situation and deployed the considerable forces at his disposal to stamp out each ember of the northern revolt, and to make an example of the Gordon lairds in such a way as to deter any others who might also be rash enough to contemplate rebellion against the new government in Scotland. His regiment of Campbells went down Deeside–Aboyne, Abergeldy, Birs, Cromar, Glentanner and Glenmuick–and plundered Covenanter and non-Covenanter with complete impartiality, while Lothian's Irish eventually had to be bought off by Aberdeen for the sum of £20,000. 18,000 merks were offered for Huntly's head and bounties were promised for the other Gordon lairds. Haddo was besieged at Kelly. He surrendered, and was dragged to Edinburgh and executed after a mockery of a trial. The younger Gight escaped, but Drum was betrayed by Sinclair and imprisoned with his brother Irving in the tolbooth. However, Nathaniel Gordon also got away. Hearing of Haddo's death he had no mind to give himself up, and he took to brigandage, and raised a band of outlaws to prey upon the northern Covenanters. But as Argyll's grip tightened round the North and his garrison kept the countryside to heel, there was little that a small force could do. And so he retired to the safety of the high country and ran with the other broken men.

Now that Montrose was able to assess the full extent of the Gordons' ruin, he must have realized that his whole concept of a conventional war in the East of Scotland would have to be abandoned. The Gordon force was no longer a military nucleus round which to fuse the Angus gentry and their small bands of retainers. Yet without such a nucleus there could be no army, and moreover without the cavalry, which would have been the Gordons' most valuable single contribution, no army–even if there was one to command–could in theory hope to campaign successfully or indeed survive in the flat lands where the decisive battles against the Covenant would undoubtedly have to be fought.

The unconventional alternative was almost impossible to gauge, but at the same time it offered the only chance remaining. Montrose knew the Grampians. His own estates bordered on the Highland line, and

Napier had inherited a quarter of the earldom of the Lennox. The Highland clans still looked on Charles as their titular chieftain, and though remote from the constitutional struggle, a common hatred of the Campbells' greed might now serve to foster a unity where none had hitherto existed. Few chiefs were more detested by the clans than the MacCailein Mhor—not so much because he was dictator now, but rather as the head of an inferior race of gael whose encroachments were steadily ruining them, and whose ambition prophesied their ultimate extinction. The component factors of Scottish Royalism in the peculiar sense of the term—the hatred of Argyll, and the hatred of the equalizing power of the Kirk—might be so in parallel as to bridge the other differences between the Royalist gentry on either side of the Highland line. The problem was one of leadership, and again of finding a viable nucleus on which to build. To bind the clans together for a political object was, in theory, an impossible task, since no clan would ever agree to defer voluntarily to its neighbour, nor would one chief submit to the leadership of another. But there was a chance that they would find it no dishonour to fight beside the King's lieutenant—were he a Graham. In the last analysis it might depend upon the spirit of his command. For the rest, it had been his constant prayer, more hopeless and yet more persistent: would Antrim, that vain man 'of marvellous weak and narrow understanding',[14] who had offered much and performed so little—dear God, Antrim—send but half the men he had promised! But even set against the other failures, this was the slimmest chance of all.

And so it was significant perhaps, that of all his prayers, it was this one that was answered.

For some weeks there had been vague rumours carried by shepherds in the hills that an army of Irishes had landed in the West and were laying waste the Highlands. Argyll received a dispatch by courier from Dunstaffnage and knew for certain that a force of Scoto-Irish—MacDonalds for the most part—had landed in the Sound of Mull on 5 July. The Committee of Estates immediately empowered him to levy troops to repel the invaders, and, confident after his triumph over the Gordon rebels, he marched westwards towards his own country with 500 Campbell swordsmen at his back.

The war band of Scoto-Irish, numbering about 1,600 in all, had been sent by Antrim who had finally overcome the objections of the Supreme Council and now honoured at least the part of his promise. Their leader epitomized the ideal of the antique Highland fighting man: Alastair MacDonald, 'the red-armed horse-knight, the brave and courageous son of Coll Kietache, son of Gillespie, son of Colla, son of Alastair, son of John Cathanach';[15] and on the Campbell's tongue, 'Alastair, son of Colla—The Devastator'.[16] He was the younger son of the fierce old Coll Kietache MacGillespick MacDonald of Iona and Colonsay—a cadet of Clan Ian Ivor—whose ability to fight with either hand Alastair had inherited together with his name. He was cousin to the Marquis of Antrim, Ranald Og, son of Ranald of Arran,[17] but he could claim too the blood of the old berserkers and descent from Conn of the Hundred Fights who had ruled in the halls of Tara. He was half a head taller than most men, with the great thews and shoulders of a swordsman; violent, valorous, already a legend among his clan and praised in the poems of MacVurich. As a boy he had wrestled Highland bulls in Colonsay, and full-grown he was accounted the greatest warrior among his father's people. He was sullen- tempered, proud like Achilles, and he drank 'strong waters'–sometimes too deep.[18] In front of Antrim he had drawn his claymore to demand the leadership of the expedition as of right–'For my sword is wielded by the best hand in Ireland!'–and when an Irish captain, moved perhaps to dispute the matter, had asked him which was next best, Alastair tossed the sword from right to left hand and replied 'It is there!'[19]

Alastair MacDonald had his own quarrel with the MacCailein Mhor. Some time past, Argyll had forced his claim to the family's lands, and because the old chieftain gave him trouble, he had incarcerated Coll Kietache and two of his sons in the dungeons of one of his remote fortresses. Alastair, however, had escaped across the Irish Channel and taken service under his kinsman the Marquis of Antrim. When Leven visited Ireland he had marked the huge MacDonald for his courage and rising reputation, and seeing in him a dangerous adversary, offered to broke with Argyll for the release of his father and the restitution of his inheritance. But Argyll, unfortunately, refused to disgorge either the chief or his patrimony, for having successfully chained up old Coll Kietache he was not fool enough to let him loose again. Alastair, who had returned temporarily to Scotland in order to treat with the MacCailein Mhor, was incensed at this additional affront, and went back to Ireland swearing to exact a vengeance in Campbell blood.

He now had his opportunity. Antrim had originally planned to send an army of 6,000 men into western Scotland, but when he had difficulty in raising such a number it was agreed that Alastair, restless for revenge, could lead an advance expedition of about 1,600 Scoto-Irish[20]–the greater part MacDonalds–to establish a bridgehead in front of the main invasion force which was to follow. At the same time he was to carry with him letters from the King to the Earl of Seaforth and to such chiefs among the Clan Donald as would no longer tolerate the oppression of Argyll and might join the Royalist cause. If by some chance the main force did not appear within the time agreed, Alastair would merely lead a foray along the western march of the Campbells' country and then return to Ireland.

The war band embarked at Hac in three ships–one Irish, and the other two chartered from the Flemings–but in mid-channel they were able to augment their fleet by capturing two Covenant vessels laden with supplies for Monro's forces in Ireland. On 5 July 1644 they landed at the Rhu of Ardnamurchan, a promontory in Morven near the mouth of Loch Sunart, and in accordance with the plan raised a battery known as 'the Trench' at the entrance to Ceanloch harbour in preparation for the landing of a larger force later.

Alastair now turned his attention to the personal object of the enterprise–'to bring a highland vengeance upon a highland foe'–and began by slaying the wretched Malcolm MacPhie whom Argyll had designated to Colonsay. He then beleaguered his ancestral castle of Mingarry on its basalt rock above the sea, but having no cannon with him he tried first to smoke out the defenders by burning wood in the fosse against the gates, and then, more successfully, to starve the garrison into surrender. He also laid siege to the square tower on the rock at Kinlochaline and took it in the assault. Since by this time he had already acquired a creditable amount of booty, he selected one of the small islands off the coast as a corral where the sheep aed cattle which his men had reived could be kept safely against the day when, assuming Antrim did not come, they could be carried back to Ireland with consequent profit. Then, having left garrisons in the two captured fortresses to guard this line of retreat, he led the army up the wild shore to the Isle of Mist and the hills of Kintail, while the ships sailed along the coast to rendezvous with him again at Loch Eishort in Skye. From the Sound of Mull to Kyle Rhea the Irish MacDonalds now visited their ancestral enemy with fire and sword and exacted a terrible reckoning from the race of Diarmid who had dispossessed them. The lands of the western Campbells were devastated along the line of their march, the livestock butchered, the houses burned and peasants killed, or homeless left to starve on the scorched mountainside.

In his plan to recruit the local clans, Alastair was disappointed. MacDonald of Skye, on whose influence he had counted, had been dead six months or more,[21] and others of the Clanranald thought the Irish force too small to have any chance of surviving the inevitable retribution of Argyll–who was even now gathering his power and raising all the country against them. Nor did letters to the MacLeods, the MacLeans of Skye, the Stuarts of Appin or the Clan Cameron bring any positive response. If the Gallows Herd held back for fear of the MacCailein Mhor, the other clans would not agree to fight under a MacDonald chieftain. Having waited a month the while continuing his depredations, Alastair prudently decided to return to Antrim with his loot intact before he could be drawn into an unequal fight with Argyll's army.

But it was already too late. Argyll had contrived to deploy his forces behind the Irish so as to hold the passes between them and the sea, and three parliamentary men-of-war had been diverted to Loch Eishort where they surprised the MacDonalds' squadron as it lay at anchor. In a short engagement the Flemings–hirelings anyway–struck their colours at the first broadside, but the Irish, who asked and gave no quarter, put up a fierce resistance until their master was killed and the ship sunk under them. Alastair could no longer return to Ireland.

He was in a parlous position, being no great strategist for all that he was a bonny fighter. But he bethought himself of the King's war and the possibility of linking up with Huntly whom he had heard was in the field. Turning their backs on the sea and the western straths where the Campbells were consolidating to block their retreat, the Irishes crossed Kyle Rhea and marched over the mountains of Quiach in the direction of Lochaber, only to learn at the last that the Gordons had disbanded long since and there was no sanctuary for them in the North-East. They were getting short of ammunition and the Campbells were still behind them. Alastair prayed for a loophole to the north-west and cut back through Glengarry, sending a messenger ahead to Seaforth with the King's letter and a formal request for help. But Seaforth, who might have held all Ross, Caithness and Sutherland for Charles, had also been unnerved by Huntly's failure and now sided with the Covenant majority, while his clan – the MacKenzies from Kintail and Loch Duich – recalled their past feud with the MacDonalds and regarded Alastair's approach with conspicuous unease. Seaforth was civil enough at first, but excused himself on the grounds that the King's cause in Scotland had been lost in the spring, and any present association with the Irish renegades would be an act of grave imprudence. Alastair was almost at the end of his resources. It was the Irish custom for the women and children to follow the army, and these were now in a sorry condition, ragged, weakening from hunger, exhausted by the long march and without hope of Campbell mercy. Now he begged only for free passage to the North and safety, but the MacKenzies grew hostile, and when Seaforth himself raised the country against them the Irish wearily prepared to fight. Fortunately, however, Seaforth's prudence also prompted him to hesitate on the brink of battle with such desperate men who had no thought to yield whatever the hazard and who, brought to bay, would sell their lives more dearly than he dared. At a parley between the two forces, he agreed finally to give the Irish some victuals and other necessaries with free passage towards Badenoch, which adjoined Lochaber to the east and had also been part of Huntly's country. So the band turned back and trudged over the mountains towards Lochaber once more – fortified somewhat by the MacKenzies' beef, but in the knowledge that there would be no one willing to offer them a refuge or rash enough to cheat Argyll of his revenge.

Since they could look only to themselves for chance of survival, and because the letters from the King had proved less potent than he had been led to expect, Alastair now adopted more violent measures to obtain recruits. During the night he sent patrols into the towns and villages along his route to kidnap the chief men of the locality, to whom he showed the royal commission and demanded aid under pain of pillaging crops and property. This technique brought him about 500 men, and he also had some small success among the Gallows Herd. He was joined by Clan Vurich of Badenoch led by Ewan Og son of Andrew, son of Ewan, who was a chieftain of MacDonald blood, and by Clan Finlay of Braemar with another chief of his own kin–

Donald Og, son of Donald, son of Finlay. These, together with a number of broken men who had attached themselves to the warband, swelled Alastair's numbers to over 2,000; and somewhat elated by this he now resolved (rather optimistically) to raise the whole of Huntly's country. But he was brought abruptly to a halt in Strathspey by the Laird of Grant who held the crossing in strength against him, supported by the gentry of Moray and a force of horse and foot out of Ross. Seaforth too reappeared with 1,000 of his highlanders to lend conviction to his lately professed Covenanting beliefs.

The Irish again retreated south, and wandered back towards Badenoch, but without hope, trapped in a steel vice that was closing slowly tighter. To the West Argyll, implacable, was bent on their destruction, and his Campbells blocked the only route to Ireland. Grant and Seaforth barred them from seeking safety in the North. Aberdeenshire had been engorged into the maw of the Covenant since the Gordon insurrection; and in the Lowlands to the South-East the levies of Fife, Perth and Angus were mustering against them under Lord Elcho. As these hostile forces converged, so the area in which the Irish could still move was contracting slowly, and even in the wild country they were outcasts, marked down for savages with every man's hand against them. The end was inevitable, and those who survived the last fight would still be wolfsheads, lost in a strange tract of land, conspicuous, without friends, and with no future but to hide like beasts until Argyll's highlanders should hunt them down at leisure. The Irish knew that they could expect no mercy.

Alastair had done everything he could, and as he later told the historian Patrick Gordon of Ruthven, the only chance now was in divine intervention. He had appealed to the Clanranald but they had hesitated. He had sent the fiery cross around the western clans but all hope of co-operation had foundered upon their jealousy of a MacDonald chieftain. He had been led to expect a Royalist army already in the field, but it had been disbanded and the Gordon country overrun. He had sent a courier with a frantic message to find Montrose, the King's Lieutenant, he knew not where, but of the promised help from England there was no sign, and the King's Lieutenant had answered never a word.

According to Patrick Gordon of Ruthven, who always maintained that he had had the story from the Graham himself, Montrose learned of Alastair's presence in Badenoch by pure chance:

> As he was one day in Methven Wood, staying for the night because there was no safe travelling by day, he became transported with sadness, grief and pity to see his native country thus brought into miserable bondage and slavery through the turbulent and blind zeal of the preachers, and now persecuted by the unlawful and ambitious ends of some of the nobility. . . .

While he was in this thought, lifting up his eyes he beheld a man coming the way to St Johnstoune [Perth] with a fiery cross in his hand, and, hastily stepping towards him, he inquired what the matter meant. The messenger told him that Coll MacGillespick— for so was Alastair MacDonald called by the highlanders—was entered into Atholl with a great army of Irishes, and threatened to burn the whole country if they did not arise with him against the Covenant, and he was sent to advertise St Johnstoune, that all the country might be raised to resist him.[22]

Wishart's version, which is possibly as accurate, states that Black Pate had intercepted Alastair's desperate message which had been received by a local Royalist who had no inkling of Montrose's presence in the heather above Tullibelton, but passed the letter on in the hope that Inchbrakie would find means of forwarding it to the King's lieutenant in Carlisle. Montrose replied as if from the borders, calling Alastair to a rendezvous at Blair.

He had been in hiding six days in all when he got definite news of the Irish at Atholl, and was characteristically prompt to seize this last chance of the hour. He put the King's commission in his pocket and retrieved the royal standard from the lining of his saddle. Then, assuming Highland dress, in plaid and trews, with a targe on his arm, his broadsword and a sprig of oats in his bonnet, he set off with Black Pate to walk the twenty miles or so over the hills to Atholl—and got there in time to save the situation by a hairsbreadth.

Alastair had received Montrose's message, and guided by a Clan-ranald man—Donald the Fair[23]—he marched south to Atholl and seized the castle there. Then all he could do was to wait upon events. But the local clans—Stuarts and Robertsons—who lived in the valleys of the Garry and the Tummel had no cause to love the Irish, and banded together to resist him. The two forces confronted each other across the red waters of the Tilt, and although some Badenoch men and Donald Robertson, the Tutor of Struan, tried to mediate between them, the situation grew steadily worse.

By 29 August matters had come to a head. The Athollmen were no Covenanters but they had an inalienable right to protect their land against any party who intruded upon it, and this territorial instinct urged them on from mutterings to threats, open hostility and ultimately to shake their weapons in grim earnest. But for their part the Irish were too desperate and too far gone to yield their ground. The women and children were ragged and near starvation, outlandish, and wild-eyed from travel. The men were lean and wolfish, and past hope of safety. Even Alastair himself was resigned. Destruction seemed inevitable, and the war band prepared itself to fight to the finish.

It may have seemed an inauspicious beginning, but it had the qualities of high drama. Across the river, the tension increasing towards flash-point; two figures on the hillside hurrying over the heather, down to the Garry and across the tumbling water; into the no-man's land between the threatening armies; faces turned towards them, towards Alastair; a pause—peering now—and suddenly a great shout taken up by the Irish and rolling through the ranks as the fierce caterans cheered and fired their matchlocks in the air; but among the Atholl-men, sharp fear and instinctive movement for defence; and then Black Pate of Inchbrakie, whom they knew, wading across the Tilt and calling out that it was the King's Lieutenant come at last, so that they too tossed their bonnets in the air and shouted for Montrose!

It is not recorded just what Alastair had expected of the King's Lieutenant when he came—a vision perhaps of a cavalry escort with trumpeters to herald his approach; a famous warrior riding a snorting war horse beneath the King's oriflamme. In the event, he settled for one aide de camp, and a slight man in Highland dress, with command in his voice and calm grey eyes, who walked out of the hills in answer to his prayer. A tide of relief broke over the camp, and the two Grahams were able to restore the situation for the moment before going to the house of Lude, where they spent the night.[24]

The next morning Montrose, who always insisted on observing the strict proprieties of war, formally raised the royal standard. For this ceremony he selected a small mound called the Truidh, not far from Blair Castle and about three-quarters of a mile from Lude, at a spot that was the natural hub from which to command the Strath of Atholl, Glenfender and the immediate vicinity of Glen Tilt.[25] The Irish mustered in three regiments with the remnants of Huntly's broken men from Badenoch, and 800 of the Athollmen under the Tutor of Struan put aside the quarrel of yesterday and came in to fight beside the Graham.

Having unfurled the royal banner to the breeze, and displayed the King's commission, Montrose then read out the personal declaration which he had prepared for this moment:[26]

... WHERFOR, to justifie the dewtie and conscience of his Majestie's service, and satisfie all his faithfull and loyall hearted subjects, I, in his Majestie's name and authoritie, solemnelie declare, that the ground and intention of his Majestie's service heir in this King-dome (according to our owne solemne and national oath and covenant) only is for the defence and maintenance of the trew Protestant religion, his Majestie's just and sacred authoritie, the fundamentall lawes and priveledges of Parliaments, the peace and freedom of the oppressed and thralled subject; and that in thus far, and no more, doeth his Majestie require the service and assistance of his faithful and loveing hearted subjects, not wishing them longer to continew in there obedience than he persisteth to maintaine and adhere to those ends. And the farther yet to remove all possibility of scruple,—lest, whilst from so much dewtie and conscience I am protesting for the justice and integritie of his Majestie's service, I my selfe should be unjustly mistaken,—(as no doubt I have hitherto beine, and still am), I doe again most solemnly declare, that knew I not perfectly his Majesties intention to be such and so reall as is already exprest, I should never at all [have] embarked myselfe in this service. Nor, did I but sie the least appearance of his Majesties change from those resolutions, or any of them, should I ever continue longer my faithfull endeavours in it; which I am confident will prove sufficient against all unjust and prejudicial malice, and able to satisfie all trew Christians, and loyall hearted subjects and countriemen who desyre to serve their God, honour their Prince, and injoy there owne happie peace and quyet.

MONTROSE.

This was not the language of the Court at Oxford. It was Montrose's personal standpoint, the statement of his consistency, and a recommitment to those ideals of the first Covenant that had once represented a just cause and one that he still held to be true. The ideals had tarnished, and he with them, among the pulpits and the backstairs of the preceding years. They had been foresworn and perjured in the committees, and finally lost to simple men among the dark labyrinths of the Covenanters' ambition. In politics, he too had served them poorly. But the clean air of Atholl in the space between the mountains seemed to renew that early purity; the rough, fierce men who followed him did not equivocate with honour; and the sharp blade of his broadsword could restore the clear-cut resolution of a faith that had blunted on lawyers' argument and clever men's deceit.

But it was characteristic of him that, having made this public declaration, he should have also directed a personal challenge to Argyll himself:

MY LORD,—I wonder at your being in armes for defence of rebellion, yourself well knowing his Majestie's tenderness, not only to the whole countrie, whose patron you would pretend to be, but to your own person in particular. I beseech you therefore to return to your allegiance, and submit yourself, . . . as to the grace and protection of your good King. . . . But if you shall still continue obstinate, I call God to witness that through your own stubbornness I shall be compelled to endeavour to reduce you by force. So I rest

Your friend, if you please,

MONTROSE[27]

But there could be no margin of delay. This was not the army he had planned for—not the Gordons with the Angus gentry, and not the full 10,000 troops that Antrim had so easily promised him at Oxford. Instead he had a gaelic war band come out of the mist, uncouth, half-armed, and marked down for destruction. But he knew the value of the moment—the heroic instinct and the reserves of courage which the standard could conjure from the highlanders. The army, shabby and disparate as it was, needed a blooding to unite its various elements. And it needed also to survive. The Campbells were coming over the mountains to avenge their burning homesteads. The MacKenzies, resentful for their slaughtered cattle, with the Frasers, the Forbeses and the Grants, were banding benorth the Grampians. Lord Burleigh was at Aberdeen, and Lord Elcho mustered the Lowland regiments at Perth. There were no tactical alternatives to ponder. It was time to fight and to break out of the steel ring that encircled them. In boldness lay their sole defence—in wresting the initiative from a stronger enemy, and staking all hope of the future on a single desperate throw.

Montrose had no illusions. The first defeat would be the last. But he had the genius to know that men's courage will rise with the occasion, and he was fey enough to understand how fortune demands that a man should be prompt upon his hour.

And it was time to begin the legend. He pointed his half-pike towards the South, and in companies, to the fierce skirl of the pibroch, set his army marching down the brae.

Tippermuir
(1 September 1644)

God of battles, was ever a battle like this in the world before?
Alfred Lord Tennyson

Montrose did not march to Perth by the straightest route, but made a slight detour to the west, perhaps to listen for Argyll's approach, and perhaps in the hope of retaining some measure of surprise or a chance to recruit more adherents near his own lands in Strathearn. The Highland army swung down the Strath of Garry and past the narrow gorge of Killiekrankie before striking west through the cleft in the hills where the River Tummel flows into the wider valley by the falls at Fascally, and skirted the northern shore of Loch Tummel until they reached the bridge at its further end. There they turned south along the old raiding road and the track of the broken men that crossed the flanks of Schiehallion, and with Fortingall and Glen Lyon on their right hand descended through the Strath of Appin to the Tay and the lands of the Clan Menzies of Weem.

Alexander Menzies, the Laird of Weem, was a staunch ally of Argyll and maltreated Montrose's herald almost to death. The Menzies also began to harass the Royalist rearguard as it passed; and, although he had neither the time nor the ordnance to batter his way through the walls of Castle Weem where it stood grim against the hillside, Montrose took a summary reprisal by firing a number of dwellings in the brae and destroying a quantity of corn which the Menzies had freshly harvested.[1] By nightfall he had the bulk of his army safely over the Tay at Aberfeldy, and next morning Grandtully Castle, the other strongpoint in the area, surrendered without a fight.

On the second day (31 August) Montrose detached a picked force of some 300 Athollmen under the command (at their specific request) of Black Pate to form an advance guard and reconnoitre the route some distance ahead of the main body. In this fashion the army marched with Highland speed from Aberfeldy over the hills into Glen Cochill and down through Strath Braan, Amulree, and by the Sma' Glen to Glen Almond.

Turning east along the Almond, the forward company were approaching Gorthie Moor when they saw the sun glinting on a formidable body of armed men drawn up across the slope of Buchanty Hill, apparently with the hostile intention of barring the way. The Royalists halted and the matter was reported back to Montrose, who ordered Black Pate to deploy the Athollmen while Sir William Rollo rode out under a flag of truce to discover what was toward.

The enemy turned out to be a force of about 400 bowmen commanded by Lord Kilpont, the eldest son of William Graham Earl of Airth and Menteith, with Sir John Drummond – a younger son of the Earl of Perth, The Master of Madertie – Montrose's brother-in-law,[2] Stewart of Ardvoirlich, James Muschat of that ilk and others of the local Perthshire gentry. They told Rollo that they had been summoned by the Covenanting authorities to repel a band of marauding Irish, but had known nothing of Montrose's arrival, and that they would not be called upon to fight against the King's Lieutenant in Scotland. They therefore sent Graham of Gorthie and another to learn Montrose's intentions, to whom he formally replied:

> . . . that he acted by the King's authority, and had undertaken to defend it to the utmost against an abominable rebellion. Further he required them, by the affection they owed him, not to refuse their aid to the best of Kings. Such service became their birth, and would be acceptable to the King; it would redound to their present advantage and future honour both at home and abroad, should they hasten to be the first to support a tottering throne.[3]

Having confirmed the validity of the King's commission, Kilpont brought over his entire force to join Montrose.

Kilpont also brought intelligence of the Covenant dispositions at Perth, and with the possibility of having to fight on the morrow Montrose halted his men a few miles further on and camped at the Moor of Fowlis. The next morning – Sunday, 1 September 1644 – he crossed the Almond and led the ragged army down into the fertile valley of Strathearn.

There, on the wide plain between Tippermuir and Cultmalindy, Lord Elcho was waiting for them with 7,000 men.

The troops who had mustered at Perth under David Lord Elcho,[4] while naturally of a lower calibre and with less experience than the front line regiments that had marched south with Leven, were nevertheless raised and equipped on the same basis, drilled, paid and well appointed. The foot-soldiers numbered about 6,000 in all[5] and were drawn mainly from Fife and Perthshire, staunch Covenanters, with the lowlanders' hatred of the gael and a fierce faith in the justice of their cause.

Although technically second-line regiments, their drill and training would have been identical with that of regular front-line troops. Each regiment was divided between musketeers and pikemen in the ratio of three to two. The latter wore steel corslets and headpieces and carried both pike and sword, their business as heavy infantry being to deliver the final charge or to repel a cavalry attack when the regiment formed the ring.[6] The musketeers wore no body armour, and carried matchlocks, each with an elaborate rest, which could shoot a 1½-ounce ball a distance of something over four hundred yards. A regiment in order of battle was usually drawn up in files six deep, with the pikemen in the centre and the musketeers on either flank, the drill being for each rank to fire in turn before falling back to reload—one rank firing at a time—until the opposing forces were close enough for the pikemen to begin the mêlée.

The flower of this Covenant army were from the Carse of Gowrie—about 800 troopers officered by the local gentry who formed the cavalry division under the command of Lord Drummond. In Scotland the horse were still equipped and drilled in the old fashion. Troopers carried a lance, four pistols and a carbine, were trained to advance five deep at a trot and deliver a volley from the saddle.

In addition, Elcho could deploy nine small cannon, each probably capable of throwing a five-pound ball, while his strength on the day was further augmented by the local Perth militia under their captain, David Grant, who marched to Tippermuir displaying the banner of the Ancient Corporation of Glovers.

The morale of the Covenant army was understandably high. The men were well drilled in their ideology and in the use of their weapons. Their equipment and organization were good: they were well armed, practised, clothed and fed. Many of them had seen action against the highlanders during the Bishops' War and had not been greatly impressed by the fighting qualities of the enemy. This would be a different thing from raiding undefended shielings, and at Harlaw, Corrichie, Glenlivet and a score of smaller encounters it had been proved beyond doubt that Lowland discipline, steady spearmen and heavy cavalry would disrupt and defeat a Highland charge even when delivered by greatly superior numbers.

If there was a flaw in this argument it would become apparent only in the retrospect. Fifty years of peace had softened the lowlander. The peasants now tilled their land without having constantly to defend it, and the burghers, who once had formed a substantial part of every Scottish battle-line, had fattened on the intervening years of ease. The weakness was an intangible thing—amounting perhaps to a loss of that native battle-sense which their forefathers had preserved—and since the change was gradual it passed unnoticed at the time.

But even had such doubts been voiced on the morning of 1 September 1644, they would have gone unheard or been caustically dismissed. They marched out of Perth that Sunday to exterminate 'a pack of naked

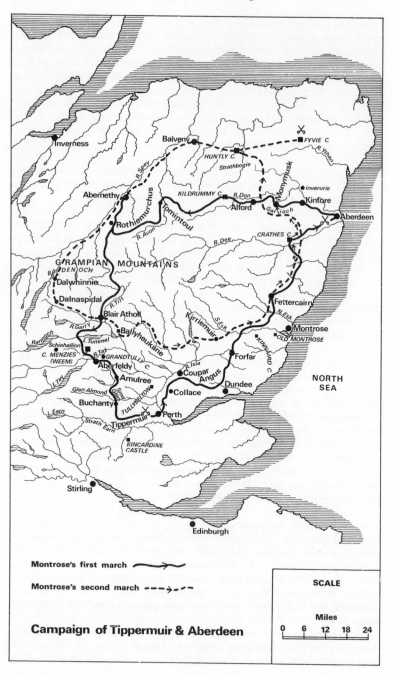

Inverness

Balveny

FYVIE C.

R. Ythan

HUNTLY C.

Strathbogie

R. Spey

inverurie

KILDRUMMY C.

R. Don

Monymusk

Abernethy

Tomintoul

Alford

Kinfore

Rothiemurchus

R. Avon

Gar loch

Aberdeen

GRAMPIAN MOUNTAINS

R. Dee

CRATHES C.

BADENOCH

Dalwhinnie

Dalnaspidal

R. Tilt

Fettercairn

N. Esk

Blair Atholl

Kirriemuir

S. Esk

Montrose

R. Garry

L. Rannoch

Ballyheukane

OLD MONTROSE

Schiehallion

L. Tummel

KINNAIRD C.

C. MENZIES
(WEEM)

R. Tay

GRANDTULLY C.

Forfar

Aberfeldy

R. Isla

L. Tay

Amulree

Coupar Angus

Dundee

NORTH
SEA

Glen Almond

Collace

Buchanty

TULLYBELTON

L. Earn

Tippermuir

Perth

Strath Earn

KINCARDINE
CASTLE

Stirling

Edinburgh

Montrose's first march

Montrose's second march ---►-·-

Campaign of Tippermuir & Aberdeen

SCALE

Miles

0   6   12   18   24

runagates',[7] ill armed, undisciplined and beyond hope of God's redemption. They were spurred on by an ancestral hatred of the highlander, and imbued with the present joy of doing the Lord's work. They went confident in their righteousness, in their superior discipline and weapons and in the overwhelming odds of three to one in their favour. Finally, the presence of the cannon–'the musket's mother'– which the highlanders feared above all things, resolved the issue beyond any doubt, and the burghers of Perth also travelled to Tippermuir in small parties to enjoy what promised to be the spectacular annihilation of Montrose.

Lord Elcho had chosen his position well–an open waste called Tippermuir within sight of the church of that name and on the northern boundary of the parish of Aberdalgie, about three miles west of Perth. The broad plain to his front enabled him to deploy his force so as to take the fullest advantage of superior numbers and wider frontage, while the flat open ground offered excellent opportunities for the Covenant cavalry.

Hearing of the highlanders' descent into Glen Almond, the Covenanters had left Perth in the small hours of the morning, and in the early light the foot regiments were drawn up in three main divisions near the foot of Methven Hill. Behind them loomed the bulk of Huntingtower, stronghold of the Gowries of sinister memory, and to their front the open plain stretched westwards towards Fowlis whence the enemy would come. Elcho himself commanded the right wing of the army. The centre he entrusted to James Murray of Gask, while the left wing was led by Sir James Scott of Rossie, a professional soldier of considerable reputation and experience who had fought in the service of the Venetian Republic in the war of the Capelleti against the Germans. While the centre consisted entirely of infantry–musketeers and pikemen drawn up in ranks six deep in the accepted manner–each wing was reinforced by a body of 400 cavalry who were stationed on the extreme flanks where they would have greatest scope for manoeuvre. In front of the army Elcho placed seven of his cannon (two were left behind in Perth[8]) together with a line of supporting skirmishers.

The highlanders debouched swiftly on to the plain and began to approach the Covenant army where it stood massive and menacing against Methven Hill. The gaels had risen that morning in the expectation of battle, and the savage thrill of their pibroch carried across the valley in the clear autumn air. In the forefront, Clan Donnachaidh–the Robertsons, under Donald, Tutor of Struan, displayed the *Clach-Nan-Brattich* on the point of their standard–the stone of the banner that made them invincible in the fight. There had been talk of the *Taghairm*, and it was said years afterwards that they had killed a herdsman early in the morning to ensure the first blood.[9] The sight of the covenant host and the terrible odds in the enemy's favour did not dismay them. The highlanders retained their ancestral contempt for the pease-eating Lowland *bodachs* and the spirit of the army was fierce and high. In Mark Napier's phrase, they were already 'hanging their bonnets on the horns of the moon, and devouring in the throat of their hopes all the promised luxuries of the glorious fertile Tay and the sad fair city of Perth'.[10]

Montrose stopped briefly at the house of Alexander Balneaves, the minister of Tippermuir, where he asked for a cup of water. He then set about making his own dispositions for the battle.

The Highland army now numbered something under 3,000 men and 3 emaciated horses. An immediate problem was therefore posed by the superior length of the Covenant battle-line which necessarily forced Montrose to find some means of extending his own front in order to prevent both his flanks from being automatically overlapped by the opposing wings of Elcho's army. This could only be achieved by drawing up the clansmen in a long thin line, three deep as against the enemy's files of six.

On the left wing, confronting Elcho, he stationed Lord Kilpont and his 400 archers together with a company of the men from Lochaber. The northern bowmen were renowned for their skill. By tradition the best Highland long-bows were cut from the yews of Glenmure, while the wood for the shafts came from the forest of Esragoin in Lorne, and the flights from the eagle feathers of Loch Trieg. The wax for the bow-strings was furnished by Baill-Na-Gail-Bhinn, and the forked arrowheads were forged by smiths of the race of MacPheidearin. The Lochaber men were armed with the deadly *tuagh,* or Lochaber Axe, the pike and hook of which as well as the blade made it a useful weapon against cavalry.

Alastair commanded in the centre. The Irish, numbering about 1,100 in all, were armed with old matchlocks and an assortment of knives, clubs and other makeshift weapons. Powder and ammunition was down to a single round per man. Their numbers were augmented by the body of Keppoch MacDonalds who had thrown in their lot with Alastair, but although some could boast a pike or claymore many of the irregular caterans were unarmed. Montrose drew up the three regiments side by side in the unusual formation that had been pioneered by Gustavus of Sweden, with the front rank kneeling, the second stooping and the third standing erect. He instructed them to hold their fire until the last moment, and then, on the word of command, all three ranks were to shoot simultaneously at pointblank range before charging the enemy with clubbed muskets or whatever other weapons were to hand. Montrose, in this as in other things an innovator, thus counted on a single devastating volley to check the Covenant advance and gain the initiative in the middle of the field. His choice of the Irish to compose the centre of the Royalist line was practical, not only because without pikes or swords they had not the means to withstand the cavalry attacks which would certainly be delivered against the wings, but also because, in an army of irregulars, they were the most experienced of his soldiers, hardened campaigners and inured to the discipline of battle. In the centre he would need men who could hold under terrible pressure and these were the steadiest troops he had. Nor if the line broke did the Irish have anywhere to run to.

Montrose led the right wing in person and thus opposed the experienced Sir James Scott of Rossie. He had elected to fight on foot at the head of the clansmen—Stewarts of Atholl and Lochaber—and carried a half-pike, at that time esteemed the 'Queen of weapons', and a Highland targe.[11] A proportion of the Athollmen were armed with claymores, while as on the left the gaels from Lochaber carried their long axes. Sir William Rollo rode one of the horses, and a second was designated to the Master of Madertie who had been appointed the official herald. The highlanders had no artillery.

It was by now almost noon. The day was very fine with hardly any cloud in the sky, and quite hot but for a light breeze off the mountains. Preparations on both sides were almost complete, and when the last companies had taken up their appointed positions there was a pause while, in the classical manner, the respective commanders addressed their troops.

On the Covenant side the ministers had for some hours been exhorting the Army of God to its sacred duty of inflicting His punishment upon the heathen. Foremost of them, the Reverend Frederick Carmichael of Markinch in Fife—'a man of great learning and holiness'—was now moved in spirit to prophesy: 'If ever God spoke certain truth out of my mouth, in His name, I promise you today, a certain victory.' Elcho's army stood confident in its God and in its strength: the battle cry was to be 'Jesus and no quarter!'

In front of the shabby little gaelic army, Montrose's speech to the fierce Kerns was by contrast short and to the point:

> Gentlemen: it is true you have no arms; your enemy, however, to all appearance, have plenty. My advice therefore is, that as there happens to be a great abundance of stones upon this moor, every man should provide himself, in the first place, with as stout a one as he can well manage, rush up to the first covenanter he meets, beat out his brains, take his sword, and then I believe, he will be at no loss how to proceed![12]

A great howl went up when he had finished, and the gaels began chanting the *Cathghairm*—the battle shout—and pressed forward in their eagerness to engage the enemy. Montrose however was bound in honour to restrain his army until one other formality had been completed.

The Master of Madertie rode out under a flag of truce and, approaching Lord Elcho, declared in the name of the King's Lieutenant in Scotland:

> . . . that he, as well as his royal master, whose commission he bore, had the utmost abhorrence of shedding his countrymen's blood, and

most earnestly desired a bloodless victory. Such a victory both armies might gain if they would return to their duty and allegiance without the hazard of war. He [Montrose] was neither covetous of honours for himself nor envious of other men's preferment, and had no designs against the lives of his fellow countrymen. All he desired was that in God's name they would at length give ear to sounder counsels, and trust to the clemency, faith, and protection of so good a King. Hitherto His Majesty had fully complied with all the demands of his Scottish subjects, both in civil and religious matters, though to the great prejudice of his Royal prerogative, and was still ready . . . though provoked by unspeakable injuries, to embrace his penitent children with open arms. If notwithstanding they persisted in rebellion, he called God to witness that their stubbornness forced him into the present strife.[13]

Despite the possibility that Argyll and the Campbells were coming through the hills behind him, Montrose also asked if the battle might be postponed for one day so as to avoid the shedding of blood on a Sabbath.

Contrary to what was the internationally accepted convention of the time, the Covenanters did not respect the flag of truce or the immunity of the envoy. Young Madertie was seized, bound and led back to Perth a prisoner, to be hanged after the battle was over. As to Montrose's request for a postponement, the ministers declared that 'they had made choice of the Lord's Day for doing the Lord's work'. In all probability they thought that the highlanders might slip away into the mountains under cover of darkness.

While the Covenanters were abusing his messenger, Montrose began to realign his division slightly further to the right in order to gain the advantage of a slight rise in the ground.[14] Thinking perhaps that this might be the first move in a general withdrawal, or wishing to harass the undisciplined highlanders while they performed the manoeuvre, Elcho sent out two troops of horse and about 160 foot under Lord Drummond and the young Laird of Reires to 'intangle' them. However, Rollo and Alastair saw the move develop and ordered forward some 120 skirmishers to intercept the Covenant advance. A sharp fight ensued in which Reires was probably killed and Drummond's detachment was driven back in disorder against the Covenant line.[15] Montrose immediately seized the opportunity offered by the temporary confusion, and gave the signal for a general advance. With a great shout the entire gaelic army swept forward and began to run towards the enemy.

The Covenant soldiers who served the cannon panicked before the solid mass of caterans tearing across the open ground towards them, and discharged their pieces ineffectively over the heads of the attackers. Seconds later the guns were overrun and the highlanders hardly paused to kill the bombardiers before racing on to assault the main Covenant position. Elcho's musketeers, who had been moving forward to meet the charge, had barely time to fire a single volley when the gaels ran at them out of the smoke, stooped under the bullets with heads down and targes high, and, hurling rocks, clubs and other missiles, burst into the Covenant files to grapple and hamstring individual opponents in a savage mêlée of knives and teeth. In the centre, the Irish paused a pike's length from the enemy line to pour a concentrated volley into the dense mass of pikemen before clubbing their muskets and breaking through the great gaps which their shot had torn in the Covenant ranks. Following them, the unarmed clansmen ran in behind a shower of stones, clawed men down to throttle them on the ground and snatched up their swords to join the execution going on around them. Simultaneously, on the flanks, the brute strength of the gaels had brought them immediately to close quarters, and their claymores cleared a path through the pikes to where the unprotected musketeers were easy victims to the slaughter. Where the press was thicker, the axemen of Lochaber howled their terrible war-cry and, swinging the huge *tuaghs* in great arcs, hacked a way through the mass of flesh and bone. In front of them, Elcho's regiments recoiled and began to panic as in the smoke and din confused soldiers looked for officers who had already perished, and young Perth apprentices, transfixed with terror, saw their friends fall dead beside them and faces they knew disintegrate in a hideous mess of brains and blood.

Elcho's army had learned the ritual of war–to load, present or fire on command and to march and manoeuvre to the shouted order–but the white-hot violence and the dreadful savagery of close-quarter fighting surpassed the scope of any simple practice for mêlée. If as soldiers they had contemplated death on the battlefield, it had been impersonal, and fancifully detached from the barbarous reality that engulfed them now. A comrade cloven to the teeth, a skull bursting under a Lochaber axe or the screams of a human being disemboweled were horrors beyond their most fearful preconception. The Covenant line reeled under the ferocity of the highlanders' attack, and within minutes began to fragment as terror seized the Fifeshire levies and in whole companies they started to throw away their weapons and run. The road to Perth became jammed with a frantic sobbing herd of fear-crazed men whose only thought was to escape the carnage of that ghastly battlefield, and as the panic spread the whole battle-line disintegrated and the foot ran to save themselves if they could while the cavalry, more fortunate and more craven, spurred through the rabble and galloped for their lives. Behind them the maimed and wounded were deserted to the fury of the gaels or the doubtful mercy of the cateran women, who came later to strip the corpses and leave them naked on the moor.

Only on the left did the Covenanters attempt to stand and fight. There, Sir James Scott of Rossie rallied his wavering troops and tried to gain the shelter of some ruined cottages on the higher ground. But Montrose himself anticipated his resolve, and led the Athollmen in a race for the crest. Scott's followers were decimated as they struggled for the position and were driven back into the mass of fleeing men.

A terrible slaughter now took place. A picked force of highlanders had hauled the captured guns around to sweep the front of what had been Elcho's army, but the rout was so complete already that Montrose countermanded the order to fire. The Kerns had gone after the fugitives in a pack and pulled them down or killed them as they ran. Those who left the track to find safety in the scrub were hunted down like beasts and dragged from their hiding places to be butchered on the road. Fear itself killed more. Terrified burghers, who could not survive the exertion, ran till they tore the tissues of their lungs, or haemorrhaged and fell retching blood like gutted fish until the gaels finished them off. Others died of apoplexy, or 'bursten in their corslets' so that after the battle they were discovered dead without a mark upon them. One of Alastair's officers later recalled that a man could walk from Tippermuir to Perth on the bodies of the slain.[16]

The city was surrounded later in the afternoon. Its walls, with *portes* and bastelhouses, were capable of defence, but within the gates only twelve men could be found to man the ramparts and these were unarmed and only bellicose with drink. The survivors of the battle had locked their doors and hidden in the cellars. When summoned, they cried out 'that they would fight no more—although they should be killed for it'. They had thrown away their weapons during the flight: their captain, David Grant, was among the dead on Tippermuir, and they would not be persuaded again to face the wild caterans: '. . . drawn up like so many hell-hounds before the gates of the town; their hands deeply dyed in blood recently shed, and with hideous cries demanding to be led to fresh slaughter'.[17] In the event, Perth surrendered without a fight, while in the country round about the gaels continued to hunt down fugitives till nightfall.

Elcho's army had ceased to exist, and all the cannon, colours, baggage, arms and ammunition accrued to Montrose's highlanders. Covenant casualties were computed to be in the order of 2,000 dead and 1,000 prisoner.[18] Of Montrose's army many had been hurt in varying degrees, but only one man was killed outright, and Henry Stewart, Ardvoirlich's son, would die of wounds thereafter.

Aberdeen and Fyvie
(September–November 1644)

In a rebellion,
When what's not meet, but what must be, was law,
They were chosen.

Coriolanus

Montrose entered Perth on the evening of 1 September with a token force of 600 men. Since he was anxious to reconcile people to the King's cause by acts of clemency, he accepted without demur the conditions upon which the city authorities had offered to surrender, and as one of these was 'that no Irishes should get entry or passage through the town',[1] Alastair's men were accordingly quartered across the river at Kinnoul where they desecrated the old church of St Constantine III by cooking their food in it and breaking up all the seats and communion tables for firewood.[2] No looting was permitted within the city, however, and one of Montrose's first acts was to commandeer the secretarial services of the sheriff clerk, Patrick Maxwell, and issue a 'General Protection' for the town of Perth and the lands round about, which he formally signed 'Marquis of Montrose, Lieutenant General of the King's Armies in Scotland'.[3] The royal commission was duly proclaimed at the Market Cross.

On the first evening there seems to have been some confusion as to the proprieties that ought to have been observed when the city was formally occupied by the victorious army. Montrose had received the keys of the High Gate Port from the magistrates when he entered Perth, but at nightfall the town guard turned out as usual to man the gates, and only after Black Pate had knocked up the provost at midnight to complain were they discharged and Royalist soldiers set upon the walls.[4] Next morning, the three or four hundred men of the Fifeshire regiment who had survived the battle and taken refuge within the city were also rounded up and imprisoned in the Kirk.

The King's lieutenant established his headquarters in the house of Margaret Donaldson and for the next three days directed his attention to the administrative requirements of the army. The most pressing need was for clothing, and the burghers of Perth were compelled to yield up 4,000 merks worth of cloth for the ragged Irish regiments. The magistrates were also commanded to pay out a further £50 sterling for Alastair's use, but given that the Royalists must have been exceedingly short of money the city seems to have got away thus lightly. Weapons and ammunition were collected from the battlefield or confiscated from the town's arsenal, and Royalist captains in Highland dress hurried about the town 'in ane furious way' ordering and equipping their men.

Montrose also lingered at Perth in the hope that some of the local gentry who in the past had boasted of their loyalty to the King would be persuaded to join the army, but in this he was disappointed. A formal summons was copied to the principal gentlemen in the area. But although his own lands in Strathearn might have given the Graham some influence in the region, the majority hung back, and it was clear that one victory at Tippermuir was not enough to encourage them to risk life and property in a still doubtful cause. Some came in to talk, but no more; a number to offer their congratulations, but not material support. One hurried to administer the estate of a relative killed in the battle; another to complain of damage done to his land. The gallery of Margaret Donaldson's house was frequented by petitioners of varying degree, but the only recruits of note were Lord Dupplin (soon to become Lord Kinnoul) and Alexander, Master of Spynie, who was the son of the hero of Stralsund and held the office of muster-master-general. With them came a few troopers from the Carse of Gowrie.

On the Monday night Montrose sent for his old tutor, Master William Forrett, to become his secretary and to take charge of all financial matters relating to the army. This business kept Forrett some days in Perth even after Montrose had left, but he later caught up with his erstwhile pupil at Forfar and served him in this capacity throughout the following campaign. Another happy reunion took place on the Tuesday, 3 September, when Graham of Braco rode in from Kincardine with Montrose's two eldest sons, John Lord Graham (now aged fourteen) and James (nearly twelve). (The youngest, Robert, was still only six and clearly too young to go campaigning.)

Meanwhile, some 400 Athollmen had left the standard, and thus Montrose was at the outset confronted with the greatest problem attendant upon an army that contained a substantial proportion of highlanders. Whatever the outcome of a battle, it was their custom to return to their own districts in order to lodge their booty (and especially the four-footed kind) in safety. This they held to be an undoubted right, and, because they were irregulars who fought without pay and were not sworn to the colours, they could not be forced to serve for a whole campaign. It was therefore always difficult for a general in Montrose's position to exploit a victory. In the longer term, however, it cast grave doubts on the possibility of leading a Highland force against the borders, and it again emphasized how crucial would be the support of the Gordon levies in the North if any permanent advantage was to be gained. In the campaigns that followed, Montrose's strategy was constantly governed by the shifting composition of his Highland contingent, which fluctuated in accordance with events, the season, the area of operations or the loyalty of individual chieftains, and by necessity was too often subordinated to the local ambitions of the clans who were reluctant or unable to act in a cause that transcended their own Highland feuds and traditions. The courage of the highlanders in battle was superlative, but their endurance outside their immediate geographical area of interest was always suspect.

The 400 departed with the spoils of Tippermuir and a vague promise to return when the harvest at Atholl had been gathered in, and the King's Lieutenant had no recourse but to resign himself to the loss of their claymores and watch them go. It was not prudent to linger at Perth in the unlikely hope that some might return, and he decided to march north into Angus to look for recruits among his own neighbours in the Mearns. Accordingly he left Perth late on Wednesday, 4 September, and, having destroyed all the small boats in the vicinity of the town to impede Argyll's crossing the Tay after him,[5] he marched seven or eight miles in the direction of Coupar-Angus and camped for the night near the kirk of Collace by the stream at the foot of Dunsinane Hill.

As the army lay at Collace, in the early hours of Thursday, 5 September, a terrible tragedy occurred. Some time before dawn, a sudden uproar in the camp caused the Royalists to snatch up their weapons and shout the alarm. Montrose and his officers, fearing that a quarrel had broken out between highlanders and Irish, drew their swords and ran towards the noise in order to restore order among their men before the situation could get out of hand. Pushing their way through the press until they reached the cause of the confusion, however, they were horrified to find instead the mutilated body of Lord Kilpont, who had been foully murdered only a short time before, and two of the Irish sentries with him. For a space Montrose, exceedingly distressed and with tears running down his cheeks, repeatedly embraced the corpse of his friend and kinsman. Then he sadly committed the body to the care of Kilpont's followers with instructions that they should carry it home to the young man's parents to be buried with honour and in accordance with the traditions of his family.

The killer was James Stewart of Ardvoirlich, but the motive behind the murder was never altogether clear. The Royalist version, published soon after in *A True Relation . . .*, suspected Ardvoirlich of some sinister but thwarted intention to murder Montrose himself:

> While he was on his March, one morning by the break of day, Captain James Stuart did withdraw the Lord Kilpont to the utmost Centry, where he had a long and serious discourse with him; at the end whereof, my Lord knocking upon his breast, was overheard to

161

say these words: 'Lord forbid man, would you undoe us all?' upon which immediately the Captain stob'd him with a durke, and my Lord falling with the first stroke, he gave him fourteen more through the body as he lay upon the ground: that he might be sure as is probable, that he should not reveale what had past between them: for it is conceived that he had intended so much for the Marquisse, and that he had disclosed his purpose to my Lord Kilpont, [whom] he thought to have engaged in the plot in regard of the familiarity [that] was between them. After the villain had committed this barbarous act he ranne to the Centry, and shot him through the body; and so by reason of a thick fogge, made an escape to the Rebells, of whom he was well received.[6]

This allegation was also reported by Wishart, and Bishop Guthry in his *Memoirs*[7] explicitly charges Ardvoirlich with intent to assassinate Montrose and Alastair. The accusation, however, appears to have been based more on suspicion than on any positive proof.

Having committed such a crime, the murderer had little alternative but to escape to Argyll (who made him a major in his regiment), and it was to their advantage that the Covenanters immediately praised him for the bloody deed and made what propaganda they could out of it. Baillie, writing from London,[8] commented: 'Kilpont's treachery is revenged by his death, justly inflicted.' During the parliamentary proceedings of March 1645 ratifying Stewart's pardon[9] it was stated that Ardvoirlich and his friends had joined up with Montrose at the same time as Kilpont but that:

. . . heartily thereafter repenting of this error in joining with the said rebels, and abhorring their cruelty, [Ardvoirlich] resolves with his said friends to forsake their wicked company, and imparted this resolution to the said umquhile Lord Kilpont. But he, out of his malignant dispositions, opposed the same, and fell in struggling with the said James [Stewart], who, for his own relief was forced to kill him at the Kirk of Collace, with two Irish rebels who resisted his escape, and so removed happily with his said friends and came straight to the Marquis of Argyll and offered their service to their country. Whose carriage in this particular being considered by the Committee of Estates, they by their act of 10 December last, find and declare that the said Stewart did good service to the Kingdom in killing the said Lord Kilpont and two Irish rebels aforesaid being in actual rebellion against the country, and approved of what he did theirein.

As Gardiner has commented in his *History of the Great Civil War*:[10] 'The favourable reception given by Argyll to the supposed murderer was a sign that all who joined in a Highland rising might be assassinated with impunity as far as the Covenanting authorities were concerned.' The pardon was a licence to bounty-killers, and it was the logical sequel now formally to set a price upon Montrose's head.

Kilpont's untimely death was not only a great personal loss. Ardvoirlich's vassals now also deserted to Argyll, and the bowmen who had followed Kilpont marched home with the body of their chief to bury him at Menteith among his ancestors. Montrose thus lost another 400 men.

He broke camp and marched towards Dundee, but on approaching the town learned that it had been put in a state of defence by the Earl of Buchan and Lord Coupar. The garrison had been augmented by the survivors of Lord Elcho's Fifeshire regiments, and the burghers, confident in numbers and in the strength of their fortifications, refused to surrender when summoned by a drummer. With Argyll gathering his power somewhere behind him, Montrose did not dare hazard the reputation snatched at Tippermuir by attempting to lay siege to a strongly defended town. After camping the night at Dundee Law he turned north towards the Esks, to where his own lands principally lay, in the hope of finding support among the loyal gentry of Angus and the Mearns.

But in this he was again disappointed. A number who had met him on the march and whom he had sent home to prepare for the campaign now thought better of it and withdrew. Others, cowed or cautious, waited upon events. The Ogilvie family were the honourable exception. As Wishart later commented with pride and bitterness: 'Amidst the almost universal defection, Airlie and Montrose were all that remained to adorn the Scottish nobility.'[11] The Ogilvies served the King; and Lord Airlie, though already sixty and old for such campaigning, brought his two younger sons, Sir Thomas and Sir David Ogilvie with 40 troopers to join Montrose. These were men of tried courage and would stay to the end. And another welcome arrival was Nathaniel Gordon, who rode in with 30 well armed cavaliers and gave up brigandage to fight under the King's Lieutenant. Though few enough, the calibre of such recruits could hardly have been bettered.

For the rest, lists later compiled by the Covenant authorities from the testimony of eye-witnesses show them to have been for the most part smaller gentry or younger sons. The greater landowners remained aloof. (At Forfar, Graham of Braco and Graham of Orchill left their chief, 'coming off', as they later told their Covenant inquisitors, 'without goodnight', although given their undoubted loyalty to Montrose for which they suffered later, it is unlikely that they defected. Their presence among the Graham lands about Strathearn was probably of greater value than their service among the soldiers as gentlemen volunteers.) In all, the army at this time numbered some 1,500 foot-soldiers composed mainly of Alastair's MacDonalds and the Irish regiments, and about 80 horse, together with baggage animals, camp followers and 300–400 prisoners from Tippermuir.

In London the news of the disaster at Tippermuir had caused consternation among the Covenanting delegation. In a private letter to his cousin William Spang, Baillie repeated the dismal news from Scotland:

A lamentable disaster. Montrose after fell on Perth: it abode the first assault: what next we know not. Lothian and his regiment are to guard Stirling Bridge. All the West and South-East are running to Stirling. Argyll is marching, Callander, Lindsay, Montgomerie, Dalhousie, Lawers, are posting from Newcastle, with their regiments of horse and foot. Had this calamity befallen two months before, when Prince Rupert, with his six thousand horse might easily have fallen on Edinburgh, and was so resolved, had not the King called him South on other fruitless employments, they, by appearance, had drawn all our forces out of England and at once had put all Scotland in a hazard. But God is our watchman: this whipp, I hope shall do us good.[12]

Sadly for Montrose, this last was fair comment.

Inevitably there was a post-mortem and consequent recrimination. Baillie blamed Lord Drummond for the defeat at Tippermuir, and accused him of premeditated treachery:

. . . they were but a pack of naked runagates, not three horse among them, few either swords or musquetts. But the villany of my Lord Drummond, and his friend, in the point of joining, exhorting to flee, according as by his letters he had appointed the night before, struck the rest with a pannick feare. . . .

But such letters, if they existed, have not survived to substantiate the charge. In Perth the clergymen seem to have been in some way held responsible for the loss that had been sustained. John Robertson and George Halybirton, ministers, were obliged to produce a written deposition accounting for the surrender of the town, which action they defended on the grounds that, once the battle had been so disgracefully lost despite the numerical and material superiority of the Covenant forces, the city had no alternative but 'honest and honourable capitulation.'[13] Halybirton and Robertson, however, were in deeper trouble yet. Montrose, in cavalier style, had invited the ministers to dine with him and Halybirton, because 'he was surprised upon a sudden and was urged thereto',[14] had even said Grace at his table. He was 'deposed' by the Commission of the General Assembly for 'haunting the company' of an excommunicate and reinstated only after his near relation Dame Margaret Halybirton, Lady Coupar, had exerted herself strenuously on his behalf. Robertson, however, was less fortunate in having no great person to speak for him. Alexander Balneaves, the minister of Tippermuir, was charged with conversing with Montrose on the morning of the battle and with giving him a cup of water, and the ministers of Errol, Abernethy and Kinnoul were also subsequently censured. The following January the Committee of Estates was still pursuing its investigation and collecting depositions from individuals who were known to have been eye-witnesses to events in Perth immediately after the battle. Apart from the Town Provost and the Sheriff-Clerk, these included such persons as Madertie, Braco, William Forrett and Ramsay of Ogill who had been with the Royalists at Tippermuir or later but had subsequently either withdrawn or fallen into Covenant hands. (However, by that time too, Montrose's depredations had somewhat further advanced.)

On 12 September Montrose was formally excommunicated by the Committee of Estates and a reward of £20,000 (Scots) was offered for his capture dead or alive.[15] In the meanwhile, 800 troops under Lothian had reached Perth on 10 September, and Argyll arrived with the main body of his army the following day. His lieutenants were already scouting in Atholl and Badenoch for detailed intelligence on Montrose's strength and intentions, or preparing for the Committee a list of the local gentry who had turned out to support the Royalist general. But the pursuit was inevitably delayed on account of the organizational problems attendant on the muster of so large a force. The converging elements of the Covenant army had to be supplied and their actions co-ordinated, while not least among Argyll's logistic difficulties was the requirement for more boats to replace the ferries across the Tay which Montrose had destroyed as he left.[16] After a short pause, the Covenanters started into Angus after the Royalists, following, in Baillie's curious phrase, 'as armed men might, which was four or five day's journey behind them'.[17]

In the North, news of Montrose's march into Angus prompted the Estates to commission Lord George Gordon, their lieutenant-general in the region, to gather an army for the defence of Aberdeen. Gordon was a somewhat reluctant Covenanter and chary of the order, but he accordingly called a muster at Kildrummy where a number of his friends joined him. However, this did not suit the other northern barons of the Covenanting party, Lord Forbes and his kin, Fraser, Crichton and the like, who either suspected Gordon of latent Royalism or saw an opportunity to gain credit for the action without deferring to the house of Huntly. Lord Gordon was possibly quite relieved and did not resist when they refused to follow him and instead called up their own forces to Aberdeen. As a somewhat equivocal gesture of good faith he sent his younger brother, Lord Lewis Gordon,[18] with eighteen or twenty troopers to enlist as a gentleman volunteer, while at Kildrummy he disbanded his main force, keeping only 300 horse whom he led southwards at a leisurely pace so that the Committee could not later accuse him of outright desertion.

Without the Gordon levies, the Covenant army in the North numbered about 2,500 foot and 500 horse. Of these, the Covenanting clans of Forbes and Fraser with the levies of Banff and Aberdeenshire comprised some 1,500 foot and 300 horse. The Committee of Aberdeen ordered in the elements of the Fifeshire regiments dispersed on garrison duty at Auchindoune, Gight, Kelly and Drum[19]–about 500 in all–while on the Sunday (8 September), after the morning sermon a proclamation in front of the Old Town Kirk called on all persons between the ages of sixteen and sixty to turn out next day in arms with provisions for fifteen days–under pain of death. Similar notices were published throughout the shire and in the parishes within the sheriffdoms of Kincardine and Banff, but without much result, as Spalding later recalled: 'Bot littill obedience wes givin to thir untymelie warningis.' Aberdeen town chose four captains for the four quarters, and the city militia was placed under the command of a Major Arthur Forbes. Some of the conscripted citizens were not over-enthusiastic at the prospect, but the sixteen-to-sixty-year-olds were rigorously drilled on the links and elementary fortifications were hastily constructed at the Bridge of Dee.

However, the main problem was one of leadership, none of the principal Covenanters in the North having had any experience of general command. Some now regretted the snub so hastily given to Lord George Gordon, and in an attempt to make amends offered the command of the army to Lord Lewis. But he cannily refused on the grounds that he had enlisted with a small train as became a private individual, and the post was properly due to his brother who must first formally refuse it before he himself could accept. In the event, the responsibility devolved upon Lord Burleigh, president of the Provincial Committee of Aberdeen,[20] with the Lords Fraser, Crichton, Frendraught and Lewis Gordon and Sir William Forbes of Craigievar as his principal lieutenants. They took the precaution of sending their money and 'best gear' to Dunnottar Castle for safe-keeping, and planned to stop Montrose at the Bridge of Dee.

The King's Lieutenant got news of the muster at Aberdeen as he was marching through the Mearns. At Forfar he issued a proclamation calling the lieges to the standard under pain of fire and sword,[21] but the passage through Angus brought in few recruits. Since his army still numbered considerably less than 2,000 men all told, it was clearly necessary for him to strike at one of the two Covenant armies that were now in the field against him and to do it without delay. If Argyll and Burleigh joined forces their resulting superiority would have made the odds too great for there to have been any reasonable hope of gaining the initiative, while if he hesitated much longer and allowed Argyll to get too close, there was the obvious danger that the two Covenant commanders might concert and crush his small force between them.

Montrose decided, logically, to attack Burleigh. The apathy of the Angus gentry and his failure to win any appreciable following in support of the King now made it imperative that he should gain access to Gordon territory. If the Royalist cause in Scotland was to triumph, or indeed survive, the key to success or failure lay ulti- mately at Huntly. This was the truth of it, and the fact could not escape him. It was also true that a substantial number of the Gordons had followed Lord George Gordon into the Covenant ranks, and that otherwise, with the Marquis absent, the clan was leaderless. But this had always been the breeding ground for opposition against the Covenant. The men who had rebelled with Huntly had been made to suffer for it. Some were in prison; many were outlaws; almost all were malcontented; and enough might take the chance of getting

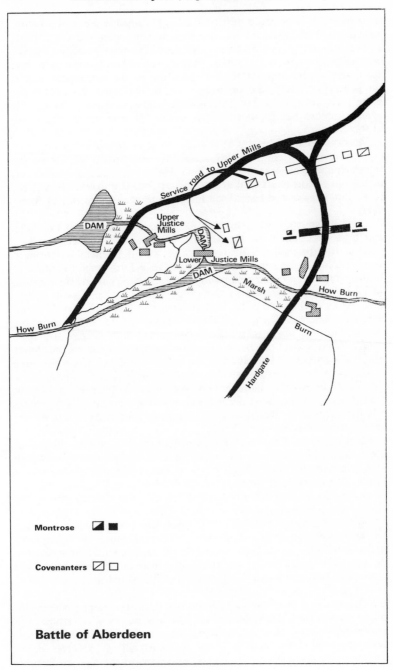

Battle of Aberdeen

their revenge. If he could destroy Burleigh's army at Aberdeen before Argyll got there, the road to Huntly would be open and the Covenanters' military grip on Banff and Aberdeenshire temporarily broken—long enough perhaps for him to appeal to the Gordon lairds to rise again with some hope of their responding to the summons. And if the gentry were reluctant or hung back, he carried in his pocket the King's commission to Huntly himself, whose command, though *in absentia*, could bring out the Gordon cavalry and revive the cause in the North.

Montrose paused briefly at Brechin to send young Lord James to Old Montrose to continue his schooling and Spynie on an errand to Finavon with orders to join him later. He also sent a formal summons to his old friend Marischal at Dunnottar, but the Covenant earl returned no answer and passed the letter on to the Committee at Aberdeen.

Then he struck north, through Fettercairn in the lee of the hills, and by a pass called the Cryne's Corse Mounth[22] to Deeside. Suspecting rightly that the Bridge of Dee would be held in strength against him, he turned swiftly up-river to a ford near the Mills of Drum which he crossed against light resistance,[23] and on the evening of 11 September camped in the grounds of Crathes Castle, where with Airlie and his sons he 'soupit with the Laird of Leys'. Their host, Sir Thomas Burnett of Leys, was of an old and honourable family who had taken their title from a small loch nearby and their charter from Robert the Bruce. He was, strangely, both a Covenanter but yet a friend of Huntly, and he knew Montrose from the time of his first expedition to Aberdeen as a Covenanting commander. Now he offered the King's Lieutenant hospitality and 5,000 merks as ransom for his castle—a gracious offer graciously refused though the Royalists felt the need of it. But next day Montrose with equal courtesy did relieve him of his arms and horses.

Meanwhile the Covenant detachment outflanked at the Bridge of Dee retired hastily upon the main body of Burleigh's army which stood to arms for a night and a day at the Crabstane outside Aberdeen. Then, when it seemed probable that the Royalists did not intend to fight until the thirteenth (Friday), the Covenanters withdrew once more into the city.

Montrose duly left Crathes sometime on the Thursday and marched to the place known as the Two Mile Cross, where he halted and ordered his men to prepare for battle on the morrow. In Aberdeen people later recalled that on that night the moon rose blood red above the mountains and two hours before the usual time.

On the morning of Friday, 13 September, Montrose sent a messenger accompanied by a drummer boy to beat the parley and demand the surrender of Aberdeen in the King's name. The good weather had broken meanwhile, and a drop of rain falling on the paper smudged the fresh ink on the formal summons to the city authorities:

Loving Friends:

Being here for the maintenance of Religion and Liberty, and his Majesty's just authority and service, these are in his Majesty's name to require you, that immediately upon the sight thereof, you render and give up your town, in the behalf of his Majesty; otherwise that all old persons, women and children, do come out and retire, and that those who remain may expect no quarter.

I am as you deserve,

MONTROSE

The envoys approached the town and were conducted to the Bowbridge where Burleigh, Fraser, Frendraught and others, together with the provost Patrick Leslie and the magistrates, were holding a council of war in the house of one Alexander Fyndlater. The Covenanters were civil enough and 'caused the Commissioner and drummer drink hardly', and one of the magistrates even gave the boy a coin valued at £6 (Scots). But they were determined to fight and refused to evacuate the old men, women and children as Montrose had suggested. Their answer to his summons, though written in haste while the messenger waited, was drafted with some care, but the last minute crossings-out and amendments may nevertheless have betrayed their nervousness before the coming battle:

Noble Lord:

We have received yours with a gentleman and a drummer, whereby your Lordship signifies to us that you are for the maintenance of Religion, Liberty, and his Majesty's just authority; and that we should render our town, otherwise no quarter except to old persons, women and children. We acknowledge likewise our obligation to maintain the same which your Lordship professeth you are doing; and we shall be most willing to spend the last drop of our blood therein, according to the Covenant subscribed and sworn by us.[24] Your Lordship must have us excused that we will not abandon nor render our town so lightly; seeing we think we deserve no censure as being guilty of the breach of any of the aforesaid points; and specially of that latter article; but have ever been known to be the most loyal and dutiful subjects to his Majesty; and by God's grace, shall to our lives' end strive to continue so; and in the meantime to be,

Your Lordship's as ye love us[25]
Provost and Baillies of Aberdeen,
in name of the Burgh.

This letter was dated 'Aberdeen, 13 September 1644, at eleven o'clock', and already the Covenant divisions were marching out of the city to the Crabstane where the army was being marshalled into line. Montrose's deputation also hurried back this way to deliver the magistrates' answer, but as they passed by the Fife regiment a trooper, regardless of their flag of truce, callously shot down the young drummer boy.

This act of wanton cruelty took place in full view of the Royalist army now drawn up by the How Burn. Montrose, particularly, was incensed at the pitiless killing of a mere child in flagrant and treacherous breach of the acknowledged code of war, and in bitter and savage anger he swore aloud that the boy's death would not go unavenged.

The Covenanters' position was a strong one, and well chosen. Burleigh had drawn up his army along the crest of the brae in front of the town, facing south towards the How Burn. The road from Aberdeen ran parallel to his rear, and on his right flank it continued behind the crest down to the Upper Justice Mills. From the centre of his position a lane (the Hardgate) descended the slope to his front through a cluster of detached cottages and gardens which he also occupied in strength.[26] On the left the ground levelled out slightly and was ideal for cavalry. The Covenanting foot, amounting to about 2,500 men, were marshalled in three divisions with 250 horse on either flank.[27] The 500 Aberdeen musketeers were probably to the right of the line, displaying the famous banner of 'Bon Accord' which had been their ancestors' battle standard at Harlaw two hundred years before. Lord Burleigh himself nominally commanded the right wing and Lord Lewis Gordon the left. The cannon were sited in front of the main battle-line, and having the advantage of the higher ground could direct a plunging fire on the Royalists massing by the Burn.

Alastair led his men across the stream and attacked the cottages and gardens that abutted on to the Hardgate, dislodging Burleigh's pickets and driving off a body of lancers who had been posted there in support. The Royalists then advanced some way up the slope and deployed into line, facing the Covenant army. Montrose now commanded about 1,500 foot and 80 horse. The Irishes in their three regiments again formed the centre with Alastair's small band of MacDonalds and the remaining men of Atholl and Lochaber. The slender cavalry force he divided into two, placing 40 troopers on each flank and strengthening them after the manner of Gustavus with 100 musketeers dispersed by platoons chequer-fashion between the squadrons.[28] With 80 horsemen against Burleigh's 500, cavalry shock tactics were out of the question. Their stance was defensive, relying on mobility and firepower to protect the vulnerable flanks of his shorter battle-line and repulse the attacks of the Covenanting lancers which would be directed against them. The cannon captured at Tippermuir were positioned in front of the army, but trained uphill, their fire was less effective than that of the enemy. Nathaniel Gordon and Colonel James Hay commanded on the left wing with a Captain Mortimer directing the musketeers. Sir William Rollo with Colonel Sibbald had the right wing, and Alastair the centre. Montrose himself, with Airlie and others of his staff, was on horseback, mobile and in overall command. To distinguish themselves from the enemy, the Royalists wore a rip of oats in their bonnets—the Graham's new whimsy—but clothed and equipped from the spoils of Perth, and with fewer highlanders among their number, the army presented a rather more regular appearance than at Tippermuir, and the two forces squared up to each other in anticipation of a conventional set-piece battle.[29]

The action began with a stand-off cannonade, the Covenanters having slightly the better of it, before Lord Lewis Gordon led his eighteen troopers down the hill in a wild attack against Montrose's right wing. They charged in the old style, advancing in line to fire at the gallop before peeling off 'in caracole' to re-form and come on again,[30] but although it was done with courage and panache they did not get so close, nor were their volleys at that pace accurate enough, to shake Rollo's men. Lord Lewis withdrew, having made no impression but with Gordon honour satisfied.

Behind him, however, a more serious attack was developing as the Lords Fraser and Crichton of Frendraught ordered their squadrons for a major assault on Montrose's right. But their 200 lancers advanced at a trot, checking to fire their carbines and reload, rather than charging home at the gallop. The Royalists stood them off with volleys of musketry and, as they milled indecisively about the perimeter of Rollo's position, the 40 cavaliers counter-attacked and drove them back up the hill in confusion. Already the deficiencies in the Covenant leadership were becoming apparent. On the bluff, the other lairds of Forbes and Buchan, who might have charged at the critical moment to support this first attack, continued to look on, as the Gordon historian recalled: 'Not for want of good will to feght, but for want of experience, not knoweing that it was there tyme to charge; and this errour came chiefly for want of a generall commander, whose ordoures they should obey.'[31] Fraser re-formed his men and came on again but, after a confused and unprofitable mêlée, was once more repulsed with loss. This time he withdrew altogether, and Rollo's men could lean on their arms.

But the danger was not past. The Covenant right and centre had remained inactive while their cavalry attacked on the left, but under cover of this diversion a force of 100 horse and 400 foot had been detached from the main body with orders to march along the service road behind the crest and work their way round to a position a little to the rear of Montrose's left flank. Having arrived at this point unseen, a determined assault might have rolled up the Royalist line and decided the battle there and then, but the Covenanters halted on a slight eminence, apparently awaiting a general order to attack. In these brief moments of hesitation Nathaniel Gordon saw the threat, and while Mortimer swung his musketeers into a line to hold them off, he sent urgently to Montrose for help. Rollo had by now beaten off the last of Fraser's attacks, and the King's Lieutenant, having no reserve at all, promptly ordered the whole of his right wing to cross over to the left at the double. Thus reinforced, Gordon and Mortimer stormed the hillock and dislodged the flanking force from their position of vantage. The Covenant cavalry fell back in confusion, but the foot were caught scrambling in the open and Nathaniel Gordon's troopers cut them to pieces.

On the Covenant side, meanwhile, Sir William Forbes of Craigievar, who had studied war on the continent and knew the value of shock tactics, had watched impatiently as Fraser's squadrons withdrew in disorder. Seeing that Nathaniel Gordon and the rest of the Royalist cavalry were heavily engaged on the flank, he now called out his own troop of horse and led them at full gallop into the Royalist centre. Alastair's seasoned Irishes had met cavalry before. When Forbes's horsemen charged home they opened their ranks to let them through, and, facing quickly about, shot the Covenanters down as they passed or chopped them out of the saddle with axes. Unsupported, Craigievar's single troop lost their momentum and were swallowed up within the Royalist centre as the Irishes closed their files again behind them. Craigievar himself and Forbes of Boyndlie were dragged off their horses and made prisoner.

There was now a pause in the manoeuvring although the cannonade resumed. The battle so far, owing mainly to the inadequacies of the Covenanting commanders, had been episodic and uncoordinated. The Covenant horse had not yet re-formed and were still disorganized, while their centre had not moved from the crest of the hill. But although the Royalists had successfully beaten off every attack which the enemy had sent at them, it was apparent to Montrose that the issue was still hanging very much in the balance and that, unless he could initiate some decisive action – and that soon – time itself would tell in favour of the enemy's superior numbers and swing the battle against him. He had no reserves. The wings of his army were nearly exhausted; men and horses winded and blown; many wounded to a greater or lesser degree. Clearly they could not continue to fight off overwhelming numbers indefinitely, and sooner or later the Covenanters would learn to attack on both flanks at once so that he would not be able to hold them back by sending one wing to help the other as he had done hitherto. In the centre the Irishes had fretted impatiently under a galling cannonade for nearly two hours. Irregular infantry were always nervous before cannon, and their steadiness and fortitude under fire had been remarkable. There were no doubt many heroes among Alastair's men who waited anxiously for the order to attack as cannon balls tore up the turf in front of them, but almost every account of the battle mentions the courage of one Irishman in particular:

> . . . that had had his legge shot with a canon bullet with which he neither shrunk nor fell; only leaned himselfe on his next neighbour and called for the Surgeon's saw; wherewith he saw'd off hos own legge after he had cut the flesh round about with a knife; which being done 'I hope' said he 'my Lord Marquisse will give me a horse to be a dragooner since I can fight no more on foot, and within a fortnight I shall be as able for service as any of you'.[32]

and so saying, he handed the amputated limb to a friend with instructions to 'Bury that lest some hungry Scot should eat it!'[33]

But even the Irishes would waver under continuous bombardment.

Their way of fighting was to attack, and they asked only to get to close quarters with the enemy.

Since the Covenant cavalry were temporarily out of the action–though possibly massing somewhere behind the enemy's position–their absence afforded the best opportunity for rushing the crest. Montrose galloped along his battle-line shouting to Alastair and a Major Lachlan of the Irish regiments that there was nothing to be won from this fighting at a distance, but that they should charge at once and fall on with swords and musket butts–'for resolution must doe it!' At the sound of the trumpet the Irishes at once began running up the slope yelling their war-cries, and hurled themselves at the Covenant formations. Burleigh's regiments took the shock of it, recoiled, and then slowly disintegrated as the Royalist attack splintered through the mass of falling men. When once their line was pierced the Covenant divisions began to fragment as units broke and ran, and the Irishes clubbed their way through the crumbling ranks and closed around any isolated groups that tried to stand and fight. Within minutes all order disappeared and the Covenant army was in full flight.

The cavalry did not return to salvage anything from the rout, but having seen the foot regiments break up rode hell for leather for their lives. Burleigh and his staff, well mounted, fled likewise to the Bridge of Don and so into Buchan, and left behind them the Fifeshire levies to be decimated on the field. The last to fall back were the regular garrison of Aberdeen, who alone retired in good order and tried to break out to the south by crossing the Dee. But Alastair guessed at their intention and 400 of his Irishes cut them off and killed them at the river.

The town militia, to the grief of Aberdeen, ran back towards the city. Their standard of 'Bon Accord' was trampled and taken, their captains dead or fled, and Provost Leslie, as he escaped (for he was mounted), had shouted to them to hold the town or all was undone. The conscripts did not comprehend that their homes would afford them no sanctuary. They fled down the road to Aberdeen with the Irishes bounding after them so that the running slaughter continued through the gates, and the streets of the city itself became part of the general killing area.

Covenant casualties were afterwards put at about 1,000 men killed, the greater part during the rout. According to Royalist accounts, Montrose lost less than a dozen men killed outright with rather more than a score wounded. Of these last, Innerquharitie had taken a lance through the thigh, Sir John Drummond had been wounded in the head and James Farquharson, son of Farquharson of Craignitie, also had to be carried off the field. Others had had lucky escapes. Sir Thomas Ogilvie had been unhorsed in the mêlée, and Kinnoul's horse was killed under him by a cannon ball, but both came off unhurt.[34]

Those Aberdonians who had survived the battle itself now had to live through the horror of its aftermath. Montrose's men burst into Aberdeen:

> . . . Hewing and cutting down with their broadswords all manner of men they could overtake (within the town, upon the streets, or in their houses, and round about the town, as our men were fleeing) without mercy. The cruel Irishes, seeing a man well clad, would first strip him and save the clothes unspoiled, and then kill the man. We lost three pieces of cannon with much good armour besides the plundering of our town houses, merchant booths and all, which was pitiful to see . . . [Montrose] had promised to them the plundering of the town for their good service. However, the Lieutenant stayed not but returned back from Aberdeen to the camp this same Friday night, leaving the Irishes killing, robbing, and plundering the town at their pleasure. And nothing could be heard but pitiful howling, crying, weeping, mourning, through all the streets.
>
> Thus the Irishes continued Friday, Saturday, Sunday, Monday. Some women they raped and deflowered, and others they took by force to serve them in their camp. It is lamentable to hear how the Irishes who had got the spoil of the town abused the same. The men they had killed they would not suffer to be buried, but stripped them of their clothes and left the naked bodies lying on the ground. The wife dared not cry nor weep at the slaughter of her husband before her eyes, nor the mother for the son, nor daughter for her father; for if they were heard then they were presently slain also.

This is one of the most graphic passages in Spalding's *Memorials*,[35] and, coming from an Aberdonian, probably an eye-witness, and a Royalist as well, it has proved damning evidence and left an indelible stain on the honour of Montrose. It is possible that Spalding exaggerated in point of degree, and that, in a sense, having lived through the event, he continued to survive off the horror of it. Parliamentary propaganda, particularly those aspects that dwelt on the unspeakable barbarities of the Catholic rebellion, had led to the Irish being regarded with especial abhorrence in Scotland. They were considered sub-human, worse than animals, and this prevailing attitude was reflected in the treatment accorded them by several contemporary Royalist historians as well. Patrick Gordon in his *Britane's Distemper* gave the following description:

> . . . the Irishes in particular were too cruel; for it was everywhere observed they did ordinarily kill all they could be master of, without any sign of pity nor any consideration of humanity; rather, it seemed to them that there was no distinction between a man and a beast; for they killed men with no more felling of compassion and with the same careless neglect as when they kill a hen or capon for their supper. And they were also without shame being most brutishly given to uncleanness and filthy lust; as for excessive drinking, when they came where it might be had, there was not limit to their beastly appetite; as for Godless avarice and merciless oppression, and plundering the poor labourer. Of those two crying sins the Scots were also as guilty as they.

The view was much the same in England. Early in 1644, when one, Captain Stanley, captured a boatload of Irish reinforcements on their way to join the King's army, he made prisoners of such Englishmen as there were, but tied the Irish back to back and drowned them in the sea. Later, when thirteen of his Irish auxiliaries were hanged by the Roundheads, Prince Rupert promptly hanged thirteen prisoners in retaliation, and received a pained letter from the Earl of Essex damanding to know by what law he had treated Englishmen like Irishes. The latter thus suffered perpetually from the double standard affected by their more sophisticated neighbours. The Covenanters killed all Irish prisoners mercilessly enough, but as Gardiner remarked: 'It is seldom indeed that a civilized community metes out to a less civilized one the measure by which it judges itself.' So to an Aberdonian, atrocities at the hands of an Irish army may have been somehow logical, and perhaps in some degree the written account later justified the expectation.

Spalding also stated that the bulk of Montrose's army remained 'standing clois unbrokin' on the battlefield, so that only a comparatively small portion could have actually been on the rampage within the town. His *Memorials* lists the names of 118 townsmen who were killed that day, but no women. Alexander Jaffray, who fought with the Covenant cavalry, later recorded that 'about seven or eight score men besides women and children were killed'.[36] Baillie put the number at seven score.[37] Others who witnessed the taking of Aberdeen may well have been led to exaggerate by the fear, widely voiced at that time, that the Thirty Years War then raging in Europe would be extended to England, and that such events were representative of the horrors then said to be commonplace in Germany. But these figures do not suggest a general massacre. Aberdeen was not Magdeburg, and Montrose was certainly no Tilly.

Those witnesses who were later examined by the Committee of Estates were, understandably, fairly cautious in their recollection. Master William Forrett deponed the following January that after the battle he:

> . . . saw several slain men laying at the entry of the town of Aberdeen and within the town . . . that to the deponer's knowledge there were several houses spulzied [spoiled] and robbed by the rebels. . . .

Sir William Forbes of Craigievar recalled that:

> When we were brought in prisoner to the town of Aberdeen after the conflict, that he saw several of the inhabitants and citizens of the town lying killed upon the streets.

and the Master of Spynie, that when he went into Aberdeen:

> . . . the evening after the fight, he saw several of the King's lieges to the number of twenty or thirty lying slain in the streets. Depones that the deponer saw the rebels, numbers of them with plundered and spulzied goods that were spulzied from the townsfolk but did not see the spulzie committed.[38]

In rather different vein, an Irish officer later stated in his dispatch to the Lord Lieutenant in Ireland:

> . . . the enemy were altogether cutt off, unless some few that hid themselves in the city. The riches of that time, and the riches they got before, hath made all our soldiers cavaliers. . . .[39]

As against these several accounts, the Town Council *Record* of Aberdeen may provide the 'official' version:

> . . . and of the townsmen were slain that day, Mr Mathew Lumsden, bailie, Thomas Buck, Master of Kirk-work, Robert Leslie, Master of Hospital, Messrs Andrew and Thomas Burnet, merchants, with many more to the number of eight score; for the enemy, entering the town immediately did kill all, old and young, whom they found on the streets, among whom were two of our town officers called Gilbert Breck and Patrick Kerr. They broke up the prisonhouse door, set all warders and prisoners to liberty, entered in very many houses, and plundered them, killing such men as they found therein.

On the evidence then, it appears that the latter stages of the battle extended into Aberdeen itself, and that, during the subsequent street fighting, numbers of innocent citizens were possibly caught out of doors and killed along with the fleeing militia. Although the main Royalist force remained outside the city, some elements at least – Irishes or highlanders who had been involved in the pursuit – thereafter got out of hand and, still bloodhot, began looting sections of the town, during which process a further number of non-combatants, including women and children, may have been maltreated or even murdered.

Most atrocities are forgotten by all but a few. A number are remembered vaguely for their enormity, or because of the publicity given them at the time: others perhaps for what came afterwards. There are some, however, that seem in a strange way to have captured the imagination of time not least because they were so uncharacteristic of the persons who were ultimately responsible for perpetrating them – though they are no less indefensible for that. Montrose was as much at the mercy of posterity as any man, and was probably sadly aware of the critical interpretation that would be put on his conduct by contemporary propaganda merchants and future memorialists. This he could come to terms with. What must have been infinitely more important at the time was the effect of such an event upon himself and upon his conscience, since his action in allowing the sack of Aberdeen – or his inaction in not preventing it – was a direct denial of some of the very principles that moved him. By the standards of the time, Montrose was beyond any doubt a merciful man. Considering that his men were irregulars, unsworn, unpaid, and therefore not bound by any formal discipline, his leadership and control over them was truly exceptional. Later, while taxing him with needless slaughter, Lauderdale yet acquitted him 'of any but what was done in the field' and the Cromwellian Richard Frank who visited Aberdeen in 1657, when recording the fact that a great battle had been fought there, took the occasion to praise the 'incomparable conduct' of the King's general.[40]

Montrose had learned that his own chivalry could be tainted by the cruelty of the meanest elements under his command. Yet the lesson of Aberdeen must have been more than this. Civil wars can have peculiar ironies of their own. Aberdeen had been the most loyal of the Scottish cities, and in times past had especially welcomed the young Earl of Montrose. He had now become the instrument by which such misery was inflicted upon its people, most of whom had been reluctant Covenanters, 'harllit out sore against thair willis to fight', with little or no say in the decisions that had set them in rebellion against the King and brought them finally to this disaster. Montrose could not have been immune to the suffering of the city that once had honoured him with its freedom; and if, as is often supposed, he was indeed obliged to keep a promise made to Alastair in anger that he should have the sack of the town in revenge for the murdered child, when the thing was done he had the wit and the compassion to understand too well that blood for blood would not give peace of mind, nor would a hundred dead Aberdonians bring back to life a single Irish drummer boy.

Montrose entered Aberdeen the day after the battle and was appalled by what he saw. The remaining Aberdonians, for the most part women and the very old and young, were still in a state of shock after the catastrophe of the previous day, hiding in their houses and too terrified to show themselves outside or to bury the corpses which stiffened in the streets. Many had fixed a sprig of oats to their front doors hoping that by such a token they might be safe and that the savage highlanders would recognize the Graham's whimsy and pass on. Montrose ordered the main body of his army to Kintore and Inverurie, sixteen miles off, while with a number of senior Royalist officers he took lodgings in the house of one Skipper Anderson and set about restoring order in the town. The townsfolk were commanded to bury the dead and clear the mess of battle off the streets. Those prisoners in the Tolbooth who had been gaoled for their part in Huntly's uprising were promptly released. The royal proclamation was read at the Market Cross together with a second notice in Montrose's name calling on the King's lieges to come in and subscribe the oath of allegiance. On the Monday (16 September) those soldiers who had not rejoined their regiments but were still scavenging in the city were charged 'by touk of drum' to remove and follow the camp under pain of instant death, and at Kintore and Inverurie the jubilant Royalists sobered up and considered their future prospects. However, all further activity in Aberdeen was brought to an end by news that Argyll was at Brechin with a large army, and so on the Monday Montrose also left for Inverurie. Spynie for some reason remained in the city and was caught by Argyll soon after.

From Inverurie Montrose sent Sir William Rollo south with a dispatch for the King, reporting his two victories to date but emphasizing the need for help. (Rollo was captured before he reached the borders and unfortunately the text has not survived.) The King's Lieutenant then marched westwards through Garioch and Strathdon to Kildrummy Castle, which he occupied and made his headquarters while Nathaniel Gordon led a recruiting expedition into Strathbogie, to Huntly and the Bog of Gight. For several days the Royalist army waited in the shelter of the hills as from their base at Kildrummy Montrose and his friends tried to win over the local Gordon lairds, the while watching warily to see what Argyll would do.

The Covenant advance guard entered Aberdeen on Wednesday, 18 September, and the main army arrived next day. At Brechin Argyll had linked up with the Earl Marischal and the survivors of the Battle of Aberdeen—the Lords Gordon, Forbes, Fraser, Crichton and what remained of their following—while Burleigh, Jaffray, Cant and other prime Covenanters also reappeared as the army marched north by Drum to Aberdeen. The Campbell now commanded some 6,000 regular troops, consisting of three regiments of his own swordsmen out of Argyll and the West, Lothian's regiment, Sir Mungo Campbell of Lawers' regiment of musketeers, which had recently been withdrawn from Monro's force in Ireland, Buchanan's regiment and 1,000 cavalry under the Earl of Dalhousie. All were billeted free upon the unfortunate citizens of Aberdeen who were also made to contribute a further twenty baggage horses for the Campbells quartered in the Old Town. These, however, removed again to Drum after a few days' stay, while Argyll himself sent patrols into Strathbogie and debated what to do. On 21 and 22 September he held councils of war in Aberdeen in which he proposed to divide his force, keeping the cavalry and Lothian's and Lawers' troops with him but deploying the others to 'keep the country'. Then, taking Lords George and Lewis Gordon along with him, he marched into Strathbogie, cautious and heavy-footed after Montrose.

In an age that made scant distinction between the respective qualities of statesman and soldier, it was inevitable that the policy that Argyll now adopted should have been frequently misunderstood. Afterwards it became the fashion among historians to condemn him for a coward, 'absolutely without personal courage', who 'could not look upon a hostile array without being overcome by sheer terror',[41] and whose actions over the next months were motivated entirely by his overwhelming dread of actually facing Montrose in battle. In this he has been maligned.

Contemporary critics among the Covenanters, although still fairly circumspect in what they said out loud, smarted under the ignominy of the Brethren's defeat at Tippermuir and Aberdeen, and were perhaps over-ready to judge within the narrow perspective of engagements won or lost rather than on the real issue of what had actually been achieved or conceded thereby. The ensuing struggle between Montrose and Argyll more properly turned on the wider priorities and factors which would decide the course and nature of the campaign, and indeed the eventual outcome of the war. On 22 September 1644, Montrose's two spectacular victories notwithstanding, Argyll, with the advantage of his wide political power in Scotland, and by virtue of the superior military forces at his disposal, undoubtedly still held the strategic initiative, and he maintained it, criticism to the contrary, with a fair degree of success until the end of the year.

Subsequently, the judgement of his later detractors too often echoes the Royalist regret that he did not at some time elect to run incautiously against Montrose and perish ingloriously by his mistake, but preferred to fight in a manner and on ground of his own choosing. Though obliged to sustain the role of general also, Argyll was by nature and ability a politician. The battlefield was only a part of his arena, and, given his political talents and material influence in government affairs, it was the most chancy part at that. The Campbell had a shrewd appreciation of where victory in Scotland would ultimately have to be won, and, having the intelligence and the capacity to calculate the limits within which he himself could operate most effectively, was sensibly reluctant to hazard it in a battle where his own special abilities counted for less while the military flair of his antagonist, whom otherwise in political manoeuvre he far outclassed, could be employed to its fullest advantage. Argyll could well have argued that, without fighting, Montrose like Huntly before him must eventually lose, and the Campbell played *cunctator* out of policy and not merely out of fear. Twice in the months that followed, he conspicuously removed himself out of personal danger when threatened by Montrose. Clearly the battlefield, when it came to that, was not his element, but whether his later action in appearing to desert his men at the critical moment was prompted by sheer cowardice, or whether he genuinely believed himself to be too consequential to risk his life it is difficult to say. The one may be used to mask the other, but the two things are not necessarily the same.

The techniques that Argyll adopted were unspectacular but effective and remarkably modern in their conception. His primary aim was to prevent Montrose from obtaining the support of the local population, and in the implementation of this design it was characteristic of the time and, unfortunately, of the Campbell that he resorted to pressure rather than persuasion. A part of his force was deployed to hold down the country, and in this Argyll was able to benefit from the experience of his previous pacification of the Gordon lands earlier in the year. Sizeable concentrations of regular troops able at once to police, protect and punish within their areas of influence kept the power of the Covenanting government very much in evidence throughout the main centres of the Gordon territory and were an essential first step towards containing the 'rebellion'. Meanwhile, the main force, a flying column consisting of the cavalry and Lothian's and Lawers' front-line regiments and commanded by Argyll in person, continued to threaten the Royalist army itself, and along the line of march any area or community that had helped or harboured Montrose was punished with exemplary severity. The unfortunate population, coming under pressure from both sides, thus suffered most in their consequent dilemma. As Spalding commented: 'The country was also holden in under continual fear, none knowing whom to follow and gladly would have [seen it] resolved by a battle between them.' But against such odds Montrose could not risk a battle without Gordon support, and with the Royalists constantly having to give ground before the encircling Covenant forces, the balance of fear remained in Argyll's favour. The season also suited him. The harvest was in; stooks ready for burning, grain for seizing, and men who lost their crops and cattle in the autumn could starve during the winter that would follow. Royalist sympathizers faced total ruin.

The King's Lieutenant, branded 'traitor-rebel' in Argyll's proclamations, was indeed confronted by the problems which more usually face the leader of an insurgent movement. He had no secure base, no fixed support, no supply line. He was dependent on the local people for provisions, grain and bestial, and since his main purpose was to win over the Gordon gentry, he could not afford to lose the goodwill of the potentially Royalist population. Nor could he later succour those who previously had helped him, since his army, by comparison with Argyll's front-line regiments, was composed for the most part of irregulars—fast and mobile, but unsuited to a static defence of the territory they temporarily occupied, and demonstrably not strong enough to protect his benefactors from the revenge of the Covenanters. Those lairds who helped or supplied him today had to face the reckoning with Argyll tomorrow, while it was easy for others to blame the Royalists—foreign Irishes as many of them were—for bringing down yet further suffering on people who had already suffered enough for the politics of their own chief. Neither could Montrose cross into the richer lands of the Gordons as he would have wished, but was obliged to keep close to the shelter of the hills since with his deficiency in cavalry he dared not risk getting caught in the open by Argyll's regiments of horse. Above all, however, he needed time to negotiate with the Gordon lairds, to call a muster and, in view of that man's intransigence, to correspond with Huntly; but having constantly to move and stay ahead of Argyll's pursuing force, this necessary breathing space was also denied him.

Argyll, from his actions, was undoubtedly aware that the issue would turn finally on whether or not Montrose would be able to enlist the Gordons, and for his part was determined to ensure that the Gordon Royalists would never be able to rise against the Covenant again. Apart from the Irishes, who had nowhere left to go, the main elements of the Royalist force were essentially volatile—highlanders who would return to defend their homes, or chafe and desert at the prospect of continuous retreat and little plunder, and lowland lairds with houses and estates neglected; families at the Covenanters' mercy, and apprehensive with the approach of winter. If Montrose could not have the Gordons, he could not win the initiative in the North let alone force a passage through the Lowlands, and unless he could offer his men the prospect of further victory his army would sicken skulking in the hills, dwindle and finally melt away. In theory at least, the King's Lieutenant could not then survive. The Irishes alone would stand no chance and could be destroyed at leisure. Montrose's effort would end in a whimper just as Huntly's had done. Neither could the King's cause in Scotland profit from so dubious and deserted a martyr.

Argyll possibly gauged that Huntly hiding in Strathnaver would be largely ineffective, and from his own informants among the Gordons may have ascertained before Montrose just how intractable and obstructive that proud man would prove to be. As insurance, however, he kept beside him Lord George Gordon, who in his father's absence could most authoritatively command the clan, and through him charged the Gordons to support the Covenant and not Montrose. But to make certain, he continued systematically to ruin and ravage the land so that, even if Huntly did eventually come to terms with Montrose, the Gordons might no longer be capable of providing the main sinews of rebellion against the Covenant. In this he made a mistake, which would come home to him later, in carrying out his depredations under the eyes of the Gordon heir, whose resentment and spirit his Campbell uncle underestimated, even as he may have overestimated his personal influence over Huntly's sons. For the rest, Argyll set out to penetrate and subvert the Royalist camp, offering pardons and safe conduct to the Lowland officers who thought to return to their homes before the winter, and, mindful of the example of Ardvoirlich, renewing the promise of £20,000 (Scots) in bounty money to anyone who would kill Montrose.

If this policy was unsuccessful in that Montrose survived, it was essentially because Argyll failed in two particulars. In the first place, he underestimated the resource and determination of his adversary. Montrose was not Huntly to succumb to despair, and his quality of leadership together with the remarkable discipline and fortitude which he inspired in his soldiers, held the Royalist army together at least until Argyll himself had retired to winter quarters. In the second particular, more seriously, when Argyll did finally drive Montrose into a corner, in spite of an overwhelming superiority in numbers, the Campbell was unable to finish him off, and on this occasion his lack of ability as a battle commander did indeed prejudice what until then had been a fairly effective strategy. Nevertheless, events would show that the methods now adopted at the council of war were at least partially successful, and that, had Argyll been better supported by the Estates and other Covenanting leaders, they might perhaps have been more so.

Not one of the Gordon lairds rode in to join the King's Lieutenant at

Kildrummy. A number 'did indeed profess their great willingness but were, they said, all restrained by the example and influence of Huntly . . . who secretly thwarted Montrose',[42] and it began to appear that, although Aboyne at Carlisle had been enthusiastic, in principle at least, towards the proposal that the Graham and the Gordon might join together in this enterprise, Huntly himself was still nursing a grudge against the 'new' Marquis for his 'betrayal' in 1639, and was as yet not prepared to co-operate. (Wishart later went so far as to say that at this time Huntly 'had forbidden his friends and clansmen even with threats to have nothing to do with Montrose or help him by word or deed'.)[43] It was a great disappointment. Apart from the men whom the Royalists had released from the Aberdeen Tolbooth, the only recruits of note had been Gordon of Abergeldie and Donald Farquharson of Tulligamont. Montrose could not afford to give up hope of Huntly, but it was clear that he would need more time – to argue, ask, beg even – than he had hitherto calculated. In the meanwhile, however, with Argyll's cavalry less than a day's ride away it was not prudent to remain in such an exposed position, and so he broke camp and moved westwards into the hills.

In a morass somewhere in Strathdon the Royalists buried the cannon that had been captured at Perth and Aberdeen and, relieved of this dead weight, climbed through Glen Ernan to Tomintoul, and then by Glen Avon and the Braes of Abernethy to Rothiemurchus, where they camped along the shore of Loch An Eilean. Montrose had intended to put the Spey between himself and Argyll, but when he approached the crossing he found 5,000 men – Grants and the levies of Moray, Ross, Caithness and Sutherland – mustered in arms on the opposite bank. They had seized the ferry boats and seemed prepared to dispute the passage. The Grants, however, temporized, and sent agents across the river to assure Montrose that they were really Royalists at heart but did not want to be the only ones to declare for the King. If their neighbours, and particularly the Earl of Seaforth, could be persuaded to join at the same time, they promised that they too would come over and serve the King's Lieutenant. Montrose had indeed hopes of Seaforth, who sent word that he had heard that the Marquis of Huntly held the King's Commission for the North and so had been hitherto uncertain whom to follow, but that since 'Montrose's power was absolute in the South, in the Marquis of Huntly's absence, he might in the King's service command in the North also'.[44] 'But the highlanders, in generall, ar a subtill and craftie people', and Montrose rightly distrusted the sincerity of these several overtures, while he had no intention of loitering long enough for Argyll to catch him at the river. He therefore 'accepted their complimentes in the hope of more reall performance heirafter', and moved downstream to the wood of Abernethy.

It was by now 27 September, and Argyll meanwhile had begun to sap the Gordon wealth. The Covenanters burned their way through Cromar, Auchtersoul, Aboyne and Abergeldie, then north to waste twelve parishes around Huntly itself, and on to the spoil of Enzie, Auchindoune and the Bog. All horses and arms were seized, livestock lifted, the freshly harvested corn eaten or destroyed, and when Lord Gordon protested bitterly at the wanton destruction of his tenants' lands he was blandly told that all such requisitions were necessary for the sustenance of the government forces pursuing Montrose. Seeing only too clearly that Argyll intended the ruin of his house also, the Gordon heir to all this damage could only rage at his own impotence and settle for a note of charges to be reimbursed at some later time by the Committee of Estates.

Argyll had also sent a portion of his Campbells back through Atholl to attack Alastair's garrisons in Ardnamurchan, probably in the hope of detaching the MacDonald from Montrose, and on 27 September he called a muster of his remaining troops at the Bog of Gight, some twenty miles away from the Royalist position in Abernethy wood. His main force now numbered around 4,000 men, horse and foot.

As Montrose watched the Campbell lacerate the Gordon lands, he realized that the Covenant army would have to be lured away from Strathbogie before the country was desolated beyond recovery and its people altogether subdued. Argyll's methods were proving all too effective, and the King's Lieutenant's only recourse lay in trying to change the whole tempo of the action. He reckoned that, if the Royalists were to leave the area and turn southwards again, Argyll would be obliged to drop his prey and follow, and if he could thus be drawn into the rugged mountainous country where his cavalry advantage would be nullified, the faster moving irregulars might win time enough to circle back again and try the Gordon lairds once more. Thus began what Baillie described as 'that strange coursing as I remember, thrice round about from Spey to Atholl, wherein Argyll and Lothian's soldiers were tired out'. Montrose led his army south into Badenoch, up Spey and Truim, by Drumochter and across the high wilderness of the Grampians. Somewhere in the mountains he fell seriously ill of a fever brought on by strain and excessive fatigue,[45] and the Covenanters when they heard of it rejoiced and gave out that he was dead.[46] But he recovered, and by 4 October his army had swung down Glengarry and reached once more the long fertile valley of Atholl. The Covenanters, unsure whether Montrose would attempt to break out to the west in the hope of taking ship to Ireland or, worse, might strike at Glasgow and then head for England,[47] trudged after him, albeit at a slower pace, weighed down as they were with all the impediments and encumbrances of a Lowland army. Campbell of Lawers was detached to govern Inverness with one regiment of horse and two of foot, while Argyll, after consulting at Forres with the northern Covenanters, crossed the Spey and followed Montrose into Badenoch with 'a slow and lingering march', burning out Royalist sympathizers as he came.

At Atholl Montrose paused for a while, and the army was able to obtain fresh victuals from John Stewart of Schierglass whose place lay across the Garry from the House of Lude. He put a garrison into Blair Castle under the command of John Robertson of Inver, Lord Lude's brother, and from now on it became his headquarters, a prison for those hostages whom he hoped to exchange, and a hospital for his walking wounded. Those Atholl and Badenoch men who had fought at Aberdeen for the most part now returned to their homes, but their places were filled by another 300 fresh recruits, and Montrose was also joined by Angus MacPherson of Inneryssie at whose house he had stayed in Badenoch and who, although he did not command a company, yet 'had great power' over the men of that region. The force was further augmented by some 400 of the Clan Chattan under the 'Laird of MacLelean' who are said to have deserted from Argyll.[48]

But at Atholl there was also news of trouble in Ardnamurchan, where the Campbells were beleaguering the MacDonald outposts at Mingarry and Lochaline. Alastair at once hurried to protect his own, taking close on 1,000 fighting men (and a host of women camp followers) with him, but swearing to return just as soon as the western garrisons had been relieved. He still had hopes of raising the Clanranald and so also promised Montrose that he would send word among the western clans, who, rumour said, grew restive, that they should call a rendez-vous and come in to fight under the Great Graham. The small Royalist army, however, was dangerously weakened by their departure, although one of the Irish regiments, led by Antrim's foster brother O'Cahan—or, in his own tongue, Magnus son of the Giolla Dubh MacCathan—did remain as the nucleus of Montrose's depleted force. The King's Lieutenant, turning northwards once again, now commanded a mere 800 foot and 80 horse.[49]

He marched through Killiekrankie by the brae between Ben-y-Vrackie and Fascally Loch, then along the Tummel and over Don-a-Vourd to reach the house of William Ferguson of Ballyheukane by nightfall. The next day he continued along the River Tay to Dunkeld. For the first time in the campaign[50] Montrose now ordered the syste-matic destruction of Covenant property—an indication perhaps that Argyll's depredations were seriously damaging the morale of would-be Royalists and effectively deterring them from offering support, so that it seemed necessary to retaliate in kind. While Sibbald led 500 musketeers and bowmen up Glen Ardle to raise recruits, Nathaniel Gordon took a party of horse and went raiding into Stormont and Strathmore. In Angus they ran foul of Lord Carnegie, Montrose's brother-in-law, who set upon and killed two Irish stragglers. Hay and Gordon took off in hot pursuit and chased the Covenanters as far as Dundee itself, where they defiantly burned a few suburban houses before riding back to join the column.[51] At the house of Dun, which with Auldber was also plundered, the Royalists found the four brass field-pieces which had been captured from Huntly's men at the Bridge of Dee at the beginning of the troubles.

The Covenanters had posted 14 troops of horse under Marischal to watch the Bridge of Dee, but on 17 October Montrose again crossed the river at the Mills of Drum and lodged with Sir Thomas Burnett at Crathes Castle. On the eighteenth the Royalists burned Kirktoun of Echt,[52] and some Covenant properties in Pittodrie, Murchall and Durlathen. On the nineteenth the King's lieutenant dined with the Châtelaine of Monymusk (Sir Thomas Burnett's daughter, married to a Forbes) and, the Laird being absent, 'spared the house upon fair conditions'. The next day the Royalists fired Leslie Castle near Insch, and, obtaining fresh supplies of grain and bestial at Frendraught, marched on into Strathbogie.[53]

On 21 October Montrose camped at Huntly Castle, which became his headquarters for the next week while he tried unsuccessfully to open negotiations with the Gordon Marquis. But Huntly was still absent and his clan remained in their 'lurking places' and would not stir without the approval of their chief. Montrose passed the time in building up the morale of his small force. Almost every night his light fighting patrols forayed up to ten miles around Strathbogie, routing out the Covenant outposts in the early hours of the morning, lifting horses or taking prisoners. And Wishart recalled that 'as he always brought his men off safe, they became flushed with confidence; however few their number, there was nothing they would not dare and do with him to lead them.'[54] For their part, the Covenant soldiery came to dread these sudden raids and left the Royalists' main force alone.

But it became clear that Huntly was still not prepared to talk, and the campaign had once again lost its momentum. The week's effort had yielded only 200 Gordon recruits of doubtful quality, and it seemed that there was little to be gained by lingering imprudently at Strathbogie. To the west, the dark ridges of the mountain line offered a safe retreat, through Glen Fiddich and Glen Livet to the Strath of Avon and the Cairngorms beyond; but Montrose, either because he was still reluctant to accept defeat, or possibly because the army had run dangerously short of ammunition which could not be replenished in the Highlands, did not yet abandon the Gordon country and wandered eastwards through Tollie Barclay and Auchterlesse to the River Ythan, where on 27 October he occupied Fyvie Castle, the ancestral home of the Earls of Dunfermline. At about this time and in such circumstances he celebrated his thirty-second birthday.

In the meanwhile, Argyll with his advance guard had emerged from Badenoch about eight to ten days behind Montrose, and going via Dunnottar reached Aberdeen on 24 October. Lawers' and Buchanan's regiments remained at Inverness and so the main force of Covenant infantry still numbered about 2,500–Campbell's and Lothian's men–strung out through Angus and marching for Kintore and Inverurie where they regrouped on the twenty-sixth. At Aberdeen Argyll was joined by a further 21 troops of horse, sent north by Leven, bringing his cavalry strength to over 1,200. However, Montrose's retaliatory raiding had had its effect locally and the Covenanters of Aberdeen and Banff did not turn out to support Argyll as he had hoped. Nevertheless, for the Covenant authorities in Edinburgh it seemed, generally speaking, to be a return to the more favourable situation of September, and the latest reinforcements '. . . as with Argyll's forces in the rebels' backs and the country forces in their face, with God's help may bring these wicked men to their deserved end'. Argyll left Aberdeen on 26 October to take command of the foot at Inverurie, sending 14 troops of horse ahead as an advance force. On 27 October the ministers proclaimed a solemn fast throughout the land that all the brethren might be purged of their manifold sins and wickedness, and on 28 October, coincidentally, the Campbell's cavalry caught Montrose at Fyvie.

The Royalists were taken by surprise. Bad intelligence had led Montrose to underestimate Argyll's speed of march through Badenoch and he had consequently assumed that the pursuing force were still somewhere in the Grampians. When the outlying pickets came running in to give the alarm Lothian's cavalry were only two miles away and approaching fast. Taken unawares, and with their own single troop of horse temporarily absent on a foraging expedition, it would have been madness for the Royalists to have tried to break out across open country to Strathbogie since the Covenant dragoons would have caught them long before they reached the hills. The small force of Irishes and highlanders had no alternative but to stand at bay where they were. The Covenant force deployed into the valley and the appearance of the great black banner with a golden cross and the motto 'For Religion, Country, Crown and Covenant' confirmed that this was indeed the main army and that Argyll himself had arrived to supervise the action in person.

Fyvie Castle stands within a loop of the River Ythan. At that time the narrow valley bottom was mainly marsh and watermeadow, undrained bogland, accessible by narrow spits of hard ground which constituted the only possible lines of approach to an attacking force. The castle itself stood on a sort of terrace of firm ground, surrounded on three sides by waterlogged scrub and connected to the small village to the south by a thin spine or causeway where, again, a small band might hope to hold off a strong attacker.

But the castle itself was a trap. It had originally been the baronial keep of the Thanes of Fortmartyne, but the present more elaborate structure, with its drum-towered entrance to the south, its rich heraldic decoration, corbelling, angle turrets and crow-stepped roofs, dated from the beginning of the seventeenth century when Alexander Seton, first Earl of Dunfermline and Chancellor of Scotland, had transformed it into a magnificent dwelling house.[55] But his alterations had left it less defensible and poorly fortified, and Montrose, clearly perceiving that it could not withstand a prolonged siege, was reluctant to make it the centre of his defence.

To the east was a small loch, marsh-banked, while behind the castle and rising slightly above it, between the river and the loch, a low bluff or ridge climbed steeply for about a hundred feet. This hill-face 'was rugged, broken with ditches, and dykes raised by farmers to fence their fields, in appearance like a camp',[56] and, unusual for that time, the slope was also thickly wooded. Montrose hurriedly positioned his men up the side of this bluff, where the trees and hedges would hinder the enemy's advance in formation, while the dry stone walls and banks of earth and turf formed a natural system of breastworks and an abattis for the musketeers, who now set about digging further trenches and improving the position as best they could. Nathaniel Gordon and the horse when they returned were probably posted to the rear of the Royalist position where the bluff merged with the high ground behind it and was more accessible to troops who might cross lower down the valley where the ground was firmer and thereafter circle round to attack the ridge from this direction. It is also likely that a further body of Royalist troops were deployed to hold the narrow causeway south of the castle entrance. Montrose's men were still short of ammunition and the armourers were set to work melting down the castle pewter (of which there was plenty, especially chamber pots)[57] to manufacture musket balls. Powder, however, had to be captured from the enemy.

Argyll drew up the main body of his army out of range and sent forward a regiment of foot to force the position or draw the Royalists into the open. Lothian's infantry, who were good troops, attacked with spirit and as their initial charge went in, the 200 Gordons whom Montrose had newly recruited threw down their arms and ran, so that their fieldwork, consisting of a turf-fauld dyke, was taken in the first rush. Montrose shouted to his men to let the Gordons go and that victory would go to the bravest regardless of numbers, but the Royalists were badly rattled by the Gordons' defection and began to give ground as the perimeter of their position was quickly overrun and groups of Covenant infantry began infiltrating into the firing points further up the bluff. Montrose saw that the situation had suddenly become desperate and might be retrieved only if a vigorous counter-attack could dislodge the Covenanters from the captured trenches. Calling to O'Cahan and Donald Farquharson of Strathdee, he ordered them to get what men they could '. . . and drive me those fellows out of yonder ditch that we may be no more troubled by them'.[58] The Irishes and highlanders rallied to the call and hurtled down the slope in a wild charge that drove Lothian's men clear out of the wood and back into the flat marsh below, leaving behind their dead and disabled, and also quantities of precious gunpowder with which the Royalists replenished their empty powder-horns.

Argyll next sent in a regiment of horse who, struggling through the boggy bottom of the valley, still tried to charge up one edge of the wooded slope. But the Royalists had recovered their nerve with O'Cahan's charge, and this time withdrew intentionally to lure the horsemen into the woods among the dykes, where Montrose's musketeers waited behind cover to shoot them down as they pecked and stumbled in the ditches. As it happened, the excitement of the new Athollmen caused them to open fire before the trap was properly sprung and the Covenant troopers were able to disengage and extricate themselves, albeit with some loss. A flank attack by 500 horse, who had circled the position to engage Nathaniel Gordon's troop as they waited in a clump of fir trees where the bluff merged with the open ridge, rode into the concentrated fire of the Irish musketeers whom once again Montrose had posted among the horsemen to stiffen the defence. As they milled about in confusion and the falling horses entangled the others spurring in behind, the small body of Royalist cavalry counter-attacked and drove them off the hill. By nightfall Argyll had gained no permanent foothold at any point on the Royalist perimeter and he withdrew two miles and made camp.

Knowing that Montrose's men were short of ammunition, however, he returned to the attack next morning, and the pattern of fighting continued much as before. The boggy ground prevented the Covenanters from advancing in order and before going into action each attacking unit had to pick its way through the open marsh under a galling musket fire until it could deploy and assault the slope itself. But the bluff was a natural bastion and among the ditches and dry stone walls the Covenant regulars were unable to keep any disciplined formation. Irish musketeers among the trees shot them at close range as they scrambled up the incline, and the fighting in the trenches was confined and messy with the highlanders having the advantage in the close-quarter killing round the breastworks. Under Lothian and Ramsay both infantry and cavalry continued their attacks at intervals throughout the day, but the Covenanters' morale began to weaken as they took increasingly heavy casualties, and as each successive assault failed and the attacking units were beaten off the bluff, their troops became disheartened at having to abandon the dykes or trenches they had temporarily won at an appalling cost in dead and wounded. (In one of these unsuccessful attempts to storm the hill Alexander Keith, Marischal's brother, was killed among the rest as he was leading a charge of Covenant horse.) At length,[59] badly mauled, Argyll withdrew, and since his army had already consumed all the available provisions in Rothie and Auchterless, he ordered his troops to fall back a further two miles to Crechie where they made camp and licked their wounds.

On 30 October, Montrose had word by the wife of the bailie of Huntly that the Marquis of Huntly himself had landed 'in the Engzie'[60] and would be at Strathbogie within the day. After Argyll had withdrawn his army for the night and was camped some six miles distant, the Royalists therefore seized the opportunity to slip away from Fyvie and marched via Turriff and Rothiemay to Huntly Castle—only to find that the news had been false:

. . . for the marques was not come, nor had he anie intention, becaus his honour and credit was ingraded in it; seing that the Kinge had written to him that he had send him a full commission, being keiped up aither by his sonn, Aboyne's negligence, or the pollutick draught of those who strive to have the honor of the whole action. He was therefor resolved he would first know his Majesties will before he would yield the presidencie, or receive ordores from any benorth the Grangebean mountains.[61]

To Huntly, by whose feudal values a man was judged on the extent of his lands rather than on his ability or indeed the cause for which he fought, the Graham, though newly a marquis, was an upstart, young enough to be his whelp and his inferior in wealth, rank and pedigree. Whatever the grudge which he still held against Montrose for his imprisonment in 1639–and indeed, however justified such a grudge may have been–in the last analysis the King's cause in Scotland appears to have been subordinated to his personal jealousy of the man whom he felt had usurped his rightful office of Lieutenant of the North. And his historian, Patrick Gordon, who defended him loyally against his critics when defence was possible, was never able to provide an adequate answer to rebut or mitigate this charge. The chance of victory in Scotland was being lost because Huntly could not allow another to have the glory that he himself had so signally failed to win while it might have been in his power to do so.

Yet that Montrose should not have forwarded the King's commission which he had carried with him from Carlisle was a palpable error indeed. It should, after all, have been decisive since the wording of its command to Huntly was unequivocal:

> . . . and you yourself carefully to observe and follow such further orders and directions as you may or shall receive from us under our signet or sign-manual, or from our General or Lieutenant General of our Kingdom of Scotland.[62]

Whatever the explanation for it, the mistake cost Montrose dear enough, and he promptly sent Huntly the royal commission by hand of his bailie together with a courteous letter asking for a meeting and promising him sincere friendship. By now, however, he must have had real doubts as to whether the Gordon chief would ever be genuinely prepared to co-operate, and it is possible that he also received the following anonymous letter at about this time:

> My Lord, we need not we hope seek to ingratiate ourselves into your Excellencies favour, by informing you of our hearts, tis true we have not with that readiness as befitted us waited on you according to your expectation, with our swords in our hands, which if we had, knowing our Dependence on the Marquess of Huntly, we had been ruined, for hitherto we still hoped his integrity, but now with grief are enforced to let your honour know the contrary, for Huntly is your back-friend, and both by his example and private directions, hath witheld us all, forbidding even with threats all with whom he hath power to have any thing to do with your Lordship,

or to assist you either with their power or counsel. This we thought
fit to signifie unto you, desiring still to continue in your good favour as
Your faithfull Friends
and Servants.[63]

And in the meanwhile the Gordons would not stir.

On 31 October, Argyll pursued Montrose to Huntly and camped at
Tullochbeg. The Covenanters probed the Royalist position and, finding
it to be a strong one, did not launch a general attack. Instead, after
some skirmishing, Argyll requested a truce, proposing a conference on
mutual pledges of assurance, and in the days that followed there
was a certain amount of trafficking between the two camps.

Argyll, however, tried to use the respite to tamper with Montrose's
men by offers of reward and indemnity, attempting even to suborn the
Irishes, and putting a high price on Montrose's head in the hope of
obtaining his assassination. Sir William Rollo returned to the Royalist
camp and promptly confessed that he had obtained his release only
in exchange for a promise that he would murder the King's Lieutenant,
and Montrose, alarmed at the possible extent of this subversion, and
having nothing further to gain from the Gordons, decided to withdraw
towards the hills. The baggage had been sent off under convoy and
the troops were ready to march when it was discovered that, of all
people, Colonel Sibbald – who had ridden north from Carlisle with
Montrose and Rollo at the start of the venture – had deserted to Argyll
and possibly betrayed their plan to withdraw during the night. Montrose immediately recalled the baggage train, appearing to have
changed his mind altogether, and the Royalists remained in Strathbogie for
another four days. Finally on 6 November, having lit fires throughout
the camp and stationed such horse as remained to the rear within
sight of the enemy, the little army slipped away under cover of darkness along the moorland roads to Balvenie Castle on the west bank
of the Fiddich.

And at Balvenie the campaign ended. The Lowland lairds would
not fight through a winter in the Highlands and argued that a small
band of irregulars would not survive on the plain. The nights were
drawing in with the approach of winter, the weather was getting
colder, the hills inhospitable and forbidding. They had estates and
families at the Covenanters' mercy, and the Campbell's agents at
Tullochbeg had done their work well. On 11 November, Kinnoul,
Drummond, Drumkilbo, Hay, Innerquharitie and many other officers
accepted Argyll's promises of pardon and peace together with his safe
conduct home. Since the only refuge now was Badenoch, where there
would be no need for cavalry, Montrose appears to have detached
Nathaniel Gordon also with orders to try to win over Lord George
Gordon and others of his clan before the spring, and so the ex-
brigand left with the rest and 'having his pass also came to Aberdeen
and walked hither and thither peacably'. With the army reduced
to the Irishes and the Athollmen, apart from Black Pate, only Airlie

and his sons to their honour did not desert the King's Lieutenant.

Argyll no longer marched after them. In mid-November he sent his cavalry to winter quarters and with the remaining infantry occupied Dunkeld. In a daring raid Montrose tried to catch him there, racing south through Badenoch by Dalnaspidal and Dalwhinnie to the Garry, and covering twenty-four miles across broken country in a single night in the hope of taking the Campbell unawares. But at Blair he heard that Argyll had had word of his coming despite the incredible speed of his march, and had hastily left for Perth. Thereafter the Campbell went to Edinburgh and resigned his commission to the Committee of Estates, who gave him a formal vote of thanks with the rather malicious comment that it was the more deserved because there had been so little bloodshed.[64] But Argyll had cause to be disappointed with the outcome of the campaign, and with the construction that many had put upon the tactics that he had adopted. He felt with some justification that he had not had the support, both in men and in money, that the task had warranted and with which he might have been able to take Montrose, and in this mood retired to his castle at Inveraray for the winter season.

And at Blair of Atholl the King's Lieutenant was left to contemplate the failure of his enterprise. Two victories snatched against the odds and a brilliant defence at Fyvie had accomplished nothing in real terms. He had failed to raise the Gordons whose support was crucial to success. He had failed even to win his own neighbours in Strathearn and Angus, on whose Royalism he had counted prematurely. And above all he had failed to alter the course of the war in England. Some front-line regiments had indeed left Leven's army to reinforce the Covenant forces in Scotland, but Newcastle had fallen on 19 October and Tynemouth on the twenty-seventh, and with them Charles had lost the North of England. Montrose's own army had dwindled to a single regiment of Irishes and a few hundred highlanders, and a descent on the Lowlands was now impossible. His brief success in Scotland had been too little and too late. For himself, he was excommunicate and outlaw, his lands forfeit and £20,000 (Scots) guaranteed to any who would take his life.

As wet autumn turned to freezing winter, he waited disconsolate in Atholl and sent his men foraging up the Garry and over the bleak moors of Badenoch. But in the meanwhile his scouts were ranging to Rannoch and beyond to listen in Lochaber for word of Alastair; for if Montrose had hope, it was that the MacDonald would not forget his promise to the Graham, and that when the business in Ardnamurchan was accomplished he would send the Cross among the western gaels and come again to fight beside the King's Lieutenant.

12

Inverlochy

Heard ye not! heard ye not! how that whirlwind the gael—
To Lochaber swept down from Loch Ness to Loch Eil—
And the Campbells to meet them in battle array
Like the billow came on—and were broke like its spray!
Long, long shall our war-song exult in that day.

'Twas the Sabbath that rose, 'twas the Feast of St Bride,
When the rush of the clans shook Ben Nevis' side;
I, the bard of their battles, ascended the height
Where dark Inverlochy o'ershadowed the fight,
And I saw the Clan Donald resistless in might.

Through the land of my fathers the Campbells have come,
The flames of their foray enveloped my home;
Broad Keppoch in ruin is left to deplore,
And my country is waste from the hill to the shore—
Be it so! By St Mary there's comfort in store!

Though the braes of Lochaber a desert be made,
And Glen Roy may be lost to the plough and the spade,
Though the bones of my kindred, unhonoured, unurned,
Mark the desolate path where the Campbells have burned—
Be it so! From that foray they never returned!

Fallen race of Diarmed! disloyal—untrue,
No harp in the highlands will sorrow for you;
But the birds of Loch Eil are wheeling on high,
And the Badenoch wolves hear the Camerons' cry—
'Come feast ye! come feast where the false-hearted lie!'
                    from the gaelic of Ian Lom MacDonald[1]

In the year of The Grahame, while in oceans of blood
The fields of the Campbells were gallantly flowing;
It was then that the Stewarts the foremost still stood
And paid back a share of the debt they were owing.
Oh proud Inverlochy! Oh day of renown!
Since first the sun rose o'er the peaks of Cruachin,
Was ne'er such a host by such valour o'erthrown,
Was ne'er such a day for the Stewarts of Appin!

192

It was the second week in December when Alastair returned to Atholl, and in addition to his two Irish regiments he brought with him 800 fighting men of the western clans whom he proudly presented to Montrose as ample justification for his absence.

The small garrison at Mingarry had more than held its own against the besieging army of Campbells, their resistance watched with interest and appreciation from Castle Tirim by John Moydartach, styled MacDonald of Eyellandtirim, fiar of Moydart and captain of the Clanranald. This John was effectively leader of the most powerful of the Clan Donald septs at this time[2]–a fact that was not lost upon Argyll, who had looked to win him over against the Irish invaders. While the siege of Mingarry was in progress, Moydartach had lately visited the Campbells' camp to listen to Argyll's overture, but then, apparently inscrutable, returned safely again to Castle Tirim. However, the ability of Alastair's small force of Irish MacDonalds to resist the Campbells' might had made a deeper impression than the blandishments of MacCailein Mhor, and in the event he responded rather to the call of kindred and to the enmity that divided the race of Diarmed from his own. Taking the moment to be opportune, the Clanranald rose up at his command–fighting men from Uist and Eig, Moydart and Arisaig–to raid unopposed through Sunart until the land was stripped bare of every cow in the byre and other four-footed beast. And when they drove the *creagh* back in triumph to Tirim, John Moydartach culled out a portion and sent it with his son Donald to relieve the defenders of Mingarry. The Campbells gave up the siege two days before Alastair arrived in Ardnamurchan.

Alastair and the young Donald Moydartach met outside Mingarry–this being their first acquaintance–and, each finding himself well pleased by the other, they joined forces and removed to Castle Tirim where Alastair proposed to the captain of the Clanranald that he should lead his men to join Montrose for an all-out war in the King's name against the MacCailein Mhor. To this John Moydartach, having already flouted Argyll, readily agreed, and after Alastair had installed a fresh garrison in Mingarry they marched their combined warband to Arisaig and Morar, gathering up the rest of the fighting strength of the Moydart Clanranald along the way. From Morar they sent to John, son of Rory MacLeod of Harris, inviting him to join the venture, but he refused for reasons of his own and they passed on into Knoydart to seek out Eneas MacDonald, aspirand of Glengarry, who now led that branch of the Clan Donald (although his grandfather, the old hero Donald of Strome, was still alive, having attained a great age). Eneas declined to join them at this time, but his uncle, Donald Gorm, brought in the greater part of the men of Glengarry, and having collected also a number of MacLeans from Coll and Lochbuie (and possibly the MacNeill of Barra) Alastair decided to turn east once more to keep the tryst at Atholl. Accordingly he led his now sizeable force from the head of Glen Nevis by Clachard to Lochaber and the

Brae, gathering in the Clan Ian of Glencoe and the men of Glen Nevis as he came. Passing through Lochaber he was joined also by Donald Glas with the MacDonalds of Keppoch, most predatory of that warlike tribe, and by the Stewarts of Appin and the Clan Cameron from east of the Lochy. Almost 1,800 strong they marched into Badenoch and over Drumochter to the rendezvous at Blair.

As the wild ranting of the pipes wound down the reaches of the Garry, to the watchers at Atholl their arrival presented an inspiring if outlandish spectacle. Chieftains and petty chieftains under the gaelic battle banners with eagles' plumes and heather in their bonnets and multicoloured plaids brooched with silver, each with bodyguards and gillies as befitted his degree—sword bearer and foster brother; bladier to speak his will; bard to sing of forays past and fashion the songs of battles still to come; piper with the drones full spread; and behind each feudal chief the train of henchmen, tacksmen and tenants—fierce, hairy, red-shanked kerns from the Western Isles in yellow shirts, brogues and *breacans*—belted plaids that hung in folds upon the thigh—armed in ancient habershones, morions and steel-spiked targes made of bull's hide, with broadswords, muskets, longbows, dags and huge Lochaber axes: wild and bonnie fighting men, and in all the finest force of highlanders since Harlaw.

Montrose hurried out to greet the erstwhile prodigal with joy and undisguised relief. At a moment when the morale of the small Royalist force was at low ebb, with winter upon them and their leaders disheartened by the desertion of friends, the coming of Alastair a second time to Atholl with the Clanranald at his back brought hope of a new chance and a fresh campaign. Now the three Irish regiments, original nucleus of his army, would be together at full strength again, and when counted with the small Ogilvie contingent, Struan's Robertsons, 300 from Deeside under Donald Farquharson of Strathawin, some Gordon renegades led by Gight the Younger and others who had stayed after the last campaign, this reinforcement from the western clans meant that he might muster nearly 3,000 men, enough to take the offensive once more. And not only would this constitute a formidable army in array against the regular battalions of the Covenant, but, because it was composed for the most part of wild caterans and highlanders, accustomed to all weathers and trained to arms from birth, one able to march and fight in any season and so strike hard and without delay at the enemy in the Lowlands while their cavalry were dispersed for lack of fodder and the regular troops rested in careless security at their winter quarters.

There was time first to welcome Alastair and his warrior kindred, and for feasting in celebration of the tryst; but when the formal greetings were done, the toasts drunk and the stories told, Montrose called the chieftains to a council of war and proposed an immediate invasion of the Lowlands.

The western gaels rejected the idea utterly. Proud and factious the sons of Somerled, and their pride fed on a tradition which with time had become more mystic than substantial, while their contentiousness echoed the old ambitions of their tribe although the reality of these had crumbled long ago. They were steeped in the genealogy of their race, counting their ancestors back to Conn of the hundred battles, High King of Ireland and Fergus who had first ruled the Scoto-Irish kingdom of Dalriada: reared like their fathers and their fathers before them on the mythology of their kind—on the tales of Fingal and the Norsemen, and great Colla who had dominion over the Western Isles. And they had dreamed while this dominion dwindled and the ancient power of Clan Donald and the Lords of the Isles had been eroded by successive waves of Campbell greed and Campbell guile. In their generation they had watched while Campbell writ usurped for good what Campbell force with the royal commissions of fire and sword had stolen for a space, and they had seen their patrimony shrink to a mere memory of former glories. Yet these were men of long, long memory and they brooded over ancient wrongs. Of the struggle in England they were vaguely aware: of its constitutional ramifications dimly if at all. But while their own traditionalism and the mystery of kingship itself—or perhaps even their religion, for many among the highlanders were still Catholics—inclined them to the royal cause, it was of greater importance that this alignment brought them out against the race of Diarmid with a chance to repay the Campbells in coin of their own. The Clanranald had not gathered in hatred of MacCailein Mhor to raid into the Lowlands. They would march to Loch Awe in dead of winter, and they would burn Argyll.

The other western chiefs were of a similiar mind. The Camerons could claim descent from the first race who had inhabited the country, and harked back to Angus their progenitor who married Marion, daughter of Kenneth III and sister to murdered Banquo, or before that still to Cambro the Dane who in ancient time had taken for his bride the heiress of the old M'Martins of Letterfinlay. And the Stewarts of Appin, sprung from the Norman Fitzallans and the common stock whence came the royal Stuarts, remembered too how their forbears had once been lords of Lorne before it became a portion of Argyll's appenage.[3] Their common hatred of the Campbell and the shared pursuit of revenge long sworn served to weld the western gaels together when loyalty to a distant king in England would have alone been insufficient. They were banded in Atholl intent on plunder beyond the frozen passes of Breadalbane, and they confronted Montrose with an unequivocal statement that they would march into Argyll or they would not march at all.

Montrose was appalled. Unconventional as his approach was by the standards of the time, he had himself proposed a winter campaign in the Lowlands with the idea that, although this would be judged a hazardous undertaking, it would be so unusual as to take the Covenanters by surprise. But these highlanders were resolved on a march over some of the wildest and most desolate country in Scotland, through inaccessible mountains, trackless bogs and undrained valleys, without food or support and at the mercy of the Highland winter.

The risk was enormous. 'It is a far cry to Lochow' had long been the Campbells' boast, and it was not an empty one. At any season their country was virtually impregnable–a compact block of territory defensible on every quarter. To the south it had the protection of the sea and its coastline was guarded by a string of fortresses such as Dunskeig, Tarbet, and Armaddie. To the east it opened on the Covenanting Lowlands, the approaches barred by the strong castles of Roseneath and Dunoon, while to the north and north-east stretched the strongest natural barrier of all–a thick knot of mountains that ranged from Glenorchy in western Perthshire through Breadalbane to Loch Awe: rock walls and secret paths to which only Argyll held the key and swore 'he would rather lose 100,000 florins than that any mortal should know the passes by which an armed force might invade his country'. In time past, small bands of raiders from Lochaber might have slipped over the Pass of Meran on a wild night, but since the days of Fingal King of Selma, no one could remember an enemy to have penetrated to Loch Awe in force. In those narrow defiles a hundred could hold back two thousand, and in winter an army stopped in that desolate place would starve. And more: within these frontiers the whole was knit together by a chain of castles of which Argyll had legal or illegal possession–even as he held Corrick and Dunstaffnage as 'governor' for the King. The power of his clan aroused might reach close on 6,000 claymores and these gaelic fighting men. The Campbells, for all their wealth and fat black cattle, were still a race of predators, strong in their own warlike tradition and proud of a power built on the ruins of weaker neighbours overrun. On their own ground they would fight savagely and to advantage. If the Royalists survived the long march through the mountains and were not lost or buried in the winter blizzards, there was the likely chance that the enemy, if watchful or forewarned, would ambush and cut them to pieces as they struggled through the passes. Failure or defeat could mean the destruction of the entire army and Montrose therefore argued with the MacDonald chieftains, protesting that the risk was unacceptable.

They would not be dissuaded, however, and so it was decided to resolve the deadlock by calling a general council of war at which each side should present its argument in open debate and thereafter abide by the vote of the majority. The western gaels, confident in their numbers, pronounced this acceptable, while Montrose, who knew that he was likely to lose the vote but had probably proposed such a solution as a means of saving face, spent the intervening hours lobbying for support among his own men.[4] When the council assembled he could only try to put forward on a rational basis his several objections to the chiefs' plan for an invasion of Argyll in the hope that the more sober among them would listen to him and that some might even reconsider.

He spoke first, and began by outlining some of the practical difficulties that ought properly to be taken into account before the army became committed to a march into the mountain barrier. The main problem, he said, was that of food. Having no regular system of supply, the army would in any event have to live off the country. But it was winter, and the region to be traversed was largely uninhabited and barren. Driving along their own meat on the hoof was out of the question, since even if there were enough cattle in Atholl–which there were not–they had eighty miles to go over a route that was largely unknown, and speed would be of the essence. The going would be extremely rough–impossible even–and the soldiers would have to travel light and fast, each man carrying provisions enough for a few days only. Once they had set out, therefore, they would have to rely entirely on being able to get through and find food and bestial on the other side of the mountains. If they failed to penetrate into Argyll before their food ran out, if they got lost or stopped in a snow storm, or if the land beyond did not yield up the expected provisions, they would possibly perish of starvation and exposure.

Furthermore, the mountain ridges that defended Argyll were held to be inaccessible, '. . . the straight passes whereof might be easely keept by fyve hundreth against tuantie thousand'. They had to assume that the Campbell lookouts would be alerted from the moment the army entered Glenorchy and that an attempt would be made to seal off the defiles in front of them. And as the Royalists pushed blindly into the ambush it followed that the enemy might seek to close the route behind them as well so that '. . . if they [the Campbells] ware but of ordinaire witte and policie, altho they wanted wallour, they could bloke them upe in the waist bouelles of those desertes till famyne had consumed them every man'.

Montrose added that even if 'by Gode's assistance' they should succeed in getting safely through the mountains and breaking into Argyll, the geographic features of the country were such, and so to the advantage of the defenders, that the army might still come off with comparatively little gain while there would remain a grave risk of some disaster befalling them. The land of the Campbells, he said, comprised a series of peninsulas separated by firths or sea lochs so that from the mountains to the sea the country was divided 'like the teith of a combe'. For the Campbells, each peninsula was a refuge, because they could withdraw along it with their goods and cattle, at the same time destroying all the ferries behind them so that a Royalist force *traversing* the country would constantly have to skirt round the lochs to find a crossing point at their head. For the Royalists, however, each would be a potential trap since to pursue the enemy down any single peninsula was to risk a second force of Campbells blocking the entrance at their back. If they should be caught in this way the enemy, having sufficient boats and complete control of the coastal waters, could harass them continually while the Campbells at either end of the neck of land could be reinforced until they were strong enough to drive inward and crush the small Royalist army between them.

The western gaels conceded that all this was true and 'of great consequence', but maintained that there was still much to be said in support of the venture. For their speaker they deferred to Alastair of whom they stood in some awe, not only because of his legendary ferocity and rising reputation as a war leader, but also because of his official commission from Montrose as major-general of the army. They may well have felt that he was the most likely person to talk the King's Lieutenant round.

For his part, Alastair was rather less preoccupied with detail or with the notion of appealing to careful reason. They knew the country well enough, he declared, and one of the Glencoe men—Angus MacAlain Dubh—would lead them through the passes. And as they knew the country so they knew the Campbells for a people 'of a shallow and blunt disposition, haveing neither braines to forsee the danger, nor judgement to apprehend what was fitteing for resistance'. It was true that the land of Argyll was held to be inaccessible and that it was unknown for an army ever to have penetrated beyond the mountains because of the difficulties that Montrose had mentioned, but for this very reason there would be honour in the trial and the greater glory to him who should first succeed in the attempt. Indeed, this legend of Argyll's impregnability would rather work to their advantage since they would find the enemy in 'carelesse securitie'. The Campbells had come to trust idly in the MacCailein Mhor for everything. The fact that their territory had not been invaded for generations was 'one of the maine reasons which had made that people in generall become so stupid and doltish'.

In going on to state the purpose of such an invasion, Alastair had no need to dwell on the gaels' desire for retribution nor to rehearse the list of wrongs perpetrated against their race by the house of Campbell. Instead, he phrased his argument in terms calculated to have most appeal to Montrose himself. The Marquis of Argyll, he said, was the King's principal enemy in Scotland. His private ambition and wealth coupled with his public authority and influence had cast him as the prime mover in advancing the Covenant cause and putting down the King's interest. He was the mainstay of the present rebellion. His Campbell swordsmen enforced the writ of the Covenant government and at the same time assured his prominent position in the direction of its affairs. To smash his power in isolation when opportunity afforded was strategic common sense. Destroy him and his reputation and the Covenant would never recover. Put down his power in the Highlands and free the clans from the Campbell yoke and they would rise as one to fight for the King.

When the vote was taken, Montrose was supported by Airlie and his Ogilvies, Black Pate Inchbrakie, the younger Gordon of Gight and his following and Donald Farquharson's men of Deeside and Strathawin. Alastair, predictably, carried the rest. Before committing himself finally, however, Montrose asked to see the Glencoe man who would be their guide and put one last question to him direct: 'Was he not acquainted with the countries of MacCailein, or could an army get victuals or encampment in them in winter?' to which Angus MacAlain Dubh answered that 'there was not a town under the lordship of MacCailein but was known to him, and that if tight houses and fat cattle to feed upon in them would answer their purpose, that they would procure them.'⁵ At this, Montrose formally accepted the decision of the council and ordered the army to prepare to march next day.

But for all the enthusiasm the difficulties ahead remained undiminished. They would need Providence on their side and extraordinary luck, especially with the weather. However, among Alastair's Irishes were a number of Catholic priests, one of whom was said to have an uncanny knowledge of such matters, and him they appointed their meteorologist.⁶ This man now squinted up at the sky and told Montrose that as long as the wind blew from the east the weather would hold but that they ought to set out at once.

The army marched from Atholl on 11 December. Montrose would have probably preferred not to take his son on the raid, considering the dangers of the way ahead, but clearly the boy could not have been left behind to risk falling into the clutches of the Covenanters. But William Forrett was too old to face the journey through the mountains and could never have survived the ordeal. He now parted sadly from Montrose and would later face the Covenant inquisition. Airlie, old bones also, would not be denied, however, and as always stuck with the King's lieutenant.

They took the familiar hill road of that first march to Tippermuir, turning up the Tummel and round the loch by the shoulder of Schiehallion to the Tay. To approach Argyll by Benderloch would risk being stopped at Brander, but once through Breadalbane from the east Montrose hoped to pick up the old raiding road out of Lorne, although the MacCailein thought he had the keys of it. On Tayside they visited once more the castle of Weem, captured Argyll's creature Alexander Menzies and burned the lands about before turning westwards into Breadalbane. At the head of Loch Tay the army divided, with the captain of the Clanranald taking his highlanders to burn the Campbell dwellings on the southern shore while Montrose's men set out to reduce the island castle of Eilean nam Bannaomh, whither Sir Robert Campbell of Glenorchy, having abandoned his castle in Balloch, had withdrawn at the news of the Royalists' approach. The Campbells held out for several hours and Montrose, who was directing the assault from the castle orchard on the shore, narrowly escaped being killed when a musket ball struck the pear tree under which he was standing. After the island fell the highlanders savaged the entire glen round about from the Ford of Lyon to the Point of Lismorr, and then continued their march along the wooded slopes of Ben Lawers.

Now the going became difficult. There was no regular track and it took a long time to cover only a short distance. The army progressed by endless detours, ascents and descents, from rock to rock across the frozen pools at the water's edge, in bog and mossland, snow and ice. With each mile the country grew more desolate. They moved into an awesome stillness across a landscape that was at once majestic and yet terrible in its natural grandeur, and the column of struggling men clawing their way along the steep sides of the mountains came to seem contemptible against the huge convulsions of rock looming over them. But it did not snow, and the intense cold was in a sense their friend, since bogs that would have been impassable had frozen hard enough to bear a man's weight; and the army pushed slowly through this wilderness until they reached the broader Strath of Dochart and could see the conical peak of Ben More beyond. At Loch Dochart, however, they encountered another obstacle such as Montrose had feared, and the column came to a sudden and disconcerting halt.

A Campbell castle stood on a small island in the Loch within pistol shot of the land and overlooking the shore at a point where the track narrowed suddenly between the rocks at the water's edge and the steep shoulder of Ben More. It appeared well fortified, built on solid rock and inaccessible from the shore except by boat. The forward scouts reported that it was garrisoned by Campbells and that it mounted heavy ordnance trained towards the near shore and sited so as to command the narrow ground over which the army would have to pass.[7]

With time all-important, a siege was out of the question. The keep would have been well victualled for the winter and the Royalists had neither boats nor cannon of their own. Yet as long as the castle's guns bore on the vital stretch of shoreline the way into Argyll was effectively blocked. The army paused to reconsider.

Help came, however, from an unexpected ally. In better times the land about had belonged to the small Clan MacNab,[8] who like many others had since been subjugated by the Campbells, and a chieftain of this people with some twelve or sixteen followers approached the camp and asked if they could join the enterprise. Montrose was somewhat reluctant at first, since he was understandably distrustful of any who were known to be vassals of Argyll, but since they were familiar with the area and presumably with the routine of the garrison also, he offered them the chance to prove their good faith by finding some way to neutralize the castle.

The small group of MacNabs went down to the lochside shortly before daybreak and, identifying themselves, called to the lookout to send over the boat since they carried letters from the MacCailein Mhor to the garrison commander. The sentry, knowing them for local highlanders, suspected nothing and duly warped the boat across and the MacNabs ferried themselves out to the island. Once inside they promptly cut the throats of the guards and surprised the Campbell commander in his bed. At sunrise they formally rendered the castle to Montrose, and the army marched safely through the narrows gratefully leaving the MacNabs in possession of their old inheritance to guard the path at their back.

Their way was now along Glen Fillan, past the gifted well of the

Saint and up towards Ben Doran, the Hill of Storms, until at Tyndrum they were poised within striking distance of Loch Awe itself. Somewhere in Glen Lochy the army divided into three separate war bands so that as each penetrated independently into a different quarter of Argyll the area of devastation would be the more extensive. Alastair was to take his Irishes and ravage the North from Glenorchy to Glennoe and then by Dalmally and Cladich to a rendezvous at Inveraray. The Clanranald, the Camerons and the Appin Stewarts under John Moydartach were to strike south-west and burn the country as far as Kilmartin Glassary, while Montrose would lead his men of Badenoch, Atholl and Aberdeenshire and swoop down by Glen Shira on Inveraray itself.

Alastair had been right. They had passed through the jaws of the mountains and the weather had held; the Campbells had not stopped them. The strongest line of defence was penetrated and all Argyll lay at the points of their swords.

From his great castle of Ion-ar-aoreidh, the MacCailein Mhor was in the process of calling out his clan.

Initially, his scouts had served him well enough, and the news that the Clanranald were plundering Breadalbane had brought him hurrying back from Edinburgh to prepare a punitive reprisal for the New Year. The Campbell fighting men had been summoned to a rendezvous, and already small groups of armed clansmen were making their way towards Inveraray where their chief, not apprehending that the Clanranald would attempt an invasion of Argyll itself, thought to spend Christmas in tight security.

Suddenly came the startling intelligence that the MacDonalds were through the passes and their war-smoke had been sighted in Glenorchy. Glenure and Achloin were in flames and, most terrifying of all, from the watchtower on Duniquoich came word that Montrose himself was barely two miles away and coming fast.

Argyll hastily took to the sea. Without stopping to organize any kind of defence, he boarded ship and escaped down Loch Fyne to Roseneath, leaving his people to the mercy of the enemy and Duncan MacIvor of Asknish and Lergachonzie, hereditary captain of the castle, to hold out as best he could.

Montrose marched into Inveraray without encountering any resistance. According to tradition, the day was so cold that the edges of Loch Fyne had frozen over and seagulls were walking on the ice—a bad omen to the Athollmen, who had never conceived that the sea could freeze. But their superstitious fear must have been dispelled by the sight of the hated Campbell gallows going up in flames, and as the town itself was set ablaze the highlanders' attention was quickly diverted to the prospect of plunder. Montrose saw little point in tying down his small force to a prolonged siege of the castle, which was too strong to be taken in the assault, while for their part the defenders were unlikely to venture out from the only place of safety. He pitched his camp on the top of Creagh Dhu, a steep hill behind the town–bleak upland but ideally suited to herding a great *creagh*, since on the boggy ground there was no shortage of water, while the marsh grass and birch and fir trees guaranteed an abundant supply of provender and firewood. From here his men ranged out in small bands to pillage the Campbell lands for miles around and drive in the sleek black cattle which represented the main source of wealth among the Highlands.

Let loose in the West, the Clanranald were revenging themselves with feral savagery. Most of the Campbells had gone to earth in their 'lurking holes' at the approach of the war band, and John Moydartach's men met with no organized resistance on their march. Unmolested, they cut a swathe of destruction south as far as Kilmartin, burning lands and homesteads; and where they came upon small groups of Campbells on their way to Argyll's rendezvous, these were promptly put to death. Apart from the desolation left behind, the clan later claimed to have killed 'eight hundred four score and fifteen men' and brought in a thousand cows to the camp at Inveraray.[9]

And to the North, Alastair, most terrible of them all, added further to his reputation and earned his Campbell appellation 'the Devastator'. His Ulstermen burned their way through Glenorchy and on to Glennoe before wheeling in a great arc by Knapdale to ravage along the shores of Loch Awe. Yet strangely, many of the tales that survive in those parts recall odd acts of mercy. In Glennoe, near the head of Loch Etive, the inhabitants had fled before his coming and he ordered all the dwellings to be burned. His men seized first upon the house of the local chief and had already taken a live coal from the hearth and thrust it into the thatch when Alastair learned that the people thereabout were MacIntyres–a tribe descended of old from the MacDonalds but who had thrown in their lot with Argyll after Harlaw– and therefore distant kin to him. He promptly had the flames extinguished, and it is said that the coal was extracted from the roof and carefully preserved thereafter by the MacIntyres of that ilk.

It is also said that in South Knapdale, not far from Inverneil at the foot of the mountain where the old Tarbet road once passed, Alastair, who had been raiding along Loch Fyne and was faint with hunger, stopped at a cottage to ask for some food. The occupant, an old widow, gave him what she had–a cup of milk–and after drinking it he had the word passed down the column: 'Comhain am botham beag ain buin na beinne, far an dfhuair mi an deoch bhaine'– 'Spare the little hut at the foot of the hill where I got the cup of milk.'

He also ordered his men to spare the village of the MacCorquodales of Loch Ballenoir who had fled from their clachan to the tower of Tromlee, since their chief had held the land for the Crown and had been his friend as well as Argyll's. But as they passed, a defender on the walls of the castle shot a man of the rearguard, and the Irishes turned about and burned the place.

Passing into Lochaweside Alastair continued the work of destruction. His men burned every house except for strongly fortified castles, slew, drove off or ate every four-footed beast, and utterly spoiled all grain, goods and utensils which they found. In this way they passed round the northern end of Loch Awe and by Glen Aray to Montrose's main leaguer at Inveraray.

The army regrouped at the beginning of January. The camp was now well supplied with an abundance of food–grain and bestial–'but little drink except cold water'. In addition to cattle the gaels had acquired a prodigious quantity of loot, arms and armour and also luxuries, and could pass the winter in fine style. But although his followers now had good arms and full bellies, Montrose saw that the army had become an unwieldy thing, laden with booty and hampered on the march by the vast herd of cattle, so that moving through an aroused and hostile country they would become daily more vulnerable to Campbell counter-attacks. In the Lowlands Argyll would not have been idle, and while he was gathering the Covenant power his clansmen would be creeping from their hiding places among the smoking ruins to muster for revenge. Providence perhaps, and exceptionally good weather conditions certainly had made the campaign successful so far. But to stay too long was dangerous, and by 14 January, Montrose judged it time to leave.[10]

He marched to the northern end of Loch Awe, where the Irishes succeeded in capturing a strong castle–possibly Innischonain or Kilchurn–and released old Colkitto and two of Alastair's brothers from the dungeons.[11] Then, as they entered the Pass of Brander, the way is said to have been barred by an old woman with a scythe who killed a soldier and would have been summarily put to death but for the personal intervention of Montrose. Just as they reached Loch Etive the weather finally broke, and in the teeth of a south-westerly gale the army kept along the southern shore towards the Connel of Lorne from where they hoped to cross into Benderloch. (There is a tradition that one party went north by Glen Etive to Rannoch. Moor, but this was probably a small group who had left the army to drive their plunder home.) At Connel the wind dropped so that the sea was comparatively calm, but Montrose was forced to camp by the shore until suitable boats could be found. The position was none too comfortable with Dunstaffnage Castle on their immediate flank, but boats were eventually obtained through the agency of Campbell of Ardchattan, a MacDonald on his mother's side, who undertook to help in return for an assurance that his lands would be spared. He produced four boats, one of which when repaired could take forty men at a time and the other three five each. It took two days and nights to ferry the army across. Luck, however, was still on their side, since on their first night in Benderloch a Covenant sloop which Argyll had sent to harass their march was wrecked on the beach and the Royalists fell heirs to its armament of brass cannon.[12]

Gathering 150 recruits from among the Appin Stewarts, Montrose now marched north to the River Cona which he crossed near its mouth. In a thunderstorm the army entered Glencoe by the foot of Meall Mor and the Field of Dogs at Achnacone where they were joined by more of the MacIans who led them up the Devil's Staircase and over the high passes—probably by Mamore—and so to Inverlochy in Lochaber. But they only stayed one day there and it was not until they reached Kilcummin at the foot of Loch Ness that Montrose called a halt.[13]

As was their custom, a large number of the Highland following —the Athollmen and part of the Clanranald—now left to return home and deposit their spoil in safety, and Montrose, as he paused to take stock, found that once more he could barely muster 1,500 men. Against him he could reckon on three Covenant armies preparing to take the field—the main regular force emerging from winter quarters somewhere in the south-east; the Campbells gathering for revenge behind in Argyll; and immediately to the north the garrison in Inverness blocking the Great Glen of Albin in front of him. Of the first two he had no intelligence, and assumed that it would be some time before they could reach the scene of action. But while at Kilcummin he heard that the two veteran regiments at Inverness (Lawers' and Lothian's) had been joined by the northern levies under Seaforth—men from Moray, Ross, Sutherland, Caithness and the Clan Fraser—bringing their numbers up to around 5,000 horse and foot. Although he had been obliged to grant leave of absence to a substantial portion of his own army, Montrose felt confident that Alastair's three Irish regiments were more than a match for the Covenant regulars, while Seaforth's levies would be 'a mere rabble . . . peasants, drovers, shopmen, servants, and camp-followers—altogether raw and unfit for service',[14] and so, since they were nearest, he decided to march north and smash them at once.

First, however, he wanted to capitalize on the campaign in Argyll since news of the raid had travelled fast, and although many of the clansmen had gone home with their loot, a number of chiefs who had not taken part in the expedition now came in to offer their support. They included such names as Sir Lachlan MacLean of Duart and Eneas MacDonald of Glengarry. Montrose saw an opportunity to begin the 1645 campaign with a formal alliance, and he therefore drew up a 'Band of Union' to unite the Highlands against Argyll and the Covenant, the signatories of which pledged themselves 'with our lyves, fortunes and estates' to fight for the legitimate authority of the King against 'thes present perverse and infamous factione of deperatt Rebells now in furie against him' as 'we would be reputed famous men'. The band as it exists contains fifty-three signatures including (apart from Montrose himself) that of Lord Graham his son, Airlie and his son Thomas Ogilvie, Alastair, the captain of the Clanranald, Glengarry, Keppoch, Duncan Stewart of Appin, MacLean of Duart, MacLean of Lochbuie, Donald Farquharson, Donald Robertson

Tutor of Struan, Donald Cameron Tutor of Lochiel, the MacPherson, the MacGregor, Drummond of Logiealmond and many others. However, the original was drawn up with a number of blank spaces in which those who signed later, notably Lord George Gordon, Nathaniel Gordon and the Earl of Seaforth, added their names also. It was signed in the Church of St Coemgen on 'the penult days of January 1645'.[15]

After this formal ceremony some of the chiefs went home to call up their men and Montrose prepared to march up the Great Glen and fight Seaforth.

Meanwhile, in the Lowlands Argyll had indeed not been idle, and from Roseneath had hurried to Dunbarton to meet General Baillie, the new commander-in-chief of the Covenant forces in Scotland.

Lieutenant-General William Baillie of Letham, who, apart from Argyll, was to become Montrose's principal antagonist in the campaigns of 1645, was a natural son of Sir William Baillie of Lamington and a cousin of the Robert Baillie then with the Covenant delegation in London. He was an experienced soldier, having learned the art of war under Gustavus Adolphus, since which time he had fought at Marston Moor and the taking of Newcastle. But he accepted the Covenant command somewhat reluctantly and almost by default.

Montrose's victories at Tippermuir and Aberdeen had had their effect upon the Covenanters' morale, and in Bishop Guthry's words, 'Many who had formerly been violent in the popular cause now began to talk moderately.' Argyll had resigned his commission at the end of 1644 and was unwilling to take it up again. Nor could Lothian or Callendar be induced to do so, and the Committee of Estates was in some difficulty to find someone capable of commanding its forces in the north.

After the fall of Newcastle Baillie had returned briefly to Scotland on private business, but was already on his way back to rejoin Leven's army in the South when he received express orders to report to the Committee in Edinburgh where 'I was pressed, or rather forced by the persuasion of some friends to give obedience to the Estates and undertake the command of the countrie's forces for persewing its enemies.'[16] The army in Scotland was now reinforced by sixteen companies of foot (1,100 men)–regular troops recalled from Leven's forces in England–and with these Baillie marched to join Argyll at Dumbarton.

Unfortunately for Baillie, they apparently disliked each other on sight, since although Argyll did not want the responsibility of commander-in-chief, he made it clear from the first that he still intended to direct the conduct of the war. Baillie recalled bitterly:

> . . . bot because I would not consent to receave orders from the Marquess of Argylk (if casuallie we should have mett together,) after I had received commission to command in chieff over all the forces within the Kingdome, my Lord seemed to be displeased, and expressed himselfe so unto some, that if he lived he should

remember it; wherein his lordship indeed hath superabundantly been alse good as his word.[17]

This antagonism was to have disastrous consequences later.

Baillie was forced to hand over his 16 companies of veteran troops to Argyll. He then joined Lindsay of the Byres and Sir John Hurry with the rest of the army at Perth, while the Campbell marched north-west again with the 1,100 Lowland regulars to supervise the arming of his clan.

The next step was to send to Ireland for Sir Duncan Campbell of Auchinbreck, a veteran Highland soldier who with a standing army had occupied the towns of Antrim's country since the beginning of the war. Auchinbreck was incensed by the news that his estates had been pillaged, and quickly raised the fighting strength of the clan. The Campbells were hot for revenge and, it being an old Highland proverb that he whose house is burned becomes a soldier, by early January over 3,000 men were gathered and ready to pursue Montrose.

On 18 January the Committee of Estates received a letter from Argyll addressed to Parliament in which he said that he had disjointed a shoulder in a fall from his horse: 'bot he wold be weill: that the rebells were fled to Lochaber and that he would omitt no occasion to pursue them: and that they were now in Glenurquhare'.[18] Despite this mishap and previous reverses, the Covenant authorities were still confident that Montrose and his gallowglasses would soon be brought to book. Certainly they had the forces to do it, and from London Robert Baillie wrote: 'If we get not the life of these worms chirted out of them the reproach will stick on us forever.'

Argyll knew that Montrose could not stay long in Lochaber for lack of food, and so set out at once to follow his route north. The Campbells marched through Lorne and crossed Loch Leven by the ferry at Ballachulish. There, the story goes, they met a woman with the sight and boasted of the feats of arms they would perform, promising to give her a good account of the foe on their return. But she is said to have looked at them and answered quietly: 'Perhaps you will not return this way'. On 1 February they camped at Inverlochy, the strategic centre of the Highlands. Montrose at Kilcummin, and unaware, was barely thirty miles ahead of them.

According to the more common tradition, it was Ian Lom MacDonald, the Bard of Keppoch, who came hurrying over the hills to warn Montrose in Abertarff of the danger at his back. Guthrie in his *Memoirs* gives the man's name as Alan MacIldowie of Lochaber. Perhaps there were two messengers. Either way, Montrose is said to have at first expressed strong disbelief at the report that the Campbells were already ravaging in Lochaber, and ordered the man to be put under guard. But further reflection made him realize that this was intelligence which, doubtful or not, he could not afford to ignore. He questioned the messenger again, swearing that there were ropes spun which would hang him if his information proved false, but Ian Lom (if it was he) vehemently attested that what he had said was true, and added that if a particular tower which he named as the last he had seen on fire was not found destroyed, 'he would no longer desire life'.

Three thousand Campbells at Inverlochy put a different complexion on things. Montrose guessed that, given a choice, Argyll would elect not to fight but rather hang on his trail until he was engaged against Seaforth. Then, when the Royalists were committed on that front, or had exhausted themselves in a battle, the Campbell would close in for the kill. Caught between two armies at either end of the Glen, the better strategy was to turn about and attack Argyll even though this meant taking on odds of almost two to one. But the trick would be in bringing him to battle. If the Campbells were indeed at Inverlochy their scouts would already be ranging up the Great Glen and Argyll would have ample warning of any Royalist approach along the valley. Yet to force a fight it was imperative for them to catch him unawares.

After talking further with Ian Lom about the alternative paths through the mountains by which he had come undetected to warn of the Campbells' approach, Montrose called a hurried council of war at which he proposed that they should attack Argyll immediately and destroy the myth of the MacCailein Mhor's omnipotence in the Highlands once and for all. To avoid the enemy advance parties moving up Glen Albin, he suggested that Ian Lom should guide them by a circuitous route over the high plateau of Lairctuirard to the Spean. From there they could swoop down on Inverlochy and, with luck, surprise the Campbells with their backs to the loch and so force an issue on the shore.

It was a plan of exceptional daring. No army had ever traversed that region, and such paths as crossed it were known only to drovers or hunters after deer in the mountains. At this time of year the whole area was covered by deep snow. But the Highland chiefs were fired by the idea of confronting their ancestral enemy in battle strength face to face, and after some argument as to the best route to follow they voted unanimously in support of the venture.

Montrose ordered the army to break camp at once. The prospect before them now was if anything more daunting even than the December march into Argyll. For two days they would be struggling over a high trackless waste, exposed to the intense cold of the Highland winter without pause for rest or shelter, and without food except for what little they could carry or kill along the way. For Thomas Ogilvie's precious troop of horse the going would be truly terrible. And they would have to fight an uneven battle at the end of it. But he believed that if they could catch and engage Argyll at Inverlochy, the superb martial qualities of his men would bring them victory at any odds, for although they numbered only 1,500, the core of the army were Alastair's proven Irish veterans and the rest the flower of western gaeldom. If many of the highlanders were temporarily absent, the small contingents who now marched under their respective chieftains were the hardest fighting men of the loyal clans–Glengarry, Clanranald, Keppoch, Glencoe, MacLean, Cameron of Lochiel, Stewart of Appin, Robertson of Struan–and their fibre made possible the most incredible flanking march in the battle history of Scotland.

They started early on the morning of Friday 31 January, and it took them two days and a night. They climbed abruptly eastwards out of the Great Glen up the lower reaches of the River Tarff and thence onto the high bleak plateau that stretches towards the Pass of Corrie-yarack and the remote headwaters of the Spey. At the narrow entrance to the Glen a picked force of highlanders remained to seal the path behind them and prevent any word of their movements from getting to the Campbells in the valley. Somewhere above Cullachy[19] the main force waded the river and turned south across the moors, moving parallel to Glen Albin until they struck the Calder Burn and then climbed up the steep hollow to its source. From here their route was probably over the shoulder of Carn Dearg (2,500ft) along Alt na Larach (the Burn of the Pass) to the headstreams of the Turret and by Turret Bridge down into Glen Roy. Traditionally they are supposed to have bivouacked briefly at Achvady. This was Keppoch country, but a bare eighteen miles from Inverlochy, and they could now expect to run into Campbell patrols at any time. On the second day the army cautiously descended Glen Roy by the Parallel Roads. On the way they got timely warning of an enemy force out plundering in the area of Bohenie and so kept high on the slopes of Bohenture Hill above the burning village and hurriedly forded the Spean at the shallows below Corriechoille where the Cour flows into the main river. Very close now, they shunned the open Dalach, striking up the Shallow trough of the Cour and along the Altan Loin to the cover of Leanachan and the skirts of Ben Nevis. At five o'clock on the evening of Saturday 1 February they finally halted at the base of Meall-an-t'suidhe, and peering down through the gathering dusk saw below them the castle of Inverlochy and the watchfires of the Campbells. Ian Lom had earned his brogue money.

Nothing could be done at once. The army was strung out along the march and the rear contingents did not arrive until after eight o'clock. The men were falling from fatigue. For even the toughest of the gaelic hillmen the march had been a terrible ordeal. 'The most part had not tasted bread these two days, marching over high mountains in knee-deep snow, wading brooks and rivers up to their girdle.'[20] All were suffering from the extreme cold. The army could not fight without a rest.

Below in Inverlochy, the Campbells were hurriedly standing to arms as word spread around the camp that there was a hostile force of highlanders somewhere on the ridge above them. Shortly before night-fall some of Montrose's men had stumbled into a Campbell patrol and had killed almost all of them, but the one or two who escaped

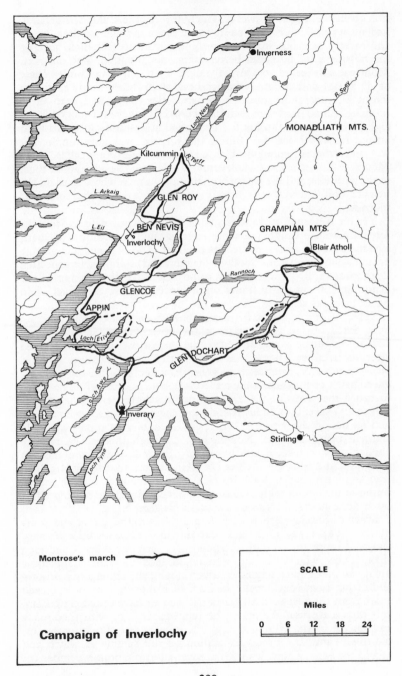

Inverness

MONADLIATH MTS.

Loch Ness

R. Spey

Kilcummin

R. Tarff

GLEN ROY

L. Arkaig

L. Eil

BEN NEVIS

GRAMPIAN MTS.

Inverlochy

Blair Atholl

L. Rannoch

GLENCOE

APPIN

Loch Etive

Loch Tay

GLEN DOCHART

Loch Awe

Inverary

Stirling

Loch Fyne

Montrose's march

SCALE

Miles

0   6   12   18   24

Campaign of Inverlochy

209

had given the alarm. However, Auchinbreck, the Campbell general, had no way of telling the strength of the war band on Ben Nevis and merely sent out small skirmishing parties to feel their way up the hillside until he could better assess the situation. For his part, Montrose still feared that Argyll might try to slip away under cover of darkness, and ordered the freshest of his men to form a thin screen in front of his position to harass the enemy and keep them confused. Small parties on each side were thus engaged throughout the night, and while the musket fire continued at desultory intervals both armies remained wakeful. But if the surprise was not complete, it was nevertheless enough. The Campbells had not realized that Montrose himself and his whole army by some miracle were above them in the darkness, and the weary but triumphant men who waited on the heights now knew that a bloody reckoning was certain come the morning.

Yet for the small Royalist army it was an awful pause. After the terrible march, the night was a long freezing vigil. According to Wishart, 'the moon shone almost as clear as daylight', and they could count the enemy's campfires strung out along the shore and multiplied by reflection in the waters of the loch. They could watch too the stirring in the camp, and in the early hours of the morning saw the MacCailein Mhor leave his army.

Subsequently, Argyll's detractors have been quick to impute this apparent desertion of his clan at the critical moment to personal cowardice. But it is arguable also that Argyll was still incapacitated after his fall from a horse, and could not effectively manage a sword or pistol, while Auchinbreck was generally accepted as the most experienced battle commander among the Campbells and therefore best able to order the army in the fight. Argyll's safety was crucial to the Covenant cause, as both his friends and enemies realized well enough, and so he—or the kinsmen who persuaded him to leave—was only right in being cautious. Nonetheless, although this was a rational enough view to take, it was based on Lowland values, and the fact remains that Argyll was the head of a Highland clan, and by Highland tradition for a chief to leave his clansmen on the eve of battle was an action of dishonour which cannot but have had a demoralizing effect upon some among the gaelic element in his army.[21]

Dawn of Sunday, 2 February, found the Royalists gaunt and wolf-hungry. There was nothing to eat but *drammachs*—a little oatmeal and cold water mixed with the point of a dirk—for officers and men alike. Those who lived and won could feed thereafter. Sometime before daybreak the commanders began moving their men into position—all but Ian Lom MacDonald the Bard of Keppoch, who now walked apart from the rest so that Alastair is said to have asked 'Ian Lom, wilt thou leave us?' To which he replied: 'If I go with thee today and fall in battle, who will sing thy praises and thy prowess tomorrow?'—and so took up his station on the heights to watch and record the fight. There, his presence was an inspiration, for under the eye of the Bard of Keppoch, win or lose today, they would be numbered among the heroes of their race: 1,500 men and a galaxy of chieftains–these would be remembered as the men who fought the Clan Campbell at Inverlochy in Lochaber on the Feast Day of St Bridget 1645.

Montrose deployed his army in four divisions. The right wing, commanded by Alastair, was composed of the musketeers and pikemen of Ranald Og's Irish regiment. Magnus O'Cahan led on the left, his regiment possibly slightly forward of the battle-line and destined to be the first into action, since by engaging the Campbells' right wing from the outset the Royalists could hope effectively to block the rest of the enemy army from escaping south. The Highland contingents held the centre–the Clanranald with the men of Glengarry, Keppoch, Glencoe, Appin, MacLean, Atholl and Lochaber, drawn up in two main battle-lines under their respective chieftains, while behind them Colonel James (O'Neill) MacDonald's regiment of Irish musketeers formed the reserve. Montrose himself took up a position in the centre close to the royal standard which was guarded by Thomas Ogilvie's single troop of horse. The Royalists had no cannon.

It was Candlemas, the first day of Spring, and the Catholics among them knelt silently in their ranks as the Irish priests passed along the files granting absolution and signing their arms with the cross. Gathering in the pickets who had been skirmishing throughout the night, the army then moved down from the heights and took up a position on the lower slopes overlooking the flats of Inverlochy.[22] It was now only a short time to sunrise.

In their camp, the Campbells had passed the night under the impression that the war band above them was merely a party of raiding caterans possibly under one of Montrose's lieutenants.[23] But as it grew light they began to realize that this was a more formidable force than they had at first supposed. Among the dark mass on the hillside they could make out dimly the famous green banner of the Clan MacLean, and when the howls of hatred and defiance started to carry down into the valley the gaelic war-cries that summoned them to death and the savage Cameron *pibroch* calling dogs to eat their flesh enabled them to distinguish separate contingents of their enemy. But full knowledge came only at sunrise, when the fanfare of trumpets to salute the royal standard proclaimed that Montrose himself was upon them with his power.

The word spread swiftly through Argyll's army. They had not thought it possible; had not thought to fight the battle here. Yet the Campbells were no cowards, and though taken by surprise were keen enough to fight. They too had waited for such an hour. They too could recollect a multitude of wrongs perpetrated against their kindred, their cattle taken, homes burned and crops destroyed. All winter the Clan Donald had pillaged unopposed through their land, but now they too were gathered in strength: 3,000 had come to Inverlochy for revenge and among them the prime swordsmen of the

Campbell race. This, then, would be a battle in the antique High-land manner, sword to sword between the clans in might—the final gaelic 'burial blent' that would resolve the issue between the heather and the gale.[24]

Sir Duncan Campbell of Auchinbreck, whom Argyll had left to bear the command, now had cause to regret the careless insecurity in which the Campbell leaguer was sprawled around the estuary where-by one contingent of the army had been allowed to camp on the further side of the Lochy in the angle between Loch Linnhe and Loch Eil. They were thus effectively cut off from the main body, and as the River Lochy then ran rapid and deep would not have time to negotiate the difficult crossing before the battle began. However, if it was a basic error it was not necessarily a fatal one, since the bulk of the force who had bivouacked on the eastern shore still substantially out-numbered the Royalists and could be deployed at once.

Auchinbreck also drew up his army in four divisions along a ridge of firm ground running roughly north–south and rising slightly above the flat alluvial soil of the estuary. The Lowland troops were posted on the wings—about 500 men and 2 cannon in each detachment. These were the companies taken from General Baillie, tried and disci-plined soldiers from Stirlingshire who had marched south with Leven and seen action at Marston Moor and Newcastle. In the centre, the main battle-front comprised the prime Campbell fighting men commanded by the Lairds of Lochnell and Rarra, and the provost of Kilmun, drawn up in a solid mass around the standard and supported by two culverin. In front of them and slightly in advance of the main battle-line the rest of the Campbell clansmen, armed with an assortment of guns, swords and axes, formed a vanguard led by Gillespie son of Gillespie Og, Laird of the Bingingeadhs.[25]

On the extreme left front of the army, almost within pistol shot of the Campbells' flank, stood the old castle of Inverlochy, once the seat of the ancient kings of Caledonia. It was immensely strong, some ninety feet square inside, with a curtain wall thirty feet high and nine feet thick and circular loopholed towers at each of the corners. The whole quadrangle was surrounded by a ditch some forty feet across. Here Auchinbreck stationed 50 musketeers of the Lowland regiments so that from the embrasures their fire would enfilade Montrose's men as they advanced.

It looked a formidable disposition, but the weakness—if Auchinbreck realized it—was two-fold. Out of deference perhaps to the Lowland infantry whose disciplined volleys were expected to stand off a Royalist attack in the conventional manner, he had adopted a static and defensive position. This would mean that if Montrose's highlanders made a charge—as they would surely do—the Campbell clansmen would have to meet it standing. But this was bound to cause unease among his own gaelic contingent who instinctively understood the excitement gener-ated in the charge and the value of its impetus when driven home. The natural Highland mode of fighting was to move to the attack. Secondly, by confining his battle-line to the ridge of firm ground, Auchinbreck seriously restricted the actions of his soldiers. The clansmen in the centre were packed too tight to fight or move effectively.

While the Campbell army was being hastily marshalled into line in front of them, Montrose's highlanders on the hill above could hardly be restrained from rushing down the slope. When Gillespie's vanguard began to advance onto the open ground below the ridge, the whole Royalist battle-line started to edge forward in their impatience to charge, yelling the old war shouts and lashing at the turf in fury with their broadswords. The general action began when O'Cahan's regiment set upon Gillespie's division, holding their fire until the muzzles of their firelocks were in the very faces of the enemy, and then smashing through the ensuing chaos to hurl themselves in a solid wedge against the Lowland troops on the Covenant right. Simultaneously, Alastair threw his Irish division at Auchinbreck's left, and behind him the whole army came streaming headlong down the slope in a wild charge that drove Gillespie's disordered remnants back into the Campbell centre.

On the wings, the Covenant regulars tried to maintain their front and fire in line, but the Irishes ran in low under the volley to discharge their pieces in the very faces of the enemy. The lowlanders had no time to reload before the attack was into them and the gaels went storming through the files with swinging swords and musket butts. In England, Leven's troops had never experienced this butchery at close quarters. Those behind watched the front rank tossed and spitted on the Irish pikes and could stand no more. The flanks of Auchinbreck's army simply disintegrated under the ferocity of the attack, and as the formations broke up in complete disorder the Irishes turned inwards to converge upon the centre. On the Campbell left, some 200 of the Lowland infantry tried to reach the safety of the castle, but Sir Thomas Ogilvie, who was following up the attack, guessed at their intent and led his troop of horse in a charge that drove them back onto the open shore where they could find no hiding place. Tragically, Ogilvie was desperately wounded in the action and was not there to see them make an end.

In the centre, the Campbells on the ridge were packed too tight to open their files and let the fugitives through. The fleeing men were thus brought up short in confusion in front of their own culverin, and as they faltered the gaelic whirlwind engulfed them. They were at once overborne by the whole weight of Montrose's army striking home, and died horribly before the eyes of the watching Campbells who now braced themselves to meet the final charge. The impact, when it came, buckled the line, but for a brief space the Campbell swordsmen held the ridge and a savage mêlée developed along the battle-front. But they were outflanked and unsupported, and the issue was resolved when Alastair himself led his berserkers in an assault against the standard. When the banner finally dipped and fell, the Campbell rank and file turned to flee. Behind them in the loch, the Dubhlinnseach, black galley of Argyll, spread its dark sails like a bird of ill omen and headed out to sea. The MacCailein Mhor left his stricken army to its fate.

Some tried to swim to the ship and were drowned. Others searched hopelessly for a ford across the Lochy. On the beach few if any survived. Here and there a few scattered groups bravely tried to make a stand but were quickly overrun by the exulting MacDonalds. One party of Lowland officers succeeded in reaching the temporary safety of the castle and presently surrendered to Montrose. Most fled along the shore hoping to escape by the way they had come and find refuge in Lochaber, and a running slaughter continued for fourteen (English) miles as the clans chased after them. In all, 1,500 are said to have been killed, and only sheer exhaustion prevented Montrose's highlanders from pursuing them further.

At Inverlochy the Campbell gentry fought to the end, and Wishart later acknowledged their bravery as 'stout and gallant men worthy of a better chief and a juster cause'. Some were taken prisoner, but Auchinbreck himself and forty barons of the clan perished in the battle.

The Royalists had lost less than a dozen men killed outright,[26] but Sir Thomas Ogilvie had been mortally hurt and would die of wounds within a few days. A son of Airlie and a truly gallant cavalier, he had earlier won distinction in the King's service under his father-in-law, Ruthven Earl of Forth, an officer of world-wide renown. He was one of Montrose's closest friends. His body was carried to Atholl by his people to be buried there.

The day after the battle Montrose sent a dispatch to the King. Inverlochy seemed a significant victory and he hoped that the news of it would revive Royalist spirits in both countries. There had been disturbing rumours that Charles was considering negotiation with the Covenant Scots, and after reporting the course of his Highland campaign, the General urged the King to make no concession:

> . . . When I had the honour of waiting upon your Majesty last, I told you at full length what I fully understood of the designs of your Rebel subjects in both kingdoms, which I had occasion to know as much as any one whatsoever, being at that time, as they thought, entirely in their interest. Your Majesty may remember how much you said you were convinced I was in the right in my opinion of them. I am sure there is nothing fallen out since to make your Majesty change your judgment in all those things I laid before your Majesty at that time. *The more your Majesty grants, the more will be asked, and I have too much reason to know that they will not rest satisfied with less than making your Majesty a King of straw.* I hope the news I have received about a treaty may be a mistake, and the rather that the letter wherewith the Queen was pleased to honour me, dated the 30th of December, mentions no such thing. Yet I know not what to make of the intelligence I received, since it comes from Sir Robert Spotiswood, who writes it with a great regret; and it is no wonder, considering no man

Montrose in 1644,
from the portrait by
Dobson (*above*), and
Montrose in 1649,
from the portrait by
Honthorst (*below*),
both in the possession
of the Scottish
National Portrait
Gallery

Archibald, 1st Lord Napier, from an engraving of the portrait by Jameson in the possession of Lord Napier and Ettrick

Archibald, 2nd Lord Napier, from an engraving of the portrait by Jameson in the possession of Lord Napier and Ettrick

George Gordon, 2nd Marquis of Huntly, from an engraving of the portrait by Vandyke in the possession of The Duke of Buccleuch

George, Lord Gordon, from an engraving of the portrait in the possession of The Duke of Hamilton

The Marquis of Argyll in 1652)
from the 'Newbattle Portrait' in the possession of the Marquis of Lothian

living is a more true subject to your Majesty than he. Forgive me, Sacred Sovereign, to tell your Majesty that, in my poor opinion, it is unworthy of a King to treat with Rebel subjects, while they have the sword in their hands. And though God forbid I should stint your Majesty's mercy, yet I must declare the horror I am in when I think of a treaty, while your Majesty and they are in the field with two armies, unless they disband, and submit themselves entirely to your Majesty's goodness and pardon.

As to the state of affairs in this kingdom, the bearer will fully inform your Majesty in every particular. And give me leave, with all humility, to assure your Majesty that, through God's blessing, I am in the fairest hopes of reducing this kingdom to your Majesty's obedience. And, if the measures I have concerted with your other loyal subjects fail me not, which they hardly can, I doubt not before the end of this summer I shall be able to come to your Majesty's assistance with a brave army, which, backed with the justice of your Majesty's cause, will make the Rebels in England, as well as in Scotland, feel the just rewards of Rebellion. Only give me leave, after I have reduced this country to your Majesty's obedience, and conquered from Dan to Beersheba, to say to your Majesty then, as David's General did to his master, 'come thou thyself lest this country be called by my name.' For in all my actions I aim only at your Majesty's honour and interest, as becomes one that is to his last breath, may it please your Sacred Majesty,—

Your Majesty's most humble, most faithful, and most obedient Subject and Servant,

MONTROSE.

Inverlochy in Lochaber,
February 3d, 1645.

13

Dundee
(4 February–6 April 1645)

I will lift up mine eyes unto the hills: from whence cometh my help.
Psalm 121

Whether these things will gain credit abroad, or with after ages, I cannot pretend to say: but I am certain that this narration is taken from the best information, and the most credible evidence. And truly I have often heard those who are esteemed the most experienced officers, not in Britain only, but in France and Germany, prefer this march of Montrose to his most celebrated victories.
Wishart, (1819 edn)

The Marquis of Argyll reached Edinburgh on 11 February and appeared before Parliament the following day, 'having his left arm tyed up in a scarf as if he had been at bones-breaking'.[1] His account of the defeat at Inverlochy was less than full, but the House expressed itself 'fully satisfied' and moved that the President in their name should 'rander him hartly thankes for his greate paines and trauells takin for the publicke, and withall intreated to continew in so laudable a course of doing for the weill and peace of his countrey'. Next day Lord Balmerino contributed further to the public deception by stating 'that the great loss reported to be sustained in that fight was but the invention of Malignants who spake as they wished it . . . and that upon his honour, Argyll had not thirty persons killed in the whole'.

But the true facts could not be suppressed indefinitely and the extent of the disaster soon became widely known.

The news added to a general mood of despondency which had settled over a large proportion of the Scottish people. Initially, the Covenanters had been pleased to contemplate a civil war fought south of the border, across English land and with English money, but now that they were forced to maintain a second front against Montrose, the burden fell directly on the Scots themselves and the true cost of supporting a war on their own soil was being brought home to them. It was not only a matter of the northern lands torn up and devastated by the contending forces–although there was much more of this to come–but in the shires as yet untouched, the citizens had to bear the cost of quartering and equipping troops destined for the North, pay taxes and contribute to war loans–tenths and twentieths to help victual the armies–until some had paid out in a few months more than they could reasonably hope to earn in three years of peace and pros-

216

perity. Letters from Scotland intercepted by the Governor of Newark (and subsequently printed in Oxford for the satisfaction of cavaliers[2]) told the same story. 'For anything that I can see, Scotland shall drink as deep in the cup of the Lord's wrath as either England or Ireland' wrote one correspondent.[3] 'For unless there be some middles found to save the miserable distractions of this kingdom, we and our posterity shall be miserable at best' declared Patrick Maule in a letter to the Earl of Loudoun;[4] and a Mistress Dorothy Spense to an unknown confidant wrote: 'Truly we can promise ourselves nothing but misery. . . . I think that we must drink of that cup England hath begun to us, and I fear we must drink it to the dregs.'[5] Indeed, it would be worse yet.

The General Assembly of the Kirk, meeting in parallel with the Scottish Parliament, reacted to the news of Inverlochy by demanding immediate revenge. A delegation of five ministers which included Andrew Cant, James Guthrie and David Dick, were sent before Parliament to press for the speedy execution of Royalist prisoners then in Covenant hands. They were particularly anxious to secure the deaths of Lord Ogilvie and the Earl of Crawford,[6] at that time incarcerated in the tolbooth of Edinburgh, but there were by now a substantial number of other prominent Royalist prisoners whose lives were also threatened by the ministers. Several of the Grahams–Braco, Orchill, Young Fintry and the elder Inchbrakie–were confined in the Castle, while among others, Harry Graham (Montrose's natural brother[7]), the Lords Maxwell and Reay and Dr Wishart[8] languished in the tolbooth.

Parliament, however, while commending the brethren for this demonstration of 'great zeal and Piety', demurred. They had just received Montrose's cartel despatched after Inverlochy offering an exchange of prisoners, and were understandably frightened lest, with so many prominent Campbells in his hands, the King's lieutenant might choose to retaliate in kind. They therefore suggested that any execution of captured Royalists should be deferred until Montrose 'could be brought lower'.

There was also the question of money. The Commissary-General, Sir Alan Hepburn of Humbie, had presented the army accounts amounting to £1,991,576 and there are indications that the Covenant war chest was short of ready funds at this time. Robert Baillie travelling north spoke to Wariston of a 'dangerous and great' mutiny among the Scottish army at Newcastle, while Master Mowet (one of the Advocates of the Sessions) writing to a London merchant on 12 March, stated that 'parliament before it rose . . . made all the haste it could to provide for monies to our army, which is making against these rebels, for without present pay no souldiers could be moved to advance.'[9] A move was made to divide all Royalist prisoners into three categories– those who from their depositions and other evidence were clearly innocent, those whose involvement was such as to have them permanently confined, and those who could be safely let off with a heavy fine and payment of an additional 'surety'. Sentences of forfeiture were passed on Montrose, Airlie, Black Pate and other principal Royalists still

with the army (Southesk and Dalhousie being the only lords cour-
ageously to vote against the motion). Their coats of arms were deleted
and publicly torn on 11 February,[10] and their estates put up for sale
at twelve years' purchase. Huntly (and subsequently Lord George
Gordon) were also attainted.

The lot of those prisoners not released upon a fine or caution
became increasingly grim. Drum's younger brother, Robert Irving,
died in the foetid tolbooth cell (Drum was given fourteen days in
the better atmosphere of the Castle as a special privilege); Wishart
petitioned Parliament for maintenance since his wife and five children
were on the point of starving; Ogilvie, obdurate as ever, loudly protested his status as a prisoner of war, and the process against him
toiled endlessly on; the Napiers, suspect from the first, were put
under house arrest at their lodgings in Holyrood upon a surety fixed
at £1,000 sterling. Plague was creeping through Edinburgh.

The Covenant authorities had now accepted the fact that Montrose's
army could no longer be passed off as 'a pack of naked runagaits',
but rather that they had a major campaign on their hands in the North.
'Before this time our people did not well awake,' wrote Robert Baillie.[11]
Now priority was given to dealing with the deteriorating situation
in Scotland. In Lieutenant-General Baillie and his subordinate Sir
John Hurry (of whom more anon) they had appointed battle commanders of considerable experience to lead their northern armies. These
were to be reinforced by veteran regiments withdrawn from the South,
while with the war chest augmented by the fines exacted from Royalist
sympathizers, Parliament proposed to raise 10,000 foot and an additional
600 horse. A further 1,400 infantry were recalled from Ireland and 1,500
from Leven's army in England. Finally, a new, more dynamic committee under Lindsay[12] and Lanerick was instructed to assist Baillie
in his operations (an appendage which that soldier would have rather
done without).

All this was not likely to be popular with the English Parliament,
however, and Lanerick wrote to reassure Maitland (now Lauderdale[13])
in London:

> . . . A solid course was taken for maintaining our forces at home
> against our as yet prevailing enemies and recalling such from England
> and Ireland as our Danger and Necessity forced us to; which I
> hope will in no way be misunderstood where you are, seeing the
> only way to make us useful to our friends and considerable every-
> where abroad is to preserve ourselves entire at home.[14]

But this letter, had it ever arrived, would have been of little comfort, since in London the affairs of the Scottish commissioners were
going none too well. The English were less concerned with the fetish
which the Scots had made out of their National Covenant than with
the practical possibility of bringing the Scottish army south as the
nucleus of a new force to be used against the Royalists in the West.
With an army to back them, the Scots had been listened to – a fact of
which Robert Baillie and his colleagues, declarations of brotherly con-

formity notwithstanding, were uncomfortably aware. Indeed, at the outset Alexander Henderson had confessed that 'my hopes are not great of their conformitie to us before an army be in England'. But the depletion of his forces through regiments drafted north to fight the 'rebels' in Scotland and the growing possibility that the King might try to link up with Montrose was keeping Leven close to the Cumberland border. The influence of the Scottish commissioners declined as the English grew more dissatisfied. Initially, the Scots' invasion of the northern counties had saved the situation for the Parliament in England. This had been appreciated. But from their point of view the situation now required that a Scottish army should march south at once, and the English were becoming increasingly impatient of their ally's failure to deliver.

At the same time, although the Scottish commissioners had succeeded in getting a Directory of Public Worship[15] ratified by both houses in England, this did not conceal the further rift that was developing between them and the Independents whose insistence on lay predominance in religious affairs had in the first instance brought them into sharp conflict with Presbyterian ideals. 'The sooner all the reformed declare against them the better,' Baillie wrote,[16] although it had previously been agreed among his colleagues not 'to meddle in haste with the question of Independence till it please God to advance our army which we expect will much assist our arguments'.[17]

At York in 1644, Vane had made a number of proposals to the parliamentary generals which indicated that the Independents were now aiming at the exclusion of the King from any future form of government. The Scottish commissioners had already rejected such an idea and Leven refused to listen to Vane. But Cromwell's quarrel with the Scots appears to date from this time when he became, in Baillie's phrase, 'the darling of the Sectaries'. Manchester, writing in November 1644, spoke of Cromwell's growing dislike of Scots and Presbyterians: 'Against these [the Scots] his animosity was such, as he told me, in the way they now carried themselves, pressing for their discipline, he could as soon draw his sword against them as against any in the King's army.'[18] And Cromwell's star was in the ascendant. In December 1644 the Scottish commissioners attempted to have him impeached, but they were not successful.

Although by January 1645 the split between Presbyterians and Independents was open and possibly irreparable – the first yet hoping to be reconciled to the King; the second seeing in such a reconciliation 'the abandonment of everything worth fighting for at all' – the Presbyterians, or Peace Party, could still command enough support, particularly in the House of Lords and in London, to secure the agreement of Parliament to the opening of negotiations with the King at Uxbridge on 31 January. The Scots were the prime movers in this. It was to be a supreme effort on their part to bring about a Presbyterian settlement, and, if they knew it, it was probably their last chance.

But the conference was doomed to failure. The three propositions (under the headings of 'Religion', 'The Military' and 'Ireland') which the parliamentary commissioners were empowered to lay before the King were totally unacceptable. Charles was to take the Covenant, agree to the abolition of episcopacy and the Prayer Book, to the establishment of Presbyterianism in England and the introduction of the new Directory of Public Worship. The militia and the navy were to be permanently under the control of commissioners appointed by Parliament. The Irish cessation was to be made void by Act of Parliament and the war was to be continued by Parliament without interference from the King. Furthermore, sixty prime cavaliers, including Rupert, Maurice, Montrose, Sir Ralph Hopton and Sir Richard Grenville, were to be excluded from any Act of Oblivion. The historian Gardiner later commented: 'Such demands could only have been made with the object of trampling upon the King's feelings as well as upon his political authority, and it would have been far more reasonable to ask his consent to an Act of Abdication than to such articles as these.'[19]

Discussion on the first of the propositions concerning religion – the most important of the Presbyterians' conditions for peace – developed inevitably into a theological wrangle and subsequent stalemate. Conceiving episcopacy to be a divine institution, the King could not agree to its abolition, but surprisingly it was the royal commissioners who on 13 February tried to break the impasse when they offered a compromise solution proposing that, while episcopacy was to be maintained together with the Book of Common Prayer (subject to such alterations as might be agreed on), there was to be liberty of conscience in matters of ceremony '. . . and all the penalties of the laws and customs which enjoin those ceremonies [were to] be suspended'. Whether or not Charles himself was fully in agreement with such a concession, the suggestion was remarkable in being the first scheme ever to be publicly put forward which embodied the principle of toleration. But the Presbyterians rejected it completely. Their hands were tied by a Covenant which did not permit of negotiation or of any other proposal being considered. The terms for peace were presented for acceptance as they stood, and the Scots could not go even a quarter of the way towards a compromise. Their other propositions were equally unacceptable and equally rigid.

It has sometimes been suggested that Montrose's dispatch from Inverlochy was instrumental in persuading the King to reject the propositions of Uxbridge. But this is not correct. It is true that Charles had been greatly heartened by the news of Montrose's early successes in Scotland. Baillie was to write in April 1645 that 'New divisions at London and the great alterations in Scotland have so far revived the malignitie of the court [and] that which hath been the great snare to the King is the unhappy success of Montrose in Scotland.'[20] Charles had been aware that any settlement at Uxbridge would have affected Montrose, and had previously instructed Secretary Nicholas to write to him '. . . not being ashamed to avow that I shall be much guided by what I shall hear from him, and should be much more ashamed to treat in those things [i.e. concerning Scotland] without at least communicating with him who hath hazarded so freely and generously for me'.[21] But letters written by the King before the arrival of Montrose's dispatch show that he had already given up hope of a successful outcome to the negotiations. News of Inverlochy probably did not reach the Court until 19 February. (Charles wrote to the Queen on that day informing her of the victory.[22]) The talks had bogged down long since and were formally broken off on the twenty-second.

After the fiasco at Uxbridge the situation in England could only deteriorate. Many who had hitherto hoped for reconciliation put the failure of the talks down to the King's obstinacy. The progress of the New Model Ordinance was smoothed through Parliament, and the Presbyterians were compelled to make common cause with the Independents for the prosecution of the war. Scottish influence in England, at its zenith in 1643 and early 1644, now went into ultimate decline. In his Public Letter of 25 April 1645, Robert Baillie admitted to the increasing impotence of the Scottish commissioners in London:

> This long time, the reputation of our nation hath been much lower than before. The lasting troubles which a handful of Irish hath brought upon our whole land, was the beginning of our disgrace. The much talked of weakness of our army in England did add unto it; our necessity to lie upon the Northern Shires, almost exhausted by the King's army before, and their daily outcries of oppression, made it to increase. But that which hath highly advanced it, is our delay to march Southward, after all their importunate calls. These things have made us here almost contemptible. . . .[23]

To retrieve their sinking fortunes in London and in Edinburgh, the Covenanters desperately needed a victory over Montrose. They nearly got it at Dundee.

Montrose was loose in the North again.

After the battle at Inverlochy he rested his army for a few days and then resumed the march towards Inverness–to the relief of many Covenanters, who had expected him to invade the Lowlands. Robert Baillie afterwards maintained: 'I verily think that had Montrose come presently from the battle he should have had no great opposition in all the highlands, in the Lennox, in the Sheriffdoms of Ayr, Glasgow, Clydesdale, scarce till he had come to Edinburgh. But God in mercy to us put other thoughts in his heart; he went incontinent Northward.'[24] But then the Rev Robert Baillie was no general. Montrose could not attempt a descent on the Lowlands with a single troop of horse and had little alternative but to continue his search for cavalry among the Gordon lands–though with greater expectations than heretofore. He had hazarded battle at Inverlochy on the supposition that a victory would attract to his standard those among the loyal clans and families who had previously been deterred by fear of Argyll, and it was logical that he should now put that supposition to the test. Inverness was strongly fortified and garrisoned by two regular regiments of the Covenant. Montrose had neither the time nor the manpower to waste on a siege, and so continued into Moray with a view to seizing Elgin where he had heard that Seaforth, Pluscardine, the Laird of Innes and other Covenanting barons were gathering on 17 February to concert measures for the safety of the North. But this group hurriedly dispersed at the news of the Royalists' approach, and Seaforth, with Pluscardine, his brother Losslyne and Sir Robert Gordon of Gordonstoun, rode in to make their peace. Others, notably the Laird of Innes, 'who for his wit and policy was esteemed an oracle in all that country', and Grant of Ballindalloch, fled to the tower of Spynie, an ancient seat of the bishops of Moray, where they successfully held out until the Royalists had left the area. The Laird of Grant, whose wife, 'that sweet nightingale', was niece to Huntly and a strong Royalist, also joined the army with 300 of his men, attracted mainly by the prospect of plundering Elgin, and he and Seaforth together signed the Kilcummin Bond. Seaforth and his friends were at best doubtful allies, however, and Montrose was content to let them return to their own lands where they promptly resumed their Covenant affiliations.

The Royalist army reached Elgin on 19 February. The magistrates sent a deputation to propitiate Montrose with a gift of 4,000 merks as an inducement not to fire the town, but he answered only that 'he would accept any who would join with him in his Majesty's service and obey him as his Royal Lieutenant'. Elgin was not burned, but Grant's men looted it from end to end.

From the neighbourhood of Elgin Montrose sent proclamations throughout Moray summoning all able men between the ages of sixteen and sixty to enlist under the King's banner under pain of fire and sword. 'This bred gryte feir', and a number of recruits were accordingly forthcoming. Against such as stood out, the King's Lieutenant carried out his threat with the utmost rigour. The lands of the prime Covenanters were systematically pillaged and their property destroyed. The houses of Grangehill, Burgie, Brodie, Cowbin, Innes, Reidhall, Foyness, Pitcash and Ballindalloch were burned. The village of Garmouth was plundered as were the lands of Burgie, Letham, Duffus and the district around the old Abbey of Kinloss, once called the Garden of Scotland. Along Speyside, the fishing boats were scuttled and stakes and salmon nets destroyed. Such ravages were carried out in a comparatively disciplined manner and unauthorized looters were often summarily hanged.[25] It was calculated cruelty. Montrose had come to learn that war, once started, was something total, and could not be limited within any certain degree by only one of the antagonists. It was a stern application of the lessons of 1644.

At Elgin, Nathaniel Gordon rejoined the army, and with him from the Bog of Gight came Lord George Gordon and his younger brother Lewis. They brought 200 well mounted troopers, personal friends and dependants. No welcome could have been too enthusiastic. The Gordon was an experienced soldier, having fought in Alsace and Lorraine under the Mariscal de la Force, and if his escort was small, his influence among his father's people promised much for the future. That night Montrose and Huntly's heir 'supped joyfully together' and discussed the campaign to come. The young Lord Lewis was made welcome too, having proved his courage in the fight at Aberdeen, though he was considered more volatile than his brother and at times perverse. (Huntly's second son, Aboyne, was still cooped up in Carlisle.)

Hope of recruits kept the army in Moray for another week while the Gordon officers, who, with their young chief had watched impotent while Argyll spoiled their lands the previous summer, now seized the chance to pay off old scores in kind. Young Gight and Harthill, who had proved adept raiders during Huntly's rising, pulled off a spectacular if somewhat humorous *coup* as far away as Inverurie, where, on the night of 23 February, they surprised ten Covenanters of Craigievar's troop in their beds, took their horses, money, clothes and weapons, and turned them naked loose into the town – 'whariat Craigievar was heghlie offendit'. By 4 March, however, it was clear that not much was to be gained from the gentry of Moray, but a great deal in Banff and Aberdeenshire, where Lord Gordon's influence would assure him of more substantial reinforcements, and Montrose crossed the Spey and camped at Gordon Castle in the Bog of Gight.

Here personal tragedy overtook him. John, Lord Graham, now only fourteen years of age, fell sick of a fever and died within a few days. He was buried in the kirkyard of Bellie just beyond the castle grounds near the east bank of the Spey.[26] The boy had marched beside his father to Argyll, and through Lochaber to the fight at Inverlochy, and perhaps the long winter campaign had overtaxed his strength. It was a tragic instance of promise unfulfilled. But Montrose, with the weight of the war upon him, had little time to indulge in sorrow, although he must have mourned in private for his eldest son. The army marched again almost immediately.

The news of their approach had caused panic in Aberdeen. The provost, Robert Farquhar, had left for Edinburgh, and the Covenanting ministers all fled the town. The burgesses lived in terror of the Irishes, and now sent a delegation of four 'discreet' commissioners to meet the King's lieutenant in Turriff and ask for mercy. They spoke of the unhappy situation of Aberdeen, preyed upon by both sides in this war, and said that if the Royalists were proposing to occupy the town again, fear of further Irish depredations would spark off a general evacuation of the remaining inhabitants. Montrose had no desire to witness a repetition of the ghastly events of the previous year. He listened sympathetically to their tale of distress and expressed his genuine sorrow for all that they had suffered, giving a personal assurance that the Irishes would not come within eight miles of the gates and that if he or his officers should enter Aberdeen they would seek only entertainment at their own expense. He intended to do no further wrong to

223

this unhappy town, and faithfully kept his promise. The army marched south through Inverurie and camped at Kintore where they were joined by a body of militia and once more by Lord George Gordon who had raised 500 foot and 160 horse from among his father's people.

But here another disaster occurred. On 9 March, Nathaniel Gordon had ridden into Aberdeen with 100 troopers to receive the keys of the town. He released a number of Royalist prisoners who had been warded in the tolbooth, and then raided the Covenant arsenal at Torry where he surprised the guard and carried off a large quantity of pikes and muskets. Then on 12 March Nathaniel Gordon, Donald Farquharson and a number of other cavaliers returned to Aberdeen, apparently for no other reason than to enjoy themselves. They posted no guards at the gates and took no measures for defence, but dispersed through the town, eating, drinking and taking their ease. Certain Covenant sympathizers, seeing this, quickly sent word to Sir John Hurry, who with General Baillie and the main Covenant army was camped at North Water Brig.

Sir John Hurry was nothing if not an opportunist. He was a soldier of fortune who had first won distinction abroad before joining the parliamentary army in England and subsequently deserting to Prince Rupert. He had been knighted by Charles I for bringing the intelligence of Parliament's intention to convey £21,000 to Thame which had occasioned the Battle of Chalgrove Field where Hampden died, but he was captured by Fairfax's men in Lancashire in July 1644. Seeing how the wind drifted, he had successfully changed sides again in August and taken service under the Estates. He came from Pitfichie near Monymusk, and was therefore on familiar ground.[27]

Hurry hastily assembled 160 troopers of Balcarres's horse and dashed to Aberdeen, arriving before the undefended gates at about 8 p.m. on 15 March. The Covenant dragoons burst into the town and galloped through the streets cutting down any Royalists whom they caught in the open. Experience of such raids perhaps kept Nathaniel Gordon safe indoors, but Donald Farquharson went into the street to find out the cause of the sudden commotion and was at once attacked by several of Hurry's men. He tried to defend himself with his sword, but they shot him down with their pistols and stripped his body where it lay. Then, having secured a number of prisoners, most of them wounded, and all the Royalists' horses, the Covenanters withdrew. Not content with this successful *coup de main*, Hurry rode next to Old Montrose where he seized Montrose's second son, the twelve-year-old James (now Lord) Graham, with his 'pedagogue' and carried them off to Edinburgh to be imprisoned in the Castle.

The King's Lieutenant was understandably furious with Nathaniel Gordon for his carelessness. Donald Farquharson had been one of the best and most popular of his captains, and a man whom he could ill afford to lose. Farquharson's naked corpse was found in a gutter and placed in the Old Chapel of St Ninian on the Castle Hill until it could be buried in the Laird of Drum's aisle in St Machars. The magistrates of Aberdeen were terrified that the Royalists would take indiscriminate revenge for Farquharson's betrayal, and came again to the camp to protest their innocence in the affair. Montrose, almost beside himself with anger and grief, returned them an indifferent answer, but in fact he did not intend to confound the innocent with the guilty. Alastair was sent with 1,000 of his men to arrange the funeral, but he stationed the bulk of them at Bridge of Dee and the Two Mile Cross, and he and Lord Lewis Gordon entered the town with only a bodyguard. But this time the gates were kept strongly guarded. The cost to Aberdeen was a levy of £10,000 (Scots) to clothe the Irish regiments who on this occasion behaved with almost complete sobriety. When Alastair left on 18 March a few Irishes thought to remain behind and exact private levies of their own, but on hearing of this he promptly went back and 'callit all the rascallis with sore skinis out of the towne befoir him'.

At Kintore, the old Earl of Airlie also fell ill with a fever and was carried to Lethintie where his daughter was the châtelaine. When his condition did not improve, Montrose sent him with a strong escort to Strathbogie (Huntly Castle).

Continuing southwards, the Royalists again spared Monymusk and the Burnett lands about Crathes, and Montrose crossed the Dee to join with Alastair at Durris which was burned together with Covenant estates in Fintray. On 19 March Montrose led the army by Elsick Mounth to Stonehaven, and, having tried unsuccessfully to negotiate with Marischal, he devastated the area around Dunnottar before moving on through Fettercairn and Arbuthnott destroying Covenant properties as he went. However, the King's Lieutenant gave express orders that the town of Montrose was to be left unspoiled and it thus escaped damage. At Fettercairn the Manse was burned and, more regrettably, a band of Irishes went to the house of Middleton nearby and pitilessly killed the old laird, John Middleton of Cadham and that Ilk, as he sat with his family at the fireside. This was a wanton murder. The young Middleton, who had fought under Montrose at Bridge of Dee, was by now a senior Covenant cavalry officer, and when the time came he would repay. They encountered little opposition. At Halkerton Wood a detachment of Covenant cavalry under Sir John Hurry were severely mauled by the Irish musketeers when they attempted an ambush, and on 25 March, the Royalists continued unmolested to Brechin where they burned sixty houses and plundered the castle. The town had been occupied by the enemy only a few days previously, and Montrose now obtained detailed intelligence of the main Covenant army. Hurry's daring raids, the Halkerton skirmish notwithstanding, had been a clear indication of a new and more enterprising spirit among the Covenant commanders. Present news of Baillie's appointment confirmed this. The Covenant army had been reinforced by Lothian's and Loudoun's regiments, and by the 1,400 men recalled from Ireland, bringing their numbers up to something over 3,000 foot and 700 horse–and these veteran troops with experienced generals. Against this Montrose now had 3,000 foot and only 300 horse, but despite this inferiority in cavalry and the improved calibre of his opponents, the King's Lieutenant decided that the time had come to carry the war south. In fact, he was under considerable pressure to do so since a Scottish gentleman named James Small had recently got through the Lowlands disguised as a beggar to deliver a letter from the King in which Charles spoke of coming north to the border in person and promised to send Musgrave ahead with 500 cavalry to link up with Montrose somewhere in the Lothians.[28] But before he could cross the Forth and break through to the Lowlands it would be necessary to bring Baillie to battle and defeat him.

The Covenant general roughly guessed as much and decided to defend the river crossings. Shadowed by Baillie, the Royalists moved South, keeping close to the safety of the Grampians where the Covenant cavalry could gain no advantage. There was a brief confrontation across the River Tay, but Montrose dared not risk a crossing under fire, and with Baillie still hovering cautiously on his flank he withdrew to Inverquharity Castle and subsequently to Alyth. On 29-30 March the two armies again faced each other across the River Isla, but having stood-to all night neither would attempt a crossing for fear of being attacked at a disadvantage. Montrose could least afford this delay and sent a challenge to the Covenant general offering to withdraw two miles and allow him safe passage of the ford if he would agree to fight thereafter. But Baillie would have none of it and answered that 'he would mind his own business himself and would fight at his own pleasure and not another man's command.'

After two days of this frustration, Montrose decided to try to elude Baillie altogether and decamped to Dunkeld, while the Covenanters, keeping always to the south of him, moved off in the direction of Perth. But the King's Lieutenant was now in a serious dilemma. In the North, the Forbeses, Frasers and other Covenanting tribes were banding together for a grand retaliatory foray against the house of Huntly, and he was compelled to grant leave of absence to many of the Gordons who wished to protect their own lands.[29] As against Baillie's growing forces his army was once more reduced to a bare 2,000 men. As usual, the highlanders would not submit to the restraint of remaining continuously with the army, and a number had gone home. Others, impatient to fight, had wearied of the constant marching and manoeuvre and deserted also. And as 'many of them shrunk dayly away' it became clear that the descent on the Lowlands would again have to be postponed. Montrose was coming to the conclusion that, if he was ever to get the Gordon cavalry to ride south in force, it would first be necessary to win a decisive battle in the North itself to secure their lands from future Covenant reprisals, the fear of which was making them unwilling to venture far from home. But Montrose was also uncomfortably aware of the probable boost to Covenant morale if he were simply to withdraw north again without having accomplished anything, and he now looked around for something to do which might in some way redeem the campaign and prevent it from appearing altogether ineffectual.

On 3 April his scouts brought word that Baillie's army had crossed the Tay to seize the fords of Forth against his coming, and thus reckoning that the Covenanting forces were marching away from him, he decided to make an 'infall' or surprise attack on Dundee which Baillie's movement had left unprotected. It was an enterprise calculated to raise the spirits of his men, since Dundee was a fat target, being a Covenant stronghold and, if not the largest, probably the most opulent city in Scotland. What he could not know was that his scouts' information had been incorrect. They had seen only a part of the Covenant army cross the Tay–the main force had gone no further than Perth.

Unaware of the danger, Montrose detached the wounded, the women and those who were less well armed, with orders to march with the baggage to Brechin where he would rejoin them later. Then, with a picked force of 300 Irishes, 300 Gordon foot and 150 horse, he left Dunkeld at about midnight and set out for Dundee. They arrived in front of the town at 10 a.m. the next morning (4 April), and John Gordon, one of Rothiemay's men, was sent under a flag of truce to demand its surrender in the King's name. The Covenanters according to their custom, arrested him, and perhaps hoping to gain time, sent no reply. After a suitable interval, Montrose climbed Dundee Law from where he could overlook the fight, and ordered his men to begin the assault.

At that time the street plan of Dundee somewhat resembled a parallelogram, with a church and market place at the centre of the town converged on by four main streets, two from the east and two from the west. In the north-west corner, within the walls, cannon mounted in the bastion on Corbie Hill[30] commanded the entire town and its defence works. Other cannon were positioned to fire along the streets. The encircling walls had been built by the French troops of Mary of Lorraine and were correspondingly strong and well designed with eight main portes each mounting heavy ordnance. But there was one weak spot, at the point closest to the Corbie Hill where the wall was under repair, and municipal indecision had delayed the work. In April 1645 there was no regular garrison and the ramparts were manned by militia and by the townspeople themselves led by a Lieutenant Cockburn, who had been lying ill with gout but had had himself carried out in a chair to direct the defence.

The Royalists invested the perimeter at three different points, but not surprisingly the main assault was directed at the weak section of the wall. Overcoming the spirited but unprofessional resistance of the town militia, the Irishes did not take long to force an entry and then promptly stormed the Corbie Hill where the cannon were swung round to bear on the West and Nethergate Ports. Bombarded from behind, the other defenders were forced to fall back into the streets, and elsewhere the main strongpoints were quickly overrun. From Corbie Hill a hundred-yard dash and some sharp fighting brought the Irishes to the market place where they were joined by the other Royalist contingents who had also fought their way inward, and the centre of the town was in Montrose's hands. The church of St Mary and a number of houses along the Bonnethill went up in flames almost at once, but in general the Royalists were now intent on plunder before anything else and wanted to loot the town before burning it. Although sporadic fighting continued in the alleys and side streets, more and more men broke off to begin the spoil, and many to undertake a thorough investigation of the citizens' wine cellars. Before long the bulk of Montrose's force were squabbling over vast quantities of booty and the most part were in a state described by Wishart as '*vino paululum incalascentes*' or in other words, moderately drunk.

The process of pillage and outrage in varying degrees had continued well into the afternoon when suddenly scouts came galloping in with news that the entire Covenant army including a large force of cavalry was barely two miles away and that Hurry's troopers would be on them in less than half an hour. Something close to panic gripped Montrose's officers as he hastily called a council of war. Opinion was divided as to what should be done, though no one believed that the situation could be saved. The troops now scattered through the town, partially drunk and out of control, could not possibly be dragged off their prey in time. Quite apart from the exertions of plunder, they were exhausted after a march of twenty miles and the fight on the walls, while it was a clear thirty miles or more to the hills and safety. Some friends urged Montrose to abandon the army and save himself. They argued that this was only a portion of his total force and its loss would still be less numerically than the casualties already inflicted on the Covenant in his previous victories. He, however, was the very heart and mainspring of the royal cause in Scotland, and if the King's Lieutenant was taken all would indeed be lost. Others, more hot-headed, declared that all was lost save honour, and advocated one final charge against the enemy in the certainty of finding death and glory on the battlefield.

But Montrose would accept neither course. He exclaimed that nothing would induce him to desert the bravest of his men in their hour of utmost peril, while to charge headlong into Hurry's dragoons was nothing less than an act of despair. Shouting to his officers 'to do their duty manfully, and leave the issue to God and the means to him', he galloped down into Dundee to rally his drunken scattered army.

At that time, to call off irregular soldiery from their privilege of plunder and debauch was considered impossible. But it was done. As drummers frantically beat out the instant recall, officers and sergeants moved eastwards through the town, dragging their dazed and bewildered troops into the streets and driving them towards the Seagate and East

Ports which were furthest from the Covenanters' approach. Drunk or sober, wounded and encumbered, many reluctant and some in panic, Montrose somehow got his men out of the death trap, and the last Royalist staggered through the seaward gate just as Baillie entered the West Port of Dundee.

If his men could still march, Montrose knew he was in with a chance. Even in their present state, his highlanders could outdistance heavily armed regulars. The danger was Hurry's cavalry, but it was by now 6 p.m. and would soon be dark. It was a question, then, of surviving until nightfall. Four hundred of the more inebriated were set marching straight away with instructions to keep close order and not break ranks, closely followed by 200 men in better condition and able to fight if need be. Montrose himself commanded the rearguard, composed of the cavalry riding in open order and interspersed with light musketeers. The column headed eastwards along the coast away from the town.

In Dundee, Baillie soon ascertained Montrose's weakness and the direction of his escape, but delayed until the infantry had arrived before ordering the pursuit. The Covenant army divided into two. Hurry was to take a division of the cavalry and attack the Royalists' flank and rear, while Baillie himself led the bulk of his force to circle inland parallel to the fugitives' line of march and cut them off from the safety of the hills. Even in the event of Hurry's failing to rout the column in retreat, the Covenant commander-in-chief confidently expected to trap Montrose against the sea and destroy him in the morning. To encourage the troops, 20,000 gold pieces were offered for the King's Lieutenant's head.

Hurry's troopers quickly overtook the Royalist rearguard but were repulsed with loss. This discouraged them, even as it raised the spirits of Montrose's men who gained in confidence as each attack was successfully beaten off. Baillie afterwards complained that, although he had expressly ordered Hurry to charge the column on numerous occasions, the latter had refused to do so, and his failure to keep up the attacks may possibly be ascribed to a disagreement with his commander-in-chief. Certainly the two men disliked each other, and Baillie suffered from an almost paranoid belief that Hurry and others had conspired to deprive him of the credit due. At any rate, Hurry lost his chance to finish with the Royalists and was obliged to break off the running fight at nightfall leaving Montrose's rearguard still intact.

During the early part of the night the Royalists continued along the coast by Carnoustie and at about midnight arrived at Eliot Water near Arbroath. Montrose guessed accurately that somewhere to his left Baillie's main army was marching to block his way to the Grampians, and now adopted one of those daring stratagems that marked his genius as a soldier. He halted the column and swiftly doubled back on his tracks as far as Panbride, where he took the small road west to Carmyllie and thence by Guthrie and Melgund to Careston Castle on the South Esk, having passed around Baillie's force during the small hours of the morning.

Careston Castle, a Carnegie property, could offer only temporary sanctuary, but at this point the men could go no further. In thirty hours they had marched something over sixty miles, stormed a town, got drunk and fought innumerable skirmishes. Many were virtually unconscious on their feet, and now they collapsed in heaps around the castle lawns and slept like dead men. Montrose sent a messenger to Brechin and was relieved to learn that the remainder of his force which had waited for him there had had warning of Baillie's approach and were already moving into the shelter of the hills. A large part of the army at least was safe.

However, dawn found Baillie at Forfar, where he discovered that Montrose had eluded him in the dark, and immediately the Covenant cavalry began to sweep the area in search of the Royalists. It did not take long for Hurry's patrols to discover their position and lookouts shortly brought word to Montrose that a large force of enemy cavalry with infantry in support was converging on the castle. Careston was barely three miles from the hills and safety, but it seemed at this point that those last three miles would still be their destruction. The exhausted men would not awake. The officers finally had to jab them with their sword points before they would stir, and then the column was somehow formed again and the retreat continued. Once more the rearguard fought doggedly mile by mile to hold off Hurry's horsemen as the battered little army stumbled on towards the mountains—until, incredibly, they got to safety. And when he saw the Royalists slipping away into the upper reaches of the Esk, Baillie called off his forces and prepared to answer for his failure.

The Covenant authorities had a pamphlet printed for distribution in Scotland and London optimistically entitled *An Exact Relation of the Victory obtained by the Parliamentary Forces of Scotland against the Rebels under the command of the Earl of Montrose*. In this they claimed that between 400 and 500 Irishes had been killed—including two of high rank:

> . . . for when they fell there was a terrible howling among them and they fought desperately to recover their bodies; one of their faces was so disfigured and mangled by the Irish themselves, not being able to carry away his corpse, that it was not possible to discern who it was. Some say it is Colonel Kittoch; others say it is O'Cain. . . .

As against this, the Covenanters were said to have lost 17 or 18 persons killed altogether.

During the retreat, the broadsheet maintained, Sir John Hurry attacked the Royalist rearguard 'and did good execution upon them'. Many stragglers had been cut down by the cavalry, and some had been killed by the country people. Hurry had annihilated 80 more

near Edzell. The Royalists had abandoned all their baggage and ammunition.

In London this propaganda was successful initially, and on 25 April
Robert Baillie wrote to his cousin that

> It was a matter of exceeding great joy unto us to hear of the
> great and first real disaster that Montrose got at Dundee and of the
> posture of our country at last, according to our mind, after the
> flight of the enemy, the killing of four or five hundred of the
> Irishes, the dissipating of most of the Scots highlandmen, the loss
> of their ammunition and most of their arms, the returning of the
> remnant to the hills and woods.[31]

But among the Covenant leadership in Scotland, where people knew
better, there was recrimination and dispute. General Baillie was particularly incensed at Sir John Hurry's part in the affair, believing that
the latter had deliberately mishandled the situation: 'Yet he was
exonered there and I charged with their escape.'[32]

And in Glenesk, the small Royalist army was exhausted but un-
beaten. A few men had fallen prisoner at Dundee but none had been
lost during the retreat. Alastair and O'Cahan, contrary to report,
were very much alive, and for Montrose, in Sanderson's archaic phrase:
'And now being safe, he leids his soldiers sleep, whilst his noble and
unwearied soul sits awake with resolves of warlike affairs.'

14

Auldearn
(7 April–9 May 1645)

Many were the warlike feats performed on that battlefield by the MacDonalds and the Gordons; many were the wounds given and received by them without mentioning the casualties and great slaughter; as Montrose had stated in treating of that day in another place, that he himself saw the greatest feats performed and the greatest slaughter by six men that he has seen performed by himself or any other person since: and of these six were Nathaniel Gordon, Ranald Og son of Alaster son of Alaster son of Angus Uaibhreach, and Lord Gordon himself, and three others whoever they are.

The Book of Clanranald

In Glenesk, while the Royalists rested, the King's Lieutenant paused to think. The threat of fresh Covenant depredations in the North was drawing his Gordon contingent home again, and it is possible that Lord Lewis deserted the army at this time, having persuaded a number of his people to do likewise. With something less than 2,000 men remaining, Montrose was now too weak to risk a head-on clash with the main Covenant forces under Baillie, and a descent on the Lothians was clearly no longer practicable. There seemed to be no alternative, therefore, but to begin all over again, and he set himself once more to the wearisome task of recruiting another army around the old nucleus of the loyal Irish regiments.

The small force split up. Lord George Gordon led his men north again to raise recruits in Banff and Aberdeenshire against the Covenanting barons, Forbes, Frendraught, Fraser and their kin, who were banding together for an attack on the Gordons' lands. He crossed the Dee at Mills of Demetty on 8 April (rumour of his coming having caused a number of Covenant gentry who were conferring with Marischal at Aberdeen to disperse hurriedly) and went on to consolidate the defences of his father's principal castles at Huntly, Auchindoun and the Bog of Gight.

Alastair took a war band into the Braes of Mar and through Glen Tanar to beat up recruits and create a diversion in that area, while Black Pate returned to Atholl to call in the Stewarts and Robertsons and others of the Badenoch men who, according to their custom, had gone home on furlough after the victory at Inverlochy.

Montrose himself retained a small force of 500 foot and 50 horse. He seems to have had little or no intelligence of Covenant dispositions after the successful retreat from Dundee, but he heard that

Aboyne with 16 other cavaliers had broken out of Carlisle (then under siege) and so thought to march in the direction of Strathearn where it would be easier for them to find him. He stayed hidden in the mountains for something over a week, possibly hoping that the Covenanters' attention would be diverted by the movements of Alastair and Lord George Gordon, and then led his small force south to Dunkeld. By 17 April he was at Crieff, camped in MacCallum's Wood near the castle of Inchbrakie and uncomfortably close to Baillie's army which was occupying Perth barely seventeen miles away. (According-ing to a tradition in the Graham family, Montrose at this time escaped from a Covenant patrol by hiding in a large yew tree which stood in the courtyard of Inchbrakie Castle.)

When Baillie was informed of Montrose's approach, he hastily as-sembled his regiments and marched all night with the intention of surprising the Royalists at daybreak. But he was not to be given another chance so soon, and long before the Covenanters had got within striking distance, Royalist lookouts saw them coming and gave the alarm. While his men stood to, ready to fight or retreat, Montrose himself rode forward to reconnoitre the enemy's advance, and seeing that the entire Covenant army was deploying against him quickly ordered the infantry to withdraw westwards up Strathearn while with his remaining 50 troopers he fought a series of rearguard actions to cover the retreat. The Covenant cavalry chased them for ten miles through Comrie and almost as far as Loch Earn until the Royalists reached and occupied the narrow pass into the hills and Baillie was forced to call off the pursuit.

Montrose now continued along the southern shore of Loch Earn, spoiling the house and lands of Kilpont's murderer, Ardvoirlich, and then by Lochearnhead, Balquhidder and Strathyre into the Trossachs, recruiting from among the outlawed Clan MacGregor. On 19 April the small band of fugitives from Carlisle successfully found them at Loch Katrine, having crossed the Forth at the Ford of Cardross—Aboyne with a badly dislocated shoulder injured during the escape, but seemingly none the worse for it.[1] On the same day, passing through Menteith, Montrose was joined by his nephew, the Master of Napier, who had escaped from Holyrood together with John Alexander, a younger son of the Earl of Stirling.

But although the calibre of these friends and the warmth of the reunion, especially with young Napier, of whom he had always been extremely fond, must have gladdened Montrose's heart, reinforcements in any numbers still eluded him. The 500 English cavalry under Musgrave had not come—nor would ever. It seemed his fate always to be disappointed. From Doune on 20 April, he wrote again to the King:

> . . . Only this much I must tell you (to decline in short all your doubts) that had I had but for one moneth the use of those 500 horse, I should have seene you (before the time that this can come to your hands) with twenty thousand of the best this Kingdome can afford; though I may justly say I have continued things this

halfe yeare bygone without the assistance of either Men, Armes, Ammunition, or that which is the Nerffes of warre; so that had we not been supported by divine providence Our Army could not have subsisted, and I cannot chuse but think it strange that this unhappy Country which had beene the bane and cause of all your woes, being now in so faire a way of reducing, that not only the ordinary but easy meanes should have been neglected. Howsoever though you have not assisted me, I will yet still do my best to barre all assistance coming against you, and to the better; for besides all their new levies and recruits are barr'd, they have beene forced presently to draw 4 Regiments of Foote from Newcastle downe here to oppose me, notwithstanding the weakness of their numbers there already. So (though above all things I should wish an happy Accomodation 'twixt his Majesty and His Subjects) let nothing that may be apprehended from this, move the King to any thing that is dishonourable; for so long as it pleases God I am alive and free, there shall nothing trouble His affaires from this: Wherefore let him be pleased to make His Conclusions from the face of things here, which I pray God give an happy aspect to, and so I will caste me into your hands and seigne myselfe,

Your most faithfull and humble Servant
MONTROSE.[2]

Understandably he was discouraged. There was no longer any mention of marching to the border. The victory at Inverlochy seemed to have achieved little or nothing. Unsupported, and still looking for an army, he could only fight to contain the forces of the Covenant in Scotland.

As usual, the letter was carried by James Small. But unfortunately, this gentleman's luck had run out. He was caught near Alloa and hanged in Edinburgh on 1 May. From Montrose's point of view the capture of his courier was arguably a disaster of considerable proportions. From the papers found about his person the Covenanters were able to deduce that the King's position in England was more critical than they had hitherto been led to suppose, while they were made more fully alive to the danger of Charles's attempting to come north to join with Montrose—a move that was clearly under consideration, and one that would shift the seat of the war to Scotland with the possible result that the Estates themselves would be obliged to seek some kind of accommodation. In retrospect, Civil War historians such as Carte would maintain that, had the King succeeded in marching North, his presence would have removed the principal difficulties which then beset Montrose. Huntly's opposition on the grounds, real or pretended, that he held the King's commission as Lieutenant in the North of Scotland would have ceased abruptly had Charles been there to command in person, and the entire Gordon clan would have ridden out in the King's service. In potentially Royalist areas the power of the Covenant, dependent as it was on terror, would have been broken. Lowland Royalists, cautious hitherto, could have been sure of support. A large proportion of Leven's army, already discontented through lack of pay promised by their English confederates, might have changed sides. In Montrose, with Rupert in concert, Charles would have had a general superior to any in England. All this might have been. Royal indecision let slip the chance, and Naseby would finally end the hope that the King might be able to lead his army into Scotland. But at this time, even the prospective advantages were to a large extent annulled by the seizure of Small. Charles did not receive Montrose's letter and hesitated for lack of news and clear-cut advice, while for their part the Covenant authorities, having correctly interpreted the intelligence that had thus fallen into their hands, at once put measures in train to prevent any junction of the Royalist armies in the Lowlands. South of the border the disposition of Leven's forces was rearranged so that when Charles did eventually come slowly north he found the way barred against him. In Scotland the Estates ordered a new levy of 8,800 infantry and 485 cavalry from the counties south of the Tay, and sent for another 1,000 regular troops from Ireland. After Dundee the Covenant army in Scotland had divided. Baillie kept his main force at Perth to block the passes to the capital and the southern shires, and he was now given specific instructions to contain Montrose within the Highland line until the fresh levies arrived. Sir John Hurry had gone north with two regular regiments of foot (Loudoun's and Lothian's) and Hackett's regiment of horse with orders to link up with the two regiments at Inverness (Lawers's and Buchanan's). The Estates also reckoned on being able to raise substantial forces north of the Grampians in Moray, Nairn and Sutherland. Baillie and Hurry would then concert to grind Montrose between them.

A messenger from Lord George Gordon found Montrose near Loch Katrine and gave him news of Hurry's march. The Covenant general had reached Aberdeen on 11 April. A mutiny in Lothian's regiment concerning clothes and pay kept him there until 19 April, when he marched north to Engzie, bypassing the Gordon strongholds for the moment, and camped by the Over and Nether Bukies. So far he had succeeded in raising only 400 dragoons, but at Engzie he was joined by the Lords Finlater, Crichton and Boyne with their followers, bringing his numbers to around 1,000 foot and 600 horse. Lord George Gordon had withdrawn to Auchindoun and was expecting Hurry to attack at any time.

Montrose could not risk the Gordons being defeated, and decided to march north at once. At the same time it suited him that Baillie and Hurry should have split their forces. Combined he could not hope to match them on the battlefield, but divided, there was a chance that he might be able to engage and defeat each in turn.

Alastair now made a diversionary raid into Angus. He had succeeded in raising a number of recruits in Cromar including Forbes of Skellater with 200 of his followers, and with these, together with his own war band, he swooped down on Coupar Angus, regrettably killing the minister, Patrick Lindsay, and burning the lands of Lord Coupar (Balmerino's brother). Baillie, who might have blocked Montrose's route at Atholl, was drawn away eastwards, but after routing a troop of Balcarres's horse Alastair's men swiftly disappeared into the hills again.

Montrose seized this opportunity to slip back through Balquhidder to Loch Tay, and then by the familiar road across the shoulder of Schiehallion to Loch Tummel and thence to Atholl. There Black Pate rejoined him with his men, and he continued north with characteristic speed, probably by Glen Isla, Clova and Capel Mounth to Glen Muick, emerging onto Deeside by Knock Castle and so to Aboyne. Alastair came in from Glen Tanar, and Lord George Gordon from Auchindoun, and the army thus reassembled leaguered at Skene. It was the last day of April.

The Royalists now numbered about 2,500 foot and 250 horse, thus over-matching Hurry's force at Engzie. However, they were desperately short of ammunition once more and so paused for a day while Aboyne, who had inherited his full share of the Gordon raiding spirit, led 80 troopers into Aberdeen and carried off 20 barrels of gunpowder from two ships that were moored in the harbour. Having obtained the wherewithal to fight, Montrose marched to Strathbogie on 2 May.

Hurry had believed the King's Lieutenant to be still south of the Grampians, and at the startling news that a superior Royalist force was barely six miles distant he hastily decamped and crossed the Spey into Moray. Montrose followed him on 3 May, and his advanced patrols came in contact with the Covenant rearguard next day. A running fight developed along the road to Inverness as the Royalist cavalry pressed Hurry on the march, charging whenever he made a stand, and constantly skirmishing around his flanks. But the Covenant general knew what he was about, and while his forward units stayed safely ahead of the pursuing force it suited him to keep up a series of rearguard actions which drew Montrose further into Moray and away from the hills and friendly Gordon territory. For six days he was content to retreat along the coast, by Elgin and Forres towards Nairn, always in contact but never giving battle–and waiting for Montrose to over-reach himself as he was sure he would.

On 8 May Hurry successfully linked up with reinforcements from Inverness and turned round to strike. He now had four veteran front-line regiments (Loudoun's, Lothian's, Lawers's and Buchanan's), two of lesser calibre (Seaforth's and Sutherland's) whom he had previously ordered to muster at Inverness, besides several irregular bodies of Frasers, Forbeses, Rosses, Monroes, MacIntoshes, MacLennans and other Covenanting clans, and the armed followers of Innes, Finlater, Boyne, Birkenbog and others of the Morayshire gentry–about 4,000 foot and 600 horse all told–and the hunted was become the hunter.

By the evening of 8 May the Royalists had reached the little village of Auldearn, an ancient seat of the Deans of Moray, about four miles east of Nairn. Moving deeper into hostile country, Montrose had been unable to obtain any precise intelligence of Hurry's army. He knew in general terms that there was a plan for a rendezvous at Inverness, but he did not know that this junction had already taken place. His own forces had been somewhat reduced during the previous few days by the departure of the Athollmen who had returned home on hearing that Baillie had marched into Atholl and was burning their lands, but in his anxiety to bring Hurry to battle this had not deterred him from continuing the pursuit. The night was wild and wet, and the Royalist scouts, in unfamiliar country, did not go far from the camp. Only a freak of the wind gave them warning of Hurry's approach.

The Covenanters had marched all night by Culloden Muir and Kilravock, hoping to surprise the Royalists at daybreak–and would have succeeded but for the fact that it had been raining continuously during the march so that near Nairn the infantry were ordered to clear their muskets in case the powder in the barrels had been soaked and spoiled. Rather than go through the laborious process of drawing the charges, the musketeers cleared their weapons by firing them into the air (a common practice then and later), thinking that on so wild a night the sound would never carry as far as Auldearn. But by some chance of the wind one of Nathaniel Gordon's advanced outposts heard the volley and gave the alarm. The Royalists had almost an hour in which to prepare.

Montrose was suddenly in a perilous situation. Now that Hurry had been joined by the Inverness regiments, his army of Irishes and Gordons was outnumbered by a clear two to one in unfamiliar and unfriendly country and on unreconnoitred ground. Under normal circumstances he would have preferred to retreat while he still could, at least as far as the Spey, but he had had news that General Baillie was also marching northwards and realized that if he withdrew now, not only would he have lost his chance to engage Hurry's army in isolation, but he would also run the risk of being caught between two Covenant armies acting in conjunction, each of them numerically superior to his own. He decided therefore to stand and fight.

At that time the village of Auldearn consisted of a number of cottages built along a ridge running roughly south from the church of St John on the line of the present Boath Road. At its northern end the ridge merged into a steep circular mound called the Castle Hill (the present site of Boath Dovecot). The steep side of the ridge itself faced west, almost at right angles to the road along which Hurry would approach, and on this slope below the cottages, the gardens and enclosures of the villagers, fenced in by a series of dry stone walls, formed a natural system of defence works. Beyond, the ground over which the Covenanters would attack was at first comparatively flat, though covered by bushes and rough undergrowth, but it then sank away gradually into a marsh. This was caused by a burn that flowed south-westwards from near the Castle Hill before curving back into a ravine which thus protected the southern end of the ridge where it continued behind the village. At the southern edge of the hamlet, behind the ridge, the ground sloped gently back into a large hollow which was masked by the higher ground from anyone looking eastwards from the direction of Inverness. Thus, while the burn and marshland

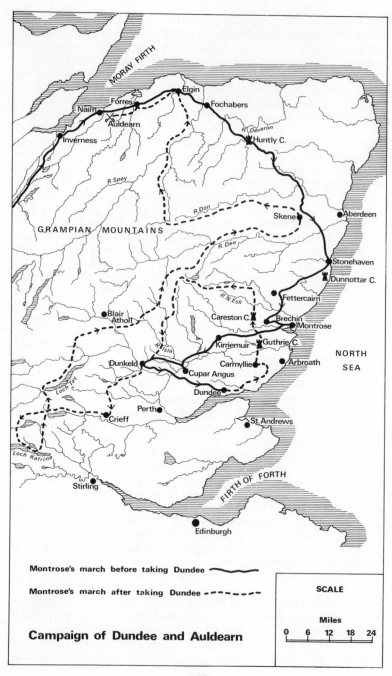

Montrose's march before taking Dundee ——————

Montrose's march after taking Dundee ----------

Campaign of Dundee and Auldearn

SCALE

Miles

0   6   12   18   24

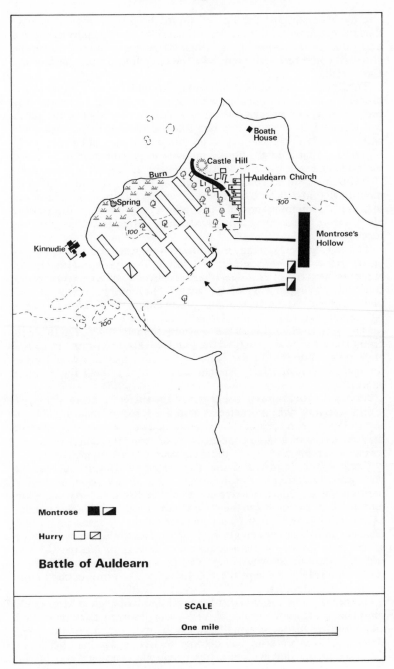

Boath
House

Castle Hill

Burn

Auldearn Church

Spring

100

Montrose's
Hollow

Kinnudie

100

100

Montrose

Hurry

Battle of Auldearn

SCALE

One mile

effectively constricted the line of approach and prevented any out-
flanking movement, the steep slope of the ridge broken up by the walled
enclosures would constitute a strong defensive position. The whole
situation could be overlooked from the church tower just back of the
Castle Hill.

The Royalists are said to have camped 'commodiously',[3] and it seems
probable that a large portion of the army, strung out in pursuit the
previous day, had leaguered short of Auldearn itself. When the alarm
was given Montrose had only two full regiments at hand–one Irish
and one made up of Gordon levies (about 600 men altogether)–and
he realized that it might not be possible to get the rear units on to
the ridge and into battle order before Hurry arrived. Moreover, even
if the other regiments could be brought up in time, he had insufficient
infantry all told to defend the whole of the ridge in strength. (He seems
to have had something short of 2,000 foot on the morning of Auldearn.[4])
He therefore decided to adopt an extremely daring and unusual battle
formation.

The two regiments already in Auldearn were sent to take up a position
on the slope of the Castle Hill and among the dykes and enclosures
at the northern end of the ridge, where in conventional terms they would
constitute the right wing of his army. They probably kept in two
divisions,[5] with Nathaniel Gordon[6] commanding the Gordon regiment
on the extreme right, while Alastair, who was in overall command,
led his Irish MacDonalds on the Gordons' immediate left. On the high
ground near the church, behind the MacDonalds, Montrose placed the
great yellow standard of the King in the hope that this would draw
the main Covenant attack. Alastair was ordered to hold the position
at all costs.

Among the enclosures in the centre of the ridge, Montrose deployed
a thin screen of light musketeers[7] with a disproportionate number of
battle standards and orders to move about and keep up a brisk fire to give
the impression of a large concentration of men. In reality his centre
was non-existent, and 'left to the imagination of the enemy'.

While Alastair's men and the royal standard conspicuous behind
them gave the appearance of the army drawn up in a strong defensive
position on the ridge, the remainder of the Royalist force hurrying
into Auldearn assembled in the hollow[8] out of sight of the approaching
enemy. Montrose himself took command of the infantry–about 800
Gordons and Irishes in a single large formation–while the cavalry force
of 250 was divided into two companies under Lord George Gordon
and the Viscount Aboyne. There was no reserve. Mounted couriers
stationed on the ridge kept the two halves of the army in communication with each other.

On the logical assumption that the royal standard marked Montrose's
command post and the centre of his position, Hurry was to be tricked
into directing his main assault against Alastair's men on the ridge.
When the Covenant army had become heavily engaged on that front,
the force in the hollow would burst over the southern end of the

ridge to wheel right and attack the exposed flank of the enemy. The crucial factor, however, would be Alastair's ability to hold on against such odds.

Unfortunately, at this point Alastair and Lord George Gordon added an individual touch of their own. Recalling the amicable relations that had long existed between their two clans, the latter sent to Alastair suggesting that, as a token of present friendship and past alliance, they should formally exchange a portion of their followers before the battle. Put in this way it was a request which in all chivalry Alastair felt that he could not refuse, and he duly sent to Lord Gordon 90 of his MacDonalds, receiving in return 300 Gordons. But whereas Alastair's contribution was made up of veteran fighting men who could be relied on in the crisis (which is why they had been placed on the ridge), many of the Gordons were raw levies who had never been in action before and were already showing distinct signs of nervousness. The exchange left Alastair with only 50 of his own MacDonalds, and to keep the Gordons in the battle line he was obliged to draw up his force with 25 of these veterans in the front rank to give a lead to the levies behind, and the remaining 25 in the rear to drive them on or stop their running away during the fight. It did not augur well for the coming battle.

At Kinnudie, Sir John Hurry drew up his army in order of battle. Looking across the flat ground towards Auldearn, he could distinguish the royal standard near the northern end of the ridge and, as anticipated, took it to mark the core of Montrose's defence and therefore his objective. He determined on a frontal attack.

As they started to advance the Covenanters immediately began to experience considerable difficulty on account of the boggy ground. The heavy rain had swollen the burn and filled the marsh, and even on the higher ground thick mud made the going heavy. Constricted by the bog, Hurry could not extend his battle line to take full advantage of his superior numbers, and the Covenant army was forced to advance on a narrow front with Lawers's regiment of Campbells forming the vanguard supported closely by the other four regular regiments in echelon two abreast. The northern levies were on the left of this thick formation and slightly withdrawn. On the right flank Hurry positioned a detachment of horse under a Major Drummond, while to the rear the main cavalry division under his personal command formed the reserve. Although the nature of the ground would not let him deploy and attempt to overlap what he presumed to be Montrose's position, the Covenant general was probably confident that the sheer weight of his attack would drive a wedge through the Royalist defences.

At the foot of the ridge, Lawers's regiment inclined slightly to the left and began to assault Alastair's perimeter. Under covering fire from musketeers and archers, the Covenanters launched a series of attacks across the broken ground, but although these were pushed home with considerable spirit and determination, the dykes and dry stone walls split up the formations as they advanced and prevented Lawers's men from being able to concentrate the full weight of their numbers at a single critical point. As one wave of attackers tired another moved forward to take their place, and for a while fierce hand-to-hand fighting continued along the slope and around the MacDonalds' enclosures. But after two major assaults had been successfully beaten off, the Covenanters at length withdrew to the foot of the ridge to re-form.

Then Alastair made the dangerous mistake of leaving his position. He had been given the battle's anvil–to sustain the repeated blows which Hurry would deliver against the standard, and hold out at any cost until Montrose could spring the trap. But as a Highland fighting man, the defensive posture made him uneasy, and the Covenant regiment in front of him was composed of Campbells. It is possible that the taunts of the enemy stung him into retaliation, or perhaps he was driven to take the initiative because of the unsteadiness of the Gordon levies. He left the safety of the enclosures and started down the hill–not in a wild Highland charge, but walking backwards with his face towards his own men, beckoning to the reluctant Gordons to follow. Their counter-attack, when delivered, halted the Covenanters for a moment, but Lawers's men were accounted the finest regiment in the Scottish army and would not flinch from a claymore. They absorbed the shock of it and then the pikemen started forward again, and the solid weight of their formation now drove the MacDonalds back. The Royalists' situation became suddenly extremely desperate. Alastair shouted to them to regain the enclosures before they could be surrounded and cut off, and his men gave ground before the long pikes, moving backwards step by step under a hail of arrows from the Covenant archers while a few MacDonalds covered their retreat. Alastair himself was out on his own and fighting berserk:

> . . . the last to retire, and covering himself with a huge target, single handed he withstood the thickest of the enemy. Some of the pikemen by whom he was hard-pressed again and again pierced his target with the points of their weapons which he mowed off by threes and fours with his broadsword.[9]

In the hand-to-hand fighting among the dykes the great sword finally broke, but his brother-in-law, Davidson of Ardnacross, threw him another, and the desperate mêlée continued around the enclosure as Alastair and his few MacDonalds held the entrance until the rest could get through.

The gaels put up a heroic defence. One of the highlanders, Ranald MacDonald son of Donald, son of Angus MacKinnon of Mull, is said to have found himself cornered against the wrong side of the wall by a body of Covenant pikemen. He carried a target on his left arm while he held them off with a hand-gun as he tried to edge his way towards the enclosure entrance. An archer who had been firing at the Gordons saw him, and changing his aim shot the retreating MacDonald through the mouth, the arrow skewering his tongue and coming out a fist's breadth through his cheek. Ranald paid the archer no attention, however, but coolly fired his pistol into the face of the foremost pikeman and stretching out his shield to ward off the spears of the others, reached for his broadsword. But the claymore was stuck, perhaps with clotted blood, and would not budge from its sheath. He tugged at it again but the cross hilt whirled loose in his hand and he was forced to lower his shield arm to grip the scabbard while he drew the blade out. In this brief moment he took the points of five pikes in his chest and chin, but he kept his feet and sliced through the shafts with his freed broadsword and again started edging sideways with his back against the wall. Fortunately for him the pikemen now broke off the attack to prick down easier prey, except for one who kept after the wounded MacDonald and continued to thrust at him with his spear. Ranald fought him off with sword and shield until the doorway was behind him. Then he sprang away, turned, and ducked quickly through the entrance, and when the pikeman incautiously followed, Alastair, waiting on the other side, decapitated him with a downward stroke of his broadsword so that his body fell across the doorway and his head bounced off Ranald's shins into the garden. Someone cut the arrow out of the MacDonald's cheek and it was found that he could still speak – somewhat to his own surprise. Of such were Alastair's fighting men, but 50 could not hold out indefinitely against 500.

The Covenanters now sensed victory. Lawers's men again stormed the enclosure and it seemed certain that it must soon be overrun. Seventeen of Alastair's MacDonalds were dead or disabled around the doorway. Of the rest, many were wounded and could not fight on much longer. The right wing of the Royalist army might still hold out for a few minutes, but little more.

One of the mounted couriers saw the desperate situation on the ridge and, galloping back to the hollow, whispered to Montrose that Alastair was done for. From where they stood in the depression, the rest of the army could not see what was happening on the further side of the hill. Rumour of Alastair's defeat might well have caused a panic among the levies, and so with admirable presence of mind Montrose called to where the cavalry were waiting – 'Come my Lord Gordon, what are we waiting for? Our friend MacDonald on the right has routed the enemy and is slaughtering the fugitives. Shall we look on idly and let him carry off all the honours of the day?'[10]

The Gordons needed no urging. They burned to avenge the death of Donald Farquharson in Aberdeen, and more immediately the murder of young James Gordon of Rynie, wounded in the fighting a few days previously and killed by the Laird of Innes's men as he lay helpless at the house of Strudders.[11] Now was their moment, and these names became their battle-cry. The squadrons galloped over the ridge and wheeled right to charge against the broad flank of the Covenant regiments which Hurry's formation had exposed to their attack.

This was the first time that Montrose had had a sizeable force of cavalry to command in battle, and he called the charge as Rupert might have done. The Gordons did not check to fire their carbines nor peel off in caracoe. It was cold steel driven home at full gallop, and the shock of it was irresistible. Hurry's cavalry on the flank could offer no resistance. Major Drummond saw them coming, but either panicked or in the heat of the moment gave the wrong word of command, and instead of wheeling to meet the charge the Covenant horse turned inwards and began to ride down their own infantry. The Gordons smashed their way into this confusion, broke the right-hand regiments and turned to charge again. Covenant formations, outflanked and caught from the rear, panicked and disintegrated under the horsemen, and tried to flee across the muddy open ground with the Gordons after them in full cry.

Montrose, meanwhile, had led his infantry across the battlefield, sweeping away the remnants of the battalions in his path, to reach the defenders in the enclosures. On the ridge Alastair saw him coming, saw the Gordons' brilliant charge, and called on his beleaguered company to make one final effort. To face the new danger from the right, the Covenanters began to disengage, and once more the Royalists broke out of the dykes and charged down the slope. At the foot of the ridge Alastair and Montrose joined up and with their combined forces closed relentlessly around Lawers's men. The Covenant vanguard was now isolated and without support, but the Campbells would not run. A bloody fight ensued and the regiment was annihilated almost where it stood.[12]

Most of the Covenant cavalry got safe away owing to a misunderstanding among the Royalists. Aboyne's troop, brandishing some captured standards, were taken for the enemy and attacked by their own men. The mistake was quickly discovered, but the delay was long enough for Hurry's dragoons to get clear. The Covenant foot were not so lucky, and with Farquharson and Rynie on their minds the Gordons took few prisoners and gave less quarter. The pursuit continued for fourteen miles.

Covenant casualties were afterwards put at about 3,000 killed. The dead included Sir Mungo Campbell of Lawers – 'a good christian and expert commander' – Sir John Murray (son of Murray of Philiphaugh), Sir Gideon Murray, two Gledstanes of Whitelaw, nine nephews of Douglas of Cavers, Colonel James Campbell, Major Garchore, seven captains and five lieutenants. Of the Frasers, 'besides what fell unmarried, there were eighty-seven widows in the lordship of Lovat'.[13] The MacLennans who guarded the Caber Feidh – Seaforth's banner – were wiped out. (Some say that eighteen of their widows married MacReas and the two tribes amalgamated.) The Covenanters lost sixteen colours and all their baggage. Hurry blamed the luckless Major Drummond for the terrible defeat. This gentleman was immediately court-martialled and executed by firing squad on the road between Inverness and Toam na-Leurich, 'standing on his feet but not at ane post'.

The broken army withdrew into Inverness and Montrose did not pursue them there, having no wish to become drawn into a protracted siege. Royalist casualties in the battle have been variously estimated—some authorities giving as low as only 15 or 24 killed. Gordon of Sallagh, however, put the figure at 22 gentlemen and 200 private soldiers and this would seem more likely. There were a large number of wounded, particularly among Alastair's division, and those whose hurts were serious were sent next day to Gordon Castle in the Bog of Gight.[14]

Among the music of the Graham family is a piece called the Blar Aultearn, in celebration of this victory. Certainly in tactical terms, it was the most brilliant of Montrose's battles. His detractors have sometimes maintained that his victories were obtained over poor and undisciplined troops—second-line regiments with no experience and little training. Whether this may have been true to some extent of Tippermuir and Aberdeen, at Auldearn it was clearly not so. Apart from the northern levies who took no part in the battle, and excluding also Seaforth's MacKenzies, the Covenant army included four regular front-line regiments, and one of them (Lawers's) was held to be the best that Scotland could show.[15] Sir John Hurry was a commander of considerable experience, and moreover the Royalists were outnumbered by two to one.

Montrose may have been overbold in pursuing Hurry into Moray, and it could be argued that the occasion to fight was not of his own choosing. But the dispositions at Auldearn were brilliantly conceived, especially when one considers the short time available in which to choose his ground. The tactics used were truly indicative of his genius and his daring, the timing cool and judged to a fine moment. It was also the first time that he had had sufficient horse to direct them in attack, and, readily adopting the new style that had been pioneered by Gustavus in Europe and Rupert in England, at Auldearn Montrose clearly demonstrated his ability to employ cavalry as a tactical arm.

But it yet remained to be seen whether any strategic advantage would accrue from this battle. One-half of the Covenant army in Scotland had effectively ceased to exist, but on the day Auldearn was fought Baillie's main forces crossed the Grampians. It was not a matter yet of riding south tomorrow.

15

Alford
(10 May–2 July 1645)

Let thy rich soule for ever be blist,
Whose sacred aishes heir doth rest:
Since none can give thee thy due praise,
Let learned penns and poets' layes
Be silent now, and learne to wonder
That Jove's decree has brocke asunder
The Fabrick where pure wertue stood,
Perfectit heire in flesh and blood;
> *To show us that earthe's greatest glorie,*
> *Lyke lightening, is but transitorie.*

Epitaph on Lord George Gordon[1]

In England, news of Auldearn made Leven the more reluctant to quit his station near the border. Fairfax had ordered him to march south out of Yorkshire and support Brereton at Manchester (the parliamentarians having been forced to withdraw out of Cheshire by Charles's advance on Droitwich), but the Scottish general proposed to move by a circuitous route through Westmorland which he said was easier for his artillery but which also covered the road into Scotland. Clearly, the alliance with the English Parliament notwithstanding, his first duty was to put himself between Charles and Montrose and, if possible, frustrate any attempt they might make to join forces. Moreover, Leven, like many other Scots, was becoming heartily sick of his English allies. Despite repeated requests, the Scottish army had received neither the pay nor the supplies that had been promised them. Assessments had been made on paper, but in practice no money had been raised, while by contrast Fairfax's men were regularly in receipt of their pay every fortnight. In London the Scottish commissioners presented a Remonstrance to the English Parliament, complaining of the shabby treatment afforded to Leven and arguing strongly against the plan of campaign adopted by the Committee of Both Kingdoms which proposed to tie the English army down to an unprofitable siege of Oxford while the Scots did all the hard work. The rift between the Scots and English, to which Montrose's victories had contributed in no small measure, thus continued to grow, although it would be some time yet before a formal break would result.

In Scotland, however, Montrose had cause to be concerned lest his most recent victory might prompt the Committee of Estates to take reprisals against the Royalist prisoners in Edinburgh.

246

Predictably, the treatment being meted out to the Napier family was especially severe, and the Master of Napier's escape was promptly and heavily visited upon his near relations. On 21 April Lord Napier and Sir George Stirling of Keir had been arrested and imprisoned in Edinburgh Castle, and their situation was further endangered when in the first days of May Lord Napier's elder brother, John Napier of Easter Torrie, was caught carrying messages from Montrose to the King. On 5 May Lanerick, Sir John Hope of Craighall[2] and Sir James Stewart, Provost of Edinburgh, were ordered to interrogate him (together with his wife and son who had also been arrested) '. . . as also to call for the Lord Napier, Mistress of Napier, and the Lord Napier's daughter Lilias,[3] Riccartoun, Drummond, or any other they think fitting, and to examine them upon such interrogators as they think expedient, or may arise upon the papers and letters taken with John Napier'. Lady Elizabeth Erskine (Mistress of Napier) and Lilias were arrested two days later and also imprisoned in the Castle 'with the benefit of a serving maid'. The plague was now raging through Edinburgh, and six people had already died of it within the prison. Together with James, Lord Graham, who was also confined there, the Napiers petitioned to be moved from the Castle on the grounds that their lives were in danger from the disease, but no immediate notice was taken. However, by an order of 23 May, the constable of the Castle was permitted to give the two ladies 'the benefit of the air once or twice in the day' provided that he always remained in attendance to prevent anyone from communicating with them, and that at such times Lord Napier and Stirling of Keir were 'keeped close in their chambers'.

On 27 May Lord Napier was temporarily released so that he could raise the fine of £10,000 (Scots) which was the forfeit for his son's escape. An old man of seventy now, ruined and in failing health, he wrote privately to Lord Balmerino protesting at the way in which he had been treated, and begging yet again that the members of his family still in prison might be moved to some place outside of Edinburgh which was not threatened by the plague.[4] As an old friend, Balmerino was probably sympathetic, but the letter did no good. Lord Napier was rearrested on 6 June and placed in solitary confinement in the Castle. Keir was sent to Blackness.

On 9 May, the day of Auldearn, Margaret Napier, Lady Stirling of Keir, was summoned to appear before the Committee of Estates in Edinburgh 'to answer for keeping intelligence and correspondence with James Graham, sometime Earl of Montrose, the time of his late and present rebellion in Scotland'. She went before the tribunal on 15 May dressed in deep mourning, as she said, for John, Lord Graham, Montrose's eldest son who had been her cousin-german, but steadfastly denied the charges that she had corresponded with the dead boy's father. As to the Master of Napier's escape, she admitted that John Alexander of Gartner, the Earl of Stirling's son, had been at her house on the night in question, but denied having had any knowledge of the escape itself. She had sent a servant afterwards to ascertain the extent of some damage to her Highland properties and to inquire in passing if her brother was safe, but she had not asked Montrose to send an escort to bring him off. She was placed under house arrest in Edinburgh, but because of the plague was subsequently permitted to move to Merchiston and thereafter to Linlithgow where she was allowed out only to attend the kirk.

Montrose himself had always been extremely close to the Napiers, and his peculiar bond with that family would continue in a strange way even after his death. However, at this time his most immediate concern was over the fate of John Napier of Easter Torrie, since it followed from the recent death of James Small that, as a courier to the King, he was likely to be executed without further trial or ceremony. In a letter of 27 May to Robertson of Inver, his castellan at Blair, who was already engaged in negotiating an exchange of prisoners, he stated that the Covenanters were to be informed that should they think to execute Napier in 'ane seiming legall way . . . I will use the lyke severitie against some of ther prisoners', among whom Colin Campbell, brother of Campbell of Crinan, was made chief hostage against Napier's safety. This threat had the desired effect, and on 13 June the Estates released John Napier into the custody of Sir Archibald Campbell to be disposed of as he saw fit. Similar arrangements were in hand concerning a possible exchange of lesser prisoners. In a letter to his brother who was confined at Blair, Glamis[5] wrote that Argyll had agreed to his being exchanged for Harry Graham,[6] Murray of Gask for Dr Wishart and others one man for another. However, these negotiations appear to have progressed only slowly and Montrose was constantly pressing Inver for more news.

But what of Montrose's own family? James, his second son and now his heir, was imprisoned in Edinburgh Castle and stalwartly refused to be exchanged lest he should cost his father the benefit of an important prisoner.[7] On 19 April 1645, in obedience to an order issued by the Committee of the North, the Earl of Southesk presented himself before the Estates in Edinburgh together with Montrose's third son Robert (then aged seven or eight) to answer 'on what occasion he met with Montrose, and what passed betwixt them'. Southesk made a verbal statement which he was ordered to submit in writing 'under his own hand'. He produced this declaration on 21 April, and having read it the Committee ordered the clerk to keep it *in retentis*, allowing Southesk to return home 'for doing his lawful affairs at his pleasure' provided that he would again appear if or when it was thought necessary. The appropriate passage in the original Register concludes:

The Committee of Estates ordains and allowes the Earl of Southesk to deliver Robert Graham, sone to the late Earl of Montrois to————Carnegie his mother to be keeped and interteinned by her; and being delivered to his mother, exonners the Earl of Southesk of him.

In strange contrast to the persecution suffered by the Napiers, and in particular by the ladies of that family, it seems from this that Montrose's wife and father-in-law were left relatively unmolested, and biographers have been quick to infer that the Carnegies, valuing property above honour, had come to terms with the Covenanters and disowned Montrose. This is indeed one hypothesis, but there are others as good and much less harsh. All, however, are pure supposition.

Unfortunately, Southesk's deposition to the Committee has not been recovered, and there is no primary evidence as to what sort of contact he had maintained with the Graham. But contact there must have been since it is reasonable to suppose that during his several marches through Angus, Montrose would have slipped away from his army secretly to visit Kinnaird or Old Montrose, to see his wife and youngest children, or to talk over matters of family administration with his father-in-law. The very fact of Southesk's being summoned to answer to 'what had passed betwixt them' would suggest as much, although the Covenanters' inquiry may have been based on suspicion rather than on knowledge, and they appear to have been satisfied with whatever account he gave them.

It seems likely that Montrose and Southesk were not a match–the first a soldier, man of action, romantic, idealist; the second an administrator, conservative, conventional, pragmatic–and each in his own way was possibly impatient of the other. How prolonged or deep-rooted was the quarrel that began at the Glasgow Assembly of 1639 none can say, but Montrose's action there, apart from directly contravening the law that his father-in-law had helped establish, may well have been taken by Southesk as an open affront to the Carnegie family. After the Solemn League and Covenant, Southesk certainly appears to have submitted to the Covenanters' authority, at least to some extent, and continued to take his seat in Parliament among the other lords. He was never one of the party, however, and it should be remembered that when Montrose was attainted Southesk voted openly against the forfeiture when prudence might have suggested abstention or non-appearance as the wiser course. This was not the action of a man who lacked a sense of honour. While Montrose was fighting in the mountains, it seems to have been Southesk who took responsibility for his wife and children, and it was Southesk who preserved his charter chest and salvaged what he could from the ruins of the Graham's fortune. Overall he was a man who preferred to work within existing institutions, however imposed, since such service made up his experience. To this role he was possibly better suited, and perhaps it was enough.

It is also possible to suppose that at this time any break between Montrose and the Carnegies may have been as much contrived as real. The King's Lieutenant would have been naturally vulnerable through his wife and family, and he may have thought it best to leave Magdalen Carnegie under the care and protection of her father (who better?) and so arranged a separation for safety's sake which he hoped might deter the Covenanters from striking at him through her, or from persecuting the wife because of the activities of the husband. In this context it is interesting to consider that, although Montrose's charter chest as it is now preserved is remarkably complete, and contains family charters, royal commissions, correspondence, drafts and even memoranda, no single letter between Montrose and his wife appears to have survived, either from the time of their courtship, his three years on the continent, the period of his imprisonment, or while he was on campaign. This omission is stranger even than the disappearance of Southesk's deposition in Edinburgh, since letters must at some time have passed between them, and one could suppose that for some reason they were destroyed.

It seems strange too that the Earl of Southesk and not Magdalen Carnegie should have been commanded to produce the child Robert Graham before the Committee of Estates in April 1645, and that the clerk when completing the Register should have left her Christian name blank as if he did not know it—an unusual lapse of memory in view of her husband's notoriety. This might suggest that she had become something of a recluse if not an invalid. According to the Diary of James Burn (and oddly there is no other definitive record[8]) she died just six months later.

But of Magdalen Carnegie herself there is no word or portrait, and nothing is known about her life at this time. Yet from what may only be guessed of her circumstances, she is more to be pitied than criticized. In 1629 she had been a child-bride, in a marriage which certainly had the appearance of a love match, and during those first calm years at Kinnaird she could not have known that her only future was to be mistress of an empty castle. She had waited while Montrose wandered over Europe; had seen him return restless and searching for a cause. She had borne him four sons and yet missed the years of his maturing. She had sat with her children while he was caught up in the ferment of Scottish politics, and she had endured when his impetuosity threatened to divide him from her family and later led to his being hurt and disillusioned and almost broken by Argyll. She had watched him ride away to England possessed of a vision she could not share, and she had heard of his return an outlaw, branded murderer and Antichrist. It is no small thing to be a hero, but it is harder yet to be the wife of one. What sort of life could she have had, though his gauntlet rang with honour and his battles endowed him with some barren glory, if all that this could bring to her was loneliness? These things are cruel for a woman to endure, and it would not have been surprising if gradually she withdrew.

> *Tristan, expect no more of me*
> *Sadly I go, I know not where,*
> *To make an end of Minstrelsy*
> *And hide myself from Love and Cheer.*

And this strange silence which hides the most personal aspect of his affairs may cover a deeper tragedy in Montrose's life. He was not a 'family man' in the conventional sense, though at times he may have longed to be one. But he had had his own vision of the grail. Perhaps in youth it made him love Magdalene Carnegie for her beauty; perhaps in life it drove him to neglect her. In this he was not the first: nor would he be the last.

I have left her behind in her warm musk-scented home,
  Talking of trifles and toys which I, too, once held dear,
Left all Beauty, all Wisdom behind me to roam
  Over the cold, bare hills, where the wind whistles Death in my ear.[9]

Too many men had been wounded at Auldearn for Montrose to think of fighting again immediately, and on 11 May he occupied Elgin where surgeons and medicines were more readily available. Aboyne, presumably suffering from his injured shoulder still, left on sick leave, and as usual a number of the highlanders drifted off home. The Gordon contingent were intent on further revenge for the murder of young Rynie, and in Elgin the houses of those responsible were looted and burned. The village of Garmouth, which was chiefly the property of the Laird of Innes (whose men had done the killing), was this time destroyed, and raiding parties plundered and burned the estates of Caddell (a Campbell), the Earl of Moray (then in England) and Forbes of Thornbeg, together with sundry other properties in Kinstery and Lethen. On 14 May, Montrose moved to the Bog of Gight and from Gordon Castle continued to conduct a series of punitive operations against the local Covenanters as far as Cullen of Aboyne.

Baillie, meanwhile, having made 'ane unnecessarie voyage into Athole' at the insistence of the Committee, crossed over Cairn o'Mounth on the day of Auldearn and camped at Birse in the district known as Cromar. On 19 May he marched to Coklaroquhy Wood, about two miles from Strathbogie, where he was joined by Sir John Hurry, who had slipped through Montrose's patrols disguised as one of Lord George Gordon's men, with 100 troopers that had survived Auldearn.

News that the Covenanters were threatening Huntly Castle reached Montrose at Birkenbog, and he hurried to get there before them and began constructing earthworks as if he would make a stand. He was still reluctant to offer battle but hoped that, once engaged, Baillie could be drawn away from Strathbogie and then outmanoeuvred in Strathspey. The Covenant general later recorded the action:

> At our approach the rebells drew into the places of advantage about the yards and dykes, and I stood imbattled before them from four o'clock at night untill the morrow, judgeing them to have been about our own strength. Upon the morrow, so soone as it was day, we found they were gone towards Balveny. We marched immediatelie after them, and came of in fight about Glenlivett, bewest Balveny some few miles; but that night they outmarched us, and quartered some sex miles from us. On the next day early, we found they were dislodged, but could find no bodie to informe us of their march;

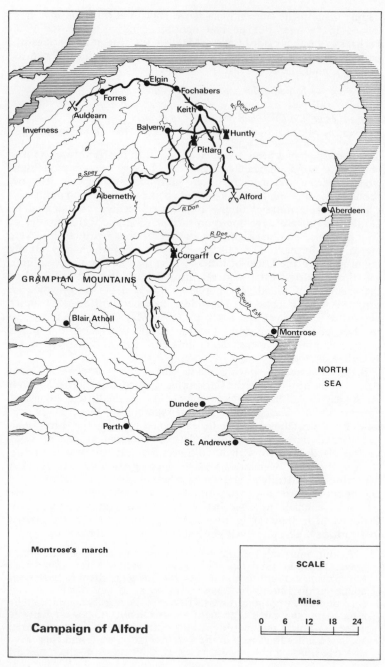

Montrose's march

Campaign of Alford

SCALE

Miles

| 0 | 6 | 12 | 18 | 24 |

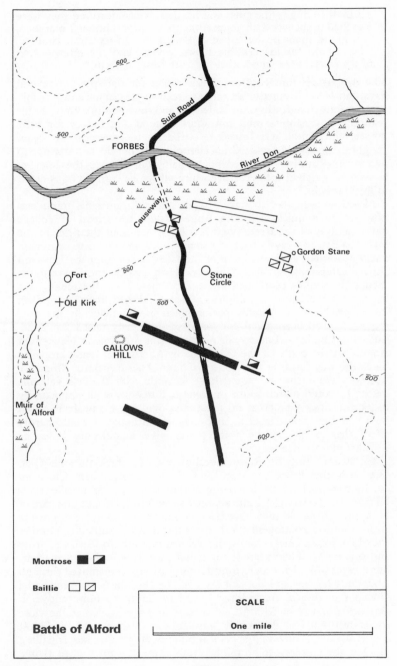

Battle of Alford

Montrose ■ ◪

Baillie ☐ ◨

SCALE

One mile

yet by the lying of the grass and heather, we conjectured they were marched to the wood of Abernethie upon Spey. Thither I marched, and found them in the entrie of Badenoch, a very strait country, where, both for inaccessible rocks, woods, and the interposition of the river, it wes impossible for us to come at them.[10]

The two armies thus confronted each other for the space of several days, but while Montrose was able to receive provisions and possibly even recruits from Ruthven in Badenoch and the friendly country to his rear, the Covenanters soon ran short of food and fodder for their horses, and Baillie was forced to withdraw to Inverness to obtain supplies. Having reorganized his commissariat he did not attempt to follow the Royalists into Badenoch again, but crossed the Spey in boats and marched into Aberdeenshire where he camped at Newton in the Garioch.

Montrose was glad to have shaken him off, since his mind was now set on a quick raid into Angus where his friend of college days, Lindsay of the Byres (who had lately acquired the titles of the forfeited Earl of Crawford), had recently been appointed to command a new Covenant army made up of the latest levies from the Lowland shires. Lindsay, who held a high position among the Covenanters (being Hamilton's brother-in-law and the new Lord President), was by his own account a military genius, and had been outspoken in his criticism of Argyll's performance in the field. At his own request he had been given command of the newly raised regiments (his own, Cassilis's, Lauderdale's) and was at this time at Newtyle of Angus, an old castle of the Oliphants of Aberdalgie, ready either to block the way south or to second Baillie in Aberdeenshire. Montrose was well aware that he would have to settle with Baillie's veterans before he could march south in earnest, but he saw an opportunity to gain a quick victory at no great cost over these raw levies with their vain but inexperienced general, which, although it would hardly affect the course of the war, would give a welcome boost to Royalist morale generally.

He struck south by Rothiemurchus and the track through Glen Dee into the Braes of Mar, and thence along Glen Clova to Auchtertyre, where he leaguered about a quarter of a mile from Kirktoun of Newtyle.[11] Lindsay, only seven miles off and unaware of his approach, would now have been literally at his mercy had not the entire Gordon contingent (with the exception of Nathaniel Gordon and their young chief) chosen this critical moment to leave the army and ride home. Their reasons for doing this are not altogether clear, but it is possible that orders from Huntly secretly transmitted through Aboyne (who was still on sick leave at the Bog) had summoned the Gordons to return. According to Wishart, Huntly's only motive in this was jealousy of Montrose's success and annoyance at the close friendship that had developed between the Graham and his eldest son. However, to do him justice, it is more likely that he was unwilling to allow the Gordons to go too far from home at a time when Baillie was shaping to attack Strathbogie and the Bog of Gight. Montrose might still have attacked Lindsay with the Irishes alone, but he calculated that it was no longer worth the risk, and the new Covenant general thus 'escaped a scouring'. Disconsolately, the Royalists withdrew into Strathardle.

Once again, recruiting became the first priority. Lord George Gordon was furious over the 'desertion' of his followers, and taking Nathaniel Gordon with him he at once rode north to call them back. Montrose sent Alastair with a small band into the west to seek help from the MacLean and John Moydartach (Glengarry and some MacDonalds of Clanranald were still with the army) while with the rest of his men he marched by Glenshee into Mar and camped among the ruins of Corgarff Castle at the head of Strathdon.[12] This was a suitable place at which to pause since from here he could either retreat into the safety of the hills or descend on Aberdeenshire. Aboyne returned, but fell sick again almost immediately, and under pretence of requiring an escort to Strathbogie took away another troop of horse whom Lord George Gordon afterwards had great difficulty in persuading to rejoin the standard. A fortnight passed while the Gordon levies slowly drifted back. It was a slow, wearisome business, yet Montrose could only wait, hoping for Alastair and his western clansmen, but intent chiefly on remustering the cavalry without whom he would not be able to face Baillie in the field.

The Covenant general, however, was having troubles of his own. In fact, he had become thoroughly sick of the business and would willingly have resigned his command. One of the factors that had prevented him from pursuing Montrose into Badenoch was that his veteran regiments, notably Hume's 'Redcoats' from Ireland, were on the verge of mutiny, and were openly saying that they had no cause to fight against the King's lieutenant. At the same time, the Committee for the War in Edinburgh, made up of defeated generals such as Argyll, Elcho, Burleigh and the rest, were bombarding him with orders to be more belligerent.

> By my letters likewise I returned answer, that I wes in no way enabled to performe that which they required of me; that I wes altogether unwilling to ruine the forces committed to my charge in wayes both against reason and common sense; and therefore my humble intreaty wes, that I might be recalled and some one imployed who would undertake more and perform better.[13]

At Mills of Drum he joined up with Lindsay, to whom by order of the Committee he was compelled to transfer Hume's 1,200 veterans and 100 of Balcarres's horse in exchange for Cassilis's new regiment of 400 raw recruits. With the Irish veterans, his own and Lauderdale's regiments and four or five companies of Perthshire levies, Lindsay now marched off to wage a purposeless war in Atholl where he did a lot of damage but achieved little else. Baillie, though his army had been much reduced, was commanded to seek out Montrose, and somewhat reluctantly he returned north to threaten Gordon Castle in the Bog of Gight.

News of his march reached Montrose at Corgarff on 25 June. Gordon Castle was well defended and strong enough to withstand a siege, but since it was clearly in his interest to do everything possible to placate Huntly, he decided to march to its relief. He had also heard about the transfer of Baillie's veterans to Lindsay, and was reasonably confident that, even without Alastair, he could now match the Covenanters in the open. Hurrying north, probably by the Lecht Road and Glen Rinnes, he caught up with Baillie's army at Keith on the Deveron.

The Covenant infantry were drawn up on a hill with the cavalry occupying a narrow pass in front of them. The position was too strong to risk a frontal attack, especially as Baillie had moved up his artillery to cover the defile, and having probed for a weak spot but found none, the Royalists merely skirmished around the gap until nightfall. Next day (28 June) Montrose sent a herald to offer battle on level ground, but Baillie was still too canny for that and answered 'that he did not take his orders to fight from the enemy'. Once again, the Covenant general had achieved a stalemate, and knowing that he could not force the position without incurring heavy losses, Montrose now decided to simulate retreat in the hope of enticing Baillie out of the area altogether, and accordingly withdrew to Pitlarg. On 29 June he continued south as if contemplating a descent on Angus, and marched by the Suie Road to Druminor Castle where he paused long enough to receive the intelligence that the Covenanters had left Keith and were advancing through Strathbogie. In fact, Baillie had learned of the absence of Alastair with many of the Ulstermen of whom his levies were so afraid, and was coming after them in hot pursuit. On 1 July Montrose crossed the River Don by a ford known as the Boat of Forbes[14] and halted his army on Gallows Hill near the hamlet of Alford which at that time comprised a few buildings including a kirk, a smithy and an alehouse two miles west of the site of the present village. He himself spent the night at Asloon Castle about a mile to the south-west.

The Boat of Forbes was the main ford on the Upper Don which then flowed broad and deep through long stretches of undrained marshland. The Covenanters, if they came, would almost certainly cross the river here. Emerging from the ford, the Suie Road ran almost due south to traverse the marsh by a short causeway before continuing in a straight line up the side of Gallows Hill at its steepest point.

The original Royalist position was slightly behind the crest, facing north astride the road. To the immediate front the northern face of the hill overlooking the ford sloped steeply down to the causeway, but on the right the gradient was less severe and the ground fell away north-eastwards in a long gradual slope towards the bog. On the left the Leochel Burn flowed down to the main river through a marshy ravine which effectively precluded any flanking attack from that quarter. To the rear of the position, the steep crest of the hill concealed a shallow table-land which subsided gently towards the Leochel Marsh along the line of the Suie Road.

Early on the morning of 2 July,[15] scouts from north of the river brought word that the Covenanters were marching towards Forbes. At daybreak the Royalist army was ordered to stand to arms while Montrose himself rode out with a cavalry patrol to reconnoitre for any other smaller fords in the area which the enemy might attempt to use. Further reports however made it clear that, as he had originally anticipated, Baillie was heading for the Boat of Forbes, and leaving the patrol to scout the Covenanters' approach he returned alone to make his final dispositions.

Montrose now conceived the idea that the Covenant general would probably not risk a direct ascent of the steep northern face but after crossing the causeway might attempt to outflank the position by turning left along the edge of the marsh to circle the crest from the east in the hope of cutting the Suie Road to the Royalists' rear. He therefore realigned his army to face north-east down the more gradual slope towards the bog, with his left flank resting on the point of Gallows Hill and with the Leochel Burn to his rear. He then withdrew his men slightly behind the crest so that his strength and disposition would not be apparent to the Covenanters approaching the ford.

An accurate assessment of the numbers engaged at Alford is virtually impossible, but Montrose probably had about 2,500 infantry and 250 cavalry. He drew up his army in four main divisions. On the left, Aboyne commanded 100 of the Gordon horse with a small force of Irishes under O'Cahan in support. Lord George Gordon led a similar division of cavalry on the right with another body of light musketeers under Nathaniel Gordon. The centre was composed of Gordons and Irishes, a small detachment of the Clanranald, Farquharsons under Inveray,[16] 200 men from Strathavon under William Gordon of Minimore and his three sons, the MacPhersons of Badenoch and a number of Athollmen. These were drawn up in files six deep, and in Alastair's absence were led by Eneas MacDonald of Glengarry, with Drummond of Balloch (Lord Napier's nephew) and the army quartermaster, George Graham, in subordinate command. The Master of Napier commanded the reserve which was concealed in a slight depression some way behind the main battle line.

Approaching the Boat of Forbes, Baillie was still under the impression that the Royalists were in full retreat. From the ford he could not see Montrose's army drawn up behind the crest, and such detachments as were visible on the top of Gallows Hill he took to be a rearguard posted to cover the withdrawal. To engage them on the steep slope was clearly not to his advantage, while any turning movement to the right would bog down in the marsh and the Leochel Burn.

Under these circumstances a flank march round the eastern slopes of the hill with the object of cutting Montrose's line of retreat seemed sound enough, and any doubts that he may have voiced were probably dismissed by the attendant committee and by Sir David Lindsay of Balcarres, who commanded the forward detachment of cavalry. Almost certainly, Baillie did not expect Montrose to seek a fight with Alastair away.

With Balcarres's horse leading, the Covenanters crossed the river and, having passed over the causeway, bagan deploying to their left along the edge of the marsh, very much as Montrose had calculated that they would. Balcarres was already committed to the flank march before Baillie realized that he had walked into a trap and that his projected turning movement was actually taking him across the front of the entire Royalist army which now had him pinned against the bog. Had it been possible at this stage he would have withdrawn, but the forward cavalry squadrons had already advanced on to the slight ridge that formed the glacis of Montrose's position and it was too late now to extricate them. If the Royalists were determined to fight, battle was unavoidable.

The Covenanters halted irresolutely on the fringes of the marsh. Although his force probably included the remnants of Hurry's army gathered in from Inverness, Baillie was slightly inferior to Montrose in infantry.[17] However, his two regiments of horse (Hackett's and Balcarres's[18]), amounting to 600 troopers, still gave him a clear advantage in cavalry. Seeing that he would be forced to fight, the Covenant general made what hasty dispositions he could. Balcarres's squadrons, whose march had brought them nearest to the enemy, were already ranged against Lord George Gordon and the Royalist right, and he now stationed Hackett's regiment at the other end of his line to confront Aboyne's division. In the centre, the foot were drawn up three deep among a series of dykes and small enclosures along the edge of the boggy ground.

For a while neither side seemed eager to take the initiative. Baillie would not storm the hill, and Montrose was understandably reluctant to leave an advantageous position to assault the defence works in the bog. However, the Covenanters had driven with them a quantity of cattle lifted from Strathbogie, and the sight of these stolen beasts herded behind Balcarres's division so infuriated the Gordons on Montrose's right that finally they would be restrained no longer and started charging down the slope. Balcarres, confident in his superior discipline and numbers, and unwilling to fight a purely defensive cavalry action, led out his front two squadrons to meet them, and the two forces crashing together at a gallop were soon locked in a tight mêlée along the edge of the ridge over the area now called Feight Faulds. There for a space, the fight swayed back and forth with neither side able to make any ground, while the thick press of men behind prevented those in front from disengaging or attempting to manoeuvre. Individual antagonists with little or no room to swing a sword took to grappling with each other at close quarters – 'seizing each other's heads with their left hands and striking one another on the heads with pistols'. The light musketeers advancing in support could not fire into the struggling mass for fear of hitting their own horsemen, and a Clanranald man, Alaster, son of Ranald, said afterwards that he had stood for a time with his sword point resting in the earth 'not knowing on whom he could strike a blow' being unable to distinguish friend from foe. Balcarres himself was caught up in the very thick of the fight and had had his helmet struck off in the first onrush,[19] but he rallied his men and came on again so that the Gordons could make no swordway. Baillie, watching the battle in the balance, now commanded the squadron in reserve to advance and charge the Royalist flank, but his order was misunderstood and they galloped in behind their fellows and were in their turn drawn into the murderous scrimmage. Even so, it seemed that by weight of numbers the Covenanters might have 'wronge back the victorie', and seeing the Gordons checked, Montrose ordered a general attack on the Covenant centre.

On the right, the deadlock was finally broken by Nathaniel Gordon who cut his way out of the fight to call up Lachlan's Irishes, shouting to them to throw away their useless muskets and kill or hamstring the horses with their swords. The Irishes dropped their matchlocks and ran light-footed among the Covenant horse, butchering the animals, slashing at legs and girths, and dragging Balcarres's men out of their saddles to dirk them on the ground.[20] Beasts and men started to panic, and, disconcerted by this new form of attack, Balcarres's troopers broke. The victorious Gordons were now able to cut their way through and charge inward to roll up Baillie's centre, already embattled with Montrose. From the rear, the young Napier flung his reserve into the attack, and even the 'peddies'–fourteen-year-old boys left to guard the baggage–jumped on nags and sumter mules and rode to join the fight. Deserted by their cavalry, the Covenant foot fought on doggedly until almost 1,600 had been killed among the dykes, but when the Royalist reserves came streaming down the hill they also threw away their weapons and tried to escape. Royalist bands pursued them to the Howe of Alford and beyond. At Tough, four miles to the east, the Blaudy Faulds recall the last stand of some who could run no further.

But Alford was Lord George Gordon's death-field, and the victory was turned to ashes. He had sworn during the battle that he would bring out General Baillie himself and when the Covenanters broke and ran he had gone seeking his adversary among the fugitives, charging rashly deep into the press. At the very moment, it is said, that he was reaching out for Baillie's belt to drag him from the saddle, a musket ball, fired by an unknown marksman, struck him in the back. The wound was mortal, and as word that he had fallen spread around the battlefield Gordons and Irishes alike broke off their pursuit and hurried back to gather round his corpse.

Conquest and plunder were forgotten as they crowded round his lifeless body, kissing his face and hands, weeping over his wounds, praising the beauty of his person even in death, and extolling a nature as noble and generous as his birth and fortune. They even cursed a victory that was bought so dearly.[21]

In their grief the Royalists had more the appearance of a beaten army than victors on the battlefield. This had been the best of the Gordons, the one great hope of the North. He was only twenty-seven years of age, cut off in his prime 'before time or nature had granted him the ornament of a beard'. How much they had lost by his death, time would surely show.

For Montrose, the tragedy was deeply personal as well as politic. In the short time that they had campaigned together a great friendship had grown between them, so much so that contemporary historians went out of their way to remark upon it:

> For never two of so short acquaintance did ever love more darkly. There seemed to be a harmonious sympathy in their natural disposition, so much were they delighted in mutual conversation. And in this the Lord Gordon seemed to go beyond the limits which nature had allowed for his carriage in civil conversation. So real was his affection and so great the estimation he had of the other that, when they fell into any familiar discourse, it was often remarked that the ordinary air of his countenance was changed from a serious listening to a certain ravishment or admiration of the other's witty expressions. And he was often heard in public to speak sincerely, and confirm it with oaths, that if the fortune of the present war should prove at any time so dismal that Montrose for safety should be forced to fly into the mountains without any army or any to assist him, he would live with him as an outlaw, and would prove as faithful a consort to drive away his malour as he was then a helper to the advancement of his fortunes.[22]

Wishart, in speaking of their relationship, called him Montrose's 'dearest, only friend'.

The time would come when in retrospect, Montrose would probably reflect that, in allowing Lord George Gordon a glorious death on the battlefield, fate had in one respect been kind.

On the evening of the battle, the Royalist army marched by Donside to Cluny Castle and thereafter to Craigton near Corrichie Field and camped on the south side of the Hill O'Fare where the old earthworks were later known as Montrose's Trench. From there the body of Lord George Gordon was carried to Aberdeen Cathedral where he was buried with all honour beside his mother, the Lady Anne Campbell.

On the battlefield of Alford a monolith was left to mark the spot where he fell. Known as the Gordon Stane it stood as a memorial for three hundred years until in more recent times it was seen fit to wall in the place with corrugated iron and use it for a rubbish dump.[23] In Aberdeen Cathedral, no inscription signifies his tomb.

Kilsyth
(July–August 1645)

It was a braw day Kilsyth! At every stroke I gave with my broadsword that day, I cut an ell o' breeks![1]

I profess to you, I never did look upon our business with that assurance that I do now, of God's carrying us through with His own immediate hand, for all this work of Montrose is above what can be attributed to mankind.

Digby to Jermyn, 21 September 1645[2]

Montrose had no time to contemplate this misfortune. In England Naseby had been fought and lost, and although the full implications of Parliament's victory were as yet not apparent, Montrose realized that, if he was to intervene effectively on the King's behalf, the march south could not be delayed much longer. After Alford many of the highlanders had gone home to deposit their spoil, but with another fight in prospect it was possible that some at least would soon rejoin the army. Black Pate was back in Atholl raising the loyal Robertsons and Badenoch men, and there was hope of Alastair's imminent return with the western clans. Aboyne was sent north to recruit cavalry in Buchan but made slow work of it, and when he rejoined the army at Craigton with only a small following Montrose sent him back with orders to do better. It was rumoured that Huntly himself contemplated a return from exile, and he may have been reluctant as before to let his clan go south, while Aboyne, though not wanting courage, was closer to his father and lacked the constancy that had so endeared his dead brother to Montrose. Recruiting proceeded with maddening slowness. The time called for a supreme effort, but clearly it was going to take several weeks to muster enough men, and particularly cavalry, for an invasion of the Lowlands.

In the meanwhile there was little to keep them benorth the Grampians. Montrose crossed the Dee and marched into Angus where Inchbrakie joined him with his Athollmen, and at Fordoun in the Mearns, Alastair himself came in with the rest of his Irishes and a war band of 1,500 gaels. From Argyllshire to the Western Isles, the Rough Bounds and the coast, the loyal clans had answered his call in strength. Young Donald, son of John Moydartach, led 500 fighting men of the Clanranald. Lachlan MacLean of Duart with MacLean of

Lochbuy and the captain of Cairnburgh–MacLean of Treshnish–brought 700 gaels from Mull, new to the war but old enemies of the Campbell, and marching with them tribe by tribe came MacPhersons from Badenoch, Camerons and MacSorleys from Lochaber, Appin Stewarts, Farquharsons from Braemar, MacNabs from Glen Dochart and MacGregors from the southern Highlands. (Glengarry and his MacDonalds were already present, having fought at Alford.[3])

Such an army would not thrive on idleness waiting for Aboyne. Baillie had regrouped the main Covenant forces at Kilgraston near Bridge of Earn where he could cover the main routes south. Montrose now commanded some 4,400 foot but he had only 100 horse and was not yet prepared to face the Covenant general for what he knew would be the decisive battle for the Lowlands. He got news however that, because the plague in Edinburgh had reached epidemic proportions, the Covenant Parliament had removed to Perth and were due to meet on 24 July. Probably as much with a view to harassing them during their deliberations, he marched to Dunkeld and, crossing the Tay, moved south by Amulree to the Almond and camped in Methven Wood.

Baillie's foot regiments were posted south of the Earn, but Perth was protected by 400 cavalry under Hurry, who in the open might have given the Royalists considerable trouble. However, by parading his 100 horse in view of the town together with a large number of light musketeers mounted on baggage ponies, Montrose successfully deceived them into thinking that he was equal to their strength in cavalry so that they adopted a purely defensive posture within the walls while his highlanders skirmished along the northern bank of the Earn as far as Dupplin and even forded the river in places to reconnoitre the infantry emplacements on the other side. This ruse could work for a few days only, however, since Aboyne and the Gordons still did not arrive; and when eventually the Covenanters realized that they had been fooled into overcaution, they plucked up courage and sallied out of the town. Montrose drew up his men as if to make a stand until his baggage was safely away and then retreated through Methven Wood towards Dunkeld, leaving a score of Highland sharpshooters to pick off the foremost troopers and check the pursuit in the passes. Hurry's cavalry broke off the chase and occupied the abandoned camp in Methven Wood. But somewhere close by they rode down a band of Irish women who unfortunately had straggled behind the column and whom, perhaps with some notion of injured morality, they massacred with great brutality. (Irish depredations during the weeks that followed were possibly inspired in part at least by revenge for the wives and dependants who were butchered in this incident.[4]) Baillie, meanwhile, was content to stay between Montrose and Stirling, and both armies now paused in expectation of reinforcements.

During this time Montrose had repeatedly sent courteous messages to Aboyne urging him to hurry south, and finally, after a week's waiting at Little Dunkeld, the Gordon arrived with 200 horse and 120 mounted musketeers[5]–fewer than the King's Lieutenant might have hoped, but clearly all that he was going to get. However, another arrival, as welcome if not more so, was the old Earl of Airlie (now recovered from his illness) with his son, Sir David Ogilvie, young Alexander Ogilvie of Innerquharitie and 80 cavaliers. With these reinforcements Montrose could muster 4,400 foot and 500 horse–the largest army he had yet commanded–and was now determined to seize the initiative. Accordingly, he circled south by Logiealmond to cross the Earn by the Bridge at Nethergask and advanced to the Kirk of Drone on the northern slopes of the Ochils to threaten the main Covenant leaguer at Kilgraston. Hearing of his approach Baillie withdrew his outposts from Bridge of Earn and hastily constructed a series of earthworks along his threatened quarter, being unwilling to take the offensive himself until his own fresh levies arrived. Montrose was forced to concede another stand-off situation, since although he was aware that he would have to fight and defeat the Covenant army before marching on the borders, he did not want to risk a frontal attack against prepared positions. However, he was now able to obtain more detailed intelligence of the Covenanters' intentions which determined his next moves in the campaign.

Fresh orders had been sent to the Lowland Covenanters and an Act had been passed to levy a new army of 10,000 foot and 500 horse. After Alford Baillie had tried to resign his commission, but the Parliament at Perth had passed a vote of thanks to him for his services and pressed him to retain command–albeit with the help of a new committee of sixteen which included Argyll, Burleigh and Tullibardine. Baillie, still discontented, had subsequently blamed Hurry for failing to catch Montrose at Perth, had resigned again, and had again been forced to withdraw his resignation. He was currently awaiting the arrival of three new regiments of Fifeshire levies and 1,200 of Argyll's highlanders. In the West, meanwhile, the 'Solemn' Cassilis and 'Grey Steel' Eglinton were raising another Covenant force in alliance with Glencairn, and, more important, Lanerick had collected 1,000 foot and 500 horse from among the Hamilton tenantry of Clydesdale and was about to march east to concert with Baillie.

In determining his own strategy Montrose could afford to discount Cassilis's and Eglinton's efforts in the West since whatever body of troops they might raise would not be able to reach the scene of operations in time to affect the issue. He saw that the vital factor which could swing the odds too heavily against him was the possibility that Lanerick would join forces with Baillie before he could force the latter to battle, and to prevent this his immediate tactic had to be to place himself between them. That in the meantime Baillie would be reinforced by the Fifeshire levies was of lesser importance. Experience led him to expect that these would be of poor quality[6]–raw levies, apprentices or sailors who had not fought on land before–and predictably reluctant to march beyond the boundaries of their own county. The expectation of their arrival had kept Baillie on the Fife border and thus away from Lanerick, and this now probably prompted Montrose to feint east as if to strike them as they mustered in the hope of luring Baillie even further in that direction. On 10 August he skirted the Covenanters' camp and marched down Glen Farg to Kinross on Loch Leven, while Baillie (with the consent of his attendant committee) followed by Lindores and Rossie.

Next day the Covenant general had successfully joined up with the Fife regiments[7] when he got news that the Royalists were turning his southern flank. From Kinross Montrose had wheeled west and marched along the south side of the Ochils by the Yetts of Muckart into Dollar, where the MacLeans, in revenge for ancient wrongs, had burned Castle Campbell (known as Castle Gloom). The army had then continued along Devonside and the Irish were said to be plundering in Alloa,[8] though reportedly Montrose and his officers had been sumptuously entertained at Tullibody Castle by the Earl of Mar and his son Lord Erskine. Baillie now saw the issue clear enough, and set out in pursuit, but his troops could not match the speed of Montrose's highlanders and his march was further delayed by Argyll and the Committee who insisted on burning Castle Menstrie[9] and the Graham house at Airth[10] as a reprisal for the destruction of Castle Gloom. As they approached the Forth at Stirling the Fifeshire men began to grumble and threaten mutiny, but the ministers were set to work on them and with tales of Lanerick's advance to aid them from the West they were induced to march for one day more.

Montrose was soon aware that Baillie was hurrying after him.[11] Knowing that it was vital to keep a day's march ahead, he did not want to become entangled with the Covenant garrison at Stirling–or with the pestilence that was raging there also–and crossed the Forth some eight miles further up at the Fords of Frew.[12] On 14 August he passed over the field of Bannockburn, and crossing the Carron at Denny reached Kilsyth[13] on the Garrel and camped on an upland meadow near old Colzium Castle about a mile north-east of the village. Baillie, taking the easier route, crossed the Forth at Stirling and, marching also by Denny, halted the same night at Hollanbush about four miles off.

Having got this close, Baillie's intention in all probability was to wait for Lanerick. Next morning, when Argyll and the Committee rode up from Stirling where they had passed the night, he pointed out the difficulties of marching directly to Kilsyth since the only road would bring them out immediately below Montrose's position. But Argyll, who wanted to get closer to the Royalists, argued that the army should leave the road and advance in a more direct line through the cornfields, and since he was supported by the Committee the Covenant general was obliged to yield, albeit reluctantly, to his authority. The Covenanters marched over the rough braes of the Campsie Hills to

Auchinclogh where bogland made further progress difficult; and, judging the position to be virtually impregnable, Baillie again halted the column, still intending that the army should dig in and wait for Lanerick who was by now barely twelve miles distant.

This, however, did not suit the Committee, whose one thought was to attack. They had convinced themselves that the King's Lieutenant was finally at their mercy, since now that he had left the shelter of the hills he would be forced to fight on their terms. To the north, the River Forth cut him off from the Highlands which hitherto had been his sanctuary. They held the high ground above him to the East. Lanerick was behind him, and south were the open Lowlands where his irregulars could not survive against superior cavalry. Since the Covenant army of 6,000 foot and 800 horse already far outnumbered the Royalist force in the meadow below they saw no real need to wait for Lanerick's reinforcements and argued that these would be better employed in rounding up the fugitives afterwards. But delay might give Montrose a chance to escape even now, and their anxiety to prevent this and to seal off all possible avenues of retreat inspired the battle plan that these military experts accordingly devised.

The projected battlefield in some way resembled a huge amphitheatre with the Royalists in the arena below and the Covenanters on the eastern ridge above them. To stop Montrose from trying to break north towards Menteith, the Committee proposed that the army should circle northwards along the ridge and take possession also of the high ground on the Royalists' left flank. Once this was occupied Montrose would be hemmed in on two sides and the trap would be sealed shut.

In vain Baillie argued against the folly of initiating a battle when reinforcements were only a matter of hours away. The action at Kilsyth would be decisive and the stakes enormous. He pointed out the inherent dangers of a flanking march directly across the enemy's front, particularly since Montrose would surely anticipate the movement, and in exasperation tried to explain the technical difficulties of performing such a complicated manoeuvre with heavily armed troops over rough and broken ground. To reach the hill to the north the army would have to cross the Banton Burn which, flowing down the hillside to the edge of the meadow beneath, had cut for itself a deep rough-sided ravine which was almost impassable for cavalry and would be a formidable obstacle for the foot soldiers to cross without losing their formation and exposing themselves to the highlanders' attack. Moreover, as against the risks involved in attempting such a manoeuvre it was even arguable whether possession of the hill in question would yield the advantage that Argyll and his colleagues so confidently predicted.

But the Committee would not be gainsaid. They had the hill reconnoitred and pronounced the plan acceptable. Baillie's arguments were brushed aside. That the foremost of them – Argyll, Burleigh, Tullibardine, Elcho, Balcarres – had all been individually or collectively

265

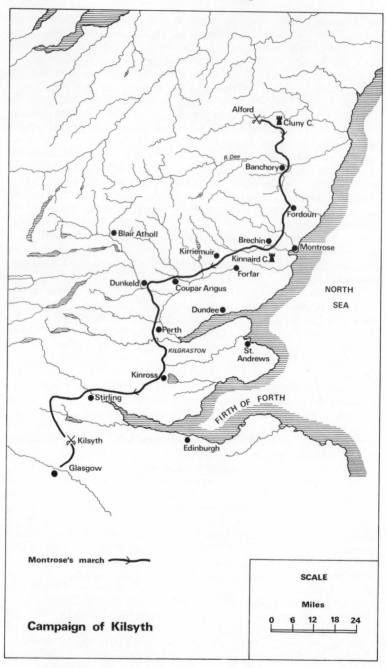

Alford
Cluny C.
R. Dee
Banchory
Fordoun
Blair Atholl
Brechin
Kirriemuir
Kinnaird C.
Montrose
Forfar
Dunkeld
Coupar Angus
NORTH
SEA
Dundee
Perth
KILGRASTON
St.
Andrews
Kinross
Stirling
FIRTH OF FORTH
Kilsyth
Edinburgh
Glasgow

Montrose's march

SCALE

Miles

| 0 | 6 | 12 | 18 | 24 |

Campaign of Kilsyth

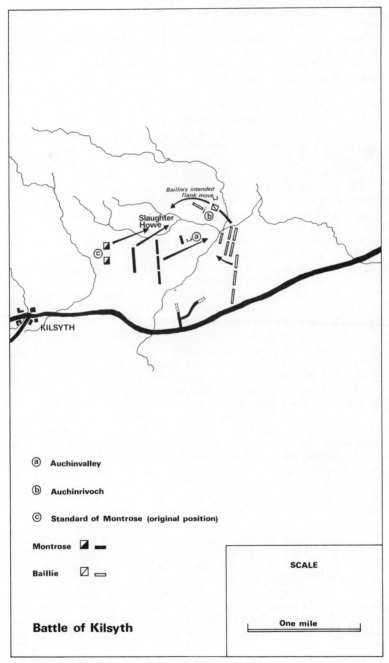

Battle of Kilsyth

beaten by Montrose (Lindsay had escaped through no fault of his own with only a fright), did nothing to shake their confidence in the scheme. Balcarres, who was the only competent soldier among them, alone sided with the General.

At this point Baillie gave up. In what must have been by all accounts a memorable outburst, he confronted Argyll with the accumulated grievances of the previous months. The Committee had bypassed his authority whenever it had suited them. Prisoners had been exchanged without his knowledge; fire raised without his consent. Now he washed his hands of the whole affair. Henceforth he would do only as the Committee explicitly demanded, and if they wanted the direction of the battle they could also bear the responsibility for it.

The Committee ordered him to commence the flanking movement.

The Covenant army was drawn up in line. The division on the extreme right, which now became the vanguard, was to be guided by a certain Major Haldane (he who had made the reconnaissance) to a position among some enclosures on the side of the northern hill which was their main objective. On their left were Balcarres and his cavalry, then Lauderdale's regiment, Hume's Redcoats, Argyll's, Cassilis's, Glencairn's, Lindsay's, and then the three regiments of Fifeshire levies. Baillie's intention was that the army should turn right into column of march – keeping the appropriate distances between divisions – until the movement was completed. The regiments would then face left into line again towards the enemy. Success depended on their keeping behind the crest of the ridge and out of sight of the Royalists waiting below. It also depended on the regiments maintaining their formation, but Baillie, in his Vindication, later recalled that as he galloped down the column he discovered that already numbers of musketeers were straying from their units.

After the army had been set in motion, Baillie, Lindsay and Burleigh rode over the brae to view the dispositions of the Royalists in the meadow, and from the ridge noticed that a number of highlanders were already moving up the glen. Returning from this reconnaissance the Covenant general saw to his horror that, instead of keeping behind the ridge as ordered, Haldane had left the line of march and was leading a company of musketeers against some cottages at the head of the glen. A galloper sent to call off the attack was ignored by that officer, and even as Baillie watched the highlanders counter-attacked.

Hurrying back towards the main body Baillie next discovered that the foot regiments had misunderstood their orders, and instead of forming a column of march had only inclined to the right before advancing at a trot towards the enemy. Lauderdale's regiment was out on its own, and Hume's, Argyll's, Cassilis's and Glencairn's had taken up a position in a large enclosure on the slope of the ridge from which they could no longer be withdrawn. Baillie was frantically trying to bring up Lindsay's regiment to plug the gap on Lauderdale's left when the Royalists charged.

The Covenant army was already fragmented and in confusion before the battle had properly begun.[14]

Montrose had selected the position at Kilsyth with a view to keeping his options open. If Baillie chose to try to join up with Lanerick, one or other of them would have to pass along the road through the village and would thus expose themselves to attack from the high meadow above. If, however, the Covenant general decided to occupy the eastern ridge–as in the event he did–then Montrose was still content to hold the lower ground. The Covenant cavalry would not be able to charge down the rough and broken hillside. Nor was the marsh meadow at the bottom suitable for horse, while regular infantry descending the steep slope would also lose their discipline and formation before reaching the level plain below. By contrast, an uphill charge was nothing to highlanders, and it was Montrose's intention to attack should an opportunity present itself. However, in the event of accident he calculated on still being able to retreat northwards over the hills. He was under no illusions but that a battle at this juncture would be decisive. Whoever lost, lost Scotland, and it was perhaps with this in mind that he called a council of war and asked his officers whether they wanted to retreat or fight. The chiefs' fierce answer assured him of the high spirit of his men.

Early in the morning of 15 August[15] (the Royalists had not yet breakfasted[16]), it became clear that the Covenanters did not intend to wait for Lanerick, and the army stood-to in expectation of battle. It promised to be a scorching summer day and the highlanders discarded their plaids to fight only in their shirts–coarse linen stiffened and stained yellow with mud and cattle dung–which they knotted between their legs. Remembering the confusion at Alford, Montrose ordered his cavalry to wear their white shirts over their buff coats so that in the mêlée they would be easily distinguishable from the Covenant troopers. He then made his dispositions for the battle.

At the head of the glen, some way in front of the Royalist position, were a number of cottages with gardens ringed about with dry stone dykes. They constituted a natural strongpoint between the two armies[17] which any experienced commander would be anxious to seize, and he sent MacLean of Treshnish with 100 men of Alastair's advance guard to occupy the position. (These were probably the highlanders whom Baillie saw moving up the glen.) Behind, and within sight of the cottages, the Royalist vanguard was composed of the main gaelic division under Alastair with the MacLeans and the Clanranald drawn up independently under Lachlan of Duart and the young Moydartach–each determined to outdo the other in the battle. To their rear the cavalry and the other infantry detachments were still being marshalled into line when Haldane's musketeers attacked. With Lord George Gordon's death on his conscience, Montrose was unwilling to risk Huntly's new heir in the forefront of the battle, and Aboyne was ordered to remain among the reserve with only a small escort of Gordons.

When the Covenanters attacked the cottages, Treshnish drove them off and then promptly counter-attacked. Haldane's undisciplined action uncovered the movement of the Covenant column, but Montrose's initial reaction was quite possibly one of sheer surprise that a general of Baillie's calibre should have attempted a flank march directly across the Royalists' front. Before he could make any formal move to exploit the situation, the main body of MacLeans, animated by Treshnish's success and without waiting for orders, started to charge up the ravine of the burn towards some enclosures where four regiments of the Covenant centre (Hume's, Cassilis's, Glencairn's and Argyll's – who had misunderstood Baillie's instructions) were taking up a position. The Clanranald, equally inspired and not to be outdone, also broke from their station and raced them to the ridge. The wave of highlanders swept up to the outer dykes with young Moydartach half a stride ahead of the MacGregor (surnamed Caoch for his mad ferocity) and MacLean of Duart close behind. The Covenant musketeers, with time only for a single volley, fired too soon, and the gaels ran in low under their shot and gave them no pause to reload. Screaming half-naked caterans rushed the enclosure and started leaping the walls with heads down and targes high to get immediately to close quarters. Helpless musketeers with their now useless weapons were quickly butchered as the perimeter disintegrated, and when they saw their forward companies overborne and the men in the front ranks cut down or dismembered under the terrible swords and axes of the highlanders, Covenant veterans and levies alike started to break for the ridge. Within minutes the enclosures were overrun and the regiments in flight, looking in vain for flank support which was not there to check the gaelic attack.

Baillie hurriedly threw Lindsay's regiment and 200 fresh cuirassiers into the gap and a desperate fight developed along the centre of the ridge. The impetus of the highlanders' charge had carried them to the crest itself, but here they found themselves confronting the greater part of the Covenant army and were now in their turn dangerously isolated and exposed. Rash and blood-hot, they charged on but were checked by the arrival of fresh Covenant formations and were soon in peril of being cut off and overwhelmed by sheer weight of numbers. From the meadow below Montrose saw their predicament and would have supported them if he could, but a critical development on the Royalists' left was forcing him to turn his immediate attention to the flank.

A part at least of Baillie's vanguard had succeeded in crossing the ravine of the burn, and rounding the head of the glen had reached a point roughly equivalent to the site of the present farm of Wester Auchinrivoch. Their objective was clearly the northern ridge, and, quickly realizing the danger, Montrose sent 200 Gordon foot to seize the position before they could reach it. Unfortunately, probably because a large part of the leading Covenant division had followed Baillie's orders in keeping behind the shelter of the crest, he gravely underestimated their numbers. The Gordons reached the slope to find themselves engaged against a vastly superior force of infantry backed by Balcarres's regiment of lancers. They were surrounded almost immediately, and if not supported at once it seemed likely that they would be killed to a man.

Watching from a distance, Aboyne saw his Gordons cut off and threatened with imminent annihilation and, regardless of Montrose's orders that he was not to risk his person, led out his small bodyguard in a gallant but mad attempt at rescue. On reaching the hill he found the way blocked by a solid phalanx of Covenant pikes, but he wheeled left and led his troop at a gallop into the exposed flank of a body of musketeers. The charge brought momentary relief to the hard-pressed Royalist infantry, but Aboyne's small following were far too few to tip the scale, and he too was soon swallowed up in the struggle and encircled by Balcarres's horsemen.

Montrose saw the issue suddenly in the balance and called urgently on the Royalist horse to advance. But at this critical moment the cavalry baulked and would not move, though it was clear that in minutes the battle could be lost through their default. He then galloped furiously over to where Old Airlie and Ogilvie of Baldovie sat their horses in front of the family troop, and appealed to the Ogilvies to save the day:

> You see my Lord, those rash men have plunged into desperate danger and will soon be cut to pieces by the Covenant cavalry unless they are supported at once. All eyes and hearts are on your Lordship, as the only man fit for the honour of beating back the enemy to save our comrades, and repairing by cool veteran courage the error of headstrong youth![18]

The Ogilvies did not hesitate as Airlie called the charge, and 80 horses wheeled for Slaughter Howe. The old earl drove full gallop into the side of Balcarres's squadrons and the Covenant lancers recoiled and began to fall back. Shamed by this courage and inspired by its success, the Royalist cavalry took heart again and, following Nathaniel Gordon in a fresh charge up the slope, drove the Covenanters off the hill. Montrose caught the impulse of the moment and now ordered a general attack on the eastern ridge where Alastair's highlanders were still holding their own in the vicious struggle around the Covenant centre.

Baillie saw his vanguard breaking up, and galloped back across the burn to call forward his reserves. But at the rear of the column the Fifeshire levies had seen their cavalry give ground and were already starting to desert the field. Collecting together a few of their officers, Baillie made a last vain attempt to check the rout, but all along the ridge the Covenant regiments were falling back as the Royalist advance swept over the crest. The cavalry, as so often before, left the wretched foot-soldiers to shift for themselves and rode for Denny. The Committee also fled in several directions, and finally, seeing that all was lost, Baillie too left the field and galloped for his life.

Behind him the Covenant infantry stood no chance and were butchered without mercy as they tried to escape. Weighed down by their equipment, and already tired from the route march of the early morning, they could not hope to outdistance the highlanders' terrible pursuit. The gaels ran them down over eighteen English miles, and as usual the killing during the aftermath far exceeded the slaughter of the battle. But the carnage after Kilsyth was more unsparing and extreme than any hitherto. The highlanders cut down every living thing in their path. The names later given to the hills and hollows of the area – Slaughter Howe, The Bullet, Kill-the-many Butts – recall the several massacres where isolated Covenant units were brought to bay and slaughtered without quarter. In the confusion of the rout innocent peasants were cut to pieces together with the fleeing enemy, and whole families were later thrown into common graves. Airlie spared a man who clutched at his saddle bow and saw him promptly spitted through by a common soldier of his troop who was less easily persuaded to mercy. Only a few gentlemen fortunate enough to surrender to Montrose in person were spared. Although they had not been involved in the battle itself and were the first to flee the field, the Fifeshire levies suffered with the rest and were virtually annihilated in the pursuit. In Kirkaldy alone it is recorded that two hundred women were made widows on that day. Entire companies who had marched away to join the army were simply never heard of again, and for years afterwards the battle was remembered with horror by the Covenant communities of Fife.[19]

In all, Covenant casualties were computed at the time to have been in the region of 6,000 dead – the greater part of them infantry. A number of horsemen were drowned trying to escape across the Dullater Bog, but most of the cavalry, the mounted officers and the Committee got away. Baillie, with a Major-General Holbourn and a few dragoons, reached Stirling where they were joined by Burleigh and Tullibardine. Lindsay fled to Berwick, his entire regiment with the exception of himself and his major having perished. Balcarres fled into Lothian, to Colinton near Edinburgh. Argyll rode twenty miles to Queensferry and escaped by ship to Berwick and the protection of the Scottish garrison there. All the spoil of battle – colours, arms and baggage – fell to Montrose's soldiers. Wishart later claimed that the Royalists lost only 6 men killed outright – 3 of them Ogilvies. However, there were a large number incapacitated by wounds, most of them from musket shot.

Montrose rested his army for two days at Kilsyth while the wounded were cared for, and then marched on Glasgow. The city was defenceless since Lanerick, on hearing that Baillie's army had been totally defeated, had hastily disbanded the Hamilton levies and fled to join Argyll at Berwick. Two commissioners came to the camp to plead for the citizens, and, accepting their offered tribute of £500 sterling to placate his army, Montrose sent them back with assurances that he would not permit his highlanders to sack the town. He made a formal entry into Glasgow the following day and was enthusiastically received by the populace. Strict orders were issued against looting and offenders were summarily hanged. But highlanders went to war for spoil, and the temptation was so great that it was clear that if they stayed in the town the army was all too likely to get out of hand. He therefore withdrew from Glasgow itself, allowing the citizens a garrison of their own, and set up his main leaguer six miles away at Bothwell Brig. From there, Alastair and his war band were sent off to put down the dissidents in the West, but they met with no resistance. Cassilis and Glencairn fled to Ireland, and Eglinton's recruits hurriedly dispersed at news of their coming. Alastair was even lavishly entertained at Loudoun Castle by the Covenanting Countess – the Chancellor having escaped to England.

Kilsyth had changed the face of affairs throughout Scotland, and now Montrose was for the first time able to enjoy the positive results of victory. The main towns and shires sent commissioners to tender their submission to the King and plead for favour. The nobility, so conspicuously absent hitherto, rode in to acclaim the King's Lieutenant – Erskine, Seton, Fleming, Wigton, Airth, Carnegie, Maderty, Drummond and others; would-be Royalists till now afraid to declare openly for Charles, waverers and even erstwhile enemies flocked to Bothwell to recognize the new power in the land. And most important to Montrose, the list included also the powerful Lowland lairds who had previously hesitated or stayed aloof or uncommitted in the struggle – the Douglas, Roxburgh, Home, Hartfell, Charteris, Dalziel and even Traquair (who sent his son, Lord Linton) – with whose support, now pledged, he could carry the war south at last.

His most immediate concern, however, was to procure the release of Royalist captives still in Covenant hands – an action which to the mind of Wishart (who was one of them) made him 'the friend of prisoners forever'. Dispatched east with a squadron of light cavalry, on 20 August the Master of Napier and Nathaniel Gordon rode to Linlithgow, first to liberate Lord Napier and Sir George Stirling of Keir with the ladies of these two families who had been kept under house-arrest within the town. They then continued to Edinburgh and formally demanded the submission of the city in the King's name, together with the surrender of the Castle and the release of all Royalist prisoners warded in the tolbooth. A deputation from the burghers met them in front of the gates and on behalf of the town council humbly submitted to the authority of the King's Lieutenant. In extenuation of their late rebellion they explained, predictably, that they had been subverted from their true duty and traditional loyalty by the ambition of a few seditious men. They offered to pay a fine in compensation for the crimes committed and implored the King's mercy – which was granted on the condition that they returned to their allegiance.

About 150 Royalists were released from the tolbooth, including

Crawford, Ogilvie, Wishart, Reay, Drum and Ogilvie of Powrie. All were weak, gaunt and in a pitiful condition. As a policy of reinsurance, perhaps, the Covenant authorities had previously made provision for the release of some but this had not been carried out. The city was so stricken by the plague that many of the gaolers were dead or fled, and the prisoners, abandoned to the pestilence in foetid and rat-infested cells, had survived on food brought in by friends outside. Wishart bore the marks of the rats' teeth on him to the grave. The Castle stayed in Covenant hands, however, and it seems that those unfortunate enough to have been incarcerated there–including Montrose's son, Lord Graham, were not released at this time. The others recovered health and spirits with their freedom, and as they could, went to Bothwell Brig to join their deliverer.

Montrose had need of them since he was now preparing to invade England. Sir Robert Spottiswoode had arrived with a letter from the King in which Charles stated that he had sent Sir John Belle with 1,500 horse with orders to rendezvous with Montrose on the border, and that he had written also to Home and Roxburgh urging them to give every possible assistance to his Lieutenant in the North–which they had promised to do. On 28 August Montrose sent urgently to Ogilvie, now fit again and hot for action, telling him to come quickly–'. . . for Home and Roxburgh long for you and have sent me this day for a party. Hasten to them and acquaint me with your opinion of my advance and what you are able to do, and where you think we may best join you.'[20]

Spottiswoode also brought the King's Commission appointing Montrose Captain-General and Deputy Governor of Scotland with power to summon Parliament in the King's name. Though intent on preparing for his border campaign, Montrose was clearly also thinking about reconstruction in Scotland, and responded by issuing a summons for Parliament to meet at Glasgow on 20 October. It may be that he had it in mind to use such an occasion to promulgate the constitutional theories by which he had always claimed to stand, since he now began to correspond again with the mentor of his own most formative years. A Protection was sent to Drummond of Hawthornden, and when the scholar wrote that he could produce a Remonstrance drafted at the beginning of the troubles 'for persuading His Majesty's subject to obedience towards him', which he had originally intended for publication when Charles visited Scotland in 1641 but had then suppressed owing to the eclipse of royal authority at that time, Montrose at once told him to bring or send any such papers which vindicated monarchy, including 'Irene', to Bothwell so that they could be printed.[21]

He also used the authority inherent in the new royal commission to reward the foremost of his officers. The Royalists paraded at Bothwell and after a brief ceremony, during which he formally thanked his soldiers for their outstanding valour and high achievement, Montrose knighted his major-general, Alastair, in front of the assembled army.

Time might prove that the MacDonald was no great strategist, but as a battle commander he had no equal. He was accounted the greatest swordsman among the gaels, and no Campbell had withstood his terrible ferocity. He had held the ridge at Auldearn against overwhelming odds; had led the Highland charge at Tippermuir, Aberdeen and Inverlochy, and commanded the gaelic division at Kilsyth. For this, he would be known by the MacDonalds henceforth as 'Sir Alastair, the Red-Armed Horseknight' and like the heroes of the old northern sagas would become a legend among his people in the Western Isles.

For Montrose it was a brief moment of glory, and as such it was surely justified. A bare twelve months previously he had crossed the border with two followers. He had found a vagabond army wandering in the hills, fugitive and close to destruction, and with this small and improbable nucleus he had set out to conquer a country. In one year, with few troops poorly armed, with little help or support of any kind and against a background of faithless friends, dubious allies, broken promises, disappointment and intense personal sorrow, he had fought and been victorious in six pitched battles. Five times he had seen his army melt away, and each time he had made another army and risen phoenix-like to fight and win again. In six battles his soldiers had killed 16,000 of the enemy for the loss of less than 200 of their own. The power of the Covenant in Scotland had been broken, its armies annihilated and its leaders driven into exile. Courage and sheer ability had achieved the seemingly impossible. And so he had kept the first part of his promise. 'From Dan to Beersheba' he was undisputed master of Scotland. Now he would honour the rest of the pledge. The road to the borders lay open. Beyond, there was one more army of the Covenant–the last one, and the biggest–to be fought and beaten, but 'though it should rain Leslies from heaven' he would ride South tomorrow.

And yet, it was a delusion.

PART IV

Philiphaugh

17

Philiphaugh

A meteor wert thou crossing a dark night,
Yet shalt thy name, conspicuous and sublime,
Stand in the spacious firmament of time,
Fixed as a star; such glory is thy right.
Alas! it may not be, for earthly fame
Is Fortune's frail dependant; yet there lives
A Judge who, as man claims by merit, gives.

Wordsworth

Highlanders have beaten lowlanders in battle, but they have rarely
been able to 'fix' their conquest. It was always difficult to attach
clansmen permanently to a cause—this was never the way in the
Highlands—and a century later not even Bonnie Prince Charlie could
prevent his men from returning home with their loot. Booty was held
to be the rightful reward for victory, but after Kilsyth there was
little booty to speak of—and certainly not the spoil of Glasgow, on
which they had hopefully set their minds. In this, Montrose undoubtedly gave offence. But Kilsyth had changed many things, his
own role among them; since in direct contrast to the destructive war
that he had waged against the Covenanters and all their works, he
was now obliged to build and consolidate a civil authority corresponding to that which he had won in battle. The people upon whom he
had encouraged the gaels to prey, as the King's representative in
Scotland, he now had to protect—from pillage by his own men. But the
highlanders, understandably, had difficulty in appreciating this nice distinction. Nor did they even have the consolation of sharing out the
£500 sterling with which the magistrates of Glasgow had ransomed
their city. If Montrose was to consolidate the North behind him, he
needed above all things to placate the middle class, and when the citizens of Glasgow complained that the Parliament which he had called
for October would be a costly affair, he returned the money to defray
some of the expenses which he knew would be involved. The gaels got
only what they had picked off the battlefield.

Discontented, the highlanders began to drift away: disillusioned by
Montrose's 'failure' in denying them the sack of Glasgow, the invasion
of England did not attract. The constitutional struggle between a
distant king and an English Parliament did not concern them and there

were other ploys and a more immediate feud nearer home. Many felt slighted that the Graham, whom they had come to follow as a chieftain after their own kind, now consorted with the lowlanders whom they despised and had so recently defeated. The Athollmen and the MacLeans asked leave to return and rebuild their homes which had been burned down during the punitive raids of the Covenanters, promising to return when this was done. It was a fair excuse and they would not be gainsaid. It was September already and winter came early in the Highlands. Provisions must be got in, and so they would be on their way. The campaign was over.

Alastair went too, though having for so long been close to Montrose he more than any must have known what this would mean. But he had learned that his father and kinsmen had retired to the islands of Rachlin and Jura pursued by the Laird of Ardkinglass under orders from Argyll. Old Colkitto had a mind to revive the ancient MacDonald pretensions to Kintyre and from the mist was beckoning him to the family quarrel. Alastair would have been no true highlander had he preferred the King's cause to that of his own blood and kindred. Montrose argued with him to no avail. He even promised to march west himself when once the King's war was won and told the MacDonald outright that his desertion would be the ruin of them both.[1] But Alastair also would not be gainsaid, and in the end Montrose could only stand and watch him go. On 3 September the highlanders left the camp at Bothwell and with Alastair went 500 MacDonalds and most of the Irishes who joined his 'lifeguard'. Their coloured plaids melted gradually into the September heather, the music of the pipes dwindled slowly away, and Alastair led them back to that other older world and into oblivion. Only Magnus O'Cahan and his regiment to their eternal honour elected to stay with the King's Lieutenant.

In the short space of a week Montrose lost 2,000 men, but although this was a severe blow it did not cause him to alter his plans. He was under strong pressure from the King to march south with all speed (Digby wrote to Jermyn in terms of 20,000 men[2]), and he may have felt himself committed beyond recall. However, it was also the opinion of many of his friends that Kilsyth had made him dangerously over-confident.[3] Clearly he had been aware that a loosely compacted High-land army would not have been able to hold down Scotland let alone attempt the conquest of England, but at the same time he seems to have deluded himself into thinking that he could conjure out of the borders an army of lowlanders, weary of Argyll and the tyranny of the Kirk, who, though passive hitherto, would now declare for Charles and join the royal standard. Douglas and Ogilvie were re-cruiting in Annandale and Nithsdale, the plan being for them to link up with Traquair, Roxburgh and Home (whose support the King had promised) and then to meet the main Royalist force as it marched south. Douglas, it is true, raised a considerable number of recruits but he had difficulty in keeping them with the standard. From Galashiels he wrote asking Montrose to come himself, saying that his presence was absolutely necessary to inspire the levies, but Montrose for some reason did not move from Bothwell. Perhaps he was too concerned with arrangements for the Parliament, or perhaps he felt that Douglas's presence was sufficient. Yet the truth of it was that Douglas was no longer the name it had been once, while the old Moss troopers and the border robbers had vanished as a breed. Kinmont Willie and the Carleton brothers were dead and gone, the days of reiving and Hot Trod with them, and their descendants had grown timorous on peace and porridge. Douglas's recruits were herdsmen and shepherd boys who had never heard a shot fired in anger.

In Bothwell, while preparing for an invasion of the border counties, Montrose was also turning his attention to the administration of government—a preoccupation which in retrospect seems somewhat premature, and may in some measure reflect the degree to which he overestimated the decisiveness of Kilsyth. The Parliament called for 20 October was intended 'for settling religion and peace, and freeing the oppressed subjects of those insupportable burdens they have groaned under this time bygone', but if it was to accomplish anything at all much would have to be done to restore the reputation of the royal cause as represented by himself in the minds of a populace who had for so long been subjected to the virulent propaganda of the Covenanters. He had already asked Drummond of Hawthornden to send to Bothwell such of his essays as vindicated monarchy, and he now also prepared a personal 'Remonstrance' justifying his own actions which he possibly intended to present to Parliament when it assembled. The document[4] as it has survived is in old Napier's handwriting but from certain biographical details that emerge from the text, the author is clearly Montrose.[5] Napier had come to Bothwell after his release and it is quite possible that, just as in earlier times, Montrose turned to him for advice, so he may have had a hand in drafting it. Alternatively he may merely have made a copy of the original.

The Remonstrance is a complete confession of faith. It has often been the fashion to assess Montrose's political philosophy on the basis of the 'Essay on Sovereignty'—and this probably did reflect his views in the early days of the Troubles, even though it is doubtful whether he was indeed the author of it. But when all the accusations have been made and the much mooted questions of his integrity and consistency are put to trial, the Remonstrance, although it allows him the advantage of justification in the retrospect, must be taken as the main speech for the defence.

He begins by reaffirming his allegiance to the first and true Covenant. This bond he had never broken. He had opposed the pretensions of prelates, their interference in civil government, their Court of High Commission—'the quintessence of popery and arminianism'—and the foisting of a 'dead Service Book' upon a national Church. Like others he had attempted to resist by constitutionally acceptable methods—through 'Supplications, Declarations, and Protestations'—and when these failed, through 'the *renewal* of o*u*r Covenant as the only safest and fairest way for preservation of Religion and Liberty'. Yet still Charles had continued to be misled by the prelates and especially by Hamilton–'the prime fomenter of misunderstanding betwixt the King and his subjects'–and the Scots finally had to resort to armed defence against invasion until at Berwick and then at Ripon the mission of the Covenant was accomplished and Charles gave way to all of their demands. But by this time it was already becoming apparent that some, 'having found the sweetness of government', had far deeper designs, ultimately intending nothing less than the total abrogation of the King's prerogative, and Montrose describes himself as 'wrestling between extremities'–suspicious of the Covenanters' ambitions and yet frightened lest the King might retract the concessions he had granted. Rather than give way to Charles 'in what still seemed doubtful', he continued with the Covenant faction. 'For the settling of Religion and the peace of our disturbed nation we gave way to more than was warrantable.' Eventually, events had decided for him. The King came to Scotland and ratified in person the concessions they had won, but now the extremists wanted more. Finding them

> . . . to intend more than they did pretend, which we do perceive tends greatly to the prejudice of our reformed Religion, ruin of lawful authority, and liberty of the subject, *contrary* to our national covenant–we were constrained to suffer them to deviate without us, with the multitude misled by them, whose eyes they seal in what concerns Religion, and hearts they steal away in what concerns loyalty, *and there we left them.*

Afterwards, he had been imprisoned even, as a potential servant of the King, and this too he had borne until the true Covenanting movement was finally perverted beyond redemption by the signing of the Solemn League with England. This was the greatest outrage of all– '. . . In which league we perceived Presbyterian Government, sworn to by us, to be esteemed loose, and subjects obliged to take arms against their prince for maintaining the liberties of the Parliament of England–which they knew not.' The Covenant, conceived in all honesty as an instrument of national and religious liberty, had, through the agency of ambitious men, been prostituted to a political bargain, while the Kirk, in coercing the people to blind obedience, pretended to a tyranny more autocratic in design than ever the bishops had dared to represent. Obliged to sign or go to prison, Montrose, 'not daring to make shipwreck of conscience', had decided to leave his country and live in England, but even there he was still 'bound in honour to those same principles of the Covenant' to which he had not lightly sworn. And so he had taken up arms to fight for three things: for 'the middle way of our reformed Religion'; for a strong central government–'maintaining the King's honour and greatness'; and for a political system which granted liberty to the subject. Now he defends himself against the accusations of the Covenanters. He had not rebelled against the Covenant but fought only to preserve its original ideals. He was not 'an enemy to Religion' and they were hypocrites that said so–for if he had used Catholic Irishes the Covenanters had done the same in Ireland. He was not a 'Malignant' since he had not come *against* his country but *for* it–and when many had not been prepared to hazard anything 'for Religion, King, or Country'. Nor, most of all was he a 'Traitor'.

> Traitors we are not, to God, nor King, nor Country. Not to God because we stand or fall, by God's assistance, for the reformed religion. . . . Traitors to the King we are not for we go about His Majesty's expedition according to his express mandate. . . . Traitors to our Country we are not but we endeavour the liberties thereof. . . . And as for shedding of blood–we would by all means shun the same: neither ever did we shed the blood of any but of such as were sent forth by them to shed our blood, and to take our lives, whose blood we shed in our defence.

This is not an expression of blind royalism: rather it is true Montrose. But, on the assumption that the Remonstrance was intended as a political manifesto, it was also true of Montrose in that it reveals too clearly the fatal weakness which would ultimately cause him to lose it all, even as it reflects more truly than any other surviving document those principles which moved him in the first place. It is the work of an idealist, not a politician. Whereas the latter tends to work on the basis of existing facts and compromises where necessary to suit the realities of a situation, Montrose had fixed his eye on an organization of Church and State which had no reality in seventeenth-century Scotland. He fought rather for something that could one day be–but not in his time–and his preoccupation with this ideal led him to misjudge completely the temper of the Scottish Lowlands.

He gravely underestimated the power of the ministers. The Kirk had given power to the people because its power over the people was absolute. 'The Lowlands had no other voice or ear than the ministers. They were the sole interpreters, teachers, and guides.' And their power was as much temporal as spiritual. Once the Kirk had identified itself with a political cause, had allied itself with the political power predominating and had maintained that power with the sword, it was logical that it should have come to regard its political opponents as the enemies of God. The same damnation horrifyingly depicted from the pulpits with lurid images of hell-fire and eternal agony awaited alike the witch, the adulterer and the man who joined the excommunicate Montrose. The weapon of excommunication (once regarded as a Romish practice and much abhorred by the Godly until they found a use for it) assured the Kirk of a temporal authority from which there could be no appeal. What the ministers bound on earth, their God would surely bind in heaven.

To these Montrose presented a reasoned appeal for a central authority. But the ministers did not deal in reason. In seventeenth-century

Scotland reason had smothered under the terrifying demagoguery of an untaught Kirk. Cromwell in his time would try to reason with them—once—beseeching them 'in the bowels of Christ to believe it possible that they might be mistaken', and failing this would thereafter drum them out of their Assembly with brusque instructions to concern themselves with the glory of God and not the iniquity of governments. But Montrose saw himself as a true Covenanter and a Presbyterian, and could not do this even had he had the power and time to do so. He saw the common people as being in subjugation, yet did not see that the religious fear of hell-fire lent a strange elation to this oppression. At best, the Remonstrance appealed to the anti-clericalism of the gentry, and these made up the bulk of his recruits at Bothwell. But even among the aristocracy, too many had already elected to join the Kirk rather than risk taking sides against it.

Nor did Montrose seem to realize just how much the use of Alastair's Irishes had damaged his cause in the Lowlands. To draw a parallel with Monroe's forces in Ulster was totally to miss the point since the Lowland Scots would admit of no such comparison. Savages set to butcher savages was acceptable in their way of thinking, but Montrose had loosed the gaels—ancestral enemy—upon a civilized people and the tales of pillage and violence had aroused their ancient hatred of the highlander—16,000 of their kindred had been slaughtered in his battles, and for this they would never forgive him.

To these, Montrose defended his ideal. Charles i—and there is the irony of it—should be king, to rule constitutionally over a free people and an unpolitical presbytery. The clergy were to renounce their political pretensions and content themselves with fulfilling their spiritual duties. The nobility were to put aside individual ambition and support the royal authority—constitutionally defined. As an ideal it had great force—Montrose proved it so. As a political concept it was profound and generations ahead of its time. But in seventeenth-century Scotland it was all fools' gold.

Montrose broke camp at Bothwell on 4 September and began the march South. Next day at Calderhouse there occurred the most serious defection yet.

Since the victory at Kilsyth, the cancer of jealousy had been eating at the heart of Aboyne. From his father he had inherited in large measure the uneasy ambition of the Gordons, and he felt slighted by Montrose's reception of the Lowland gentry who had flocked in such numbers to Bothwell when what seemed the decisive battle had been won. It had angered him that a pamphlet by Sir William Rollo recounting the campaign had largely ignored the Gordon contribution. Although, when he complained, Montrose claimed to have known nothing of the document, nor did he repudiate it; and since Rollo was known to be close to the King's Lieutenant, Aboyne suspected that Montrose had even connived at belittling the role which he and his dead brother had played. He felt personally wronged when Crawford was given command of the cavalry instead of himself and he possibly resented also the reappearance of Ogilvie, who, released from prison, now seemed to threaten his favoured place in the counsels of the General. These were fears upon which Argyll's creatures, easily penetrating the open leaguer at Bothwell, could play with some effect, and Ogilvie, who saw all too clearly that he was becoming the object of Aboyne's envy, tried to warn him in a letter.

> Argyll leaves no wind unfurled to sow dissention among you and draw your Lordship off . . . notwithstanding of any oaths or promise that he will seem to make to you [he] does intend nothing but your dishonour, the utter extirpating of all memory of your old family, and, give it should be in your hands, the ruination and betraying of the King's service . . . for they are studying to draw your Lordship off . . . I know your Lordship's gallantry to be such that I will not presume to go further faithfully than render up my commission to you.[6]

Unfortunately, the warning appears to have had no effect. Aboyne claimed that he had received letters from his father, now returned from exile, summoning him back to Huntly, and, despite all Montrose's protests, he left, taking all the northern levies with him.[7] Of his clan, only Nathaniel Gordon remained with the army.

Montrose's force was now reduced to 700 foot and 200 mounted gentlemen, but, apparently still inspired by the vague expectation of obtaining substantial reinforcements in the borders, he continued south of Edinburgh to Cranstoun Kirk. The sixth of September being a Sunday, Wishart was to preach to the army, but here the Royalists suddenly got word that David Leslie (later Lord Newark)[8] was at Berwick with a strong force hurriedly withdrawn from the main Scottish army in England. An intercepted letter also revealed that Argyll had ordered Tullibardine to take an army and block the route north.

Lord Erskine and others now urged Montrose to withdraw again beyond the Highland line before it was too late, but he felt bound still to carry the war into England, and, counting possibly on Douglas's levies and the support promised by the border earls, he persisted in his adventurous course and hurried on down Gala Water. At Tordwoodlee, Douglas and Ogilvie joined him with a body of horse from Nithsdale, but these were mainly bonnet lairds and their half-hearted followers were deserting daily in large numbers. Traquair met them at Galashiels, outwardly friendly, and sent his son Lord Linton as a pledge for his loyalty with a well-equipped troop of horse to join the army. Thus reinforced, on 8 or 9 September Montrose continued to Kelso where he had agreed to rendezvous with Home and Roxburgh–only to find that they had become prisoners of the Covenant the day previously, and probably by their own contrivance–a measure of caution which enabled them to preserve their apparent fidelity to the King while simultaneously ingratiating themselves with Argyll. (Royalist historians have even claimed that they deliberately 'enticed' Montrose south, and that, unconvinced by the victory at

Kilsyth, they like many others preferred the part of passive sedition to one of empty heroics in a steadily unfolding tragedy. Roxburgh certainly is supposed to have sent himself to Berwick for the troops of horse which allegedly 'surprised' him.)

Montrose's own state of mind up to this time is difficult to assess. To retreat once more beyond the Highland line would have been to surrender to Leslie everything that he had won at Kilsyth, while to begin recruiting among the clans again would have meant an intolerable delay–and time was against him. He may still have hoped for help from England–so often promised yet never delivered–or, having won so often against the odds, he may have deluded himself into thinking that he could go on doing so and that courage alone could achieve the impossible. It was said that his over-confidence after Kilsyth was overweening, but the decision to continue south after his main forces had deserted him bears rather the mark of a man who was becoming desperate.

On 10 September Sir Robert Spottiswoode, who was with the army, wrote to Digby describing their predicament (the letter was still in his coat pocket when he was captured):

You little imagine the difficulties my Lord Marquis hath here to wrestle with. The overcoming of the enemy is the least of them; he hath more to do with his own seeming, friends. . . . He was forced to dismiss his highlanders for a season who would needs return home to look to their own affairs. When they were gone, Aboyne took a caprice and had away with him the greatest strength he had in horse. Notwithstanding whereof he resolved to follow his work and clear this part of the Kingdom of the rebels that had fled to Berwick, and kept a bustling there. Besides he was *invited here unto* by the Earls of Roxburgh and Home; who, when he was within a dozen miles of them, have rendered there houses and themselves to David Leslie, and are carried in as prisoners to Berwick. Traquair hath been with him and promised more than he hath yet performed. All these were great disheartenings to any other but to him, whom nothing of this kind can amaze. With the small forces he has presently with him, he is resolved, to pursue David Leslie, and not suffer him to grow stronger. If you would perform that which you lately promised. . . .[9]

That Montrose should have contemplated 'pursuing' Leslie, who could not have had less than 5,000 men, sounds like over-confidence indeed (unless, as is probable, he was misinformed as to the Covenanter's strength), but Spottiswoode was writing also to revive failing hearts in England and may have felt that some exaggeration was justified under the circumstances. Yet even for Montrose there had to come the point of disillusion. At Jedburgh not a man would join him, and he abandoned the march south to turn wearily westwards towards the Tweed in the hope of gaining recruits among the Douglas tenantry of Annandale. Evening on 12 September found him at Philiphaugh near the village of Selkirk.

The Royalists leaguered at the further end of a level meadow about a quarter of a mile wide along the northern bank of Ettrick Water, a short way below its junction with the Yarrow. Strategically, the place seemed well suited for defence, since here the 'Haugh' formed a deep recess in the hills, protected to the south and east by the Ettrick Stream itself, to the north by high inaccessible ground and to the west by the Yarrow and a steep wooded slope known as the Hareheadshaw. The army camped with the left wing resting on the edge of Harehead Wood while on the level plain below the Irish dug a line of shallow trenches to protect the right which faced up the narrow expanse of Philiphaugh. Behind them the strait passes of the Ettrick and the Yarrow afforded a secure line of retreat. The cavalry were billeted across the stream in the village of Selkirk itself which stood on a height overlooking the meadow about a mile from the camp.

Montrose also established his headquarters in Selkirk and prepared to pass the night in writing dispatches to the King. By now he had probably reached the bitter conclusion that the drive south would have to be abandoned, at least for a time, and he faced the difficult and distressing task of finding words to tell Charles that unless he received cavalry support–and urgently–he would be forced to withdraw again to the Highlands. This seems to have so distracted him that for the first time in the entire campaign he neglected to set the watch or brief the scouts in person, but left all such camp duties to his officers. They were still in hostile country, and Leslie could not be far off, so he intended to march early in the morning. Reveille was set for dawn.

In fact, David Leslie was closer than the Royalists thought.

After the fall of Carlisle this Covenant commander had taken his cavalry south to assist Leven, who was then besieging Hereford, and he was subsequently sent to pursue the King in the Midlands. After hearing of Kilsyth, however, his troops refused to continue in England while Scotland lay defenceless. Leven raised the siege of Hereford and David Leslie hurried north with every mounted man he could muster. Charles might have caught him at Rotherham, where his troops were too exhausted from the forced march to have defended themselves, but the King was suffering from a general paralysis of will, and Leslie was allowed to escape.[10] Nor, having let him loose, did Charles send any force to follow him. Collecting reinforcements from the garrisons at Newcastle and Berwick (where he was also joined by a Covenant committee which included Argyll, Lanerick and Lindsay) he crossed the Tweed on 6 September with an army now grown to 5,000 horse and 1,000 foot.[11] A flying column under Sir John Middleton (who had been Montrose's subordinate at Bridge of Dee and whose aged father had been murdered by the Irishes during their march through the Mearns) raced to Kelso where they captured Home and Roxburgh while the main force took the coast road north to circle round behind Montrose and cut him off from the Highlands.

On 11 September, when Montrose was at Jedburgh, Leslie held a

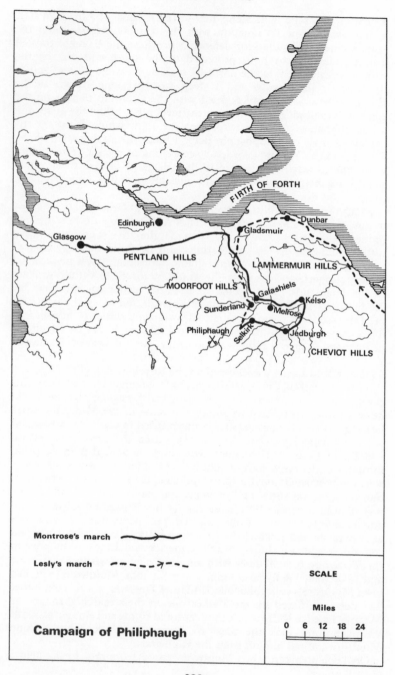

Montrose's march

Lesly's march

SCALE

Miles

0   6   12   18   24

Campaign of Philiphaugh

council of war on Gladsmuir in Lothian where he received a letter (it is generally presumed from Traquair) apprising him of Montrose's whereabouts and of his weakness in numbers. Leslie promptly turned in his tracks and struck south down Gala Water, crossing the ridge at Rink by the old Edinburgh–Selkirk road. He forded the Tweed just below Rae Weil and by nightfall on 12 September he was at Sunderland Hall, barely four miles from the Royalists' camp at Philiphaugh.[12]

Montrose wrote his dispatch unaware of the danger. During the night there were vague rumours of the enemy's approach. Around midnight a troop of horse under Charteris of Amisfield stationed in Sunderland were suddenly attacked. Amisfield and two others escaped but they were thought to have been engaged in a drunken brawl with hostile country folk and possibly the officer of the watch did not want to disturb the General. In the early morning scouts under Powrie-Ogilvie were sent out to reconnoitre the surrounding countryside but they returned saying that for ten miles about there was no sign of any enemy. Yet the patrols were made up of Traquair's men from Peebleshire and their loyalty was questionable. Or perhaps those who rode east and blundered into Leslie's pickets did not return to report. A dense autumn mist filled the valleys and visibility was down to a few yards. The army awoke and began to cook breakfast. It was discovered that Lord Linton had left in the night.

By a strange irony, 13 September was the anniversary of Aberdeen. In Paris Queen Henrietta Maria is said to have been singing a 'Te Deum' for the victory which heaven had vouchsafed her husband's arms at Kilsyth.

Shortly before first light Leslie closed in for the kill. He split his army into two. The main force, led by himself, headed up the left bank of the Ettrick under cover of the dense mist, while 2,000 dragoons under Middleton, guided, according to tradition, by a local Covenanter, crossed the water and, approaching the Selkirk road by way of Will's Nick, circled round behind the camp to seal the trap shut. Half an hour after dawn, Leslie launched his thunderbolt.

Montrose was eating a breakfast of boiled sheep's head[13] when his scoutmaster, Captain Blackadder, burst in with the news that the entire Covenant army was less than half a mile away and coming fast. Simultaneously a ragged fusilade of musket shots announced that the Royalist vedettes were being driven in. Rushing out into the street, Montrose threw himself onto the first horse he saw and galloped furiously down the hill towards the camp, his officers following as best they could. But even as he reached the stream Leslie's bugles were sounding the charge and the advancing Covenant squadrons threatened to cut him off from the main body of his army.

On Philiphaugh everything was in complete confusion. Most of the Royalist cavalrymen were still in Selkirk and separated from their horses which had been turned loose to graze in the meadow and neighbouring fields. As a result they could not be brought into action at all. The Douglas levies fled at the first shot, and, making for the woods, most got safe away. But with their flight the Irishes had no chance. Leslie's cavalry were the cream of the Scottish army,[14] heavy cuirassiers encased in steel, who charged confident in numbers and superior discipline and with the advantage of surprise. Twice O'Cahan's Irish counter-attacked and momentarily checked the advance, but overwhelmed by odds of almost ten to one they were driven back into the trenches and beset on all sides. Here and there a few isolated groups who had been separated from the rest fought their way out and reached the safety of the woods, but the fate of the rest was sealed by the arrival of Middleton and his 2,000 dragoons.

To the right of the shattered line, Montrose rallied 150 horsemen around him and hurled himself in the path of Leslie's squadrons. They took the full brunt of the Covenanters' charge, checked it and, regrouping, tried hopelessly to fight their way through to the beleagured Irish. Montrose led them like a man demented. For him, who had never experienced it before, defeat came hard, and seeing in his disintegrating army the ruin of everything that he had striven for, he now seemed intent only on finding an honourable death on the battlefield. His small band was soon reduced to less than 50 cavaliers, but with these he repeatedly charged the enemy, and all would probably have died at the last had not the Douglas, with Sir Thomas Dalziel and others of his officers, finally persuaded him to leave the field while it was still possible. Insistently they argued that Philiphaugh was not necessarily the end. The troops lost were only a fraction of the army which he had so often led to victory. The clansmen, the Gordons and the bulk of the Ulstermen were still loose in Scotland and would fight again with him to lead them. But if the Captain-General were killed, the royal cause was down for ever. Flight now was no disgrace.

> They implored him with tears, wrung from them by deep affection, by the memory of his past achievements, for the sake of his friends, his house, his sweet wife and children, for the King, country, and church, to have a care for his life. Next to God, he was their only hope; with him they must live or die.[15]

For better or worse, Montrose allowed himself to be constrained by their arguments. The fifty split up. Montrose went one way; Douglas and Airlie another, and the two groups cut their way through Leslie's troopers, who, fortunately, were now more intent on plundering the baggage than on trying to apprehend small bands of desperate fugitives. Montrose with his party, escaped up the Yarrow and on to Minchmuir, heading north-west, pursued by only a small detachment of enemy horse whose captain had recognized him as he fled. Some distance from Philiphaugh the Royalists turned on their tormentors, killing some and capturing the rest together with two standards, and were then able to continue unhindered. On Minchmuir they caught up with large numbers of other fugitives, and having brought these into some form of order again Montrose led them on to Traquair where he stopped to beg help from the Earl. But Traquair was not at home to defeated generals[16] and they continued through Peebles towards Tweeddale and Biggar.[17] Next morning at daybreak they forded the Clyde and linked up with Douglas and Airlie, and another 200 horse who had also survived the battle. About 500 strong, they continued north towards the Highlands, crossing the Forth and the Earn, and reached Buchanty on 19 September.

Montrose now took stock of the situation. He himself was for Atholl to raise the highlanders again while Douglas and Airlie were sent to Angus to try the Mearns once more. Erskine went to Mar. Dalziel (who had married a Carnegie) was sent to ask Lord Carnegie for help, and couriers were dispatched to Alastair and Aboyne begging them to return. Of his friends many were still missing, but more than he could have hoped, perhaps, survived. Douglas, Airlie, Crawford, Erskine, Wishart, Dalziel, Black Pate and the Napiers were still with him. Out of the army of 2,000 that had been surprised at Philiphaugh, some 500 were left who would still fight, and as many of the Douglas levies had escaped before the battle began. In the strictly military sense some honour too remained since neither of the two royal standards had fallen to the enemy. (Indeed, it was a strange coincidence at Philiphaugh that the victor lost more standards than the vanquished. The infantry standard was saved by an Irish soldier who tore the cloth from its pole and wrapped it round his body. He fought his way out of the press and next day brought it to Montrose, who made him one of his life guard and appointed him to carry it thereafter. The cavalry ensign was preserved by its bearer, the Hon. William Hay, brother of the Earl of Kinnoul, who escaped to England, and after lying low for a while subsequently found his way back to the army.) And so Montrose began again.

But at Philiphaugh, O'Cahan and 500 of his Irishes had been left to die and their fate would haunt him hereafter.

Surrounded, and with no hope of rescue, the Irishes defended the breastworks for an hour[18] until over half their number were dead, and finally, on being offered quarter, the army adjutant, Stewart, as the senior surviving officer, surrendered to Leslie.

According to Covenant estimates,[19] 1,000 died at Philiphaugh, but not more than 500 of these could have been soldiers under arms. Some 200 camp followers, cooks and house boys were slaughtered. The rest were women and children who had followed the Irish. Much has been said about the brutality of Alastair's gaels at Aberdeen. It was now the turn of the Covenant troops to show what they could do:

> With the whole baggage and stuff, which was exceeding rich, there remained now but boys, cooks, and a rabble of rascals, and women with their children in their arms, all those without commiseration were cut in pieces; whereof there were 300 women, that being natives of Ireland, were the married wives of the Irishes;

There were many big with child, yet none of them were spared, but all were cut in pieces with such savage and inhuman cruelty. . . . For they ripped up the bellies of the women with their swords, till the fruit of their womb – some in the embryo, some perfectly formed, some 'crouling' for life, and some ready for birth, fell down upon the ground, weltering in the gory blood of their mangled mothers.[20]

Eighty more women and children who escaped the initial massacre were later rounded up by the local people and taken to Linlithgow, where they were thrown from the bridge into the River Avon. Those who survived the fifty-foot drop and tried to reach the bank were spitted or pushed back into the deep water by lines of pikemen until all were drowned.[21] The countryfolk around Selkirk murdered dozens more.

The surviving Irish soldiers were taken to Newark Castle and placed under guard until their fate should be determined. David Leslie was a professional soldier and not accustomed to murdering unarmed men in cold blood, but the Kirk triumphant was set on a tour of vengeance, and the ministers were 'rowping like ravens'. Quarter, they argued, had been offered to Stewart alone and did not include the rank and file. By showing clemency towards prisoners, Leslie offended the Almighty, for had not Samuel so rebuked Saul for sparing the Kine of the Amalekites? 'What meaneth the bleating of sheep in my ears and the lowing of oxen which I hear?'—and they pointed at the waiting captives and howled for blood.

Leslie succumbed (as he would do many times thereafter) and the Irishes were taken out to be shot in rows and their bodies thrown into a mass grave which came to be known as 'Slain-Man's-Lee'.[22] O'Cahan and McLachlan, as officers of rank, were taken to Edinburgh and hanged without trial from the south wall of the castle. Only Stewart, seeing that his own execution would follow—promise of quarter or no—managed to escape and subsequently rejoined Montrose.

It had been a feature of the Civil War in England that no commander had ever descended to such terrible extremes. In Scotland, Montrose's clansmen had slain thousands in hot blood and during the immediate pursuit, but the mass killing of unarmed prisoners had never been counted among their virtues. Leslie had set an awful precedent, and in years to come, when the Covenanters themselves had to endure the so-called 'Killing Time', men would remember the quality of mercy which had been extended by the brethren.[23]

A number of prominent Royalists had also been taken prisoner at Philiphaugh including Hartfell, Drummond Earl of Perth and his son Spottiswoode, Sir William Rollo, William Murray (brother of Tullibardine), Sir Philip Nisbit, Andrew Guthry, Alexander Ogilvie of Innerquharitie and Nathaniel Gordon—all of whom had surrendered upon promise of quarter. Ogilvie, unlucky as ever, was also recaptured. On being urged to quit the field he had cut his way through the Covenant lines, crossed the river and ridden blindly into the mist. But his horse had been severely wounded and it foundered under him after three miles. Completely lost, he wandered on through the fields until he reached a peasant's cottage where he was 'graciously received, kindly treated, hospitably entertained, and basely betrayed'.

Rollo, Nisbit and Innerquharitie were taken to Glasgow where they were tried and condemned by a Committee of Parliament. Rollo and Nisbit were hanged at the Market Cross on 28 October, and young Innerquharitie was executed the following day. As a boy only eighteen years of age he might have been considered worthy of a pardon, but he was an Ogilvie and Argyll's hatred of that family was implacable. The scaffold was graced by the presence of that renowned Covenanter Mr David Dick, who expressed his satisfaction with the famous comment – 'The work gangs bonnily on.'

Owing to rumours that Montrose had raised a new army in the North and was threatening reprisals, the rest of the executions were temporarily postponed. The lay element among the Covenanters were showing signs of developing scruples, but the Kirk would not be denied its revenge. Synods and presbyteries throughout the land presented petitions to Parliament praying that 'the sword of justice may be impartially drawn against those persons now in bonds who have lifted up their hands against the Lord, the sworn Covenant, and this afflicted Kirk'.[24] On 26 November the General Assembly and Parliament met concurrently at St Andrews, and Wariston addressed the Estates in a tone of ferocious superstition. Previous reluctance to shed the blood of the wicked, he maintained, had brought God's two great servants against them – the sword and the pestilence – with which they were now afflicted. Let them remember the sea of blood that lay before Jehovah's throne, crying out for vengeance on these butchers of innocent souls. If the promise of quarter were sustained, the whole nation, and especially the Estates of Parliament, would be violating the sacred oath of the Covenant. God had shown his anger unto them, and only blood could propitiate the terrible deity.[25] Wariston's was the voice of the Kirk in full cry.

A very few escaped. Sir John Hay of Barro, a senator of the College of Justice, bribed Lanerick with the rents of his estates in Galloway and survived to die a pauper in 1654. Young Drummond also lived to become the third Earl of Perth. Ogilvie escaped the night before his execution by changing clothes with his sister and became the only man ever to have broken out of the famous bottle dungeon in St Andrews. Argyll felt cheated by his escape and, suspecting the connivance of the Hamilton faction, reacted by arranging the pardon of Hartfell on whose death they had counted.

But there was no hope for the others. Nathaniel Gordon offered to obtain an exchange of prisoners with Montrose – counting perhaps on the fact that the Chancellor's own son was among those held at Blair Atholl. But Loudoun replied that all his brethren and children were in like hazard and he would not be the means of hindering the course of justice. The surviving cavaliers were tried by a self-appointed committee who presumed to be both their accusers and their judge. Tullibardine made a half-hearted attempt to save his brother, William Murray, who was only nineteen, but he was unsuccessful and the youth was eventually executed on 29 January 1646. Nathaniel Gordon, Andrew Guthry and Sir Robert Spottiswoode had died under the Maiden three days previously.

Nathaniel Gordon, uncharacteristically, is said to have repented at the last and signed a declaration admitting to a life of adultery and drunkenness (the Covenanters were particularly keen on securing such confessions) as well as to having shed innocent blood.[26] Adventurer to the last, he may have hoped thereby to cheat the Maiden, but although they lifted the ban of excommunication and sententiously welcomed his outward signs of penitence, 'the auld rusty lass' had her victim nevertheless. He wrote a will before he died leaving two hundred dollars to the Minister of Deir and the rest to his widow, Grizelda Seton, but the Covenanters made certain deductions for 'prison expenses', and it is doubtful whether the lady saw much of her inheritance.

Sir Robert Spottiswoode and Andrew Guthry died as they had lived – 'full of malice against the cause and and Covenant' – despite the ministrations of Robert Blair and Andrew Cant who were sent to torment them in their latter hours. Spottiswoode's death was judicial murder. A civilian all his life, he had never actually been in arms against the Covenant, but he had been taken at Philiphaugh with a sword in his possession – to defend himself, as he said – and this had doomed him. Before his death he had an interview with the young Lochiel, who was then Argyll's ward, and the conversation fixed the highlander's future as a Royalist. (He dissociated himself from Argyll immediately thereafter.) Spottiswoode also wrote a last letter to Montrose 'to recommend the care of my orphans to you', and he urged the general not to lose heart, but to continue 'by fair and gentle carriage to gain the people's affection to their prince, rather than to imitate the barbarous inhumanity of your adversaries'.[27]

Montrose honoured the request. The Royalists took no reprisals.

Rattray
(October 1645–August 1646)

If man you are, then be a man,
Keep principle, keep trust,
And be prepared to pay for both
If pay with blood you must.
Rather a hundred times your life,
But not yourself disdain;
And let your life be forfeited
If honour still remain.

Petöfi Sandor[1]

Philiphaugh was not the end, but somehow the magic had gone. Montrose had lost his aura of invincibility, and to add an element of futility to his own sense of failure there arrived a letter from the King, written before news of the battle had been carried south to England. The march to Tweed had been for nothing, since the plan to send a force of cavalry to join Montrose on the border had been temporarily abandoned. 'And indeed it is no small part of my misfortune,' wrote Charles, '(though the more for your glory) that this *shall be* is yet all my song to you; and it were inexcusable if real impossibility were not the just excuse.'[2] The letter was dated: Ragland, 9 September 1645. The next day Prince Rupert surrendered Bristol, and in England the shadows lengthened on the royal cause.

Montrose, characteristically, was not deterred, and now began with renewed energy to piece together another army. Sir John Hurry chose this moment to change sides again and offer his services to the Royalist cause. The Captain-General was possibly reluctant to put much trust in so notorious a soldier of fortune, but it was significant perhaps that even at this stage Hurry thought that Montrose was in with a chance.

In terms of casualties, Philiphaugh had been a defeat of minor proportions only. Tragic as was the loss of O'Cahan and his Irishes, and of Nathaniel Gordon and the other veteran officers soon to die at Covenant hands, they represented only a fraction of the force which had been victorious at Kilsyth. Alastair and his war band were still somewhere in the West and might yet return as they had promised. Airlie was mustering horsemen in Angus. Erskine was in Mar. And if in Atholl the harvest season made recruiting slow, when the corn was in the Robertsons too would render up their tale of tried fighting men.

But Montrose's main hope, as always, was for the Gordon cavalry, and 7 October found him at Drumninor Castle near Strathbogie where Aboyne and Lord Lewis Gordon, their quarrel apparently forgotten, joined the army with 1,500 foot and 500 horse. The Marquis of Huntly himself, however, now reappeared on the scene, having emerged from hiding after Kilsyth, and Montrose wrote courteously to him, looking for his help and co-operation in the King's cause, and concluding: '. . . and for times to come I am absolutely resolved to observe the way you propose; and in everything, upon my honour to witness myself as your son and faithfull servant. . . .' No doubt his intention in this was to allay Huntly's jealousy or to placate him for past wrongs real or imagined, but it was a rash thing to write nonetheless. In other men it might have succeeded in arousing some finer feeling, but in the case of the Gordon it unfortunately served only to fan his already overbearing conceit. Nevertheless, for the first few days things seemed to promise well.

With the Gordon reinforcements, Montrose was able to field a sizeable force of some 2,200 foot and 700 horse, and could consider taking the initiative again. Tactically he had two alternatives. After Philiphaugh a large part of the Covenant army had been sent back to England. The rest had split. Middleton had gone north to Turriff with 800 cavalry, while David Leslie with the main force of 3,000 horse remained at Glasgow to protect the Committee of Parliament who were sitting in judgement there. Montrose's most obvious course of action would have been to fall on Middleton and destroy him there and then. Apart from restoring some of his prestige at no great cost, by first protecting the Gordon lands he might have done much to establish himself in Huntly's good graces, and certainly, with the advantage of retrospect, this would probably have been the wiser course to take. However, for a number of reasons less easily apparent, Montrose preferred to strike at Leslie.

In the first place, it was always his rule when confronted by two hostile forces to attack the stronger. Secondly, a victory over Leslie at Glasgow (and with the Gordons this was a feasible proposition) would at one stroke have wiped out the defeat at Philiphaugh, while (according to the Gordon historian) Montrose still hoped that if he could take Glasgow before the end of October he would be able to force a sitting of the Parliament which he had summoned after Kilsyth, and thus recoup much of what had been lost in political terms as well. Middleton, weak and isolated in the North, could be destroyed at will thereafter. Finally, and more personally, he was intensely preoccupied with the fate of the Royalists who had been captured at Philiphaugh and whom for honour's sake he could not abandon. Having learned of the deaths of O'Cahan and his Irishes, he knew that the rest stood in peril of their lives and he hoped that, by threatening to take reprisals against the Committee in Glasgow, he might make them stay their hand and force an exchange of prisoners.[3]

The Gordons, understandably, were not at all happy about this, being reluctant to leave Middleton loose in Aberdeenshire (although as it happened his men were unwilling to fight and he was obliged to retire temporarily to Banff). Lord Lewis Gordon left the army forthwith, taking as many of his followers as would go with him. Aboyne, to do him justice, was prepared at least to discuss the matter, but on the second day of the march, having received peremptory orders from Huntly, he too left and took the rest of the Gordon contingent with him. Montrose sent Lord Reay (Huntly's son-in-law) and young Irving of Drum (another intimate friend) to reason with the Gordon and argue that by moving south he would draw Middleton after him and away from the Gordon lands. Huntly remained obdurate and the precious days slipped by in useless recrimination and barren argument.

Finally, on 22 October, Montrose would wait no longer, and he led his remaining troops (about 300 horse and 1,200 foot) from Castleton in Braemar down Glenshee to Lochearnside. Somewhere in Perthshire, Ogilvie of Powrie and Captain Robert Nesbit reached him with dispatches from the King. Digby was riding north with 1,500 cavaliers, and Charles ordered Montrose to meet him at the border. In the hope that this news might convince Huntly of the need to move south, Montrose sent the messengers on to Strathbogie.

Unfortunately, Digby did not get through. He had left Welbeck on 14 October, and the following day successfully routed a force of parliamentary infantry under Poyntz at Sherburn. But the Royalists were subsequently surprised and defeated in their turn and driven north to Skipton. Digby with Nithsdale and Carnwath resolved on a desperate dash through the Lowlands, and despite a further mauling at Carlisle reached Dumfries on 22 October. But they could get no word of Montrose (who was still in Braemar), and their men were deserting in large numbers. Digby decided to abandon the attempt, and fled to the Isle of Man. Montrose did not learn of Charles's pathetic effort to keep faith until some time after it had failed.

Still preoccupied with the fate of the prisoners, he moved through the Lennox and camped at Buchanan on Loch Lomondside. The first executions took place in Glasgow at the end of October. For the rest he could gain only a temporary respite. Leslie lay in Glasgow with 3,000 regulars and Montrose could not risk a set-piece battle in the open. No help came from the Gordons. Nor would Alastair leave his quarrel in the West. Montrose's small force of Athollmen and Ogilvies could accomplish nothing by staying longer, and wearily he turned north again and marched through Menteith back to Atholl.

According to James Burns, a Glasgow baillie who recorded the event in his Diary, Magdalen Carnegie died sometime in November, and Montrose rode alone into Angus to bury her near their home. Her mystery remains unsolved. 'It is all unknown how loved, how lived, how died she.' Even the fact of her death at this time is in dispute.[4] All that is left is an echo of unspoken tragedy. A cry in the night and she is no more. But Middleton came seeking him in Angus and Montrose had little time to mourn. Returning to Atholl he found that

Old Napier too was dead – at Fincastle – and they buried him in the kirk at Blair.[5] Too many of the best were gone, and the world seemed to be growing old.

At Atholl Montrose received another letter from the King who had by now learned of the disaster at Philiphaugh and wrote in considerate terms to console the best of all his generals. Charles had conceived a real affection for Montrose and genuinely intended to keep faith with him – if, and as, he could:

> As it hath been none of my least afflictions, nor misfortunes, that you have hitherto had no assistance from me, so I conjure you to believe that nothing but impossibility hath been the cause of it: Witness my coming here [Newark] (not without some difficulty) being only for that end; and, when I saw that could not do, the parting of 1,500 horse under the command of Digby to send unto you. And though the success (which I have here ever since expected, and that with some inconvenience to my other affairs) hath not been according to my wishes, yet that, nor nothing else, shall discourage me from seeking, and laying hold upon, all occasions to assist you; it being the least part of that kindness I owe you for the eminent fidelity, and generosity you have shown in my service. And be assured that your less prosperous fortune is so far from lessening my estimation of you, that it will rather cause my affection to kythe the cleerlier to you: For . . . no hardness of condition shall ever make me slacken my friendship towards you; in despite of all the specious shows of cunning, base propositions, against which (if there were nothing else) your letter to Digby of 24th September[6] (which I have opened and read) is to me a sufficient antidote . . . upon all occasions and in all fortunes you shall ever find me your most assured, faithful, and constant friend,
>
> CHARLES R.[7]

But it was clear that he could no longer count on any help from England, and Montrose had no alternative but to turn once more to Huntly. Powrie and Nesbit had failed in their turn to hammer any sense into the Gordon, and losing patience Montrose now sent Dalziel to Strathbogie to deliver the most strongly worded letter yet:

> I hope I need not inculcate to your remembrance the danger the King and the kingdom at present is in, and the misery that hangs over his, and all faithful subjects' heads. Blame me not, My Lord, if I can lay the fault on none but yourself and son; first for hindering the supplies which the King sent; and next for the loss of those gallant and faithful men lately with so much cruelty butchered. Yet nevertheless since things past cannot be recalled, I beseech you to recollect yourself for the future, and if you will not assist, yet at least grant the favour of a conference to the King's Governor.[8]

And when Dalziel too returned with nothing that could be called an answer, Montrose decided to have it out with Huntly face to face. In December he marched north over the frozen hills into the Gordon country. It was the worst winter of a generation[9] and the dejected little army suffered appallingly as it struggled across rivers that had become icy torrents and through passes made treacherous by heavy snowfalls and sub-zero conditions. But Montrose drove relentlessly on, and quartering his main force at Keith rode with a small escort to Strathbogie. Huntly had word of his coming, however, and, rather than face him, fled to his castle at the Bog of Gight. But there his horse went lame, and Montrose, who would not give up the pursuit, finally forced the confrontation which he sought.

Montrose in person was an infinitely more disquieting prospect than Montrose at a distance, and Huntly quickly tried to compromise. He suggested first that they should divide Scotland between them, with himself in charge of all operations in the North (by virtue of his own royal commission) while Montrose with the Athollmen and the clans, and a force of 500 Gordons lent to him for the purpose, should pursue the campaign in the South. When Huntly had subdued the northern Covenanters he would march to the Graham's assistance. Such a proposal, however, implied tacit recognition of Huntly's claim to supremacy in the North, and Montrose 'passed the offer over in silence', suggesting instead that they should both work in concert to pacify the North and then march south together–as equals.

Huntly pronounced this idea acceptable, and a plan of campaign was agreed. Their primary target was to be Inverness, where the Covenant garrison was known to be short of ammunition and supplies and would be unlikely to hold out against their combined strength. By seizing this strategic centre they would gain a harbour suitable for receiving assistance by sea from France where the Queen was working to obtain money and war materials. And with the capital of the North firmly in Royalist hands there was also a fair chance that the Earl of Seaforth would be induced finally to declare for the King (he was already in close touch with Glengarry) and bring his Mackenzies and others of the northern clans with him. Montrose was to take his small force (now 800 foot and 200 horse) and advance by Strathspey, while Huntly would lead his Gordons (1,400 foot and 600 horse) through Moray where he could effectively cover Montrose's rear and prevent any supplies from getting through to Inverness. They would then converge and lay siege to the town.

At first all seemed to promise well. News of the reconciliation was greeted with great enthusiasm in both camps and the Gordons 'wished damnation to themselves' if they failed the King in the future. (In the months to come they would do their best to earn it.) At the beginning Montrose at least appeared hopeful and on 23 December was writing to Huntly from Kinnermony on the Spey: 'I have received your Lordship's and do congratulate your good beginnings.' But as the days passed and the delays increased, it became clear that the Gordon did not intend all that he had promised. Montrose's letters remained courteous but soon the frustration which he must have felt began to show through:

10 January; My Noble Lord,
  It being necessary we should now take the opportunity of the
season and employ the time that so favourably offereth unto us. . . .
For it concerns us now *really to fall to work*.[10]

For himself, Montrose was scrupulously careful to honour the agreement and even forebore to recruit among the Clan Grant since Huntly
reckoned that he had a prior claim to their services. The Gordon,
however, not only neglected to contribute much needed powder and
money to the joint war kist, but even dug up the cannon that Montrose
had buried in 1644 and kept them for himself. While Montrose could
only wage an ineffective guerilla war along Speyside, Huntly diverted
his resources and attention to pursuing a number of private vendettas
against his enemies in Moray. According to Wishart, he had learned
that there were stores of gold in certain 'obscure castles', and as so
often before the Gordon strength was frittered away on minor raids
and plundering expeditions. The precious time was wasted in attacking
small isolated strongholds such as Burgie, Moyness and Rothes. Huntly
spent three whole months besieging Lethin alone, and in this manner
the initiative was thrown away.

  For Montrose, these first months of 1646 were possibly the most
frustrating of his whole career. Unable to take any decisive action
on his own account for lack of troops, he could only hover between
the Findhorn and the Spey and reflect bitterly on the selfish obstinacy
that was preventing the initial promise from being fulfilled. At the
end of January he heard that Spottiswoode and Nathaniel Gordon
had been executed at St Andrews. While Huntly dawdled the Covenanters strengthened and resupplied their forces in Inverness, and
Middleton came north to join with the garrison at Aberdeen and
threaten the Royalists' flank. A ship from Brittany laden with stores
and ammunition sent by the Queen was captured by the Covenanters
at Teignmouth. It seemed as if nothing would go right for him any more.

  By April Huntly had given up all pretence at co-operation and
reverted to his previous tactics of open obstruction. Knowing that
all the Captain-General's personal papers had been lost at Philiphaugh,
he had earlier questioned the Graham's authority in the North on the
grounds that he could not actually produce the King's commission
as proof of his appointment. But when Montrose now sent him a new
authenticated copy of the document and ordered him by virtue of the
authority vested in the patent to advance on Inverness as they had
agreed, Huntly simply ignored the summons and the commission as
well. Quite clearly he could not endure the role of subordinate and
he even began to negotiate with Seaforth on his own account. But
Seaforth was a shrewd man. He replied tactfully saying that he hoped
Montrose and Huntly would be able to reach some agreement but that
for the moment he assumed that Montrose, as viceroy, was supreme
in all things—which must have been gall to the Gordon's soul. But it
was obvious to a keen observer that Royalist hopes were foundering
on one man's vain conceit.

Only two minor but heroic Royalist actions relieved the gloom of these otherwise profitless months.

In early February, Campbell of Ardkinglass and 1,200 of his clan who had been driven from their own lands by Alastair's independent war band[11] joined up with the Menzieses and the Stewarts of Balquhidder under Ardvoirlich (the murderer of Kilpont) and went raiding into Menteith. Black Pate Inchbrakie and Drummond of Balloch (whom Montrose had sent to recruit in Atholl) led 700 Athollmen against the marauders and on 13 February attacked and killed 500 of them at Callander.

Shortly after this, young Napier with 50 men garrisoned Montrose's castle of Kincardine in Strathearn where on 2 March they were attacked by Middleton with 1,400 regulars and a large number of heavy cannon brought up from Stirling. The Royalists held out for fourteen days until the tremendous concussion from the continuous Covenant bombardment caused the castle well to dry up. Napier, Drummond and the Laird of MacNab escaped at night by jumping their horses over the enemy barricades. The garrison surrendered next day. Middleton sent 35 of the prisoners to the tolbooth in Edinburgh and, possibly as a sop to the attendant ministers, had the rest executed by firing squad. The castle was battered to ruins.

In mid-April Middleton was preparing to move from Aberdeen and Montrose sent to Huntly suggesting that they should join forces and smash the Covenanters before they became a serious threat to the operations in the North. Huntly replied, however, that he was satisfied with things as they were. Montrose therefore decided to attempt the siege of Inverness on his own while there was still time, and by 29 April he had invested the town from the west (where he had a line of retreat into the hills and his men could live off the Fraser country). He suspected (correctly) that Middleton might try to come to its relief, and although Huntly's substantial forces lay between them and could have intercepted any Covenant advance, Montrose no longer trusted the Gordon and sent three troops of horse to Speyside to watch the crossings. Unfortunately they were not enough. Either through carelessness or the treachery of Lord Lewis Gordon (who, according to some accounts, having assured them that the enemy were not coming, deliberately enticed Montrose's officers to Rothes until the Covenanters were across the river[12]), Middleton was allowed to slip through the protective screen unopposed. On 5 May he fell on the Royalists before Inverness who had almost no warning of his approach, and Montrose was forced to fight a rearguard action across the Ness and up Caiplich abandoning all his stores, ammunition and the two brass cannon which constituted his only ordnance. Huntly, instead of trying to draw Middleton off, took advantage of the diversion to march on Aberdeen which, after much hesitation, he took with little profit and considerable casualties.

By 8 May, Montrose had succeeded in shaking off Middleton's pursuit and doubled back by Strathglass and Errick to Speyside again. The only achievement of the ill-starred Inverness campaign was a dubious Bond of Confederation which he had forced Seaforth, Sutherland and other northern chiefs to sign on pain of ravaging their lands. The Committee of Estates at once published a condemnation of the Bond and most of the signatories soon retracted. Sutherland wrote a penitent letter to the Committee and others even went to Edinburgh to disclaim their part in it.

On 27 May Montrose made one last attempt to come to terms with Huntly, and having sent a messenger on ahead to inform him that fresh instructions had arrived from the King, set out with a small escort to ride the twenty miles to Strathbogie. But as before, the Gordon preferred to leave by the postern gate rather than face the Captain-General, and Montrose rode the twenty miles back to his camp resolved to have no further dealings with the man who in everything but name was now also his enemy.

The Gordon clan was irrevocably lost to him. Alastair and his MacDonalds, abetted by the futile Antrim, would not abandon their feud with the Campbells in the West. Huntly's behaviour was causing other potential Royalists to waver, and the prudent watched the royal cause go down and looked to their own estates. Largely because there seemed no other course left to him, Montrose decided to turn towards the highlands once more in the hope of enlisting help from among the northern clans. It was not in the nature of the man to give up. But despair was becoming an almost tangible thing and failure was now a darkening shadow at his elbow. The fortune which had earlier favoured him seemed at the last to have deserted his cause. The flame of victory which had gleamed so bright in those months before Kilsyth was burning cold, and like a man at the end of his resources he cast about for some way that might rekindle it. But there was no turning back. In Montrose there was always hope – or faith – and determination in adversity remained his greatest quality. And in the army too there was hope, since if his soldiers were disappointed their spirit was not broken. Those who had stayed by the Graham believed in him, in what he had done, and in what he could do again. There were untapped reserves in the North. Somewhere there was another army which would emerge to defeat the Covenanters in the field. At some time and in some place they would reach the final battle – and if need be, the one beyond. Weary but not hopeless, they prepared for the march into the hills.

Then on 31 May, a man called Sir Robert Kerr arrived with a letter from the King. It was written from the Scottish camp at Newcastle.

MONTROSE,

I am in such a condition as is much fitter for relation than writing. Wherefore I refer you to this trusty bearer Robin Kerr for the reasons and manner of my coming to this army; as also what my treatment hath been since I came, and my resolutions upon my whole business. This shall therefore only give you positive commands and tell you real truths, leaving the *why* of all to this

bearer. *You must disband your forces and go to France,* where you
shall receive my further directions. This at first may startle you;
but I assure you that if for the present, I should offer to do more
for you, I could not do so much: and that you shall always find me
　Your most assured, constant, real, faithful friend,
CHARLES R.[13]

Newcastle, 19 May, 1646.

After so much had been won—and so much of it lost—Charles
had taken what was left and for some inexplicable reason thrown
that too away. For Montrose, who had come so close to succeeding,
who had lost everything—lands, fortune, family—in the service of the
King, who had suffered such neglect, and lived through so much
disappointment, and who was even now forcing himself to believe
that all could be begun—and won—again, this was the bitterest moment
of all. In the few seconds which it took to read the letter it must
have seemed that the King too had betrayed him.

But to do him justice, Charles had not intended it so. This is not
the place to relate in detail the declining fortunes of the King. Sufficient
to say that Charles had reeled from plot to plot and plan to plan.
The various possibilities of obtaining help from France, Spain and
even the Vatican had all been tentatively explored—and to his ultimate
cost, since this apparent inclination to conspire with foreigners and
papists against his own subjects, even though they were in rebellion,
was turning many Englishmen away from the unfortunate king. But
as the remaining Royalist strongholds fell or capitulated one by one,
the room for manoeuvre grew correspondingly less, and when the last
of his armies under Sir Ralph Hopton surrendered in March 1646,
Charles was finally left with a bare and unpalatable choice between
the Scots and the Independents. In fact, preliminary negotiations
were already *en train* with both—sufficiently maladroit for each to be
uneasily aware of the King's 'secret' correspondence with the other.

That Charles chose the Scots was in large part due to a French
intrigue undertaken by the French ambassador—Jean de Montereul—
an able and ambitious young abbé who had arrived in England in
August 1645 with instructions from Mazarin to open secret tripartite
negotiations between the French, the Scots and the King. The French
tactics were based on the assumption that the Scots would be willing
to come to some sort of accommodation with the King because they
were by now thoroughly disenchanted with their English allies and
realized that if the Independents were victorious in England there
was comparatively little chance of their ever being paid in full what
they had originally been promised. It was Montereul's view that
any agreement between Charles and the Independents ought on
principle to be prevented since it would ruin the Scots, whom it
was in France's best interest to maintain as a power to oppose England.
It seemed an excellent opportunity to revive the concept of the
Auld Alliance.

Montereul also calculated that the Scots' desire to enforce Presbyterianism on England sprang from political rather than purely religious motives, since a Presbyterian government in London would be friendly and to some extent dependent on Edinburgh. This was part of the truth but by no means all of it.

> I could not well understand how they wished to establish in the Church of England a form of government that the King did not wish, that the English rejected, and which even those who were most attached to their interest did not even desire in the manner they proposed to introduce it: and I could not but express my great surprise at the strong stand they took on a matter which did not concern them but their neighbours. Whereupon they replied that without taking into account the dictates of conscience . . . there were two reasons which obliged them not to give up the idea of introducing their form of government into the English Church. First the maintenance of their League . . . and again their security which they could only maintain by this means having always to fear England as long as the people were not activated by the same spirit in matters of religion as prevailed in Scotland.
> These are the reasons they brought forward which, as you will no doubt consider, have no great weight.[14]

To the Scots Montereul offered the cynical answer that uniformity of religion had not guaranteed peace in the past, while an agreement with France would be of practical and material assistance in the present. But this was to underestimate Presbyterianism as a stumbling block, and the Catholic diplomat was too detached from the consciences, ambitions and religious scruples of a people whom he was otherwise ready to dismiss as heretics.

Nevertheless, at first an agreement did seem a possibility—to an outsider. In October 1645 the Scottish commissioners in London sent a note to Montereul in cypher by which they declared that the Scots and Presbyterian English would act together 'if the King would condescend to establish ecclesiastical affairs as it may be resolved in the Parliaments and Assemblies of the two countries and according to what is established in the other reformed Churches'.[15] If the King accepted but the English refused, the Scots would employ the best means compatible with the safety of the King to obtain peace. Thus a compromise did seem feasible and the Frenchman may be forgiven for believing initially that, if this was what they said, it was also what they meant. It was his first mistake.

Unfortunately Montereul did not understand the King either. He reckoned that Charles's main preoccupation should have been his own survival, and the casuist's mind saw nothing wrong and indeed everything that was sensible in the King's agreeing to Presbyterianism under duress on the sure calculation that when matters were finally resolved (with the help of France) there would be little difficulty in persuading an English Parliament to abolish it again. This was his second mistake. Montereul did not realize that, although Charles was quite capable of explaining away a previous promise when it suited him to do so, and indeed at times would deliberately phrase a promise in such a way as to enable him to explain it away later, he would never consciously enter into a binding contract with the express intention of breaking it thereafter. In a strange way he allowed that there could be many shades of honesty but yet clung to a kind of integrity which was peculiarly his own. Such a fine distinction was not readily understandable to a cynical French diplomatist. Montereul continued to look for a compromise on the basis that religious matters might 'remain established as they had already been and might be established in future by both Parliaments and by the Assembly of the clergy of both Kingdoms', and proposed that Charles should not sign the Covenant but merely approve it in a letter (arguing in his way that what Charles did not actually sign he did not later have to keep). Neither side was being honest with the other.

Under pressure from the Frenchman and from his Queen, who was also deeply involved in the negotiations, Charles was prepared to compromise to the extent of granting toleration to Presbyterians in England. He offered to pay the wages of the Scottish army out of the Irish fund, and promised not to attempt to alter the Scottish Kirk. He was not prepared, however, to sanction the destruction of the Church of England any more than he was prepared to ratify the destruction of the monarchy itself. Nor, in reality, had the Scots moved from the propositions of Uxbridge. They 'had taken up arms to put down every other form of worship' and they did not intend to be 'tolerated'. They wanted to be supreme.

By the time Montereul realized that the affair was turning sour it was too late to turn back. Charles had many (too many) irons in the fire, and was still treating abroad for Catholic help. France's interests had to be served, and the King was offering himself (with the reservation of his conscience) to the highest bidder. He therefore proceeded on the basis that Charles should seek the safety of the Scottish camp in anticipation of an agreement which would be worked out later, and the King in going was persuaded to consent 'to be instructed according to Presbyterian Government and to satisfy them as far as his conscience would permit'.

Unfortunately, Montereul's third mistake was in assuming that the word of the Scottish commissioners in England would be honoured by their masters in Edinburgh. Sensibly cautious, he asked for a written assurance that if the King were to go to the Scottish camp he would be safe 'in person, honour, and conscience'. The Covenanters, however, were prepared to give a *verbal* assurance only 'on account both of the danger they would individually incur by giving such writing, and of the disadvantage in which it would place them of being reproached by the English Parliament with having broken their Covenant by entering into a separate agreement with their King'.[16] It was with this 'ghost of assurances' that Charles finally threw himself on the mercy of the Scots.

But although the negotiations turned mainly on the religious issue, almost from the outset Montereul was acutely aware that a second major obstacle was likely to be the Marquis of Montrose. At his first interview with the King in January 1646 Charles made it quite clear that his Captain-General in Scotland was not to be treated as a mere pawn in the game:

> He showed also much anxiety about the safety of the Marquis of Montrose and told me he wished to be not only securely but honourably reconciled to him, and went so far as to say he would in future consider him as one of his children, and that he wished to live with him henceforth as a friend rather than as a King.[17]

Montereul broached the subject with his Covenant contacts but did not elicit a very positive response. As he reported to Mazarin:

> I wished also to have it specified that terms would be made with Montrose as Sir Robert Murray had stated to me it might be done, but the last proclamation issued against him by the Scottish Parliament, together with the circumstance that the Commission here consists of some of his worst enemies, has rendered it necessary to delay this point until the King will himself be with their army, when Sir Robert Murray assures me that the King will be able to provide for him a good part of what he may wish. He fears, however, that Montrose may be included in the number of those who will require to absent themselves for a time.[18]

A further suggestion by Montereul, that Montrose should be made ambassador to France, was rejected by the Scots, but under pressure Sir Robert Murray apparently promised, on whose authority none can say, that although the King's General would have to leave the country, he would in all other respects be given generous terms:

> As for Montrose, terms will be made for him at the army, but he will be obliged to leave the country for a short time; and it is promised that on his engaging to do so, he will have all his estates and all his offices restored to him. As I saw how much the King gave heed as to what might be in the interests of this Montrose—and as I did have some doubt as to whether the King would agree to go to the Scottish army without having informed him beforehand, I proposed to the Scots, in order to allay any suspicion they might have, that Sir Robert Murray might be sent to Montrose, but they replied that the King should send a certain Sir ****** Fleming . . . who is a relative of Montrose and his particular friend . . . and who might leave as soon as the King would be with the army.[19]

Unfortunately (though perhaps for obvious reasons), Montereul did not report all this in like detail to Charles, and the King appears to have proceeded meanwhile on the incredibly naïve assumption that when he arrived in the Scottish camp, the Covenanters would be obliged to make common cause with Montrose and that their forces would thereafter work in conjunction. In anyone other than Charles this might have been taken as symptomatic of an impaired intellect, but the King was undoubtedly sincere. Among the Evelyn Papers is a short Memorandum endorsed by the secretary, Nicholas: 'A note written with the King's own pen concerning his going to the Scots':

> . . . And before I take my journey, I must send to the Marquis of Montrose to advertise him upon what conditions I come to the Scots' army, that he may be admitted forthwith into our conjunction, and instantly march up to us.

The letter referred to was duly written on 18 April, a week before Charles left Oxford.

> MONTROSE,
>
> Having, upon the engagement of the French King and Queen Regent, made an agreement to join with my Scots subjects now before Newark, and being resolved upon the first opportunity to put myself into that army–they being reciprocally engaged by the intervention of M. de Montereul, the said King's Resident, now in the said army, to join with me and my forces, and to assist me in the procuring of a happy peace–I have thought it necessary to acquaint you herewith . . . desiring you, if you shall find, by the said M. de Montereul, that my Scots army have really declared for me, and that you be satisfied by him that there is by them an amnesty of all that hath been done by you, and those who have adhered to me . . . that then you take them by the hand, and use all possible diligence to unite your forces with theirs for the advancement of my service, as if I were there in person; and I doubt not but you, being joined, will be able to relieve me here, in case I shall not find any possible means to come to you.[20]

This text was sent in cypher through Secretary Nicholas to Montereul who was instructed to 'use his discretion' as to whether to forward it to Montrose. Needless to to say, *the letter was never delivered.*

Charles had no sooner arrived in the Scottish camp than he was informed in stark and brutal terms of the true state of affairs. Sir James Turner, who was an eye witness to the King's reception at Newark, later recorded in his *Memoirs*:

> In the summer of 1646, the King's fate driving him on to his near approaching end, he cast himself in the Scots' arms at Newark. There did the Earl Lothian as President of the Committee, to his eternal reproach, imperiously require His Majesty (before he had either drunk, refreshed or reposed himself) to command my Lord Bellasis to deliver up Newark to the Parliament's forces; to sign the Covenant; and to command James Graham to lay down arms: all which the King stoutly refused, telling him that he who had made him an Earl had made James Graham a Marquis.[21]

But Charles was a prisoner, and despite his brave face he soon realized that he had no alternative but to order Montrose to disband his army. He had hopes (long-standing) of being able to win over Leslie, but this was known to the Covenanters, and when it came to the point they could offer more. Charles, still looking for a way out, steadfastly refused to sign the Covenant, and the miserable episode drew inexorably to its dishonourable conclusion. The Scots would get their money and they would give away their King. The French got nothing out of it. With commendable prescience their representative Bellievre (Montereul having been temporarily arrested by the English) wrote to Brienne on 31 August/10 September:

> The strong inclination the King has to go to London and the hopes in which he is maintained by the Scots, prevent him from thinking seriously of placing himself in a position wherein he may command consideration, and he thus attempts every plan, hoping well of them all, without really attempting any of them: such conduct in the present juncture in which matters are conveys within itself, in my opinion, the fatal necessity of perishing.[22]

In France, no blame was attached to Montereul.

Some of this, at least, Montrose learned from Robert Kerr. But after reading the King's order he was convinced that it had been written under duress. On 2 June he returned a formal reply in which he offered no comment on Charles's disastrous decision to surrender to the Scots–'I shall not presume to canvass, but humbly acquiesce in Your Majesty's resolutions'–but he did feel justified in asking what was to become of the soldiers who had served him so long and so faithfully: 'Only I must beg Your Majesty to consider there are nothing remembered concerning the immunity of those who have been upon your service.' He asked that those who returned to their homes might be free from persecution and that any who chose to go abroad might be allowed 'freedom of transport'. He also formally requested that all prisoners should be released–'so that no characters of what has happened remain'. For himself, he accepted banishment, though he may have had some doubts as to whether the Covenanters really intended to let him escape alive: 'And as for my own leaving this Kingdom, I shall in all humility and obedience *endeavour* to perform Your Majesty's command, wishing (rather nor any should make pretext of me) never to see it again with mine eyes.'[23]

At the same time, however, he sent another private letter by a separate courier[24] asking the King if it was his genuine wish that he should disband, since if it was not he would continue to fight for as long as he could.

The immediate answer came in the form of a second *public* order to disband. Then, on 15 June, Charles wrote again from Newcastle.

> I assure you that I no less esteem your willingness to lay down arms at my command for a gallant and real expression of your zeal and affection for my service than any of your former actions. But I hope that you cannot have so mean an opinion of me that for any particular or worldly respects I could suffer you to be ruined. I aver it is one of the greatest and truest marks of my present miseries that I cannot recompense you according to your deserts. . . . For there is no man (who ever heard me speak of you) that is ignorant that the reason which makes me at this time send you out

of the country, is that you may return home with greater glory; and in the meantime to have as honourable employment as I can put upon you. . . . Wherefore I renew my former directions of laying down arms unto you, desiring you to let Huntly, Crawford, Airlie, Seaforth, and Ogilvie know. . . .[25]

But what of his soldiers? On 7 July the terms of surrender were published at Dundee, but they were couched in the form of a limited pardon and Montrose felt that his army deserved a more honourable capitulation. He wrote again to the King, objecting that the conditions were unjust and asking that the ban of excommunication might be lifted from his men so that after they had surrendered the magistrates would not be able to proceed against them on religious grounds (by custom an excommunicate was automatically forfeited regardless of what the treaty might say). He asked also that any amnesty should include Royalists who were already in exile, and again that Royalist prisoners should be released. And meanwhile he waited.

But the King was in no position to bargain on his behalf. Charles replied on 16 July:

The most sensible part of my many misfortunes is to see my friends in distress, and not to be able to help them. And of this kind you are the chief. Wherefore, according to that real friendship that is between us, as I cannot absolutely command you to accept of unhandsome conditions, so I must tell you that I believe your refusal will put you in a far worse estate than your compliance will. This is the reason that I have told this bearer Robert Kerr, and the Commissioners here that I have commanded you to accept of Middleton's conditions; which I really judge to be your best course . . . for if this opportunity be let slip, you must not expect any more treaties; in which case you must either conquer all Scotland, or be inevitably ruined. That you may make the clearer judgement. . . . I have sent you here enclosed the Chancellor's answers to your demands; whereupon if you find it fit to accept you may justly say I have commanded you; and if you take another course you cannot expect that I can publicly avow you in it until I shall be able . . . to stand on my own feet; but on the contrary seem to be not well satisfied with your refusal which I find clearly will bring all the army upon you; and then I shall be in a very sad condition, such as I shall rather leave to your judgement. . . .[26]

Submit to the King's public order or fight on alone—it was up to Montrose then to decide. But whatever his own personal feelings, it was really no choice at all. If he fought on, Charles would have to disown him. Huntly and Seaforth were said to be disbanding, and without resources or hope of help his own defeat must follow. There was, moreover, the real threat that the Covenanters would seize on any pretext to retaliate against the person of the King and remove what few liberties were still allowed him. To ignore the King's order, however reluctantly it may have been given, was to put himself and his soldiers beyond hope of amnesty, and although either way Montrose himself was ruined, he could not, in honour, wilfully sacrifice his followers in a cause that was clearly lost. If hope remained it was only for the future, and a later, better time when an opportunity might come to renew the struggle. But for the present his first duty was to his men, and the only practical–and honourable–course left was to try to obtain the best possible terms for his army.

On 22 July Montrose met with Middleton and for the space of two hours they conferred secretly and alone in a small meadow on the banks of the River Isla in Angus. In this almost romantic way their war ended and the terms were agreed. Montrose's followers, including those who had been declared forfeited (with the exception of Graham of Gorthie), were free to go back to their homes with lives and fortunes safe and without fear of further persecution. The surviving Irishes too could return without hindrance to their own country. But for Montrose, Crawford and Sir John Hurry, there could be no pardon and they had until the last day of August to leave Scotland and go into exile beyond the sea. Nor would Royalist prisoners be released, since the sentences that Parliament had passed upon them could not be superseded by the treaty.

The little army paraded for the last time at Rattray near Blairgowrie. In a scene highly charged with emotion, Montrose thanked them for the gallantry and fortitude which they had shown in all their campaigns together and tried to explain to them that 'their present submission was as essential to the King's cause as their past achievements'.[27] There were many who asked to be allowed to stay with him and fight on whatever the cost, but he ordered them, as it was their duty, to return to their homes and live in peace. For both General and soldiers it was a long farewell.

Airlie and the rest of the Scottish loyalists returned to their own estates. Crawford led the surviving Irishes west to Kintyre and from there transported them back to Ireland at his own expense before going to the Queen's Court in France to await the arrival of the other exiles. Montrose returned to his house at Old Montrose to settle his affairs, and presumably much of his remaining time was spent at Kinnaird where his youngest children were being cared for by Southesk. Something had to be put in hand for their future, and a month was a short time for a father to make up for the years of neglect.

Charles wrote one more letter–of farewell–and the friendship which he expressed was undoubtedly sincere. A whole lifetime had passed since the day he had first snubbed the young Montrose at Court. They would not meet again–though neither guessed it then.

MONTROSE,

In all kinds of fortunes you find a way more and more to oblige me. And it is none of my least misfortunes, that all this time I can only return to you verbal repayment. But I assure you that the world shall see that the real expressions of my friendship to you shall be an infallible sign of my change of fortune. As for your desires, they are all so just, that I shall endeavour what I can to have them all satisfied, not without hope to give you contentment in some of them. . . .

    Your most assured, real, faithful, constant friend,

CHARLES R.

P.S. Defer your going beyond seas as long as you may without breaking your word.[28]

Yet Charles had added a dangerous postscript. It had been specified in the agreement that the port of Montrose should be the exile's point of embarkation, but throughout August the harbour, which usually sheltered a score or more ships, had been ominously empty. It began to look as if the Covenanters, while agreeing to abide by the letter of the treaty, would nevertheless try to arrange it so that Montrose would overstay his period of grace. Finally, on 31 August, the promised ship arrived, but it was neither seaworthy nor victualled for a voyage. The master, who was a rogue, stated that he needed at least three days to refit, and bragged openly in the taverns that he had been instructed to sail along the coast of England where parliamentary men-of-war were lying in wait to intercept the fugitives. Some of Montrose's remaining friends now urged him to take to the Highlands again rather than trust to this treacherous peace, but he dared not endanger the safety of the King. A bargain was struck with the captain of a vessel anchored at Stonehaven, and despite the efforts of the local Covenanters, who cut the mooring ropes in the hope of sending it aground, on 3 September a small group, including Sir John Hurry, Drummond of Balloch, Montrose's natural brother Harry Graham, John Spottiswoode and George Wishart, got safely aboard and sailed for Norway. The same night, Montrose, disguised as the servant of his private chaplain, James Wood, slipped out of the harbour in a cock-boat and made a rendezvous with another ship anchored in the roads whose master (a friend to Wood) agreed to take them to Bergen in Norway. The seas were running high, and it was a stormy crossing.

PART V

Passion

Le Chevalier en Deuil
(September 1646–January 1649)

Who comprehends his trust, and to the same
Keeps faithful, with a singleness of aim;
And therefore does not stoop, nor lie in wait
For wealth or honours, or for wordly state.
Wordsworth, *Happy Warrior*

At Bergen in Norway the exiles were hospitably received by Thomas Gray, a Scot, who was governor of the royal castle there.[1] Montrose's immediate intention was to seek an audience with Christian IV of Denmark who had always been a staunch friend to his nephew Charles I, and whom he hoped would be the first to pledge material support for a new expedition on the English king's behalf. On 15 September he set off by the overland route across the mountains to Christiania and took ship from the port of Marstrand. When he arrived in Denmark, however, he learned that Christian was in Germany and so, crossing the Baltic, he travelled by Holstein as far as Hamburg where he temporarily established himself and waited for further news of the King in Scotland.

He waited also for some communication from Queen Henrietta Maria. The Earl of Crawford had gone direct to the exiled Court in Paris with a detailed assessment prepared by Montrose (presumably at Rattray or shortly before the disbandment) of the potential Royalist strength in Scotland. It named those loyal chieftains who would declare for the King, and listed the numbers of fighting men whom they could put into the field–amounting, if each could honour his promise, to close on 20,000 men all told.[2] Crawford was under instructions to emphasize the need for some immediate encouragement to be given directly to the chiefs by the Queen and the Prince of Wales if their loyalty was not to waver or be tampered with by Argyll and the Covenanters. But such a proposition involving the possibility of armed intervention was not enthusiastically received. When Crawford arrived at the Court in October, Charles was still with the Scots army, and the Queen, who had also been in communication with the Covenant leaders for some considerable time, was inclined to trust more in compromise and negotiation than to the sort of bold stroke that Montrose obviously had in mind. She sent a dispatch to the Scottish chiefs, ostensibly to 'check their ardour', but in terms that virtually declined their offers of help. To the King she wrote: 'My Lord Crawford is arrived, who brings me very great offers on the part of your adherents in Scotland: with respect to which I shall take all necessary steps.' She did not write to Montrose until five months after Crawford had laid the details before her.

Charles wrote to Montrose in January (1647[3]), telling him, for want of a cypher, to refer to the Queen for instructions, and in early February the long awaited letter from Henrietta Maria finally arrived.[4] In this she referred briefly to his propositions as put to her by Crawford:

> . . . of which I approve exceedingly; and as I hold it to be of great importance to the service of His Majesty I shall do all I can to further it and labour therein with all my power . . . and also . . . assure you that I shall never be contented until I am able to prove by deeds, the estimation in which I hold yourself and the services which you have rendered to the King.[5]

Fair words, but there was no reference to the Letters of Credence which he had also been expecting and to which he attached some importance. Charles had promised him honourable employment on the continent—in the role of Ambassador Extraordinary with the task of seeking aid from the other European monarchies—and Montrose wanted to be about the work without delay. Left to herself, the Queen might have dealt more honestly with the man who had proved himself one of the most loyal of her husband's servants, but she was governed by her favourites and in particular by the Lord Jermyn, a courtier distinguished for his cupidity rather than for any political flair. And Jermyn had especial cause to dread the arrival of the Ambassador Extraordinary since, as he was only the King's Envoy Ordinary in France, he stood to lose a portion of his emoluments.

A week later (12 February) the Queen wrote again, assuring him of her favour—'I shall always have your interests more deeply at heart'—and saying that Jermyn would be writing in greater detail. Montrose, however, was himself in no hurry to get to Paris. He was already aware that he would have enemies at Court among 'the courtiers and parasites, the plague of princes on whom they fawn' who might try to exclude him from the Queen's counsels, and he was also conscious of the fact that, as long as Charles was with the Scots, his presence would be an embarrassment so that he might not get the hearing that he wanted. His own experience of Covenanting integrity led him to believe with absolute certainty that they could not be trusted to honour any agreement with the King should it suit them to break it, and he was convinced, as in 1642, that armed intervention would in the end be the only solution. If and when events clearly demonstrated the perfidy of Argyll and his colleagues, the futility of negotiating with the Covenanters would have to be recognized, and then his advice might be listened to. But this was to underestimate the personal antipathy of Jermyn and his faction who had little intention of allowing their follies to be interrupted by a military zealot.

The news from Britain, when it came, was possibly even worse than Montrose had expected. The Scots had betrayed their King to the English, ostensibly in return for a promise that Presbyterianism would be established in the South. They also received a substantial proportion of the money owing to them, and the coincidence was not missed:

Traitor Scot
Sold his King for a groat!

The sum involved was £200,000 down payment with another £200,000 to follow–and many thought it cheap for a nation's honour. It was also a mistake. By giving up the King, the Covenanters lost all chance of enforcing Presbyterianism south of the border, and they would later pay dearly for this persistent piece of bigotry.

It was now time for Montrose to be seen in public, and in March 1647 he set out for Paris. Somewhere in Flanders he was intercepted by John Ashburnham, a Gentleman of the King's Bedchamber, who had accompanied Charles to the Scottish camp. Ashburnham brought instructions, as he said, from the Queen, although it is more likely that he had been put up to it by Jermyn, and he urged Montrose not to proceed to Paris but to return at once to Scotland and renew the war–an enterprise which he imagined could be undertaken without money, arms or other support.

Montrose had learned patience in a hard school. He told Ashburnham that in principle the service proposed was acceptable, but that it could not be done unless the Queen would provide the wherewithal. He personally had lost everything and no longer had the private resources to support an army. The spirit of many of his friends had been broken by the humiliating surrender at Rattray. Huntly had been crushed and other would-be Royalists cowed into submission. The main Scottish army had returned from England. Any new expedition would have to be planned, paid for and supported from the continent. In the meantime he had been commanded by the King to go to France, and the Queen surely did not intend that he should disobey. When he had paid his respects to her–in person–he would 'esteem it a new honour and distinction to undertake any task, however perilous and difficult, in the service of so excellent a Queen'.[6]

Having failed to dissuade Montrose from going to Paris, Ashburnham then begged him at least to make his peace with the Covenanters, 'and save himself and his friends for better times'. It was, he said, a matter of policy–a sort of reinsurance–and he personally undertook to obtain the King's permission, or command, if that was preferable, for Montrose to treat with them 'on any terms'. Montrose's reply was typical. 'No man', he told Ashburnham, 'was readier to obey the King's instructions in all that was just and honourable; but not even the King could command his obedience in what was dishonourable, unjust, and destructive to His Majesty himself.'[7] He continued to Paris and received a cold welcome.

Anne of Austria had put the Louvre (which had not been used since 1643) at the disposal of the English queen and this vast palace now housed her tinsel Court. Henrietta Maria was concerned with keeping up appearances, and if money was short for the King's war, there was enough for the extravagant round of balls and masquerades that were the courtiers' main preoccupation. It was as vicious as any and more artificial than most of the contemporary European courts, and had little appeal for a man whose bearing Burnet sneeringly described as 'stately to affectation'. Montrose was never a courtier: his concept of chivalry was antique. But he had also changed, and the years of campaigning and the spartan life of an armed camp had marked him as a soldier. The easy acceptance of youth had gone, and his judgement was severe. While his army had fought without supplies, money desperately needed for the war had gone to the carpet knights who now postured at him in the anterooms and simpered behind their delicately scented handkerchiefs. The King's cause, for which honest men had fought (and died), was daily bartered on the backstairs by mountebanks who had the presumption to cloak their shallow intrigues under the name of statesmanship. The antipathy was mutual. The courtiers openly resented the interference of the soldier whose untimely zeal threatened to interrupt their life of ease and shorten their hope of profit. The stern presence of the man was an accusation.

On arriving at the Louvre, Montrose asked if he could now be given the Letters of Credence which the King had promised. Jermyn affected surprise, and said that no orders to that effect had been received from Charles. This, however, was a blatant lie and the Court knew it. Ashburnham himself admitted privately to Montrose that he personally had brought the relevant instructions from the King in England. But 'Lord Jermyn by his address and interest got everything rejected that tended to lessen his power or obstruct his profit.' Montrose soon saw that if he was to achieve anything at all he would have to deal directly with Henrietta Maria. He obtained an audience, but 'the Queen answered him with a heavy heart and failed to explain herself sufficiently'.[8] He found her attitude inconsistent and perplexing. She appreciated what he had done for the King, but the expense of an armed expedition did not appeal and the Jermyn faction were constantly at pains to impress her with reports concerning the power and influence of the Covenanting party in Scotland. The Queen was by nature extravagant where the Court was concerned, but in Clarendon's phrase she was 'not open-handed'. She was gracious to those who had served her husband well in the past, but her material favours were dispersed rather with an eye on services to come. It was a policy that encouraged the mercenary and inhibited the faithful. Apart from the money obtained from the sale of her jewels (about £900,000), she lived on a French pension of 30,000 livres a month. Money was certainly not plentiful, but a sizeable proportion of what there was went on the upkeep of a large household–and to the courtiers who scavenged on her favour–while she was not averse (on one occasion at least[9]) to lavishing 2,000 pistoles on the wedding of two of her French servants. The royal purse was officially in Jermyn's hands and his fingers were busily deep inside it. At one time he had a mind (military inexperience notwithstanding) to command the Royalist fleet, and his agent Goffe was sent to tell the ships' crews: 'You should all petition the Lord Jermyn may be your Admiral. He will be able to supply you with money and whatever else you want.' The sailors were rightly suspicious and chose Rupert instead (who was financed by John of Braganza), but the incident was a fair indication that there might be money enough if the favourite's interests were engaged. Montrose asked the Queen for 6,000 pistoles.[10] With this he offered to raise and equip a force of 10,000 men whom he could lead back to Scotland to form the nucleus of a new army. The money was not forthcoming, and the offer was coldly declined.

Many attempts were made to discredit Montrose both during his lifetime and for posterity. This period of his career was no exception, and within the Court he became the object of petty slander and malicious gossip. Bishop Burnet, a devotee of the Hamiltons and the author of *A History of his own Times*, apart from alleging that Montrose was a personal coward, recorded the following account of what happened at the Louvre:

> The Queen-mother hated him mortally; for when he came over from Scotland to Paris, upon the King's requiring him to lay down his arms, she received him with such extraordinary favour as his services seemed to deserve, and gave him a large supply in money and in jewels, considering the straits to which she was then reduced. But she heard that he had talked very indecently of her favours to him; which she herself told the Lady Susanna Hamilton, a daughter of Duke Hamilton, from whom I had it. So she sent him word to leave Paris, and she would see him no more. He wandered about the courts of Germany but was not esteemed so much as he thought he deserved.[11]

Even had Burnet not been biased, the story was hearsay at third hand from the daughter of one of Montrose's enemies, and the passage was so suspicious that the original editors of the book suppressed it altogether. The 'History' was intended for posthumous publication, and despite Macaulay's somewhat equivocal assertion that 'though often misled by prejudice and passion he was emphatically an honest man', Burnet has long been discredited as an historian, not least because his account does not stand up against other contemporary and more authentic records–or indeed with his own previous writings. Montrose was not ordered to quit Paris, and subsequent correspondence between him and the Queen in no way reflects this alleged affront which in any event would have been totally at variance with the known character of the man. As to the esteem in which he was held in the courts of Germany, that he was made a marshal of the Holy Roman Empire is a matter of record.

Nor did he receive 'a large supply in money and in jewels'. As he told the Cardinal de Retz: 'He would conform himself to the conditions in which the King, his master, was: that he would set up no equipage for appearing at court; that he had a Great Family [i.e. those officers who had accompanied him into exile or joined him there] but had little left for maintaining it'.[12] Yet considering that he had given his own fortune to the service of the King, he would have been justified in feeling that some sort of financial subsistence was his due.

While the Jermyn faction openly snubbed him and made it clear that his continued presence was not welcome at the Court, for his part he found the atmosphere of levity and vice that pervaded its society personally abhorrent. There had been some suggestion that his niece, Lilias Napier, who was nineteen and unmarried, might become a maid of honour but he sharply rejected such an idea: '. . . For there is neither Scots man nor woman welcome that way; neither would any of honour and virtue (chiefly a woman) suffer themselves to live in so lewd and worthless a place.'[13] While many of his officers took lodgings in the Academy, he himself retired to the country and lived quietly outside Paris.

But if the English Court would not recognize his merit, there were many in Paris who did. He was given precedence over regular ambassadors, while the French, who had followed his amazing campaigns with admiration, ranked him as the equal of Condé in military ability. He was able to deal directly with Mazarin who offered him a dazzling career in the service of France, and he became a friend of the Coadjutor of Paris, Cardinal de Retz, who looked upon him as some antique hero returned to a corrupted world:

> Le Compte de Montrose, Ecossais, et chef de la maison de Graham, le seul homme du monde qui m'ait jamais rappelé l'idée de certains héros que l'on ne voit plus que dans les vies de Plutarque, avait soutenu le parti du roi d'Angleterre avec une grandeur d'âme qui n'en avait pas de pareille en ce siècle.

Another consolation was the arrival in Paris of his nephew Napier (with permission from the Estates to *see* his uncle but not converse with him!), who now became his closest companion.

In the meanwhile, events were taking a strange twist in Scotland. The English had not honoured their part of the infamous bargain. The second instalment of £200,000 was not paid, and in June the King was forcibly abducted by the sectaries of the army whom the Scottish Presbyterian faction had especial cause to fear. This latest example of English faithlessness, and a widespread feeling of shame for the dishonourable transaction that had preceded it, revived a latent royalism among the more moderate Scots. The Covenant faction began to split. Dog was ready to eat dog, and many of the laity were becoming increasingly alarmed at the theocratic pretensions of Wariston and the extreme faction of the Kirk who, since the death of Alexander Henderson the previous August, were now in complete control of the General Assembly. Private ambitions and religious bigotry were producing the divisions which would ultimately bring the country to ruin. 'By that confusion my thoughts become distracted,' Argyll would later write to his son. 'Whatever therefore hath been said by me or others on this matter you must repute and accept them as from a distracted man . . . in a distracted time wherein I lived.'[14] Argyll was in thrall to the Kirk, and the extremists would have no further dealings with the King. But Hamilton (who had regained his freedom when Cariston Castle was captured by the parliamentary forces), with the more moderate Covenanters behind him, was now actively competing for the leadership once more and the divisions began to harden. Montereul reported cynically to Mazarin:

> It is to be remarked that the more the King's affairs are depressed the more the division between the Duke of Argyll and the Marquis of Hamilton . . . increases, so that they are of opposite opinions in everything but what concerns the ruin of the King; and that although they speak to each other and dine together very often, it is seen that they look upon themselves as the only persons who can mutually destroy each other, and that while the Marquis will not brook having a master, the Duke will not have a companion.

The Royalist reaction in Scotland gave Hamilton a temporary edge, and although the Kirk declared against him he gained a large majority in the Scottish Parliament. In November 1647 Charles escaped from Hampton Court to Carisbrooke Castle in the Isle of Wight, and there Lanerick, Lauderdale and Loudoun concluded a new secret treaty with the King, pledging armed support against the promise that Presbyterianism would be given three years' trial in England. The Hamilton faction (known thereafter as the Engagers) also sent a delegation to Paris to obtain sanction and support from the credulous Queen.

Details of these negotiations were deliberately kept from Montrose, but the news leaked out and he went to Court to argue against any new treaty with the Covenanters (of whatever brand) whose untrustworthiness had been so clearly demonstrated by their betrayal of the King. Avarice, ambition and a guilty conscience were hardly the ingredients of loyalty as he conceived it. For Hamilton himself he had nothing but contempt. True, he had protested to Parliament at the 'selling' of the King, but £30,000 of the 'blood money' had fallen to his share. As a military commander he was incompetent, and in the cypher that he used at this time, Montrose refers to him as 'Captain Luckless'. (Argyll was 'Ruling Elder', and himself, not untypically, was 'Venture Fair'.)[15] Even without the advantages of retrospect, to the clear-cut Royalist the Engagement was a dishonest bargain from the beginning, and as such was doomed to fail. It sought to combine those very elements that had been shown to be incompatible, and while it professed to be Royalist in aspiration, it still tried to attach Charles to the Covenant in accordance with the Presbyterians' ambition to force their religion upon a reluctant neighbour–thereby alienating the English Royalists on whose support it would ultimately have to depend. To the 'court politicians' in Paris it may have had the attraction of disuniting the Covenant party in Scotland, but they seriously overestimated the short-term advantages that might accrue. Hamilton was inept, and as always shrank from an open confrontation with the Kirk, so that when he finally marched on England he would leave a large proportion of his worst enemies behind him. Argyll was clever, and for the sake of power was getting ready to do a deal with Cromwell. Clarendon later commented that the Engagement contained 'so many monstrous concessions that except the whole Kingdom of England had been likewise imprisoned in Carisbrooke Castle with the King it could not be imagined that it was possible to be performed'.

Montrose did not know the details of Charles's own foolish plotting with the Engagers. Just as in 1642, he saw himself competing against Hamilton for the ear of the Queen–and as before, he lost. He was made to understand that his presence at Court was an embarrassment, and the more resented in that the first part of Wishart's biography, *Res Montisros*,[16] which had just been published in Holland and was achieving a wide circulation, had caused considerable offence among the Covenant party with whom Her Majesty was intriguing. The Queen rejected his advice, and the King's fortunes were entrusted instead to a sick Presbyterian faction whose half-hearted blundering (though no one guessed it then) would ultimately bring Charles even to the block.

When he saw that nothing he could say would alter the Queen's decision, Montrose offered to return to Scotland in person and raise those other Royalists who like himself suspected the honesty of the Engagers and would not fight under Hamilton. He promised that such a force would play an auxiliary role only. If the Engagement was successful the credit would go to Hamilton. But if the Covenanters had any thought of breaking the agreement, the presence of his Royalist army would ensure their good behaviour. The Hamilton party, however, stipulated that Montrose was to have no share in the business. He was the object of general aversion in Scotland, having shed the blood of his own countrymen, while the Engagers (piously) would be marching against a foreign enemy.

In March 1648 the Queen replied favourably to the propositions of the Engagers and the fateful negotiations went ahead. 'That he might not seem the impious partner or idle spectator of such villainy',[17] Montrose decided to leave Paris.

Europe was still in the throes of the Thirty Years War, and both the main protagonists were understandably interested in securing the services (if only nominal) of the man whom many considered to be one of the great military geniuses of the age. For some time already, Mazarin had been negotiating with Montrose on a personal basis, and a contract was drawn up formally offering him the command of the Scots in France, the rank of Lieutenant-General in the royal army with authority over all the Mareschals du Champ, and the post of Captain of the Gens d'Armes with an annual pension of 12,000 crowns besides his pay. In addition, Mazarin gave a verbal promise that after one year he would be made a Marshal of France and captain of the King's Guard (a post which at that time normally sold for 150,000 crowns). It was an extremely tempting proposition, offering the possibility of a private command, wealth, rank, privilege and personal access to the King of France, and Napier was very keen that Montrose should accept it. Montrose himself certainly agreed that, since Henrietta Maria did not seem to require his services, there was little point in remaining idle and unemployed in Paris. Nor would his financial circumstances permit it. But he was doubtful of Mazarin's offer and even wrote to the Prince of Orange asking his advice.[18] He distrusted the French, having not forgotten their role in persuading Charles to join the Scots in the first instance, and he suspected with good reason that they were now less interested in helping the English king than in trying to prevent him from obtaining aid from the Spanish whom he was thought to favour. He noted with unease their cordial relations with the English Parliament, and he argued with Napier 'that if he did engage with them [the French] he would be forced to connive and wink at his Prince's ruin'.[19] In the second place, it is probable that the degree of commitment involved was not acceptable. Montrose's sword was temporarily for hire but it was not for sale. The day might come when Charles himself would call him back, and he had to be free to go. In the meanwhile he was looking for a patron, not a master. At that time it was possible for a general to obtain a commission to levy troops on his own account, and, having failed to get any support from the Queen, Montrose's aim now was to raise a number of independent regiments, or at least an officer corps, which though temporarily at the disposal of a friendly European prince could become at short notice the nucleus of a new expeditionary force to be led back to Britain when the right opportunity presented itself. The French offer may not have contained this release clause and Montrose may have felt that he would not be guaranteed the necessary independence of command.

At the same time there were other political factors to be taken into account. If he committed himself actively to the cause of France it was unlikely that he would be able to obtain any help from the Empire with whom France was at war. But the prospect of an independent commission under the Emperor—if possible in Flanders and close to the Channel—was if anything more attractive and might allow him a greater freedom of action than the French would permit.

When, therefore, he received an invitation to visit the Imperial Court he decided to let the French negotiation lapse. But his departure from Paris had to be kept secret since it was possible that if they got to know of his intended destination the French would try to prevent him from leaving. It was agreed that he would travel via Switzerland while Napier was to remain in Paris and merely give out that Montrose had retired to the country to recuperate his health. 'Which', Napier wrote to his wife, 'was always believed so long as they saw me; for it was ever said that Montrose and his nephew were like the Pope and the Church, who would be inseparable'.[20]

As soon as Napier got word that Montrose had reached Geneva, he and the other Scottish Royalists who preferred still to attach themselves to the Graham rather than accept commissions in one or other of the continental armies[21] left Paris for Flanders, where they could live less expensively and with greater freedom to correspond with their chief.

From Geneva Montrose wrote to the Queen, begging to be excused for not having previously informed her of his departure and stating his intention to seek help from among the German states. He then travelled through the Tyrol and Bavaria to Austria, and finding that the Emperor was not in Vienna continued to Prague where Ferdinand III received him with great honour. Their negotiation was completely successful. Montrose was appointed a Marshal of the Holy Roman Empire and granted a commission to raise forces with sole command under the Emperor himself. Ferdinand agreed that the Flanders border would be best suited to his purpose, and wrote to his brother, the Archduke Leopold of Austria, who was governor of the Spanish Netherlands, recommending Montrose and asking him to render every possible assistance.

This was exactly what Montrose had been hoping for, and he set off for Brussels at once. However, the direct route across Europe was blocked by contending armies, and he was obliged to make a long detour–by Presburg (then Pozsony in Hungary, now Bratislava), Tyrnan, through Poland to Cracow and then across Prussia to Danzig where he boarded a ship sailing for Denmark. There he was kindly received by Christian IV before continuing to Jutland and thence by sea to Groningen in Friesland, and so to Brussels. He arrived just in time to hear that the Archduke Leopold had been heavily defeated by Condé at Lens (20 August 1648) and was falling back on Tournay– where Montrose eventually met him. Leopold was clearly in no position to offer any immediate help since Lens had cost him upwards of 6,000 casualties and the matter was deferred until both should have returned to Brussels when the problem could be laid before the Estates. It was another disappointment.

At Brussels, Montrose also got detailed news of the collapse of the Engagement. On 17 August (thereafter called 'St Covenant's Day' by the kirk precisians) the Scots army had been totally defeated at

Preston and the incompetent Hamilton taken prisoner by the English. Scotland was in confusion. The Estates had capitulated to the Kirk, and Cromwell was marching north to meet Argyll. Though appalled perhaps by the extent of the disaster[22] (which in some degree he had predicted), Montrose now had greater cause to hope that the King would be willing to sanction the 'clear gallant design' which he had hitherto advocated so earnestly and without success, and he began to seek the support of the younger active Royalists who were of a similar mind. He maintained a long and courteous correspondence with Prince Rupert to whom he offered his services stating frankly that he did not propose to return to the Imperial Court since 'there is nothing of honour among the stuff here and that I am not found useful for His Majesty's service in the way of home'.[23] He also expressed the hope that at some time he and Rupert might have the opportunity to mount a joint expedition, for 'we may have a handsome pull for it and a probable one, and either win it or be sure to lose it fairly'. The correspondence came to nothing, however, since Rupert was preoccupied with quelling a mutiny in the Royalist fleet, and when this was done, in January 1649, he set off on a cruise which would take him first to Ireland and subsequently to the West Indies. It was unfortunate perhaps that these two Royalist commanders never took the field together since in theory at least they would have made an invincible combination.

Montrose also wrote to the Duke of York (in his youth a competent soldier), who replied in friendly and courteous terms, and to the Prince of Wales who had escaped from the restrictive atmosphere of his mother's Court and was now established at The Hague. The young Charles was interested, and on 20 January 1649 he replied, suggesting that his chancellor, Edward Hyde (later Clarendon), would meet Montrose 'in any place you shall appoint, and by him you shall understand my mind upon the whole. I need not tell you', he added, 'that there must be great secrecy in this business.'[24]

Montrose at once agreed to the proposed meeting–'Till when I only beg Your Highness to believe that, as I never had passion on earth so strong as that to do the King your father service, so shall it be my study, if Your Highness command me, to show it redoubled for the recovery of you.' And he begged the Prince to distinguish between his true and false friends–'If Your Highness will but vouchsafe a little faith unto your loyal servants and stand at guard with others, your affairs can soon be whole.'[25]

Hyde had also written by the same courier as Prince Charles, urging the utmost secrecy and suggesting that, since Brussels and Antwerp were now crawling with ex-Engagers and 'inquisitive men', they should meet in some small out-of-the-way town where there was less risk of their being recognized.[26] Montrose replied proposing Sevenbergen as the best place.

But events were to intervene. On 30 January 1649, Charles I was publicly executed in London.

When Montrose heard the news he appears to have collapsed in a
dead faint. Then, according to Wishart, who was an eye witness
to the scene: '. . . after many deep groans he broke into these words:
"We must die, die with our gracious King. May the God of life
and death be my witness, that henceforth life on earth will be
bitterness and mourning." '[27] On the third day Wishart entered
his bedchamber and found a piece of paper on the table on which
Montrose had written this poem:

> *Great, Good, and Just, could I but rate*
> *My griefs and thy too rigid fate*
> *I'd weep the world to such a strain*
> *As it should deluge once again.*
> *But since thy loud-tongued blood demands supplies*
> *More from Briareus' hands than Argos' eyes,*
> *I'll sing thy Obsequies with trumpet sounds*
> *And write thine epitaph in blood and wounds.*[28]

When he eventually emerged, Montrose was a changed man.
To his friends he later described the remaining period of his life
as his 'Passion'. The King's death had come as a terrible shock,
but it was the manner of it that so appalled him. Kings had been
killed before. In England four at least had been secretly assassinated,
one had been killed in battle, one by accident. The history of
Scotland was bloodier yet. But Charles I had been publicly murdered,
and the formal hypocrisy of his trial did nothing to mitigate the
inherent barbarity of the act. Montrose had never been a blind
believer in the divine right of kings to which the early Stuarts
aspired, but he had fought for a personal concept of a constitutional
monarchy which he believed to be benevolent and right. The execution
of the King shattered this ideal. It was an end to philosophy and an
end to compromise. Any victory now must be absolute and unconditional. The idealist was gone, and in his place was the avenger.
In February he wrote to Hyde:

> The griefs that astonish speak more with their silence than
> those that can complain. It will be no more time now to dally.
> For if affection and love to the justice and virtue of that cause be not
> incitement great enough, anger and so just revenge methinks should
> wing us on.[29]

From now on, Montrose is a sombre figure—a soldier in black armour,
the cavalier in mourning. Instead of hope there is a brooding sense
of destiny. Hope, determination and sorrow are turned to bitterness
and anger. Stern honour alone remains his inspiration.

Venture Fair
(February 1649–March 1650)

Who, rowing hard against the stream
Saw distant gates of Eden gleam
And did not dream it was a dream
Tennyson

On 28 February 1649, Hyde wrote to Prince Rupert from The Hague:

> Our court is full of Scots. The Earls of Lauderdale and Lanerick
> are here, being as they say, driven out of their country by the power
> of Argyll who is in firm league with Cromwell. Here is likewise the
> Marquis of Montrose, who is in truth a gallant person and very
> impatient to be doing; and though the Presbyterians are as busy as
> ever, yet I believe the next news I shall send you will be, that His
> Majesty entirely trusts Montrose and puts the business of Scotland
> wholly into his conduct.[1]

On 4 March, Charles II appointed Montrose his Captain-General in
Scotland and Commander-in-Chief of all his forces in that country.

However, he was not yet able to act on this commission. The Hague
was thick with Scottish intrigues, and in such a situation the young
King, whose concept of integrity was never of the strictest, had
inherited the fatal Stuart predilection for treating with both sides
simultaneously. The Marquis of Hamilton was a prisoner of the
English, soon to be executed after his master, but the remnants of his
faction led by Lauderdale still aimed at a *coup de partie* and sought to
entice the King to Scotland. Against these, the failure of the Engagement and the subsequent execution of the King had tipped the scales
in Montrose's favour, and though Hyde argued caution, he was determined to confront them openly at Court: 'For they know if we once
engage the business is half done; and that in a few weeks they
must be honest men or have no knaves left to take their places.'[2]

But the failure of the Engagement and the execution of the King had
also forced Argyll back into the game. On 5 February Charles II had
been proclaimed king at the Mercat Cross in Edinburgh, the
proclamation being couched in the traditional form but with the

added proviso that he would not be allowed to exercise royal power until he had signed the Covenant. On 20 February, Sir Joseph Douglas and others of Argyll's creatures reached The Hague to announce that Covenant commissioners would soon follow.

The execution of Charles I had destroyed the prospective alliance between Argyll and Cromwell by rekindling the nationalist feelings and loyalist impulse of the Scots. It was a matter of sentiment that aligned Covenant and monarchy against the English, sectarianism and regicide; and Argyll, as a politician, adapted to the mood of the country. The English had buried the Covenant—none too decently—and the Scots, against all logic, thought still to rejuvenate it for their own ends. The situation was unreal. The original aims of the Covenant would no longer bear practical examination, and it stood as a hollow pretext for espousing the new king's cause with intent (never relinquished) to interfere with the domestic affairs of another nation. But above all, it remained the sole sanction for their policy, and Argyll and the Kirk clung to it with a tenacity that would otherwise be inexplicable. Amnesty for the sake of unity thus had no place in their creed, and the day before the commissioners left (22 March) the Marquis of Huntly was beheaded at Edinburgh[3]—an object lesson for the young King as to what happened to Royalists who were not Covenanters. Not surprisingly the outstanding feature of the subsequent negotiations was the spirit of utter insincerity in which they were conducted.

The Scottish commissioners, who included Cassilis and the Rev. Robert Baillie, arrived at The Hague at the end of March. They appeared before Charles II dressed in deep mourning for his father, but the written proposals which they laid before him were the most arrogant to date. The King was to sign and ratify the Covenant and the Solemn League and Covenant. He was to agree to the establishment of Presbyterianism in his three kingdoms of Scotland, England and Ireland, and he himself was to adhere to the Presbyterian form of worship both publicly and in private. He was to give his assent to all acts and ordinances of past, present and future parliaments and the General Assembly.

The commissioners also made it clear that any negotiated settlement was conditional upon Charles's getting rid of Montrose, and on 9 April they delivered a petition representing the Kirk's 'earnest desire that such as lie under their censure of excommunication may be discountenanced by Your Majesty and removed from your court. Especially James Graham, the late Earl of Montrose, being a man most justly if ever any, cast out of the Church of God'. The King's duty, they told him, was to maintain the discipline of the Church and not associate with excommunicates '. . . least of all at this time in the hopeful beginning of your reign, for gratifying of a person upon whose head lies more innocent blood than for many years has done on the head of anyone:—the most bloody murderer in our nation'. They themselves refused to meet Montrose in conference, and if he entered the chamber they ostentatiously left by another door.

Montrose had a powerful ally, though possibly not a personal friend, in Chancellor Hyde, who believed 'his clear spirit to be most like to advance the King's service'. Hyde also hated the Scots with their 'damnable Covenant', and had little time for Engagers, either, since he and Lauderdale were enemies of old. Lauderdale was particularly virulent in his denunciations of Montrose, whom he accused of committing the most unspeakable atrocities during the war in Scotland. But when Hyde asked him whether Montrose, like the Covenanters, 'had ever caused a man to die in cold blood or after the battle was ended', he was obliged to admit 'that he did not know he was guilty of anything but was done on the battlefield'. Lauderdale hastened to add, however, that 'though he wished nothing more in this world than to see the King restored, he had much rather that he should never be restored than that James Graham should be permitted to come into the court'. Hyde merely saw to it that such sentiments were duly reported to the King.[4] Of the other lords of the Engagement, Lanerick (who became Marquis of Hamilton after the execution of his brother) was more moderate, and even offered to serve 'as a sergeant' under Montrose, but was prevented by Lauderdale–'who haunts him like a fury'.[5] It seems likely that, through the agency of the ubiquitous William Murray, who had also arrived at The Hague, Lauderdale was already in cryptic alliance with Argyll.

Unfortunately, Hyde saw no profit in the business, and he later seized an opportunity to leave the King's Court on an embassy to Spain. His departure was to be a severe blow to Montrose, Napier and the other Royalists *sans phrase*. By assiduous lobbying the Scots commissioners had secured the support of the Prince of Orange as well as the Jermyn faction at St Germain who were constantly pressing Charles to agree to the Covenanters' terms. For the time being Charles was personally inclined to favour the Royalists' proposal that he should lead an expedition to Ireland while Montrose made his attempt on Scotland,[6] but he was not averse to bargaining with the other side, and the Royalists were soon to lose their ablest and most influential advocate at the crucial discussions in the King's Council Chamber. Hyde's embassy to Spain brought no profit, but his presence on the Council during the latter months of 1649 and early 1650 might have preserved the balance for Montrose.

In the meantime, however, Montrose had made another ally who was also a friend. Elizabeth of the Palatine, Queen of Bohemia, was one of the most celebrated personalities of Europe. Her husband, the Winter King, was dead; her second son Prince Rupert was the most famous of the cavalier generals; and though she was now in her fifties, poor and in permanent exile, age had not dimmed the vitality of her earlier beauty, nor misfortune withered the spirit or that charisma which throughout her life had so drawn men to serve the Queen of Hearts. Hers was an old-world chivalry in which Montrose epitomized the true knight at arms, and if she was extrovert, extravagant, flamboyant and many things that he was not, yet they were strangely kindred spirits in a calloused world. Her friendship was possibly his greatest comfort in the difficult months ahead. It was she who now supported his cause and guarded his interests. She warned him of the intrigues of his enemies, and encouraged him when things went badly. Her letters were direct and personal and she always referred to him as Jamie Graham. Unfortunately his letters to her have not survived but he gave her a portrait of himself, painted between February and May 1649 by Gerard Honthorst,[7] which she hung in her chamber–'to frighten away the Brethren' as she told him. It is the most famous of the portraits of Montrose, the most romantic, and perhaps the best in that it reveals the personal charm, and captures in some strange way the calm magic of his presence. He is wearing coal black armour and clasps the red baton of a Marshal of the Empire. The grey eyes are wide and clear, with a hint of sadness, the face strong and thinner than in earlier portraits. His hair is long and combed in the fashion of the cavaliers. He stands beside a cliff. Behind him is a stormy sea, and beyond there is a promise of sunrise.

Elizabeth of Bohemia spent her time between The Hague and her country house at Rhenen. The Palatines were a large and talented family. Carl-Louis, her eldest son but the runt of the litter, was in England as the guest of Cromwell. Rupert was in the process of changing from cavalry leader to cavalier pirate. Maurice, soon to drown, was with him. At The Hague the Queen held court with her four daughters–Elizabeth, an intellectual and friend of Leibnitz; Henrietta, who would marry the Prince of Transylvania; Sophia, who became Electress of Hanover; and Louise, the painter who studied under Honthorst and later became a nun and abbess of Maubuisson. The Princess Sophia in her Memoirs, written forty years after, recalled of Montrose:

> Since he was a very brave soldier and a man of high merit, he thought nothing impossible to his management and courage. He was sure he could restore the young King if His Majesty would make him Viceroy of Scotland, and, if he did him so great a service, the King could not refuse him the hand of my sister Princess Louise.

It is a sentence that tantalizes. Perhaps in the story of the princess who left home in secret to become a nun there is some suggestion of unspoken tragedy. But there is no other reference, and the mystery of Montrose's second love, if indeed he had one, remains unsolved. It is rather the stuff that novels are made of.

The negotiations at The Hague dragged on from February to May 1649. Reconciliation between the contending factions was clearly impossible. The precious months slipped by. In northern Scotland a premature rising under Mackenzie of Pluscardine, Seaforth's brother, was put down by the Covenanters. It confirmed Montrose's opinion that the mood was right, but they were too early, and he was in danger of becoming too late.

Finally Charles, despairing of any reasonable conference between the various parties, asked Montrose and the Engagers to state their views on the Scottish conditions in the presence of the Council. Lauderdale was reluctant to commit himself publicly, but Montrose immediately agreed to comply with the request–being willing to deliver his opinion concerning things or persons before anybody or in any place'.

He therefore submitted his comments in the form of a letter to the King, in which he examined the precedents for the Covenant, tracing it back to the original document which had been signed by James VI in his nonage. But this first Covenant, he explained, had been a 'negative confession' against 'the exorbitances and abuses of the Roman hierarchy', never formally approved by act of Council, and certainly not intended for 'a snare and stumbling block to all posterity'. The Covenant of 1638, which, it was true, had professed to be the renewal of the earlier one, was not in itself objectionable, though it had since been turned into a 'religious pretence' and a charter for sedition. It had been signed by many (including himself) 'who meant rightly enough for His Majesty's service' and, provided that it was confined to the kingdom of Scotland, Montrose saw no harm in the King's signing it if he was willing to do so.

The Solemn League and Covenant, however, was a different thing entirely, though 'they always strive to twist along at with the other':

It is so full of violence, injustice and rebellion that, in my humble opinion, it were Your Majesty's shame and ruin ever to give ear to it: it being nothing but a condemning of your father's memory, joining all your dominions by your own consent against you. . . .
They would also force Your Majesty to quit the form of service and worship in your own family. And yet they made it a ground of rebellion against your royal father that they but imagined he intended to meddle with them in like kind.

Against the bigotry of the Covenanters' demands, Montrose argued for a realistic policy and one that would attract the maximum support in both Scotland and England–the restoration of a monarchy along constitutional lines with each country free to choose its own form of religion. Contrary to the claims made by the Scots commissioners, by acceding to the Covenanters' terms the King would lose the support of Royalists in his other dominions–'For have they not still totally declined the Royal Party in all your Kingdoms?' And with a biting sarcasm he continued:

Whereas they promise to continue the same faithfulness unto Your Majesty as they have done to your Royal father, it appears they do not at all dissemble at this point. Their selling of him to his enemies, their instructions to their Commissioners, and all their public and private carriages with his murderers doth sufficiently declare it. . . .
As for their pretence in proclaiming Your Majesty King, it is the greatest argument can be given of their disloyalty. For while Your Majesty is the hereditary and undoubted heir of that kingdom . . .

in place of declaring your right, they question it, and rather would make it null by turning your hereditary right to a conditional election of *ands* and *ifs*.

And further they desire that Your Majesty would consent and agree that all matters civil should be determined by Parliament, and all matters ecclesiastical by the Assembly; by which Your Majesty does clearly see they resolve that *you* should signify nothing. . . .

And besides all this, they have been the fountain and origin of all the rebellions both among themselves and all others of Your Majesty's dominions. And after they had received all full satisfaction in order to their whole desires both touching Church and State, within their own nation, they entered England with a strong army and there joined themselves to the rebel party in that Kingdom, persecuted the King your Royal father, till in a kind they had reduced him to deliver himself up into their hands. And *then*, contrary to all duty, gratitude, faith, and hospitality, they sold him even into the hands of his merciless enemies–complotted his death–connived at his murder–and have been the only rigid and restless instruments of all his saddest fates. Of all which past horrid misdemeanours they are so little ashamed, that they make it their only business now to preserve their conquest . . . murdering those of your best subjects [i.e. Huntly] while they pretend to treat with Your Majesty. . . .

Against all which, in my humble opinion, I know no other remedy than that the contraries should be quickly applied; and that Your Majesty should be pleased resolutely to trust the justice of your cause to God and better fortunes; and use all vigorous and active ways, as the only probable human means that is left to redeem you.[8]

This document was read in Council on 21 May 1649, and it proved decisive. Montrose was confirmed as Viceroy of Scotland and Captain-General of the forces in that country, and appointed Admiral of the Scottish seas. The terms of the Scottish Estates were rejected and the commissioners left The Hague at the beginning of June. The King appeared to have made up his mind and given his approval to Montrose's 'Venture Fair'.

Charles also left The Hague on 15 June. His presence there had become increasingly embarrassing to the Dutch who, for reasons of maritime interest, did not wish to offend the English. Rupert's appropriation of English ships had already caused considerable friction, and the matter came to a head when the Commonwealth envoy, a Dr Dorislaus, was murdered on the night of his arrival by a group of men who were afterwards said to have been Scots and adherents of Montrose. Charles removed to Breda and from there wrote to Montrose on 22 June confirming his decision to entrust the Scottish venture to his command:

The more to encourage you to my service, and render you confident of my resolutions, both touching myself and you, I have thought fit by these to signify to you, that I will not determine anything touching the affairs of that kingdom without having your advice thereupon. As also I will not do anything that shall be prejudicial to your commission.[9]

But despite such assurances, Montrose still had cause to be uneasy. Almost simultaneously he received another letter from Elizabeth of Bohemia warning him not to leave the King:

> By great chance I have found that the Prince of Orange will again extremely press the King to grant the [Scots] Commissioners' desires and so ruin him through your sides. I give you warning of it that you may be provided to hinder it. . . . For God's sake leave not the King as long as he is at Breda, for without question there is nothing that will be omitted to ruin you and your friends and so the King at last. It is so late I can say no more; only believe me ever your most constant, affectionate friend,
>
> ELIZABETH[10]

He followed Charles to Breda and thereafter to Brussels and was somewhat reassured when the King renewed and extended his commission as Ambassador Extraordinary to foreign courts. The ink was barely dry, however, before Charles was also writing to the dominant party in Scotland in terms that clearly indicated to Argyll that the way to further negotiation was still open.

Nor was the Jermyn faction idle. In April Henrietta Maria had renewed her former correspondence with Montrose–'Having an esteem for you that can never be diminished'–in which she continued 'with the greatest possible sincerity' to express her desire 'to convince you of the reality of my gratitude; and believe me when the time comes I will rather prove it by deeds than words.'[11] But he was not deceived by this, knowing all too well the notions of policy that prevailed at St Germain, of which Elizabeth of Bohemia continued faithfully to keep him informed:

> I do not desire that you should quit Brussels while there is a danger of change. I hear Jermyn has orders to get your commission for Hamilton. If that be true, sure they are all mad or worse. I write this freely to you; wherefore I pray you burn this, for I do not desire to have it seen. You may well know why.[12]

It was an ominous background against which to plan a desperate adventure. However, although Charles himself was now in Paris (*en route* as he hoped for Ireland) and under considerable pressure from the Queen-Mother, the King appeared to be remaining constant after his fashion, and, notwithstanding the dangers posed by these intrigues, Montrose began to prepare in earnest for his attempt on Scotland. In Holland he found no shortage of potential recruits, at least as far as officers were concerned, but the overriding problem was the lack of money to purchase stores, arms and ordnance, and procure the necessary ships to transport an army to Scotland. For its initial success the enterprise would depend on substantial foreign help.

In August he met the Earl of Kinnoul at Elizabeth of Bohemia's country house at Rhenen, and together they planned the forthcoming campaign. It was decided that Kinnoul should lead an advance force of 80 officers and 100 Danish recruits (the sum total of those enlisted so far) and seize the islands of Orkney. There he was to establish a base in preparation for the arrival of the more substantial forces that would follow, and in the interim to raise and train men from among the islanders. Messengers were to cross to the mainland to warn the loyal chiefs of Montrose's imminent return, so that when the main invasion took place the clans would be ready to rise in arms.

The plan was strategically sound. The Orkneys were outside the Covenanters' control. Their feudal chief, Lord Morton, was Kinnoul's uncle and a known Royalist who could be relied on to give his support. A subsequent landing in the very North of Scotland would place the invading army conveniently close to the northern clans – Mackays and Mackenzies – who were expected to join the rising, and with these reinforcements Montrose hoped to be strong enough to take the direct mountain route to the central Highlands where his chief support principally lay. The Mackenzies under Pluscardine had already rebelled in the spring, and Seaforth, now in Paris, was party to the scheme. Letters from other Royalists in Scotland indicated that the moment was auspicious. Finally, the chances of reaching the Orkneys unintercepted were better than average since the English navy was currently occupied with blockading Rupert in Ireland and would have few ships to spare for the wild north-eastern approaches. With this agreed, at the end of August Montrose bade farewell to Elizabeth of Bohemia and went with Kinnoul to Amsterdam where the latter took over command of the advance force. Montrose continued to Hamburg to begin negotiations with the German princes.

The Royalists' preparations were conducted in the greatest secrecy, but the intention was well known and the movements of Montrose and his officers were followed with great attention by English, Covenanters and Hamiltonians alike. The reports of their spies often reflected the bias or fears of a particular faction, but word leaked out, and in the case of the English particularly their intelligence was commendably accurate. On 2 September Strickland, the new parliamentary envoy in Amsterdam, was able to report to London:

> Since Montrose, his absence, those who appeared so much in designs against me are seen no more. I believe most of them are gone, so I am more at liberty than I was. . . . Montrose hopes to raise a thousand horse and three thousand foot, and with them to visit his countrymen. My Lord Kinnoul who is well known in England, I hear, is gone to take possession of some island in Scotland. . . .

and on 6 September:

> There is in Amsterdam a ship in which is much arms and ammunition bound for Scotland for the use of Montrose as I am informed. If there be any in Scotland who desire such an information, it were well they knew it. It is to be sent to some of the Isles, some say the Orkades. Those of that nation are so excessively my enemies here that it is high charity for me to do anything which may lend to their service. Montrose is expected in Hamburg.[13]

(It is possible that Strickland's masters in London knew of this already. As will transpire, their intelligence on what was happening at St Germains was better still.)

This bad security and the poor condition of the ship were not without their effect on the morale of some of the troops who were to sail with Kinnoul. Captain John Gwynne, whose *Military Memoirs* provide the only eye-witness account of the campaign to follow, recorded this of the period immediately prior to Kinnoul's departure:

> At Amsterdam before we went over with the Earl of Kinnoul. . . .
> I was told by those who condoled us (as knowing our business better
> than some of ourselves did) that we were all betrayed; and by our
> proceedings it appeared to be so as thus; First we were to have a
> small fleet vessel with 12 guns; and instead of that we had an old
> one, new vamp't without a gun. . . .[14]

But despite such gloomy premonitions the little ship evaded three parliamentary men-of-war which had been lying in wait, and after a long and stormy voyage made a successful landfall at Kirkwall in the Orkneys where Kinnoul was warmly received by Lord Morton. He immediately seized the castle of Birsay for his headquarters and 500 men of Orkney were quickly raised for the island's defence. The Covenanters had word of the landing soon afterwards and Leslie marched North as far as Ross, but stormy seas prevented him from mounting any attack on the Orkneys. Kinnoul wrote to Montrose in enthusiastic terms reporting his safe arrival and urging his general to follow as soon as possible. The Scottish Royalists, he said, were ready to rise,

> . . . if you fall upon them [the Covenanters] at this nick of their
> distemper you shall find assistance beyond all expectation and that
> sufficient to effectuate your intentions. Your Lordship is gaped after
> with that expectation that the Jews had for their Messiah, and
> certainly your presence will restore your groaning country to its
> liberties and the King to his rights.[15]

For the moment all seemed to be going well. Unfortunately however, on 12 November Lord Morton expired and a few days later Kinnoul himself was dead of pleurisy—leaving the advance detachment without a leader.

Montrose meanwhile, preoccupied with raising the main invasion force, was using his commission to seek material and financial assistance from the rulers of northern Europe. But the business of negotiation proved slower and less rewarding than he had hoped. In theory at least, the defence of monarchy was a matter of importance to all European princes whose own position was made precarious by the English precedent, but in practice their past experience of Stuart incompetence and the present wrangling among the English Royalists in exile was making them reluctant to throw good money after bad. The Duke of Holstein had offered ships—'three or four very fair vessels and well manned . . . which Prince would willingly have contributed more in that service but that he perceived that which he had given before to be so misemployed: wherein both he and the Marquis were grossly abused'. In some cases Montrose found himself forestalled by Covenant representatives who were also touring the European courts predicting the certain failure of his forlorn mission and advocating their easier (and cheaper) plan for a negotiated settlement. In others he was deceived by the men whom he was obliged to use. From Hamburg the King's political agent in the North, Sir John Cochrane (whom Charles I had once described as 'a man who had many discourses, most of his own praises') was sent to the Duke of Courland (who promised six large ships laden with corn) and thereafter to King John Casimir of Poland, but, according to the *Montrose Redivivus*, 'having procured very considerable sums of money . . . and other provision for the furthering of Montrose's expedition–disposed of the money for his own uses, made sale of corn and provisions, together with the vessels provided for the transportation of it, and did himself turn tail to the quarrel. . . . This did much retard the Marquis's affairs'.[16] Another, Colonel Ogilvie, sent to Amsterdam 'to entertain such strangers as might be to his purpose', forgot his commission and 'bestowed both moneys and pains in entertaining himself'. Others were more honest but unsuccessful. Sir William Johnstone, Cochrane's deputy, was sent to negotiate with the Dukes of Brunswick, Celle and Hanover, but he appears to have achieved little of substance. Harry Graham went to Brandenburg where the elector Frederick William promised a large sum of money but did not in fact disgorge it. The Duke of Friesland was more helpful in offering free quarter in his country for the troops who had already been enlisted and were waiting to embark.

Montrose himself had hopes of obtaining help from the new King of Denmark (Christian IV having died shortly after their last meeting) and in September he met Frederick at Flensburg in Schleswig. The Danish king was willing to promise much, but effectual power was in the hands of a Council of Nobles and Montrose was obliged to wait in Copenhagen for a decision. Their debate was lengthy and unproductive and his growing frustration at this time is apparent in a letter which he wrote to Frederick on 19 October in which he begs to know his intentions, stressing that in a venture of this kind 'delays are the worst of all evils' and 'a refusal that sets us free is better than a promise that ruins us'. He did not come away altogether empty handed, however, since apart from the Danish troops who had accompanied Kinnoul and a further detachment who were recruited later he had previously formed a friendship with the powerful Danish nobleman Korfits Ulfeldt, the 'Maître du Royaume' who was married to Frederick's half-sister and had been his country's representative at The Hague. Ulfeldt advanced Montrose upwards of £10,000, much of it from his own resources. (Charles II subsequently repudiated the debt.[17])

But at Copenhagen Montrose also received a disquieting letter from the King in St Germain dated 19 September:

> I entreat you to go on vigorously and with your wonted courage and care in the preservation of those trusts I have committed to you, *and not to be startled by any reports you may hear as if I have otherwise inclined to the Presbyterians than when I left you.* I assure you that I am upon the same principles I was and depend as much as ever upon your undertakings and endeavours for my service, being fully resolved to assist and support you therein to the uttermost of my power.[18]

There was an ominous inference of duplicity and double-dealing, and he suspected Henrietta Maria of having a hand in it. On 2 October Elizabeth of Bohemia wrote again to tell him that Jermyn was on his way to The Hague as some thought 'to meet with Hamilton, Lauderdale, and *your other friends* to have new commissioners sent to the King from the Godly Brethren to cross wicked Jamie Graham's proceedings'. But, she assured him, 'it will do no good, the King continuing still most constant to his principles as you left him'.[19]

Nevertheless, he had cause to be uneasy. There were already rumours that Charles was playing a double game, and Montrose was understandably alarmed lest reports of an accommodation between King and Covenanters might paralyse his own efforts on the Continent and dishearten the Scottish Royalists whose support would be crucial to the success of the enterprise. It was clearly worrying him that Seaforth, who should by now have returned to Scotland to gather his clan in readiness, still lingered in Paris and appeared as ever to play his own kind of waiting game.

It was possibly in order to pre-empt or counteract such rumours that he now issued a premature Declaration in which he publicly defended the justice of his cause and called on all loyal Scots to rise against the Covenant authority. It is perhaps the most famous of his declarations, rehearsing in strong and incisive language the treasonable practices of the Covenanters from the beginning and offering pardon in the King's name to all except proven regicides.[20]

This paper was circulated in Edinburgh during December 1649, and on 2 January 1650 the Estates published their formal reply. In it they damned Montrose 'in the blindness of his mind and hardness of his heart as being given up of God as Pharaoh was'. He was called 'perfidious traitor', 'impudent braggart', 'Child of the Devil', 'dissembling hypocrite' and 'that viperous brood of Satan whom the Church hath delivered into the hands of the Devil and the nation doth generally detest and abhor' (this from the pen of Wariston). Apart from this string of abuse and a studied misrepresentation of Montrose's motives from the commencement of his career, the document also went to great lengths to defend all the past actions of the Covenanters (including their combination with the parliamentary army in 1643) as having been 'for the honour and *happiness* of the King' and 'for the defence and preservation of His Majesty's person and his just greatness and *authority'*. Despite the extreme virulence and personal animus of the attack, the Covenant reply was an effective piece of propaganda at the time, while even subsequently it was to influence the judgement of some later historians whose own political opinions led them to accept it without undue investigation as a fair assessment of Montrose. The contemporary English, however, had few such illusions and Commonwealth pamphleteers accused the Scots of blatant hypocrisy in venting their indignation on the servant while still pretending to be loyal to the master upon whose orders he had acted. *An English Translation of the Scottish Declaration Wherein Many Things are set Right between the Kingdom of Scotland and the Commonwealth of England* was published in London shortly after, and though a poor defence of regicide, it put the question plain enough:

> Let the world judge who deals more candidly with the King, the Parliament of England or the Committee of Estates: the one tells him He hath no rights but what he gets by the sword: and the other proclaims his right but will not let him exercise it without either he gives them their own terms or conquer them.[21]

In London, Scottish protestations of loyalty fooled nobody.

On 10 November Montrose left Copenhagen and went to Gothenburg in Sweden. The Swedish service was full of Scottish officers who had fought under Gustavus Adolphus, and he hoped that many of these could be induced to join the expedition. He also had good reason to believe that Gustavus's daughter, Queen Christina, would be sympathetic to the royal cause since she had previously written to Charles, assuring him 'that she will join with any Prince in assisting him to recover his crown and just rights'. However, she had gone on to advise His Majesty 'to forbear as yet to send any Extraordinary Ambassador to her for some weighty reasons', and unfortunately these weighty reasons also made her unwilling openly to support Montrose's enterprise. In this she was advised by her minister Oxenstierna. Holland and Denmark had recently concluded a treaty to Sweden's disadvantage and to counter-balance it she would need the friendship of a strong sea power such as Commonwealth England. She gave Montrose 1,500 stands of arms. All other war stores, and the small frigate the *Shepherdess*, which became his flagship, he was obliged to purchase. At the same time, however, she directed her officials to turn a blind eye to the preparations that were taking place in Gothenburg.

This port was well suited to Montrose's purpose, having a deep commodious harbour, well sheltered from the Atlantic and rarely closed by ice. He established himself at the house of John Maclear, a wealthy Scottish merchant with strong Royalist sympathies, who advanced £25,000 for the purchase of stores and ammunition and became Montrose's official buying agent and consignee for the arms and military equipment which began to arrive from other parts of Europe. Negotiations with Denmark continued in the interim, while in

Hamburg, Napier and other senior Royalist officers were still treating with the German princes.

The small invasion force began to take shape. Numbers of officers and men recruited in northern Europe arrived and were billeted in Gothenburg. Quantities of arms and ammunition including artillery pieces accumulated in Maclear's warehouses ready for loading into the ships that lay anchored in the sound. A constant stream of messengers came and left. Throughout, an atmosphere of secrecy prevailed, but although Montrose observed the strictest security as to his immediate intentions, such preparations could not pass unnoticed in a seaport crawling with Commonwealth spies. The provincial governor in the town, Per Lindormson Ribbing, who had received no official guidance as to what action if any he should take, was also becoming increasingly alarmed at the possible political consequences and wrote to his superior, Field-Marshal Count Leonard Torstenson, the Governor-General of West Sweden, reporting the Royalists' activities and begging for instructions:

Your Excellency, I cannot fail to inquire (being my duty) about the activities of this Scottish Count of Montrose, as it seems to me that this has been going on for so long without my having received any instructions either from Her Majesty the Queen or from Your Excellency in person. As I have already several times informed Your Excellency, the aforementioned Count arrived here on 15 November and kept secretly to himself, but presently he began to assemble a number of officers who are quartered in different parts of the town. Because of this I was obliged to ask him if he had received any permission from Her Majesty to arrange such a rendezvous here without informing her servants. Thereupon he sent Maclear to me with Her Majesty's letter in which she ordered me to pass [for examination] the ammunition and other items purchased by Maclear or his representatives and then also to provide him with shipping at low cost here from the town. This was the whole content. Consequently I wrote to Her Majesty that the Count was here in person but that he kept out of sight and would not talk with anyone [which he is still doing]. I also wrote that he was expecting a ship from Denmark with 200 men . . . which is [now] anchored at Billinge, and he has also acquired one small ship from the Crown called the *Shepherdess* which is anchored here and which Admiral Ankerhielm had been ordered to deliver, along with guns and two months provisions for 50 men. This ship has now been sent to Strömmen and it is said that they will be leaving one of these days. But about the Count nobody has any information. Sometimes he claims that he intends to go to Stockholm, sometimes to Denmark, and sometimes elsewhere. If a [Swedish] official meets him in the street or anywhere, he immediately turns about or aside, so I cannot understand this man or his designs. . . . And as I do not know Her Majesty's wishes concerning this, and since almost everyone in the town is worried about their own ships and it has even gone so far that the local Parliament have made it a subject for debate. . . . I therefore urgently request Your Excellency to inform me of your high opinion as to how I should best behave. . . .[22]

Torstenson's reply was briefly to let Montrose alone. Ribbing therefore continued to report all his movements, wishing only that this Scottish Count would hurry up and leave, and concluding nervously:

> I hope for Your Excellency's kind consideration as to whether I should just let everything pass unheeded. Up to now I have behaved as if he were none of my concern. What he will do from now on only time can show. God help me to do what pleases Her Majesty.[23]

Montrose himself was equally anxious to leave Gothenburg. Early in December a small sloop arrived from Kirkwall in the Orkneys with news of Morton's and Kinnoul's deaths. The messenger was James Douglas, Morton's brother, and he urged Montrose to sail for the Orkneys at once with what men he had leaving the rest to follow: '. . . for his own presence was able to do the business, and would undoubtedly bring 20,000 men together for the King's service, all men being weary and impatient to live any longer under that bondage, pressing down their estates, their persons and their consciences'.[24]

But a number of factors were keeping Montrose in Sweden. Unaware perhaps of Cochrane's deceit, he may have been waiting for the promised help from the Duke of Courland and the Polish king. Material assistance from other European sources was falling far short of his original expectations and his overriding problem was still shortage of funds. Things in fact, were going badly. Napier and his other lieutenants had recruited numbers of soldiers at Bremen and Hamburg, but lack of passage money was preventing them from reaching the rendezvous at Gothenburg. At the same time, there were other distinguished Scots serving abroad whom Montrose still wanted to win over, in particular General James King, Lord Eythin, who had retired to Sweden after Marston Moor. According to the *Montrose Redivivus*, he had been led to expect that General King would join 'with a considerable body of horse', and in his reports to Torstenson Ribbing recorded that he was expected any day. This possibility of a cavalry reinforcement was cause enough to linger and Montrose also wanted Eythin for his second in command.[25] But for some reason the General did not appear. In the meanwhile three full months had slipped by since Kinnoul made the crossing and with his death the forces in Orkney had no accredited leader. Every report from Scotland indicated that the time was ripe, but it was a moment to be seized, and if the venture was to have a fair chance of success he could not afford to delay much longer.

In the second week of December, a number of transports carrying the main body of troops with stores of arms and ammunition sailed for the Orkneys. According to reports subsequently circulated in Edinburgh, the ships encountered floating ice shortly after putting to sea, and many of them foundered with considerable loss of life. Such tales of disaster, however, were probably grossly exaggerated since

Ribbing's dispatches make no mention of it. It may well be that Montrose had only two ships to send. Certainly, the Danish troops who eventually landed at Kirkwall on this occasion could not have numbered more than three or four hundred men.

On 15 December Montrose wrote to Seaforth that he proposed to embark next day. But he had missed his opportunity since the winds turned contrary and pack ice blocked the entrance of the harbour. He boarded the *Shepherdess* on 10 January (according to Ribbing) and made as if to sail, but then apparently changed his mind since 18 January found him once more ashore at Maclear's house in the town. Ribbing could no more understand this further delay than the English and Covenant spies who had been watching the elaborate preparations of the previous months. But a letter from Secretary Nicholas to the Marquis of Ormonde indicates that Montrose had been warned to expect an important express from the King (who was now in Jersey and hoping for an opportunity to land in Ireland). He could not have known that Charles would hesitate until 16 January before dispatching the messenger and so this otherwise inexplicable delay must be attributed in large part to the King's vacillation. The Royalists had become very reluctant to send letters which might have been intercepted at sea, however, and at the same time it appears that Charles was by no means clear in his own mind as to the exact timing of Montrose's attempt. Poor communications were to have serious consequences later.

But by early March Montrose would wait no longer, and at the beginning of the month the *Shepherdess* sailed for Marstrand. Montrose himself travelled overland to Norway, and, having arranged for Napier, Ruthven and others to remain behind to bring on the stragglers as soon as there should be funds and numbers enough, he joined the ship at Bergen. By 26 March he was in Orkney where Harry May, the King's courier, finally caught up with him and delivered two letters from Charles together with the George and Blue Riband creating him a Knight of the Garter.

Regrettably, no eye witness has recorded which of the King's two letters Montrose read first. One was a private message for his eyes only:

My Lord of Montrose,
My public letter having expressed all that I have of business to say to you, I shall only add a word by this, to assure you that I will never fail in the effects of that friendship I have promised, and which your zeal to my service hath so eminently deserved; and that nothing that can happen to me shall make me consent to anything to your prejudice. I conjure you therefore not to take alarm at any reports or messages for others; but to depend upon my kindness and to proceed in your business with your usual courage and alacrity; which I am sure will bring great advantage to my affairs and much honour to yourself. I wish you all good success in it, and shall ever remain, your affectionate friend,
CHARLES R.

The immediate suspicions which this must have aroused (if indeed he read the private message first) were confirmed by the King's principal dispatch dated 12 January. Charles wrote officially to inform Montrose that further negotiations were in hand with the Scots commissioners, and he enclosed copies of the relevant correspondence which had so far passed between them:

> ... And to the end you may not apprehend that we may intend, either by anything contained in those letters, or by the Treaty we expect, to give the least impediment to your proceedings, we think fit to let you know that, as we conceive that your preparations have been one effectual motive that hath induced them to make an Address to us, so your vigorous proceeding will be a good means to bring them to such moderation in the said Treaty as probably may produce an agreement, and a present union of that whole nation in our service. We assure you therefore that we will not, before or during the Treaty, do anything contrary to that power and authority which we have given you by our commission or consent to anything that may bring the least diminution to it. And if the said Treaty should produce an agreement, we will with our uttermost care so provide for the honour and interest of yourself and of all who shall engage with you. . . .

Better perhaps for the King's honour if this letter had never been written. Charles added, with incredible *naïveté*, that although he was now addressing himself formally to the Committee of Estates, this was for the purpose of securing a treaty only, and did not, in his view, imply formal recognition of the legality of that body.

> We require and authorise you therefore, to proceed vigorously and effectually in your undertaking . . . wherein we doubt not, but all our loyal and well affected subjects in Scotland will cordially and effectually join with you. . . .[26]

Charles hoped to win either way, it seemed. Cromwell's successes in Ireland had brought an end to Royalist hopes in that country, leaving the King with a straight choice between Montrose and Argyll. It was characteristic of him that he thought to choose both, or rather that, having chosen one, he believed that it was politically adroit to reinsure with the other. If Montrose's expedition was successful and he won a decisive victory on the battlefield, this would present the best of all solutions. But such a result was by no means sure—and Charles was not only thinking of Scotland. The idea (which was still being cultivated by Argyll and the Covenanters) of an invasion of England linked to a Royalist rising in the South was too tempting to pass over, and if Montrose could not conquer Scotland outright, Charles deluded himself into believing that, with skilful diplomacy, he could still use the presence of a Royalist army in the North to extract favourable concessions at the conference table. The more realistic policy which Montrose had advocated was thus to be sacrificed to a political ploy, and the young King was too inexperienced (and possibly too conceited) to realize the degree to which he had miscalculated the calibre of his opponents or indeed the reactions of those 'loyal and well affected subjects' to whom he so casually referred.

Copies of this 'public letter' would reach Scotland within a matter of days, and the effect would be to hamstring Montrose. The enterprise depended on an immediate rising by the Scottish Royalists, but the announcement that a treaty between King and Covenanters was pending was hardly likely to induce men to take up arms and risk life and fortune in the royal cause. As Buchan aptly put it, 'It is one thing to fight in a crusade; it is another to share in a campaign whose avowed purpose is no more than to create an object to bargain with. On such mercantile terms you cannot conjure the spirit that wins battles.'

The King was to learn his lesson the hard way. Dunbar and Worcester were yet to come. In the meantime he seriously underestimated the ability and the ruthlessness of the men with whom he was dealing. To say that he personally did not consider formal negotiation with the Committee of Estates as implying recognition of that body as the government of Scotland was a piece of pointless conceit. It was what Covenant propaganda made of it that mattered. The authorities in Edinburgh promptly issued a statement that Charles had recognized their authority and that Montrose's commission was invalid. They then put a price of £30,000 on Montrose's head, and did it in the King's name.

Montrose replied formally to the King's dispatch in a brief letter dated 26 March:

> Sir,
> I received yours of 12 January with that mark of favour wherewith you have honoured me, and for which I can make no other acknowledgement but with the more alacrity to abandon my life for your interests, with that integrity that you and all the world shall see that it is not your fortunes, but you, in whatsoever fortune, that I make sacred to serve. . . .[27]

The words 'abandon my life . . .' have a certain significance.

21

Carbisdale–The Last Campaign
(26 March–2 May 1650)

My life I never held but as a pawn
To wage against thine enemies; nor fear to lose it.
King Lear

Sweete ar the thoughtes, wher Hope persuadeth Happe,
Great ar the Joyes, wher Harte obtaynes requeste,
Dainty the lyfe, nurst still in Fortunes lappe
Much is the ease, wher troubled mindes finde reste.
These ar the fruictes, that valure doth advaunce
And cuts off Dread, by Hope of happy chaunce.
Sir Walter Raleigh

During the latter part of 1649, John Thurloe, Cromwell's Secretary of State, had succeeded in placing a spy called Henry Manning within the small entourage of Charles II. As a supposed courtier, Manning was singularly well placed to observe the events leading up to, and the negotiations connected with, the Treaty of Breda, and in addition he appears to have been either well trusted or to have had access to highly placed and accurate sources of information, since on 2 February 1650 he was able to write to London giving a summary of the King's fateful dispatch to Montrose of 12 January, fully two weeks before the text was 'leaked' in Paris. Manning's weekly reports were published in a regular broadsheet called *A Brief Relation*, which for a time was the official organ of the English Council of State,[1] and although some of the comments included in them reflect a strong republican and anti-Scottish bias, as an eye-witness account of the intrigues within the exiled Court they provide a valuable insight into Charles's behaviour and the pressures he was under during these first months of 1650.

Far from callously 'betraying' Montrose and throwing him to the Covenant wolves, as he has sometimes been accused of doing, the reports indicate that, initially at least, Charles himself regarded Montrose's venture as the pivot upon which everything turned. He was convinced that only Montrose's presence in Scotland with a Royalist army at his back would induce the Covenanters to moderate their terms, and in ordering his Captain-General to 'proceed vigorously' he intended them to know that he was prepared to resort to force if they persisted in their unreasonable demands. This position was well short of that of Montrose, who from the start had advocated an armed solution amounting to nothing less than the conquest of Covenant Scotland, but the difference was essentially one of degree, and it was

344

not the King's intention, just as it was not in his interest, to abandon Montrose or stultify his mission. In the event this was what it came to, but the fault was due as much to inexperience as mere lack of principle. Once Charles's Public Letter had compromised Montrose's position in Scotland, Argyll called the bluff and himself took the offensive by setting a deadline to the negotiations. Now bad communications played a part. Montrose was behind schedule. Time began to run out and there was no news from Scotland. Deprived of the quick military success for which he had hoped, Charles found it expedient to sign the treaty, but it is clear from his subsequent instructions to Montrose (which were not delivered) that he still hoped to keep his options open and was quite ready to repudiate it should it have suited him to do so.

The internal divisions among the Scots were of considerable interest to the English Government, who realized that a further war between the two countries was a distinct possibility, and many of Manning's reports are devoted to the struggle between the 'Montrossians' and the 'Argyllians' at the King's Court – in which the former ultimately went down. He appears to have had considerable sympathy for Montrose but an English contempt of the rest – including the Lauderdale faction who were prepared to combine with King or Covenanters for 'Montrose's undoing'. Of Argyll's commissioners he remarked: 'Tis evident that he [Charles II] perfectly hates them and neither of them can so dissemble it but that each knows it: and 'tis a matter of pleasant observation to see how they endeavour to cozen and cheat each other'. The Queen Mother and Jermyn were pressing Charles to reach an agreement with Argyll, and she was incensed at the behaviour of Montrose's agent in Paris when he published a French translation of the King's letter authorizing his Captain-General to make war on the Covenanters (although there was reason to believe that he had acted on secret instructions from Charles in Jersey). In early March Charles met his mother at Beauvais, and she urged him to settle with the Scots on any terms and avoid 'the rock on which his father split himself'. Any such agreement signed under duress could, she argued, be repudiated later. She objected only to his signing the Solemn League and Covenant which she felt would antagonize the Roman Catholic courts of Europe. Charles II was less scrupulous than his father and more receptive to such arguments, but he looked for a better bargain. After being closeted with him for three hours, the Queen Mother emerged from their conference 'very red with anger', and their subsequent parting was so cold that 'the party of Montrose was very joyful'.

At Court, Montrose's supporters were led by Ralph Lord Hopton, Sir Edward Nicholas and Elizabeth of Bohemia, who came herself to Breda to argue with the King on his behalf. 'The Queen of Bohemia will not be content to stay away from the Treaty,' wrote the English spy. 'She is passionately affected to Montrose his ends and will leave no wind unsailed to this effect.' Charles, for the moment, remained resolute and still faithful to Montrose, and even talked at times of going to join the army in Scotland. But this was youth speaking. In reality he was growing desperate and it would be 'necessity or chance that would guide his course'. It was plausible to argue that the easier way was also the more astute. The Prince of Orange, Lauderdale and all his councillors but two urged a settlement with the Scots commissioners. Under their continued pressure the young King eventually gave way and banished Hopton and Nicholas from the council table. From then on the descent was easy. If Montrose was the victim, Charles II was the dupe.

The King's final messages to Montrose, though overtaken by events, were also revealing of his intention not to abandon his Captain-General just as they were redolent of his continued hesitation and distrust of the Covenanters even after signing the draft of the Treaty of Breda on 1 May.

On 3 May he instructed Sir William Fleming to proceed to Orkney and inform Montrose that an agreement had been reached with the Scottish Estates. Fleming was to explain that, after the failure of the Irish expedition, Charles had had no choice but to negotiate. Adequate help had not been forthcoming from the continental powers, and though the King had appealed to the Emperor, the German princes, Spain, France, Denmark and Italy, he had 'obtained only dilatory and general answers'. Montrose's own undertaking 'had not answered to his or our expectations, neither to point of time of his being in Scotland, nor in supplies assistances and numbers of men we expected'. No blame was attached to Montrose for this since it had been due rather to 'unexpected accidents', and Fleming was to assure the Marquis that Charles hoped to be able to secure good terms on his behalf, including if possible the restoration of his estates, and that in the meanwhile he was to have 'honourable subsistence'. The King added a short private letter to Montrose saying that Fleming would explain everything and informing him that 10,000 Rix dollars had been deposited with Sir Patrick Drummond for his use.

It is generally supposed that, before signing the Treaty of Breda, Charles had obtained some private assurance that Montrose and his officers would receive complete indemnity, although it is probable that any such guarantee was not given by the official Scots commissioners but by William Murray acting as Argyll's agent. A private deal between Argyll and the King which circumvented the Kirk was not inconceivable, and the contemporary notes of Secretary Long would seem to confirm that Charles did secure some such promise at this time.

On 5 May Charles signed a *public* letter to Montrose ordering him to cease hostilities and withdraw his forces from Scotland, leaving all his arms and military equipment at Orkney where they would be easily available should the King require them later. When delivering this letter Fleming was to assure Montrose of His Majesty's 'affection'. He was also to take counsel with William Murray (who travelled with him) 'concerning any further treaty with Montrose in order to our service, than what your public instructions do bear'. The inclusion of William Murray in such a discussion is ominous. It seems incredible that, notwithstanding all evidence of previous treachery, Charles II, like his unfortunate father, seems to have placed some trust in this man.

On 8 May the King gave Fleming (who still had not sailed) a letter addressed to the Scottish Estates in which he informed them that he had formally ordered Montrose to withdraw his army, and asked that they should permit him to depart without hindrance.

Then on 9 May Fleming received a further set of instructions, which considerably modified and even contradicted his original orders. If it seemed that the Covenanters did not intend to honour the terms of the Treaty, or, more specifically, if there was good reason to suspect that they had engineered the Treaty for the sole purpose of getting the King to call off Montrose, then the Captain-General was not to disband but carry on the campaign. 'In case my friends in Scotland do not think fit that Montrose lay down his arms then as many as can may repair to him.' Fleming was to consult with William Murray on this point and advise accordingly. If Montrose's position was strong he was to continue: if weak, he was to withdraw as ordered.

On 12 May rumours reached the Court that Montrose had been defeated, and in yet another order from the King Fleming was instructed to find out if this was true. If it was, or if Montrose was not in Scotland, Fleming was to suppress the letter to the Estates of 8 May already cited. If, however, there had been no battle, or if Montrose was still at the head of a considerable force, it was to be delivered as originally ordered. Fleming obeyed his instructions and concealed the letter.

The accusation that Charles now betrayed Montrose to the Scottish Parliament is based on a *second* letter, dated 12 May (the same date as Fleming's last instructions), which, according to Balfour's account, was read out to the Estates on 20 May. In this the King is alleged to have '. . . earnestly desired the Estates . . . not to believe he was an accessory to the said [Montrose's] invasion in the least degree'. This was Montrose's death warrant, and if he did indeed write it then Charles stands guilty as charged. However, the provenance of this letter is extremely doubtful. Fleming's instructions say nothing about delivering an alternative letter in place of the one which he was ordered to conceal, and though reportedly handed to the Committee of Despatches to be answered, no copy of the document was ever found in the Register House despite a thorough search. A separate and quite harmless version of it appeared in an English newspaper, *Several Proceedings*, on 6 June (to which it had been sent by William Murray), in which the King merely asks for information. Charles was fully aware that his previous public letters of 12 January and 5 May had been printed in the newspapers and that these demonstrated quite clearly that Montrose was acting on his command. The public letter of 5 May was read out in Parliament at the same time as the alleged 'denial' of 12 May. The King could not have been so stupid or so forgetful as to provide his enemies (in England as well as Scotland) with such proof of perjury. It therefore seems almost impossible that Charles could have written the letter described by Balfour, and it was more probably a forgery, fabricated by William Murray or by Argyll himself, with a view to expediting the proceedings against Montrose—whom they wanted condemned and executed before the King arrived in Scotland. Charles does not emerge with honour, but the principal charge must remain unproven.[2]

If Montrose indeed foresaw the ruinous effect which news of Charles's negotiations with the Scots might have in causing men to think twice before taking up arms against the Covenant authority, why then did he not abandon his attempt, or at least remain in Orkney and wait upon events? He would have been justified in doing so. It has been the fashion to describe the Carbisdale campaign as doomed from the start, and Charles's apologists have been quick to argue that as the sole architect and prime mover in this forlorn venture, Montrose alone was responsible for bringing about his own ruin and that of his friends by allowing a misconceived sense of destiny and personal hatred of Argyll to cloud his better judgement.

But without the advantage of retrospect, the decision was not so simple. In the first place, Montrose went ahead with the invasion because the King had explicitly ordered him to do so in his dispatch of 12 January. Charles had limited the objective of the campaign, but Montrose appears to have accepted this—or at least so he claimed at his trial.

Secondly, the situation in Scotland had never been more favourable. The collapse of the Engagement had left all political power in the hands of the Kirk extremists, and theocratic government had proved itself to be corrupt, incompetent and oppressive. Dissenters had been purged from every public office. The burghs had been bled white by taxation. Money was scarce; food was dear; the North was on the verge of famine; heavy fines and sequestrations had done little to ease the burden and much to fan the popular discontent. Pluscardine's rebellion had been a symptom of this distemper. It needed only the spark to kindle a new revolt, and the Mackenzies, Gordons, Mackays, Monroes, Ogilvies, the loyal clans of Badenoch and Atholl—all the North—would rise again.

The military situation was equally advantageous. Cromwell was occupied in Ireland. No longer in receipt of English pay, the Estates had disbanded a large proportion of their forces, and in March 1650 there were only 3,000 foot and 1,500 cavalry under arms, strung out to garrison a thin chain of fortresses across the Highlands. There was a shortage of competent general officers to lead them. Leven was too old for active campaigning; Baillie had been an Engager and was therefore excluded from command; Middleton was suspect since Pluscardine's rising; and Hurry was with Montrose. There remained David Leslie, the victor of Philiphaugh, and Colonels Holbourn and Strachan. Holbourn had been on the losing side at Kilsyth, while Strachan was a sectarian fanatic who could not be trusted by his commanding officers.

Against this, the possible damage done by Charles's public letter of 12 January was difficult to quantify, and Montrose was not the sort of person to accept a negative judgement without first putting it to the test. The campaign ahead could be envisaged as falling into two distinct stages, of which the first was undoubtedly the more crucial. The small expeditionary force was to land in the North of Scotland and link up with the Mackenzies and Monroes who would march to meet them. These two clans, together with the Rosses, could put over 1,000 fighting men into the field, and provided this reinforcement was secured Montrose could then embark on the second stage and move south through the Highlands counting on initial success to produce a momentum that would to some extent counteract the prejudicial effects of the peace rumours. If he got half the support he hoped for it would be enough, and even if the Royalists did not rise as he marched south he would still be able to withdraw in good order.

It all depended therefore on the Mackenzies. But if the temper of the other Royalists was doubtful, they at least were the surest element in the plan. Pluscardine and the clan had already risen once and were reportedly ready to do so again. Whereas in Badenoch and the southern Highlands Montrose would be dependent on a spontaneous uprising among the loyal clans, the junction with the Mackenzies had almost certainly been prearranged. Seaforth had been party to the scheme from the beginning and had promised everything (except possibly himself). He had also been close to the Court in exile and was less likely in theory to be affected by speculation about the impending Treaty. It was not too difficult therefore, to argue 'on the sunnier side of doubt'. The risk (and it was greater than perhaps he imagined) lay in the fact that Seaforth had never been renowned for constancy, and if the Mackenzies should fail them, the small invasion force was too weak to fight the Covenanters alone.

Finally it must be admitted that, in making this decision, Montrose was influenced by certain intensely personal factors. He still believed that outright victory was the only solution, for he saw with awful clarity that King and Kirk could no longer co-exist. A negotiated settlement with Argyll would gain Charles nothing—neither in practical terms, since it would lose him friends in England, nor in honour, since it was done in the knowledge that each would not hesitate to break his bond. It was for Charles to parley with the men who had destroyed his father. For Montrose they had put themselves beyond the reach of Treaty. He also realized that this was the last chance. The old cause was going down; the old ideals died with it. Withdraw, and there would be no second 'Venture Fair'. Go on, and there was a chance, if only a very slim one. In the last analysis it was a question of commitment. As a young man he had signed the Covenant to moderate a tyranny, not exchange it for another. Now, the fey mood was still upon him and he was too far gone to compromise.

The seventeenth century was an age of strange devices. Armies marched to battle beneath huge embroidered banners which signified the cause for which they fought. Montrose was no exception. His cavalry standard was black, showing three pairs of clasped hands holding drawn swords with the superscription '*Quos pietas, virtus, et honor fecit amicos.*' The foot marched also behind a black banner on which were depicted the bleeding head of the murdered King and the motto: 'Deo et victricibus armis'. By contrast, Montrose's personal standard was of white damask. It showed two steep rocks with a river between, and a lion poised to spring across the chasm. His motto was '*Nil medium*'.

At Orkney two weeks were spent in organizing and equipping the small expeditionary force which now numbered about 1,500 all told, of whom nearly 1,000 were local Orcadians recruited to the colours. The main weakness was in cavalry. Montrose had only a single troop of horse – about 40 mounted men – made up of gentry and officers who had accompanied him from Gothenburg. They included Viscount Frendraught (the Earl of Sutherland's nephew who had fought on the Covenant side at Aberdeen), Sir William Johnstone and Colonel Thomas Gray (veterans of the continental wars), Harry Graham (Montrose's half-brother), William Hay (the new Lord Kinnoul), Drummond of Balloch, Powrie Ogilvie, Major Lisle (an English Royalist) and the turncoat General Sir John Hurry.

A bond of allegiance was signed with the ministers and gentry of Orkney and Shetland, and Sir William Johnstone was appointed to remain behind as governor. On 9 April 1650 the army broke camp at Kirkwall and marched to Holm Sound where a fleet of fishing boats had been assembled. An advance force of 500 picked men under Sir John Hurry were sent ahead to make a landing in Caithness and seize the narrow Pass of Ord. They made the crossing safely, and bypassing the Covenant stronghold at Dunbeath took the position in the first assault. The road south to Sutherland was thus secured. Montrose with the rest of his army crossed the Pentland Firth on 11 and 12 April, and landed at Duncansby Head near John O'Groats. From there he marched to Thurso and set up his headquarters in an old house near the church.

There was no spontaneous Royalist rising in Caithness, despite his appeal, but a number of gentry came forward – mainly Sinclairs and Mackays, who were partisans of the Reay interest against the encroachments of the Earl of Sutherland. The Reays were strong in the North-West, and three of these volunteers – Alexander Sinclair of Brims, Mackay of Dirlot and Mackay of Scourie – were sent to Tongue, which had been abandoned by its Covenant garrison, to assemble what followers they could and rejoin the army further south by way of Loch Naver and Loch Shin. Then, having left Harry Graham with 200 men to raise recruits in Caithness by whatever means he could, Montrose marched south by the road that strikes the coast at Latheron, and appeared before Dunbeath Castle on about 17 April.

The commander of the garrison, Sir John Sinclair, had hurried south to warn the Earl of Sutherland of Montrose's landing, and the castle was defended by his wife. Dunbeath occupied a position of great natural advantage on a rocky cliff overhanging the sea, and though the garrison

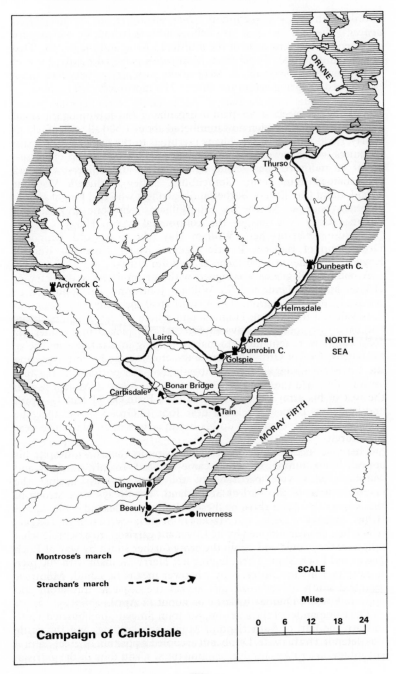

ORKNEY

Thurso

Dunbeath C.

Ardvreck C.

Helmsdale

Lairg

Brora

NORTH
SEA

Dunrobin C.

Golspie

Carbisdale

Bonar Bridge

Tain

MORAY FIRTH

Dingwall

Beauly

Inverness

Montrose's march

Strachan's march

Campaign of Carbisdale

SCALE

Miles

0   6   12   18   24

was small it put up a spirited resistance and the fortress was reduced only after a siege of several days. It had never been Montrose's practice to waste time in the investment of isolated castles, but Dunbeath commanded his line to Harry Graham and his way of retreat to Orkney, so he was obliged to detach a further 100 men under Hay of Dalgetty to hold it secure behind him.

In the meanwhile the Earl of Sutherland, as commander of the Covenant forces in the far North, had sent messengers to the Estates with news of the Royalists' advance. Two troops of horse stationed at Ross refused to come to his assistance on the excuse that their commanding officers were in Edinburgh, and Sutherland withdrew into Ross-shire with 300 men, leaving strong garrisons at Dunrobin, Skelbo, Skibo and Dornoch.[3]

The initiative still lay with Montrose. Gathering up Hurry's force at Ord of Caithness, he continued south by Helmsdale and Kintradwell, and three days after entering the county of Sutherland arrived before Dunrobin and summoned it to surrender. But the garrison refused to yield, and the Royalists were not strong enough to take the fortress by assault. Several men were lost prisoner when they ventured between the castle and the sea, and Montrose was obliged to retire to the slopes of Ben Braghie overlooking Golspie where he camped for the night. He had no time to waste on another protracted siege, nor was he strong enough to force his way through the Covenant garrisons of the Dornoch Peninsula, and so next day he turned inland and marched westwards up Strathfleet to Rhaoine. On 23 April he continued past Lairg to Gruids where he was probably rejoined by Sinclair of Brims and Mackay of Scourie since the roads from Tongue and Assynt converged at this point. He then crossed the hills to Rosehall, where he forded the Oykell above its junction with the Casseley, and from there marched down Strathoykell as far as Carbisdale, which he probably reached on the evening of 25 April.[4]

Now began the fatal delay. If Montrose had continued south he might have been in Badenoch within the week and the Covenant forces would not have caught up with him. But he preferred to wait for Pluscardine and the Mackenzie war band from the West, and, according to Menteth, he also instructed Hurry to look for a force from south of Dornoch under Ross of Balnagowan who had previously pledged his support.[5] At the same time, he may have been reluctant to attempt the mountain route with an army of foreign mercenaries unused to Highland warfare. It is equally possible that a general rendezvous at Carbisdale had been part of the original plan. Certainly, he had no premonition of danger. Robert Monro of Achness and his three sons, who acted as the army's scoutmasters, had informed him that there was only one troop of horse in all of Ross, and there was no other information to indicate that a substantial Covenant force was within striking distance.

It is true that the Covenanters seem to have been strangely unprepared. In the South, David Leslie mustered 4,000 horse and foot at Brechin on 25 April and began hurrying north by forced marches.

But in the meanwhile he had sent instructions to Colonels Strachan and Hackett who commanded the Covenant detachments in Banff and Moray to do what they could to delay Montrose.

Strachan, though distrusted as a fanatic, had nevertheless acquired a reputation as a dashing cavalry officer. He disliked David Leslie and looked for an opportunity to show that 'there shall be no need' of the General and 'his levy of knavis to the work'.[6] On receipt of Leslie's orders he immediately advanced with his own troop of horse and that of Colonel Ker, then stationed at Brahan and Chanonry, to Tain, where he was joined by Montgomery's troop, Hackett's troop, an Irish troop under a Captain Cullace, and 36 musketeers of Lawers's regiment, bringing his force to 256. His men were experienced, well mounted and under competent officers.

As ill luck would have it, at Tain he also linked up with a force of 400 Rosses and Monroes under David Ross of Balnagowan and Colonel John Monro of Lemlair, both of whom had been 'out' with Pluscardine the previous year. This was almost certainly the reinforcement that Montrose was expecting, and they were probably on their way to the rendezvous when Strachan overtook them. Faced with a strong force of cavalry in open country, Balnagowan and Lemlair took discretion to be the better part of valour and attached themselves to the Covenant column. Strachan was probably not deceived, and though as a means of ingratiating themselves they offered to reconnoitre Montrose's position, their doubtful services received no mention in his subsequent dispatch.

Strachan paused at Tain long enough to hold a brief council of war, at which it was decided that the Earl of Sutherland, who was possibly unwilling to fight, should take his force across the Kyle and stand ready to block the advance of Harry Graham and the Royalist rearguard, who were reported to be moving south along the coast road. He then marched to Wester Fearn opposite the Dun of Criech. It was Saturday, 27 April, three o'clock in the afternoon.

The Covenanters were now about four miles from Montrose's position. Ahead of them the Kyle narrowed suddenly by the alluvial beds at the mouth of the River Carron. Beyond was a long heathy slope rising on the left into a low range of hills which curved north towards the heights of Craigcaoinichean. Two miles above the Carron the track crossed the Culrain Burn, which flowed into the Kyle by a deep channel fringed with broom and scrubland. With the hills to the north and the Kyle estuary to the east, the burn enclosed a triangle of level ground admirably suited to cavalry. At the northern point of this triangle was Carbisdale Loch, and beyond, a narrow defile overhung by Craigcaoinichean. Here, in the jaws of the pass, was Montrose's camp. His left flank rested on the Kyle. His right and rear were protected by the hills, and on the bluff facing south-east towards the open ground the Royalists had thrown up a formidable breastwork. The position was a strong one and could not be taken by cavalry in a frontal assault.

At this point the Rosses and Monroes detached themselves from the Covenant force as diffidently as they had joined it. Crossing the Carron, they took up a position in the lea of the hills flanking Carbisdale, and waited to see what would happen.

Once he was apprised of the situation, Strachan realized that he would not be able to force a successful action unless he could tempt Montrose out of his entrenchments and on to the open ground. He therefore sent a single troop of horse forward to act as a decoy, and concealed the rest of his force among the tall broom which was at this time thick with blossom. The appearance of the advance troop was reported to Montrose by Major Lisle who commanded the Royalist cavalry, and the Captain-General, thinking this to be the single troop referred to by Monro of Achness, was completely deceived. He ordered Lisle to halt and then advanced with the main body of foot to reconnoitre. Sir John Hurry commanded the Royalist vanguard.

Strachan waited until Montrose's men were committed to the open ground and then sprung the trap. At the head of 100 troopers he charged out of the scrub closely followed by Hackett and his 80 dragoons. The 40 Royalist horse were cut to pieces in the initial onslaught and the survivors driven back on to the stumbling foot. Lisle, Guthrie, Gordon, Douglas, Powrie-Ogilvie and Menzies of Pittfoddells, who carried the royal standard, died within the first few minutes. Montrose, Hurry, Frendraught and a score of others were wounded. The Orcadians panicked, and flinging away their arms ran for the Kyle where 200 in one company perished in the water. A few got across in a small boat pursued by a single trooper – who drowned, the only loss sustained on the Covenant side. The Danish and German mercenaries tried to make a fight of it and retreated to a 'scroggie wood'. Their ragged volley brought down two troopers and a bullet hit Strachan on the buckle of his belt but did no harm. Despite the 'ill riding ground', the dragoons pursued them into the birch, and the Rosses and Monroes now hurried to join the slaughter and the looting that came after. The killing continued for two hours and more than 450 were slain on the field or in the flight. Sir John Hurry was taken prisoner, together with 61 officers, 386 soldiers, and 2 ministers from Orkney who had served as chaplains to the army.

Montrose's horse had been killed under him, but Frendraught, himself severely wounded in two places and hopeful of clemency through the agency of his uncle Sutherland, gave him his, and urged him to escape if he could. Montrose though hurt was able to ride, and, throwing off his sword belt and his coat with its conspicuous Star of St George (which was later found under a tree near the battlefield), he swam the Kyle on Frendraught's horse accompanied by a Major Edward Sinclair (an Orcadian), Sinclair of Brims and 'four or five others' who probably included Monro of Achness and his three sons. Near Oykell Bridge the fugitives split up into two groups, Achness's party turning south by Glen Einig for Kintail, while Montrose and the rest abandoned their horses and headed north up the Oykell towards Strathnaver and the friendly Reay country. 'They wandered upriver the whole of the ensuing night and next day', but 28 April found them still barely thirty miles from the battlefield. Somewhere on the borders of Assynt one of the party succumbed to wounds and exhaustion and had to be left 'there among the mountains where it is supposed he perished'.[7] The others decided to separate, and Montrose now went on alone. The country was utterly desolate and unfamiliar, and he became lost in the wilderness of barren hills. After two days and nights without food or rest he was close to starving, and hunger forced him to eat his gloves. On 29 April he stumbled into a small *sheiling* in Glaschyle where the tenant gave him bread and milk and hid him under a sheep trough when a Covenant search party rode up to inquire after fugitives. He emerged conscience-stricken at the danger which he had brought upon his host and 'determined never to do the like again to avoid death, of which, he thanked God, he was not afraid'.[8]

Shortly after leaving this cottage he was overtaken by a gillie of the Laird of Assynt, accompanied, it is said, by his recent benefactor, who asked him whither he was headed. Montrose told them that he wanted to reach the Reay country but had lost his way, and the gillie undertook to guide him. After nine miles they came to Ardvreck Castle, the house of Neil MacLeod of Assynt, where by tradition Montrose was received at the door by the laird's wife. Shortly afterwards Major Edward Sinclair was also brought in, having been found hopelessly lost in the mountains.

Ardvreck stands on a small peninsula extending into Loch Assynt. The castle was very small, only two storeys high, but strong, and the cornerstones of the single tower were chisel-dressed, an ornament rare in the Highlands. Below were two vaulted cellars in which Montrose and Sinclair were now accommodated.

Four days later they were delivered up to the Covenanters.

This chapter of Montrose's life began with a suspicion of betrayal, and it was his fate that it should also end with one. According to tradition, Montrose revealed his identity to the Laird of Assynt – 'a pretended old friend'[9] – and offered to pay a high ransom if he would help him to escape. Despite all his entreaties, however, MacLeod 'betrayed' him to the Covenanters, 'being greedy of the reward'.[10] The case against Neil MacLeod was exhaustively examined by Morland and Simpson in an appendix to their edition of Wishart, and they found against him on every count, not least because the main evidence of his guilt rests on the authority of contemporary accounts whose authors were if anything biased against Montrose.[11] Nevertheless, Neil has found many apologists from among his own clan and the controversy is by no means dead.

That MacLeod seized and delivered up Montrose is in itself beyond doubt. It is also certain that he claimed and was granted a reward of £25,000 (Scots) (£1,360), of which £20,000 was to be paid in cash and the rest in 'sour meal'. More than a dozen references in Balfour's *Annals* and the Acts of the Parliaments of Scotland attest the fact.[12] MacLeod would later maintain that he could not be held personally responsible for the capture of Montrose since he was '60 miles away' from Ardvreck at the time, yet this alibi only serves to brand him as a liar, since in 1650 he was happy to claim full credit for the deed. In 1660 he was formally indicted and put on trial for his life, but after spending over two years in the Edinburgh tolbooth he was released by order of Charles II under the terms of the Act of Indemnity. No judgement was therefore ever given.

Whether MacLeod actually 'betrayed' Montrose in the worst sense is another matter. The word 'betrayal' can be too easily used; and it can be taken to mean too much. Consequent argument becomes overladen with emotion and contemporary perspective disappears.

There were two good reasons why Montrose should have thought that MacLeod was a potential friend. But there are two equally good reasons why this was not in fact the case. According to some Royalist accounts, MacLeod had actually served under Montrose. This may have been true, but the circumstances were unusual. In 1645, when Neil was sixteen and a minor, he had attended his 'superior', Seaforth, at Brahan. This was the custom in the Highlands, but it seems that MacLeod had good reason to hate Seaforth and the Mackenzies who unscrupulously used their advantage to prey upon his lands. When Seaforth joined Montrose at the siege of Inverness his followers included 100 men from Assynt, and Neil, as their titular chief, may have been among them. It is quite possible that Montrose remembered the young man from that time and so took him for Seaforth's client and a Royalist. He could not have guessed that MacLeod had probably been there under compulsion.

When he came of age it was not unnatural that Neil should have looked to the Earl of Sutherland for protection against the encroachments of the Mackenzies, whose depredations during his minority had already impoverished his estates. In 1650 Sutherland was nominally in command of Covenant forces in the far North and MacLeod was his sheriff depute at Assynt. Despite the claims of his apologists, religious conviction does not appear to have played any part in his decision, since not even Wodrow could later make a saint of him. Nor was the main struggle so important. Politically he was not so much for the Covenant as against Seaforth. And Seaforth was associated with Montrose.

The second reason why Montrose may have expected hospitality at Ardvreck was that MacLeod's wife was a daughter of Monro of Lemlair, and this may explain why some versions of the story shift the blame from Neil and seek to portray her as a seventeenth-century Lady Macbeth. Lemlair was with Ross of Balnagowan (who, on Menteth's evidence, had specifically pledged his support) and they were possibly marching to the rendezvous when Strachan overtook them. Montrose was probably unaware of the Monroes' presence at Carbisdale. Had he been so he would have tried to make contact with them, and when they finally emerged to join the rout he had already been ridden down by Strachan's troopers. Nor could he have known that after the battle Lemlair, no doubt fearful as to how Strachan might choose to interpret his behaviour before the fight, sought to ingratiate himself by writing a letter to his son-in-law urging him to search his country for fugitives 'and chiefly James Graham'. Family came first in the Highlands, and Neil was 'no laggard to the business'.

There are two other aspects of the story, however, which are more puzzling. Montrose probably reached Ardvreck on 29 April, but the Covenant patrol did not arrive from Tain to arrest him until 4 May, which would suggest that MacLeod's messenger did not set out until the second or third. He seems therefore to have hesitated before deciding to deliver up his prisoner. There are several possible explanations—that he was indeed away when the fugitive was brought in and his wife waited until his return before taking any action herself, or that he did not at first recognize Montrose for who he was. Nevertheless, the delay is interesting.

Secondly, the only contemporary account that does not specifically mention MacLeod by name is that of Menteth, who stated that Montrose was betrayed by Sinclair of Brims. Four men fled north from Oykell Bridge. One, wrongly presumed to have been Kinnoul, was abandoned in the mountains. That left three. Montrose and Major Edward Sinclair were taken. Who then was the third, and what became of Alexander Sinclair of Brims?[13]

Neil MacLeod's subsequent career was stormy and in a sense tragic. In 1674 he was again put on trial for his life, charged with having abetted the English, with harrying Seaforth's lands and with various acts of piracy along the coast of Assynt. It was further alleged that in 1671 he had fortified Ardvreck against the sheriff of Sutherland, and that when summoned to surrender the garrison had declared they 'could not give a plack for the King'. The fortress capitulated after fourteen days but Neil fled to the mountains with 300 men and was put to the horn for rebellion. His 'betrayal' of Montrose was again introduced against him albeit as an 'aggravation', but the jury acquitted him and the charges remain unproven.[14]

The impression that remains is of a man not untypical of his time and of the wild northern country in which he lived—a petty robber baron bred of 'the seed of John the Grizzled', a predatory sept of the Clan MacLeod, preying upon the weak just as he was preyed upon by Seaforth and Sutherland and those who were more powerful than he. Neil MacLeod did not survive, and in 1690 he lost the lands of Assynt. Ardvreck crumbled, and it stands a picturesque ruin against one of the most spectacular and desolate landscapes in the Highlands. Two old cannon, inscribed 1587 and possibly relics of the Spanish Armada, until recently lay abandoned among the fallen masonry accumulating slowly the patina of three hundred years.[15] Earth now fills the vaulted cellars. It has a forlorn beauty, as if there were some curse upon the place.

The stigma remained. Among the loyal clans where the story passed from generation to generation, the Laird of Assynt was the highlander who sold a suppliant for gold, and Ian Lom, the Bard of Inverlochy, wrote the Clan Donald's Lament for Montrose which in the gaelic memory branded Neil MacLeod for ever with the mark of shame:

I'll go not to Dunedin
Since the Graham's blood was shed,
The manly, mighty lion
Tortured on the gallows.

That was the true gentleman,
Who came of line not humble.
Good was the flushing of his cheek
When drawing up to combat.

His chalk-white teeth well closing,
His slender brow not gloomy! –
Though oft my love awakes me,
This night I will not bear it.

Neil's son of woeful Assynt,
If I in net could take thee,
My sentence would condemn thee,
Nor would I spare the gibbet.

If you and I encountered
On the marshes of Ben Etive,
The black waters and the clods
Would there be mixed together.

If thou and thy wife's father,
The householder of Lemlair,
Were hanged both together,
'Twould not atone my loss.

Stript tree of the false apples,
Without esteem, or fame, or grace,
Ever murdering each other
'Mid dregs of wounds and knives!

Death-wrapping to thee, base one,
Ill didst thou sell the righteous,
For the meal of Leith,
And two-thirds of it sour![16]

22

Ne Oublie

*Only those few black swans I must except who behold
death without dread and the grave without fear, and embrace
both as necessary guides to endless glory.*

Sir Walter Raleigh

David Leslie reached Tain at about the same time as MacLeod's
messenger, and at once dispatched Major General Holbourn with a
troop of horse to secure Montrose. (Strachan meanwhile had ridden
south to receive his reward.) Holbourn arrived at Ardvreck on 4 May,
and next day brought his prisoners to Skibo Castle on the north side
of the Kyle.

Montrose could expect no favours; nor was it in the nature
of the Covenanters to respect a fallen enemy. For six years they had
gone in terror of his name and it seemed that only in his complete
humiliation could they find release. The captive was led south in
triumph to be exhibited to public scorn in every town and village
along the route, while the ministers exulted in their pulpits and
urged the brethren to insult and jeer at the traitor as he passed.
But in this they miscalculated. Many came to stare, but few to revile,
and sympathy rather than bitterness was the predominant emotion
even in those towns that had suffered most on account of his wars.
There were many who thought that the Covenanters in abusing him
debased themselves and would have no part in it–not least among
them the dowager Lady Gray of Skibo Castle:

> On the arrival of the Marquis and his guards, she prepared a
> suitable entertainment for them. She presided at the dinner-table,
> at the head of which, and immediately before her, was a leg of
> roasted mutton. When Montrose entered the room he was
> introduced to her by the officers who escorted him, and she
> requested him to be seated next to her; but Holbourn, still retaining
> the strict military order he observed in his march, placed the
> Marquis between himself and another officer, and thus he sat down
> at Lady Skibo's right hand and above his noble prisoner, before the

Lady was aware of the alteration. She no sooner observed this arrangement than she flew into a violent passion, seized the leg of roasted mutton by the shank and hit Holbourn such a notable blow on the head with the flank part of the hot juicy mutton as knocked him off his seat, and completely spoiled his uniform. The officers took alarm, dreading an attempt to rescue the prisoner; but the Lady, still in great wrath, and brandishing the leg of mutton, reminded them that she received them as guests; that as such, and as gentlemen, they must accomodate themselves to such an adjustment of place at her table as she considered to be correct; and that although the Marquis was a prisoner, she was more resolved to support his rank when unfortunate than if he had been victorious; and consequently, that no person of inferior rank, could, at her table, be permitted to take precedence over him. Order being restored, and the mutton replaced on the table, every possible civility was thereafter directed by all present towards the Marquis.[1]

On 7 May he was ferried across the Kyle and delivered to Leslie at Tain and from here the story is taken up by a number of eye-witnesses whose accounts are more vivid than any paraphrase. The first of these was James Fraser, then a boy of sixteen, who joined the march at Lovat, and later remembered:

He was conveyed with a guard over the river Conan towards Beauly. Crossing that river they refreshed at Lovat; such scurvy base indignities put all along upon him as reached the height of reproach and scorn. . . .
But now I set down that which I was myself eye-witness of.
The 9th May,[2] 1650, at Lovat, he sat upon a little shelty horse, without a saddle, but a quilt of rags and straw, and pieces of rope for stirrups; his feet fastened under the horse's belly with a tether; a bit halter for a bridle; a ragged old dark reddish plaid, a *montrer* cap, called *Magirky,* on his head; a musketeer on each side, and his fellow prisoners after him.
Thus conducted through the country, near Inverness, under the road to Muirtown, where he desired to alight, he called for a draught of water, being then in the first crisis of a high fever. And here the crowd from the town came forth to gaze. The two ministers . . . wait here upon him to comfort him; the latter of which Montrose was well acquainted with. At the end of the bridge, stepping forward an old woman, Margaret MacGeorge, exclaimed and brauted saying–'Montrose look above! View these ruinous houses of mine which you occasioned to be burnt down when you besieged Inverness!' Yet he never altered his countenance; but with a majesty and state beseeming him, kept a countenance high.
At the cross, a table covered. The Magistrates treat him with wine, which he would not taste but allayed with water. The stately prisoners, his officers, stood under a forestair and drank heartily. I remarked Colonel Hurry, a robust, tall, stately fellow with a long cut on his cheek. All the way through the streets Montrose never lowered his aspect. The Provost, Duncan Forbes,

taking leave of him at the town's end, said–'My Lord, I am sorry for your circumstances.' He replied–'I am sorry for being the object of your pity.' The Marquis was conveyed that night to Castle Stewart where he lodged.

From Castle Stewart the Marquis is conveyed through Moray. By the way some loyal gentlemen wait upon his Excellency, most avowedly, and with grieved hearts: Such as the Laird of Culbin, Captain Thomas Mackenzie Pluscardine, the Laird of Cookstoun, and old Mr Thomas Fullerton his acquaintance at college. He was overjoyed to see these about him; and they were his guard forward to Forres, where the Marquis was treated; and thence, afternoon, convoyed to Elgin city, where all these loyal gentlemen waited on him, and diverted him all the time, with allowance of the General.

In the morning Mr Alexander Symons, parson of Duffus, waited on him at Elgin, being college acquaintance with the Marquis; four years his co-pupil at St Andrews. This cheered him wonderfully as the parson often told me. Thence they convoyed him all the way to the River Spey and a crowd of royalists flocked about him unchallenged. Crossing the Spey, they lodged all night at Keith; and next day, May 12th, being the Sabbath, the Marquis heard sermon there. A tent was set up in the fields for him in which he lay. The Minister, Master William Kinanmond, altering his ordinary, chose for his theme and text the words of the Prophet Samuel to Agag, the King of the Amalekites, coming before him delicately: 'And Samuel said, As thy sword hath made women childless, so shall thy mother be childless among women etc. . . .' This unnatural merciless man so rated, reviled, and reflected upon the Marquis in such invective, virulent, and malicious manner, that some of the hearers, who were even of the swaying side, condemned him. Montrose, patiently hearing him a long time, and he insisting still, said–'Rail on Rabshakeh[3]' and so turned his back to him in the tent. But all honest men hated Kinanmond for this ever after. Montrose desired to stay in the fields all night, lying upon straw in the tent till the morning.[4]

Thus they traversed the scene of his former victories, the Covenant herald ever pacing before to proclaim 'Here comes James Graham, a traitor to his country!' Entering the Mearns, on 15 May the cavalcade passed by Kinnaird where he saw Southesk and his two youngest children, Robert and Jean, for the last time. 'But neither at meeting or at parting could any change of his former countenance be seen, or the least expression heard which was not suitable to the greatness of his spirit and the fame of his former actions, worth, and valour.' The fey mood had passed from him, and he seemed to have become careless of life. The old ties were broken, the old cause down, the old friends dead–or, like him, on their way to execution. The time of struggle was over, and the certainty of his end bestowed a peace which in life had been so long denied him. 'Death had no terrors for one who had nothing to live for.'

That night they reached the house of Grange, five miles short of Dundee, and here an attempt was made to effect his escape:

It was at this Lady's house that that party of the Covenanters' then standing army that guarded the Marquis of Montrose after his forces was beat and himself betrayed in the North, lodged him whom this excellent Lady designed to set at liberty, by procuring his escape from her house; in order to do this, so soon as their quarters were settled and that she had observed the way and manner of the placing of the guards and what officers commanded them, she not only ordered her butlers to let the soldiers want for no drink, but she herself, out of respect and kindness as she pretended, plied hard the officers and soldiers of the main guard (which was kept in her own hall) with the strongest ale and aquavite, that before midnight all of them (being for the most part highlanders of Lawers's Regiment) became stark drunk. If her stewards and other servants had obeyed her directions in giving out what drink the outer guards should have called for, undoubtedly the business would have been effected, but unhappily when the Marquis had passed the first and second sentinels that were sleeping upon their muskets, and likewise through the main guard that were lying in the hall like swine on a midden, he was challenged a little without the outmost guard by a wretched trooper of Strachan's troop that had been sent at his taking. This fellow was not one of the guard that night, but being quartered hard by, was come rammelling in for his bellyfull of drink when he made this unlucky discovery, which being done, the Marquis was presently seized upon and with much rudeness (being in the Lady's clothes which he had put on as a disguise) turned back to his prison chamber. The Lady, her old husband, and all the servants of the house were made prisoners for that night and the morrow after when they came to be challenged before those that had command of this party. . . .

The Lady, as she had been the only contriver of Montrose's escape, so did she avow the same before them all; testifying she was heartily sorry it had not taken effect according to her wished desire. This confidence of hers, as it bred some admiration among her accusers, so it freed her husband and the servants from being further challenged; only they took security of the Laird for his Lady's appearing before the Committee of Estates when called, which she never was. Their worships got somewhat else to think upon than to convene so excellent a Lady before them on such an account as tended greatly to her honour and their own shame.[5]

On 16 May Montrose entered Dundee, where the citizens had especial cause to remember him with bitterness. But 'the whole town expressed a great deal of sorrow at his condition and furnished him with clothes and all other things suitable to his place, birth, and person.'[6] Of the subsequent progress through Fife, however, there is no record, although it was probably the hardest to endure, since here the widows of Kilsyth and Tippermuir would have flocked to enjoy a barren revenge on the man whose caterans had killed their kindred. On the afternoon of 18 May he reached Leith—and on the same day and at the same port, by some perverse twist of fate, Sir William Fleming also arrived with the King's equivocal order of disbandment.

In Edinburgh meanwhile, the Covenanters had been making preparations for his immediate execution, since they wanted him dead before Charles II could set foot in Scotland and ask clemency for the man who had carried his commission. Accordingly, they decided to pronounce sentence upon him even before he could be brought before Parliament, and he was condemned *in absentia* to be 'hanged on a gibbet at the Cross of Edinburgh till he died, and his History and Declaration hanged about his neck, and to hang three hours thereafter in the view of the people; and thereafter he should be beheaded and quartered, his head to be fixed at the prison house of Edinburgh, and his legs and arms to be fixed at the ports of the towns of Stirling, Glasgow, Perth, and Aberdeen; And if he repented that the bulk of his body should be buried . . . in Greyfriars, if not, to be buried in the Burgh-Moor'. The arrangements for his actual entry into Edinburgh included as particular refinement of cruelty as they could devise. He was to be met by the hangman, hooded, with a villainous little cart on which 'there was framed for him a high seat in fashion of a chariot upon each side of which were holes: through these a cord being drawn crossing his breast and arms, bound him fast in that mock chair'.[7] The purpose of this elaborate contraption was 'the hope that the people would have stoned him and that he might not be able to use his hands to save his face'.[8]

On 18 May, at about four o'clock in the afternoon, Montrose was brought to the Water Gate of Edinburgh where he was met by the magistrates who ordered him to climb up on to the hangman's cart. 'Without betraying the slightest emotion he inquired if their instructions were to compel him to do so. They answered in the affirmative and that such were the orders of Parliament. "Oh," he said immediately, "If that is the way they mean to treat us, let us mount!".'[9]

. . . thus was he led to prison. In all the way there appeared in him such majesty, courage, modesty and even somewhat more than natural, that these common women who had lost their husbands and children in his wars, and who were hired to stone him, were upon the sight of him so astonished and moved, that their intended curses turned to tears and prayers, so that the next day all the ministers preached against them for not stoning and reviling him. It is remarkable that, of the many thousand beholders, only the Lady Jean Gordon, Countess of Haddington, did publicly insult and laugh at him; which, being perceived by a gentleman in the street, he cried up to her that it became her better to sit upon the cart for her adulteries. The Lord Lorne and his new Lady were also sitting on a balcony joyful spectators; and the cart being stopped when it came before the lodging where the Chancellor, Argyll, and Wariston sat that they might have time to insult, he, suspecting the business, turned his face towards them, whereupon they presently crept in at the windows; which being perceived by an Englishman, he cried up, that it was no wonder they started aside at his look, for they durst not look him in the face these seven years bygone.

After he was loosed from the cart, he gave the hangman gold, saying 'Fellow there is drink money for driving the cart.' It was past seven o'clock at night before he entered the Tolbooth, and immediately the Parliament met and sent some of their own number and some ministers to examine him; but he refused to say anything to them until he should know in what terms they stood with the King; which being reported to Parliament, they continued [postponed] the proceedings against him until Monday, and allowed their commissioners to tell him that the King and they were agreed. He desired that night to be at rest for he was wearied from the long journey, and . . . the compliment they had put upon him that day had been somewhat tedious.[10]

The next day being Sunday, he was visited by a number of ministers and members of the Parliament. But he would give them no satisfaction, and referring to the ugly procession of the previous afternoon told them 'that if they thought they had affronted him . . . by carrying him in a cart they were much mistaken, for he thought it the most honourable and joyful journey that he had ever made'.

Early on the Monday before he was brought into Parliament to hear his sentence, several ministers again came to his cell, including James Guthrie, Robert Trail (the minister at Edinburgh), Mungo Law and a young man, the Rev. Robert Simpson, who later recorded his impressions of the interview. They began by reproaching him for his 'personal vices' (alleging that he was 'given to women') and then accused him of using 'Irish papist rebels and cut-throats' to kill his own people. He answered them lightly, 'intermixing many Latin apophthegms', and only when they went on to accuse him of breach of the Covenant was he provoked to retort in anger–'The Covenant I took, I adhere to it. Bishops, I care not for them. I never intended to advance their interest.' And in his turn he now accused them of conceiving the Solemn League as an instrument of rebellion against the King. To this one of them hypocritically replied: 'That was a sectarian party that rose up and carried things beyond the true and first intent of them'–a piece of casuistry which drew the sad rejoinder, 'Error is infinite.' They made one more effort to induce him to repent. They had come, they said, with power to release him from the sentence of excommunication if only at the last he would admit the error of his ways. He answered them gently: 'I am very sorry that any actions of mine have been offensive to the Church of Scotland, and I would with all my heart be reconciled with the same. But since I cannot obtain it on any other terms–unless I call that my sin which I account to have been my duty–I cannot, for all the reason and conscience in the world.'[11]

When they had gone he took some breakfast of bread dipped in ale and, because they would not allow him a knife in case he should try to commit suicide, asked for a barber to shave him. This was refused:–'I would not think but they would have allowed that to a dog'—and he was led out to face his judges unwashed, but with spirit enough to comment to his captors, 'It becomes them rather to be hangmen than me to be hanged!'

The subsequent scene in Parliament was briefly described by Sir James Balfour:

> The Parliament met about 10 o'clock, and immediately after the down-sitting, James Graham was brought before them by the Magistrates of Edinburgh, and ascended the place of delinquents. And after the Lord Chancellor had spoken to him, and in a long discourse declared the progress of all his rebellions, he showed him that the House gave him leave to speak for himself, which he did in a long discourse, with all reverence to the Parliament (as he said). . . . To him the Lord Chancellor replied, punctually proving him by his acts of hostility, to be a person most infamous, perjured, and treacherous, and of all that ever this land brought forth, the most cruel and inhuman butcher and murderer of his nation, a sworn enemy to the Covenant and peace of his country, and one whose boundless pride and ambition had lost the father, and by his wicked counsels done what in him lay to destroy the son likewise.
>
> He made no reply; but was commanded to go down on his knees and receive his sentence, which he did: Archibald Johnstone [Wariston] the Clerk Register, read it, and the Dempster gave the doom: and immediately arising from off his knees, without speaking one word, he was removed thence to the prison. He behaved himself all this time in the House with a great deal of courage and modesty, unmoved and undaunted, as it appeared, only he sighed two several times, and rolled his eyes amongst all the corners of the House, and at the reading of the sentence he lifted up his face without any word speaking.
>
> He presented himself in a suit of black cloth and a scarlet coat to his knee trimmed with silver galouns and lined with crimson taffeta; on his hand a bever hat and silver band. He looked somewhat pale, lank-faced, and hairy.[12]

Balfour passed lightly over Montrose's defence, but the whole has been preserved. 'As I hear you are in some manner reconciled to the King, I regard this Assembly just, as if His Royal Majesty were here in person. For this reason only do I appear before you bareheaded and plead my cause. . . .' Once more he defended his loyalty to the first and true Covenant, but as to the Solemn League:

> I thank Almighty God that I never approved it, never acknowledged it as lawful or honourable. I cannot therefore be justly accused of having broken it. What profit it has been to the cause of religion . . . these three distressed kingdoms can witness! . . . What my carriage was in this country many of you here may bear witness. Even the greatest of generals have rarely succeeded on all occasions in preventing the licence of their soldiers, but where such crimes were known . . . I took care that they should be punished at once. . . . Never was any man's blood spilt but in battle; and even then many thousand lives have I preserved. And I dare here avow in the presence of God

that never a hair of a Scotsman's head that I could save fell to the ground. . . .

And as for my coming at this time, it was by His Majesty's just commands, in order to accelerate the Treaty betwixt him and you; His Majesty knowing that whenever he had ended with you I was ready to retire upon his call. I may say that never subject acted upon more honourable grounds, nor by so lawful a power as I did. . . .

And therefore I desire you to lay aside all prejudice; and consider me as a Christian in relation to the justice of the quarrel; as a subject in relation to my royal master's command; and as your neighbour in relation to the many of your lives I have preserved in battle when I lacked neither power nor occasion but only the will to destroy. And be not too rash; but let me be judged by the laws of God, the laws of nature and of nations, and the laws of this land. If otherwise, I do here appeal from you to the righteous Judge of the World, who one day must be your Judge and mine, and who always gives out righteous judgements.[13]

Back in the tolbooth cell, the Ministers gathered to torment his final hours and 'aggravate the terror of his sentence'. He remained defiant, and told them that he was much beholden to the Parliament for the honour they had put upon him, 'for I think it a greater honour to have my head standing on the ports of this town than to have my portrait in the King's bedchamber: I am beholden to you lest my loyalty should be forgotten, ye have appointed four of the most eminent towns to bear witness of it to posterity.' Then, after talking for a while in a corner with Robert Baillie, he asked them all to leave–'I pray you gentlemen, let me die in peace.'

But this was hardly their intention. The gaolers were instructed to allow him no privacy or rest, and to blow tobacco smoke in his face since it was known that he disliked the smell of it. Sometime in the night his thoughts returned to Raleigh–his sonnet 'Even such is fine'–and with a diamond, it is said, he scratched a similar epitaph on the window of his cell.[14]

In the early morning of 21 May he was roused by the sound of drums and trumpets and was told that the soldiers and citizens were being called to arms since Parliament feared the possibility of rescue at the eleventh hour. 'What, am I still a terror to them?' he asked, and with a touch of malice, 'Let them look to themselves, my ghost will haunt them.'

He began to prepare for his execution, and when, later, Wariston came to the prison, he found him combing out his long hair. The fanatic began to rebuke him for such vanity in the face of death, but Montrose told him sharply, 'While my head is my own, I dress and arrange it. Tomorrow, when it is yours, you may treat it as you please.'

At 2 o'clock they came to fetch him to the gallows.

In his going down from the Tolbooth to the place of execution, he was very richly clad in fine scarlet, laid over with rich silver lace, his hat in his hand, his golden hat band, his bands and cuffs exceeding rich, his delicate white gloves on his hands, his stockings of incarnate silk, and his shoes with their ribbons on his feet; and *sarks* [embroidered linen] provided for him, with *pearling* [lace] about, above ten pounds the elne. All these were provided for him by his friends:[15] and a pretty cassock put on upon him, upon the scaffold, wherein he was hanged. To be short, nothing was here deficient to honour his poor carcase, more beseeming a bridegroom than a criminal going to the gallows.

A scaffold had been erected at the Mercat Cross: above it the gibbet, thirty feet high, and in plain view the table with the axes for the subsequent mutilation. It was the privilege of a condemned man that he should be allowed to address the people before his execution, but even this was now denied him. His words, which have been preserved, were therefore not so much a set speech as a series of answers to questions put by those who stood by:[16]

I am sorry if this manner of my end be scandalous to any good Christian here. Doth it not often happen to the righteous according to the way of the unrighteous? Doth not sometimes a just man perish in his righteousness, and a wicked man prosper in his wickedness and malice? They who know me should not disesteem me for this. Many greater than I have been dealt with in this kind. But I must not say but that all God's judgements are just, and this measure, for my private sins, I acknowledge to be just with God, and wholly submit myself to Him.

But in regard of man, I may say they are but instruments. God forgive them, and I forgive them. They have oppressed the poor, and violently perverted judgement and justice, but He that is higher than they will reward them.

What I did in this kingdom was in obedience to the most just commands of my sovereign, and in his defence, in the day of his distress, against those who rose up against him. I acknowledge nothing, but fear God and honour the King, according to the commandments of God and the just laws of Nature and nations. I have not sinned against man, but against God: and with Him there is mercy, which is the ground of my drawing near unto Him.

It is objected against me by many, even good people, that I am under the censure of the Church. This is not my fault, seeing it is only for doing my duty, by obeying my prince's most just commands, for religion, his sacred person, and authority. Yet I am sorry they did excommunicate me; and in that which is according to God's laws, without wronging my conscience or allegiance, I desire to be relaxed. If they will not do it, I appeal to God, who is the righteous Judge of the world, and will, I hope, be my Judge and Saviour.

It is spoken of me that I should blame the King. God forbid! For the late King, he lived a saint and died a martyr. I pray God I may end as he did. If ever I would wish my soul in another man's stead it should be in his. For His Majesty now living, never any people, I believe, might be more happy in a king. His commandments to me were most just, and I obeyed them. He deals justly with all men. I pray God he be so dealt withal that he be not betrayed under trust, as his father was.

I desire not to be mistaken if my carriage at this time, in relation to your ways, were stubborn. I do but follow the light of my conscience, my rule, which is seconded by the working of the Spirit of God that is within me. I thank Him I go to heaven with joy the way He paved for me. If He enable me against the fear of death, and furnish me with courage and confidence to embrace it even in its most ugly shape, let God be glorified in my end, though it were in my damnation. Yet I say not this out of any fear or mistrust, but out of my duty to God, and love to His people.

I have no more to say, but that I desire your charity and prayers. I shall pray for you all. I leave my soul to God, my service to my prince, my goodwill to my friends, my love and charity to you all. And thus briefly I have exonerated my conscience.

They asked him if he had any wish to pray apart, but he said that he had already poured out his soul before God–'Into His hands I commend my spirit, and He has deigned in grace and mercy to assure me of full forgiveness for my sins, and peace and salvation in Jesus Christ, my Redeemer.' He then gave some money to the hangman, who stepped forward and pinioned his arms behind him. His Declaration and Wishart's *History* were hung about his neck and he was led to the foot of the gallows. His last words on mounting the ladder were: 'May Almighty God have mercy on this afflicted country.'

The final seconds of his life were recorded by an Englishman who was among the crowd around the scaffold:

It is absolutely believed that he hath overcome more now by his death in Scotland, than he would have done if he had lived. For I never saw more sweeter carriage in a man in all my life. I would write more largely if I had time, but he is just now a turning off from the ladder: but his countenance changes not. . . .[17]

After being left to hang for a full three hours, the body was cut down so that it fell upon its face. The head was severed and placed on a spike above the tolbooth, the limbs hacked off and sent to the appointed cities. The trunk was thrown into a rough wooden box and taken to the Burgh-Moor.

No man kills his enemy therefore, that his enemy might have a better life in heaven; that is not his end in killing him; it is God's end. Therefore he brings us unto death, that by that gate he might lead us unto life everlasting.[18]

368

PART VI

Postscript

23

Full Circle

Thou hast drawn together all the far-stretched greatness, all the pride, cruelty, and ambition of man, and covered it all over with these two narrow words: HIC JACET.

Sir Walter Raleigh, *A History of the World*

Although it had long been the custom to dismantle the scaffold almost immediately after a public execution, on this occasion the blood-stained platform beside the Mercat Cross was kept standing for several weeks to become known in time as 'the altar of Argyll and the ministers' whereon, it was remarked, the Kirk 'delighted not in unbloody sacrifices'.[1] The Lord had appointed that the men of blood should die, and eight days after Montrose's execution Sir John Spottiswoode, grandson of the dead archbishop, and Major-General Hurry were beheaded by the Maiden, followed on 4 June by Hay of Dalgetty and Colonel Sibbald. The cycle was finally concluded with the death of Captain Alexander Charteris on the very eve of Charles II's arrival in Scotland.

It was the end of Montrose's company. Some had perished in the early wars; many after Philiphaugh; a number lay in Carbisdale; a few languished in exile on the continent. The best of the Irish were buried under Slain-Man's-Lee, and of the remainder the most part had fallen in a smaller cause. The old Royalists had disappeared.

Alastair had died by treachery with a knife in his back.

The campaign in Kintyre for which he had deserted Montrose was violent and undistinguished. For a year the highlanders had been elevated into the greater perspective of the national struggle, but they never fully understood it. Now the old forces were again predominant and the western clans returned to their particular kind of war against the hereditary enemy. The old Coll Kietache and his sons were on the loose again, bent on a predatory war in Argyll and the Western Isles, and with a mind to bleed Diarmid and scorch the lands of the MacCailein Mhor. With this intent they cleared Clan Campbell

371

out of Islay and fortified a number of strongpoints on the Kintyre peninsula including Dunavertie.

But the MacCailein Mhor would have revenge, and he was not alone. Of the Scottish army that had returned from England, a sizeable proportion was still under arms and had been campaigning against the Gordons in the North. When the principal strongholds at Huntly and the Bog of Gight finally capitulated to the Covenanters, Middleton stayed to hunt down the Marquis in Lochaber while David Leslie was free to march south for the reckoning with Alastair. At Dunblane he joined up with Argyll and on 21 May 1647 their combined forces reached Inverary. By 24 May they were ready to counter-attack in Kintyre.

The brief campaign that followed would reveal only too clearly Alastair's incompetence as a strategist. Access to Kintyre depended upon the control of the narrow passes at the neck of the peninsula where a small determined force could have surprised an army as it straggled through the defile. But Alastair's pickets were caught unawares, and Leslie's troops were able to penetrate into Kintyre without great hindrance. After a day's skirmishing against superior forces, Alastair left 300 of his clan to hold the castle of Dunavertie and withdrew to Islay. There he also posted his old father to garrison Dunneveg, and himself retired to Ireland with the rest of his men.

At Dunavertie the three hundred prepared to die. The castle might have been defensible but for the fact that it had no water supply and could not hope to sustain a prolonged siege against a determined attacker. The dreadful story of what happened there was later told by Sir James Turner, at that time Leslie's adjutant, and afterwards a witness at Argyll's trial:

> We besieged Dunavertie which held out well enough, till we stormed a trench they had at the foot of the hill whereby they commanded two strips of water. This we did take in the assault. Forty of them were put to the sword. We lost five or six with Argyll's Major. After this, inexorable thirst made them desire a parley. I was ordered to speak with them: neither could the Lord Lieutenant be moved to grant other conditions than that they should yield on discretion or mercy: and it seemed strange to me to hear the Lord Lieutenant's nice distinction that they should yield themselves to the kingdom's mercy and not to his. At length they did so: and after they were come out of the castle they were put to the sword, every mother's son, except one young man Mackonnel whose life I begged, to be sent to France with a hundred country fellows whom we had smoked out of a cave as they do foxes, who were given to Captain Campbell, the Chancellor's brother.[2]

Responsibility for the massacre must rest ultimately with David Leslie, who both ordered and permitted it. Many have since blamed Argyll, but in his evidence given under oath, Turner later insisted that to his knowledge he never openly advised the killing, and maintained that, even had he done so in private, 'counsel is not command', and on this campaign Argyll only held the commission of a colonel of foot. Whether he could have actively prevented it is another matter. It is more likely that Leslie acted under pressure from his chaplain John Nevoy, a Covenanting fanatic, who threatened to curse the General as God had cursed Saul for sparing the Amalekites. As it was, Leslie hesitated for two days before allowing the prisoners to be slaughtered, and in the end, may rather have given way to the demands of his soldiers. Some months before the Macdonalds had filled a barn at Lagganmore with men, women and children before setting it alight, and the Campbells would not be denied their revenge. They would have lynched the Macdonald commander on the spot but that the gibbet was too short and his feet dragged on the ground, so they shot him instead. Leslie, for all his faults, seems to have been genuinely sickened by what occurred, and when next day he and Argyll were contemplating the charnel-house, he is said to have turned to Nevoy and exclaimed 'Now Mr John, have you gotten your fill of blood?'[3] Nevertheless, he had earned for himself the sobriquet of 'Executioner'.

After Dunavertie the Covenanters crossed to Islay and laid siege to Dunneveg. The fierce old Coll Kietache of Colonsay was tricked into accepting a safe-conduct to visit his friend the governor of Dunstaffnage Castle, was captured, and promptly hanged from the yard of his own galley. Ranald Og, who had commanded one of the original regiments under Montrose, was also taken at this time and hanged at Inverary. Argyll and Leslie then continued to Jura and Mull where the Maclean delivered up his son as hostage and another fourteen 'very pretty Irishes' who 'had all along been faithful to him', whom again the Covenanters executed. In Mull, news arrived of Charles II's abduction from Holmby House, and Argyll hurried back to Edinburgh. Macdonald pretensions in Kintyre had been totally destroyed.

In Ireland Alastair and his dwindling band fought on–but with the losing side. Four hundred of the Irish who had marched under Montrose were butchered after the defeat at Dungan Hill, and the remainder perished after the Battle at Mallow in Munster when Murdoch O'Brien, Lord Inchiquin, broke the Royalist forces under Lord Taaffe. Alastair yet survived, since, as an officer, he was granted quarter. Unsuspecting, he went to the parley at Cnoc-na-n-Dos to negotiate the surrender, and Inchiquin's captains murdered him there.

The year 1647 had also seen an end to effective Gordon resistance in the North.

When Charles I ordered the Royalist armies in Scotland to disband, Huntly, like Montrose, had been ready to obey, but it seems that the King later changed his mind and sent a second message to the Bog of Gight, countermanding the first and asking Huntly to rearm in the event of his being able to escape from the Covenanters. Huntly raised between 400 and 500 horse and about 1,500 foot, and, reasoning that if Charles were to escape altogether it would probably have to be by sea, he marched to the coastal town of Banff and occupied it.

But Charles did not break free, and Huntly, by not disbanding his men as the King's public order required, had now placed himself outside the law and so prejudiced his chances of obtaining an amnesty. Fearing also that any hostile action on his part might lead to reprisals against the person of the King, he therefore remained under arms but inactive, so that when a force under Bickerton advanced on Banff, the Gordons merely withdrew behind their fortifications and did not offer battle. Even when the Covenanters retired in some disorder, Huntly restrained his men from pursuing or harassing them, although such an opportunity was presented. Instead, he now garrisoned Huntly and the Bog of Gight, and moved at a leisurely pace into the high country where he thought to live as an outlaw. David Leslie was already marching north with the bulk of the Scottish army and it was not long before both the Gordon strongholds surrendered to him. Middleton, with another force, tracked Huntly into the hills.

In Badenoch the Gordons disbanded, and Huntly moved on into Lochaber with only Aboyne and an adequate bodyguard.

In December 1647, the Marquis was betrayed to the Covenant authorities in Edinburgh who threw him into the common jail. Aboyne escaped to France where he died of an ague about a year later.

While Hamilton retained some ascendancy over Argyll there was still a chance that Huntly's life might be spared. However, instead of releasing him, Hamilton merely had him moved to a more comfortable confinement in the Castle, and in the Committee of Estates his condemnation was delayed by one vote until the meeting of Parliament. When this body eventually convened, many of the members had no mind to exact the death penalty, but they yielded to pressure from the extreme faction of the Kirk. When the nobles realized that they could not get a majority of votes in favour of mercy, they absented themselves from the chamber. Of the Lords of the Realm, only the Chancellor was present as Huntly was condemned to death.[4]

But it seemed as if he might cheat the executioner at the last, for his health had been broken by the long incarceration, and in early 1649 he was slowly dying of dysentery. His sister, the Marchioness of Douglas, together with the Ladies Haddington, Seton and Drummond, Argyll's nieces, went to their uncle and implored him to use his influence to obtain a few days stay of execution so that the old man might be allowed to die of his illness rather than on the scaffold. But Argyll said that nothing could be done. His position was equivocal. At his own trial he later protested: 'I may truly say I was as earnest to save him as possibly I could, which is very well known to many in this honourable House, and my not prevailing may sufficiently evidence that I had not so great a stroke nor power in the Parliament as is libelled.'[5] On Huntly's death his forfeited estates accrued to Argyll, but the property was in debt to the sum of £55,560, and he was the principal creditor. It could be said that by taking over the estates with their financial burden he had effectively saved them for the family. He had also assured himself of feudal jurisdiction over the Highlands.

Huntly went to the scaffold on 22 March 1649. He was dressed in mourning and pitifully weak. The ministers urged him to repent his crimes and asked if he desired at the last to be released from their sentence of excommunication. But the old man would not speak with them for he was long since resolved with his God.

It is difficult to look back over Huntly's career without a feeling of regret. He was not a lucky man. The Royalist cause in Scotland, which had once promised so fair, foundered on his jealousy and inability to forgive. He undoubtedly possessed many good qualities, but his greatest and most apparent fault was that of selfishness, and it all too often alienated those who served him.

> Service done was forgotten, and old servants for whom there was no use [were mostly] brushed or rubbed off as spots from clothes: so as this fault, if it may be termed a fault was truly a noble one, for it attended always on nobility: and yet the hard construction which was made of this did more harm to himself than to those castaways, for it did, little by little, insensibly alienate the hearts of his followers. . . . For this slighting of his followers bred him great prejudice because, with a certain kind of reserved inclination, he seemed desirous to maintain a distance with his inferiors without distinction of quality: for friends and followers were equalled with domestics and common observance, unless his affairs required it, and then he could be both familiar and obsequious.[6]

Coming from the contemporary historian of his own clan, this is a sad indictment. To his credit, he had kept rebellion smouldering in the North, but his military operations were ineffective and the Gordon power was frittered away on a series of futile and unproductive excursions on a local scale. This ineffectiveness was in part due to his lack of ability as a strategist (although he himself was always convinced of his talent) and in part to his own inconstancy of purpose. As Patrick Gordon put it, 'Perhaps the contemplative faculty did so far exceed the active.' His great courage was never in doubt. The lesson is a hard one: that, too jealous of his place in history, he came eventually to lose it.

The Duke of Hamilton had been executed a month after his King. After his capture at Preston, in December 1648, he was taken to Windsor and saw the King for the last time. 'My dear Master,' Hamilton exclaimed, much moved. 'I have been so indeed to you,' replied the King embracing him.[7]

In his own cell, he underwent continuous interrogation. Cromwell himself visited him, to promise his life in return for the names of the Englishmen who had supported the Engagement. To his honour, Hamilton refused to betray them, and seeing how the wind shifted, dipped his pen in lemon juice to warn his brother Lanerick in invisible ink: 'I under the power of the sword and merciless men, no favour to be expected: oft examined but nothing discovered being ignorant: perhaps you will abide the same trial: beware if you do.'[8] But

375

Lanerick was temporarily safe and would die of wounds at Worcester. There was still a chance. He had a faithful servant, one Cole, who arranged for him to escape, warning him however to avoid the City of London where the armed patrols would be certain to pick him up. Hamilton broke free successfully enough, but he ignored the warning. Towards morning he was arrested in Southwark for infringing the curfew, but even then might not have been recognized had he not attempted to destroy an incriminating document by trying to light his pipe with it. The suspicions of his captors were aroused. They searched him and found proof of his identity, and Hamilton went back to prison resigned to the will of God.

On 30 January 1649 Charles I went to the block. The English authorities sent to Argyll, again supreme in Scotland, to know his pleasure concerning their other prisoner. Hamilton's daughter and members of his family begged Argyll to intervene, but he replied that it was not fitting that he should address himself to regicides. Hamilton's trial dragged on until 6 March, when, although he was a prisoner of war who had surrendered upon promise of mercy, he was finally condemned to death. At the eleventh hour Cromwell's officers made a last attempt to persuade him to divulge the names of his English associates, but he replied that 'if he had as many lives as hairs on his head he would lay them all down rather than redeem them by such base means'.[9] He died on 9 March, and on the scaffold stated that he owed everything to the late King's favour. Indeed, he had had much reason to love him.

Others would die hereafter. At the Restoration there was considerable apprehension in Scotland lest the young King should decide to revenge himself upon those persons who had particularly harmed his father's cause. But Charles II, whatever his other faults, was not openly vindictive. The time was coming when the Covenanters would be driven out into the mosses and hunted down like beasts, but for the moment only four of his old enemies were called to account: the Marquis of Argyll, the Reverend James Guthrie, Archibald Johnston Lord Wariston, and a little-known renegade called Giffan, who seems unfortunate to have been thus distinguished.

The result of the débâcle at Preston was that within a short time Argyll and the Kirk, with its supporters Eglinton, Elcho, Loudoun and the rest, were back in power and in temporary alliance with Cromwell. Gathering the extreme Covenanters of the West, from Ayrshire and Dumbarton, together with a mustering of Campbells who had survived Montrose's wars, they descended on Edinburgh and Stirling in what has later come to be known as the 'Whiggamore Raid'. The Engagers might still have resisted to good effect, and indeed had some success in skirmishing with Argyll, but the Committee of Estates now cravenly regretted their patronage of Hamilton and capitulated to the Kirk. On 22 September 1648 Argyll met Cromwell on the Tweed. On 4 October

Oliver came to dine at Edinburgh, and their compact established the new balance of power. In January 1649, again supreme in the Scottish Estates, Argyll and Wariston passed the Act of Classes which excluded Royalists and Engagers from public office for a number of years according to their degree of guilt. It was a matter, they said, 'of breaking the Malignants' teeth'.

However, in February came news of the King's execution, causing a widespread reaction in Scotland and a general demand to treat with the young Charles II on the continent. Argyll's position was suddenly undermined. His association with Cromwell had placed him in a difficult situation, and it was even said, although wrongly, that they had discussed and agreed the King's death the previous October. Many of his old allies in the Kirk had disliked the idea of an alliance with the English Independents in the first place, while at the other end of the political spectrum the breach between himself and the Engagers was quite irreparable. It was the beginning of a schism which would destroy them all.

Negotiations with Charles II began. Montrose landed, failed and died. The young king signed the treaty at Breda out of *force majeure*. Scotland was worth a Covenant—or two.

When Charles eventually landed at Speymouth the common people greeted him with enthusiasm, but the Covenanters were indignant because he brought some of the old Engagers in his train. These were made to do public penance, and other Royalists like old Carnwath, who wished to kiss the new king's hand, were not permitted to do so. Charles's retinue was carefully purged, those dismissed being deemed insufficiently godly. He travelled slowly south. At Aberdeen they gave him lodgings opposite the tolbooth from which to contemplate the severed arm of Montrose impaled upon the Justice Port. Towns which offered him gifts of money were severely rebuked, and along the route crowds who cheered were sharply restrained. Thus Argyll, Lorne and Lothian brought their new king to Falkland.

Argyll now approached Charles with a scheme of his own. The King should give some 'undeniable proof of a fixed resolution to support the Presbyterian Party',[10] and one way of doing this would be to marry his daughter Lady Anne Campbell. On Legge's advice, Charles stalled by saying that out of common courtesy he must first consult his mother, and Henrietta Maria, as an expert in such things, could be relied upon to complicate the issue for as long as would be necessary. Argyll suspected Legge's part in the affair and had him confined in the Castle of Edinburgh. In the meanwhile much reverence was shown to Charles at Falkland, but he was never admitted to the Committee's counsels. Nor would Argyll himself yield to any of the King's propositions.

But the Covenanters would pay a terrible price for not attempting to come to terms with the Engagers. Cromwell had completed his subjugation of Ireland and now turned his baleful glance to the northward. Scotland faced a war in which her very survival was at stake, but among the brethren an atmosphere of total unreality prevailed. The Lord Jehovah was with them even as he had been with Joshua and Gideon, and the army of saints would drive the English sectaries before them even as Joshua and the judges smote the enemies of Israel. But first Jehovah had to be placated, for the Scottish host itself was tainted and they must rid themselves of the evil in their midst. Accordingly they purged the army. Many of the Engagers who retained a cynical and ungodly faith in cold steel as the effective antidote to the English offered to raise a separate force for the country in case the Covenanters should be defeated. But this was unthinkable, and the brethren purged the army again. Even the King, who had signed the Covenant twice already, was asked for purgative purposes to sign a new Declaration stating that he desired to be 'deeply humbled and afflicted in spirit before God because of his father's opposition to the work of God and to the Solemn League and Covenant, and for the idolatry of his mother'.[11] Charles indignantly refused, even when Argyll told him that nothing else would please 'these madmen'.[12] The pulpits rattled with sermons against 'this very Root of Malignancy', and the extremists drew up another Declaration dissociating themselves from the King's cause unless he agreed thus to revile his father's memory. On 16 August he gave in, but he would never forgive.

Such was the uneasy prelude to Dunbar, where the Scottish army, superior in numbers despite the purges, and from what should have been a decisively advantageous position, was sacrificed by the incompetence of its officers and the pretensions of the civilian committee that accompanied it. The ministers upbraided the Almighty for failing them on the field of battle, and howled for a scapegoat. The King should examine his own soul: the army had been insufficiently purged: the defeat resulted from the neglect of family prayers by great ones and many others. But the Kirk would never be the same, and from this moment the Covenant began to devour its own. On hearing the news of Dunbar, Charles II is said to have fallen to his knees and thanked God.

Even now the extremists would not accept the need for a united front against Cromwell. In a provincial synod at Glasgow, they framed the Western Remonstrance, disowning the King and maintaining that an offensive war against England was contrary to the terms and spirit of the Solemn League and Covenant. Fear of Strachan, Ker and others prompted Charles to make an abortive bid to escape on 4 October 1650,[13] the failure of which encouraged them to publish a second Remonstrance a fortnight later which went so far as to demand the resignation of Argyll, Lothian and others who had treated with the King. They had now clearly rejected all authority other than their own, and such government as there was in Scotland was trapped between these Remonstrants on the one hand and the erstwhile Engagers on the other. The very extremism of the former operated in Charles's favour since he now emerged as the only possible rallying point for a stand against Cromwell who was still ravaging the South. On 26 October the King and the Committee of Estates published an indemnity for the northern Royalists who had connived at his unsuccessful escape, and others who had been involved in the Engagement. The Kirk was thus completely split between the extremists who held for the Covenant, and the moderates who perforce now stood for King and country. In the West, Ker and Strachan would not submit. Ker's force dashed itself to pieces against Lambert's Ironsides, but Strachan disbanded and deserted to the English. He was promptly excommunicated by the moderates, went mad, and later died.

On 1 January 1651 Charles II was crowned at Scone. Argyll himself placed the crown upon his head, and it may have seemed for a moment at least as if, king-maker, he was at the zenith of his career. In fact, his position was becoming increasingly lonely. The division within the Kirk, from which he had once drawn his main support, had sapped his power also. At Stirling, soon after the Coronation, he made a last attempt to win Charles away from the Malignants and Royalists to whom he now turned more and more, and one night followed the King to his closet and dealt freely with him. Charles was:

> ... seemingly sensible, and they came at length to pray and mourn together till two or three in the morning, and when at length Argyll came home to his Lady she had never known him so intimous. He said he never had such a sweet night in the world and told her all; what liberty they had in prayer and how much concerned the King was. She said plainly they were crocodile tears and that that night would cost him his life.[14]

It was a shrewd judgement. As Argyll himself observed later, 'Princes do not love those who are acquainted with, see, and reprehend their vices.' He had done all of these. He was virtually isolated, hated by Royalists, the Engagers and the common people alike, while the extreme Remonstrants blamed him for having allowed Charles to come to Scotland in the first place. Nor could help come from the English as heretofore: Cromwell was also an enemy now.

The King meanwhile, was mustering an army for a new attempt upon England, and despite the advice of several of his friends, took no overt steps against Argyll, shrewdly reasoning that 'he would not attempt anything while the army was entire: if it prevailed, he neither would nor could do any harm; and if it were defeated, it would be no great matter what he did'.[15] Charles was obviously learning, and he gained a signal victory when the barons and burgesses asked him to command the army in person. When they marched south in July towards Worcester and disaster, Argyll did not go with them. He was now held in some contempt. 'A Royalist success could not improve his position; a Royalist defeat he did not wish to share. Politics conducted on theocratic principles with the temporary aid of the Lairds and Burgesses had broken down beneath his feet.'[16] He would never retrieve his former place.

The old fox went to earth in Inverary, and it was as well for him that he did so, for on 28 August, Monk (whom Cromwell had left behind in Scotland while he himself hurried to intercept Charles) swooped down on the Committee of Estates who were meeting at Alyth, and carried off the lot. Argyll and Loudoun were suddenly the only persons of former importance still at liberty.

On 3 September the Scottish army was destroyed at Worcester and the country submitted to what Laing was later to call 'a period of ignominious yet not intolerable servitude'. Argyll made a separate peace with the English (he could have been troublesome to them) but remained in his Highland fastness on Loch Awe. In October 1652 resentment of the invader flared into open revolt when the Highland clans formed an association and Glengarry wrote to Charles II (now safe abroad) asking him to send Middleton to lead the rising. The movement was joined by a host of younger sons, including Lord Lorne, whom Argyll subsequently disowned to Lilburne. He had promised to keep his country and his clan at peace, and now performed his part of the agreement by supplying the English with information and intelligence on the Royalists' movements. Written as part of a calculated design or for reasons of pure self-preservation, these documents sent under his hand would ultimately kill him.

The rising itself was a comparatively feeble affair, lacking a leader of genius, and the Royalist potential was squandered in a number of unproductive raids. Lord Lorne quarrelled with Glencairn and would have betrayed him but that his messenger delivered the letter in question to Lord Kenmure instead. Middleton landed in Sutherland in February 1654 to be joined by Glengarry, Glencairn, Atholl, Kenmure and others, but the leaders soon fell out and the movement began to disintegrate.

On 4 May Cromwell was proclaimed Protector at the Cross of Edinburgh, and in June the English moved decisively against the rebels. Argyll, with English garrisons at Glasgow and Dumbarton, secured the South-West of Scotland, while Monk ravaged the Cameron and Glengarry country, linking up with the Campbells again at Loch Lochy. 'The Marquis of Argyll is resolved to engage with us in blood,'[17] wrote Monk to Cromwell before going on to burn Invergarry. Middleton and the Royalists rode to catch Argyll in Breadalbane, but they missed him and were thereafter routed at Lochgarry by the English under Morgan. The rising was at an end, but after this latest treason Argyll had cause to dread a Restoration.

Between 1655 and 1657 he visited England, sat in the joint Parliament and succeeded in recovering some of the money which he had lost during the wars. On 15 July 1657 he was one of the few Scottish lords who consented to be present at the second proclamation of Cromwell as Protector, and on Oliver's death he returned to London to sit as member for Aberdeenshire in Richard Cromwell's short-lived Parliament. At this time he recovered another £1,000, and his claim for a further £12,000 in reparations was charged against the Excise of Scotland. He also made an effort to regain the support of

Wariston and others of the extreme faction by using his new influence in London to obtain employment for them under the English, but in Scotland as a whole his old power had quite disappeared and 'the hate of the country was heavy upon him'.

In 1660, when Charles II came into his own again, Argyll seems to have deliberately staked everything on one desperate, and in the event suicidal, throw. Possibly on the advice of Lorne, but more probably on his own initiative, he left the security of Inverary, where it would have taken an army to smoke him out, and went to London resolved upon an interview with the King himself. His friends had all manner of dreadful premonitions. One of his kinsmen claimed to have had a terrible vision of 'My Lord with his head cut off and his shoulder full of blood'. His hounds at Roseneath behaved strangely on the day Charles landed, and at least five other stories were told concerning strange and supernatural warnings. Argyll must have known the risk. The Act of Indemnity did not cover his actions of 1652 and later, and to his betrayal of Glencairn's rising there could be little defence. Charles had no cause to love him. He had tormented the young king with his preaching and abused his power over him. He had ruined the Engagement. He had killed Montrose.

On 8 July he called several times at the lodgings of the new Lord Chancellor to ask that an audience with the King might be arranged. Although Clarendon refused to see him, he importunately hung about in the street outside, and when the Chancellor eventually emerged with Lord Lorne, he started forward and caught Clarendon's sleeve, but was immediately repelled: 'Not a word my Lord!' Argyll hurried straight away to Whitehall by water, and arriving before the others waited to intercept his son in the ante-room as he would have passed into the chamber of presence. But when he waylaid Lorne with a message for the King, Clarendon drew the young man aside and whispered 'That is a doomed man'.[18] Minutes later, Argyll suffered the awful ignominy of being arrested for high treason by the Garter King of Arms in front of the Court. He was taken to the Tower and remained there until December, when he was conveyed to Edinburgh by ship to stand trial for his life before Parliament.

It seems certain that Charles II had it in mind to destroy Argyll, but he also wanted the process and subsequent judgement to appear as just and as constitutional as possible. Trial before Parliament was not an unfair procedure, and the prisoner was allowed counsel – a luxury which few men accused of treason were ever permitted. However, Middleton was the new Chancellor in Scotland who would preside over the court, and he had long been a bitter enemy to Argyll. That he was determined upon his death was no secret and there was talk that Glencairn and he had already planned to divide the accused's estates between them.[19]

As it turned out, the trial was not well managed. The indictment had been drawn up by the King's Advocate, Sir John Fletcher, and it rambled through Argyll's career since his first association with the

Covenanting movement. A large proportion of the charges were based upon hearsay, and as Lang later commented: 'The indictment itself was mainly a deluge of irrelevancies introduced to excite prejudice.'[20] Possibly under the influence of Lauderdale, whose niece was married to Lord Lorne and who hated Middleton in any event, the King now decreed that the charges were to be restricted to alleged offences committed after 1651, and that the record of the entire trial should be sent to London for scrutiny before sentence was pronounced. However, Middleton objected to this last request on the grounds that it would indicate a lack of trust in the court's competence, adding that he had therefore not made the royal instruction public pending further confirmation, which, if forthcoming, would be certain 'to discourage this loyal and affectionate Parliament'. Charles dropped the matter,[21] and the restriction on the charges was thought to be practically nullified when Middleton sent Glencairn and Rothes to Whitehall to work against Argyll's interest there. During the numerous sittings of the court at Edinburgh, the prosecution particularly pressed the charge of acceding to Charles I's execution, but was unable to prove its case, and the issue finally turned on his abetting of the English during 1654–5 to which he could only plead 'common compliance wherein all the kingdom did share equally'. Even here, the evidence was inconclusive, or at least insufficient to kill a man, and for a brief moment it seemed as if Argyll might yet escape with his life. But then came the dramatic moment of the trial. As recorded by Sir George Mackenzie:

> After the debate and probation was all closed and the Parliament ready to consider the whole matter, one who came post from London knockt most rudely at the Parliament door, and upon his entry with a packet, which he presented to the Commissioner, made him conclude that he had brought a remission, or some other warrant in favour of the Marquis, and the rather because the bearer was a Campbell.[22]

But the fellow came from Monk and in the packet were the letters which Argyll had written to the English over the period of Glencairn's rising. This latest evidence was incontrovertible.[23] On 25 May 1661 he was brought before the court to hear sentence pronounced upon him.[24] His lands were forfeit, and he himself was to be executed upon the Monday following. His arms were to be torn before Parliament and at the cross (a heraldic procedure customary in cases of treason), and his head was to adorn the tolbooth spike where that of Montrose had been formerly.

That evening the Marchioness of Argyll went to Holyrood to intercede with Middleton that he might grant a brief stay of execution to allow time for an appeal to the King. She found the Lord Commissioner drunk, and in his cups he informed her that help from that quarter was out of the question. He had come to Scotland with three instructions from His Majesty: to rescind the Covenant; to take off the Marquis of Argyll's head; and to sheathe every man's sword in his brother's breast.[25] No one was going to save Argyll.

The Marquis himself rejected a possible opportunity to win free. His wife had been permitted to visit him in prison, and, inspired perhaps by Ogilvie's escape from the bottle dungeon at St Andrews, they hastily changed clothes so that Argyll might have a chance to leave the Castle in her covered sedan chair. However, at the last moment he suddenly demurred, and refused to make the attempt. His enemies put this hesitation down to cowardice, while his friends always maintained that, like Socrates, he had declined to break prison.

Argyll's courage had ever been suspect, and his resolution or lack of it became the morbid preoccupation of his friends and foes alike. Their speculation was such that his doctor was required to feel his pulse as he laid his head upon the block, and after his death, as a final indignity, they even dissected his stomach to pronounce upon the digestion of his last meal. But he surprised them all by making a good end. As he told Sir George Mackenzie, his advocate, 'he would not die as a Roman braving death, but as a christian, without being affrighted' – and indeed, he seemed to have resigned himself to the scaffold and the old ghosts who would be waiting there. On 27 May, having passed the morning with his friends, dined and taken his customary after-dinner nap, he walked to his death in the afternoon, quite freely, in his hat and cloak, and hardly seeming like a condemned traitor on his way to execution. By the Maiden, he showed some slight signs of nervousness, speaking at all four corners of the platform and fidgeting with his doublet so that his chaplain Hutchison whispered: 'My Lord, hold now your grip sicker!' But Argyll replied: 'Mr. Hutchison, you know what I said to you in the chamber. I am not to be surprised with fear.'

The warrant for his execution was not signed in London until the following day.

Argyll's body was carried to the little church of St Magdalene in the Cowgate, and thereafter to Newbattle Abbey. A month later it was taken by night to the family vault on Holy Loch. Three years after, by permission of Charles II, the head was restored to the trunk and the remains of the Marquis thus collected were finally laid to rest at Kilmun.

Of all men in Scotland, Wariston was now the most abominated. Like Argyll, his power had foundered on the schism within the Kirk, and all the troubles and the sufferings of the country were laid to his account. He had passed the infamous Act of Classes; he had purged the army of its finest troops; and he had given the fatal order to leave the hills before Dunbar. It seemed as if every man's hand was turned against him, and even God had withdrawn His favour.

In 1650 he was bankrupt with seven or eight young children to feed. His small estate near Edinburgh was burdened with debt and ruined by years of mismanagement and neglect. Many of his friends had taken service with the English, who needed men of experience to staff their new administration, but Wariston shrank from betraying those early fierce ideals. His situation grew worse. His house was plundered by a roving band of highlanders. English troops were billeted on him. The children grew sick, and he was threatened with legal proceedings for debt. He was haunted by nightmares and oppressed by the consciousness of his own failure, and when, in May 1656, Argyll wrote from England offering employment with the new government, Wariston finally put aside his principles and became Cromwell's man.

In October Argyll could tell him that he had been granted £300 sterling per annum, and Wariston gradually came to conquer his conscience. The Protector was the man whom the Lord had appointed to govern, and was not Cromwell without the Malignants better than Charles with them? Perhaps there was a future for him in England: 'I dreamed that these nations were become a united city and that I was appointed to be governor over them, which left an impression upon me.' In June 1657 he had an interview with Cromwell himself and sold his soul for ever. He obtained the coveted position of Clerk Register with a down payment of £3,000 and an annual pension of £400. In return, the Protector: '. . . desired me to give him from time to time full information of matters and persons, their carriages in Scotland, and it should not meet with me again'.[26] He also secured a position in Cromwell's 'Other House', and sat as an MP in Richard Cromwell's Parliament. When the military again seized power he was appointed to the new council of state, and in July 1659 even presided over it. But the recokoning was at hand, for as the people turned against this government, so was he ruined by association, and on 27 March 1660 he returned to Scotland 'hated of all sort of the people of this kingdom for being resident in England and of the Committee of Safety, and for his great oppression in Scotland in raising the prices of all suits and great extortion of the subjects'.[27] Guthrie and his other old friends turned their backs, and Monk marked him down for punishment.[28]

On 14 July 1660, after the Restoration, he was riding into Edinburgh when a friend warned him that his arrest was intended. Wariston turned and fled for his life. He went into hiding and eventually escaped to Holland where his wife joined him. The sentence of forfeiture and death was passed in his absence.

In the meanwhile, the Committee of Estates (captured by Monk at Alyth) had been restored, and met for the first time on 23 August 1660. On the same day, and in a neighbouring house, ten protesting preachers and two elders also gathered under the leadership of the Reverend James Guthrie. As Baillie recalled, it was 'to my sense exceeding dangerous as showing a resolution to keep up a schism and a party of the godly as they will have them called, for themselves that will obey no Church judiciary further than they please'. These

Protesters were a dangerous element, for at any 'counter assembly' they might have attracted the support of numerous other dissidents, and it behoved the government to take some sort of action. Guthrie himself was doomed. He had tormented the last hours of Montrose. He had excommunicated Middleton himself, and all men remembered how he had 'preached the poor little army down' after Dunbar. But he was undeterred. Like the early Covenanters, the group drew up a formal Supplication. The Cromwellians, they said, had done many evil things including the barbarous murder of Charles I, but beyond all else they had established 'a vast toleration in religion'. After protesting their loyalty to the new king, they therefore denounced those Malignants who now thought to bring back the Service Book. Never again, said Guthrie, must 'the vomit of toleration be licked up'. Charles II must enforce Presbyterianism upon his three kingdoms. He must appoint only Covenanters to official positions, extirpate prelacy, abstain from the Liturgy in his private chapel, and publicly approve the Covenants.[29]

It was a supplication for the renewal of civil war and a return to chaos, and the Committee of Estates at once took the practical if illegal step of arresting all those who had had a hand in it. They hanged Guthrie on 1 June 1661. It was reported of him that after his condemnation 'he would willingly have redeemed his life by a submission but that the multitude of ladies upbraided him with the very aspect of what would strike at the root of religion, and so thrust him violently upon his death'.[30] He spoke at the gallows for a full hour, but the hangman was very patient.

In 1663 a Scottish spy called Crooked Murray recognized Lady Wariston in Rouen and followed her to her lodging where Wariston himself lay recovering from an illness that had struck him down in Hamburg some months before. By courtesy of the French King he was extradited and sent to Edinburgh, but it was a broken man whom they dragged bareheaded up the High Street to the Council House.

> The Chancellor and others waited to examine him: he fell upon his face roaring, and with tears entreated they would pity a poor creature who had forgot all that was in his Bible. This moved all the spectators with a deep melancholy and the Chancellor, reflecting upon the man's great parts, former esteem, and the great share he had in all the late revolutions, could not deny some tears to the frailty of silly mankind. At his examination, he pretended that he had lost so much blood by the unskilfulness of his chirurgeons, that he lost his memory with his blood, and I really believe that his courage had indeed been drawn with it. Within a few days he was brought before Parliament where he discovered nothing but much weakness, running up and down upon his knees begging mercy. But the Parliament ordained his former sentence to be put into execution at the Cross of Edinburgh. At his execution he showed more composure than formerly, which his friends ascribed to God's miraculous kindness for him. But others thought that he had only formerly put on this disguise of

madness to escape death in it, and that, finding the mask useless, he had returned, not to his former wit which he had lost, but from his madness which he had counterfeited.

Before his death, Wariston recovered sufficiently to read aloud a Declaration which he had prepared long since against this hour, and in which he repented deeply of his association with the English. The crowd around the gallows was surprisingly sympathetic, and from this he seems to have drawn some comfort. His composure at the last was extremely placid, although when they made him climb the ladder he experienced some difficulty with the bandage about his eyes. It was soon adjusted for him, however, and he stepped off into his particular eternity with few convulsions of any kind.

The last word was left with Argyll, who in those final days glimpsed a greater truth and penned it to his son:

> I charge you to forget, and not harbour any animosity or particular anger against any man concerning me. Such heartburnings have been the destruction of many a Noble Person in this kingdom. I know not of any person so given, but that the very same measure has been meted to him again. The Cup has gone round, and therefore content yourself.

24

Montrose Redivivus

Let them bestow on every airth a limb,
Then open all my veins, that I may swim
To Thee, my Maker, in that crimson lake;
Then place my par-boil'd head upon a stake,
Scatter my ashes, strew them in the air;
Lord! since thou knowest where all these atoms are,
I'm hopeful thou'lt recover once my dust,
And confident thou'lt raise me with the just.

Montrose [said to have been written with the point of a
diamond upon the window of his cell]

Two things yet remain: the story of Montrose's heart, and the recollection of his 'True Funerals'.

In the seventeenth century, the area immediately to the south of
the city of Edinburgh, which in later times came to be called the
Meadows, was occupied by the Burgh-Moor, or South Loch.[1] At one
corner of this space was a walled-in Golgotha, where generations of
common felons had been hanged and left to bleach under the city
gibbet. It was a place of putrefaction, a square of unhallowed earth;
and, because by dying excommunicate he had forfeited the right to
Christian burial, the mutilated trunk of Montrose was carried here and
thrown into a shallow pit.

Merchiston Castle stood at the south-western extremity of the Burgh-
Moor, about half a mile to the east of the common gallows. Montrose's nephew, the second Lord Napier, was in exile on the continent, but his wife, Lady Elizabeth Napier, had remained in Edinburgh
for the trial and execution. Together with Lilias Napier and her sister
Margaret Napier the Lady of Keir, who had also suffered for their
devotion to Montrose during his wars, she had been responsible for
providing him with necessities while he was in prison, and had given
him the fine suit of clothes that he had worn to confront Parliament
and to his execution. By custom the victim's clothing was a perquisite
of the hangman, but when the body was cut down and dismembered
Lady Napier succeeded in recovering the fine satin cap and incarnate
stockings which were to remain in the care of the Napier family for
more than two centuries.[2] In his lifetime, Montrose had been particularly
fond of the young Lord Napier and his wife, and had always promised
to bequeath his heart to Lady Elizabeth Napier for her steadfast and
unremitting kindness to him through all the vicissitudes of his career.

387

Two days after the execution, therefore, on 23 May 1651, she sent two of her servants from Merchiston with instructions to find the body in the Burgh-Moor and extract the heart. The names of these 'adventurous spirits'[3] who dared the spectres of that noisome place[4] have not been officially recorded, but from their subsequent inclusion in the account of Montrose's 'True Funerals' it seems possible that this gruesome task was undertaken by the secretaries William Ord and Thomas Sydserf. The two men found the body and succeeded in cutting out the heart which they wrapped in fine linen and carried to Lady Napier. For their part, the authorities subsequently discovered that the corpse had been tampered with, and were obliged to order the Locksman's (hangman's) men to cover the grave over again and to make it deeper— at a cost of thirty-six shillings to the civic purse.[5]

Lady Napier took the heart to James Callender, a skilled chirurgeon and apothecary, who secretly embalmed it. It was then enclosed in a steel case fashioned from the blade of Montrose's broadsword and said to have been similar in size and shape to an egg. It opened on the depressing of a small catch, like a watch-case. This was placed in a small gold filigree box which the Doge of Venice had presented to John Napier of Merchiston when the great philosopher and mathematician had visited Italy, and this in its turn was put into a silver urn which Montrose himself had given to the young Lord Napier.

It seems possible that Lady Napier's original idea may have been to keep the relic as Montrose had intended, and at about this time she commissioned a portrait of herself holding the silver urn. However, if this was the case, she must have come to change her mind, because later she joined her husband in Flanders and gave the urn with its precious contents to the second Marquis of Montrose who was his companion in exile. The young Lord Napier had been exempted from pardon or amnesty by both the Covenanters in 1650 and Cromwell in 1654, and so could never return to Scotland, but Lady Napier was soon obliged to travel back for the sake of their five small children, and until the Restoration she lived in miserable circumstances upon the pittance granted to her by the Covenanting authorities. Her husband did not see her again, for he died sadly at Delfshaven in the spring of 1660 before the Restoration, and it was Archibald, third Lord Napier, and still a minor, who witnessed the 'True Funerals' of Montrose.[6] James Graham, second Marquis of Montrose, returned prematurely from exile to join the northern Royalists in 1654, and in 1659 was imprisoned by Parliament. After the Restoration, when preparations were being made for his father's state funeral, he again took the heart to the chirurgeon whose accounts for 11 May 1661 record that it was carefully re-embalmed with odoriferous powders and oils.[7]

On the basis of the Lord Lyon's account, it has sometimes been assumed that the heart was then interred in St Giles together with the rest of Montrose's remains, and that the subsequent history concerns only the empty steel case and the casket.[8] However, on this occasion the veracity of the Lord Lyon's manuscript cannot be accepted without question (there is also a possible discrepancy concerning the right arm) and, apart from the Marquis's stated desire to bequeath it to Lady Napier, there is written evidence to maintain that a hundred years later the steel case still contained a small parcel wrapped in coarse cloth and done over with a glutinous substance which successive guardians of the casket quite definitely took to be the heart of Montrose.[9]

What is certain however is that, some time after the state funeral in 1661, the casket and whatever it contained was lost to both the Graham and the Napier families until it was recognized in a Dutch collection by a gentleman from Guelderland who procured it for Francis, fifth Lord Napier. Unfortunately, only the steel case and the gold filigree box were recovered. The silver urn was never found.

The heart then remained in the possession of the fifth Lord Napier until he died at Lewes in Sussex while journeying to France. As he was taken suddenly ill and had a premonition of death, he was much concerned lest the Castle of Merchiston might be sold by his executors and its contents dispersed. The Napiers had suffered considerable losses in lands forfeited to Cromwell, while a large portion of their remaining capital was invested in plans for the Caledonian Canal. To ensure therefore, that Montrose's heart would remain within his family, he gave it to his sixteen-year-old daughter Hester Napier, who had been his constant companion during his last years, and who with his wife was beside him when he died.

Hester Napier grew up to marry Samuel Johnston of Carnsalloch, an officer in the East India Company. They had a son, Alexander, who was later to become Chief Commissioner and Chief Justice of Ceylon, and who in 1836 recorded the following history of Montrose's heart in a letter to his two daughters.[10]

When Alexander Johnston was still a child of five, the family sailed for India in a merchant ship attached to a squadron under Commodore Johnston. Some distance off the Cape Verde islands the English vessels were attacked by a French squadron under Suffrein, and as their captain prepared to fight his ship, Samuel Johnston obtained permission to take command of the four cannon which were on the quarterdeck. At the same time, his wife went below and packed all their valuables including the heart into a large velvet reticule, lest, in the event of capture, the cabins would be plundered by the enemy. Then, as a French frigate bore down towards the East Indiaman, she took her stand beside her husband with the child Alexander in one hand and the reticule in the other, resolutely declaring that no wife should quit her husband in a moment of such peril. As the Frenchman opened fire, a shot struck one of the quarterdeck guns, killed two of the crew and ploughed a splinter out of the deck with such force as to knock down Samuel Johnston and wound Lady Hester Johnston severely in the arm. Upon inspection, however, it turned out to have been the reticule which had absorbed the major force of the impact as it hung loose in her hand, and on opening it she discovered with considerable dismay that the Venetian filigree box had been shattered to pieces. But the steel case containing Montrose's heart survived intact.

Fortunately also, the French frigates broke off the action and the Johnstons were able to continue their voyage to India without further incident. When they reached Madura, where Samuel Johnston was to be stationed, his wife sought out a celebrated Indian goldsmith who, partly from the remaining fragments and partly from her description of the original, fashioned another beautiful filigree casket as similar as possible to that which had been destroyed in the naval engagement. She also commissioned him to make another silver urn and to engrave on it in Tamil and Telugu a short account of Montrose's life and the circumstances of his death. When the work was completed, the heart in its steel case and new box was placed inside the urn together with a certificate signed by her father's friend from Guelderland explaining how the relic had been rediscovered and by what characteristics it could be shown to be genuinely the heart of Montrose. Alexander Johnston recalls that the remaining fragments of the Venetian casket were also put into the urn, which was then set on a small ebony table in the drawing-room of the Johnstons' house in Madura.

But Lady Hester Johnston's preoccupation with the relic had become the subject of much gossip among the local Indians, who came to believe that the silver urn contained a great *pusaka* or powerful talisman which so protected its owner that whoever possessed it would never be wounded or taken prisoner in battle. It was perhaps because of this report that the urn was stolen from the house and the family later heard a rumour that a tributary chief of the Nabob of Arcot had purchased it for an enormous sum.

Samuel Johnston was in the habit of sending his son to stay with some of the chiefs in the neighbourhood of Madura during the four months of the hunting season so that he could learn the language and the practice of Indian yoga exercises. It happened that, not long after the robbery, the young Alexander Johnston found himself in a hunting party with that same chief who was said to have obtained the heart of Montrose, and by good fortune was given an opportunity to distinguish himself. Johnston's own account of the incident states rather modestly that during the hunt his horse was attacked by a wild hog but he succeeded in wounding it with his pike so that the chief was able to kill it soon afterwards. However, it seems likely that he in fact saved the chief's life,[11] because immediately after the hunt the Indian nobleman asked him in front of the whole party in what way he could demonstrate his respect and regard. The young Johnston at once recounted all the circumstances of the heart and his mother's anxiety when it had been stolen and asked, if it was indeed within the chief's power, that it might yet be restored to her. The Indian admitted that he had bought the relic in ignorance of the fact that it had been stolen, and added that, as 'one brave man should always attend to the wishes of another brave man whatever his religion or nation might be', he would willingly return the heart of Montrose to its rightful guardian. The next day he stood by this promise and sent the young man home with six of his finest hunting dogs, two matchlocks, a gold dress and some shawls for Lady Johnston and the silver urn accompanied by a letter apologizing for having innocently been thus the cause of her distress.

This chief was probably Velli Murdoo who, together with his elder brother Cheena Murdoo and other members of his family, joined the men of Punjalumcoorchy and Catabomia Naig in the Poligar War against the Nabob of Arcot in 1801. Their rebellion was put down by a British detachment under Colonel Agnew and Major Colin Macaulay, and the Murdoo brothers were captured and hanged in chains. In 1807 Alexander Johnston revisited the ruined palace in the now desolate capital of Sherewele where the dead prince's surviving servants told him that when their master had been condemned to die, he had recalled the story of the Scottish hero and expressed the hope that some of his own friends or kindred might also think to preserve and revere his heart in a similar manner.

In 1792 Samuel Johnston and his wife returned to Europe and chanced to be in France when the revolutionary government there decreed that all gold or silver plate and ornaments were to be surrendered to the authorities to finance the war effort. The Johnstons thus lost all their valuables (for which their son received reparation some twenty-five years later), but in an attempt to preserve the silver urn and its contents, they entrusted it to an Englishwoman living in Boulogne called Mrs Knowles, who promised to hide it until such time as it could be sent safely to England. Unfortunately, shortly afterwards Mrs Knowles suddenly died, and although Lady Johnston and her son made every possible effort to trace the urn the heart of Montrose was never recovered.

On the 4 January 1661, the Restoration Parliament in Scotland formally resolved that the body of Montrose should be redeemed from the Burgh-Moor and its several limbs recovered from the towns which had displayed them. In recognition of his service to the Royalist cause Charles II also ordered that he should be given a state funeral at the Crown's expense to be attended by the Lord High Commissioner, the northern baronage and all the members of the Scottish Parliament. In a solemn pageant, led by Montrose's heir, with others of the Grahams, 'the whole nobility and gentry, with Provost, Bailies and Council', the body was recovered from the 'Burgh Muir' (together with that of Francis Hay of Dalgetty which lay beside it) and the head retrieved from the steel prick above the tolbooth where it had weathered the intervening years. A special scaffold was mounted by the young Lord Napier and the chiefs of the Grahams–Morphie, Inchbrakie (Old Black Pate), Orchill and Gorthie–with certain other 'noble gentlemen'. 'With sound of trumpet, discharge of many cannon from the castle, and the honest people's loud and joyful acclamation' Mungo Graham of Gorthie took down the head of Montrose, kissed it and placed upon it the coronet of a marquis. The various limbs were also recovered, and the remains thus reunited with the trunk conveyed to Holyrood House to lie in state until the funeral.[12] (For Mungo Graham it was almost his last act, for he died the same night.) This was set for Saturday, 11 May 1661, when the remains of Montrose and Sir William Hay of Dalgetty were carried in solemn procession from the chapel at Holyrood House to the Great Church of Edinburgh. Ironically, the General Assembly was in session, somewhat crestfallen, though its members would not attend the funeral of the two Royalists lest, in Sydserf's phrase, 'the bones of both should bleed'. But from all accounts the rest of Edinburgh was there, and the people who had once called him bloody murderer and excommunicate now packed the streets to render a belated homage to one of the greatest soldiers of their age. Above them in the castle, Argyll lay under sentence of death, enduring till the moment when his own skull would decorate the tolbooth spike for another grisly symbol of justice and revenge.

The day began overcast and stormy, but as the cortège left the abbey church the sun broke through and the procession continued under a square of blue until, strangely, after all was over it came on to rain again. From the West Port of the city, from Leith, Leith Wynd and Cannongate, first marched twenty-six companies of foot in the livery of the city Trained Bands, and from the Abbey Close itself to the Mercat Cross they lined the route with swords drawn. While the bells of Edinburgh and the Cannongate pealed incessantly, the great Common Bell tolling over them all, and the guns of the castle thundered their salute, the slow procession made its way towards St Giles in the High Town and the solemn pageant was begun.

From the Abbey Gate to the Luckenbooths, people crowded on the stairs, the balconies, at the windows and on the roofs to watch the body of the Marquis carried by. There may yet have been a few old Royalists among them who wondered at the strange reunion with his late opponents Eglinton and Callendar, peered perhaps at Home, or Marischal that once held Dunnottar against the King's Lieutenant, and looked askance at Roxburgh and Tweeddale (the latter in Dalgetty's) cortège) who ten years earlier had cast their votes for Montrose's death and mutilation. But he had left his love and charity to them all.

Slowly, to the muffled beat of the funeral drums, the party approached the High Kirk. Before the great doors they paused, and as the Trained Bands drawn up around the Mercat Cross fired their final volleys to salute the honoured dead, the body of Montrose was carried into St Giles and laid in the grave beside his grandfather, who also had once been Viceroy of Scotland. The service was read, the last respects were paid, and the mourners turned away. Outside it began to rain.

No stone or inscription was placed upon the spot, although it is said that a suitable epitaph was intended.[13] Some crude attempts at verse have survived, and at some time his name was incised into one of the pillars in the cathedral, but the present marble effigy dates from the nineteenth century when the notice of Queen Victoria and the respect of a later generation caused a more fitting memorial to be erected. In 1879, when restoration was in progress, a search was made for his remains, but they were never found–although perhaps this was not altogether surprising since the aisle that once formed the tomb of Montrose is said to have been used as a coal cellar during the previous restoration work of 1829.[14]

In his official account of the 'True Funerals', published in the *Mercurius Caledonius*,[15] Montrose's old adherent, Thomas Sydserf, concluded by recording that 'The solemnities being ended, the Lord Commissioner with the nobility and barons, had a most sumptuous supper and banquet at the Marquis of Montrose's house, with concerts of all sorts of music.' The Lord Commissioner who had been responsible for the pageant was that Earl of Middleton who had first fought under Montrose at the Bridge of Dee, and against him as Leslie's second-in-command at Philiphaugh; who in 1646 had reduced Montrose's castle of Kincardine to a heap of rubble and sent his remaining servants in front of a Covenant firing squad. With other soldiers of fortune he had turned his coat to serve under Hamilton, survived the destruction of the army at Uttoxeter, and latterly connived so successfully at the more extreme tenets of royalism that at the Restoration he was thus rewarded with the unique experience of presiding at once over the policy of revenge upon his previous associates, and over this splendid gesture to the memory of his erstwhile enemy and predecessor. (He would later acquire the lands of Old Montrose.) In the retrospect, this appointment of a common adventurer to be Viceroy of Scotland, responsible alike for the distribution of present justice and posthumous honour, may perhaps seem unlikely or even tragic, but the character and fortune of Middleton were not exceptional in his time. Sir Walter Scott, whose descriptions were sometimes scathing and often to the point, would later write of him:

> He was a good soldier, but in other respects a man of inferior talents, who had lived the life of an adventurer, and who, in enjoying the height of fortune which he had attained, was determined to indulge without control all his favourite propensities. These were, unhappily, of a coarse and scandalous nature. The Covenanters had assumed an exterior of strict demeanour and precise morality, and the Cavaliers, in order to show themselves the opposite in every respect, gave in to the most excessive indulgences in wine and revelry, and conceived that in doing so they showed their loyalty to the King, and their contempt of what they termed the formal hypocrisy of his enemies. When the Scottish Parliament met, the members were, in many instances, under the influence of wine, and they were more than once obliged to adjourn, because the Royal Commissioner was too intoxicated to behave properly in the chair.[16]

Lauderdale, who next succeeded to the office of Lord Commissioner, although a man of much greater talent, was equally unscrupulous, and in his turn did not allow a previous zeal for the Covenant and all its works to obstruct his rise to political pre-eminence.

But Middleton's was not the only face to conjure up discordant memories. In April, while the ruins of the great Marquis still lay in state, there had been a general celebration to mark the restoration of the monarchy for which Montrose had fought so gallantly. The Lord Commissioner and his Lady had given 'a banquet, a concert, a bonfire, and a ball' at Holyrood House—a lavish affair at which their hopeful son Lord Clermont had to be physically restrained from acts of excessive immoderation—while in the upper city itself the Lord Provost and the magistrates conducted a no less extravagant revel. On the spot by the Mercat Cross, where the grim Maiden had spilled the blood of Montrose's friends until it ran down the gutters and into the shambles, a symbolic hogshead of claret was broken open so that streams of wine gushed from all the conduits.[17] Queen at this carousal was the immortalized Jenny Geddes who had survived her Covenanting principles and now, making a cheerful recantation, suffered them to burn her stool, 'she herself countenancing the action with a high-flown claret and vermilion majesty'.

For Montrose, the dream had been true while it and he had lasted, and a fragile gleam of honour faded also with their passing. But whatever the inspiration that had once sustained him, or the antique ideal for which he fought, in reality he was little kin to this 'rabble of the Restoration'. '*Vivit post proelia Magnus, sed fortuna perit*'—perhaps that cynic Rothes would have smiled.

Appendix

TWO POEMS BY MONTROSE

'I'LL NEVER LOVE THEE MORE'
Part First

My dear and only love, I pray
This noble world of thee
Be governed by no other sway
But purest monarchie.
For if confusion have a part,
Which vertuous souls abhore,
And hold a synod in thy heart,
I'll never love thee more.

Like Alexander I will reign,
And I will reign alone,
My thoughts shall evermore disdain
A rival on my throne.
He either fears his fate too much,
Or his deserts are small,
That puts it not unto the touch
To win or lose it all.

But I must rule and govern still,
And always give the law.
And have each subject at my will,
And all to stand in awe.
But, gainst my battery if I find
Thou shun'st the prize so sore,
As that thou set'st me up a blind,
I'll never love thee more.

If in the empire of thy heart,
Where I should solely be,
Another do pretend a part
And dares to vie with me;
Or if committees thou erect,
And goes on such a score,
I'll sing and laugh at thy neglect,
And never love thee more.

But if thou will be constant then,
And faithful of thy word.

I'll make thee glorious by my pen,
And famous by my sword.
I'll serve thee in such noble ways
Was never heard before;
I'll crown and deck thee all with
bays,
And love thee evermore.

Part Second

My dear and only love, take heed
Lest thou thyself expose,
And let all longing lovers feed
Upon such looks as those.
A marble wall then build about,
Beset without a door;
But if thou let thy heart fly out,
I'll never love thee more.

Let not their oaths, like volleys
shot,
Make any breach at all;
Nor smoothness of their language
plot
Which way to scale the wall;
Nor balls of wildfire love consume
The shrine which I adore;
For if such smoke about thee fume,
I'll never love thee more.

I think thy virtues be too strong
To suffer by surprise;
Those victual'd, by my love,
so long,
The siege at length must rise,
And leave thee rulèd in that health
And state thou was before:
But if thou turn a commonwealth,
I'll never love thee more.

395

Or if by fraud, or by consent,
Thy heart to ruin come,
I'll sound no trumpet as I wont,
Nor march by tuck of drum;
But hold my arms, like ensigns, up,
Thy falsehood to deplore,
And bitterly will sigh and weep,
And never love thee more.

I'll do with thee as Nero did
When Rome was set on fire,
Not only all relief forbid,
But to a hill retire,
And scorn to shed a tear to see
Thy spirit grown so poor;
But smiling sing, until I die,
I'll never love thee more.

Yet, for the love I bare thee once,
Lest that thy name should die,
A monument of marble-stone
The truth shall testifie;
That every pilgrim passing by
May pity and deplore
My case, and read the reason why
I can love thee no more.

The golden laws of love shall be
Upon this pillar hung,—
A simple heart, a single eye,
A true and constant tongue.
Let no man for more love pretend
Than he has hearts in store;
True love begun shall never end:
Love one and love no more.

Then shall thy heart be set by mine,
But in far different case;
For mine was true, so was not thine,
But look't like Janus' face.
For as the waves with every wind,
So sails thou every shore,
And leaves my constant heart
      behind,—
How can I love thee more?

My heart shall with the sun be fix'd
For constancy most strange,

And thine shall with the moon be
      mix'd,
Delighting aye in change.
Thy beauty shin'd at first most
      bright,
And woe is me therefore,
That ever I found thy love so light
I could love thee no more.

The misty mountains, smoking
      lakes,
The rocks' resounding echo,
The whistling wind that murmur
      makes,
Shall with me sing hey ho!
The tossing seas, the tumbling boats,
Tears dropping from each shore,
Shall tune with me their turtle
      notes,
I'll never love thee more.

As doth the turtle, chaste and true,
Her fellow's death regrete,
And daily mourns for his adieu,
And ne'er renews her mate;
So, though thy faith was never fast,
Which grieves me wond'rous sore,
Yet I shall live in love so chast,
That I shall love no more.

And when all gallants ride about
These monuments to view,
Whereon is written, in and out,
Thou trait'rous and untrue;
Then in a passion they shall pause
And thus say, sighing sore,
Alas! he had too just a cause
Never to love thee more.

And when that tracing goddess,
      Fame,
From east to west shall flee,
She shall record it, to thy shame,
How thou hast lovèd me;
And how in odds our love was such
As few have been before;
Thou loved too many, and I too
      much,
So I can love no more.

ON FALSE FRIENDS

*Unhappy is the man, in whose
    breast is confined
The sorrows and distresses all of an
    afflicted mind;
The extremity is great—he dies if
    he conceal—
The world's so void of secret
    friends—betrayed if he reveal.
Then break, afflicted heart, and
    live not in these days,
When all prove merchants of their
    faith none trusts what other says.
For when the sun doth shine, then
    shadows do appear,
But when the sun doth hide his face
    they with the sun reteir;
Some friends as shadows are, and
    fortune as the sun—
They never proffer any help till
    fortune hath begun;
But if in any case fortune shall
    first decay,
Then they, as shadows of the sun,
    with fortune pass away.*

Footnotes

CHAPTER 1

1 *Montrose Redivivus*: Saintserf's description of Montrose.
2 Wishart (*Deeds of Montrose* [Numerous translations have been made of Wishart's original biography in Latin which have been published under various titles. All references here are to the 1893 edition, edited by Murdoch and Simpson.]) also traces Montrose's line back to this original 'Graym', having presumably read Buchanan and Fordun. For a more detailed analysis of Graham ancestry see I. G. Graeme, *Or and Sable : A book of the Graemes and Grahams*, xvii–xlii.
3 Eighth in line from William de Grame.
4 Fourteenth in line.
5 Seventh in line.
6 His age may be computed from Jameson's portrait (q.v.) and subsequent statements by Wishart. In October 1632, he signed a number of legal documents, which suggests that in that month he entered his twenty-first year and, as was fairly common practice at that time, began to exercise the rights of a major.
7 Napier, *Memorials*, I, p. 140 (vi) (found by Mark Napier among the Southesk Papers).
8 St Salvator's had been founded by one of his ancestors.
9 'A Historical, political, allegorical romance' which was translated from Barclay's original Latin by order of Charles I in 1628.
10 Napier, *Memorials*, I, p. 158. From Mr. John Lambye's 'Comtes' (Southesk Papers): Item, 12 May 1628.
11 For their ancestry see Fraser, *History of the Carnegies, Earls of Southesk and their Kindred*.
12 See chapter 2.
13 In 1626 Carnegie bought Farnell from the Earl of Airlie, and it has remained the property of the Earls of Southesk ever since.
14 See Wilson, *The House of Airlie*, I, pp. 12–14.
15 Strangely, the matter was never referred to by contemporary writers nor did the Covenanters later try to use the scandal against Montrose.
16 The Hamilton biographer, *Lives of the Dukes of Hamilton*.
17 These early books belonging to Montrose were rediscovered by Mark Napier at Innerpeffray. See Napier, *Memoirs of Dundee*, I, Introduction.
18 Buchan, *Montrose*, p. 42.
19 *Life of Laud,* and *Commentary on L'Estrange.*

CHAPTER 2

1 Edward Walford in the Whitehall Debates of 1648.
2 Smout, *History of the Scottish People*.
3 Donaldson, *Scotland : Church and Nation through the Sixteenth Century*.
4 Mathew, *Scotland under Charles I*.
5 Wilson, *James VI and I*.
6 At Dunfermline, on 19 November 1600.
7 Barker, *Religion and Politics 1559–1642*.
8 Hume, *The History of Great Britain : The Reigns of James I and Charles I*, p. 331.
9 Rochets and white sleeves. White vestments were considered by the Presbyterians to be pagan in origin from the white robes worn by the Priests of Isis.

10 Lang, *History of Scotland*, III, p. 26.
11 Mathew, *Scotland under Charles I*.
12 Clarendon, Nicholas and Echard mention the places where the plotters met.
13 Spalding, *History of the Troubles*, pp. 45–6.
14 ibid. pp. 46–7.

CHAPTER 3

1 Spalding, *History of the Troubles*, I, p. 46.
2 e.g. 'A Dispute against the English Popish Ceremonies obtruded upon the Kirk of Scotland'. Many of these pamphlets had been printed in England (Baillie, *Letters and Journals*, I, p. 23).
3 Baillie, *Letters and Journals*, I, p. 17.
4 Guthry, *Memoirs*, p. 20.
5 Elspa Craig is said to have been a relative of Wariston.
6 Baillie, *Letters and Journals*, p. 23.
7 ibid., p. 32.
8 Wariston, *Diary*, I, p. 271.
9 Napier, *Memoirs*, I, p. 136; Guthry, *Memoirs*, p. 24.
10 See chapter 7.
11 He was writing retrospectively in 1642.
12 Burnet, *History of His Own Times*, 15.
13 Clarendon, *History*, I, p. 278.
14 Napier, *Memorials*, I, p. 70.
15 See chapter 2; Napier, *Memorials*, I, p. 73.
16 Guthry, *Memoirs*, p. 27.
17 Hope ruled that a supplicant party might meet and choose commissioners 'for any public business'.
18 So-called after boards, or tables, of green cloth.
19 A contemporary wit had coined an anagram on his name: 'Ho what an affronted liar!'
20 Gordon of Rothiemay, *Scots Affairs*, I, p. 33.
21 Cook, *History of the Church of Scotland*, II.
22 Buchan, *Montrose*, p. 74.
23 Baillie, *Letters and Journals*, I, pp. 67–8.
24 On learning of the Covenant, Spottiswoode exclaimed: 'All that we have done these thirty years past is thrown down at once'.
25 Morris, *Montrose*, p. 35.
26 Gordon of Rothiemay, *Scots Affairs*, I, p. 45.
27 Burnet, *Lives of the Dukes of Hamilton*, pp. 55–6.
28 ibid., p. 57.
29 On Traquair's advice, the King had sent a ship laden with munitions to Leith. The stores were intended for Edinburgh Castle, but the Covenanters would not allow them through, and there was talk of seizing the vessel. To prevent this, Traquair had the ship unloaded and the gunpowder, stores, etc. taken by cart to the palace of Dalkeith. All this happened in the week before Hamilton was due to arrive.
30 Baillie, *Letters and Journals*, I, p. 84.
31 Guthry, *Memoirs*, p. 35.
32 Baillie, *Letters and Journals*, I, p. 99.
33 Spalding, *History of the Troubles*, p. 57.
34 See chapter 23.
35 Gordon of Rothiemay, *Scots Affairs*, p. 151; see also Baillie, *Letters and Journals*, I, p. 132.
36 Hardwicke Papers.

CHAPTER 4

1 Baillie, *Letters and Journals*, I, p. 144.
2 Gordon of Ruthven, *Britane's Distemper*, pp. 56–7.
3 Burnet, *History of his Own Time*.

4   See Wilcock, *The Great Marquess*, p. 11, for an analysis of the evidence suggesting that this was the true year of his birth.
5   Mathew, *Scotland Under Charles I*, pp. 225 ff.
6   Montereul, *Correspondence*, II, p. 556. Argyll could not speak French.
7   'Children', or the 'Seed of Diarmid'.
8   Mathew, *Scotland Under Charles I*, p. 226.
9   Clarendon, *History*, II, p. 55.
10 See chapter 2.
11 Gordon of Rothiemay, *Scots Affairs*, I, p. 192.
12 Baillie, *Letters and Journals*, I, p. 146.
13 ibid., I, p. 153.
14 Charles I, *The Large Declaration*.
15 Buchan, *Montrose*, p. 87.
16 Gordon of Rothiemay, *Scots Affairs*, II, p. 165.
17 ibid., II, pp. 171–2; Guthry, *Memoirs*, p. 41; Baillie, *Letters and Journals*, I, p. 485.

CHAPTER 5

1   Spalding, *History of the Troubles*, I, p. 870.
2   Baillie, *Letters and Journals*, I, p. 213.
3   Pinkie, 1547.
4   Essex, the parliamentary general of the Civil War, held only a subordinate command.
5   Gordon of Rothiemay, *Scots Affairs*, II, p. 218 n.
6   i.e. raising of troops and money for war.
7   Which contained an unqualified abjuration of episcopacy as unlawful.
8   The *Paris Gazette*, imperfectly informed, carried an article entitled 'The siege and taking of the great town of Turriff by the Marquis of Huntly'.
9   Father of Gordon of Rothiemay.
10 Spalding, *History of the Troubles*, I, p. 104.
11 Montrose's banner carried the motto: 'FOR RELIGION, COVENANT, AND THE COUNTRY'. Marischal and Kinghorn each had personal banners and the town of Dundee, whose levies were engaged, had two.
12 Montrose got the idea from the Royalists, who wore flesh-coloured scarves around their 'craigs' (necks).
13 They are said to have had high words at first and then, on Straloch offering to mediate, calmed down.
14 Gordon of Rothiemay, *Scots Affairs*, II, p. 233.
15 Spalding, *History of the Troubles*, I, pp. 119–22.
16 Gordon of Rothiemay, *Scots Affairs*, II, p. 238.
17 ibid., II, p. 235.
18 Spalding, *History of the Troubles*, p. 47.
19 During Montrose's absence in the North, Napier, supported by the Privy Council including Sir Thomas Hope, had advocated sending an embassy to the King to negotiate. But Rothes and Loudon, who probably had Argyll behind them, squashed the idea since from their spies at court they were aware of the true weakness of Charles's position.
20 '. . . with playing of the ordnance at every toast' (a Danish custom).
21 Gordon of Rothiemay, *Scots Affairs*, II, p. 264.
22 A soldier of fortune whose career was to be strangely tangled with that of Montrose. He was one day to become Viceroy of Scotland, and then later Governor of Tangiers.
23 Baillie, *Letters and Journals*.

CHAPTER 6

1   The Scots were to disband within forty-eight hours; the King, after the royal castles had been restored to him.
2   Hardwicke Papers, 141–2.
3   Montrose's *Remonstrance*; see chapter 17.
4   Wariston described Montrose's action as 'noble'.

5   Original: Hamilton Charter Chest; Napier, *Memorials*, II, p. 102.
6   Wariston to Hepburn of Humbie (20 April 1641).
7   Gordon of Rothiemay, *Scots Affairs*, III, p. 182.
8   Spalding, *History of the Troubles*, I, p. 236.
9   Napier, *Memoirs*, II, p. 477.
10 The details of the narrative are drawn from Montrose's defence at his trial in 1641.
11 Napier, *Memorials*, I, p. 254, from a copy found by Mark Napier among Balfour's MSS.
12 A practice favoured by the Covenanters since it had Biblical precedent and resolved difficult problems of precedence among the nobility.
13 Baillie, *Letters and Journals*, I, p. 264.
14 *Dictionary of National Biography*.
15 Baillie, *Letters and Journals*, I, p. 262.
16 e.g., in January 1641, when riding from Chester to Newcastle, he spoke to General Leslie and Colonel Cochrane. Cochrane later testified that he had been acutely embarrassed by the conversation in front of the General and had asked Montrose to change the subject.

CHAPTER 7

1   Now the National Library of Scotland.
2   Napier Charter Chest; Napier, *Memorials*, II, p. 54.
3   ibid., I, p. 286.
4   ibid., II, p. 43.
5   Clarendon's description.
6   The narrative of the Plot and relevant quotations are drawn from the Proceedings of Montrose's 'Trial' in 1641 and the depositions of Montrose, Napier, Keir, Blackhall, John Graham, Robert Murray, Lindsay of the Byres, Colonel Cochrane, Walter Stewart, Stewart of Ladywell, Lord Ogilvie and others. These may be found in the Wodrow MSS, Traquair Papers, Napier Charter Chest and Napier, *Memorials*, I, pp. 264–368.
7   Montrose Charter Chest.
8   He concluded his defence with a couplet from Ovid (*Tristia*, II, 9): *Hoc pretium vitae vigilatorumque laborum cepimus ingenio est poena reperta meo.*
9   Gardiner, *History*, IX, p. 411.
10 Townsend, *Life and Letters of Endymion Porter*, p. 192.

CHAPTER 8

1   See Appendix I: Montrose's Poetry.
2   Napier, *Memorials*, II, p. 56.
3   ibid., II, p. 70.
4   At York an incident occurred which led Montrose to express this contempt in a short verse. Hamilton was disturbed by two dogs which were fighting in the garden and in a fit of temper killed one of them, belonging to the Marquis of Newcastle. Montrose composed a sarcastic epitaph for the animal:
> 'Here lies a dog whose quality did plead
> Such fatal end from a renowned blade;
> And blame him not that he succumbed now
> E'en Hercules could not combat against two;
> For whilst he on his foe revenge did take
> He manfully was killed behind his back
> Then say to eternize the cur that's gone
> He fleshed the maiden sword of Hamilton!'

(The poem is preserved among Sir James Balfour's MSS in the National Library of Scotland).
5   Napier, *Memorials*, II, p. 77.
6   Wishart, *Deeds of Montrose*, 37.
7   Appointing Carnwath lieutenant of Clydesdale.

8 Sinclair had been responsible for searching Montrose's houses and charter chest during the process of 1641.
9 A full account of the siege of Morpeth is given in Lord Somerville, *Memorie of the Somervilles*, pp. 306–31.
10 Napier, *Memorials*, II, p. 138.

CHAPTER 9

1 Blakhal, *Brieffe Narration.*
2 MS copy (Advocates' Library, Edinburgh); given also in Wilson, *The House of Airlie*, II, p. 28 f.; Napier, *Memoirs*, II, pp. 406 f.
3 Accounts of the action are given in Rushworth's *Collections*, V, p. 745; Fairfax's letter to Leven (15 August 1644); Napier, *Memoirs*, II, pp. 405 f.
4 The eldest son, Lord Gordon, was still on the Covenant side.
5 Wishart, *Deeds of Montrose*, p. 51.
6 Wishart, *Deeds of Montrose*, p. 51.
7 *Wigton Papers*, p. 80–1.
8 Gordon of Ruthven, *Britane's Distemper*, p. 48.
9 Provost Leslie, Robert Farquhar, Alexander Jaffray and his brother John Jaffray (Spalding, *History of the Troubles*, II, p. 196).
10 William Moir.
11 Spalding, *History of the Troubles*, II, p. 205.
12 ibid., p. 211.
13 But some accounts say that he was killed by a highlander.
14 Clarendon's description.
15 Alaster MacColkeitach Vic Gillespie (*The Black Book of Clanranald*).
16 Alaster MacColla fear tholla nan Tighean.
17 Alastair's father, Coll Kietache MacGillespick MacDonald of Colonsay, was the grandson of Coll, a brother of James MacDonald of Dunyveg and the Glens, and the celebrated Sorley Buy MacDonald who was father of the first Earl of Antrim.
18 Sir James Turner.
19 The story is given in Grant, *Memoirs of Montrose*, p. 168.
20 In a letter to Nicholas dated 22 July (Carte, *Ormonde Papers*, VI, p. 178), Ormonde put the figure at 2,500, but from Antrim's own letter to Ormonde of 27 June, it appears that only 1,600 actually sailed with Alastair.
21 *The Black Book of Clanranald.*
22 Gordon, *Britane's Distemper*, pp. 71–2.
23 Forbes-Leith, *Memoirs of Scottish Catholics during the seventeenth and eighteenth centuries*, I, p. 291.
24 The Laird of Lude, a minor, was Inchbrakie's nephew. The Tutor of Struan was Black Pate's brother-in-law.
25 Napier, *Memoirs*, II, p. 420.
26 Napier Charter Chest; also given in Napier, *Memorials*, II, p. 146.
27 *'Blood for blood and murther avenged'* by T.M., Esq., Bk 7, 1661, p. 323. (British Museum has the only copy in the U.K.) T.M.'s essay is the only known source for this letter. It is undated, but from the context would seem to fit in at this point.

CHAPTER 10

1 In 1645 Alexander Menzies of Weem petitioned Argyll for compensation and was granted Scots £10,000. (*Acts of the Parliaments of Scotland*: VI, Pt 1, pp. 387, 791.)
2 He had married the Lady Beatrix Graham.
3 Wishart, *Deeds of Montrose*, p. 57.
4 Eldest son of Sir John Wemyss of that ilk whom Charles had made an earl in 1633.
5 Different authorities give different figures for the size of the Covenant army:
    Wishart 6,000 foot and 700 horse.
    Spalding 6,000 foot and 800 horse.
    P. Gordon 6,000 foot and 1,000 horse.
    A True Relation (pamphlet) 6,000 foot and 1,000 horse.
    Irish officer (*Ormonde Papers*) 8,000 foot and 800 horse.

6   The seventeenth-century version of the square. For a discussion on tactics and equipment of the period, see:
     Elton, *The Complete Body of the Art Military*;
     Terry, *Papers relating to the Army of the Covenant*;
     Spalding, *History of the Troubles*, I, p. 154;
     Rogers, *Battles and Generals of the Civil War*;
     Lord Somerville, *Memorie of the Somervilles*, II, p. 307.
7   Baillie's description of Montrose's army.
8   *A True Relation of the Happy Success of His Majesty's Army in Scotland under the conduct of Lord James, Marquis of Montrose, His Excellence against the rebels there*.
9   A custom known as 'The Oracle of the Hide'. It was part of Highland superstition that the fate of a battle could be anticipated by observing which side drew the first blood on the day. See Sir Walter Scott, *The Lady of the Lake*, footnotes XLIV and XLVIII.
10 Napier, *Memoirs*, II, p. 423.
11 Grant, *Memoirs of James, Marquis of Montrose*, refers to a portrait of Montrose at some time in the possession of M. Vachee (*Marchand de Curiosités*) in Paris, which had once belonged to Lord Nairn, (whose ancestor had married the daughter of Patrick Graham of Inchbrakie) and had been discovered after his death in the attic of his house in St Germain. Montrose is said to have been depicted leaning on an ancient claymore, in a high-plumed bonnet, slashed doublet, trews, plaid, brogues, powder horn, dirk and pistols.
12 Report of an eye-witness quoted in *Gentleman's Magazine*, XVI, p. 153.
13 Wishart, *Deeds of Montrose*, p. 60.
14 *A True Relation* . . .
15 Later allegations as to Drummond's treachery cannot be fully substantiated. The younger brother was fighting with Montrose, and his own heart was probably not in the Covenant cause. However, it is unlikely that he *deliberately* created the confusion or collaborated previously with Montrose. Nor did he join Montrose in person until after Kilsyth.
16 'News from His Majesty's Army in Scotland . . . to the Lord Lieutenant in Ireland: written at Inverlochy by an Irish officer in Alexander Macdonnel's forces' (*Ormonde Papers*).
17 Deposition of Mr John Robertson 'Reasons for the Surrender of Perth' (Wodrow MS., Advocates' Library).
18 Spalding gave Covenant casualties at 1,300–1,500 dead and 800 prisoner; Wishart, 2,000 dead and 'a large number captured'; Patrick Gordon, 2,000 dead and 1,000 prisoners; *A True Relation* . . . 1,500 dead and 2,000 prisoner.

CHAPTER 11

1   Wodrow Collection, National Library of Scotland: 'Copie of a paper given in by Mr John Robertson and Mr Geo Halybirtoun, Ministers at Perth', quoted also in Napier, *Montrose and the Covenanters*, II, p. 306.
2   *Old Stat. Acct. Scotland.*
3   Deposition of Patrick Maxwell.
4   Deposition of Robert Arnott.
5   In 1621 floods had swept the old bridge away and no other had yet been built in its place. At this time the Tay was crossed by ferry boats plying between the city and the Hill of Kinnoul.
6   *A True Relation of the Happy Success of His Majesty's forces in Scotland under the conduct of the Lord James Marquis of Montrose His Excellence, against the rebels there*, p. 9.
7   Guthry, *Memoirs*, p. 166.
8   Baillie, *Letters and Journals*, II, p. 233; letter to his cousin William Spang of 25 October 1644.
9   *Act Parlt Scot.* VI, pt i, p. 359: the original record of Acts and Proceedings of the rescinded Parliaments from 1640 to 1651 were discovered (5 vols.) in the State Paper Office, London, during the last century (cf. Evidence of Thomas Thomson, Esq. in the *Report of the Record Commission* 1936).

Footnotes

10 Gardiner, *History of the Great Civil War*, II, p. 142.

11 Wishart, *Deeds of Montrose*, p. 65.

12 Baillie, *Letters and Journals*, II, p. 225: letter of 13 September 1644.

13 Wodrow Collection, National Library of Scotland: 'Copy of the Paper given in by Mr John Robertson and Mr Geo Halybirtoun, Ministers at Perth'.

14 Extracts from the Register of the Presbytery of Perth as transcribed by the Rev. James Scott, MS National Library of Scotland; Napier, *Memorials*, II, pp. 312 ff.

15 Montrose Charter Chest; Napier, *Memorials*, II, pp. 163–4. (£20,000 (Scots) was the equivalent of £1,666 13s. 4d.)

16 Breadalbane MSS., cf. items 853–60 incl.

17 Baillie, *Letters and Journals*, II, p. 233: letter to Spang of 25 October 1644.

18 Huntly's third son, and later the third Marquis. In 1641 he had absconded to Holland with his father's jewels, and in 1644 was recorded as having been in Edinburgh under the care of Lady Haddington and in alliance with Argyll, his uncle. Shortly after this he married the Laird of Grant's daughter.

19 A number of writers have taken Spalding's phrase 'about 400 Fyf men and other dispersd soldiouris' as meaning fugitives dispersed after Tippermuir. This is incorrect. After Tippermuir the survivors of Elcho's Fifeshire levies escaped to Dundee or Fifeshire. The soldiers referred to by Spalding had been 'dispersed' on garrison duty by Argyll when the Gordon uprising was put down earlier in the year. See chapter 11.

20 Robert Arnot of Ferney, who had married the heiress of Burleigh. A supporter of Argyll, he was twice president of the Scottish Parliament, and also served on the Covenant commissions of war. He held the honorary rank of colonel of Fife Regiments, but had no previous military experience.

21 Montrose Charter Chest.

22 Fraser, *Old Deeside Road*, p. 75.

23 Baillie is the only authority who states that the Royalists met with resistance at the crossing. In his letter to Spang dated 25 October 1644 he wrote: 'The Bridge of Dee was manned, so he went over a hard dispute, where Elcho's regiment had a hot dispute and killed many of his men; but prevailing in number he forced the passage'. Baillie, *Letters and Journals*, II, p. 234.

24 This written instead of 'without prejudice of the first and latter Covenant', which has been scored out.

25 Instead of 'Your Lordship's faithful friends to serve you', which has been crossed out. Facsimiles of Montrose's summons and the magistrate's answer are printed in the 1851 (Spalding Club) edition of Spalding's *History of the Troubles*.

26 The area is now built over. The battle took place in the present Bridewell district of Aberdeen. Bon Accord Terrace lines the bluff roughly where Burleigh drew up his army.

27 Wishart gives Burleigh's strength as 2,000 foot and 500 horse: Guthry gives 2,500 as the number of foot; Gordon of Ruthven gives 3,000 foot and 600 horse.

28 This was essentially a defensive formation. As an attacking formation, the disaster on Rupert's right wing at Marston Moor (where the Prince's cavalry were thus marshalled by Hurry) had demonstrated its inadequacy for horsemen trained to charge at a gallop. Contrary to the claim that is sometimes made, Gustavus did not reintroduce shock tactics. His cavalry advanced together with musketeers firing volleys until the very last minute. It was Rupert who really revived the cavalry charge. In the Battle of Aberdeen, Montrose used Gustavus's method in taking up a defensive position. His later use of cavalry (at Auldearn and Alford) would show that he was also abreast of Rupert's new techniques.

29 The account that follows is drawn mainly from Gordon of Ruthven. However, certain discrepancies between the various sources are resolved on the basis of what later happened or what went before. Most authorities give Montrose's cavalry at 25–30 troopers on each wing, but Ogilvie had brought in 40 and Nat Gordon 30 more, so that with the gentry of Strathearn who did join the army he must in fact have had upwards of 80. Gordon states that Nat Gordon, James Hay and Mortimer commanded on the left wing, but Wishart and others put them on the right. In view of the fact

that it was their men who first noticed the Covenant flank attack on the Royalist left, Gordon's version is the more likely to be correct.

30 This was sometimes known as the 'interrupted charge' and was practised by Cromwell but never by Rupert. An illustration is given in *De Militia Equestris* by Hermannus Hugo (1630).

31 Gordon of Ruthven, *Britane's Distemper*, p. 82.

32 The passage continues: 'The Marquisse took special note of the fellowe's courage and had a particular care of him ever after'. (*A True Relation* . . .) Wishart also confirms that the man recovered and did subsequently become a trooper.

33 Sanderson, *Raigne of Charles I*.

34 *A True Relation* . . . gives the number killed as 4: *The Irish Despatch* (Carte) also gives 4: Gordon of Ruthven gives 7.

35 Spalding, *History of the Troubles*, p. 161.

36 Jaffray, *Diary*, p. 50.

37 Baillie, *Letters and Journals*, II, p. 265.

38 Original depositions in Montrose Charter Chest.

39 'News from His Majesty's Army in Scotland to be presented to the most Honourable the Lord Lieutenant-General of Ireland': written at Inverlochy in Lochaber, 7 February 1645 by an Irish officer in Alexander Macdonnel's forces (Carte, *Ormonde Papers*).

40 Frank, *Northern Memoirs*, p. 226.

41 Gardiner, *History of the Great Civil War*, CIII, p. 372.

42 Wishart, *Deeds of Montrose*, p. 70.

43 ibid.

44 Gordon of Ruthven, *Britane's Distemper*, p. 85.

45 Monteth, *A History of the Troubles of Great Britain*, p. 176.

46 According to Wishart, *Deeds of Montrose* (p. 72), the Covenanting authorities 'ordained a day of public thanksgiving for this deliverance', but there does not appear to be any corroborative evidence for this.

47 Baillie, *Letters and Journals*; letter to Spang of 25 October 1644.

48 *A True Relation* . . .

49 Wishart gives 1,500 foot but, as Buchan remarked in his biography, he would appear to have forgotten the force that Alastair took to Argyllshire.

50 'Which before he had not done in this country': Spalding, *History of the Troubles*, II, p. 278.

51 *A True Relation* . . .

52 Near Conchie, the ditches of the Royalist camp came to be known as 'Montrose's Dyke'.

53 Details of Royalist depredations in Angus and Aberdeen are taken from Spalding, Gordon of Ruthven, *A True Relation* . . . and the original depositions of Forrett and Forbes of Craigievar.

54 Wishart, *Deeds of Montrose*, p. 73.

55 Grant, *Memoirs of Montrose*, p. 200.

56 Wishart, *Deeds of Montrose*, p. 73.

57 'Matula': the cause of some amusement among Montrose's men, one of whom is reported to have exclaimed as he fired his musket: 'Sure as a gun, I have broken another traitor's face with the pot!'.

58 Wishart states that the counter-attack was led by O'Cahan, while Patrick Gordon attributes it to Farquharson.

59 There is some question as to how long the fighting at Fyvie actually lasted. Patrick Gordon gives one day; Wishart says several days. Buchan, in his reconstruction, favours the former account, partly because 'Montrose could not afford to make too long a business out of it'. However, with his deficiency in cavalry it is unlikely that Montrose would have been prepared to break cover. Argyll's withdrawal to a point four to six miles away must rather have been the decisive factor in prompting him to slip away during the night. If Argyll left Aberdeen on 26 October, he is unlikely to have located Montrose at Fyvie before the twenty-seventh, and so the fight probably began on the twenty-eighth. Montrose left Fyvie on 30 October (Spalding), and so

this reconstruction of the fight assumes it to have lasted two days. The Irish officer who wrote the Inverlochy despatch (see 39 above), though not present himself (he went with Alastair to Mingany), states that the fight took place on 28 October.

60 Gordon of Ruthven, *Britane's Distemper*, p. 92.
61 ibid.
62 MS 'History of the Gordons', National Library of Scotland.
63 T.M., Esq. *'Blood for Blood and Murther Avenged'*, Bk 7, p. 325. The letter is given without any date and does not appear to have been printed in any other collection. There does not seem to be any record of the original. (See also chapter 11, note 40.)
64 Guthry, *Memoirs*, p. 172.

CHAPTER 12

1 Translated for Mark Napier by James Robertson, a lineal descendant of the Tutor of Struan.
2 Skene, *History of the Highland Clans*, II, and Philips, *The Grameid*.
3 ibid.
4 For the account of this council, see Patrick Gordon of Ruthven, *Britane's Distemper*, pp. 94 ff.
5 *The Book of the Clanranald*.
6 Forbes-Leith, *Memoirs of Scottish Catholics*, I, p. 308.
7 Gordon of Ruthven's description in *Britane's Distemper* (p. 96) is not recognizable as being Loch Dochart.
8 Their original name is given by Gordon of Ruthven as 'M'Enabotes', their having descended from an abbot.
9 *The Book of the Clanranald*; Guthry in his *Memoirs* maintained that no one was killed which is extremely unlikely. However it is true to say that the highlanders were more keen on plunder, victuals and cattle than on killing. Wishart (p. 81) states that Campbells bearing arms were put to the sword.
10 Wishart gives 28 January, but the date can be more accurately computed from Argyll's letter to the Estates of 18 January (Balfour, *Annals*, III, p. 256), in which he states that 'The rebells' had fled into Lochaber.
11 Father MacBreck's account. Forbes-Leith, *Memoirs of Scottish Catholics*, I, p. 323. *The Book of the Clanranald*, strangely, does not mention it.
12 Forbes-Leith, *Memoirs of Scottish Catholics*, I, pp. 308–19; Father MacBreck's account.
13 Now Fort Augustus.
14 Wishart, *Deeds of Montrose*, p. 85.
15 The Band is printed in Napier, *Memorials*, II, p. 172: the original is in Montrose Charter Chest.
16 Baillie, *Letters and Journals*, II, p. 417 (Lt.-Gen. Baillie's Vindication for his own part, etc.).
17 ibid.
18 Balfour, *Annals*, III, p. 256. See note 10 above.
19 The old tradition that Montrose passed over the Pass of Corrieyarack, though once popular, was probably wrong since it would have taken him many needless miles eastwards on a longer climb than was necessary. It seems more likely that he would have kept along the ridge parallel to, but out of sight of, the main route through the Great Glen. Nor is it likely that, as recorded in some versions, he reached Inverlochy by way of Glen Nevis, since this would have meant another long circuit via Loch Trieg and Glen Trieg to the head of Glen Nevis, and it seems impossible that he could have accomplished this distance within the time. See Dr Cameron Miller, *Montrose in Lochaber 1645* and also Morland and Simpson's footnote to Wishart, *Deeds of Montrose*.
20 Gordon of Ruthven, *Britane's Distemper*, p. 100.
21 Monteth, *A History of the Troubles of Great Britain*, said that Argyll and his companions went on board the galley 'under pretence of going to order Ammunition' (p. 197).

22 The army faced north-west from the area now occupied by the aluminium works. The Campbell position was along the spine of ground in line with the present road.
23 Wishart, *Deeds of Montrose*, on the basis of statements made by prisoners after the battle.
24 The heather was the badge of Clan Donald; the gale (or bog-myrtle) of Clan Campbell.
25 *The Book of the Clanranald*.
26 Wishart, and Montrose in his dispatch, say 4 were killed. The Clanranald MS says 8, including Ogilvie, a Captain Brain and 6 soldiers. Monteth says 3 of these were killed 'inadvertently' by their own men.

CHAPTER 13

1 Guthry, *Memoirs*, p. 141.
2 Printed in Oxford by Henry Hall, printer to the University in 1645. The only known copy of this pamphlet is in the Bodleian Library.
3 ibid., John Wood to John Campbell, 14 March 1645.
4 ibid., 8 March 1645.
5 ibid., 13 March 1645.
6 Captured at Newcastle.
7 Captured in the North of England.
8 All three captured at Newcastle.
9 Letter intercepted by the Governor of Newark, 12 March 1645.
10 In Covenant documents he is no longer given his title and is usually referred to as James Graham or the Late Earl of Montrose. If captured, on the basis of this sentence he could (and would) be executed without further process.
11 Letter to Spang, 25 April 1645; Baillie, *Letters and Journals*, II, p. 258.
12 Who had aspired to the honours and titles of the captured Earl of Crawford.
13 The old Earl of Lauderdale had died during the first days of the January Parliament.
14 Letter intercepted by the Governor of Newark, 13 March 1645.
15 This was not a detailed order of worship, but rather a series of principles to be followed. When laying it before the General Assembly, Baillie begged that there might be no quarrelling over slight divergences in absolute uniformity.
16 Baillie, *Letters and Journals*, II, p. 254.
17 ibid., II, p. 111.
18 Terry, *Alexander Leslie*, p. 344.
19 Constitutional Documents of the Puritan Revolution, xlii.
20 Baillie, *Letters and Journals*, II, p. 258.
21 *Evelyn Papers*.
22 'I cannot but tell that even now I have received certain intelligence of a great defeat given to Argyll by Montrose, who upon surprise, totally routed these rebels, killing 1,500 upon the place'.
23 Baillie, *Letters and Journals*, II, p. 267.
24 ibid., II, p. 263.
25 *Fraser Papers*, p. 61.
26 Bellie Kirk has long ceased to exist but the churchyard and the tomb are still there.
27 He figured in the 'Incident' as Captain Hurry. His brother had been killed fighting for Parliament. Hurry was later described as 'a robust tall stately fellow with a long cut on his cheek'.
28 This was a scheme of Digby's which would be foiled by Cromwell. The King's letter has not survived, but Montrose's reply, which was intercepted by the Covenanters, does—see chapter 16.
29 Lord Lewis Gordon left the army for about three days on business for his father. Wishart wrongly accuses him of inducing the Gordons to desert at this time on the basis of letters, real or counterfeited, from Huntly. Spalding and Patrick Gordon, however, record his being with the army at Dunkeld and after, and an eye witness recalled that he distinguished himself in the fight at Dundee and during the retreat that followed: Gordon, *History of the Illustrious Family of Gordon*, II, p. 453. His defection possibly came later.

Footnotes

30 Since quarried away.
31 Baillie, *Letters and Journals*, II, p. 264.
32 ibid., p. 118 (General Baillie's Vindication).

CHAPTER 14

1 Aboyne and his sixteen companions, who included Robert, Earl of Nithsdale (called 'The Philosopher'), his son, Lord Herries, and Hay of Dalgetty, broke out of Carlisle on a wild night. Aboyne injured his shoulder when his horse fell into a deep ditch. They rode to Morpeth in Annandale but the town was in Covenant hands and the alarm was given, and so they were forced to ride another sixty miles to Crawford in Douglas where Aboyne had his shoulder tended to (the Marchioness of Douglas was Huntly's sister). They later crossed the Forth at Cardross and, narrowly escaping betrayal at Isle of Menteith, reached Montrose's camp near Loch Katrine.
2 Letter published in *Mercurius Aulicus* on 10 May 1645.
3 Spalding, *History of the Troubles*, II, p. 319.
4 Different accounts vary: Spalding–Hurry 4,000 foot, 500 horse against Montrose's 3,000 horse and foot; Gordon of Ruthven–Hurry 3,000 foot, 700 horse. Montrose estimated the enemy at 4,000–5,000 and his own force at about 1,400. Assuming that he had about 900 Irishes and as many Gordons, these with other odd bands would seem to give about 2,000 foot as a fair figure for Montrose. However, various detachments may have been sent out raiding and so did not reach Auldearn in time.
5 Contemporary accounts, while they agree on the general shape of the battle, differ enormously on points of detail. The Clanranald historian saw it as another clan battle against the Campbells (Lawers's). Gordon of Ruthven extols the virtues of his own clan. Such accounts were certain to be biased.
6 Nathaniel Gordon got on very well with the Irishes and MacDonalds by whom he was called Gordonach Caoch (*Book of Clanranald*).
7 And cannon, if he had any, which seems unlikely.
8 Now called Montrose's Hollow (Ordnance Survey).
9 Wishart, *Deeds of Montrose*.
10 ibid.
11 Young Rynie had been wounded on 5 May. His father, George Gordon of Rynie, had been taken prisoner by Forbes of Craigievar the previous week but was later exchanged.
12 There must have been some survivors, however, as the regiment is later mentioned as having been at Alford: *Acts Parlt Scotland*, VI, i, p. 469.
13 *History of the Family of Fraser*, p. 348. MS at the National Library of Scotland, V.7.29.
14 Montrose's letter to the garrison commander, Gordon of Buckie, dated 10 May 1645. This confirms the date of the battle as 9 May–sometimes erroneously given (Guthry, *Montrose Redivivus* and 1756 edition of Wishart's biography) as 4 May. Wishart's original Latin text gives 9 May.
15 Lord Somerville, *Memorie of the Somervilles*, II, p. 315. Lawers's regiment is described as one of the two 'stoutest regiments in the Scots army'.

CHAPTER 15

1 Gordon of Ruthven, *Britane's Distemper*, p. 134.
2 A Lord of Session and the Lord Advocate's eldest son.
3 Born 15 December 1626; Lord Napier's youngest daughter; unmarried.
4 Dated 3 June 1645. Original draft, Napier Charter Chest: Napier, *Memorials*, II, p. 212.
5 John, Earl of Kinghorn, Lord Lyon and Glamis.
6 Montrose's natural brother.
7 This is stated by Thomas Sydserf (a son of the Bishop of Galloway) in dedicating to the second Marquis of Montrose his translation of a French work entitled *Entertainments of the Course etc.* rendered into English by Thomas Sydserf, gent., London 1658.

8 Maidment, *Historical Fragments*. Buchan, however, draws attention to the fact that, in the disposition of Montrose's lands by the Committee of Estates to Sir William Graham of Claverhouse on 21 February 1648, provision is made for her life rent. But this may have been further confused by the additional fact that Sir William Graham of Claverhouse's wife was also called Magdalen Carnegie (a daughter of Lord Northesk).

9 The two quotations are from 'Melancolie' by Bernat de Ventadour, and 'Visraminiani' (twelfth-century Georgian epic).

10 Baillie, *Letters and Journals*, II, pp. 417–18 (General Baillie's Vindication).

11 Traces of the entrenched camp are still visible.

12 The castle had not been repaired since its destruction in 1571.

13 Baillie, *Letters and Journals*, II, p. 418.

14 Now the Bridge of Alford.

15 An auspicious day for the Catholics in Montrose's army, being the Feast of the Visitation of the Holy Mother of God.

16 James Farquharson, cousin-german to Donald, killed at Aberdeen.

17 Baillie estimated the enemy at 'a little above our strength in horsemen, and twice as strong in foot'. Probably Gardiner is right in regarding this as 'the exaggeration of a beaten man'.

18 One hundred of Balcarres's horse had been sent south with Lindsay.

19 Forbes-Leith, *Memoirs of Scottish Catholics*, II, p. 344.

20 *Stat. Acct.* of the parish of Alford. In about the mid-eighteenth century, 'some men in casting peats near the village dug up the body of a man on horseback and in complete armour who had been drowned either in the pursuit or flight from the engagement'.

21 Wishart, *Deeds of Montrose*, p. 111.

22 Gordon of Ruthven, *Britane's Distemper*, p. 135.

23 For information as to the fate of the Gordon Stone, I am indebted to the Secretary of State for Scotland and the Scottish Development Department, and am most grateful for their inquiries on my behalf. The stone is now somewhere under the rubbish tip at Alford, which came into use some years before any sort of planning permission was required. There was no inscription on the stone and it was not shown in the Ordnance Survey as 'the site of', etc. Consequently it was not listed when the parish was visited for this purpose a number of years ago. According to the Scottish Development Department, since the stone was unsculptured it would not have qualified for listing 'as it could not properly be regarded as a building'.

CHAPTER 16

1 The Jacobite, Sir John Sinclair of Longformacus, used to tell that he heard an old highlander who had fought at Kilsyth make this remark about seventy years after the battle when he himself was a very young man (see Chambers, II, ch. IV, footnote 21).

2 Bankes's MSS, cited by Gardiner, *History of the Great Civil War*, II, p. 344 n.

3 There was considerable rivalry between the various clans. Each camped independently and was responsible for finding its own forage etc.

4 Wishart is the only authority to record this incident (*Deeds of Montrose*, p. 117). Monteth repeats the story after him.

5 Wishart, *Deeds of Montrose*; Patrick Gordon of Ruthven gives Aboyne's contingent as 400 horse and 800 infantry but he was prone to exaggeration where the Gordons were concerned. Montrose had 100 horse already. Airlie brought 80 more. At Kilsyth he had about 500 horse all told. (Hope, the Lord Advocate, gives him as 3,500 foot and 600 horse—*Miscellany of the Scottish History Society*, SHS I, 128. Gordon was probably counting the mounted musketeers as cavalry, and on the generally accepted figures for Kilsyth, Wishart's estimate is probably the more accurate.

6 Wishart called them 'Minus bellicosi'.

7 Three regiments under the Lairds of Cammo, Ferny and Fordel Henderson.

8 It is interesting to note that the Irishes were careful to spare two houses in the area because they thought they were church property—one in Dollar, which they thought

belonged to the Abbey of Dunfermline, and the other in Muckart because they thought it pertained to the parish of Fossaway. This reverence for church property was also noticeable before: see Spalding, *History of the Troubles*, II, p. 300 when after Auldearn they 'plundered the Friary of Elgin but would not burn it being Church lands'. This would seem to speak for the influence of the Catholic priests who were with the army.

9   Belonging to the Earl of Stirling who was the King's secretary.

10   Belonging to Graham of Braco. Argyll later denied responsibility for their destruction at his trial.

11   According to Monteth, the Royalists caught an enemy scout who said that Baillie intended to pursue them all night to prevent them from crossing the Forth.

12   At the confluence of the Teith.

13   Then sometimes called Monaeburgh.

14   This version of what happened is based on General Baillie's Vindication (Baillie, *Letters and Journals*, II, pp. 420 ff.).

15   An auspicious day for the Catholics in the army, being the Festival of the Assumption of the Holy Mother of God.

16   *The Book of Clanranald.*

17   Compared by some writers to the position of Hougomont at Waterloo.

18   Wishart, *Deeds of Montrose*, p. 124.

19   It was recorded in the Statistical Account of the parish of Anstruther–'There are few old inhabitants of the parish who do not talk of some relations that went to the field of Kilsyth and were never afterwards heard of. Ever since the people here have had a strong aversion to a military life; and in the course of twenty-one years, there is only a single instance of a person enlisting, and he went into the train of artillery'. (1790.)

20   Napier, *Memorials*, II, p. 229.

21   ibid., pp. 225–6.

CHAPTER 17

1   Wishart, *Deeds of Montrose*.

2   Bankes MSS (21 September).

3   Gordon of Ruthven, *Britane's Distemper*.

4   Printed in Napier, *Memorials*, I, pp. 215 ff.

5   The addition of a list of casualties at Kilsyth at the end of the text would seem to fix it as having been written at this time. It was quite possibly seized along with Montrose's other papers at Philiphaugh.

6   September 1645. (Napier, *Memorials*, II, p. 234.) Ogilvie claimed to have had information as to Argyll's intention to suborn Aboyne from Lady Drummond while he was still in prison.

7   At Haccartoune on the way north, Aboyne captured Marischal with other Covenanting barons of the Mearns, but somewhat incontinently let them go again.

8   Son of Leslie of Pitcairly and not related to Lord Leven.

9   Napier, *Memorials*, II, p. 233.

10   'He came tired and weary, with his troops into Rotheram; and he confessed afterwards that if the King had fallen upon him, as he might easily have done, he had found him in a very ill fortune to have made resistance, and had absolutely preserved Montrose'. Clarendon.

11   Horse regiments: Dalhousie's, Eglinton's, Middleton's, Leven's, Fraser's Dragoons, Kirkudbright's Dragoons, Sir David Barclay's independent troop of horse; Foot from regiments of: Clydesdale, Tweedale, Galloway, Montgomery, Strathearn, Kenmure.

12   Some versions state that Leslie spent the night of 12 September at Melrose, but this, having come from Gala Water, would have been an unnecessary detour. cf. Elliot, *The Trustworthiness of Border Ballads*, p. 906, and Buchan's footnote on the subject.

13   See Craig-Brown, *History of Selkirkshire*, I, p. 185. It is said that the woman of the house was putting the sheep's head into a pot when Montrose passed by the kitchen door, and she was heard to exclaim that she wished it was Montrose's head, for in

that case she would be careful to hold down the lid. Selkirk was notoriously hostile.

14 Lord Somerville (who had held Morpeth against Montrose in 1644) saw the muster on Gladsmuir the previous day, and later recalled that the sight of so many men clad in steel, back and breast, with helmets, and moving in such regular order and with such a fearless demeanour was the most terrifying thing that could be conceived (see *Memorie of the Somervilles*).

15 Wishart, *Deeds of Montrose*: the reference to Montrose's 'sweet wife' would seem to refute the theory that Montrose and Lady Carnegie had become estranged. Wishart, of course, was present at Philiphaugh.

16 There is a tradition (see Scott's *Minstrels of the Scottish Border*) that Traquair was actually on his way to Philiphaugh with money for Montrose when he heard the sound of gunfire. When he came upon the first fugitives who told him all was lost, Traquair fled also, but, weighed down by all the coin he was carrying, he gave the money to his servant, who, subsequently pursued by the Covenanters, threw it in a pond near Hangingshaw. Traquair later welcomed the victors. (He subsequently died in penury.)

17 See Buchan, *Montrose*; Peebles was only sixteen miles from Philiphaugh, and although Wishart records that he spent the night there it seems most likely that he would have pressed on to Tweeddale which was more favourably disposed towards the royal cause.

18 Leslie's account to Level: 'I never fought with better horsemen and against more resolute foot'.

19 Baillie, *Letters and Journals*.

20 Gordon of Ruthven, *Britane's Distemper*, p. 160. See also Wishart, *Deeds of Montrose*, XVI, and Guthry, *Memoirs*, p. 203.

21 Sir George MacKenzie, *Vindication of the Government of Scotland*, p. 20; Wishart, *Deeds of Montrose*; Gordon of Ruthven, *Britane's Distemper*.

22 The mass grave was excavated and the skeletons unearthed at the beginning of this century.

23 MacKenzie, *Vindication*.

24 Synod of Galloway; Napier, *Memorials*, II, p. 248.

25 Balfour's *Annals*, III, p. 311; *Acts of Parliament of Scotland*, VI, p. 514.

26 Spottiswoode's *Miscellany*, I, p. 205.

27 Napier, *Memorials*, II, p. 254.

CHAPTER 18

1 Translated from the Hungarian by E. B. Pierce and E. Delmar.

2 Original: Montrose Charter Chest; also in Napier, *Memorials*, II, pp. 213–22

3 See Montrose's letter to Robertson of Inver, his Castellan at Blair, of 2 October 1646: '. . . Meanwhile you will be doing what you can; and be extremely careful of the prisoners, especially of Archibald Campbell'. Napier, *Memorials*, II, p. 237.

4 This part of Burns's Diary is among Maidment's *Historical Fragments*. Buchan, however, points out that in the disposition of Montrose's lands by the Committee of Estates to Sir William Graham of Claverhouse on 21 February 1648, provision was made for her life-rent. Yet a further cause of confusion may have been that, while Montrose's wife was Magdalen Carnegie, daughter of Lord Southesk, Sir William Graham of Claverhouse's lady was Magdalen Carnegie, daughter of Lord Northesk.

5 The Covenanters ordered the body to be disinterred so that a sentence of forfeiture could be passed on the corpse, but finally accepted a payment of 5,000 merks from young Napier to leave his father's grave alone.

6 This letter has not been recovered, but it presumably contained Montrose's own account of Philiphaugh.

7 Original: Montrose Charter Chest also in Napier, *Memorials*, II, p. 242.

8 First printed in T.M., Esq., *Blood for Blood and Murther Avenged* (British Museum) also in Napier, *Memorials*, II, p. 244.

9 Wishart, *Deeds of Montrose*, p. 160.

10 Napier, *Memorials*, II, p. 263.

11 By displacing such large numbers of Campbells, Alastair was in fact hindering Montrose, since these refugees now went raiding in their turn into areas where the

Royalists might have hoped to gain recruits had the local Royalists not had to stay and protect their homes against the latest threat.

12 Wishart, *Deeds of Montrose*, pp. 177–8.
13 Original: Montrose Charter Chest; also in Napier, *Memorials*, II, p. 277.
14 Montereul's *Correspondence*: Montereul to Mazarin, 18/28 September 1645.
15 Gardiner, *History of the Great Civil War*, III, p. 3.
16 Montereul to Mazarin, 28 February/8 March 1646.
17 Montereul to Mazarin, 15/25 January 1646.
18 Montereul to Mazarin, 28 February/8 March 1646.
19 Montereul to Mazarin, 12/22 March 1646.
20 Clarendon Papers, II, fo. 224, also in Napier, *Memorials*, II, p. 275.
21 Turner, *Memoirs*, p. 41.
22 Montereul, *Correspondence*, I, 255.
23 Napier, *Memorials*, II, p. 278: Montrose to Charles, 2 June 1646.
24 Guthry, *Memoirs*, p. 177.
25 Original: Montrose Charter Chest, also in Napier, *Memorials*, II, pp. 279–80.
26 Original: Montrose Charter Chest, also in Napier, *Memorials*, II, pp. 282–3.
27 Wishart, *Deeds of Montrose*, pp. 84–5.
28 Original: Montrose Charter Chest, also in Napier, *Memorials*, II, pp. 283–4.

CHAPTER 19

1 10 September 1646. The event was recorded in *Oprignelser*, a chronicle written by H. Hofnagel, a local schoolmaster.

2 Viz: Marquis of Antrim in the name of Clan Donald 2,000

MacLean	2,000
MacRanald	1,300
MacLeod of Harris	1,000
Sir James MacDonald	2,000
Earl of Seaforth	2,000
The Lord Rea	1,200
The country of Atholl and Badenoch	3,000
ClanGregor and Farquharson	1,200
Grant	1,000
Clanchattan and Strathearn men	1,000
Marquis of Huntly	1,500
Earl of Airlie	400
Earl of Airth	700
MacNiel of Barra	500
Glengarry	500
Earl of Nithsdale	1,000
Marquis of Montrose	1,000
The Lord Dalkeith (horse)	100
Total	23,400

3 21 January 1647. Original: Montrose Charter Chest (also in Napier, *Memorials*, II, p. 299).
4 5 February 1647. Original: Montrose Charter Chest (also in Napier, *Memorials*, II, p. 300–translated from the French).
5 Original: Montrose Charter Chest (also in Napier, *Memorials*, II, p. 301–translated from French).
6 Wishart, *Deeds of Montrose*, p. 192.
7 ibid.
8 ibid., p. 194.
9 Secretary Nicholas to Clarendon, 8 May 1647: *Clarendon State Papers*, II, fo. 344.
10 Wishart, *Deeds of Montrose*, p. 195.
11 Burnet, *History of His Own Times*, I, p. 89.
12 Monteth, *A History of the Troubles of Great Britain*, XII, p. 509.

13 Montrose to George Stirling of Keir, 26 July 1647. Original: Keir Charter Chest (also in Napier, *Memorials*, II, p. 304).

14 Argyll, *Instructions to his Son*, p. 5.

15 Callander was 'Almanach'; Lindsay, 'Judas'; the General Assembly, 'The Goodwife that wears the breeches'.

16 *De Rebus Auspiciis Serenissimi et Potentissimi Caroli etc sub imperio illustrissimi Jacobi Montisrosasorum Marchionis*. A second edition appeared in Paris in 1648, a third in Amsterdam the same year, and a fourth in 1649. The first English translation was published by Samuel Browne at The Hague probably in 1647. Wishart's book was dedicated to Prince Charles, who wrote to Montrose disclaiming it: 'Right trusty and right entirely beloved cousin, We greet you well. We have seen a book which hath been published and dedicated to me, containing a relation of your proceedings in the late unhappy war in Scotland, and are well pleased that your actions and conduct therein be made known to the world with such advantage as they deserve; but finding a liberty used by the author of that discourse concerning ye actions and carriage of several persons of quality whereby they are respectively charged with many crimes of a high nature, we conceive we cannot in justice offend our Patronage to accusations which render persons of honour infamous before they be heard, and we therefore desire that the said book be suppressed, and that there be no further publication made thereof; and to ye end that our desire herein may be accordingly affected, we think fit to recommend the doing of it to your care and endeavours rather than to ye Author being a person altogether unknown to us. Given at La Germaines ye 5th March 1647/8'.

17 Wishart, *Deeds of Montrose*, p. 198: Clarendon later maintained that Montrose left for reasons of wounded vanity, but Clarendon's retrospective remarks about Montrose are unreliable since they do not reflect his comments at the time. Moreover, by the time he wrote his *History* there was much to justify where Montrose was concerned.

18 The Prince's reply dated 17 February 1648 is among the papers in the Montrose Charter Chest. The Prince of Orange was married to Princess Mary, the eldest of Charles I's daughters.

19 Napier to his wife. Original: Napier Charter Chest (also in Napier, *Memorials*, II, pp. 306 ff).

20 ibid.

21 e.g., Napier was offered a regiment in Spain (the Jesuits hoped to convert him to Roman Catholicism).

22 3 December 1648: Napier, *Memorials*, II, p. 360.

23 Surviving letters are: Montrose to Rupert (7 September, 7 October, 3 December, 14 December, 1648, 8 January, 27 February, 8 March, 1649); Rupert to Montrose (20 September, 13 October, 17 October, 6 December, 1 April). See Montrose Charter Chest and Napier, *Memorials*, II.

24 Napier, *Memorials*, II, p. 364: First printed in Berkeley's *Literary Relics* (1729) without historical reference.

25 28 January 1649: *Clarendon State Papers*, II, fo. 470.

26 20 January: *Clarendon State Papers*, II, fo. 467. It seems that Clarendon's first inclination was to reject Montrose's offer of service since there is a previous draft given in *Clarendon State Papers*, II, fo. 466, entitled 'The Earl of Brentford to the Marquis of Montrose' declining in the Prince's name. It was presumably redrafted on the instructions of the Prince of Wales.

27 Wishart, *Deeds of Montrose*, pp. 228–9.

28 Napier, *Memorials*, II, p. 368: based on Guthry's MS in the Scottish National Library.

29 15 February 1649: appendix to vol. II of *Clarendon State Papers*.

CHAPTER 20

1 See Grant, *Memoirs of Montrose*, p. 345, and *Memoirs of Prince Rupert*.

2 *Clarendon State Papers*, II, p. 472.

3 See chapter 23.

4 Clarendon, *History*, VI, p. 290.

Footnotes

5 Lord Byron to the Marquis of Ormonde, The Hague, 30 March 1650 (Carte, *Ormonde Papers*).

6 Secretary Nicholas to the Marquis of Ormonde, Jersey, 12/23 October 1649 (Carte, *Ormonde Papers*).

7 Gherardo dalla Notte: The original is now the property of the Earl of Dalhousie and hangs in Brechin Castle. I take the portrait in the Scottish National Gallery to be a copy or a second portrait by Honthorst. The two have often been confused. At least two other copies were made of the painting in Brechin Castle, one for the Montrose family when they lived at Buchanan Castle and another which is at present in Wemyss. The picture described in the text is the Brechin Castle portrait.

8 Original draft, Montrose Charter Chest, entitled 'My opinion to His Majesty upon the desires of the Scots Commissioners at The Hague'. A version is also given in the Appendix to the last volume of *Clarendon State Papers*; cf. also Napier, *Memorials*, II, pp. 376 ff.

9 Berkeley, *Literary Relics*, p. 2; Napier, *Memorials*, II, p. 383.

10 21 June 1649: Montrose Charter Chest; Berkeley, *Literary Relics*, p. 6; Napier, *Memorials*, II, pp. 384–460.

11 22 April 1649: Montrose Charter Chest.

12 3 July 1649: Montrose Charter Chest; Berkeley, *Literary Relics*, p. 7; Napier, *Memorials*, II, p. 385.

13 Thurloe, *State Papers*, I, p. 117.

14 John Gwynne, *Military Memoirs*, p. 84.

15 Wodrow MSS lxvii, 93; Napier, *Memorials*, II, p. 394.

16 *Montrose Redivivus*, II, p. 172. Royalist accounts of Montrose's proceedings (e.g. Nicholas to Ormonde, 20 January 1650 [Carte]) are grossly exaggerated on the side of optimism, however.

17 *Mémoires de Chanut*, III, pp. 342 ff. Ulfeldt's widow petitioned Charles again in 1663 with no success.

18 Montrose Charter Chest; Napier, *Memorials*, II, p. 393.

19 Montrose Charter Chest; Berkeley, *Literary Relics*, p. 13; Napier, *Memorials*, II, pp. 397–9.

20 Wishart, *Deeds of Montrose*, pp. 454–8.

21 Printed in London and sold at the Shop of the Sign of the Three Daggers near the Inner Temple in Fleet Street, 1650.

22 2 January 1650, from the Royal Swedish Archives. For their translation I am deeply indebted to Mr Bo Gunnar Wernström of the Swedish Diplomatic Service.

23 ibid., 22 January 1650.

24 Nicholas to Ormonde. Carte, *Ormonde Papers*, I, p. 345.

25 He was later appointed lieutenant-general by royal warrant on 19 March 1650 but never reached the theatre of operations.

26 Montrose Charter Chest; Napier, *Memorials*, II, pp. 410 ff.

27 Gardiner, *Charles II and Scotland in 1650*, p. 53.

CHAPTER 21

1 *Thurloe Papers*; Gardiner (ed.), and Gardiner, *Charles II and Scotland in 1650*; *A Brief Relation* (BM). Manning was later caught and shot after being betrayed by Thurloe's assistant, Samuel Morland, who was himself a royalist spy. After the Restoration Charles II knighted Morland for his intelligence work during the Commonwealth period (see Pepy's *Diary*, 15 May 1660).

2 The instructions to Fleming are printed in the *Wigton Papers*. See also: Gardiner, *Commonwealth and Protectorate*, I, pp. 190 ff.; Balfour, *Annals*, IV, p. 24; Lang, *History of Scotland*, III, ch. vii note.

3 Also Brahan, Chanonry, Eilandonan and Cromarty.

4 Main sources for the campaign are Gordon of Sallagh, Monteth, Gwynne and Balfour.

5 Monteth, *A History of the Troubles of Great Britain*, XII, p. 511.

6 Strachan to James Guthrie, 3 January 1650: Wodrow MSS lxvii/97.

7 Sallagh states that it was Kinnoul, but unless there was another brother also named

William Hay who succeeded to the title this cannot be true, since he lived to escape from Edinburgh Castle in 1654.

8   *Miscellany of the Scottish History Society,* I, p. 223.
9   Gwynne, *Military Memoirs,* p. 92.
10 *Montrose Redivivus,* II.
11 e.g. Sallagh (his neighbour), Burnet, Balfour, Wodrow.
12 Balfour, *Annals,* IV, p. 10; *Acts Parlt Scot.* 17, 23, 24 May; Balfour, 30 May, 4, 8 June; *Acts Parlt Scot.* 11 June; Balfour, 11 June; *Acts Parlt Scot.* 14, 21 June; Balfour, 23 June; *Acts Parlt Scot.* 25, 28 June etc.
13 Was he the Captain Breams mentioned by Gwynne as being involved in Glencairn's rising?
14 Wishart, *Deeds of Montrose,* App. XIII.
15 These cannon have recently been removed by the present owner. They were still there in 1960.
16 'Cumha Mhontroise', in Mackenzie, *Beauties of Gaelic Poetry* (1841); translated by Sheriff Nicholson.

CHAPTER 22

1   Dunrobin MS.
2   Some printed versions of the Wardlaw MS give 7 May, but this must be in error.
3   'Ra ——' (illegible in the MS).
4   Wardlaw MS: '*Polichronicon Seu Politicrata Temporum*', p. 353.
5   Lord Somerville, *Memorie of the Somervilles.* The author's father, from whom he got the story, stayed at Grange about four months afterwards.
6   Wardlaw MS.
7   ibid.
8   *Wigton Papers,* XLIII.
9   M. de Graymond, the French Resident in Edinburgh, to Mazarin. (*Archives des Affaires Etrangers de France*): see Napier, *Memoirs,* pp. 781 ff. A letter signed by the young French king was sent to the Estates, emphasizing that Montrose had been 'fulfilling the commands of the king (Charles)' and asking for clemency on his behalf. Montrose was executed the day after it was written. (Montrose Charter Chest; Napier, *Memoirs,* p. 770.)
10 *Wigton Papers.*
11 The Rev. Patrick Simpson's Testimony as preserved by Wodrow (see Napier, *Memoirs,* 785 ff.)
12 Balfour, *Annals,* IV, p. 15.
13 Summaries and versions of the speech are given in *Wigton Papers,* Wishart, *Deeds of Montrose,* and Wardlaw MS.
14 See chapter 24.
15 The ladies of the Napier family; see chapter 23.
16 Wardlaw MS. Versions also in Wishart and *Wigton Papers.* Montrose's last words are said to have been recorded in an early form of shorthand by a young man who had been detailed for the purpose.
17 British Museum: 'Relation from Edinburgh concerning the hanging of Montrose; May 21st, 1650'. Among the papers given to the BM by Van Sittart; see also Napier, *Memoirs,* p. 804.
18 John Donne (1573–1631).

CHAPTER 23

1   Forbes-Leith, *Memoirs of the Scottish Catholics,* II, p. 51; Skinner, *Ecclesiastical History,* p. 417.
2   Turner, *Memoirs of his Own Life and Times,* p. 46.
3   Guthry, *Memoirs,* p. 199; Turner, *Memoirs,* p. 47.
4   Gordon of Ruthven, *Britane's Distemper,* p. 223.
5   *State Trials,* V, p. 1426.

6   Gordon of Ruthven, *Britane's Distemper*, p. 229.
7   Burnet, *Memoirs of the Dukes of Hamilton*, p. 379; Lang, *History of Scotland*, III, p. 197.
8   Burnet, *Memoirs*, p. 483.
9   Burnet, *Memoirs*, p. 510.
10 Lane, *The Reign of King Covenant*, p. 220; Note by Lord Dartmouth–(Col. Legge's descendant) in Burnet, *History of his own Times*, p. 1823, Ed. I; p. 150.
11 Peterkin, *Records of the Kirk of Scotland*, p. 599.
12 Monteth, *History of the Troubles of Great Britain*, p. 509.
13 'The Start'.
14 Wodrow, *Analecta*, I, p. 67.
15 Clarendon, *History of the Great Rebellion*, XIII, p. 809.
16 Lang, *History of Scotland*, III, p. 256.
17 Historical MSS. Commission, VI, p. 619 (letter dated 17 July); Firth, *Scotland and the Protectorate*, pp. 145–6.
18 Maidment, *Argyll Papers*, p. 16.
19 Wilcock, *The Great Marquess*, p. 321 note; Wodrow, *Analecta*, II, p. 52.
20 Lang, *History of Scotland*, III, p. 295.
21 Burnet, *History of My Own Times*, I, p. 134.
22 Mackenzie, *Memoirs of the History of Scotland*, p. 39.
23 Wilcock, *The Great Marquess*, Appendix VI.
24 The young Marquis of Montrose did not vote on the grounds that he had too deep reason for resentment against Argyll to allow him to judge decently in the matter. A proposal to hang Argyll as Montrose had been was rejected.
25 Wodrow, *Analecta*, I, p. 66.
26 i.e., Cromwell would not disclose the source of his information.
27 Nicholl, *Diary of Public Transactions and Other Occurrences*, p. 279.
28 'I have heard of General Monk's saying that he had letters under my hand that would take off my head'. Wariston, *Diary*, 1 May 1660.
29 Wodrow, *Analecta*, I, pp. 66–71; Lang, *History of Scotland*, III, p. 290.
30 Mackenzie, *Memoirs*, p. 50.

CHAPTER 24

1   As opposed to the North Loch, which was located in the area of the present railway station. The South Loch was drained in the eighteenth century and is sometimes called Hope Park after Hope of Rankeillor who undertook the work.
2   *The Napier Relics :*
    (a) the cap of rich satin, straw coloured, lined with fine linen and turned up with lace;
    (b) the stockings, knitted from a flesh-coloured glossy thread. Above the knee they appear to have been saturated with blood. Their size would seem to indicate that they had been made for a man with small feet and well-shaped legs;
    (c) a sheet or handkerchief of fine linen, about three feet square, trimmed on all sides with tassels on the corners like a pall: very bloodstained. This was probably used either to wrap the trunk or the heart of Montrose when it was recovered.
    The relics remained in the possession and care of the Napier family until 1910 when they passed to His Grace, The Duke of Montrose.
3   Sydserf, *A Relation of the True Funerals of the Great Marquisse of Montrose*.
4   The Burgh-Moor had also been used as a mass burial ground for the plague victims of 1645.
5   Accounts of the City of Edinburgh; Napier, *Memoirs*, II, p. 813.
6   According to Sir John Scot of Scotstarvet's MS (which is not very accurate) the second Lord Napier was robbed of all his possessions while travelling on the continent, and it may be presumed that among the articles lost was the small miniature of Montrose – about the size of 'ane sixpence' – which he always carried with him.
7   Robbie, *The Embalming of Montrose*; (Book of the Old Edinburgh Club, I).
8   Buchan, *Montrose*, p. 380, fn. 2; Robbie, in *The Embalming of Montrose*, 'assumes'

that since the heart was re-embalmed at the same time as the rest of the body, it must have been for the purpose of gathering it to the rest of Montrose's remains for interment in St Giles. It does not necessarily follow that it *was* buried with the rest.

9 Sir Alexander Johnston's letter to his daughters dated 1 July 1836; Napier, *Memoirs*, II, Appendix I; also Napier, *Montrose and the Covenanters*.

10 Johnston's letter to his daughters.

11 Stephen Wheeler's articles in the *Allahabad Pioneer* (13 May 1920, 9 August 1920).

12 In their Appendix concerning the 'Relics of Montrose', Morland and Simpson state that at the beginning of the eighteenth century, a certain Yorkshire antiquary called Dr Thoresby claimed to have acquired the right arm of Montrose from a Dr Pickering, who they suggest, may have been descended from a Roundhead officer of that name who could have obtained the arm as a souvenir or in payment of a debt. The arm was examined by the anatomist Sir William Turner whose report described it as: 'Mummified, bearing evidence of having been at one time impaled. The hand is small and well proportioned and obviously not that of a big man or of one accustomed to manual labour. In the palm is a hole such as would have been made by driving a nail through it, and on the inner side of the forearm is an appearance which could have been produced by pinching up the skin when soft and flexible and driving a nail through it'. The arm was always accompanied by a sword which was double edged with a small basket hilt. On both sides of the blade were damascened the Graham Arms and the initials I.S.? (or I.G.?). Thoresby left his collection to his son, who auctioned all the items in 1764. The arm was among the pieces bought by a Dr Burton (cf. D. H. Atkinson, *Ralph Thoresby, the topographer–his town and times*, pp. 425–43). Murdoch and Simpson obtained details of the supposed relic from Mr Morkill of Killingbeck, near Leeds.

13 'Immortalis verae nobilitatis, inaequandae magnanimitatis Incontaminatis honoris, et interneratae fidelitatis MAGNI GRAMI'. (i.e., Sacred to the Memory of the immortal and true nobility, the unparalleled fortitude, the unblemished honour, and undaunted loyalty of the GREAT GRAHAME.) (Grant, *Memoirs of Montrose*, p. 396.)

14 Robbie, *The Embalming of Montrose*.

15 Sydserf, *A Relation of the True Funerals of the Great Lord Marquesse of Montrose, His Majesty's Lord High Commissioner, and Captain General of his forces in Scotland*. Also, another original MS given as a note to Appendix XXVIII in Wishart, *Deeds of Montrose*.

16 Scott, *Tales of a Grandfather*, II, ch. xlix.

17 *Edinburgh's Joy for His Majestie's Coronation in England*.

Bibliography

I SOURCES

Contemporary Mss: letters: collections:

Montrose Charter Chest
Napier Charter Chest
Southesk Papers
Traquair Charter Chest
Memorials of Montrose and His Times (Mark Napier, Maitland Club)
Hamilton Papers (Camden Society)
Wigton Papers (Maitland Club)
Historical Collections (John Rushworth)
Wodrow mss folios LXV and LXVII (National Library of Scotland)
Hardwicke Collection of State Papers
Breadalbane ms
Argyll Papers (J. Maidment, 1834)
Letters to the Argyll Family (Maitland Club)
Fraser Papers (Scottish History Society)
Dunrobin ms
Thurloe–State Papers (ed. by J. Birch, 1742)
Blair's Papers 1603–1660 (ed. Malcolm V. Hay)
Nicholas Papers (Camden Society)
The Spottiswoode Miscellany (Spottiswoode Society)
Memorials and Letters relating to the History of Great Britain in the Reign of Charles I (Lord Hailes)
Clarendon State Papers
State Trials
Calendar of State Papers (Domestic)
General Assembly Commission Records
Register of the Scottish Privy Council
Acts of the Parliaments of Scotland
Reports of the Historical Manuscripts Commission
The National Covenant of Scotland
Extracts from the Burgh Records of Aberdeen (Spalding Club)
Presbytery Book of Strathbogie (Spalding Club)
A Large Declaration concerning the Late Tumults in Scotland 1639
Diplomatic Correspondence of Jean de Montereul (S.H.S.)
Letters and Papers illustrating the Relations between Charles II and Scotland in 1650
Ormonde Papers (T. Carte, 1739)
Statistical Accounts of Scotland

Contemporary Pamphlets (from the collections in the Bodleian Library, Oxford, and the British Museum)

'Questions concerning the Earl of Montrose his Plott' (1641)

'Certain Instructions given by the Lord Montrose, L. Nappier, Laird of Kerr and Blackhall' (1641)

'A True Narration of the Happy Success of His Majesty's Forces in Scotland under the conduct of the Lord James, Marquess of Montrose . . . etc.' (1644)

'An exact Relation of the Victory obtained by the Parliament Forces of Scotland against the rebels under the command of the Earl of Montrose' (1645)

'Letters from the Marquess of Argyll, the Earl of Warwick, Lord Wariston, and others now in Edinburgh to their friends in London intercepted by Sir Richard Willys, Governor of Newark' (1645)

'Montrose totally routed at Tividale on Saturday last by Lt. Gen. Leslie' (1645)

'A letter from His Majesty's Quarters in Newcastle . . . with the proceedings of the Scots forces in the North . . . and another letter from Edinburgh of Montrose's being ship'd away and the particulars thereof. And General Middleton's marching against the Gordons'

'An English Translation of the Scottish Declaration against James Graham alias Marquesse of Montrose wherein many things are set right between the Kingdom of Scotland and the Commonwealth of England' (1650)

'The Scots Remonstrance or Declaration . . . and a more exact relation of the resolute deportment of the late Marquess of Montrose and several speeches spoken of him at the time of his execution' (1651)

'Two letters from Edinburgh concerning a message to be sent from the Committee of Estates in Scotland to their Commissioners at the Treaty of Breda' (1650)

'A True Relation of the late great and happy victory obtained by the blessing of God upon 27 April 1650 against the excommunicate and bloody traitor James Graham and his complices who had invaded this Kingdom' (1650)

'A Relation of the Execution of James Graham, late Marquis of Montrose, by H.P.'

'A Relation of the True Funerals of the Marquis of Montrose by Thomas Sydserf' (1661)

'Edinburgh's Joy as His Majestie's Coronation in England' (1661)

'Blood for Blood and Murther Avenged' by T.M., Esq.

'Mercurius Aulicus'

'Mercurius Caledonius'

Contemporary Accounts: Chronicles: Diaries: Journals: Memoirs etc.

JOHNSTON, Archibald – of Wariston: *Diary 1634–9: 1650–4: 1655–60* (S.H.S.)

HOPE, Sir Thomas – of Craighau: *Diary 1633–45* (Bannatyne Club)

BRODIE, Alexander: *Diary* (Spalding Club)

NICHOLL, John: *Diary of Public Transactions and other Occurrences* (Bannatyne Club)

BALFOUR, Sir James: *Annales* (1824)

LAMONT, John: *Diary 1649–72* (1810)

EVELYN, John: *Memoirs and Diary of John Evelyn* (1827)

BAILLIE, The Rev. Robert: *Letters and Journals (3 vols.)* (Bannatyne Club)

TURNER, Sir James: *Memoirs of his Own Life and Times* (1829)

BURNET, Gilbert: *History of My Own Times* (1897 ed.); *Memoirs of the Dukes of Hamilton*

HEYLYN, P: *Cyprianus Anglicus–or the History of the Life and Death of Wm. Laud* (1719)

FORBES-LEITH, W: *Memoirs of the Scottish Catholics* (Father MacBreck's Account)

NAPIER, Archibald, 1st Lord: *Memoirs*

HEATH, James: *A Chronicle of the late Intestine War in England, Scotland and Ireland* (1676)

GORDON, Patrick of Ruthven: *A Short Abridgement of Britain's Distemper* (Spalding Club)

GORDON, James of Rothiemay: *A History of Scots Affairs* (Spalding Club)

GORDON, Gilbert of Sallagh: *Continuation of a History of the Earldom of Sutherland by Sir Robert Gordon of Gordonstoun* (1813)

GWYNNE, John: *Military Memoirs of the Great Civil War* (ed. Sir Walter Scott 1822)

GUTHRIE, Henry, Bishop of Dunkeld: *Memoirs*

SPALDING, John: *Memorials of the Trubles in Scotland and England* (Spalding Club)

ROTHES, John, Earl of: *A Relation of the Proceedings concerning the Affairs of the Kirk of Scotland* (Bannatyne Club)

SPOTTISWOODE, Archbishop: *History of the Church of Scotland*

MONTETH, Robert de Salmonet: *History of the Troubles of Great Britain* (trans. Capt. James Ogilvie 1735)

WODROW, Robert: *Analecta* (Maitland Club); *Biographical Collections* (New Spalding Club); *History of the Sufferings of the Church of Scotland*

SANDERSON, William: *A Compleat History of the Life and Reign of King Charles* (1658)

HYDE, Edward, Earl of Clarendon: *A History of the Rebellion and Civil Wars in England* (original Mss in Bodleian)

MACKENZIE, Sir George: *Memoirs of the Affairs of Scotland from the Restoration of Charles II* (1821 ed.)

BLAKHAL, Gilbert: *Brieffe Narration* (Spalding Club, 1844)

RUPERT, Prince: *Memoirs* (edited by Warburton 1849 ed.)

WISHART, George: *Res Montisros* (1647); *Montrose Redivivus* (1652); *Montrose ed. by Murdoch and Simpson* (1893)

WARDLAW, M. S: *Chronicle of the Frasers by James Fraser* (S.H.S.); *History of the Family of Fraser* (Ms. Nat. Lib. Sc. V–7–29)

BERKELEY: *Literary Relics*

Miscellany of the Scottish History Society

Black Book of Clanranald (in Reliquae Celticae, ed. Alexander Cameron 1892)

421

II SECONDARY MATERIAL

Biographies of Montrose

WISHART, George: *Res Montisros* (1647)

CHAMBERS, Robert: *History of the Rebellions in Scotland under the Marquis of Montrose* (Constable, 1828)

NAPIER, Mark: *The Life and Times of Montrose* (Oliver and Boyd, 1840); *Montrose and the Covenanters* 2 vols. (Duncan, 1838); *Memorials of Montrose* as above – with documents – 2 vols. (Maitland Club, 1848); *Memoirs of Montrose* 2 vols. (Stevenson, 1856)

GRANT, James: *Memoirs of Montrose* (Routledge, 1858)

GREVILLE, Lady Violet: *Montrose* (Chapman and Hall, 1886)

MORRIS, Mowbray: *Montrose* (Macmillan, 1892)

PRYCE, Mrs Hugh: *The Marquis of Montrose* (Everett, 1912)

BUCHAN, John: *The Marquis of Montrose* (Nelson, 1913); *Montrose* (Nelson, 1928)

WEDGWOOD, C. V: *Montrose* (Collins, 1952)

Miscellaneous

AYTOUN, W. E: *Lays of the Cavaliers*

BARKER, W. A: *Religion and Politics 1559–1642* (Historical Association Pamphlet, 1957)

BUCHAN, John: *Men and Deeds* (Peter Davies, 1935)

BURN, Michael: *The Debatable Land* (Hamish Hamilton, 1970)

CALDERWOOD, David: *History of the Kirk of Scotland* (Wodrow Society)

CARLYLE, Thomas: *Heroes and Hero Worship*

CHAMBERS, Robert: *Domestic Annals of Scotland* (W. & R. Chambers)

CHAPMAN, Hester: *The Tragedy of Charles II* (Cape, 1964)

CRAIK, Sir Henry: *The Life of Edward, Earl of Clarendon* 2 vols. (Smith Elder and Co., 1911)

CUNNINGHAM, Archdeacon: 'The Political Philosophy of the Marquis of Montrose' (Essay – *Dictionary of National Biography*)

DISRAELI, Isaac: *Charles I* (Colburn, 1851)

DONALDSON, G: Scotland: *Church and Nation through the Sixteenth Century*

ECHARD, Laurence: *History of England*

ELTON, Richard: *Complete Body of the Art Military* (1650)

FIGGIS, J. N: *The Divine Right of Kings*

FIRTH, H. C: *Scotland and the Commonwealth* (1895)

FRASER, Duncan: *Montrose* (Montrose Standard, 1967); *Portrait of a Parish* (Montrose Standard, 1970); *Highland Perthshire* (Montrose Standard, 1973); *Four Hundred Years around Kenmore* (Montrose Standard, 1972)

FRASER, William: *A History of the Earls of Southesk* 2 vols. (Edinburgh, 1867)

GARDINER, Samuel Rawlinson: *History of England* (Longmans Green, 1886); *History of the Great Civil War* (Longmans Green, 1893 ed.)

GRAEME, L. G: *Or and Sable : A Book of the Graemes and Grahams* (Edinburgh, 1903)

GRANT, I. F: *In the Tracks of Montrose* (MacLehose, 1931)

GREGORY, Donald: *History of the Western Highlands and Islands of Scotland*

GUIZOT, F: *History of the English Revolution of 1640* (Bogue, 1844)

HALLER, William L: *Liberty and Reformation in the Puritan Revolution*

HERMANNUS, Hugo: *De Militia Equestri* (1630)

HERVEY, Lord: *Ancient and Modern Liberty Stated and Compared* (1734)

HUME, David: *History of Great Britain* (Pelican, first published 1754)

HUME-BROWN, P: *Scotland before 1700 from Contemporary Documents* (1893); *History of Scotland* (Oliver and Boyd)

INGLIS, Lord President: *Montrose and the Covenant of 1638* (*Blackwoods Magazine,* November 1887)

JERVISE, Andrew: *The Lairds of the Lindsays* (Douglas, 1882); *Memorials of Angus and the Mearns* (Edinburgh, 1885)

JOHNSTON, T. B. (ed. James Robertson): *Historical Geography of the Clans of Scotland* (Johnston, 1899 ed.)

LANE, Jane: *The Reign of King Covenant* (Robert Hale, 1956)

LANG, Andrew: *History of Scotland Vol. III* (Blackwood)

LINDSAY, Lord: *Lives of the Lindsays* 3 vols. (John Murray, 1849)

MACKENZIE, W. C: *The Life and Times of John Maitland, Duke of Lauderdale* (Kegan Paul, 1923)

MAHON, Lord: Essay on Montrose (*Quarterly Review,* December 1846)

MASSON, David: *Drummond of Hawthornden* (Macmillan, 1873)

MATHEW, David: *Scotland under Charles I* (Eyre and Spottiswoode, 1955)

MATHIESON, W. L: *Politics and Religion* 2 vols. (MacLehose, 1902)

MAXWELL, Alexander: *History of Old Dundee* (1884)

NAPIER, Mark: *Memoirs of Dundee Vol. I* (Stevenson, 1859)

NAPIER, Priscilla: *A Difficult Country* (Michael Joseph, 1974)

NOBBS, Douglas: *England and Scotland 1560–1707*

ORLEANS, Père d': *Revolt in England*

ORR, Sheriff R. L: *Alexander Henderson: Churchman and Statesman* (Hodder and Stoughton, 1919)

PETERKIN, Alexander: *Records of the Kirk of Scotland* (1838)

PHILIP, J: *The Grameid* (Scottish History Society, 1691)

PREBBLE, John: *The Lion in the North* (History Guild)

RAMSAY, A. A. W: *Challenge to the Highlander* (John Murray, 1933)

ROBBIE, J. C: *The Embalming of Montrose* (Bk. of the Old Edinburgh Club, Vol. I)

ROGERS, Col. H. C. B., O.B.E: *Battles and Generals of the Civil War* (Seeley Service, 1968)

ROW, John: *History of the Kirk of Scotland 1558–1637* (Wodrow Society, 1842)

SCOT, Sir John of Scotstarvet: *The Staggering State of Scots Statesmen* (1754)

SCOTT, Sir Walter: *Tales of a Grandfather* (Black); *Minstrelsy of the Scottish Border* (Harrap); *A Legend of Montrose,* preface (Nelson).

SEALEY, Lucy: *Champions of the Crown* (Methuen, 1911)

SKELTON, John: 'The Marquis of Montrose', from *Essays in History and Biography* (Blackwood, 1883)

SKENE, W: *History of the Highland Clans* (MacKay, 1837)

SKINNER, John: *An Ecclesiastical History of Scotland* (1788)

SMOUT, T. C: *History of the Scottish People* (Thames and Hudson)

SOMERVILLE, Lord: *Memorie of the Somervilles* (1815 ed.)

TERRY, Charles Sanford: *Life and Campaigns of Alexander Leslie* (1899); *The Army of the Covenant* (S.H.S.)

TOWNSEND, Dorothea: *Life and Letters of Endymion Porter*

TREVELYAN, G. M: *English Social History* (Longmans, 1938); *England under the Stuarts* (Methuen, 1904)

TREVOR-ROPER, Hugh: *Archbishop Laud, 1573–1645* (Macmillan, 1962)

WEDGWOOD, C. V: *The King's Peace* (Collins, 1955); *The King's War* (Collins, 1958)

WILCOCK, J: *The Great Marquess* (Oliphant, Anderson and Ferrier, 1903)

WILSON, William: *The House of Airlie* 2 vols. (John Murray, 1924)

Original Portraits of Montrose (Private Edition, 1854)

Montrose and Marvell. *Selected Poems* (Westminster/Constable, 1901)

Index

425

Index

FERGUSON, William, of Ballyheukane, 184

FIELDING, Basil, later Earl of Denbigh, 15, 17

FINLATER (FINDLATER), James Ogilvie, Lord, later 1st Earl of, 237–8

FINLAY OF BRAEMAR, CLAN, 143

FINTRY, see GRAHAM, of Fintry

FLEMING, John, Lord, later 3rd Earl of Wigton, 273

FLEMING, Sir William, 346, 347, 362 (see also 306)

FLETCHER, Sir John, 381

FORBES, Major Arthur, 166

FORBES, Duncan, Provost of Inverness, 360

FORBES, Sir William, of Craigievar, 166, 172, 175, 223, 409 (n. 11. 14)

FORBES, Lord, 73, 74, 165, 178, 232

FORBES, of Boyndlie, 172

FORBES, of Skellater, 237

FORBES, of Thornbeg, 251

FORBES, CLAN, 72, 136, 138, 147, 165, 171, 185, 226, 238

FORD OF LYON, 90–1, 102–4, 199

FORFAR, 71, 133, 137, 160, 163, 166, 230

FORRES, 183, 238, 361

FORRETT, Master William, 6, 8–9, 160, 164, 175, 199, 224

FOVERANE, see TURING, of Foverane

FRANK, Richard, 175

FRASER, Master of, also Lord, 73, 74, 165, 166, 169, 171, 178, 232

FRASER, James, 360–1

FRASER, CLAN, 72, 136, 138, 147, 165, 204, 226, 238, 244, 301

FREDERICK V, Elector Palatine, King of Bohemia, 329

FREDERICK III, King of Denmark, 336

FREDERICK WILHELM, Elector of Brandenburg, 336

FRENDRAUGHT, James Crichton, Viscount, 74, 166, 169, 171, 232, 350, 354

FRIESLAND, Duke of, 336

FULLERTON, Thomas (or William), 361

FYNDLATER, Alexander, 169

FYVIE, Battle of, (152, map), 186–8, 191

FYVIE CASTLE, 185, 186–8

GARCHORE, Major, 244

GARDINER, Samuel Rawlinson, xiii, 31, 65, 75, 162, 175, 220

GEDDES, Jenny, 42, 394

GENERAL ASSEMBLY, of 1598 at Dundee, 25; of 1600 at Montrose, 25; of 1605, 26; Convention of 1606 at Linlithgow, 26; of 1610, 26; of 1616 at Aberdeen, 5, 11; of 1617 at Perth, 11; of 1618 at Perth, 27; 34, 49, 53, 54, 56; of 1638 at Glasgow, 56–9, 65, 67, 68, 82–3, 249; of 1639 at Edinburgh, 85, 108; of 1642 at St Andrews, 116, 164, 217, 284; of 1645 at St Andrews, 293, 321, 328, 332, 392

GERMANY, 69, 78, 175, 315, 319, 320, 324, 334, 339, 346

GIBSON, Sir Alexander, 110

GIGHT, see GORDON, of Gight

GIGHT, BOG OF, (GORDON CASTLE), 73, 79, 139, 165, 178, 183, 222–3, 232, 245, 251, 254–5, 256, 372, 374

GILLESBUIG GRUAMACH, see ARGYLL, 7th Earl of

GILLESPIE, son of Gillespie Og, Laird of the Bingingeadhs, 212–3

GLAMIS, see KINGHORN

GLASGOW, 6, 7, 8, 54, 57–9, 65, 82, 91, 183, 272, 273, 274, 279, 293, 296, 297, 362, 378, 380

GLEDSTANES (GLADSTANES), Francis, of Whitelaw, Lieutenant, 244

GLEDSTANES, James, of Whitelaw, Captain, 244

GLENCAIRN, William Cunningham, 9th Earl of, 37, 263, 273, 380, 381, 382, 415 (n. 13. 21)

GLENCAIRN's Regiment, 268, 270

GLENCOE, MacDonalds of, see MACDONALDS

GLENGARRY, MacDonalds of (Clanranald), 193, 204, 208, 211, 255, 262, 380

GORDON, George, 2nd Marquis of Huntly, see HUNTLY

GORDON, George, Lord Gordon, 75–6, 134,

431